Quality Management Principles and Policies in Higher Education

Neeta Baporikar
Namibia University of Science and Technology, Namibia & University of Pune, India

Michael Sony
Namibia University of Science and Technology, Namibia

A volume in the Advances in Higher Education and Professional Development (AHEPD) Book Series

Published in the United States of America by
    IGI Global
    Information Science Reference (an imprint of IGI Global)
    701 E. Chocolate Avenue
    Hershey PA, USA 17033
    Tel: 717-533-8845
    Fax: 717-533-8661
    E-mail: cust@igi-global.com
    Web site: http://www.igi-global.com

Copyright © 2020 by IGI Global. All rights reserved. No part of this publication may be reproduced, stored or distributed in any form or by any means, electronic or mechanical, including photocopying, without written permission from the publisher. Product or company names used in this set are for identification purposes only. Inclusion of the names of the products or companies does not indicate a claim of ownership by IGI Global of the trademark or registered trademark.

    Library of Congress Cataloging-in-Publication Data

Names: Baporikar, Neeta, editor. | Sony, Michael, 1981- editor. | Business
   Science Reference (Firm) | IGI Global.
Title: Quality management principles and policies in higher education /
   Neeta Baporikar and Michael Sony, editors.
Description: Hershey, Pennsylvania : Information Science Reference (an
   imprint of IGI Global), 2019. | Includes bibliographical references and
   index. | Summary: "This book examines the implementation of quality
   management principles and policies in research, teaching, learning,
   administrative processes, and other facets of higher education"--
   Provided by publisher.
Identifiers: LCCN 2019023683 (print) | LCCN 2019023684 (ebook) | ISBN
   9781799810179 (Hardcover) | ISBN 9781799810186 (Paperback) | ISBN
   9781799810193 (eBook)
Subjects: LCSH: Total quality management in higher education. |
   Universities and colleges--Administration. | Universities and
   colleges--Evaluation.
Classification: LCC LB2341 .Q35 2019 (print) | LCC LB2341 (ebook) | DDC
   378.1/01--dc23
LC record available at https://lccn.loc.gov/2019023683
LC ebook record available at https://lccn.loc.gov/2019023684

This book is published in the IGI Global book series Advances in Higher Education and Professional Development (AHEPD) (ISSN: 2327-6983; eISSN: 2327-6991)

British Cataloguing in Publication Data
A Cataloguing in Publication record for this book is available from the British Library.

All work contributed to this book is new, previously-unpublished material. The views expressed in this book are those of the authors, but not necessarily of the publisher.

For electronic access to this publication, please contact: eresources@igi-global.com.

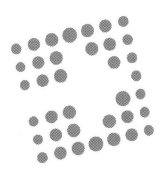

Advances in Higher Education and Professional Development (AHEPD) Book Series

Jared Keengwe
University of North Dakota, USA

ISSN:2327-6983
EISSN:2327-6991

Mission

As world economies continue to shift and change in response to global financial situations, job markets have begun to demand a more highly-skilled workforce. In many industries a college degree is the minimum requirement and further educational development is expected to advance. With these current trends in mind, the **Advances in Higher Education & Professional Development (AHEPD) Book Series** provides an outlet for researchers and academics to publish their research in these areas and to distribute these works to practitioners and other researchers.

AHEPD encompasses all research dealing with higher education pedagogy, development, and curriculum design, as well as all areas of professional development, regardless of focus.

Coverage

- Adult Education
- Assessment in Higher Education
- Career Training
- Coaching and Mentoring
- Continuing Professional Development
- Governance in Higher Education
- Higher Education Policy
- Pedagogy of Teaching Higher Education
- Vocational Education

IGI Global is currently accepting manuscripts for publication within this series. To submit a proposal for a volume in this series, please contact our Acquisition Editors at Acquisitions@igi-global.com or visit: http://www.igi-global.com/publish/.

The Advances in Higher Education and Professional Development (AHEPD) Book Series (ISSN 2327-6983) is published by IGI Global, 701 E. Chocolate Avenue, Hershey, PA 17033-1240, USA, www.igi-global.com. This series is composed of titles available for purchase individually; each title is edited to be contextually exclusive from any other title within the series. For pricing and ordering information please visit http://www.igi-global.com/book-series/advances-higher-education-professional-development/73681. Postmaster: Send all address changes to above address. ©© 2020 IGI Global. All rights, including translation in other languages reserved by the publisher. No part of this series may be reproduced or used in any form or by any means – graphics, electronic, or mechanical, including photocopying, recording, taping, or information and retrieval systems – without written permission from the publisher, except for non commercial, educational use, including classroom teaching purposes. The views expressed in this series are those of the authors, but not necessarily of IGI Global.

Titles in this Series

For a list of additional titles in this series, please visit: www.igi-global.com/book-series

Handbook of Research on Innovative Pedagogies and Best Practices in Teacher Education
Jared Keengwe (University of North Dakota, USA)
Information Science Reference • ©2020 • 422pp • H/C (ISBN: 9781522592327) • US $260.00

The Formation of Intellectual Capital and Its Ability to Transform Higher Education Institutions and the Knowledge Society
Edgar Oliver Cardoso Espinosa (Instituto Politécnico Nacional, Mexico)
Information Science Reference • ©2019 • 312pp • H/C (ISBN: 9781522584612) • US $195.00

Engaging Teacher Candidates and Language Learners With Authentic Practice
Chesla Ann Lenkaitis (Binghamton University, USA) and Shannon M. Hilliker (Binghamton University, USA)
Information Science Reference • ©2019 • 368pp • H/C (ISBN: 9781522585435) • US $195.00

Case Study Methodology in Higher Education
Annette Baron (William Paterson University, USA) and Kelly McNeal (William Paterson University, USA)
Information Science Reference • ©2019 • 393pp • H/C (ISBN: 9781522594291) • US $195.00

Workforce Education at Oil and Gas Companies in the Permian Basin Emerging Research and Opportunities
Julie Neal (Dearing Sales, USA) and Brittany Lee Neal (Axip Energy Services, USA)
Business Science Reference • ©2019 • 131pp • H/C (ISBN: 9781522584643) • US $160.00

Handbook of Research on Educator Preparation and Professional Learning
Drew Polly (University of North Carolina at Charlotte, USA) Christie Martin (University of South Carolina at Columbia, USA) and Kenan Dikilitaş (Bahçeşehir University, Turkey)
Information Science Reference • ©2019 • 459pp • H/C (ISBN: 9781522585831) • US $245.00

Preparing the Higher Education Space for Gen Z
Heidi Lee Schnackenberg (State University of New York at Plattsburgh, USA) and Christine Johnson (University of Western Kentucky, USA)
Information Science Reference • ©2019 • 253pp • H/C (ISBN: 9781522577638) • US $175.00

Competency-Based and Social-Situational Approaches for Facilitating Learning in Higher Education
Gabriele I.E. Strohschen (DePaul University, USA) and Kim Lewis (DePaul University, USA)
Information Science Reference • ©2019 • 317pp • H/C (ISBN: 9781522584889) • US $185.00

701 East Chocolate Avenue, Hershey, PA 17033, USA
Tel: 717-533-8845 x100 • Fax: 717-533-8661
E-Mail: cust@igi-global.com • www.igi-global.com

Editorial Advisory Board

Sulaiman Olusegun Atiku, *University of KwaZulu-Natal, South Africa*
Rajbir S. Bhatti, *Mount Royal University, Canada*
Deonarain Brijlall, *Durban University of Technology, South Africa*
Mukund Deshpande, *Independent Researcher, India*
Carolina Machado, *Universidade do Minho, Portugal*
Nwachukwu Prince Ololube, *Ignatius Ajuru University of Education, Nigeria*
Liphie Pereira, *University of Swaziland, Swaziland*
Maria S. Plakhotnik, *National Research University Higher School of Economics, Russia*
Jose Manuel Saiz-Alvarez, *Nebrija University, Spain*
A. M. Sakkthivel, *Skyline University College, UAE*

List of Reviewers

Loukas Anninos, *University of Piraeus, Germany*
Dileep Baburao Baragde, *G. S. Moze College, India*
Denise A. D. Bedford, *Georgetown University, USA*
Joseph Ezale Cobbinah, *University of Ghana, Ghana*
Idahosa Igbinakhase, *University of KwaZulu-Natal, South Africa*
Ngepathimo Kadhila, *University of Namibia, Namibia*
Vannie Naidoo, *University of KwaZulu-Natal, South Africa*
Rajka Presbury, *Torrens University, Australia*
Damini Saini, *University of Lucknow, India*
Steven Sena, *University of Zimbabwe, Zimbabwe*
Hylton James Villet, *Namibia University of Science and Technology, Namibia*

Table of Contents

Preface xiv

Acknowledgment xviii

Chapter 1
Quality Management Principles Application to Higher Educational Institutions 1
    Jose Manuel Saiz-Alvarez, Tecnologico de Monterrey, Mexico

Chapter 2
Higher Education Approach to Quality Management 23
    Dileep Baburao Baragde, G. S. Moze College, India

Chapter 3
Contemporary Perspectives on Higher Education Quality Management 38
    Steven Sena, University of Zimbabwe, Zimbabwe

Chapter 4
Quality Management and Higher Education Scenario in Namibia: A Critical Analysis 61
    Selma Mupeniwo Iipinge, Namibia University of Science and Technology, Namibia
    Anna M. Shimpanda, Namibia University of Science and Technology, Namibia
    Ngepathimo Kadhila, University of Namibia, Namibia

Chapter 5
Leadership and Innovative Approaches in Higher Education 83
    Sulaiman Olusegun Atiku, University of KwaZulu-Natal, South Africa
    Richmond Anane-simon, Pentecost University College, Ghana

Chapter 6
Quality Management and Academic Leadership 101
    Joseph Ezale Cobbinah, University of Ghana, Ghana
    Samuel Agyemang, Bia College of Education, Ghana

Chapter 7
Overcoming Complacency Through Quality Intelligence in Greek Higher Education: The Critical
Role of Academic Leadership 121
    Loukas Anninos, University of Piraeus, Greece

Chapter 8
Situational Leadership for Quality Graduate Research in Higher Education 141
    Hylton James Villet, Namibia University of Science and Technology, Namibia

Chapter 9
Fair Process in Assessing the Quality of University Faculty 156
    Denise A. D. Bedford, Georgetown University, USA

Chapter 10
Quality Assurance for Teacher Education in Democratic Globalized World 188
    Liphie Precious Pereira, University of Eswatini, Eswatini

Chapter 11
Professional Integrity for Educational Quality in Management Sciences 209
    José G. Vargas-Hernández, University of Guadalajara, Mexico

Chapter 12
Ethics Courses Teaching Linkage to Quality Management Education................................ 232
    Damini Saini, University of Lucknow, India
    Sunita Singh Sengupta, University of Delhi, India

Chapter 13
Higher Education Quality Improvement Strategies Through Enriched Teaching and Learning 246
    Idahosa Igbinakhase, University of KwaZulu-Natal, South Africa
    Vannie Naidoo, University of KwaZulu-Natal, South Africa

Chapter 14
Mentoring for Quality Enhancement and Fostering Industry-Ready Graduates in Higher Education 263
    Rajka Presbury, Torrens University, Australia
    Madalyn A. Scerri, Torrens University, Australia

Chapter 15
Quality Assurance and Institutional Research for University Strategic Management: A Case Study 287
    Ngepathimo Kadhila, University of Namibia, Namibia
    Gilbert Likando, University of Namibia, Namibia

Compilation of References 309

About the Contributors 354

Index 359

Detailed Table of Contents

Preface xiv

Acknowledgment xviii

Chapter 1
Quality Management Principles Application to Higher Educational Institutions 1
  Jose Manuel Saiz-Alvarez, Tecnologico de Monterrey, Mexico

Higher educational institutions (HEIs) are going through a process of structural transformation in which policies based on sound management are of growing importance. A process of change observed when the student had become a client, HEIs desire being at the top of international rankings, impulse relations with organizations outside the HEI to search new opportunities focused on socioeconomic change, and the HEI strives to achieve continuous improvement. Quality management has a fundamental role to play in this transformation process. The objective of this chapter is to reason about the application of the eight quality management principles into HEIs.

Chapter 2
Higher Education Approach to Quality Management.. 23
  Dileep Baburao Baragde, G. S. Moze College, India

The situation of higher education in India does not concur with the worldwide benchmarks. Consequently, there is sufficient defense for an expanded evaluation of the quality of the nation's instructive foundations. Traditionally, these foundations accepted that quality is controllable by intrinsic assets, for example, knowledgeable and learned faculty with an impressive set of degrees and experience detailed at the end of the institute's admission brochure, and extrinsic assets like huge library rich with number of books and journals in the library, an ultra-modern campus, and size of the endowment, etc. This chapter aims at reviewing the higher education approach to quality management from an Indian perspective and deliberates on the tools and techniques like SIX SIGMA, LEAN, and TQM, most commonly used in higher education.

Chapter 3
Contemporary Perspectives on Higher Education Quality Management 38
  Steven Sena, University of Zimbabwe, Zimbabwe

Quality management is considered a very important factor for the long-term success of each and every organization. The links between quality management and organizational performance can never be overemphasized. Quality management in both goods and services industries gives a company a distinct competitive advantage over its competitors in the market place. Market share can also be gained or lost over the level of quality management in an organization; that is if an organization's quality management process is poor, the market share is lost, and conversely, if it is quality management is good, a market share is gained. Quality is, therefore, a competitive priority for any serious organization. Quality management is the only factor that ensures an organization's survival and growth especially in institutions of higher learning and other service organizations. Quality management focuses on meeting consumers' needs, meeting the competition, improving continuously, and extending these concerns to all phases of business.

Chapter 4
Quality Management and Higher Education Scenario in Namibia: A Critical Analysis..................... 61
Selma Mupeniwo Iipinge, Namibia University of Science and Technology, Namibia
Anna M. Shimpanda, Namibia University of Science and Technology, Namibia
Ngepathimo Kadhila, University of Namibia, Namibia

The new wave in the higher education space, which includes mass access to higher education, changes in the diverse needs of the student body, economic challenges faced by many countries, societal and general stakeholder expectations, relationships with external stakeholders, and new funding mechanisms has necessitated new forms of accountability in the sector. These factors have a profound influence on the handling of quality assurance arrangements at both national and institutional levels. This chapter seeks to critically analyze the current state of quality management practices in higher education in Namibia at both national and institutional levels. The chapter identifies achievements that have been recorded so far, as well as challenges and areas for further development.

Chapter 5
Leadership and Innovative Approaches in Higher Education.. 83
Sulaiman Olusegun Atiku, University of KwaZulu-Natal, South Africa
Richmond Anane-simon, Pentecost University College, Ghana

The place of leadership support for technological innovation in advancing quality management in higher education cannot be underrated in the fourth industrial revolution. This chapter examines the role of leadership in higher education and innovative teaching and learning methods for quality assurance in higher education system. The literature review approach and author observation were adopted to cross-examine the influence of leadership on innovative teaching/learning methods and quality assurance in higher education. This chapter shows that leadership support for innovative teaching and learning methods is a benchmark for quality assurance in higher education in recent times. Therefore, no meaningful change will happen in any higher institution without a strong leadership support for innovation and quality management. Policymakers in higher education should create a climate that promotes creativity and innovation by ensuring that transformational leaders are at the helm of affairs for quality management.

Chapter 6
Quality Management and Academic Leadership.. 101
Joseph Ezale Cobbinah, University of Ghana, Ghana
Samuel Agyemang, Bia College of Education, Ghana

Quality management in higher education is one of the measures that institutions put in place to ensure that courses and programs that are offered meet international and accreditation standards. This chapter examines how academic leaders can promote and manage quality in higher education institutions. Higher education institutions and senior faculty members appear to improve performance by ensuring that quality assurance unit enforces effective delivery to increase students and parents' satisfaction. Promotion of quality and the management of quality is not about long service but an exhibition of effective leadership that will help higher education institutions to navigate through the turbulence of challenges facing higher education institutions today. To achieve this, the academic leader is supposed to assist institutions to pursue their vision and mission to enable them to effectively manage quality.

Chapter 7
Overcoming Complacency Through Quality Intelligence in Greek Higher Education: The Critical Role of Academic Leadership 121
    Loukas Anninos, University of Piraeus, Greece

During the last decade, an intensification of evaluation at the Greek universities has been noted, encouraged by the state and institutional initiatives aiming to reform, modernize, and cultivate a culture of excellence. The progress that has been reported was facilitated by global developments that gradually strengthened the cultural and scientific foundations of university performance evaluation and set the foundations for continuous institutional improvement and transformation. However, the role of academic leadership is crucial if universities wish to fully embrace the concept of excellence in their operations and services not from an obligatory, but from an evolutionary perspective that would allow them to learn and improve. As Greek universities are currently in the process of quality accreditation, the chapter briefly presents the framework for quality accreditation in Greek universities and underlines the critical role of academic leadership for achieving accreditation and establishing a culture for sustainable excellence.

Chapter 8
Situational Leadership for Quality Graduate Research in Higher Education 141
    Hylton James Villet, Namibia University of Science and Technology, Namibia

Quality postgraduate supervision is key in ensuring that postgraduate programs at institutions of higher learning produce quality graduates and in turn play an appropriate role in building a knowledge economy. In essence, the role of the supervisor is to support the postgraduate student to successfully complete specific tasks in line with the research process. Supervisors adopt a variety of styles to supervise students. Adopting an exploratory research approach the chapter deliberates the supervisor-student dyad through the lens of the situational leadership model.

Chapter 9
Fair Process in Assessing the Quality of University Faculty 156
    Denise A. D. Bedford, Georgetown University, USA

This chapter presents an exploratory research framework designed to support quality assessment of faculty in higher education. First, a neutral view of a university is developed which highlights five essential business capabilities, including teaching, research, advising, advocacy, and convening. Activity models are constructed for each capability – identifying inputs, activities, and outputs. Faculty preparation and contributions to inputs, activities, and outputs/outcomes are modeled and described. Deming's model of quality is applied to the five activity models. The quality model is applied to faculty (e.g., tenure and tenure-track, non-tenure track, adjunct, graduate students, clinical, and other specialized faculty). Finally, the research explores whether the current quality management processes are fair for faculty and effective for the university's stakeholders. The exploratory research offers six observations and recommendations. The most significant observation is that only one of the five business capabilities – research has a fair and effective quality process.

Chapter 10
Quality Assurance for Teacher Education in Democratic Globalized World 188
Liphie Precious Pereira, University of Eswatini, Eswatini

In this chapter it is argued that when determining quality assurance in teacher education there is need to take into account not only what teachers are taught but also how they are taught. New perspectives on learning and teaching at school level and the changed nature of the role of the teacher form the basis for suggesting a focus on the "how" of teacher education in addition to or more than the "what." It draws on research underpinned by a critical realist philosophy to demonstrate the changed nature of the school system and the need to adopt a sociocultural approach to learning and teaching in teacher education.

Chapter 11
Professional Integrity for Educational Quality in Management Sciences 209
José G. Vargas-Hernández, University of Guadalajara, Mexico

The objective of this chapter is to analyze the importance of professional integrity as the improvement concept and ethics in the development of professionals in administration and management sciences. The research method employed is the ethnographic, documental, and life histories, complemented with field work supported by in-depth interviews and analyzed using a comparative method. The outcomes of the research on the application in management education demonstrate that the drama of economic efficiency is centered on dysfunctional professional integrity. This chapter provides a sound professional philosophy that empowers professionals to act with integrity, increases the probability for long-term success and professional fulfillment. The results provide also the basis to develop a code of conduct and regulation policies to sustain management education for professional integrity that can positively impact on business culture through influencing the behavior of key actors.

Chapter 12
Ethics Courses Teaching Linkage to Quality Management Education.. 232
Damini Saini, University of Lucknow, India
Sunita Singh Sengupta, University of Delhi, India

Almost every management institution in India has an ethics course in their curriculum that is focused upon inculcating the value set in an individual. To understand the role of ethical education in accelerating the quality of management education, this chapter provides a discussion of implications of the questions of quality, dilemma, and pedagogy of ethical training. In the introduction, the authors emphasize on the reasons of focusing upon the ethical education, then give a brief history of ethics education in Indian management institutions. In order to show the significance, authors also show the place of ethics course in top 10 business institutions in India. Further, the authors describe the main focus of the chapter that is the contribution of ethics in management education.

Chapter 13
Higher Education Quality Improvement Strategies Through Enriched Teaching and Learning 246
    Idahosa Igbinakhase, University of KwaZulu-Natal, South Africa
    Vannie Naidoo, University of KwaZulu-Natal, South Africa

This chapter focuses on the critical analysis of evidence of higher education improvement strategies in improving teaching and learning in higher education institutions. Several higher education improvement strategies such as preparation for accreditation and student learning assessment has been utilized in the area of teaching and learning in higher education institutions with diverse outcomes. Overall and despite some recorded successes, there still exist some situations where improvement strategies create challenges and conflicts in the institutions as a result of the improvement strategies not serving their defined purpose. Some of these challenges are ineffective teacher professional development initiatives and lack of specifically developed programs designed for specific students' needs. In order to resolve higher education improvement challenges, decision makers in higher educational institutions must be willing to involve key stakeholders in designing the right approach to quality assurance in higher educational institutions.

Chapter 14
Mentoring for Quality Enhancement and Fostering Industry-Ready Graduates in Higher Education 263
    Rajka Presbury, Torrens University, Australia
    Madalyn A. Scerri, Torrens University, Australia

Mentoring programs play a valuable role in higher education. Formal mentoring processes and relationships increase the overall perceived quality of an educational program and the professional success of new hotel management graduates. To evaluate an established mentoring program in higher education, a single case study of the Blue Mountains International Hotel Management School at Torrens University Australia (BMIHMS @TUA) was developed and that is presented and discussed in this chapter. The evaluation of the mentoring program found that mentoring relationships enable mentees to build knowledge and skills, develop networking opportunities, build confidence, and gain self-reflection abilities. The chapter offers insights and recommendations for higher education institutions to consider when setting up mentoring programs. The knowledge gained through this research will assist higher education institutions to better prepare students for a transition to work through mentoring whilst enhancing the quality of educational courses.

Chapter 15
Quality Assurance and Institutional Research for University Strategic Management: A Case Study 287
    Ngepathimo Kadhila, University of Namibia, Namibia
    Gilbert Likando, University of Namibia, Namibia

Strategic management in higher education (HE) has become data-reliant. Most higher education institutions (HEIs) all over the world have implemented quality assurance (QA) and institutional research (IR) with the purpose of generating data that that would assist in evidence-based decision making for better strategic management. However, data generated through QA and IR processes have to be integrated and streamlined in order to successfully inform strategic management. One of the challenges facing higher education institutions is to integrate the data generated by QA and IR processes effectively. This chapter examines examples of good practice for integrating the data generated by these processes for use as tools to inform strategic management, using the University of Namibia as a reference point. The chapter offers suggestions on how higher education institutions may be assisted to overcome challenges when integrating the outcomes of QA and IR processes in order to close the quality loop through effective strategic management.

Compilation of References 309

About the Contributors 354

Index 359

Preface

Higher education sector needs to attract large-scale investments as that is the key to access, affordability, and equity. Yet, the core issue until the beginning of this century remained 'quality in higher education'. Education is a complex business with many interacting facets of quality in many varied contexts. To understand what is going on it is necessary to have a way of conceiving these varied facets or variables involve (Baporikar, 2015). Quality also means different things to different people; it is relative to 'processes' or 'outcomes'. Further, education is a complex system of national, local and institutional stakeholders, public and private institutions and forces, and a broad range of professionals. It also takes responsibility for conducting every student through the formal education that should enable them to attain their learning potential, for the benefit of both individuals and society. Hence, quality is the key to increasing student performance (Baporikar, 2018a).

So, what does quality mean in the context of education? Many definitions of quality in education exist, testifying to the complexity and multifaceted nature of the concept. Incessant assessment and improvement can focus on any or all of the facets. The extent to which indicators of quality have shaped both the politics of higher education and institutional priorities is not a new phenomenon.

Given the complexity of the quality concept there is no single definition to comprehensively describe the meaning of 'quality'. That is the reason why quality discussion is based on dimensions. According to (Harvey & Knight, 1996 in Becket & Brookes, 2006:127), within the higher education field, these dimensions are "different but related". They refer to "(1) quality as exceptional (e.g. high standards); (2) quality as consistency (e.g. zero defects); (3) quality as fitness for purpose (fitting customer specifications); (4) quality as value for money, (as efficiency and effectiveness); and (5) quality as transformative (an ongoing process that includes empowerment and enhancement of customer satisfaction)." Thus, the widely differing conceptualizations of quality grouping is into five discrete but interrelated categories. Quality thus can be as exception, as perfection, as fitness for purpose, as value for money and as transformative.

Many colleges and universities have looked to apply lessons from industry and adopt some type of total quality management (TQM) systems. The high level of independence historically provided to faculty also poses a serious challenge to the implementation of quality programs in higher education, and some faculty members fear a centralized adoption of TQM principles in the classroom as a means for others, particularly administrators, to dictate what they must do in the classroom (Bass et al., 1996). However, quality in higher education can be can be designed to accommodate multiple stakeholders and the varying changing roles of students in the educational process. The academic services that higher education should provide must extend beyond the acquisition of content knowledge. Arguably, the most important

Preface

skill they should strive to teach is how to learn and think critically, given the rapid rate of change in our society, instructors who focus too much on specific content, as opposed to teaching students how to learn, risk providing their customers with a service that will be obsolete in a very short time (Baporikar, 2015).

Yet, today's learners enter institutions and education with very different expectations and assumptions about their experience compared with previous cohorts (Baporikar, 2018b). Further, increased student numbers have placed exceptional strain on a system not designed to deliver mass education. The casualty than is the quality in education and the challenge posing education is quality assurance. Quality assurance is a challenge because the groups of quality assurance audits and institutional accreditations evaluate the stakeholder relations and the service to society. Therefore, the quality assurance system should include description of stakeholder relationships (Baporikar, 2016). In this, critical situation where higher education stands with greater demands made to institutions of higher learning; continuous reforms are being made regarding the policies and practices in higher education (Baporikar, 2014). Hence, quality has become an agenda issue for various academic and professional institutions of higher learning.

Further, quality is widely accepted to be a significant source of competitive advantage (Baporikar, 2016). Although the concept of quality is as old as human history, only in the last two decades is it recognized as a crucial factor for institutional success. Quality management has gained much attention from both academics and practitioners; however, as an application to higher educational organizations is still in its infancy, especially in the governmental universities and educational institutions. Unfortunately, these government universities and institutions that use quality management and practices without thorough knowledge and awareness of them will fail to reap their true and full benefits. Therefore, it is vital to understand the concept of quality management and to align it to education sector with the individual institutions' strategy when starting a quality management initiative in order to succeed. Successful implementation and the practicing of Quality Management (QM) in the education sector improves organizational performance through increased efficiency, productivity, and innovation, ultimately, QM helps institutions and universities to make better decisions, streamline processes, reduce re-work, whilst also increasing teaching-learning integrity and greater collaboration by increasing quality knowledge creation, dissemination and transfer.

The materials included in this book cover and explore the different principles, concepts, factors, strategies, that lead to the most effective and efficient ways of utilizing, managing, and sustaining quality management in education sector organizations. In particular, the chapters focus on principles, approaches, academic leadership, faculty, teaching-learning roles, ethics, integrity, research and strategic management to enhance the quality of higher education.

The prospective audiences for this book include researchers, academics, practitioners, and students from different fields of research, such as quality management, knowledge management, educational organizational performance, policy makers, government and public administration, information technology, and developmental specialists.

This book will increase QM awareness in the education sector by providing a clear direction for the effective implementation of QM program, which could improve quality implementation and education excellence. In this sense, the intended audience includes education sector employees at various levels, any policy makers already working in the education sector, or those considering working in the field.

The book consists of 15 chapters and a brief outline of each chapter is as below:

Chapter 1 focuses on application of the quality management principles into HEIs.

Chapter 2 attempts to reviewing the higher education approach to quality management from an Indian perspective and deliberates on the tools and techniques like SIX SIGMA, LEAN, and TQM.

Chapter 3's core aim is to the study, examine and elaborate the linkage between quality management and long-term success of every educational organization.

Chapter 4 seeks to analyse critically the current state of quality management practices in higher education in Namibia at both national and institutional levels. It also identifies achievements recorded so far, as well as challenges and areas for further development.

Chapter 5 examines the role of leadership in higher education, and innovative teaching and learning methods for quality assurance in higher education system.

Chapter 6 mainly aims at examine how academic leaders can promote and manage quality in higher education institutions.

Chapter 7 presents the framework for quality accreditation in Greek universities and underlines the critical role of academic leadership for achieving accreditation and establishing a culture for sustainable excellence.

Chapter 8 deliberates the Supervisor-Student dyad through the lens of the Situational Leadership Model for enhanced quality supervision.

Chapter 9 presents an exploratory research framework designed to support quality assessment of faculty in higher education and explores whether the current quality management processes are fair for faculty and effective for the university's stakeholders.

Chapter 10 argues that when determining quality assurance in teacher education there is need to take into account not only on what *is taught* to teachers but on also how they *are taught*. New perspectives on learning and teaching at school level and the changed nature of the role of the teacher form the basis for suggesting a focus on the 'how' of teacher education in addition to or more than the 'what'. It draws on research underpinned by a critical realist philosophy to demonstrate the changed nature of the school system and the need to adopt a sociocultural approach to learning and teaching in teacher education.

Chapter 11 presents the importance of professional integrity as the improvement concept and ethics in the development of professionals in administration and management sciences.

Chapter 12 explores the role of ethical education in accelerating the quality of management education and implications of the questions of quality, dilemma and pedagogy of ethical training.

Chapter 13 focuses on the critical analysis of evidence of higher education improvement strategies in improving teaching and learning in higher education institutions. It also deliberates on several higher education improvement strategies such as preparation for accreditation and student learning assessment utilized in the area of teaching and learning in higher education institutions with diverse outcomes.

Chapter 14 discusses the valuable role mentoring programs play in higher education though the case study of the Blue Mountains International Hotel Management School at Torrens University Australia. The chapter also offers insights and recommendations for higher education institutions for setting up mentoring programs.

Chapter 15 focus is on strategic management in higher education (HE) and examines good practices for integrating data generated in quality assurance (QA) and institutional research (IR) processes for use to inform strategic management, using the University of Namibia as a reference point. It also offers suggestions for higher education institutions to overcome challenges when integrating the outcomes of QA and IR processes in order to close the quality loop through effective strategic management.

Preface

On a final note, we expect the readers and users to cherish the contents as much as enjoyed putting them together and hope that this book will further the cause of *quality higher education*, which is crucial in the emergent knowledge economy.

Neeta Baporikar
Namibia University of Science and Technology, Namibia & University of Pune, India

Michael Sony
Namibia University of Science and Technology, Namibia

REFERENCES

Baporikar, N. (2014). Introduction. In N. Baporikar (Ed.), *Handbook of Research on Higher Education in the MENA Region: Policy and Practice* (pp. 1–7). Hershey, PA: IGI Global. doi:10.4018/978-1-4666-6198-1.ch001

Baporikar, N. (2015). Quality Facets in Educational Process for Enhanced Knowledge Creation. *International Journal of Service Science, Management, Engineering, and Technology*, 6(4), 1–15. doi:10.4018/IJSSMET.2015100101

Baporikar, N. (2016). Stakeholder Approach for Quality Higher Education. In W. Nuninger & J. Châtelet (Eds.), *Handbook of Research on Quality Assurance and Value Management in Higher Education* (pp. 1–26). Hershey, PA: Information Science Reference. doi:10.4018/978-1-5225-0024-7.ch001

Baporikar, N. (2018a). Educational Leadership for Quality Teacher Education in Digital Era. In N. P. Ololube (Ed.), *Handbook of Research on Educational Planning and Policy Analysis* (pp. 241–255). Port Harcourt: Pearl Publishers.

Baporikar, N. (2018b). Policy Perspectives for Technology Usage in Higher Education. In N. P. Ololube (Ed.), *Handbook of Research on Educational Planning and Policy Analysis* (pp. 295–313). Port Harcourt: Pearl Publishers.

Bass, K., Dellana, S., & Herbert, F. (1996). Assessing the use of total quality management in the business school classroom. *Journal of Education for Business*, 72(4), 339–343. doi:10.1080/08832323.1996.10116809

Harvey, L., & Knight, P. T. (1996). *Transforming Higher Education*. Buckingham, UK: SRHE and Open University Press.

Acknowledgment

We are grateful to IGI team, for their enthusiasm and support to make the publishing process smooth and enjoyable.

We thank the editorial board members for their contribution and particularly all chapter authors for their excellent contributions.

However, our sincere gratitude goes to the reviewers both - chapter authors and other academic associates who took time to review and provide constructive comments. We appreciate their time given out of their busy schedules.

Neeta Baporikar
Namibia University of Science and Technology, Namibia & University of Pune, India

Michael Sony
Namibia University of Science and Technology, Namibia

Chapter 1
Quality Management Principles Application to Higher Educational Institutions

Jose Manuel Saiz-Alvarez
https://orcid.org/0000-0001-6435-9600
Tecnologico de Monterrey, Mexico

ABSTRACT

Higher educational institutions (HEIs) are going through a process of structural transformation in which policies based on sound management are of growing importance. A process of change observed when the student had become a client, HEIs desire being at the top of international rankings, impulse relations with organizations outside the HEI to search new opportunities focused on socioeconomic change, and the HEI strives to achieve continuous improvement. Quality management has a fundamental role to play in this transformation process. The objective of this chapter is to reason about the application of the eight quality management principles into HEIs.

INTRODUCTION

The Eight Principles of Quality Management (QM) (Customer focus, leadership, employee involvement, process approach, systematic approach management, continual improvement, evidence-based decision making, and relationship management) ground the ISO 9001 certification. As well as being guiding principles for the development of the most modern quality standard designed to benefit organizations independently of their size, they are also useful resources for management professionals looking to implement or improve QM programs.

Higher educational institutions (HEIs) are organizations focused on educating future generations having in mind the importance of business survival that is guaranteed by achieving constant revenues and controlled operating costs. Divided into public and private HEIs, they follow the same QM principles as applied to other industries and sectors, both nationally and abroad. As a result, and from a manage-

DOI: 10.4018/978-1-7998-1017-9.ch001

rial perspective, students are considered clients, while professors and researchers are like managers and employees (collaborators), and as financing instruments, financial payments made by parents are, in large part, the primary source of financial sources for private HEIs, while the public administration mainly finances public HEIs at different levels (national, regional, and/or local).

The literature related to QM practices (Hong et al., 2019; Isaksson, 2019; Tenji and Foley, 2019) assumes that employee involvement is crucial to implement the process approach in the organization, the system tactic to management through *kaizen*, and the factual strategy to decision-making (core QM practices) (Bakotić & Rogošić, 2017) As a result, while managers implement QM practices, they need a global vision of the organization, as well as a motivated human team to perform transformational leadership. These processes of change take place in any sector of activity, with the ultimate goal of maximizing EBITDA within the organization and, in the case of non-governmental organizations (NGOs), maximizing social impact.

The objective of this chapter is to analyze how the eight QM principles impact on private and public HEIs to maximize their social impact. To cope with this goal, the authors will describe these eight principles briefly to propose a new strategy based on the combination of these principles and emotional intelligence.

Background

Except for some African countries defined by the (almost) nonexistence of service companies, in the rest of the world, the services sector is becoming increasingly important, especially in the G8 countries formed by the most advanced nations of the planet in terms of gross domestic product (GDP). Ibeh et al. (2018) affirm that evidence suggests the primacy of market-seeking motivations in explaining the FDI (foreign direct investment) activities of the explored nascent African multinationals located in the primary sector, with the relationship, efficiency and mission-driven motivations emerging as strong sub-themes.

The development of the service industry in the world is leading to the client becoming increasingly important, both to offer the market the products and services that best meet their needs, and to guide indirectly in the R&D plus innovation processes of the organization. HEIs defined by offering services to both their teachers and suppliers and, above all, to their students who enroll in the university, not only because of their closeness but also to develop professionally in quality programs. Therefore, today, universities must maximize the number and quality of services offered to their clients. Educational facilities that are analyzed by supervisory bodies, both internal (unofficial) and external (official), to carry out the continuous improvement.

This reality makes it increasingly urgent to adopt the vision of executives and managers of companies located at any hierarchical level so that they can face the challenges that the unique characteristics of the service offer them. One of the significant advantages of providing services to customers is personalization; that is, each client can receive the services they need individually, being several services for different clients.

This customization of the services offered to clients deals with the growing digitization of the company. This process is happening equally, except for some countries located in Africa and Oceania, and with greater or lesser intensity, in all the nations of the world. This customization is increasing the quality of services offered in the market, so new business strategies based on quality costs as tools for quality improvement teams are crucial for business success (Campanella, 1999).

In this changing process, HEIs play a crucial role. Learning more about the part of the academic departments may improve faculty (and non-faculty) selection, development, support, and retention (Pifer, Baker, & Lunsford, 2019). In addition to promotional marketing policies, professors and researchers also play a fundamental role in the process of attracting and retaining new students, as when choosing an HEI. As happens with the process of home proximity (whether familiar or not), it has a great importance (a) the academic reputation that is very hard to achieve only after decades of hard work; (b) the enrollment cost; (c) the existence of scholarships and study aids to guarantee equal opportunities independently from sex, the social group of origin, race and religion. However, unfortunately, this equality of opportunities is broken in some countries for cultural, religious and customary reasons, so only in this case, there is discrimination based on sex, race, a social group of origin, and religion. As a result, there is no equal opportunity.

The customization of the services offered to clients and the increasingly active role played by HEIs has changed the mentality of some managers of leading companies who affirm that one of the best ways to attract new clients is through the 'economy of the experience.' The 'economy of the experience' consists of giving value to a service offered to the client so that the organization can differentiate itself from the competition in its offer to the market. An offer that also has to come guided by the eight QM principles that are shown and briefly described below.

Principle 1: Customer Focus

This principle covers both customer needs (to understand and classify clients) and customer services to achieve processes defined by total QM to exceed customers' expectations. The combination of customers' needs and services defines the utility chain in services composed by quality in the internal services of the firm, focused on influencing managers and employees, and also in the external services to enhance clients' satisfaction. In this service profit chain, employee productivity has a mediating effect in this ameliorating process (Adeinat and Kassim, 2019).

When firms and HEIs are focused on clients, they classify them according to what firms desire from them. As a result, four types of clients can be distinguished (lead, iron/silver, gold, and platinum) to offer them distinct products and services to maximize EBITDA (Earnings Before Interests, Taxes, Depreciation, and Amortization). As a result of this classification among clients, the marketing policy will focus on each of the groups in a personalized manner, offering a series of advantages in services to those located at higher levels with the ultimate goal of increasing their loyalty. Following this strategy, firms will tend to increase their income to the organization, which in turn will benefit the stakeholders, especially shareholders.

As the organization improves the ability to spot new customer opportunities, customer loyalty increases, revenue rises, and as a result, waste diminishes. As a result, more effective processes result in higher customer satisfaction. One of the significant advantages of focusing the organization on clients is the decrease in the external financing of banks and financial intermediaries. This fact is fundamental in those countries in which, mainly due to the weakness of the national currency, and high-interest rates that widely exceed the two digits. In these nations, it is challenging for national organizations to survive because the payment of interests absorbs a large part of the profits. An absorption process can be total when the inflation rate is also high.

Related to this principle, the ISO organization proposes eight actions to take for making firms to grow. These actions are summarized as follows (The British Assessment Bureau, 2018),

a) Actively manage relationships with customers to achieve sustained success
b) Communicate customer needs and expectations throughout the organization.
c) Determine and take actions on interested parties' needs and expectations that can affect customer satisfaction.
d) Link the organization's objectives to customer needs and expectations.
e) Measure and monitor customer satisfaction and take appropriate actions.
f) Plan, design, develop, produce, deliver and support goods and services to meet customer needs and expectations.
g) Understand customers' current and future needs and expectations.
h) Recognize direct and indirect customers as those who receive value from the organization.

The application of these actions combined with reducing costs' strategies increases customer value, corporate reputation, customer satisfaction and loyalty, revenues, and market share. In other words, organizations retain customers because every aspect of customer interaction provides an opportunity to create more value for actual and future customers, so firms maximize their EBITDA.

In addition to the clients, with whose payments they capitalize on the organization, a second crucial factor that directly influences the results of the organization, is given by the leadership of the human team that works in the HEI. As an internal engine of the organization, it is essential to find leaders who dynamize the entire production process, whether it be products or services, carried out by the organization. This process is what will be seen in the next section.

Principle 2: Leadership

Organizations in general and HEIs, in particular, must have executives endowed with leadership to compete internationally effectively. As the organization grows, the innate leadership of the founders must be accompanied by the ability for teamwork to motivate and get the best out of the entire human resources of the firm. The mixture of leadership with good practices in human resources management leads to business growth that contributes to guaranteeing the survival of the organization in globalized and competitive environments.

A business flounders when the mission, vision, and objectives are not clear for stakeholders and managers with a lack of leadership. This situation is especially dramatic when employees are not actively involved in achieving organizational targets due to the ignorance of the mission and vision of their organization. When both are clear to all stakeholders, at this moment an authentic pride (Tracy et al., 2009) of belonging to the company begins to emerge and, as a result, the organization attracts the best human resources existing in the market. In this way, employees become the best sellers of the company, both the brand and its products and services offered to the market, which has a positive impact on corporate reputation. Reputation directly linked to pride and leadership, as Yeung and Shen (2019) show, authentic pride is associated with the use of more effective (e.g., consideration and initiating structure) and fewer ineffective (e.g., abusive supervision) leadership behaviors, and hubristic pride links to abusive practices (Tracy et al., 2009).

Also, the benefits born from satisfied stakeholders guided by leaders are higher levels of employee engagement, the attraction of clients, and increased motivation to satisfy customer needs. If employees are kept 'in the loop' and understand the firm, they will be more productive. This principle seeks to rectify employees' complaints about the 'lack of communication' between managers and employees.

To avoid the 'lack of communication' problem, Wang et al. (2019) show that positive affects partially mediate the relationship between transformational leadership and employee voice behavior. Employee voice is the way people communicate their views to their employer. As a result, this communication is crucial to the organization, as an excellent bottom-up communication can avoid future problems, especially in large organizations. In this sense, communication enhances with the intensive use of ICTs in the organization.

Communication is a crucial factor for developing transformational leadership in managers and highly over-qualified employees. At this respect, Putra and Cho (2019) show that the ideal skills to achieve sustainable leadership are respect, compassion, effective communication, experience, effective delegation, recognition, sociability, controlled emotions, and organization. A good communication process diminishes inefficiencies and avoids present and futures imbalances in production and services offered in HEIs. As a result, there is a

a) Better coordination in the organizational process.
b) Higher development process and improvement of the capability of organizations and stakeholders to deliver desired results.
c) Increased communication between organizational departments and functions of the organization.
d) Higher efficiency and effectiveness in meeting the organization's quality objectives.

To carry out this process of change, it is necessary for the existence of leaders within the organizations — leaders chosen for their professional merits and not for relationships of kinship or friendship. As a result, it is essential to combine labor flexibility with high-quality production or service offered in the market to increase productivity and improving the working environment. Especially in the HEIs, relations between academics must be based on trust and not on the imposition of a few managers, who, in many cases, have less merit than the people they lead.

Leading organizations often work with other leading organizations that work in their industry. This fact is especially palpable in universities and research centers where people tend to prevail over the institutions where they work. Therefore, there is a lot of collaboration between different universities, especially in the case of public universities, as they do not compete with each other, by providing an educational service to society. Hence, these collaborative ties extend to universities in other regions, countries and even continents, thus becoming a leader the university conducting these relationships.

Only the leading universities are capable of lasting in the long run, because the educational organizations attract students by reputation, rather than having cheaper tuitions. For this reason, the most critical asset of HEIs is the teaching staff and researchers, with the attraction of students the ultimate result of this process. A process of change that has to come from continuous improvement (*kaizen*) to stay in the forefront that is, to be in the 'crest of the wave' throughout this process.

In addition to leadership and clients, a third element that influences the quality of management is given by involving people in the organization, either directly or indirectly, as will be seen in the next section.

Principle 3: Engagement of People (Employee Involvement)

Employee involvement refers to the opportunities for employees to take part in decisions affecting their work, either in their next job (task discretion) or concerning broader company issues (organizational participation) (Eurofund, 2016). When talking about employee participation in the decision-making process, it is customary to distinguish between direct employee participation (direct interaction between managers and employees) and indirect employee participation (local trade unions or works councils).

The engagement of people increases efficiency and effectiveness in HEIs, as well-managed processes reduce costs, improve consistency, eliminate waste, and promote continuous improvement. In this ameliorating process, managers' personality plays a crucial role in deciding the strategic direction of the firm and hence the performance of the company (Shalender & Yadav, 2019). As a result, people manage the organization effectively and efficiently; it is mandatory to involve all intellectual capital (defined by the sum of human capital, relational capital, and structural capital) at all levels and to respect them as individuals. As a result, when managers and directors introduce recognition and empowerment policies in the organization, competence enhances, and the engagement of stakeholders linked to organizational quality objectives can be achieved.

At this respect, García-Torres (2019) shows that teachers' perceptions of distributed leadership are significantly and positively associated with their job satisfaction after accounting for other individual and school culture variables, with reciprocal mediation between distributed leadership and professional collaboration. It is essential to have high levels of professionalism to be successful throughout this process.

When collaborators and stakeholders fully understand the benefits derived from their participation in the organization, some essential benefits can be achieved by the HEIs. Among others, organizations can improve activities (number and quality) to benefit society, increase people satisfaction and organizational reputation, and enhance personal development, initiatives, trust, collaboration, and creativity. As a result, there is increased attention to shared values and culture throughout the organization, as well as achieving a deeper understanding of the overall organization.

By becoming a more efficient organization, HEIs will build confidence in their stakeholders by optimizing performance and excellent managerial skills. Managerial processes defined by making responsibilities clear to ensure physical and human resources used with efficiency.

To make these advantages possible, HEIs can

a) Conduct surveys to assess stakeholders' satisfaction, communicate the results, and take appropriate actions.
b) Empower people for performance and collaboration.
c) Self-evaluate against personal objectives.
d) Share knowledge and experience.
e) Understand the importance of their contribution and recognize it.

The integration of the stakeholders in the organization allows the creation of associations of former students who not only make a strong network of contacts among them but also help universities and research centers in their financing needs. So, it is very reasonable for alumni to donate a tree to the gardens of the university, and even donate money so that, e.g., some classrooms bear their names, given that they have renovated or modernized them. Alumni donations generate a snowball effect where alumni donations raise a university's reputation, which in turn creates additional alumni donations (Faria, Mixon, and Upadhyaya, 2019).

This process of improvement strengthens when activities are understood and managed as interrelated processes that function as a coherent system. This fact is what we will see in the following principle.

Principle 4: Process Approach

Independently from the industry and sector where any organization operates, the QM system consists of interrelated processes. Understanding how this system produces results enables firms and HEIs to optimize their operations and performance, so both EBITDA and social impact maximize. This process approach relates to achieving higher levels of efficiency, consistency, effectiveness, and understanding that well-designed processes also speed up activities. The application of this principle in the organization optimizes production processes, reduces costs, improves labor and production-related consistencies, eliminates waste, and promotes continuous improvement in the HEI. The main reason for this improvement deals with consistent and predictable outcomes, and optimized performances through active management and efficient use of resources focused on effectiveness and efficiency.

Organizations must define their goals and the necessary managing interrelated processes to achieve efficient educational operations after having understood the organization's capabilities and experience to take advantage of these actions. In this process, HEIs must ensure that the necessary information is available to evaluate the performance of the overall system where operating risks should be diminished or avoided.

To assure optimization in managing, initially in Japan and then worldwide, organizations use the 5S managerial technique to organize a workplace for efficiency and decrease non-value added activities with the final goal of optimizing quality and productivity through monitoring an organized environment (Singh, Rastogi, & Sharma, 2014).

When organizations combine the 5S, as shown in Figure 1, with *kaizen* (continuous improvement) and TQM (total quality management), firms increase their competitiveness and profit maximization. Deeping into the 5S, several business-related concepts and ideas can be added, as follows

a) *Seiri* (Sort). Non-profit and for-profit organizations are obliged to be efficient with the aim of achieving their goals and to satisfy stakeholders, and especially clients' wishes and desires. To do so, it is necessary to know clients' needs through relational marketing, to achieve a more significant commitment of the company towards its clients where it is essential to achieve continuous levels of contact and quality over time. The intensive use of ICT and even the analysis of big data is fundamental to achieve this aim, especially when the volume of data to be managed is considerable.

b) *Seiton* (Set in order). One of the advantages of achieving high levels of order in the organization is given because the firm avoids the waste of resources, which is why both the use of resources and labor productivity are optimized. Also, when the company is ordered, sales increase by optimally using time, avoiding duplication in purchases.

Figure 1. The 5-S as a Tool to Achieve Efficiency
Source: Author

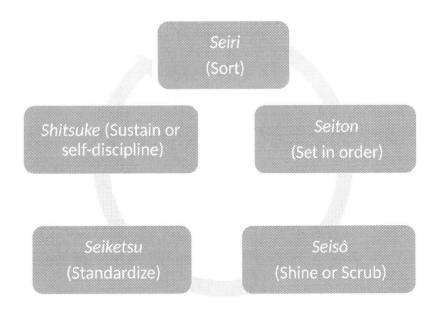

c) *Seisô* (Shine or scrub). Cluttered and dirty workplaces increase the risk of accidents (Grover, Dalal, & Singh, 2016), so it is crucial to eliminate (or at least diminish) this labor risk.

d) *Seiketsu* (Standardize). Based on the three previous "S" and visual control, managers and employees assure that everything is controlled. As a result, and from the knowledge generated above, the critical information is highlighted, meaning that the time required to understand the information reduces significantly, which avoids an overload of information so that employees can see their results and improve the working environment by creating a habit of keeping the job site impeccable permanently, which increases productivity. Also, organizations avoid errors in cleaning that can lead to accidents or unnecessary work risks.

e) *Shitsuke* (Sustain or Self-discipline). By following the previous "S" defined by established standards and policies, there is greater awareness of the job and respect for people, which increases motivation and creates a culture of sensitivity, respect, and care for the company's resources. All this leads to the client feeling more satisfied because of higher quality levels since the established procedures and rules have been fully respected.

Besides 5S, some specific methods and techniques belonging to the *Kaizen* strategy have been successfully applied in organizations, such as: Lean, Six Sigma, Balanced Scorecard, Poka-Yoke, JIT (Just-in-Time), and Kanban (Ghicajanu, 2019). As a result, organizations have tools in their hands to optimize their productive and commercial processes and thus make much more efficient structures. As a result, the application of the 5S model combined with the implementation of TQM-related techniques achieves better results, especially when the organization implements quality-related norms, as will be seen in the following principle.

Principle 5: Systematic Approach to Management

The International Organization for Standardization (ISO) norms have the goal of identifying, internalizing, and managing interrelated production and distribution processes to maximize effectiveness and efficiency in products, processes, services, and systems in firms, and it only achieves satisfactory results when the norm is applied judiciously and responsibly so that it has the expected effects (Tutida, 2019). One of the significant advantages of applying ISO norms in organizations, independently of the sector they operate, is that the ISO norms ensure quality in the archival processes, and also standardize and make flexible the complexity existing within organizational environments. A complexity level that is inherent to the metamorphosis of each's functional context (Do Nascimento, Moro-Cabero, & Valentim, 2018).

Also, complex business environments have the risk of wasting operating resources that are scarce by definition. As businesses focus their efforts on the key processes to maximize EBITDA, as well as aligning complementary processes to get better efficiency, multiple operations must be managed together as a system to achieve a higher efficiency level. As a result, it is necessary to complement the ISO norms with QM systems (Ost & Da Silveira, 2018). QM systems defined as a compilation of patterns that every organization in search of continuous improvement must apply to project an integral development (Hernández, Martínez, & Rodríguez, 2017), with the final aim of optimizing the use of resources to create synergies between HEIs, firms, and the public sector (Simonova & Fomenko, 2017).

It is crucial to deliver a systematic and grounded approach to achieve higher levels of efficient management. According to Ferreira and Lopes (2017), the implementation of ISO 9000 certification in HEIs ameliorates both internal restructuring - related to units' management and functioning, as well as with the employees' awareness of the quality of the services provided; and external restructuring - linked to the promotion of units' image/ reputation and customers' satisfaction. Regarding HRM practices, some changes were identified in the planning and managing of work, job analysis and description, lifelong learning, and educational growth, both for professors and researchers, and students. Also, the implementation of the ISO 9000 certification increased individual efficiency and efficacy in employees' job performance and in academic and research achievements. As a result, there is a more exceptional quality in orientation and control, and increased levels of motivation and accountability can be achieved, which increase the quality of the service provided to benefit HEIs.

One of the main reasons for the lack of effective operation of the quality system is the defectiveness of the information system, in particular when highlighting problems with maintaining control over the required documentation, the quality process realization that is too labor-intensive, and an inadequate way of training employees (Trąbka, 2015). Intensive use of ICTs can contribute to solving these problems, especially the work related to the exhaustive bureaucratic control of all the operations associated with the power of the teaching and research activity generating a high volume of documentation. The digitalization of such bureaucratic processes will reduce costs and will give greater flexibility to the whole process, as well as will increase the quality in the control, classification, and use of information.

Besides achieving a systematic approach to quality-related management, one of the keys for HEIs to survive is obtaining a sustainable and good academic reputation. As a result, it is mandatory for HEIs to be in continuous improvement. The following principle will describe this fact.

Principle 6: Continual Improvement

The arrival of the new industrial revolution with the universalization of the Internet has increased the competition between universities and research centers to attract the best professors and students on the planet. These efforts focused on attraction are especially more intense in private and global universities, rather than in public universities, many of which have a national focus only, especially those HEIs classified away from the first places in the QS and Shanghai rankings, among others. In this process of attraction, and given the Internet and the existence of faster means of communication thanks to the use of ICT and a quicker means of transportation, the academic and research worlds are currently producing more 'circulation of brains' than 'brain drain.' In general, this situation occurs in all sectors of those countries whose economies compete internationally, where nations endowed with stronger beliefs that climbing the social ladder can be realized by own hard work, attract a higher proportion of high-skilled immigrants over time (Lumpe, 2019).

Not only in the education sector does this process of continuous improvement occur. More than 70% of companies are currently in the service sector, so constant improvement (*kaizen*) is essential to survive. The customer (student) must always be taken into account in the sales process, especially in private universities. Since both academic and research reputation of the HEI fuel organizational prestige, it is fundamental to attract the best professors and researchers to the organization to make possible a future stronger attraction of clients (students) and capital for research. Therefore, universities and research centers that are not guided by quality, in the medium term they will be affected by a loss of academic and research prestige that, in the long run, can even cause the disappearance of the organization or, in the better case, the selling of the company.

As a result, achieving a continual improvement is a must for globalized companies, and should be a business goal for HEIs. However, many public universities worldwide are reluctant to treat their students as clients, as done for decades in almost all of the private universities in the world. Opposed to the idea that this change is leading to a process of commercialization of the university, this change of mentality favors the student who, when treated as a client, receives better and more services endowed with higher quality standards. Quality levels that, combined with reduced prices, achieve a good relationship between price and quality that is maintained over time.

In this process of improvement, the human resources play a crucial role, as shown by McCormick, Guay, Colbert, and Stewart (2019), who indicate that organizations desiring proactive employee behavior must select dynamic employees; develop transformational leaders who will motivate, inspire, and support employees, and create a climate that rewards innovation and labor flexibility.

Employee dynamic behavior is the beginning of intrapreneurship, also known as corporate entrepreneurship or corporate venturing (Burgelman, 1983). Corporate venturing is the practice of developing a new firm within an existing organization, to exploit a unique opportunity and create economic value (Pinchot, 1985, cited by Parker, 2009). Organizations defined by entrepreneurship are the leaders in their sectors because intra-enterprises make continuous improvements (*kaizen*) within the company, which in turn leads to an EBITDA increase within the organization.

In this process of change, decision making is of growing importance, especially in international team works defined by their divergence, mainly represented by their discrepancy in daily operations, as in the behavior needed in critical moments of the company. The creation of multidisciplinary teams' increases productivity provided that (a) employees know how to work in international environments; (b) the organization has leaders who are respected by all levels of the organization; and (3) employees have high levels of responsibility and are able to make suggestions for improvement at crucial moments throughout intrapreneurship.

These efforts made by the organization increase the EBITDA, which allows rewarding stakeholders, and mainly the investors of the project, who took risks throughout the investment process. Risks that must always be controlled if managers want to succeed and to obtain proper business results to benefit the organization after the activity and efforts have been made. A well-defined short-term and long-term strategy must be in place in the organization to achieve this goal. Organizational strategy adequately transmitted to the team and planned for its continuity over time and based on the evidence needed for attaining a grounded decision-making process. The next section will analyze this fact.

Principle 7: Evidence-based Decision Making

Regarding the factual approach to decision-making, Etzioni (1967) distinguishes three theories: (a) the *rationalistic approach*, defined by how decisions are and ought to be made. As a result, an individual becomes aware of a problem, posits a goal, carefully weighs alternative means, and chooses among them according to the estimation of their respective merit, with reference to the state of affairs preferred; (b) the *incrementalist theory*, which seeks to adapt decision-making strategies to the limited cognitive capacities of decision-makers and to reduce the scope and cost of information collection and computation; (c) the *mixed-scanning approach* that provides both a realistic description of the strategy used by the managing directors of the organization for achieving higher efficiency and effectiveness. Current organizations tend to adopt a mixture of the three theories due to the existence of a highly competitive global environment where providing leaders with practical information and tools can help in decision making and improving performance (Yanar et al., 2019).

Decision-making processes should be made gradually to have business success in this global environment and to avoid internal tensions that can damage the organization. At this respect, Yang and Yang (2019) affirm that any organization should increase process innovation in a moderately competitive environment, but not in a fiercely competitive environment where a stronger transformational leadership should be adopted. In other words, changes in organizations must be consecutive over time, without excessively aggressive measures that may cause the opposite effect to the desired one within the organization. Therefore, the changes have to be a fine-tuning policy, that is, following a process of gradual adjustment to go, so not only adapting the organization to changes but also to have room to maneuver to make adjustments if necessary.

As a result, a logical approach, based on data and analysis, is endowed of a good business sense. Unfortunately, in a fast-paced workplace, decisions can often be made rashly, without proper thought (The British Assessment Bureau, 2018). Implementing QM principles will allow transparent decisions that are of increasing importance as informed decisions lead to improved understanding of the marketplace. When the process is more open, there will be better reactions from the stakeholders, which will improve the pride of belonging of the human capital working in the organization, as well as improving both image and corporate reputation of the organization.

Having a quick and effective decision-making process solves problems arisen in the firms' day to day operations, as well as transforms structural issues inside the organization. The managers of any organization must avoid short-term and medium-run problems that can easily be solved in the organization to become rooted if they continue to be unsolved, which are more complicated to explain. Therefore, time is a crucial variable in the QM processes, because low quality of services (e.g., educational, after sales, or health) offered to the client, whether student, client or patient, influences decisively in the good (or bad) organizational results.

One of the keys to succeeding in this process of change is the provision of intellectual capital with sufficient training and experience (human capital), endowed with a large number of contacts around the world (relational capital) and that can be successfully developed within organizations (structural capital). At this respect, Bakotić and Rogošić (2017) show that employee involvement through different concepts (employee training, communication, empowerment and rewards, and recognition) has a positive impact on the implementation of the process approach, system approach to management, continual improvement, and factual approach to decision-making.

Employment involvement is reinforced in organizations when the commitment of the organization's stakeholders is growing. This commitment is directly related to the feeling of belonging to the organization, as well as if the employees are shareholders of the company listed on the stock exchange. Good relations with the suppliers make positive feelings even stronger, as shown in the following principle.

Principle 8: Mutually Beneficial Supplier Relations (Relationship Management)

This principle promotes the relationship between the organization and its suppliers dealing with supply chains to recognize that they are interdependent. This strong relationship enhances productivity and encourages seamless working practices that it lays the foundations for the beginning of a later process of vertical integration or, in its case, to initiate an M&A (mergers and acquisitions) process among the organizations.

As in the case of the industrial sector, the implementation of vertical integration processes in the education sector is a strategy that, in addition to diminishing (and in some cases eliminating) the risk of student recruitment, in turn, maximizes benefits. The result is the costs and resources' optimization, improving and building long-term relationships and the 'flexibility of joint responses to changing the market or customer needs and expectations.' Also, vertical integration processes reduce operating costs, which allows achieving leadership positions in the market, especially when there is a process of transformational leadership. At this respect, Afsar, Shahjehan, Shah, and Wajid (2019) show that non-national employees with a higher level of cultural intelligence are more likely to display voice behaviors. Furthermore, this relationship is partially mediated by transformational leadership.

Transformational leadership is especially intense in education. At this respect, Luyten and Bazo (2019) show that the effect of transformational leadership on teaching practices is substantial but indirect, running via professional learning communities and teacher learning, so the impact (direct and indirect) of professional learning communities on teaching practices is particularly strong. One of the problems of transformational leadership is that, when communication between stakeholders fails, it generates conflicts. At this respect, Lee et al. (2019) show that task conflict is directly and positively related to team creativity and is negatively and indirectly related to team creativity via relationship conflict. Furthermore, they find that team-focused transformational leadership moderates all paths through which task conflict affects team creativity. Specifically, team-focused transformational leadership enhances the positive direct effect of task conflict and alleviates the adverse indirect effects of task conflict on team creativity.

A QUALITY MANAGEMENT MODEL APPLIED TO HEIs

By combining the given QM mentioned above principles with emotional intelligence, the authors propose the following theoretical model, as shown in figure 2. Besides, regarding the eight QM principles, Yu, To and Lee (2012) show that both leadership and customer attention are much more focused than previously anticipated for successful implementation of a QM system.

The graphical model consists of two parts. The first part has to do with stakeholders, whether they are clients or internal personnel of the organization. This focus on the consumer turns the user into the final customer, so all efforts HEIs make must be directed towards attracting new customers and building loyalty to existing consumers. Therefore, the focus on customers has a direct impact on relationship management, together with the need to unite all the stakeholders that have a direct relationship with the firm.

When companies are customer focused, customer knowledge can form a sort of co-creation value network to benefit the firm (Bagheri, Kusters and Trienekens, 2019). Customer knowledge transfer is difficult due to some recognizable challenges (e.g., lack of trust and bad reputation), so the value chain is negatively affected. Increasing the capacity to achieve more efficient value chains is one of the organizational goals to reach new markets and to expand existing ones. Value chains are what makes companies succeed in the market, so it is always necessary to be improved and adapted to market demands continuously. Not knowing how to change to the market will lead to losses to the company and, in extreme cases, to bankruptcy.

For this reason, the four central variables (Systematic approach to management, Process approach, Continual improvement, and Evidence-based decision making) are connected (Figure 2). The process approach determines the vision and the values of the firm, without affecting the mission that, by definition, is much more general. In this process, the objective is to eliminate (or at least reduce) productive

Figure 2. A QM model applied to HEIs
Source: Author

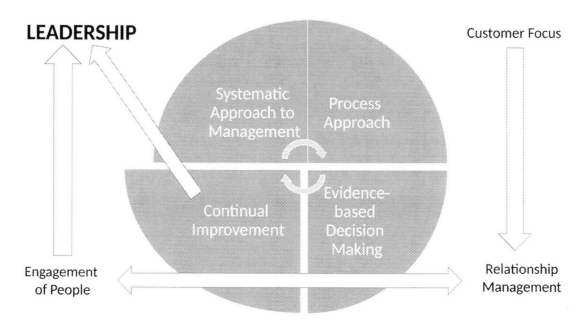

inefficiencies with the application of lean strategies and the outsourcing, if necessary, of the most inefficient products and services that are part of the company's production and distribution chains.

It is necessary to implement *kaizen* policies of continuous improvement with the impulse of strategies based on evidence-based decision-making to attract new clients and build loyalty. This evidence allows the organization to have a historical memory that is usually useful to be successful in future decision-making by having previous experience. Besides, the professional experience born of the evidence allows us to initiate a process of continuous improvement leading to leadership in the medium term.

This process approach must be grounded on evidence-based decision making. In many companies, the evidence born from labor experience and the historical data attached to them, constitute the experience of the company, so it is mandatory to have the computer systems that are necessary to keep all the information stored. In this way, bad decision-making and wrong strategies are avoided when learning from experience. A working knowledge that, when addressed to brands, generate experiential value for creating integrated resort customers' co-creation behavior (Ahn et al., 2019).

Also, this process of continuous improvement (*kaizen*) facilitates the company to increase the commitment of its stakeholders within the organization, as well as to carry out a growing development in the decision making the process and the handling of all the information available in the organization. Today, the processing of large volumes of data is possible within organizations thanks to big data, so that it is increasingly cheaper to analyze large amounts of information in less time. This fact is of particular interest in those HEIs with a large number of graduates (*alumni*) and students in training since it is possible to create an extensive database to later carry out a follow-up process of each of current and future students.

All this managerial process will be successful only if the organization designs sounded strategic policies and direct them towards the final client (student and alumni). What this group of students and alumni expects is the realization of activities related to the 'economy of the experience,' so that a lasting memory remains in each one of them who will communicate it to future and current students. In this way, the students become ambassadors of the organization, as they grow in them a vivid pride of belonging to the institution. This pride of belonging can be enhanced with the design and introduction of a smart marketing campaign defined by the sale of numerous (and preferably cheap) promotional items (merchandising) that may even be carried by other students and teachers who do not study or work in the organization. For this reason, it is always suitable for the educational institution to democratize and popularize all merchandising articles to the market, in general, so that the organization will get publicized at no cost while increasing the level of pride of its stakeholders towards the organization. This process is even faster when the sales process is carried out in an official store that may also be outside the main buildings of the organization.

When customers standardize the practice of global and shared experiences (Yoon, 2014) digitally shared using social networks, the economy of experience is quickly spread out, and more clients will be attracted. The primary reason for this fact is to know that the economy of the experience is a fruitful way of value creation (Boswijk, 2012) and that it lasts (sometimes forever) in the consumers' memory. It is precisely these good memories that feed the creation of alumni with a dual purpose: (a) to become a lobby to external stakeholders, and (b) to help each other by transforming their social and economic realities for their benefit. Hence, the creation of alumni and student groups are a way to scale socially, do business, and to achieve better living standards. And even to get married, on many occasions.

Next, to the creation of alumni, a second aspect that directly affects the production of value for the organization is given by the realization of proper relationship management. In an increasingly linked society where HEIs are increasingly known, the IoT (Internet of Things) paradigm connects the physical world and cyberspace via physical (smart) objects and facilitate the development of smart applications and infrastructures that possess information processing abilities (Roopa et al., 2019). When the IoT is socially conceived (SIoT), the new SIoT enhances information sharing, supports new applications and provides reliable and trustworthy networking solutions utilizing social networks and smart objects. As a result, SIoT improves digital and relationship management of alumni and other students' associations to benefit HEIs.

When HEIs consider both alumni and graduate students as clients, this perception fosters the culture of services to offer better attention and monitoring of students (past, present, and future). Therefore, and contrary to those who think that considering a student as a client is equivalent to commercializing the university, the reality is that when the student is viewed as a client, it usually improves the service offered to students by the organizations having the client the possibility of evaluating the service. For this reason, it has been a private university that has advanced to the public university by considering students as clients. Some clients are more demanding towards the teaching staff and towards the institution, as they pay more for the services and the educational quality they receive.

Given the current process of economic globalization, and the quick development of both MOOCs (Massive Open Online Courses) and virtual education based on social interaction (Fang et al., 2019; Weinhardt and Sitzmann, 2019), it is leading to educational opportunities on a global scale, mainly if the European educational model is characterized, opposite in the United States, by low enrollment costs (with some exceptions only). As a result, the presence of European universities in developing countries is becoming increasingly important, especially in Latin America and the Caribbean, where it is widespread the signing of bilateral (and even multilateral) agreements between Spanish Universities and Latin American HEIs.

The signing of these agreements allows organizations to achieve leadership positions, first nationally and, in some cases, internationally. Leadership positions that help to attract students and teachers, creating a virtuous circle that benefits the organization in the medium and long term. The digital economy is changing the required traits needed for sustainable leadership, as leaders must face the problem of a new dialectical co-operation between the teamwork and the market (Guryanova, Krasnov, and Frolov, 2020), so a new paradigm is emerging based on the capacity of remote control and the excellent management of new technologies.

The economic globalization in which a large part of humanity is inserted also has a direct impact on education. Due to this reason, the authors of this work add a type of university to the traditional division between public and private: the 'global university' that is defined to be known worldwide, although its impact may be not planetary. These types of universities exist mainly in Europe and the United States, although there are also global universities in Latin America, Asia and, with less impact, in Oceania and Africa. These global universities form global leaders, whose effects exceed those achieved in their countries and regions of origin. Getting this type of leaders trained should be the goal of any HEI that wants to have a highly sustainable and firmly anchored reputation in the long run.

FUTURE RESEARCH DIRECTIONS

Given the economic globalization, the organization's clients find more and more information in real time about the product or service to be acquired, so obtaining high levels of quality in the service is fundamental to attract new customers and retain loyalty. This relationship between the quality of service and customer loyalty, in any sector considered, has been little studied in the existing economic literature on QM. Quality of service that is increasingly affected by ZMOT (Zero Moment of Truth), FMOT (First Moment of Truth) and SMOT (Second Moment of Truth) consumers' decisions.

A second research direction will be how emotional intelligence interacts with QM. The five essential capacities of emotional intelligence (discover emotions and feelings, recognize them, manage them, create their motivation, and manage personal relationships)(Goleman, 2018), directly affect the excellent performance of the organization, so that it is worthwhile to delve into the psychological aspects of this interaction.

A third research line is to study how these QM principles influence on the formation of pride (authentic and hubristic). Pride directly impacts the sense of belonging to the organization, which positively affects the attraction of customers, the increase in income and, as a result, business profit generation. Also, pride loyalty to stakeholders in the medium and long run guarantees financial stability in the organization and ensures its continuity, even for generations.

CONCLUSION

The objective of any HEI is to leave a legacy in time, to have a social impact that is memorable, both in its local scope and internationally. The higher the result, the greater the heritage, prestige, and reputation the organization achieves. Some global institutions only play an essential role that is irreplaceable in the world where we live.

One of the essential rights in the Charter of the United Nations is the right to education. A dignified and quality education. All civil, cultural, economic, political and social rights can be better enjoyed if a minimum education has been received. Therefore, it is now possible to provide cheap and high-quality education with the help of new technologies. We are living in the era of communications, and it is an ethical and moral obligation for governments and HEIs to offer quality education to their students who will be the future managers of the nations where they live.

According to Azizaman et al. (2014), only four out of eight QM principles can be used to monitor quality according to the ISO 9001:2008 norm: Student focus, total employee involvement, factual approach to decision making, and continuous improvement. This last principle exerts the highest influence on the satisfaction of students, as compared to the other three QM principles. However, all HEIs should be focused on students to guarantee a minimum quality of teaching, R&D, and innovation. To achieve this goal, the best strategy is for HEI to make a solid academic reputation for attracting the best professors, researchers, and students. The educational world lives from its knowledge, the transmission of such experience and academic reputation, compliance with schedules, preparation of classes, quality of knowledge shared between professors and students, and research reputation with the publication of books, book chapters, proceedings, and papers.

HEIs' strategies aimed at continuous improvement (*kaizen*) lead to higher quality in both teaching and research, which results into better training for students, as well as the achievement of a growing social impact and corporate prestige for the HEI, where the 5S technique is of great importance. At this respect, Ramesh and Ravi (2016) show the 5S as a useful tool for improvement of organization's safety performance, but only if the top and middle managers implement the program, as they are an example for their professors and researchers (Barcia & Hidalgo, 2006). This fact is especially visible in small educational organizations where management, in many cases, is linked to teaching as it is reduced the distance between educational institution's owners, professors and administration and services personnel working in the organization. For this reason, one of the essential responsibilities of the owner of the organization is to achieve cohesion intensively to the entire organization, so that the desired goals can be achieved.

HEIs develop and survive according to their corporate reputation and leadership. A leadership that, increasingly and more than teaching, has more to do with research and the implementation of *kaizen* processes in the organization. The evidence daily generated, both in R&D and education, are the basis for the organization to be accredited by public and private bodies, both national and international. These certifications conceived to assure quality are mandatory in countries with advanced and highly-competitive educational systems.

Even more critical than in other sectors, the educational industry is defined by teamwork where training and experience are of increasing importance over time. The knowledge capacity is not limited in time and has a higher value as professors-researchers have a more significant number of publications resulting from more extensive research experience and more grounded teaching experience. Therefore, the struggle between HEIs to capture these highly-specialized human resources is growing, as they tend to be scarce, knowing that professors and researchers are the most important active in a HEIs. Because without them, with the help of administration and services staff, HEIs could not survive in a competitive environment.

The digitalization with the incorporation of new technologies in the classroom (face-to-face or virtual) is both changing the way of teaching and researching. The combination of work between interdisciplinary teams located (or not) in remote places, the constant updating of knowledge, and the use of researchers anywhere in the world in real time, is changing the educational paradigm. These means that the new learning tools existing in the market will tend to improve the educational levels of the population, but they will never replace the active presence of professors who will continue to be responsible for the education of their students. The human environment is irreplaceable, although catastrophic voices are assuming that professors will disappear after the incorporation of virtual environments in the classroom.

Throughout this process of improvement, the QM principles have a fundamental role to play if they wish to have excellent educational results. The involvement of all stakeholders towards the achievement of a common objective constitutes a united force leading to continuous improvement in the decision-making process based on evidence. Evidence that, on many occasions, are even useful for future generations, given that organizations tend to remain in time.

Working in the educational sector entails a high responsibility for professors and researchers, as they are responsible for the quality training of future generations, as well as to improve knowledge and skills in the current ones educationally. Being a professor-researcher is a vocation that requires significant effort and dedication daily, so not everyone reaches the final goal. And in this process of continuous improvement, the eight principles of quality management are of increasing importance, as the competition among HEIs is becoming stronger in a global educational market.

ACKNOWLEDGMENT

This research was supported in Mexico by a research project collaboration between EGADE Business School-Tecnologico de Monterrey, the National Council of Science and Technology (CONACYT), and the Mexican Academy of Sciences. I thank the first two institutions for their financial support, and the anonymous referees for their comments.

REFERENCES

Adeinat, I., & Kassim, N. (2019). Extending the service profit chain: The mediating effect of employee productivity. *International Journal of Quality & Reliability Management, 36*(5), 797–814. doi:10.1108/IJQRM-03-2018-0064

Afsar, B., Shahjehan, A., Shah, S. I., & Wajid, A. (2019). The mediating role of transformational leadership in the relationship between cultural intelligence and employee voice behavior: A case of hotel employees. *International Journal of Intercultural Relations, 69*, 66–75. doi:10.1016/j.ijintrel.2019.01.001

Ahn, J., Lee, C.-K., Back, K.-J., & Schmitt, A. (2019). Brand experiential value for creating integrated resort customers' co-creation behavior. *International Journal of Hospitality Management, 81*, 104–112. doi:10.1016/j.ijhm.2019.03.009

Azizaman, N., Ariff, M., Zakuan, N., & Ismail, K. (2014). ISO 9001:2008 implementation in higher education: Does it contributes to student satisfaction? The Role of Service in the Tourism and Hospitality Industry. *Proceedings of the 2nd International Conference on Management and Technology in Knowledge, Service, Tourism and Hospitality, SERVE 2014*, 45-50.

Bagheri, S., Kusters, R. J., & Trienekens, J. J. M. (2019). Customer knowledge transfer challenges in a co-creation value network: Toward a reference model. *International Journal of Information Management, 47*, 198–214. doi:10.1016/j.ijinfomgt.2018.12.019

Bakotić, D., & Rogošić, A. (2017). Employee involvement as a key determinant of core quality management practices. *Total Quality Management & Business Excellence, 28*(11-12), 1209–1226. doi:10.1080/14783363.2015.1094369

Barcia, K. F., & Hidalgo, D. S. (2006). Implementación de una Metodología con la Técnica 5S para Mejorar el Área de Matricería de una Empresa Extrusora de Aluminio. *Revista Tecnológica ESPOL, 18*(1), 69–75.

Boswijk, A. (2013). The power of the economy of experiences: New ways of value creation. In J. Sundbo & F. Sørensen (Eds.), *Handbook on the Experience Economy* (pp. 171–176). Edward Elgar Publishing. doi:10.4337/9781781004227.00014

Burgelman, R. A. (1983). Corporate entrepreneurship and strategic management: Insight from a process study. *Journal of Manufacturing Science and Engineering, 29*(12), 1349–1365.

Campanella, J. (1999). Principles of quality costs: Principles, implementation, and use. *ASQ World Conference on Quality and Improvement Proceedings*, 59.

Do Nascimento, N. M., Moro-Cabero, M. M., & Valentim, M. L. P. (2018). The adoption of ISO standards in Brazil, Iberian Peninsula and the United Kingdom in information and documentation: A comparative study. *Records Management Journal, 28*(3), 305–324. doi:10.1108/RMJ-04-2018-0009

Etzioni, A. (1967). Mixed-Scanning: A 'Third' Approach to Decision-Making. *Public Administration Review*, *27*(5), 385–392. doi:10.2307/973394

Eurofund. (2016). *Employee involvement and participation at work: Recent research and policy developments revisited*. Brussels: European Foundation for the Improvement of Living and Working Conditions.

Fang, J., Tang, L., Yang, J., & Peng, M. (2019). Social interaction in MOOCs: The mediating effects of immersive experience and psychological needs satisfaction. *Telematics and Informatics*, *39*, 75–91. doi:10.1016/j.tele.2019.01.006

Faria, J. R., Mixon, F. G., & Upadhyaya, K. P. (2019). Alumni donations and university reputation. *Education Economics*, *27*(2), 155–165. doi:10.1080/09645292.2018.1527895

García-Torres, D. (2019). Distributed leadership, professional collaboration, and teachers' job satisfaction in U.S. schools. *Teaching and Teacher Education*, *79*, 111–123. doi:10.1016/j.tate.2018.12.001

Ghicajanu, M. (2019). Techniques to continually improve business quality and performance. *Quality-Access to Success*, *20*, 503–506.

Goleman, D. (2018). *La inteligencia emocional*. Barcelona, Spain: Ediciones B.

Grover, R., Dalal, S., & Singh, A. (2016). Impact of 5S implementation. *Proceedings of the International Conference on Industrial Engineering and Operations Management*, 699-721.

Guryanova, A. V., Krasnov, S. V., & Frolov, V. A. (2020). Human transformation under the influence of the digital economy development. *Advances in Intelligent Systems and Computing*, *908*, 140–149. doi:10.1007/978-3-030-11367-4_14

Hernández, H., Martínez, D., & Rodríguez, J. (2017). Management of quality applied in the improvement of the university sector. *Espacios*, *38*(20), 29–41.

Hong, J., Liao, Y., Zhang, Y., & Yu, Z. (2019). The effect of supply chain quality management practices and capabilities on operational and innovation performance: Evidence from Chinese manufacturers. *International Journal of Production Economics*, *212*, 227–235. doi:10.1016/j.ijpe.2019.01.036

Ibeh, K. I. N., Uduma, I. A., Makhmadshoev, D., & Madichie, N. O. (2018). Nascent multinationals from West Africa: Are their foreign direct investment motivations any different? *International Marketing Review*, *35*(4), 683–708. doi:10.1108/IMR-08-2016-0158

Isaksson, R. (2019). A proposed preliminary maturity grid for assessing sustainability reporting based on quality management principles. *The TQM Journal*, *31*(3), 451–466. doi:10.1108/TQM-12-2017-0167

Lee, E. K., Avgar, A. C., Park, W.-W., & Choi, D. (2019). The dual effects of task conflict on team creativity: Focusing on the role of team-focused transformational leadership. *International Journal of Conflict Management*, *30*(1), 132–154. doi:10.1108/IJCMA-02-2018-0025

Lumpe, C. (2019). Public beliefs in social mobility and high-skilled migration. *Journal of Population Economics, 32*(3), 981–1008. doi:10.100700148-018-0708-x

Luyten, H., & Bazo, M. (2019). Transformational leadership, professional learning communities, teacher learning, and learner-centred teaching practices; Evidence on their interrelations in Mozambican primary education. *Studies in Educational Evaluation, 60,* 14–31. doi:10.1016/j.stueduc.2018.11.002

McCormick, B. W., Guay, R. P., Colbert, A. E., & Stewart, G. L. (2019). Proactive personality and proactive behaviour: Perspectives on person-situation interactions. *Journal of Occupational and Organizational Psychology, 92*(1), 30–51. doi:10.1111/joop.12234

Ost, J. H., & Da Silveira, C. G. (2018). Evaluation of the transition process from ISO 9001:2008 to ISO 9001:2015: A study focused on chemical companies in the State of Rio Grande do Sul, Brazil. *Gestão & Produção, 25*(4), 726–736. doi:10.1590/0104-530x4089-17

Parker, S. C. (2009). *Intrapreneurship or Entrepreneurship.* IZA Discussion Paper, 4195. Bonn, Germany: Forschungsinstitut zur Zukunft der Arbeit.

Pifer, M. J., Baker, V. L., & Lunsford, L. G. (2019). Culture, colleagues, and leadership: The academic department as a location of faculty experiences in liberal arts colleges. *Review of Higher Education, 42*(2), 537–564.

Pinchot, G. (1985). *Intrapreneuring: Why You Don't Have to Leave the Corporation to Become an Entrepreneur.* New York: Harper & Row.

Putra, E. D., & Cho, S. (2019). Characteristics of small business leadership from employees' perspective: A qualitative study. *International Journal of Hospitality Management, 78,* 36–46. doi:10.1016/j.ijhm.2018.11.011

Ramesh, N., & Ravi, A. (2016). The 5S route for safety management. *International Journal of Business Excellence, 10*(3), 283–300. doi:10.1504/IJBEX.2016.10000125

Roopa, M.S., Pattar, S., & Buyya, R., Iyengar, S.S., & Patnaik, L.M. (2019). Social Internet of Things (SIoT): Foundations, thrust areas, a systematic review, and future directions. *Computer Communications, 139,* 32–57. doi:10.1016/j.comcom.2019.03.009

Shalender, K., & Yadav, R. K. (2019). Strategic Flexibility, Manager Personality, and Firm Performance: The Case of Indian Automobile Industry. *Global Journal of Flexible Systems Management, 20*(1), 77–90. doi:10.100740171-018-0204-x

Simonova, A. A., & Fomenko, S. L. (2017). Evolution of integrated quality management system at higher school. *Quality-Access to Success, 18*(161), 126–134.

Singh, J., Rastogi, V., & Sharma, R. (2014). Implementation of 5S practices: A review. *Uncertain Supply Chain Management, 2*(3), 155–162. doi:10.5267/j.uscm.2014.5.002

Tenji, T., & Foley, A. (2019). Testing the readiness of an organisational culture profile to a TQM implementation. *The TQM Journal, 31*(3), 400–416. doi:10.1108/TQM-01-2018-0002

The British Assessment Bureau. (2018). *Quality Management Principles-ISO*. Retrieved from https://www.iso.org/files/live/sites/isoorg/files/archive/pdf/en/pub100080.pdf

Trąbka, J. (2015). Quality management support systems (QMSS)–definition, requirements, and scope. *Lecture Notes in Business Information Processing, 232*, 45–58. doi:10.1007/978-3-319-24366-5_4

Tracy, J. L., Cheng, J. T., Robins, R. W., & Trzesniewski, K. H. (2009). Authentic and hubristic pride: The affective core of self-esteem and narcissism. *Self and Identity, 8*(2–3), 196–213. doi:10.1080/15298860802505053

Tutida, L. (2019). ISO 9001: Comparisons, quality of life and results. *Espacios, 40*(1), 23–34.

Wang, Z., Xu, S., Sun, Y., & Liu, Y. (2019). Transformational leadership and employee voice: An affective perspective. *Frontiers of Business Research in China, 13*(1), 2–13. doi:10.118611782-019-0049-y

Weinhardt, J. M., & Sitzmann, T. (2019). Revolutionizing training and education? Three questions regarding massive open online courses (MOOCs). *Human Resource Management Review, 29*(2), 218–225. doi:10.1016/j.hrmr.2018.06.004

Yanar, B., Amick, B. C. III, Lambraki, I., D'Elia, T., Severin, C., & Van Eerd, D. (2019). How are leaders using benchmarking information in occupational health and safety decision-making? *Safety Science, 116*, 245–253. doi:10.1016/j.ssci.2019.03.016

Yang, H., & Yang, J. (2019). The effects of transformational leadership, competitive intensity and technological innovation on performance. *Technology Analysis and Strategic Management, 31*(3), 292–305. doi:10.1080/09537325.2018.1498475

Yeung, E., & Shen, W. (2019). Can pride be a vice and virtue at work? Associations between authentic and hubristic pride and leadership behaviors. *Journal of Organizational Behavior*, 1–20. doi:10.1002/job.2352

Yoon, K. (2014). Transnational youth mobility in the neoliberal economy of experience. *Journal of Youth Studies, 17*(8), 1014–1028. doi:10.1080/13676261.2013.878791

Yu, B. T. W., To, W. M., & Lee, P. K. C. (2012). A quality management framework for public management decision making. *Management Decision, 50*(3), 420–438. doi:10.1108/00251741211216214

KEY TERMS AND DEFINITIONS

5S: Formed by five Japanese concepts: *Seiri* (Sort), *Seiton* (Set in order), *Seiso* (Shine), *Seiketsu* (Standardize), and *Shitsuke* (Sustain), 5S is a systematic technique to maximize efficiency and productivity by increasingly avoiding the waste of resources.

Employee Voice: It is the way people communicate their views to their employer.

Evidence-Based Decision Making: It is formed by the decisions made from data and suitable information focused on achieving desired results.

Kaizen: Originated in Japan, it is composed of the Japanese words *kai* (change) and *zen* (for something better).

Quality Management: Also referred to as total quality management (TQM), it consists of the act to oversee all tasks and activities to achieve excellence.

Stakeholder: It is formed by the entire group affected by the activity of an organization.

Relationships Management: Managerial strategy focused on maintaining a continuous level of engagement between stakeholders.

Transformational Leadership: This is a type of leadership centered into the value-related transformation of the organization.

Chapter 2
Higher Education Approach to Quality Management

Dileep Baburao Baragde
https://orcid.org/0000-0001-9112-5535
G. S. Moze College, India

ABSTRACT

The situation of higher education in India does not concur with the worldwide benchmarks. Consequently, there is sufficient defense for an expanded evaluation of the quality of the nation's instructive foundations. Traditionally, these foundations accepted that quality is controllable by intrinsic assets, for example, knowledgeable and learned faculty with an impressive set of degrees and experience detailed at the end of the institute's admission brochure, and extrinsic assets like huge library rich with number of books and journals in the library, an ultra-modern campus, and size of the endowment, etc. This chapter aims at reviewing the higher education approach to quality management from an Indian perspective and deliberates on the tools and techniques like SIX SIGMA, LEAN, and TQM, most commonly used in higher education.

INTRODUCTION

Quality has a different definitions and ideas. For few, quality is in connection to the importance of predominance and perfection, and to others quality is a confirmation that there are less administrations or items with imperfections. Most of these definitions center on clients and their fulfillment (Takalo, Abadi, Vesal, Mizaei, & Nawaser, 2013). According to Green (1994), quality is a great and exciting challenge to Higher Education (HE). Giving quality administrations from Higher Education Institutions is the way to separate between contenders just as guaranteeing supportability for an extensive stretch (Govender, Veerasamy, & Noel, 2014). According to Nadim and Al-Hinai (2016), quality in education is a very vital issue because HEIs are accountable to several stakeholders such as students, society and other. In addition, quality of HE is a standout amongst the most of parts of the making of learning, human asset improvement and social power for any country. According to Becket and Brooks (2008) in many countries and many cultures, the issue of Quality Management has been steadily on the agenda of HEIs. The issues of QM have become one of the most basic ingredients and strengths within HEIs all over the world (Ganguly, 2015). Quality Management is about creating a quality culture where the aim of every member of staff is to delight their clients and where the structure of their organization allows them to do so. The aim of this chapter is to focus on approaches to quality management in higher education, with particularly focus on India, and to enhance the scope in the field of Quality Management in Higher Education.

This study underlines the issues that influence the successful implementation of Quality Management such as obstacles to Quality Management implementation. This is necessary because knowledge of these drives to improvement of Quality Management. One of the most known Quality Management models implemented in HE is Quality Management. SIX SIGMA has been successfully used in product and service improvement in the business environment. Lean means creating more value for customers with fewer resources, by minimizing waste. Although traditionally this concept is applied in manufacturing, the Lean management improvement principles can be also applied in the case of educational institutions. Total Quality Management (TQM) incorporates quality assurance, and extends and develops it. Here some quality tools used in higher education like SIX SIGMA, LEAN and TQM. Although SIX SIGMA has been successfully used in product and service improvement in the business environment. Lean means creating more value for customers with fewer resources, by minimizing waste. Although traditionally this concept is applied in manufacturing, the Lean management and improvement principles can be also applied in the case of educational institutions. Total Quality Management incorporates quality assurance, and extends and develops it. TQM is about creating a quality culture where the aim of every member of staff is to delight their customers and where the structure of their organization allows them to do so.

"Education should also be autonomous and free from politics. The modernization of the curriculum and skilled personnel in the profession would help India to achieve the set goals. Better qualified people should come to the noble profession of teaching to develop innovative mechanisms in Indian education system." - Montek Singh Ahluwalia, Deputy Chairman, Planning Commission. Quality in businesses could be characterized as holding fast to the expressed or suggested execution prerequisites of the customer; however with translations as fluctuated as the people, it is somewhat hard to characterize the Quality in educational institutions. Although, the Quality management concept in business and education stay same, there are sure constraints in receiving the corporate strategies for Quality management in light of the fact that instructive foundations cannot be considered as industry and the items are not their students, but rather it is the training granted to the students. Students, their parents, and their future employers are the clients of this product as education.

OBJECTIVES

This perspective of deciding Quality in higher education, prominently named as the "Value addition" approach, does not gauge the skills understudies create through the courses offered. The skills are review, comprehension, and critical thinking. "Recall" amounts to a competency of picking up information by method for reading, viewing, listening in, and demonstrating it when required. "Understanding" is comprehension, which requires clarifications and vocabulary advancement, and showing it by giving thoughts, anticipate, and assess circumstances and end results. The competency of "problem solving" can be created by taking care of reading material sort of issues and the ability so created can be utilized in dealing with genuine circumstances. The students should understand and accept these concepts, and the level of competency they are expected to attain should be defined in consultation with them. The tools also used in higher education is studied for the quality management.

LITERATURE REVIEW

According to Freeman, there is an extending need to improve the idea of innovative training since guidance is transforming into an overall component going up against troubles with resource goals. As opposed to various affiliations, propelled instruction has a couple of accomplices, for instance, understudies, guards, future administrators and society. Zhang proposed eight basic things to ask with respect to a Six Sigma look at program. Of these eight, the most critical to innovative training are "By what means can the suitability of a Six Sigma program be endorsed?" "By what means should Six Sigma be changed for different various leveled settings?", "What is the best legitimate structure for a Six Sigma program?", and "How do organization improvement and human resource practices relate to Six Sigma program?" (Zhang, 2011). The responses to these request centers around observational endorsement of ampleness and customization of the program, disconnecting the Six Sigma program from Quality Control Adaptation of six sigma approaches in innovative training requires careful idea of differentiations in accomplices' necessities and wants. Rather than business condition, propelled instruction may be seen by some as non-advantage to serve the more vital academic and societal necessities. Decisions in innovative training are not data driven and the prerequisites for data rarely taken care. An instance of a method improvement incorporates recording scores on the accounting section of the Educational Testing Service state regulated test. Additional data, for instance, work force assignments, perusing material, course arrangement, appearing, and course demand were accumulated. To improve typical test scores from 42.4% to 46.5%, the data factors were changed. These movements to the program arrangement achieved a genuine addition to 47.3%, over the perfect goal (Kukreja, 2009).

Total Quality Management is a broad and organized association the executive's approach that spotlights on ceaseless quality improvement of items and administrations by utilizing nonstop input. Joseph Juran was one of the originators of all out quality administration simply like William E. Deming. Complete quality administration started in the modern part of Japan (1954). Since that time the idea has been created and can be utilized for practically a wide range of associations, for example, schools, motorway support, lodging the board and houses of worship. These days, Total Quality Management is likewise utilized inside the e-business area and it sees quality administration altogether from the perspective of the client. The target of absolute quality administration is doing things right the first run through again and again. TQM is the craft of dealing with the entire to accomplish perfection. TQM covers all the set standards, guidelines, rules and rules that contribute in improving the association consistently. It is a nonstop procedure of progress for people, gatherings of individuals and the entire association. It is the use of quantitative strategies and HR to improve every one of the procedures inside an association to fulfill the necessities of clients reliably. TQM coordinates all the major administration methods, existing improvement endeavors, and specialized apparatuses under a restrained methodology. It covers the most quality standards and practices proposed by quality masters. Total Quality Management (TQM) is an administration approach for an association, focused on quality, in light of the support and duty of all the inside and outer clients and going for deliberately long haul accomplishment through consumer loyalty, and advantages to all individuals from the association and to society. All out Quality Management (TQM) is a top-administration methodology went for inserting familiarity with quality in every single authoritative procedure. All out Quality Management is a complete framework approach and it is a necessary piece of the vital basic leadership of the top administration. It works on a level plane over every one of the capacities and offices. It includes every one of the workers of three dimensions, i.e., top dimension, center dimension and base dimension. It expands in reverse and forward and covers production network the board just as coordination the executives moreover. It is a steady exertion by everybody in the association to meet the desires for the clients driving 100 percent fulfillment. TQM necessitates that the organization keep up the quality standard in all parts of its business.

According to Razaki and Aydin, particular methodology improvement techniques from the business world are explored for their incentive in the insightful world. Four one of a kind techniques were examined, including Total Quality Management (TQM), SIX SIGMA, Business Process Reengineering (BPR), and Lean Manufacturing. "TQM was extremely fit to improving the departmental systems to affect an advancement to flawlessness; Lean Six Sigma gave a couple anyway particularly effective procedures for departmental improvement." The usage of Lean Six Sigma was revealed from their examination of the Kukreja consider. It was seen that the data gathering cycle was too much long and a great deal of time was essential to complete the errand. Since most understudies are chosen for quite a while, this did not work splendidly with this required timespan. They propose mixing the correct bits of SIX SIGMA and Lean Manufacturing to make the system continuously fitting for the for the most part short time open to assemble data on individuals. This system uses quantifiable instruments of moderate multifaceted nature, with a short procedure length and an accentuation on end of waste.

Propelled instruction methodology can be believed to resemble a collecting system. In an amassing method, unrefined materials are dealt with through a movement of dares to make finished things. Furthermore, the propelled training foundations produce academic graduated class from moving toward understudies through a movement of steps. In cutting edge training, quality depends upon a couple of variables, for instance, instructive projects, course content, moving toward understudies, educators, showing technique, and assessment methodologies. Since one of the central purposes of Lean Manufacturing is decreasing waste, it is basic to describe waste in the propelled instruction course of action of strategies. Occurrences of enlightening waste join, "empowering topics recently instructed in various courses, over the top review of basic materials, silly and monotonous introductions, spoon-reinforcing, appearing of date subjects, and believing that not well prepared understudies will get up to speed" (Tatikonda, 2007). In order to convey a first rate graduate, tries to restrain wastes must be grasped all through the strategy with wary idea of accomplices' points of view. Quantifiable technique control can be a useful mechanical assembly in the educational condition as the institutional examination incorporates a great deal of data, for instance, enrollment designs, graduation rate, consistency norms, etc. As every system has an ordinary dimension of assortment, it is essential to make sense of what contains 'run of the mill' assortment with the objective that it might be foreseen. The more the assortment of a methodology can be restricted or controlled, the more absolutely the system results can be foreseen." When the strategy is under reasonable control, the conveyed assortments will be relentless and inside the recognized range. The technique for SPC can be endeavoring to apply outside an amassing area, for instance, an organization industry like propelled instruction. In conditions where execution parameters are not taken from significant, quantifiable things, more work is required. In an examination by Roes and Dorr of SPC (Statistical Process Control) execution in the organization business, the key traits for methodology control were described as how much the help of the customer is to make certain irrelevant, the intensity of relationship of specialists in the coordinated effort, and the level of customer sway on the organization gave. For academic condition, the customer would be a future supervisor, laborers would be school workforce, and the organization would be the given preparing. The SPC approach can be used to improve course instruction, using the following steps:

1. Identify the process to control
2. Determine quality characteristic to monitor
3. Choose the appropriate control chart based on
    a. Type of data
    b. Sample size
    c. Frequency
4. Perform process improvement using SPC tools
5. Implement continuous quality improvement on process.

Quality, with respect to innovative instruction has a couple of troubles, for instance, diligence, conformance to requirements, incessant improvement and regard notwithstanding. The methodology change exists inside the understudies, anyway inside educators too. For example, investigating by teachers may be uncommon and the instructional systems may in like manner have assortments. In an examination by Knight, educators assessed unknown assignments and after that reconsidered these assignments weeks afterward to watch the refinement in assessments got. These assessments were then presented to genuine examination, finding the ordinary range for each teacher. These were then landed at the midpoint of with each other and used to find an upper control limit for the achievers themselves. In future inspecting, in the occasion that grades outperformed this range, the assignments would then be reevaluated.

The utilization of Six Sigma DMAIC strategy to improve quality in planning educational had been productive in improving the quality perception with understudies and the organization of association. The Six Sigma system can in like manner be associated inside the course to improve constantly its quality. The Statistics part of Florida State University, associated with understudies in seven one of a kind undertakings all through a course. The chief endeavor incorporated the understudies posting two responsibilities they should need to make to their livelihoods. The accompanying five undertakings sought after the DMAIC methodology, and the last endeavor requires a report on the general system. In each endeavor, the understudies associated the DMAIC models toward achieving their target, learning the language and limit of Six Sigma as they advance. By applying DMAIC, understudies had the ability to achieve their targets and adjust themselves with the system.

The issues related with change the administrators is attempting in innovative instruction due to the possibility of the condition that propels academic chance. Academicians have been accustomed with this condition and have particular points of view towards different issues similarly as departmental authoritative issues and between departmental sharpness that development complexities related with any alteration all the while. "It is surveyed that 70% of progressive change exercises bomb completely. Of the ones considered powerful a similar number of as 75% of these disregard to achieve their proposed result." Individuals do not by and large get along in an affiliation, and, when the accomplishment of a program is dependent on joint exertion, noncooperation can be an impediment to achieving a legitimate change. Given all of these issues, there is a request in regards to whether there truly is a "best practice" for such change. "It gives that various surely understood organization practices set apart as best practices, (for instance, Total Quality Management, Six Sigma, and Lean) rely upon rambling verification rather than trial data." This perception may be required to some degree to the way that "the terms 'progressive change,' 'change the officials,' and 'best practice' emit an impression of being used in a variety of perspectives and research applications anyway the search for proclivity plans have not realized any steady ends". Moreover, with various pieces of the board, without a doubt adaptabilities must be drilled to execute changes reasonable to the earth. Beside the understudies, teachers and the organization notwithstanding, the establishment and educational resources that understudy's passage in like manner ends up being essential in achieving higher quality preparing.

RESEARCH METHODOLOGY

The examination has been led by counseling existing writing through authentic, logical and exact methodologies. Verifiable investigative strategy has been mulled over while watching the reports related with the examination and keeping in mind that inspecting the other writing significant to the investigation. Contextual analysis strategy, an exact procedure, is connected to consider the different measurements and effect of TQM on instruction part. Information investigation procedure has been mulled over to look at diagnostically routine reports concentrated worried to the TQM. The writing analyzed incorporates peer-evaluated articles (surveys and gathering procedures), monographs and reports distributed during the years 2000-2018. The lean, just in time, coordinated, college, instructive foundation, scholarly, training and advanced education. The snowball impact was utilized to soak the strategy. The pursuit was centered on titles and modified works. This can be recovered were perused and arranged based on their significance to the subject under investigation, their methodological quality. The difficulties of presenting and actualizing lean, six sigma and lean six sigma were listed at that point separated into two classifications, in particular describing fabricating settings versus experienced uniquely in the scholarly community.

The analysis gives that the different models, which are created for the ventures for overseeing quality, has been received or tried by the higher instructive foundations on a worldwide premise. There is an extraordinary utilization of idea TQM in the assembling businesses however; its application in the instruction part appears to be less. However at this point a few schools and colleges have begun utilizing the idea of TQM and its qualities with a conviction that TQM esteems are perfect with advanced education than numerous customary administration frameworks. In India, All India Council for Technical Education (AICTE) is set up as a national dimension summit warning body to direct, guarantee and control the nature of instruction in the nation. High rate or expanding rate of understudies' enrolment in the higher instructive foundations gives that the nature of training in the higher instructive organizations has been improved and is improving. Yet there is an interest of extraordinary improvement to improve the nature of training in future since India has not yet achieved superb outcomes in the TQM usage in the advanced education part. For this India need to make at least twelve colleges, universities that will agree to worldwide measures to completely partake on the planet economy. An effective TQM activity will clearly raise the standard and market estimation of the instructive establishments and furthermore these associations will wind up ready to confront any test from its rivals. The analysis uncovers the different activities embraced by higher instructive establishments or ought to be received by higher instructive foundations to introduce or execute TQM.

DISCUSSION AND FINDINGS

In Quality management, the customer is defined as next person in line. In educational institutes, students specifically get the showing administrations and teachers are the clients of the educator, though the staff and the Institute's managers are the providers of the administrations. Indeed, even the provider client idea of Quality administration cannot be connected in instruction because the clients do not comprehend what is to be gained, or what is of good Quality. The understudy's meaning of a Quality ordeal must be found through exchanges and perceptions of what gives them delight of learning, not only satisfaction without learning. In the event that the instructing and learning process adjusts to their thoughts regarding what Quality is training, understudies appreciate learning. Educators need to talk about such inquiries with the understudies as why are you here? What are you attempting to do? What does it intend to you to do it well? How the instructor can help you in doing it well? An educator needs to develop an accord in a class in regards to what comprises a Quality affair. When a commonly concurred intention is built up, the Quality administration ideas guarantee that educational modules soundness expands, instruction is enhanced, efficiency of educators is improved, and instructors and understudies find more bliss that is prominent in their work and can make positive commitments to the public. It is, in this manner fundamental that the organizations of advanced education acknowledge the mantra of 'Value' and accommodate an institutionalized appraisal of what precisely the understudies can do (that they were not ready to do previously) because of their instruction.

SIX SIGMA

Nature of instruction turned into a vital issue because of regularly expanding interest by its partners and aggressive condition. Albeit Six Sigma has been effectively utilized in item and administration improvement in the business condition, the idea has not been adjusted in the Education Industry. To improve comprehension of how Six Sigma can be utilized for Educational Institutes, we should pick up the bits of knowledge of how precisely the instruction framework functions.

Key Zones of Training System

Association

The preparation structure is held together by strategies that must run effectively and interface profitably. Six Sigma norms can reduce the distinction in these basic strategies: insistences, information development, and accreditation, surrender association, fix and upkeep and purchase demand association.

Selection

Before preparing can happen, understudies must be enlisted and set in an investigation lobby (Physical or Virtual). Six Sigma is fit to deal with a standout amongst the best weights in the educational strategy a chance to complete selection process. Streamlining the enrollment strategy can incite progressively noticeable understudy satisfaction from the very start.

Scholastics

Six Sigma can have a working effect in extending the dedication in an understudy's mind. From making a strategy, to picking the right representatives, to using benchmarking to recognize and execute the recommended methodology of various foundations, Six Sigma framework can change the idea of teaching and its movement and thusly the learning results.

We moreover need to appreciate who are the customers of this system isolated from the understudies. The summary consolidates the guards, the system, the foundations, the governing body, and the divisions inside the associations that interfaces with each other and some more. With this different summary of customers, how we can meet their necessities. Do we essentially carry on as ordinary and desire that by somehow things will work out, or do we center on the changing needs of the overall population and adjust preparing in like manner? If we are not prepared to address the issues of the customer, by then we are not expanding the estimation of the informational system and likewise we are making waste. The waste or flaw or screw up inside the structure fuses Institute's Goal Misalignment, Incorrect Assignment, Old or Not excellent Curriculum, Variations in Teaching, Treating All Students Equal anyway their individual style of learning and understanding is totally sudden, etc.

Six Sigma can help improve the systems that make up the field of Education. As gatekeepers, understudies, governments and worldwide money related conditions continue putting more weight on improving guidance, educational associations may depend extensively more seriously on Six Sigma procedure to pass on the best wellsprings of information coming to fruition into the best learning outcomes for additionally encouraging time to happen to mankind. (Mandlecha A. 2018)

Six Sigma Application in Education

The use of Six Sigma in education, essentially incorporates a strong point of convergence of improving strategies by reducing/taking out deformations/botches/waste rather than cutting cost by diminishing spending plans. This is the key response to change the methods into the gainful ones. This than requires an understanding and:

Focus on the Customers

Helping each domain of the association to grasp the estimation of their organization. This thought is vital to Six Sigma, as without an appreciation of necessities and requirements of internal and outside customers, the organization gave is non-regard included.

Data-driven Management

Individuals in educational foundations need to change the way in which they look at and supervise data. Overall, the data that is assembled is used for offering an explanation to the state, government, anyway isn't used to run the foundation. With Six Sigma, every individual or social affair ought to be almost an estimation so they will undoubtedly improve their own one of a kind execution.

Focus on Process Improvement

This thought is fundamental to Six Sigma without having the ability to recognize and portray frames they cannot improve. The thinking needs to move from one of individual blame to one of looking at methodology and course correction.. It has been seen that building technique maps and recognizing measures become the huge starting stage for educational associations. Portraying shapes ensure that the technique is clear and thus something that can be fathomed and administered.

Proactive Management

It requires the full-scale association getting away from the demeanors of finding motivations to issues, goofs and blunders. Alternatively, maybe everyone needs to push toward neutralizing activity this is another perspective.

Constant and incessant drive for faultlessness

Building the mindsets of dissatisfaction with the standard and the thought to be committed to a culture of consistent improvement.

In guidance as in, various organizations it is found that there are no sensible method limits and that the foundations have a strong utilitarian storage facility structure.

This is the real block for executing process improvement. Do we stop here and express that creation improvement is over the top? No. We begin by helping individuals to fathom and describe shapes and to perceive torment centers related with the method.

Effectiveness of Six Sigma in Higher Education

The execution of Six Sigma will address a few difficulties for improving the benchmarks of advanced education. This will likewise improve graduation rates in schools and furthermore get ready understudies to address adequately genuine difficulties. Learning Six Sigma procedure will likewise accentuation the significance of school instruction among understudies and guardians, since it very well may be changed to address any difficulties, overall, and in improving instructive gauges. Six Sigma improves quality be diminishing waste and is valuable for making understudies about impeccable in their secondary school and school ponders and furthermore causes them in their picked professions for their future.

Individuals who know about and practice Six Sigma forms figure out how to utilize controlled methodology for utilizing information to screen, oversee and improve their operational exhibitions by the aversion of deformities in items and procedures which incorporate organization, conveyance of administrations, structuring, creation/the assembling procedure and in the long run in general fulfillment. Six Sigma not just aides in the ID of deformities and the disposal of various sorts of waste (Chakrabarty and Tan, 2007)

Future Utilization of Six Sigma

Six Sigma can be effectively used for new and inventive assignments with an online system for studying the level of an understudy's learning. Perusing material can in like manner be successfully mentioned over the Internet, which is clever. The appointment books would then have the capacity to be taken a gander at over the Internet as the books are passed on to different schools. It will in like manner help in finding the vital limits that teachers are acquired for, with the objective that the educators stick to their insisted commitments and works and don't wrap up achieving something other than what's expected. For the most part, Six Sigma is basic for understudies, educators and foundations if they have to win in their presentations. (Kwak and Anbarib, 2006)

Lean Flow Eliminates Waste

Henry Ford advanced the historical backdrop of Lean Flow the Lean Flow process, likewise called Lean Manufacturing, Continuous Flow, and even more as of late, Just-In-Time Manufacturing, was advanced by Henry Ford soon after the turn of the century. He compared his idea of the mechanical production system to a waterway that streams ceaselessly. Anything that upsets the stream is squander that must be wiped out. Using this approach, Ford Motor Company could begin and complete a Model T in a little more than 30 hours. In the late 1940s, Toyota Motor Corporation put together its creation framework with respect to the Lean Flow process. Obviously, Toyota based on Ford's ideas, which were systematic and streamlined, yet very resolute. Lean Flow, as utilized by Toyota, connected its generation framework with constant client requests and material recharging prerequisites—so just the accurate amount of items and materials required were created at a particular point in time. This is like the Just-In-Time fabricating worldview that changes the customary "free market activity" model to an increasingly proficient, responsive "request then-supply" display. Toyota the executives perceived that to be powerful, Lean Flow must be deep down centered around taking out waste (decreasing stock, costs, and so forth.), yet ostensibly centered around satisfying client need (for example giving the vehicle in the ideal shading, with the ideal alternatives, and so forth.). Adaptability turned into an expansive piece of how this change was practiced. Toyota was maybe the principal organization to take freely note of: "The capacity to take out waste is created by surrendering the conviction that there is no other method to play out a given undertaking. It is pointless to state, 'It must be done that way,' or 'This would not benefit from outside assistance.' At Toyota, we have discovered that there is constantly another way."

Lean Flow Today

While Lean Flow started as an assembling model, the present definition has been stretched out to incorporate the way toward making an "enhanced stream" anywhere in an association. The main prerequisite is that this "stream" challenge current business practices to make a quicker, less expensive, less factor, and blunder inclined procedure. Lean Flow specialists have discovered that the best achievement can be accomplished by deliberately searching out wasteful aspects and supplanting them with "less fatty", progressively streamlined procedures. Wellsprings of waste generally tormenting most business forms include:

- Waste of specialist development (unneeded advances)
- Waste of making flawed items
- Waste of overproduction
- Waste in transportation

- Waste of handling
- Waste of time (inert)
- Waste of stock available

Giving Lean Flow something to do actualizing a Lean Flow requires having the correct information and realizing how to utilize it. There are various distinctive methodologies taken however in a general sense, Lean Flow is accomplished by:

- Analyzing the means of a procedure and figuring out which steps include esteem and which do not.
- Calculating the expenses related with evacuating non-esteem included advances and looking at those expenses versus anticipated advantages.
- Determining the assets required to help esteem included advances while disposing of non-esteem included advances.
- Taking activity.

Lean Six Sigma Applied to Document Management Services in Higher Education

One key area where higher education institutions seek to improve efficiency is by implementing electronic document and digital image repository to simplify and streamline document-intensive business processes, such as enrollment. Imaging and document repository solutions include scanning, organizing, and storing back files and incoming documents so they are readily available and instantly accessible to people who need them most. Institutions often look to experts in the industry to help them implement transformation, affording them the ability to concentrate on their core mission providing life-long learning to their students. What goes wrong with this approach? Many institutions look at image enabling, but not process improvements. One without the other is half a solution that does not consistently attain its goals of improving communication and information flow. Many institutions take a departmental, rather than a holistic enterprise, approach and create silos of information, resulting in information that cannot be leveraged by everyone. Institutions focus on the administrative side, but not the academic side of capturing documents, missing on opportunities to collaborate, share knowledge, and improve course work. For more than 17 years, Xerox has been incorporating a Lean Six Sigma methodology to help improve the ways in which information flows in, though, and out of colleges and universities. Specifically, Xerox Global Services imaging and repository services leverage the Lean Six Sigma-based DMAIC approach.

The Define phase of the DMAIC process is often skipped or short-changed, but is vital to the overall success of any Lean Six Sigma project. This is the phase where the current state, problem statement, and desired future state are determined and documented via the Project Charter. Xerox asks questions like what problem are we trying to solve. What are the expected results if we solve the problem? How will we know if the problem is solved? How will success be measured? In most cases where imaging and repository services are involved, the problem relates to document management and access. Schools look to improve the ways documents are created, stored, accessed, and shared so they may accelerate and enhance work processes, share information more conveniently, and collaborate more effectively. As the project progresses and more information is collected in future phases, the problem statement developed in the Define phase is refined. (Ross Raifsnider, 1997)

SOLUTION AND RECOMMENDATION

The word educational programs has been gotten from the Latin word 'currere' that signifies 'a course to be run'. The educational programs ought to be an entirety of thought of the motivations behind training, the substance of instructing, encouraging methodologies with the emphasis being on the item just as the procedure and a program of assessment of the results (Hok-Chun K., Dennis, 2002). It is a weapon to meet a challenging reality in the field of instruction named 'rivalry', which needs the structuring of compelling educational modules. By improving the past educational programs according to evolving necessities, the instructive organizations can make due in the market for quite a while and furthermore they need not to confront the test of falling enrolment rate of the understudies. Poor educational modules configuration is a noteworthy reason for quality disappointment. The procedure of educational programs structure should be indicated and collaboration ought to be there to make a need based educational modules of our clients for example our understudies (Sallis 2002).

To make TQM a triumph, today the instructive establishments are beginning their TQM activities from the grassroots level since schools and colleges actualize the undertakings however the essential promise to oversee TQM originates from top administration or high authorities like President/Chancellor/Vice Chancellor and so forth. These authorities are assuming a principal job in molding the quality culture of training and are treated as the initiator of value educating activities. These pioneers are passing on the pertinence of the entire network in the execution of the quality culture. These pioneers are additionally similar to a gatekeeper to the understudies, which are learning in their consideration (Oduro, Dachi et al., 2008).

The Six-Sigma Leadership Program. The Private Universities Council and the private HEIs have set out on a six sigma venture to understand its advantages on chosen work forms. Under the protection of this undertaking, the authority and staff of Private Universities Council and a few employees/managers from every one of the five taking an interest schools and number of colleges are experiencing six-sigma preparing. Private Universities Council is accused of the evaluation and quality confirmation of every single private college and schools. Its objectives in this task are first to sort out and work its inward procedures the six sigma way and second to safeguard that schools and colleges are following six sigma standards in their dull exercises. There are twenty-one members in all speaking to these foundations. Every establishment has chosen a six-sigma task including one of their work procedures to chip away at during preparing. In this way before the finish of yearlong preparing, the activities would be effectively finished. When the six-sigma ideas have been aced, the plan is to duplicate six-sigma on all significant work forms under the domain of their individual foundations.

CONCLUSION

This chapter has looked at the tools and techniques applied in higher education for improving quality management in higher education. LEAN and TQM plays an important role for improvising the quality in product and service based industries tried implementation in higher education weather getting same output for quality management. Different six sigma models have been made and acquainted with improve quality in innovative training. The key information sources and yield factors were perceived in the portray time of DMAIC process. The data and yield factors were assessed by social occasion the data after some time. The examination organize used SPC to perceive the variables outside beyond what many would consider possible. After unmistakable confirmation of the variable that lies outside beyond what many would consider possible, reasonable medicinal exercises can be executed for method improvement. This stage is seen as basic in academic condition, as it is essential to understudy accomplishment and quality improvement. In the control arrange, the information and yield factors require predictable seeing to ensure sensible system. The advanced education process demonstrated a three sigma (3σ) level quality that requires critical improvement to accomplish six sigma (6σ) level. The fundamental objective of innovative training is understudy achievement through higher quality guidance where disillusionment of any understudy may be considered as a distortion at the same time. In view of variability simultaneously, for instance, remarkable kind of direction by different educators, an assortment of significant worth exists. Assortments of significant worth may be a result of nonappearance of cognizance of how understudies learn and changing in accordance with different learning styles of understudies. After unmistakable verification of the issues and describing the issues, an answer can be made using six sigma strategies and models showed in this paper. A control diagram can be used with UCL and LCL close by a steady improvement mean to improve the propelled training process. This will result in higher quality and pragmatic method in the foundation with bigger measures of understudy satisfaction and accomplishment rates, for instance, graduation and benchmarks for reliability. The information and gadgets gave in this paper is an undertaking to shed a couple of lights on how special quality improvement models can be used in innovative training.

This review summarizes the documented experiences (2000 to 2016) of colleges with utilization of lean, six sigma and lean six sigma ways to deal with improve authoritative proficiency and the general nature of the instruction gotten by the understudies. We distinguished the objectives of the intercessions, colleges especially dedicated to applying this kind of methodology, the favored instruments, the discoveries (when introduced), and the difficulties experienced. We have thus, exhibited the rising character of the presentation of lean, six sigma and lean six-sigma methods of reasoning into the college setting, just as their restricted organization inside the perplexing frameworks under examination. A few difficulties obstruct their effective application, including appropriate meaning of the customer, of included esteem and of the relationship among instructing and research. Different roads for settling these troubles have been proposed. The effect of such endeavors, especially concerning OHS, is considerably less recorded, which we view as significant, given that the effect of lean assembling on OHS, as depicted in the writing, might be certain or negative, due frequently to factors that stay to be recognized. While methodologies of this sort seem to hold guarantee, it is still too soon to presume that they will enable colleges to pick up an upper hand.

REFERENCES

Al-Atiqi, I. M., & Deshpande, P. B. (2009). *Transforming US Higher Education with Six Sigma*. Abu Dhabi: International Network of Quality Assessment Agencies in Higher Education.

Al-Tarawneh, H. A., & Mubaslat, M. M. (2011). The Implementation of Total Quality Management (TQM) On the Higher Educational Sector in Jordan. *International Journal of Industrial Marketing*, *1*(1), 1–10.

Alzhrani, K. M., Alotibie, B. A., & Abdulaziz, A. (2016). Total Quality Management in Saudi Higher Education. *International Journal of Computers and Applications*, *135*(4), 6–12. doi:10.5120/ijca2016908245

Antony, J., Krishan, N., Cullen, M., & Kumar, M. (2012). Lean six sigma for higher education institutions (heis): Challenges, barriers, success factors, tools/techniques. *International Journal of Productivity and Performance Management, 61*(8), 940–948. doi:10.1108/17410401211277165

Bergquist, B., & Edgeman R. L. (2003). Six Sigma and Total Quality Management: Different day, same soup? *International Journal of Six Sigma and Competitive Advantage., 2*(2), 162–178.

Chakrabarty, T. K. C., & Chuan Tan, K. (2007). The Current State of Six Sigma Application in Services. *Managing Service Quality, 17*(2), 194–208. doi:10.1108/09604520710735191

Dew, J. (2009). Quality issues in higher education. *Journal for Quality and Participation, 32*(1), 4–9.

Freeman, R. (1993). Quality assurance in training and education. *British Journal of Educational Studies, 41*(3), 309–311. doi:10.2307/3122295

Ganguly, A. (2015). Exploring Total Quality Management (TQM) Approaches in Higher Education Institutions in a Globalized Environment-Case Analysis of UK and Sweden. *Brock Journal of Education, 3*(7), 83–106.

Govender, J. P., Veerasamy, D., & Noel, D. T. (2014). The service quality experience of International students: The case of a selected higher education institution in South Africa. *Mediterranean Journal of Social Sciences, 5*(8), 465–473.

Hallencreutz, J., & Turner, D. (2011). Exploring organizational change best practice: Are there any clear-cut models and definitions. *International Journal of Quality and Service Sciences, 3*(1), 60–68. doi:10.1108/17566691111115081

Hok-Chun, K., Dennis. (2002). Quality Education through a Post Modern Curriculum. *Hong Kong's Teachers Centre Journal, 1*(1), 56–73.

Knight, J. E., Allen, S., & Tracy, D. L. (2010). Using six sigma methods to evaluate the reliability of a teaching assessment rubric. *The Journal for American Academy of Research Cambridge, 15*(1), 1–6.

Kukreja, A., Ricks, J. M. Jr, & Meyer, J. A. (2009). Using Six Sigma for performance improvement in business curriculum: A case study. *Performance Improvement, 48*(2), 9–25. doi:10.1002/pfi.20042

Kwak, Y. H., & Anbarib, F. T. (2006). Benefits, obstacles, and future of six sigma approach. *Technovation, 26*(5-6), 708–715. doi:10.1016/j.technovation.2004.10.003

Madu, C. N., & Kuei, C. H. (1993). Dimensions of quality teaching in higher institutions. *Total Quality Management, 4*(3), 325–338. doi:10.1080/09544129300000046

Maleyeff, J., & Kaminsky, F. (2002). Six sigma and introductory statistics education. *Education + Training, 44*(2), 82–89. doi:10.1108/00400910210419982

Mitra, A. (2004). Six-sigma education: A critical role for academia. *The TQM Magazine, 16*(4), 293–302. doi:10.1108/09544780410541963

Nadim, Z. S., & Al-Hinai, A. H. (2012). Critical Success Factors of TQM in Higher Education Institutions. *International Journal of Applied Sciences and Management, 2*(12), 19–32.

Oduro, G. K., & Dachi, H. (2008). *Educational Leadership and Quality Education in Disadvantaged Communities in Ghana and Tanzania.* The Commonwealth Council for Educational Administration & Management Conference, International Convention Centre, Durban, South Africa.

Perry, L. (2004). Instructional effectiveness: A real-time feedback approach using statistical process control (spc). *Proceedings of the 2004 American society for engineering education annual conference & exposition.*

Raifsnider, R., & Kurt, D. (2004). *Lean Six Sigma in higher education: Applying proven methodologies to improve quality, remove waste, and quantify opportunities in colleges and universities.* Xerox The Document Company, White paper.

Rajesh, B. (2008). Study on Indian Higher Education: A TQM Perspective. *Researchers World: Journal of Arts, Science and Commerce, 4*(2), 53–65.

Razaki, K. A., & Aydin, S. (2011). The Feasibility of Using Business Process Improvement Approaches to Improve an Academic Department. *Journal of Higher Education Theory and Practice, 11*(2), 19–32.

Roes, K. C., & Dorr, D. (1997). Implementing statistical process control in service processes. *International Journal of Quality Science, 2*(3), 149–166.

Sallis, E. (2002). *Total Quality Management in Education.* Kogan Page Publishers.

Takalo, S. K., Abadi, A. R. N. S., Vesal, S. M., Mizaei, A., & Nawaser, K. (2013). Fuzzy Failure Analysis: A New Approach to Service Quality Analysis in Higher Education Institutions. *International Education Studies, 6*(9), 93–106.

Tatikonda, L. (2007). Applying Lean Principles to Design Teach, and Assess Courses. *Management Accounting Quarterly, 8*(3), 27–38.

Tsinidou, M., Gerogiannis, V., & Fitsilis, P. (2010). Evaluation of the factors that determine quality in higher education: An empirical study. *Quality Assurance in Education, 18*(3), 227–244. doi:10.1108/09684881011058669

Weinstein, L. B., Petrick, J., Castellano, J., & Vokurka, R. J. (2008). Integrating Six Sigma concepts in an MBA quality management class. *Journal of Education for Business, 83*(4), 233–238. doi:10.3200/JOEB.83.4.233-238

Wiklund, H., & Wiklund, P. S. (2007). Widening the Six Sigma concept: An approach to improve organizational learning. *Total Quality Management, 13*(2), 233–239. doi:10.1080/09544120120102469

Zahn, D. (2003). What influence is the six-sigma movement having in universities? What influence should it be having? *ASQ Six-Sigma Forum, 3*(1). Retrieved from http://asq.org/pub/sixsigma/past/vol3issue1/youropinion.html

Zhang, W., Hill, A. V., & Gilbreath, G. H. (2011). A research agenda for Six Sigma Research. *The Quality Management Journal, 18*(1), 39–53. doi:10.1080/10686967.2011.11918301

Chapter 3
Contemporary Perspectives on Higher Education Quality Management

Steven Sena
University of Zimbabwe, Zimbabwe

ABSTRACT

Quality management is considered a very important factor for the long-term success of each and every organization. The links between quality management and organizational performance can never be overemphasized. Quality management in both goods and services industries gives a company a distinct competitive advantage over its competitors in the market place. Market share can also be gained or lost over the level of quality management in an organization; that is if an organization's quality management process is poor, the market share is lost, and conversely, if it is quality management is good, a market share is gained. Quality is, therefore, a competitive priority for any serious organization. Quality management is the only factor that ensures an organization's survival and growth especially in institutions of higher learning and other service organizations. Quality management focuses on meeting consumers' needs, meeting the competition, improving continuously, and extending these concerns to all phases of business.

INTRODUCTION

Quality management is a very important factor for the long-term success of each organization. The links between Quality Management and organizational performance can never be over emphasized. Quality management in both goods and services industries gives a company a distinctive competitive advantage over its competitors in the market place. Market share can also be gained or lost over the level of quality management in an organisation; that is, if an organisation's quality management process is poor the market share is lost and conversely, if its quality management is good, a market share is gained. Quality is therefore a competitive priority for any serious organisation. Quality management is the only factor that ensures an organization's survival and growth especially in institutions of higher learning and other service organisations. Quality management focuses on meeting consumers' needs, meeting the competi-

DOI: 10.4018/978-1-7998-1017-9.ch003

tion, improving continuously and extending these concerns to all phases of business. In the contemporary world all managers must understand that the real price of poor quality is lost clients and ultimately, the death of an organization. Consequently organizations must pay particular attention to quality management in order to be successful in today's business environment. Hence, a systematic procedure/ standard operating procedure (SOP) has to be grown and followed. Different concepts of quality management have to be understood clearly for managers to be able to design and execute a quality management programme effectively. As the primary focus of quality management (QM) is to meet customer requirements and strive to exceed customer expectations, it follows however that, this first chapter should explains Quality Management explicitly in a practical way. It must cover the various definitions and principles of quality management, fundamental beliefs, norms, rules and values that can be used as a basis for quality management. The chapter must also show that Quality Management is an extensive and structured organization management approach that focuses on continuous quality improvement of products and services by using continuous feedback. The chapter will show the Benefits of Quality Management in institutions of higher learning and other services industries. The chapter should indicate the two main dimensions from which quality management may be viewed, that is, product dimension of quality and service dimension of quality. There are various disciplinary perspectives from which professionals view quality management from. The following perspectives will be addressed:

- Financial Perspective,
- Marketing Perspective,
- Operations Perspective,
- Engineering Perspective,
- Production Perspective, and
- Supply Chain Perspective

After considering the different perspectives of quality management, the chapter will end by looking at quality management systems where it is going to reveal how checks and balances are going to be made through quality management systems audit. After reading this chapter, readers should be able to understand the basics of this powerful management tool.

Finding the way to quality is neither easy nor smooth; people must muddle and stumble for quite a good period of hard work. Managers must reach out and listen to anyone with ideas inside and outside the organisation. According to Foster (2017) the key to achieving total quality management lays in empowering employees with the authority and responsibility to improve manufacturing processes throughout the organisation, however, before an organisation could empower its employees it needs to equip them with right and quality tools for specific jobs. Academic institutions need to have intellectual experts; people who have the correct qualifications for the correct jobs. Management should get involved in the process of reaching out in order to learn from every source they could. Dahlgaard and Kanji (2009) argued that for an organisation to have an effective quality management programme it should formulate and implement staff development policies, continuous on job re-training. Armed with teams of trained and empowered employees the organisation would be able to produce goods and services of higher quality. Management must set target levels of education and skills required of each and every job description and adhere to the policy no matter what comes. Issues of quality management must not be left to rank and file workers only, the organisation's top-management and chief executives must be compelled to be involved (Foster, 2017). Quality management programmes often fail because of lack of commitment by top-management.

UNDERSTANDING QUALITY MANAGEMENT (QM)

Stoner, Freeman, and Gilbert (2009) argued that there is no one defination of quality. They defined quality as a sense of appreciation that something is better than something else. Quality as it is used in management means more than Stoner et al's definition of a better than average product at a good price. It also means focusing on the production of increasingly better products and services at progressively more competitive prices. It also means doing things right in the organisation on the first try, rather than making making and correcting mistakes. By focusing on doing things right the first time, organisations avoid the high costs associated with rework.

Quality management is the act of ensuring that a company's goods and services are built and delivered to specifications, on time and at the appropriate cost. According to Bathie and Sarkar (2002) the common factors about the definitions of quality include the following aspects; perfection, consistency, eliminating waste, speed of delivery, compliance with policies and procedures, doing it right the first time, delighting or pleasing customers, and total customer satisfaction and service.

Quality management is the act of overseeing different activities and tasks within an organization to ensure that products and services offered, as well as the means used to achieve them are consistent. It helps to achieve and maintain a desired level of quality within the organization. Bergman and Klefsjö, (2004) posited that quality management consists of four key components, which include:

- **Quality Planning**

Bergman and Klefsjö, (2004) pointed out that " quality planning is a process of identifying the quality standards relevant to the project and deciding how to meet them". The process involves the preparation of a quality management plan that describes the processes and metrics that will be used. All stakeholders in the quality management planning process need to agree in principle in order to ensure that their expectations for quality are correctly identified (Brady, 2006). "The processes described in the quality management plan should conform to the processes, culture and values of the host organisation (Bounds, Yorks, Adam, and Ranney, 2004).

- **Quality Improvement**

According to Conti (2006), quality improvement is the purposeful change of a process to improve the confidence or reliability of the outcome. Continual improvement is the generic term used by organisations to describe how information provided by quality assurance and quality control processes is used to drive improvements in efficiency and effectiveness.

- **Quality Control**

The continuing effort to uphold a process' integrity and reliability in achieving an outcome. The tenants of quality control are; inspection, testing and measurement. It aims at verifying whether the deliverables conform to specifications, are fit for purpose and meet stakeholder expectations (Bergman and Klefsjö, 2004). Quality control activities determine whether acceptance criteria have, or have not, been met. For this to be effective, specifications must be under strict configuration control. It is possible that, once agreed, the specification may need to be modified. Commonly this is to accommodate change requests or issues, while maintaining acceptable time and cost constraints. Any consequent changes to acceptance criteria should be approved and communicated to all stakeholders.

- **Quality Assurance**

The systematic or the planned actions necessary to offer sufficient reliability that a particular service or product will meet the specified requirements. Dahlgaard and Kanji (2009) argues that "quality assurance provides confidence to the host organisation that its projects, programmes and portfolios are being well managed, it validates the consistent use of procedures and standards, and ensures that staff have the correct knowledge, skills and attitudes to fulfil their project roles and responsibilities in a competent manner". In order to the process to work it is required to be independent of any influence from the project, programme or portfolio to which it applies.

The aim of quality management is to ensure that all the organization's stakeholders work together to improve the company's processes, products, services, and culture to achieve the long-term success that stems from customer satisfaction. The process of quality management involves a collection of guidelines that are developed by a team to ensure that the products and services that they produce are of the right standards or fit for purpose. The process starts when the organization sets quality targets to be met and which are agreed upon with the customer. The organization then defines how the targets will be measured. It then takes the actions that are required to measure the quality. They then identify any quality issue that arises and initiates improvements. The final step involves reporting the overall level of the quality achieved. The process ensures that the products and services produced by the team match the customers' expectations. The quality improvement methods comprise three components: product improvement, process improvement, and people-based improvement.

Evans and Dean (2003) pointed out that, "…quality management is the act of overseeing all activities and tasks needed to maintain a desired level of excellence; it includes the determination of a quality policy, creating and implementing quality planning and assurance, and quality control and quality improvement". It is also referred to as total quality management (TQM). For the purpose of this book quality management would be referred to as total quality management (TQM). At its core TQM is a business philosophy that champions the idea that the long-term success of a company comes from customer satisfaction. TQM requires that all stakeholders in a business work together to improve processes, products, services and the culture of the company itself. All members of an organization must participate in a TQM effort process in order to; improve processes, products, services, and the culture in which they work. This was also echoed by Harvey and Green (2003) who said that "total Quality Management (TQM) describes a management approach to long-term success through customer satisfaction, all members of an organization must participate in improving processes, products, services, and the culture in which they work". In order to achieve TQM in an institution of higher learning like a university it means that each person involved in the teaching and learning process must play his/her part in order for the process to succeed. All the stakeholders like the security, services, administration and academic staff as well as the learners themselves must play their part in full for TQM to be achieved. Total quality management aims to hold all parties involved in the production process as accountable for the overall quality of the final product or service.

ORIGINS OF QUALITY MANAGEMENT

While QM seems like an intuitive process, it came about as a revolutionary idea. The 1920s saw the rise in a reliance on statistics and statistical theory in business, and the first-ever known control chart was made in 1924 (Dahlgaard-Park, 2009). People began to build on theories of statistics and ended up collectively creating the method of statistical process control (SPC). However, it wasn't successfully implemented in a business setting until the 1950s.

It was during this time that Japan was faced with a harsh industrial economic environment. Its citizens were thought to be largely illiterate, and its products were known to be of low quality (Dahlgaard-Park, 2009; Dahlgaard, K., & Kanji, 2009). Key businesses in Japan saw these deficiencies and looked to make a change. Relying on pioneers in statistical thinking, companies such as Toyota integrated the idea of quality management and quality control into their production processes. By the end of the 1960s, Japan completely flipped its narrative and became one of the most efficient export countries, with some of the most admired products. The effective quality management resulted in better products that too produced at a more competitive price.

Example of Quality Management

The most famous example of QM is Toyota's implementation of the Kanban system. A Kanban is a physical signal that creates a chain reaction, resulting in a specific action. Toyota used this idea to implement its just-in-time (JIT) inventory process. To make its assembly line more efficient, the company decided to keep just enough inventories on hand to fill customer orders as they were generated. Therefore, all parts of Toyota's assembly line are assigned a physical card that has an associated inventory number. Right before a part is installed in a car; the card is removed and moved up the supply chain, effectively requesting another of the same part. This allows the company to keep its inventory lean and not overstock unnecessary assets.

QUALITY IN EDUCATION

Quality Assurance Agency for Higher Education (QAA) (2004:1) defined academic quality as "a way of describing how well the learning opportunities available to students help them to achieve their award". It is about making sure that appropriate and effective teaching, support, assessment and learning opportunities are provided for them. Srikanthan and Dalrymple (2003:127) suggested that the definition changes according to the perspective of each customer, or stakeholder group. In a higher education and training system customers or stakeholders include; students, parents, lecturers, industry, community and government.

PRINCIPLES OF QUALITY MANAGEMENT

There are several principles of quality management that the International Standard for Quality Management adopts. These principles are used by top management to guide an organization's processes towards improved performance.

Figure 1. Principles of Quality Management
Source: Dahlgaard and Kanji, (2009)

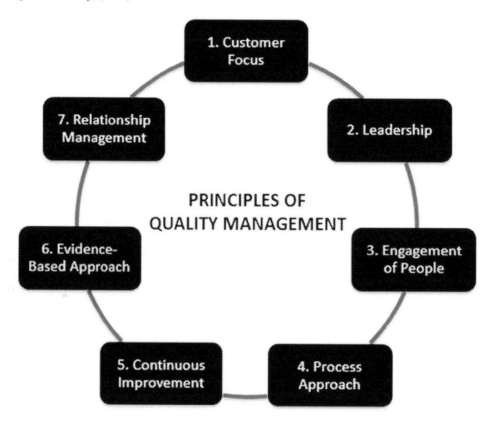

Customer Focus

The primary focus of any organization should be to meet and exceed the customers' expectations and needs. When an organization can understand the customers' current and future needs and cater to them, it results in customer loyalty, which in turn increases revenue. The business is also able to get new customer opportunities and satisfy them. When business processes are more efficient, quality is higher and more customers can be satisfied. It is the customer who ultimately determines the level of quality of goods and services they require. According to Edvardsson and Gustafsson (2008) "no matter what an organization does to foster quality improvement training employees, integrating quality into the design process, upgrading computers or software, or buying new measuring tools the customer determines whether the efforts were worthwhile".

Leadership

Good leadership results in an organization's success. Great leadership establishes unity and purpose among the workforce and shareholders. Creating a thriving company culture provides an internal environment that allows employees to fully utilize their potential and get actively involved in achieving its objectives. The leaders should involve the employees in setting clear organization goals and objectives. It motivates employees, who can significantly improve their productivity and loyalty. For management to know how well the organization is performing, it is necessary for them to measure their data on performance. The data required is obtained through market surveys and customer relationship management processes. Feigenbaum (2016) argued that "TQM requires that an organization continually collect and analyze data in order to improve decision making accuracy, achieve consensus, and allow prediction based on past history".

Engagement of People

Staff involvement is another fundamental principle. The management engages staff in creating and delivering value whether they are full-time, part-time, outsourced or in-house. An organization should encourage the employees to constantly improve their skills and maintain consistency. This principle also involves empowering the employees, involving them in decision making and recognizing their achievements. When people are valued, they work to their best potential because it boosts their confidence and their motivation. When employees are wholly involved, it makes them feel empowered and accountable for their actions. All the employees of an organisation must participate in working toward achievement of common goals. In order obtain total employee commitment fear must be driven from the workplace, employees should be empowered and proper work environment should be promoted (Feigenbaum, 2016). Continuous improvement efforts and normal business operations are integrated by High-performance work systems.

Process Approach

The performance of an organization is crucial according to the process approach principle. The approach emphasizes on achieving efficiency and effectiveness in the organizational processes. The approach entails an understanding that good processes result in improved consistency, quicker activities, reduced costs, waste removal and continuous improvement. An organization is enhanced when leaders can manage and control the inputs and the outputs of an organization, as well as the processes used to produce the outputs.

Harry and Crawford (2005) opined that "a fundamental part of TQM is a focus on process thinking; a process is a series of steps that take inputs from suppliers (internal or external) and transforms them into outputs that are delivered to customers (again, either internal or external)". These steps are defined, and performance measures are continuously monitored in order to detect unexpected variation. Even though an organization may have many different functional specialties organized into vertically structured departments, it is its horizontal processes that interconnect these functions, which is the focus of TQM. Business processes are made up micro-processes that are aggregated to work together in a coordinated whole body.

Everyone in the organisation must understand the vision, mission, and guiding principles as well as the quality policies, objectives, and critical processes of the organization in order to work with a unity of purpose. There is need to monitor and communicate business performance continuously to all members of the organisation. The Baldridge National Quality Program criteria and/or incorporate the ISO 9000 standards may be used as guidelines for modeling integrated business systems. According to Hellsten

(2000) "every organization has a unique work culture, and it is virtually impossible to achieve excellence in its products and services unless a good quality culture has been fostered; thus, an integrated system connects business improvement elements in an attempt to continually improve and exceed the expectations of customers, employees, and other stakeholders".

Continuous Improvement

Every organization should come up with an objective to be actively involved in continuous improvement. Businesses that improve continually experience improved performance, organizational flexibility and increased ability to embrace new opportunities. Businesses should be able to create new processes continually and adapt to new market situations. Continual process improvement is the major thrust of TQM. It drives an organization to be both analytical and creative in finding ways to become more competitive and effective at meeting stakeholder expectations.

Evidence-Based Decision Making

Strategic and systematic approach to achieving an organization's vision, mission, and goals is the critical part of the management of quality. The strategic planning or strategic management process includes the formulation of a strategic plan that integrates quality as a core component. Kondo (2003) argues that businesses should adopt a factual approach to decision-making. Businesses that make decisions based on verified and analyzed data have an improved understanding of the marketplace. They are able to perform tasks that produce desired results and even justify their past decisions. Factual decision making is vital to help understand the cause-and-effect relationships of different things and even explain potential unintended results and consequences.

Relationship Management

Relationship management is about creating mutually beneficial relations with supplier and retailers. Different interested parties can impact the company's performance. The organization should manage the supply chain process well and promote the relationship between the organization and its suppliers to optimize their impact on the company's performance. When an organization manages its relationship with interested parties well, it is more likely to achieve sustained business collaboration. Mehra, Hoffman, and Sirias (2001) argued that "during times of organizational change, as well as part of day-to-day operation, effective communications plays a large part in maintaining morale and in motivating employees at all levels; communications involve strategies, method, and timeliness". They further argued that, "……these elements are considered so essential to TQM that many organizations define them, in some format, as a set of core values and principles on which the organization is to operate". The teachings of such quality leaders as Philip B. Crosby, W. Edwards Deming, Armand V. Feigenbaum, Kaoru Ishikawa, and Joseph M. Juran form the basis of models for implementing continual quality improvement in and organisation.

BENEFITS OF QUALITY MANAGEMENT

Quality management poses a number of benefits to an organisation that practices it in good faith. Some of the benefits include the following:

- It helps an organization achieve greater consistency in tasks and activities that are involved in the production of products and services,
- It increases efficiency in processes, reduces wastage and improves the use of time and other resources,
- It helps improve customer satisfaction,
- It enables businesses to market their business effectively and exploit new markets,
- It makes it easier for businesses to integrate new employees and thus helps businesses manage growth more seamlessly, and
- It enables a business to continuously improve their products, processes, and systems.

TOTAL QUALITY MANAGEMENT (TQM)

(Foster, 2017; Juran, 2014) both defined TQM as "…… a management system for a customer-focused organization that involves all employees in continual improvement". It was further argued that "it uses strategy, data, and effective communications to integrate the quality discipline into the culture and activities of the organization".

DIMENSIONS OF TQM

Drury (2000) argues that different authors have defined quality differently. He further argued that quality can be seen from different perspectives. Quality is regarded as an attribute of an entity (as in property and character), a peculiar and essential character of a product or a person (as in nature and capacity), a degree of excellence (as in grade) and as a social status (as in rank and aristocracy). According to Linderman, Schroeder, Zaheer, Liedtke, and Choo (2004) the typical definitions include fitness for use, the totality of features and characteristics to satisfy certain needs, and meeting requirements. On the same line of thinking was Oakland (2008) who said that "…..quality is usually associated with words or phrases such as quality assurance, quality control, quality improvement, software quality, organizational and educational quality, food quality, air quality, and image quality as well as many others".

Product Dimension of Quality

Under this dimension much emphasis is put on the quality of physical products. Oh, (2009) argues that "consumers have a variety of different products to choose from and quality is often a determining factor when choosing which of several similar products to purchase". The customer's concern of quality provides a great reason for industries to see the importance of product quality to the survival of business. Consumers believe that, product quality is related to the fit of needs of the consumers. Garvin (2008) defined product quality in terms of the product's lifecycle and came up with eight dimensions:

- Performance – primary operating characteristics of a product,
- Features – 'bells and whistles' of a product,
- Reliability – probability of a product failing within a specified period of time,
- Conformance – degree that a product's design matches established standards,
- Durability – measure of a product life,
- Serviceability – speed and competency of repair,
- Aesthetics – subjective measure of how a product looks, feels, sounds, smells or tastes, and
- Perceived Quality – subjective measure of how the product measures up against a similar product.

On the other hand Brucks and Zeithaml (2000) identified six abstract dimensions of quality in the context of durable and physical goods. These dimensions include the following:

- Ease of use,
- Functionality,
- Performance,
- Durability,
- Serviceability, and
- Prestige.

Though the Brucks and Zeithaml (2000) classification was similar to that of Garvin's, it was argued that Bucks and Zeithaml based their argument on empirical study while Gavin was purportedly accused of not basing any empirical findings.

Service Dimension of Quality

Drury (2003) argues that "… whether the context is academia or industry, service quality is how customers interact with the business at hand". When they are able to define service quality, companies will be able to deliver their products and services with a higher level of it, giving a rise to and accomplishment of customer satisfaction. Parasuraman et al. (1985) proposed a conceptual model of service quality that is in use to current date. The model has ten perceived quality components. They suggested a definition of quality that has a multiple dimensions of service quality including:

- Reliability – consistency of performance and dependability;
- Responsiveness – the willingness or readiness of employees to provide service;
- Competence – possession of the required skills and knowledge to perform the service;
- Access – approachability and ease of contact;
- Courtesy – politeness, respect, consideration, and friendliness of contact personnel;
- Communication – keeping customers informed in language they can understand and listening to them;
- Credibility – trustworthiness, believability, honesty;
- Security – the freedom from danger, risk or doubt;
- Understanding/knowing – making the effort to understand the customer's needs;
- Tangibles – the physical evidence of the service.

Parasuraman et al. further grouped these dimensions into five major groups, which are:

- Tangibles,
- Reliability,
- Responsiveness,
- Assurance, and
- Empathy.

Page and Curry (2000) argued that, "their categorization focused more on specific services, e.g. banks, credit cards, than on general service quality". The definition of service quality used in different articles 76 K. M. Ghylin et al. varied based on the topics being discussed. One study defined excellence in business education based on students' impressions of service quality (Sohail 2004). In that study, six factors were found to have an impact on service quality:

- Contact with personnel,
- Physical evidence,
- Reputation,
- Responsiveness,
- Access to facilities, and
- Curriculum.

However in another study Robinson (1999) found that service quality was more related to attitudes than customer service, with performance perceptions differing based on the service context.

QUALITY AND ETHICS

Quality is closely associated with ethics. Good services will always be able to fulfil customer needs if it is able to follow Ethics in its true spirit (Womack and Jones, 2006). A service or product that has been poorly designed carries liability. On the other hand, if the organization has followed ethics to manufacture a product or service, it would be able to provide a quality product or service to its customer. TQM is an important concept and is followed by various departments of the organization. Accounting department measures the costs associated with a poor quality based service or product. Finance department measures the cash flows associated with various departments, the Human Resources department employs workforce, which is capable of quality based work results. Management Information Systems department design TQM based systems to ensure increased productivity, similarly, marketing department uses TQM techniques to increase the organisation's market share and customer base, last but not the least the Operations department designs and implements TQM strategies (Womack and Jones, 2006).

CONSEQUENCES OF POOR QUALITY

There are a number of negative outcomes of poor quality in both goods and services. According to Womack and Jones (2006) some of the common consequences of Poor Quality are:

- Loss of business: Loss in sales, revenues and customer base,
- Liability: A poor quality product or service comes with the danger of the organization being taken to court by an unhappy or affected customer,
- Productivity: Loss in productivity as more time is spend in rectifying the errors or short coming then producing more, and
- Costs: Increase in costs as a poor quality product is repaired, replaced, or made new.

DIFFERENT DISCIPLINARY PERSPECTIVES ON TQM

Everyone defines Quality based on their own perspective of it. One of the most determinants of how people perceive quality is the functional role they play in the organisation. Artists and scientists process information differently, so do employees who perform different functions in an organisation. Accountants are interested in information for accounting and tax purposes, operations people want information for process control and scheduling, finance people need information to manage cash flows and marketing people need information to see whether sales quotas are being made. Foster, Howard and Shannon (2002) argued that the organic view of the organisation sees the whole as the sum of different parts uniting to achieve one end. They further argued that, "….the heart and liver do not perform the same function in a body, but they each perform processes that are necessary for survival of the whole". Just as the body is subject to breakdown when different parts are not performing properly so are organisations. Recognizing fundamental differences between how different functions view quality is an important first step in understanding and resolving problems associated with mismatching of quality perceptions within organisations. The functional perceptions of quality discussed here are:

- Supply chain management perception,
- Engineering perception of quality,
- Operations management perception,
- Strategic Management perception,
- Marketing perception,
- Finance/Accounting perception,
- Human Resources perception and value added perception.

Supply Chain Perspective

Supply Chain Management (SCM) grew out of the concept of the value chain, which includes in-bound logistics, core processes and out-bound logistics (Foster, 2017). Other functions in the organisation support these core processes. The SCM develop suppliers through supplier evaluations, training and implementing systems with suppliers. This often includes the use of electronic data interchange (EDI) to link customer purchasing systems to supplier enterprise resource systems.

Engineering Perspective

According to Foster (2017) engineering is an applied science, as such, engineers are interested in applying mathematical problem solving skills and models to the problems of business and industry. Two of the major emphasis in engineering is the area of product and process design. Product design engineering involves all those activities associated with designing a product or service from conception development to final design and implementation. Product or service production is the key because quality is assured at the design stage.

Operations Management Perspective

An operation management view of quality is rooted in the engineering approach. Operation was the first functional field of management to adopt quality as its own and is the core of the global supply chain model. Like engineers, operation managers are concerned about product/service and process design. However, rather than focusing on only the technical aspects of these activities, operation management also concentrates on their management (Foster, 2017). Operations management has developed into an integrative field combining concepts from engineering, operation research, organisational theory, organisational behaviour and strategic management to address quality problems. Operations Management uses the systems view that underlies modern quality management thinking. The systems view involves the understanding that product quality is the result of the interactions of several variables such as machines, labour, procedures, planning and management (Edvardsson and Gustafsson, 2008). Operations management focuses on the management and continual improvement of conversion processes. It focuses on the interaction between the various components (i.e. people, policies, machines, processes and products) that combine to produce a product or service. The systems view also focuses management on the system as the cause of quality problems.

Strategic Management Perspective

Strategic management refers to the planning process used by an organisation to achieve a set of long term goals. The organisation establishes a planned course of action to attain their objectives. This planned course of action must be cohesive and coherent in terms of goals, policies, plans and sequencing to achieve quality improvement (Edvardsson and Gustafsson, 2008).

Marketing Perspective

Traditionally marketing referred activities involved with directing the flow of products and services from the producer to consumer. Currently with customer relations management, marketing has directed its attention toward satisfying the customer and delivering value to the customer. The marketer focuses on the perceived quality of products and services. All marketing efforts are focussed on managing quality perceptions and quality management systems. The marketing systems involve the interactions between the producing organisation, the intermediary and the final consumer. One of the ways marketing has helped to improve product and service quality has been the interacting closely with engineering and operations in product/service design. In the design process marketing has taken the role of bringing the voice of the customer into the design process (Foster, 2017; Edvardsson and Gustafsson, 2008).

Financial Perspective

When you talk of quality management in any organisation, managers are quick to ask 'will this pay the organisation financially, or what are the financial gains for the organisation'. Implemented correctly, improved quality reduces waste and can lead to reduced costs and improved profitability. According to Deming (2007) improved quality is linked to reduction in defects and improved organisational performance. Deming also stressed quality as a way to increase employment. The financial function is primarily interested in the relationship between the risk of investment and the potential rewards resulting from those investments.

Human Resources Perspective

Human Resources (HR) managers are involved in enabling the workforce to develop and use its full potential to meet the company's objectives. Understanding the HR perspective on quality is important for managers as is practically impossible to implement quality with the commitment and action from employees. Leadership and employees' involvement and participation are important antecedents to successful quality efforts; it is the rank and file that implements quality throughout the organisation. In order to achieve the desired quality in an organisation it is important to empower employees by giving them authority to make decisions at all levels. Empowerment will give the employees that feeling of belonging; they will feel as important members of the organisation (Foster, 2017). HR will play the balancing act between the personal needs of each employ and the organisational objectives. HR should endeavour to create a tight-fit between employees' and organisation's objectives. Quality management flourish where the workers' and the company's needs are closely aligned. The needs are aligned, actions that are good and compatible to both the organisation and workers become order of the day.

Value-Added Perspective

According to (Foster, 2017) a customer-based perspective on quality, which is common in services, manufacturing and public sector organisations that involves the concept of value. A value added perspective on quality involves a subjective assessment of the efficacy of every step of the process for the customer. In order to address this perspective such questions as, 'would this activity matter to the customer' are addressed. A value added activity is that which will proffer economic value to the customer.

QUALITY MANAGEMENT SYSTEMS

Any organisation that skillfully address the various perspectives discussed above will definitely improve its quality management systems that subsequently leads to better performance, profitability and gained competitive advantage (Foster, 2017). If a company has reached its best levels, gained the market share and gained the company of choice status, the next thing would be to discover that next step that will enable it to continually improve on its quality of goods and services. There are some building blocks for continual improvement of quality systems that can be employed by any organisation regardless of type and size.

Building Blocks for the System of Quality Improvement (The Quality System Model)

A quality system depends on the interaction of many different variables. Quality improvement is not a stand-alone discipline, it requires the interactions on a contingency basis of many other disciplines to create products, services, processes and systems that effectively serve customers (Edvardsson and Gustafsson, 2008; Foster, 2017). The complexity of work requires people from different disciplines to settle on standardized methods for serving customers that result in work simplification. Figure 2 depicts the building blocks in the quality service model.

People

According to Foster (2017) people represents the core of a firm's capabilities because they provide the intellect, empathy and the ability required to provide outstanding customer service. A system must be put in place to develop, train, care for and motivate people to serve the customer properly. For a quality system to function effectively, employees must understand that they are an integral part of the system. They must be made to feel important and necessary for the continued survival and growth of the company. Another people related activity involves organisational restructuring and redesigning. When properly performed, quality improvement efforts lead to improved morale and confidence among employees that the company is becoming more competitive and employees' security is improving.

Figure 2. The Quality Service Model
Source: Foster, (2017:427)

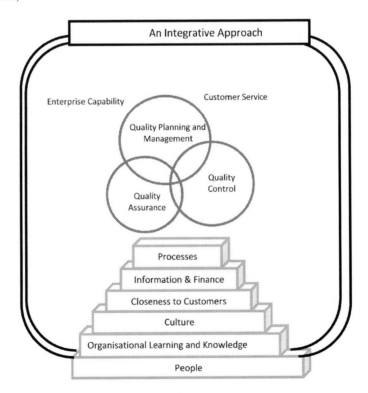

Organisational Learning and Knowledge

Organisational learning and knowledge is another building block of a quality system. Knowledge is the capital that fuels outstanding quality results and life-long learning is a key attribute for employees (Foster, 2017; (Edvardsson and Gustafsson, 2008). Managers should carefully consider the organisational and cultural aspects of their companies that inhibit and fail to reward life-long learning. Employees do not like to do a job and feel that management does not value their knowledge or opinion. One of the by-products of a quality empowerment effort is the realization by management that rank and file employees are primary sources for in-depth knowledge relating to processes and that organisational learning is the sum of the learning of individual employees. Learning needs assessment, training design and delivering of training are important for the organisation's competitive. Outstanding customer services are a result of outstanding employee knowledge and training. Organisational learning is required for consistency in operation, approaches and customer contact (Foster, 2017).

Culture

Culture refers to norms and beliefs that lead to decision-making patterns and actions in an organisation. Some organisations have cultures conducive to quality improvement and some make quality improvement very difficult. Some of the key aspects of culture include attitudes towards change, presence or absence of fear, degree of openness, fairness and trust, and employee behaviour at all levels. Many authors (Conti, 2006; Dahlgaard, and Kanji, 2009; Foster, 2017; Edvardsson and Gustafsson, 2008) are in agreement that, companies that play blame games end up with cultures in which trust is absent, and employees act in self-defence ways. Companies that work in an environment of fear will find that distrust takes root between labour and management, between middle and top level managers, and between departments. Companies must put in place control systems to manage the environment.

Closeness to Customers

Closeness to customers describes the firm's understanding of customers, their needs and wants. According to Foster (2017) the building block of closeness to customers is built on people, organisational learning and knowledge and organisational culture. All these variables result in a supportive environment in which employees can be close to customers. Companies that value knowledge will gather data about customers and will also study and understand the ever-changing customer needs. In order to achieve customer closeness, systems must be put in place for gathering data about customers, analysing the data, and implementing change systems based on the analysis (Edvardsson and Gustafsson, 2008). There is also need for understanding of competitors' customers in order to come up with marketing strategies that will attract those customers away from your competitors. Customer closeness engenders loyalty, understanding of the type of customers that a firm must serve and focusing on key capabilities.

Information and Finance

The information systems provide the core of the support systems for satisfying the customer. Foster (2017) argued that well-designed organisational information systems will automatically become the institutional memory for customer needs. If they are not well designed, and information is difficult or slow to obtain, customers will go elsewhere. Electronic Data Interchange (EDI) is of increasing importance for satisfying customer needs (Klefsjö, Wiklund, and Edgeman, 2001). These systems will allow customers and suppliers to tie their systems together in order to enhance planning, purchasing and coordination. The objective of quality information systems is to gather information relating to the key variables that affect customer services and product quality. The scope of the information system includes the entire organisation, linkages to customers and suppliers, better information leads to better customer services. Problem identification, analysis and corrective measures are the actions required to make the information systems effective. Financial resources are needed to provide the infrastructure and services needed by customers. It takes money for medical doctors to decorate their offices in a way that pleases the patients, to have state of the art technology that will result in sate of the art care, and to provide the equipment needed to achieve customer satisfaction. High quality can improve bottom line results and enhance and enhance financial stability.

Three Spheres of Quality

The building blocks of quality improvement provide the foundation to the quality system that supports the three key spheres of quality; quality planning and management, quality assurance, and quality control (Foster, 2017). The spheres are closely related to company capabilities and customer service. Enterprise capabilities are those capabilities firms have that make them unique and attractive to customers. Customer service is both a goal and outcome of systems. Processes, procedures, training and enterprise capabilities must be focused on providing good customer service.

Integrative Approach to Quality Improvement

The integrative approach provides the glue that binds together the systems that result in high-quality products and services. Since quality is not under the purview of any specific functional group and is the responsibility of everyone, cross-functional approaches are required to achieve the required results. The integrative system view recognises that all the building blocks must be in place in all the functional areas and throughout all levels of the organisation for quality improvement to be both horizontally and vertically deployed. Successful companies that provide high-quality products and services are able to take the focus away from narrow functional orientation and turn it to broad, customer-centred systems.

ASSESSMENT OF QUALITY SYSTEMS

Evans and Dean (2003) postulate that, once a quality system has been established, it must be allowed to operate effectively over a given period of time. It must be noted that the system must be in constant change as continuous improvement efforts occur throughout the organisation. At times it becomes difficult to come up with new ideas for improvement, especially when the company is operating well or is competitive and profitable. In this case Foster (2017) advises that benchmarking can be used to observe the practices of others and achieve even higher levels of performance. When the company has achieved benchmark or role model status, the ideas and initiatives for improvement must come from within the

Figure 3. The Self-Assessment Process Model
Source: Foster (2017:433)

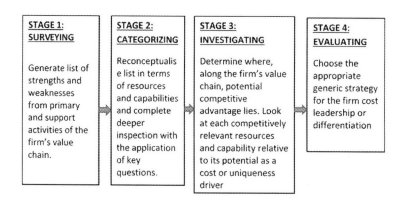

Figure 4: Quality Audit Model
Source: Foster (2017)

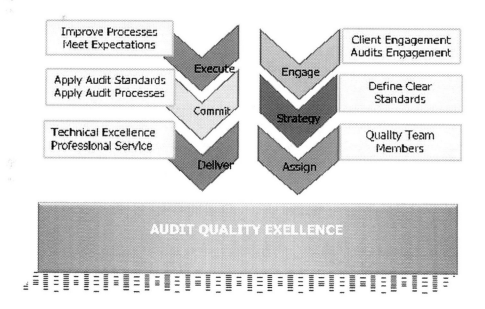

organisation. Self-assessment is a good and strategic tool to spur quality improvement. The goal of self-assessment is to observe current practices, to assess those practices and to identify gaps in deployment of resources for quality processes. Once the gaps have been identified and plugged off new levels of performance can then and only be achieved.

Stage 1: Surveying

Surveying is the means in which strengths and weaknesses of the organisation are generated and documented.

Stage 2: Categorizing

This stage involves categorizing the strengths and weaknesses of the organisation. Strengths can be categorized as strategic resources or strategic capabilities that help define the path for improvement the firm should undertake.

Stage 3: Investigation

This stage involves investigating the sources of competitive advantage that the company enjoys or that the competitors enjoy. These investigations should address questions as regard to how the firm markets itself, how the firm differentiates itself from competitors, how the firm wins orders in the market place, and how the firm achieves competitive advantage over competitors (Foster, 2017).

Stage 4: Evaluation

The stage involves evaluation of competitive advantage enjoyed by both the company and its competitors in order assess how relevant resources and capabilities are in terms of generic strategies to be employed in future. Foster (2017) pointed out that the primary question to be asked include to what extend does the alignment between resources allocation in the firm and primary marketing and operational objectives of the firm match?

QUALITY SYSTEMS AUDIT

According to Ishikawa (2008) "quality audit is the process of systematic examination of a quality system carried out by an internal or external quality auditor or an audit team; it is an important part of an organization's quality management system and a key element in the ISO quality system standard (ISO 9001)". It is a carried out periodically and the auditors must be independent of any influence. Once with the audit, quality auditors must document examine and verify all activities, records, processes, and other elements of a quality system to determine their conformity with the requirements of a quality standard such as ISO 9000. Any failure in their proper implementation may be published publicly and may lead to a revocation of quality certification. It is also called conformity assessment or quality system audit.

Foster (2017) argues that "…quality audits are typically performed at predefined time intervals and ensure that the institution has clearly defined internal system monitoring procedures linked to effective action". Quality audits will help to determine whether the organization is complying with the defined quality system processes and can involve procedural or results-based assessment criteria.

According to McAdam and Bannister (2001) quality audits focus on procedural adherence, measurement of the actual effectiveness of the Quality Management System (QMS) and the results that have been achieved through the implementation of a QMS.

They are an indispensable management tool that is regularly used for:

- Verifying objective evidence of processes;
- Assessing how successful implementation of processes has been;
- Judging the effectiveness of achieving any defined target levels, and
- Providing evidence concerning reduction and elimination of problem areas.

In order for it to benefit the organisation, quality auditing should not only report non-conformances and corrective actions, but also highlight areas of good practice. As a result of quality audit all departments in an organisation will share information and amend their working practices and positively contribute to continual improvement.

Feigenbaum (2016) argues that, "Quality audits must be an integral part of compliance or regulatory requirements". Several countries have adopted quality audits in their higher education system (New Zealand, Australia, Sweden, Finland, Norway and USA). Initiated in the UK, the process of quality audit in the education system focused primarily on procedural issues rather than on the results or the efficiency of a quality system implementation. Audits can also be used for safety purposes. Evans & Parker (2008) describe auditing as "one of the most powerful safety monitoring techniques and 'an effective way to avoid complacency and highlight slowly deteriorating conditions', especially when the auditing focuses not just on compliance but effectiveness".

Performing an internal audit first allows you to gain knowledge of what areas you need to improve upon. Internal audits are important to any business because they can evaluate your processes and ensure that you are meeting quality standards and conformance. According to Treacy and Wiersema (2013) to higher education, audits are frequently associated with examinations to verify the compliance of the accounting methods used in financial statements, the teaching and learning of university programmes, teaching and non-teaching staff compliments and qualifications, examinations and full coverage of course outlines, and examination processes. The main objective of quality audit is checking that procedures are in place to assure quality, integrity or standards of provision and outcomes. An audit is an evaluation of the strengths and weaknesses of the quality mechanisms established by an institution itself to continuously monitor and improve the activities and services of a subject, a programme, the whole institution or a theme. Treacy and Wiersema (2013) argued that there are common characteristics of all quality audit processes carried out regardless of type and size of an organisation.

The three common characteristics of audit procedures are as follows:

- **Focus on Institutional Quality Assurance**

The procedures have an explicit focus on measures and/or processes set by higher education institutions with the purpose of assuring and developing quality in teaching and learning, and (in some cases) in research and development. Audits are to be distinguished from institutional reviews, which go beyond internal quality assurance and refer more to criteria related to the programmes offered by institutions, such as study programmes, research, infrastructure and resources.

- **Enhancement Orientation**

Quality audits must support quality enhancement in higher education institutions. Unlike accreditation and affiliation, quality audits do not primarily verify the achievement of (minimum) standards with regard to the formal recognition of a (new) study programme or institution, but instead demonstrate the capacity of an (existing) institution to assure (and develop) its own quality. Although the enhancement function of external and independent quality assurance procedures may be seen to conflict with the function of accountability, audit models must combine the two.

- **Evidence Through Samples**

Quality Audits demand evidence of the existence of internal quality assurance, which is generally provided through samples, such as 'audit targets', 'selected themes', 'fields of performance', or 'exemplary study programmes'. These samples are intended to demonstrate the performance of internal quality assurance and are reviewed in more detail.

Quality audit makes use of certain parameters to measure the level of compliance with or adherence to predefined standards or requirements, in order to demonstrate the capacity of an institution to assure and develop its own quality. Stakeholder participation has become one of the key areas assessed in the quality audit process in many countries, where the institution is not only expected to involve students, labour market needs or 'society' in its strategic planning and operational activities, but also is expected to demonstrate how this involvement is actually being utilised.

CONCLUSION

TQM is a corporate culture [and/or management philosophy] characterised by increased customer satisfaction through continuous improvements with active participation of all employees (Dahlgaard et al, 2008). It is a management system containing interdependent components in order to increase internal and external customers' satisfaction with a reduced amount of resources (Hellsten and Klefsjö, 2000). Total Quality Management is a people-focused management system, which includes systems, methods, and tools that aims at continual increase in customer satisfaction at continually lower real cost (Evans and Dean Jr, 2003). It is an approach whose main objective is to improving the effectiveness and flexibility of business as a whole (Oakland, 2009). There are principles and concepts that can be identified as TQM's core values. There are many "versions" regarding the description of TQM core values, and principles. Main and most common factors of TQM as argued by most authors include:

- Management commitment/leadership,
- Customer and employee focus,
- Focus on facts,
- Continuous improvements,
- Everybody's participation/ involvement.
- Process focus,
- Innovation focus, and
- Environmental focus.

All these are included in Dahlgaard-Park's (1999) finding that TQM consists of twelve (12) principles. An extensive literature review by Mehra et al (2001) suggests that there are forty five (45) critical elements of TQM's practice, which can be grouped into five (5) main factors: human resources focus, management structure, quality tools, supplier support, and customer orientation. A successful implementation of TQM to improve the company's quality cannot neglect the contribution of performance measurements (Juran, 1993; McAdam and Bannister, 2001; Dahlgaard and Dahlgaard-Park, 2002). The importance of performance measurement can never be neglected because a performance measurement system is a part of the value management framework.

REFERENCES

Bathie, D., & Sarkar, J. (2002). Total Quality Marketing (TQMk) – A Sympiosis. *Managerial Auditing Journal, 17*(5), 241–244. doi:10.1108/02686900210429650

Bergman, B., & Klefsjö, B. (2004). *Quality – from customer needs to customer satisfaction.* Lund, Sweden: Studentliteratur.

Bounds, G., Yorks, L., Adam, M. G., & Ranney, G. (2004). *Beyond Total Quality Management: towards the emerging paradigm.* New York: McGraw-Hill.

Brady, J. A., & Allen, T. T. (2006). Six Sigma Literature: A review and agenda for future research. *Quality and Reliability Engineering International, 22*(3), 335–336. doi:10.1002/qre.769

Conti, T. (2006). Quality Thinking and Systems Thinking. *The TQM Magazine, 18*(3), 297–308. doi:10.1108/09544780610660013

Dahlgaard, J. J., K., K., & Kanji, G. (2009). *Fundamentals of Total Quality Management.* Nelson Thornes.

Dahlgaard-Park, S. (2009). The Evolution Patterns of Quality Management: Some reflections on the quality movement. *Total Quality Management, 10*(4&5), 473–480.

Edvardsson, B., & Gustafsson, A. (2008). Quality in the Development of New Products and Services. In B. Edvardsson & A. Gustafsson (Eds.), *The Nordic School of Quality Management.* Studentliteratur.

Evans, J., & Dean, J. J. (2003). *Total Quality: Management Organisation and Strategy* (3rd ed.). New York: Thomson South Western.

Feigenbaum, A. (2016). Total Quality Control. *Harvard Business Review, 34*(6), 93–101.

Feigenbaum, A. (2016). *Total Quality Control.* New York: McGraw-Hill.

Foster, S. T. (2017). *Mnaging Quality: Integrating the Supply Chain.* Cape Town: Pearson.

Harry, M., & Crawford, D. (2005). Six Sigma – the next generation. *Machine Design, 77*(4), 126–130.

Harvey, L., & Green, D. (1993). Defining Quality: Assessment and Evaluation in Higher Education. *The Quality Management Journal, 18*(1), 9–34.

Hellsten, U. K., & Klefsjö, B. (2000). TQM as a management system consisting values, techniques, and tools. *The TQM Magazine, 12*(4), 238–24. doi:10.1108/09544780010325822

Ishikawa, K. (2008). *What is Total Quality Control? – the Japanese way*. Prentice-Hall.

Juran, J. (2014). Why Quality Initiatives Fail. *The Journal of Business Strategy, 14*(4), 35–38. doi:10.1108/eb039571 PMID:10127318

Klefsjö, B., Wiklund, H., & Edgeman, R. (2001). Six Sigma Seen as a Methodology for Total Quality Management. *Measuring Business Excellence, 5*(1), 31–35. doi:10.1108/13683040110385809

Kondo, Y. (2003). *Company Wide Quality Control*. Tokyo, Japan: 3A Corporation .

Linderman, K., Schroeder, R., Zaheer, S., Liedtke, C., & Choo, A. (2004). Integrating Quality Management Practices with Knowledge Creation Process. *Journal of Operations Management, 23*(6), 589–607. doi:10.1016/j.jom.2004.07.001

McAdam, R., & Bannister, A. (2001). Business Performance Measurement and Change within a TQM Framework. *International Journal of Operations & Production Management, 21*(1/2), 88–107. doi:10.1108/01443570110358477

Mehra, S., Hoffman, J., & Sirias, D. (2001). TQM as a Management Strategy for The Next Millenia. *International Journal of Operations & Production Management, 21*(5/6), 855–876. doi:10.1108/01443570110390534

Oakland, J. (2008). *Total Quality Management*. Oxford, UK: Heinemann Professional Publishing.

Oh, H. (2009). Service Quality, Customer Satisfaction, and Customer Value: A holistic perspective. *Hospital Management, 18*(1), 67–82. doi:10.1016/S0278-4319(98)00047-4

Page, R., & Curry, A. (2000). TQM – a holistic view. *The TQM Magazine, 12*(1), 11–18. doi:10.1108/09544780010287159

Stoner, J. F., Freeman, R. E., & Gilbert, D. R. (2009). *Management*. London: Pearson.

Treacy, M., & Wiersema, F. (2013). Customer Intimacy and Other Value Disciplines. *Harvard Business Review, 71*(1), 84–93.

Womack, J., & Jones, D. T. (2006). Beyond Toyota: How to root out waste and pursue perfection. *Harvard Business Review, 74*(5), 55–65.

Chapter 4
Quality Management and Higher Education Scenario in Namibia:
A Critical Analysis

Selma Mupeniwo Iipinge
Namibia University of Science and Technology, Namibia

Anna M. Shimpanda
Namibia University of Science and Technology, Namibia

Ngepathimo Kadhila
University of Namibia, Namibia

ABSTRACT

The new wave in the higher education space, which includes mass access to higher education, changes in the diverse needs of the student body, economic challenges faced by many countries, societal and general stakeholder expectations, relationships with external stakeholders, and new funding mechanisms has necessitated new forms of accountability in the sector. These factors have a profound influence on the handling of quality assurance arrangements at both national and institutional levels. This chapter seeks to critically analyze the current state of quality management practices in higher education in Namibia at both national and institutional levels. The chapter identifies achievements that have been recorded so far, as well as challenges and areas for further development.

INTRODUCTION

Globally, quality has emerged as one of the determinants of a university's world ranking and competitiveness. The concept of "quality in higher education" is thus of immense concern for academics and academia globally, and Namibia is no exemption. In its visions of becoming a knowledge-based industrialised country, Namibia recognises quality higher education as one of the key aspects in moving towards

DOI: 10.4018/978-1-7998-1017-9.ch004

its long-term development aspiration of Vision 2030. To realise this, the acquisition of relevant skills through quality higher education remains a priority (National Planning Commission Secretariat, 2004).

Higher education in the Namibian context refers to all learning programmes that lead to qualifications equivalent to National Qualification Framework (NQF) level 5 and higher and are offered by higher education institutions as defined in the Higher Education Act, Act 26 of 2003 (GRN, Act No. 26 of 2003). This Act established the National Council for Higher Education (NCHE) to promote a coordinated higher education system, enhance students' access to higher education and ensure quality higher education. It mandates the NCHE to conduct registration of private higher education providers, programme accreditation and institutional audit. Another Act that regulates higher education is the Namibia Qualifications Authority (NQA) Act (NQA Act No. 29 of 1996), which established the NQA and mandated it to set up and administer the NQF, set standards for all occupations, evaluate international qualifications, and accredit education and training providers (GRN, Act No. 29 of 1996). The third Act is the Vocational Education and Training Act (Act No. 1 of 2008), which establishes the Namibia Training Authority (NTA) with the mandate to coordinate and ensure quality in technical vocational education and training (TVET) (GRN, Act No. 1 of 2008).

Higher education in Namibia is relatively small, with only two public universities and one private university; the rest are colleges without university status. The focus of this chapter is on higher education institutions with university status. Public universities are established by Acts of Parliament and consist of the University of Namibia (UNAM) which was established in 1992 (Act no. 18 of 1992), and Namibia University of Science and Technology (NUST) (Act no. 7 of 2015). The latter was transformed from a polytechnic. The only private university, the International University of Management (IUM), was established in 2002.

It is acknowledged that higher education plays a significant role in national socioeconomic development. For higher education to play this role meaningfully, quality becomes paramount. Although studies have identified critical issues and concerns pertaining to quality management in academic organisations around the globe, little emphasis has been placed on the quality management practices of higher education institutions in Namibia. According to Kadhila (2012), there is a lack of publicly available, transparent information on quality assurance and management processes and their outcomes in higher education institutions in Namibia. This is supported by Papanthymou and Darra (2017), who found that apart from a few studies in the field of quality management, there are also gaps in the quality models that are used by higher education institutions. Hence, the need to provide valuable information on the subject in order to improve quality management in Namibian higher education institutions.

The purpose of this chapter is, therefore, to examine the current status, challenges and practical implications of quality management in higher education in Namibia, with a specific focus on national quality assurance agencies and the two public universities, in comparison to international best practice. Based on the conclusions made and as informed by the analysis, the chapter makes suggestions aimed at the improvement of the practice of quality management in higher education in Namibia. In addition, the chapter is informed by the authors' experiences, an analysis of official institutional documents and individual interviews conducted with personnel from public higher education institutions and the national quality assurance agencies in Namibia.

BACKGROUND

The issue of quality management on a global level has been firmly on the agenda of higher education institutions for a lengthy period. Forces such as globalisation, higher education for the masses and a growing climate of increased accountability are frequently cited as rationales for a greater emphasis on quality (Becket & Brookes, 2006; Eriksen, 1995; Oldfield & Baron, 1998). Other influencing factors include students' expectations and diversity, their demand for increased flexibility in provision, and increasing levels of competition within and across national borders (Brookes & Becket, 2007). These factors demand that quality assurance processes should be both rigorous and transparent, and that quality enhancement initiatives be firmly embedded in institutional management at all levels of operation. Such processes should also be included in programme design and delivery, research and development, community engagement activities and support services. As Pierce (1995) states, people have become more critical of authority and no longer willing to place total confidence in "ivory tower" image of higher education institutions but expect evidence that higher education is providing good quality educational services and value for money.

Over the past decade, quality assurance in the higher education sector has generated much debate globally among stakeholders of higher education (Anane & Addaney, 2016). It is against this background that quality assurance has become the concern of higher education institutions; and the quality of higher education is increasingly considered as strategically important for national economic development and competitiveness (World Bank, 2009). Likewise, in Namibia, Kadhila (2012) points out that there has been increasing recognition of the importance of quality higher education in national development. This relationship between quality higher education and national economic development has therefore foregrounded existing assumptions that higher education will provide the necessary quality inputs and the expected quality outputs, that is, quality graduates.

In response to international trends and contextual needs, the Government of the Republic of Namibia (GRN) has established national quality assurance agencies to implement quality assurance systems at a national level. As seen in the introduction section, the history of quality assurance dates back to the 1990s with the establishment of the NQA, and later the NCHE and the NTA as external quality assurance agencies. Prior to the implementation of external quality assurance systems, there was no framework for quality management and each institution was managing quality in its own way (NCHE, 2009). The establishment of external quality assurance agencies brought with it the implementation of mechanisms such as institutional registration, accreditation and audits as a way of managing quality.

In the same vein, at institutional level, higher education institutions have implemented internal quality assurance systems with the establishment of quality assurance units at both NUST and UNAM in 2009 and 2010 respectively. This is in recognition of the fact that although quality assurance may be externally regulated, the primary responsibility for quality lies with higher education institutions themselves. The literature reveals that apart from unpublished official documents, there is limited empirical literature on quality management in higher education in Namibia. Hence, the need to examine the field of quality management in higher education in an effort to close the existing knowledge gap and inform policy and decision making in higher education in Namibia.

Quality, Quality Assurance and Quality Management

Quality is a contested concept; we know it when we see it. It is relative, contextual, and time bound, and absolute quality does not exist (Harvey & Green, 1993). It can be compared to beauty that lies in the eyes of the beholder. Quality in higher education is seen as a multidimensional construct which is interpreted in different ways by diverse stakeholders (Cheng & Tam, 1997; Dicker, Garcia, Kelly & Mulrooney, 2018; Pounder, 1999). It therefore creates complexity in its measurement and management. Moreover, there is still no universal consensus on how best to manage quality within higher education, although a variety of quality management models have been implemented in different higher education institutions (Kalusi, 2001; Martens & Prosser, 1998; Martin & Parikh, 2017).

The means in which quality is defined in research and put into practice have obvious implications for efforts to manage it. Yet, many stakeholders in higher education would find it difficult to define quality precisely. The differences in the way that quality management is defined and understood in various contexts thus lead to differences in the focus and coverage of tools and processes (Martin & Parikh, 2017). This supports Pounder's (1999, p. 156) view that quality is a "notoriously ambiguous term" since it has different meanings for different stakeholders.

It is clear that there is no single definition for quality. Harvey and Green (1993) proposed some of the most widely used notions of "quality" in higher education, which are categorised into five interrelated dimensions. In defining quality, higher education institutions in Namibia refer to Harvey and Green's notions summarised in Table 1 below.

Considering the notions of quality in Table 1, quality in higher education is seen as a multidimensional construct which is interpreted in different ways by diverse stakeholders. This, in turn, creates complexity in its measurement and management of quality. Therefore, to be meaningful, quality in higher education must be defined with the context in mind.

Quality assurance, on the other hand, involves the systematic internal and external management procedures and mechanisms by which higher education institutions assure stakeholders of the quality of their systems, processes, products and outcomes and their ability to manage the maintenance and enhancement of quality (Luckett, 2007). It encompasses all those planned and systematic actions such

Table 1. Quality notions

Definition	Explanation
Quality as excellence	The exceptional view of quality sees quality as something special. This view is often regarded as a traditional definition of quality which links quality to exceptionally high achievement standards. Here, quality is achieved if standards are surpassed.
Quality as "fitness for purpose"	This view judges quality in terms of the extent to which a product or service meets its stated purpose. Quality as fitness for purpose sees quality in terms of fulfilling a customer's requirements, needs or desires.
Quality as value for money	Here, quality is assessed in terms of the return on investment or expenditure.
Quality as transformation	Quality as transformation is a classic notion of quality that sees it in terms of change from one state to another. Quality is seen as a process of change and "value adding". Education is not a service to a customer but an ongoing transformation process in the student.
Quality as consistency/ Perfection	Quality as perfection sees quality as a consistency of flawless outcome, which reflects the interrelated ideas of zero defects and getting things right the first time.

Source: Harvey and Green (1993).

as policies, attitudes, actions and procedures necessary to provide adequate confidence that quality is being maintained and enhanced. Quality assurance can be externally or internally driven, or both. In the Namibian context, the quality assurance systems are characterised by internal (higher education institutions themselves) and external (quality assurance agencies) quality assurance mechanisms.

Internal quality assurance encompasses all the activities that a higher education institution must carry out internally in order to maintain and improve their quality. Internal quality assurance mechanisms may include external moderation and examination systems, self-assessment (usually followed by external peer assessment for validation), benchmarking and stakeholder feedback (Kadhila, 2012). External quality assurance, on the other hand, refers to a range of quality monitoring procedures that are undertaken by bodies outside a higher education institution (i.e. professional bodies or quality assurance agencies) in order to determine whether the institution meets agreed or predetermined quality standards. Generally speaking, the system of external quality assurance has two main purposes, namely, quality improvement and external accountability (Kadhila, 2012). In the Namibian context, external quality assurance involves registration of higher education institutions (normally private), institutional and/or programme accreditation by professional bodies and/or quality assurance agencies, and institutional audits.

Quality assurance regulatory instruments include documents such as senate regulations, admission policies, mission statements and strategic plans. Robust internal quality assurance systems instil public confidence and trust in the ability of a given higher education institution to deliver higher quality education and training. Quality assurance is thus designed to prove and improve the quality of an institution's methods, educational products and outcomes; accordingly, the quality of a higher education institution is there to be seen by outsiders.

Quality management is defined as an aggregate of measures taken regularly at a system or institutional level in order to assure the quality of higher education with an emphasis on improving quality. As a generic term, it covers all activities that ensure fulfilment of the quality policy and the quality objectives and responsibilities and implements them through quality planning, quality control, quality assurance and quality improvement mechanisms (UNAM, 2015). Quality management is further defined in research as a general comprehensive term; it covers both process and structure, and can be seen as the techniques and instruments used to improve the quality directly and also as establishing operating mechanisms by making the activities of institutions more accountable, transparent and efficient (Pratasavitskaya & Stenssaker, 2010). In a nutshell, quality management therefore focuses on achieving quality and on the acceptance and pursuit of continuous improvement in the products and/or services. In the Namibian context, quality management focuses on institutional day-to-day activities to enhance quality. Robust quality management based on a deliberate process of change may lead to a quality culture and an improvement of the student learning experience, which is the desired state of quality assurance.

MAIN FOCUS OF THE CHAPTER

Managing Quality in Higher Education: International Perspective

Higher education is observed as strategically important for national economic development and competitiveness (World Bank, 2009). Given the broad importance of higher education, concerns about the quality and relevance of its services have emerged over the years. Adding to these concerns are the new trends in higher education such as fierce full global competition, lifelong learning, student migration, rapid dissemination of knowledge, internationalisation of education and the development of higher education as an export-oriented industry. These underscore the need for continuous improvement in academic quality (Toma & Naruo, 2009, p. 575).

The introduction of quality assurance and quality management in higher education at the international level is a result of the above-mentioned factors. Therefore, many governments and higher education institutions all over the globe have adopted and put in place quality assurance and management practices of some sort. Table 2 identifies and defines the different quality management models that have been applied internationally in various higher education institutions.

From the above list of models, TQM is one of the frequently implemented quality management models in higher education.

TQM is defined as a management approach of an organisation, centred on quality, based on the participation of all its members and aiming at long run success through customer satisfaction and benefits to all members of the organisation and to society (ISO 8402, in Wiklund, Wiklund, & Edvardsson, 2003, p. 99).

Al-Tarawneh and Mubaslat (2011) define TQM as a philosophy and system for continuously improving the services offered to customers (Al-Tarawneh & Mubaslat, 2011).

As the definition implies, TQM has the potential to encompass the quality perspectives of both external and internal stakeholders in an integrated manner. It enables a comprehensive approach to quality management that will assure quality as well as facilitate change and innovation. According to Al-Tarawneh and Mubaslat (2011), TQM is both a philosophy and a system for continuously improving the services offered to customers.

Other models emulate TQM and concentrate on developing systematic business processes for achieving measurable quality outputs. The key benefit of using these models is the requirement for higher educa-

Table 2. Different models for quality management

TQM	TQM stands for total quality management. A comprehensive management approach which requires all participants in the organisation to work together towards long-term benefits for those involved and society as a whole.
EFQM excellence model	This refers to the European Foundation for Quality Management excellence model. It is a non-prescriptive framework that establishes nine criteria (divided between enablers and results) suitable for any organisation to use when assessing progress towards excellence.
Balanced scorecard	This model is a performance/strategic management system which utilises four measurement perspectives: financial; customer; internal process; and learning and growth.
Malcolm Baldridge award	Based on a framework of performance excellence which can be used by organisations to improve performance. This model has seven categories of criteria: leadership; strategic planning; customer and market focus; measurement, analysis, and knowledge management; human resource focus; process management; and results.
ISO 9000 series	International standard for generic quality assurance systems which is concerned with continuous improvement through preventative action. Its elements are customer quality and regulatory requirements, and efforts made to enhance customer satisfaction and achieve continuous improvement.
Business process re-engineering	This is a system that enables the redesign of business processes, systems and structures to achieve improved performance. It is concerned with change in five components: strategy; processes; technology; organisation; and culture.
SERVQUAL	SERVQUAL stands for Service Quality and is an instrument designed to measure consumer perceptions and expectations regarding quality of service in five dimensions: reliability; tangibles; responsiveness; assurance and empathy; and to identify where gaps exist.

Source: Becket and Brookes (2008).

tion institutions to adopt a strategic approach to quality measurement and management, and to engage in self-assessment against predetermined criteria (see, for example, Cullen, Joyce, Hassall, & Broadbent, 2003; Roberts & Tennant, 2003).

Rosa, Sarrico, and Amaral (2012) similarly maintain that although higher education institutions are not companies, some basic principles and tools can be applied as long as they are instruments at the service of the institutions' academic mission, goals and strategies. While these models are considered valuable within higher education, academics have argued that some of these models are not suitable for such institutions. This is supported by Srikanthan and Dalrymple (2002, p. 215), who view models such as TQM as industrial approaches and as inappropriate for academic functions. Srikanthan and Dalrymple further advise higher education institutions to develop a more holistic model that would serve to manage academic functions better.

In addition to quality management models, numerous bodies exist worldwide with the responsibility for quality assurance at institutional, national and regional levels, both in developed and developing countries. In many European and African countries, governments regulate higher education institutions through the creation of such bodies, in some cases independently and privately owned. This has been observed particularly in Europe and is done by enacting certain quality standards. These regulatory frameworks and structures are set to help in establishing quality control and promote access to quality higher education. Various approaches are used by quality assurance agencies in the world, but in most cases there is a combination of accreditation and audits, and these are usually conducted in a cyclical basis (Butcher, Hoosen, & Chetty, 2017). Accreditation and audits may be focused at different levels such as institutional and programme level, while audits may be conducted at the institutional level. Different quality assurance processes may also apply to public and private higher education institutions. For example, there may be programme accreditation for private providers and quality audits for public higher education institutions. In addition, programmes may be accredited by professional bodies.

According to Martin and Parikh (2017), more comprehensive and systematic approaches have been introduced in many countries over recent decades. Some of them have been guided by institutional initiatives, others by national reforms, and still others by regional policies, such as the Bologna Process in Europe with its heavy emphasis on quality management and its effect on the internationalisation activities of universities. However, Zmas (2015) points out that the transfer of the Bologna Process model around the world has proven to be complex with unclear consequences. He further argues that the outcomes of the international transfer of the BP model depend on existing policy discourses and practices, whose priorities may in fact differ from its postulates and therefore are affected by the socioeconomic, political, historical and cultural context of each region. For example, countries in Southern Africa (SADC) do not follow the Bologna Process itself, but they have benefited from exchanges with specific member states through the ad hoc initiatives of individual higher education institutions and governments on the opportunities offered by partner countries (Sintayehu, 2019).

Some quality assurance and management initiatives are cross-border by nature. For example, owing to the Bologna Process, higher education institutions in Europe are required to implement internal quality assurance systems based on the European Standards and Guidelines (ESG) that higher education institutions have to comply with. The Bologna Process encourages mobility by providing common tools for universities across Europe. Some of the most important tools include the European Credit Transfer and Accumulation System (ECTS) and the Diploma Supplement. These are all examples of good practice that Namibia could learn from. In the Bologna Process, although there are standard guidelines in place, the way in which the internal quality assurance is organised and its function is not specified. This means that it is up to each institution to define and implement its own system. Similarly, in Africa, there are different structures and initiatives set up at national, regional and continental levels in efforts to promote quality in higher education.

However, the decision is left up to the individual higher education institutions to define and implement their own quality assurance and management systems and processes in accordance with their mission, goals and institutional culture. These systems must of course also be aligned to national quality assurance requirements and beyond.

In some countries, the government exerts minimal control over higher education institutions. As an example, the United States (US) regional accreditation agencies do not impose any pre-set standards on higher education institutions. Their institutions are accredited on the basis of the institutional goals set by the higher education institutions themselves. The consequence of this autonomy is a large degree of diversity in terms of size, institutional goals, academic programmes, curricular and institutional governance structures (Teixeria, Kim, Landoni, & Gilani, 2017). Implementing such a process might, however, compromise the quality of education offered.

Managing quality in higher education has proved to be a challenging task. Literature suggests that there are two main reasons for this. Firstly, "quality" has different meanings for different stakeholders. Within the higher education sector, there are both internal and external stakeholders who have diverse views and understandings of quality. The second reason why quality is difficult to manage in higher education is the complicated and dynamic nature of higher education as a product (Soomro & Ahmad, 2012). Hence, as Cheng and Tam (1997, p. 23) argue, education quality is a rather vague and controversial concept.

As a result, its measurement and management has unsurprisingly proved to be contentious. While it is acknowledged that quality assurance and quality management improve the quality of higher education provision, it remains difficult to measure the impact of initiatives aimed at determining quality in higher education. This raises the question: how do we know whether the developments happening in higher education institutions are indeed a result of quality management?

State of Quality Management in the Namibian Higher Education System

Higher education has been recognised in Namibia as a driving force in the realisation of its developmental agenda, as stipulated in the national document Vision 2030. The national development agenda calls for quality enhancement in which the government is advocating for a well-educated Namibian workforce that will drive a knowledge-based economy (National Planning Commission Secretariat, 2004). In its effort to meet this objective, the government of Namibia has established agencies responsible for ensuring quality in higher education. Literature has shown that mechanisms for managing quality have been implemented in Namibia both at national and institutional levels. At national level, for instance, there is a combination of accreditation and audits, and these are usually conducted on a cyclical basis. Accreditation and audits may be focused at different levels. For example, accreditation may be at the institutional and programmatic level, while audits may be at the institutional level, or different quality assurance processes may apply to public and private and higher education institutions (e.g. there may be programme accreditation for private providers and quality audits for public universities). In particular, registration of private education providers is done at the institutional level, and accreditation for private providers and quality audits for public universities are done at the programme level. Other quality assurance measures used include programme validation, compliance visits, registration of institutions, and support visits to institutions. Additionally, programmes may be accredited by professional bodies.

At institutional level, there is evidence that some higher education institutions have a dedicated office or unit to monitor the quality of teaching and learning. However, higher education institutions are at different phases in developing their quality assurance policies and practices. Some are still in the planning phase, while others have a detailed quality assurance "map" that stipulates quality assurance procedures at every level. Most interview respondents noted that they have institutional plans, policies and/or other documents that describe their quality assurance approach. Some have committees at faculty level, others have introduced quality assurance in several institutional policies, and others tie in their internal quality assurance processes to meet the requirements of the external quality assurance (though some have tried to shift towards a quality enhancement or quality improvement model as opposed to just meeting external quality assurance reporting requirements). External and internal quality assurance systems are often viewed as playing conflicting roles, particularly if the two are not aligned. However, these initiatives are meant to play a complementary role (Kadhila, 2012).

All these efforts show the government's commitment to ensuring quality in higher education and training as a means to realise the national development goals as stipulated in Vision 2030. Vision 2030 calls for quality enhancement; hence, the government is advocating for a well-educated Namibian workforce that will drive a knowledge-based economy (National Planning Commission Secretariat, 2004). As alluded to above, externally quality is managed through statutory quality assurance/accreditation agencies (NQA and NCHE) and other professional bodies. These statutory institutions are responsible for

- Conducting assessments before registration or accreditation is given to the higher education institutions. This is done to ensure higher education institutions comply with minimum standards.
- The registration of private higher education providers and accreditation of qualifications and programmes in each higher education institution. This is guided by the Higher Education Act (Act No. 26 of 2003) which stipulates what institutions should put in place with regard to quality education.
- Establishing structures to manage quality, on which higher education institutions should base their quality policies and procedures. National quality assurance agencies further conduct quality audits for improvement purposes.

In addition to the national quality assurance agencies as alluded to in the background section, several statutory councils exist in Namibia that have a variety of responsibilities for the quality and quality assurance of specific professional programmes and occupations. These professional bodies include the Ministry of Education's funding division and various professional, statutory and regulatory bodies such as the Engineering Council of Namibia (ECN), the Allied Health Professions Council of Namibia (AHPCN), the Namibian Council of Architects and Quantity Surveyors (NCAQS), the Land Surveyors Council of Namibia (SURCON) and the Public Accountant's and Auditors Board (PAAB). Therefore, higher education institutions need to comply with the requirements of national quality assurance systems and also meet other stakeholders' requirements for programme quality, where applicable.

The aforementioned bodies and agencies are responsible for managing quality externally. This process entails a range of quality monitoring procedures to determine whether the higher education institutions meets the agreed or predetermined quality standards. Externally, quality assurance involves the registration of higher education institutions, institutional and/or programme accreditation and institutional audits.

Accreditation

It is worth mentioning that academic accreditation is an effective tool for evaluating and enhancing the quality of the educational process and the continuity of development and is proof of the efficiency of the scientific programmes offered by the college or university. Access to academic accreditation enhances the community's confidence in the institution and increases its chances of success and progress in the world, as well as making the college or university more attractive. It also provides a competitive research and teaching platform (Alzhrani, Alotibie, & Abdulaziz, 2016). Although programme accreditation and institutional audits follow the guidelines of the external agencies, the higher education institutions can develop their own institutional guidelines to guide both processes. Higher education institutions are therefore required to meet the standards set by the national quality assurance agencies and relevant professional bodies.

In order to gain programme accreditation, institutions and/or programmes are evaluated against set criteria. The process of accreditation requires institutions to provide proof that the process has passed through independent panels from industry, both international and local, to ensure quality. This has not, however, happened effectively because of the inability of some advisory bodies to make sufficiently authoritative judgements, while others have a tendency to develop their own view of good practice. To ensure accuracy, suitability and fairness within the academy and to meet public expectations for assuring and enhancing the quality of teaching and learning, reviews of the quality of programmes are done by neutral external parties.

Quality Audit

Quality audit in the context of higher education is a process of checking or examining what goes on in an institution to ensure that there is institutional compliance with quality assurance procedures, integrity, standards and outcomes. The audit may be internal or external. According to Winch (1996), an audit only provides answers to questions that are of a certain kind, such as an event where something happened which was not supposed to happen. Hence, an audit is concerned with what is taking place, rather than judging how well something is taking place.

Namibian higher education institutions are subject to the NCHE audit requirements for academic activities. Institutional audits include the evaluation of institutional quality assurance mechanisms in the three core areas of higher education, namely, teaching and learning, research, and community engagement against NCHE audit criteria. The NCHE audit criteria are of internationally comparable standards and were developed with regard to the country's legislative policy framework for higher education, the prevalent quality of its institutions, and its societal and economic needs.

For an audit to be successful, the institution must thoroughly prepare itself. Preparation involves the compilation of a self-evaluation report and supporting documentation. These reports provide information for the team in charge of the external audit. External audits are conducted by panels chosen by the NCHE and comprise experts on higher education issues. Institutional audit systems are improvement oriented, but accountability aspects are also integrated into the system. Therefore, such audits do not pronounce an institution as "passed" or "failed". The outcome of an institutional audit is formulated as commendations and recommendations to the institution concerned. Audit findings on institutional quality may be used by the institutions to strengthen their internal quality management systems and thereby facilitate the improvement of the quality of its core academic activities.

Although programme accreditation and institutional audits follow the guidelines of the external agencies, the higher education institutions can develop their own institutional guidelines that guide both processes to meet the standards set by the national quality assurance agencies and relevant professional bodies. Internally, quality assurance encompasses all the activities that a higher education institution must carry out in order to maintain and improve its quality. Higher education institutions in Namibia have implemented formalised internal systems for quality management through a dedicated office or unit that monitors the quality of teaching and learning, although they are at different stages in developing internal quality assurance policies and practices. These policies and practices include internal quality reviews for academics and administration departments, processes for programme design, approval and review, annual programme monitoring, graduate surveys, feedback from students and employers, and the like. The mechanisms for internal quality assurance and management include the following:

Programmes Evaluation/Review

As per the NCHE mandate, higher education institutions have regular internal quality reviews of their existing programmes in order to enhance and maintain quality. Programmes are reviewed on a regular basis to ensure their relevance and currency with regional, national and global developments. The institutional quality management framework provides guidelines to assist with programmes and departmental reviews. The review is done to assess the adequacy of learning objectives and whether the pedagogic system and the available resources of a programme enable students to reach the objectives.

In preparation for the external evaluation by the NCHE, internal evaluation is conducted according to a specific cycle for the academic and support functions through the application of self-evaluation mechanisms and procedures. Programme evaluation is conducted by academic staff but it also involves an element of student feedback whereby students evaluate certain quality dimensions of teaching and learning at the course level. For example, a new programme requires the higher education institution to first conduct a self-evaluation exercise with regard to the new programme that it wishes to offer, using the NCHE criteria for accreditation of new programmes. This culminates in the compilation of a self-evaluation report, together with a supporting implementation plan. Departmental heads are responsible for regular critical self-evaluation in preparation for external evaluation in their departments. The self-evaluation report is critical and clearly indicate, inter alia, that

- a needs analysis has been conducted, and that the outcome thereof supports the introduction of the new programme, and
- the institution is committed to ensuring the quality of provision and programme delivery.

External institutional audits/reviews complement the self-evaluation process, adding credibility to it by encompassing the judgement of independent experts from the national, regional and international academic community.

Peer Review

Peer review is a procedure that assesses the quality and effectiveness of an institution's academic programmes, staffing and/or structure and is carried out by external experts (peers). The peer experts are from comparable institutions and carry out the assessment process. The role of these peers is not inspectorial as they are involved primarily in the assessment of performance and standards rather than practices; for example, the practice of examination as it is carried out in the Namibian higher education system. In this system, assessments involve moderation by one or more external markers who also shed light on the overall standards of work seen and sometimes, on this basis, make judgements about the quality of teaching and learning on the course for which they are examiners.

Moderation

Moderation of student assessments is a critical component of teaching and learning in universities around the globe (Adie, Lloyd, & Beutel, 2013). The moderators are academics/faculty staff from within the institution and from other higher education institutions, who evaluate the adequacy, fairness and consistency of student assessment. In monitoring student assessments, the higher education institutions use the following methods:

- Internal moderation of all final assessment, which takes place during each round of examination and is the responsibility of each faculty.
- External moderation of examination papers, which takes place according to the institutional rules and regulations.
- External assessment of scripts, master's theses and doctoral dissertations, which is done according to the institutional rules and regulations.

Benchmarking

Education is a global paradigm and higher education institutions should produce graduates for the global market. As such, stakeholders of higher education expect graduates to be of the finest quality to be able to fit into any environment both in graduates' home countries and internationally (Anane & Addaney, 2016). Many HEIs around the globe use benchmarking as a tool for both improving performance and ensuring continuous improvement.

Sallis (2002) defines benchmarking as a standard against which present performance is measured. It is undertaken by seeking the best of the competition and understanding the way in which quality is produced. Educational institutions therefore need to develop tools that can be built into their own structures and which allow them to learn both from their own successes and failures and from the best practice of others. National higher education institutions have solicited quality support and engaged with different international institutions and organisations such as, among others:

- Higher Education Quality Committee of South Africa on Education (HEQC), a subsidiary of the Council on Higher Education (CHE) in South Africa
- International Network of Quality Assurance Agencies in Higher Education (INQAAHE)
- Southern African Regional University Association (SARUS)
- Association of African Universities (AAU) in collaboration with the Association of European Universities (AUA), and
- African Quality Assurance Network (AfriQAN).

Apart from benchmarking with external organisations and/or universities, the two public higher education institutions have also implemented internal benchmarking in which comparisons are made of the performance of different departments, campuses or sites within a university in order to identify best practice in the institution. This is done without necessarily having an external standard against which to compare the results.

Offering programmes without the benefit of internationally benchmarked quality standards creates a quality vacuum and, consequently, the quality may be contested. Therefore, it is beneficial for institutions to offer programmes for which the quality has been benchmarked against reputable regional and international quality assurance and management systems. In support, McKinnon, Walker, and Davis (2000) believe that good benchmarking enables university leaders to know how their institution rates in certain areas in comparison with others, to ascertain their competitive position relative to others, and to know how their institution can be improved.

Strengths and Positive Impacts of Quality Management

There is strong political support and legislation to support quality assurance and management at a national level, as evidenced by the presence of national quality assurance agencies and related policies and practices. The presence of the national qualifications framework, for example, has brought about some improvement in terms of the way qualifications are organised and interpreted; which in turn promotes the harmonisation of higher education, institutional and cross-border mobility of students and graduates, and qualification recognition and credit transfer (Kadhila, 2012). Quality management at both national and institutional levels has also increased visibility and awareness of quality assurance, leading to an enhanced quality culture. External quality assurance practices have not only brought about improvement but have also enhanced accountability and transparency within the higher education system.

At an institutional level, since there is no consensus globally on how to measure and manage quality in higher education institutions, a variety of approaches and methods have been adopted. In the Namibian context, quality is managed both internally and externally. Therefore, individual higher education institutions have formalised their own ways of managing quality. Although there is still room for further development, the presence of quality management systems at both national and institutional levels has enhanced publicly available and transparent information about the quality assurance and management processes and their outcomes in these institutions in Namibia. This has a spin-off effect on stakeholder trust and confidence in a particular higher education institution and its graduates. There are, however, various practices being implemented by these institutions in their quest to manage quality. Given the diverse nature of higher education institutions in the country in the implementation of quality management practices, the corresponding needs, demands, and priorities of institutions in Namibia are also diverse.

Challenges for Implementing Quality Management Systems in the Namibian Higher Education System

The development of quality management depends on contextual factors which include both the internal and external environment of a higher education institution. Any endeavour to induce and monitor quality in academic setting hinges on the awareness of the factors responsible for bringing about this desired attribute. However, several challenges responsible for hindering the effective implementation of quality management initiatives in the Namibian higher education system have been identified:

National Level

Some of the challenges identified at national level that inhibit effective implementation of quality management initiatives include:

- Resistance to change
- Shortage of quality assurance agency staff and budget constraints that hamper quality assurance implementation
- Lack of relevant experience and expertise in quality assurance agencies
- Multiple regulatory bodies with overlapping quality assurance mandates and requirements, which may lead to over-regulation
- Lack of coordination between the professional bodies involved in programme accreditation
- A lengthy and cumbersome accreditation process, as each body involved conducts the process at different times
- Lack of funding and financial resources
- Visibility – there is a lack of publicly available, transparent information about the quality assurance and management processes and their outcomes in the higher education in Namibia
- Lack of understanding and appreciation of the need for quality management from different stakeholders, and
- Misconceptions and misunderstanding of the work of quality assurance agencies has caused confusion of roles among different key stakeholders.

Institutional Level

There are also factors that hamper effective implementation of quality management initiatives at institutional level, of which some are by and large similar to those at the national level in nature. These include

- Lack of quality culture, which was often characterised by aversion to change, scepticism and the belief that there is no need for quality management
- Ineffective internal quality assurance processes, aggravated by budgetary constraints, under-funding of higher education institutions, lack of understanding of internal quality assurance, resistance to change, lack of accountability, and the high teaching load of academic staff, which means little time to carry out quality assurance activities
- Internal quality management processes that are not aligned to external processes, leading to duplication of effort and wastage of resources; for example, in most cases higher education institutions must complete and submit the same reports on quality management to the NQA, NCHE and other professional bodies at different occasions, leading to repetition
- Resistance to quality management and lack of commitment from both academics and administrators
- Organisational bureaucracy which causes delays in programmes evaluation, registration and accreditation
- Financial constraints due to shrinking government funding and the absence of a national funding formula

- Lack of specialised skills in the area of quality assurance and management – this is especially true with regard to the absence of professional and academic qualifications by the said quality management practitioners in the field
- Programme accreditation (delay in getting information on time from departments which in turn cause a delay in the whole process with quality assurance agencies)
- Insufficient implementation time – faculties are overloaded with day-to-day work
- Inadequate stakeholder engagement leading to difficulties achieving buy-in from stakeholders
- Lack of adequate technology infrastructure to complete quality assurance tasks.

Main Challenges and Their Implications

The identified challenges for implementing quality management systems in Namibian higher education apply to both national and institutional levels. Hence, the main issues identified focus on the following themes: role ambiguity, organisational culture, the skills gap and financial resources. Firstly, role ambiguity between the NCHE and the NQA, as well professional bodies, has caused confusion among different key stakeholders resulting from misconceptions and misunderstandings of the work of these quality assurance agencies. In addition, the apparent lack of coordination between the different bodies has resulted in delays in the accreditation process. Therefore, higher education institutions are forced to undergo a lengthy and cumbersome accreditation process, as each body involved conducts the process at different times.

The second issue relates to organisational culture. There seems to be a lack of understanding and appreciation of the need for quality management from different stakeholders. This is the result of various factors, including lack of commitment and resistance from both academics and administrators; lack of alignment between internal and external quality management processes and lack of publicly available, transparent information about the quality assurance, management processes and their outcomes.

The third issue relates to specialised skills in the area of quality assurance and management – this is especially true with regard to the lack of professional and academic qualifications held by the quality management practitioners in the field. The final issue is concerned with inadequate financial resources which hampers the implementation of some initiatives, including the implementation of the funding framework; acquisition of quality assurance subject experts; approval of some key documents and retaining of qualified and experienced personnel. The financial constraints are due to shrinking government funding and the absence of a national funding formula.

The above challenges have dire implications. Among the chief of these is the failure to have programmes accredited on time in order to meet industry and/or market needs. This may lead to lost investment opportunities resulting from the absence of an adequately skilled workforce in the country, consequently defeating the purpose of the national development agenda as stipulated in Vision 2030. Vision 2030 is a document that clearly spells out the country's development programmes and strategies to achieve its national objectives (GRN, 2004). The second implication has to do with finances. The majority of the challenges have financial consequences. By and large quality is a very expensive commodity; it costs money, time and resources.

These challenges are similar to the findings of Cardoso, Rosa, and Stensaker (2016), who state that the main obstacles to quality are related to the view of quality as culture, and especially to its structural component, including the design and functioning of institutional governance and management. Other obstacles include governance and management, internal quality assurance mechanisms, institutions' financial situation and infrastructure, as well as resources and support services.

SOLUTIONS AND RECOMMENDATIONS

There are a number of areas identified for potential capacity development in both national and institutional quality assurance systems to address the current challenges (Butcher et al., 2017). According to Butcher et al. (2017), there is a general lack of training in quality assurance and the need to develop skills in quality assurance at both quality assurance agency and higher education institution levels. There is, therefore, a need to enhance capacity building to address the skills gap in quality assurance and to enhance capacity. Some of the potential areas for capacity development include the following:

- Increase awareness and understanding of quality assurance, including understanding quality assurance concepts, approaches and processes. An understanding of quality assurance processes is important for both staff and students; for students they ensure quality education, for staff they pinpoint all the milestones that need to be passed to ensure a quality education is delivered.
- Since Namibia has multiple quality assurance agencies, there is a need to manage quality assurance processes in a more harmonised manner rather than having a fragmented and unaligned system.
- Quality assurance agencies in Namibia appear to be focused on ensuring compliance. Therefore, there is a need for adopting a more "developmental" approach or this may be more supportive in nature.
- Develop and revise policy and regulatory frameworks and create awareness of and easy access to these policies and frameworks.
- Understand how quality assurance systems work, including mechanisms and practices that can allow measurement of quality on all dimensions of higher education.
- Develop specific skills related to conducting institutional audits and site visits, conducting programme reviews, setting standards, conducting accreditation, monitoring and evaluation, conducting self-evaluation, and benchmarking.
- Design and development of quality assurance tools for assessment and analysis of data, as well as developing and implementing improvement plans.
- Incorporate quality issues in curriculum development and evaluation, and develop capacity around teaching, assessment and research skills.
- Develop research and writing skills to collect data and prepare assessment reports.
- Develop ICT skills and systems relevant to quality assurance work.
- Establish and manage quality assurance units, as well as develop and implement effective internal quality assurance systems and internal quality management (Butcher et al., 2017).

The following recommendations are, therefore, made:

- The foundation of any quality improvement is to develop a "quality culture" or mind set within the organisation and to integrate it throughout the company. There is a need to develop a culture of quality at both national and institutional levels through awareness raising and capacity development among all stakeholders.
- At national level, the processes of accreditation and registration require improvement by streamlining the processes between the quality agencies.
- There is a need to enhance existing external quality assurance processes, examples of which include maintaining high levels and standards of programmes, conducting institutional reviews, developing standards for qualifications, developing online systems to support quality assurance systems, aligning learning programmes to national frameworks, streamlining quality assurance processes, and reviewing quality assurance tools.
- Enhancement is required when it comes to financing of higher education. Accordingly, in the absence of a clear higher education funding formula, it is recommended that NCHE develops a higher education funding formula to ensure that these institutions receive adequate funding to achieve their goals and objectives.
- Since no prominence has been given to the output of higher education at national level, there is a need for the NCHE to put in place clear procedures that emphasis the type of quality they expect to get from the institutions (input vs output).
- There is a need for the NCHE to develop a framework for benchmarking activities.
- National quality assurance agencies must foster information exchange and collaboration, sharing information and experiences at workshops and conferences, increasing collaboration between quality assurance agencies in the region and internationally, sharing best practices, and collaborating in activities such as staff exchanges and peer audits.
- National quality assurance agencies must create a higher education repository and information systems for monitoring and evaluation.
- Both national quality assurance agencies and higher education institutions must source and mobilise funding to achieve quality assurance goals.
- Higher education institutions need to develop internal quality assurance processes and systems, thus creating internal quality assurance policies and structures, supporting development of institutional quality assurance processes and systems, establishing internal quality assurance units where they do not exist, developing strategies for continuous enhancement of quality such as monitoring, review and evaluation of student experiences, revising quality indicators, improving dialogue and engagement with stakeholders, and undertaking projects to support the implementation of recommendations that follow external quality assurance audits.

FUTURE RESEARCH DIRECTIONS

- Since the inception of a national quality system, not all institutions have undergone an external audit. Hence, future research could look at the outcomes of such audits and also at the impact of departmental self-reviews on the quality management of the institutions involved.

- Conceptualisation of quality in immerging countries like Namibia needs further research to check for dimensionality as a result of socioeconomic challenges.
- A limitation of this study was that it examined only public higher education institutions in the country. Further research could involve a comparison of the way quality is managed in public and private higher education institutions in the country.

CONCLUSION

Higher education institutions are the principal drivers of skills, knowledge and innovation development across the world. Therefore, quality in higher education will be achieved if universities carry out their core functions, namely, teaching and learning, research and innovation, and community engagement, in an environment that continuously and conscientiously promotes quality and learning by doing. The Government of the Republic of Namibia has established national quality assurance agencies and regulatory policy frameworks as instruments to ensure quality higher education provision. As a result, these institutions have implemented internal quality assurance mechanisms and have dedicated offices or units to monitor the quality of teaching and learning. Higher education institutions in Namibia are at different stages in implementation of their quality assurance systems and may have different priorities. Meanwhile, external quality assurance agencies have adopted registration, accreditation and audits in their quality assurance approaches, and these are conducted in a cyclical basis.

Although there are quality assurance agencies and professional bodies that regulate the quality of higher education at a national level, higher education institutions remain the main custodians of quality in Namibia and have the primary responsibility for the quality of their programmes and the assurance thereof.

However, many challenges exist including lack of capacity among quality assurance agencies and higher education institutions, and unaligned quality assurance systems owing to the presence of multiple quality assurance agencies. This chapter, therefore, suggests that more efforts need to be invested in quality assurance capacity development at both national and institutional levels, and that quality assurance systems should be aligned so as to ensure that these systems live up to their purpose of improving quality rather than creating an unnecessary bureaucratic and administrative burden.

REFERENCES

Adie, L., Lloyd, M., & Beutel, D. (2013). Identifying discourses of moderation in higher education. *Assessment & Evaluation in Higher Education, 38*(8), 968–977. doi:10.1080/02602938.2013.769200

Al-Tarawneh, H., & Mubaslat, M. (2011). The implementation of total quality management (TQM) on the higher educational sector in Jordan. *International Journal of Industrial Marketing, 1*(1), 1–10.

Alzhrani, K., Alotibie, B. A., & Abdulaziz, A. (2016). Total quality management in Saudi higher education. *International Journal of Computers and Applications, 135*(4), 6–12. doi:10.5120/ijca2016908245

Anane, G. K., & Addaney, M. (2016). Managing quality assurance in higher education: The case of the University of Energy and Natural Resources, Ghana. *Journal of Education and Practice, 7*(22), 41–46.

Becket, N., & Brookes, M. (2006). Evaluating quality management in university departments. *Quality Assurance in Education*, *14*(2), 123–142. doi:10.1108/09684880610662015

Becket, N., & Brookes, M. (2008). Quality management in higher education: What quality are we actually enhancing? *Journal of Hospitality, Leisure, Sport and Tourism Education*, *7*(1), 40–54. doi:10.3794/johlste.71.174

Brookes, M., & Becket, N. (2007). Quality management in higher education: A review of international issues and practice. *International Journal of Quality and Standards, 1*(1).

Butcher, N., Hoosen, S., & Chetty, Y. (2017). *State of play: Regional quality assurance in Southern Africa (SADC)*. DAAD.

Cardoso, S., Rosa, M. J., & Stensaker, B. (2016). Why is quality in higher education not achieved? The view of academics. *Assessment & Evaluation in Higher Education*, *41*(6), 950–965. doi:10.1080/02602938.2015.1052775

Cheng, Y. C., & Tam, W. M. (1997). Multi-models of quality in education. *Quality Assurance in Education*, *5*(1), 22–31. doi:10.1108/09684889710156558

Cullen, J., Joyce, J., Hassall, T., & Broadbent, M. (2003). Quality in higher education: From monitoring to management. *Quality Assurance in Education*, *11*(1), 5–14. doi:10.1108/09684880310462038

Dicker, R., Garcia, M., Kelly, A., & Mulrooney, H. (2018). What does "quality" in higher education mean? Perceptions of staff, students and employers. *Studies in Higher Education*, 1–14. doi:10.1080/03075079.2018.1445987

Eriksen, S. D. (1995). TQM and the transformation from an elite to a mass system of higher education in the UK. *Quality Assurance in Education*, *3*(1), 14–29. doi:10.1108/09684889510146795

Government of Republic of Namibia (GRN). (1996). Namibia Qualifications Authority Act, Act No. 29 of 1996. Windhoek: Namibia.

Government of Republic of Namibia (GRN). (2008). Vocational Education and Training Act, Act No. 1 of 2008. Windhoek: Namibia.

Government of the Republic of Namibia (GRN). (2003). Higher Education Act, Act. No. 26 of 2003. Windhoek: Namibia.

Government of the Republic of Namibia (GRN). (2004). Vision 2030. Windhoek: Namibia.

Harvey, L., & Green, D. (1993). Defining quality. *Assessment & Evaluation in Higher Education*, *18*(1), 9–34. doi:10.1080/0260293930180102

Kadhila, N. (2012). *Quality assurance mechanisms in higher education institutions in Namibia* (Unpublished doctoral dissertation). University of the Free State, Bloemfontein, South Africa.

Kalusi, J. I. (2001). Teacher quality for quality education. *Nigerian Journal of Educational Philosophy*, *8*(2), 62–72.

Luckett, K. (2007). The introduction of external QA in South African HEIs: An analysis of stakeholder response. *Quality in Higher Education, 13*(2), 97–116. doi:10.1080/13538320701629129

Martens, E., & Prosser, M. (1998). What constitutes high quality teaching and learning and how to assure it? *Quality Assurance in Education, 6*(1), 28–36. doi:10.1108/09684889810200368

Martin, M., & Parik, S. (2017). *Quality management in higher education: Developments and drivers: Results from an international survey.* Paris, France: International Institute for Educational Planning, UNESCO.

McKinnon, K. R., Walker, S. H., & Davis, D. (2000). *Benchmarking: A manual for Australian universities.* Canberra, Australia: Department of Education, Training and Youth Affairs, Higher Education Division.

National Council for Higher Education (NCHE). (2009). *Quality assurance system for higher education in Namibia.* Windhoek, Namibia.

National Planning Commission Secretariat. (2004). *Vision 2030.* Windhoek, Namibia: National Planning Commission, GRN.

OECD. (2016). Education at a glance 2016: Indicator B1 and B5. Paris, France: OECD.

Oldfield, B., & Baron, S. (1998). *Is the service scape important to student perceptions of service quality?* (Research Paper). Manchester Metropolitan University.

Papanthymou, A., & Darra, M. (2017). Quality management in higher education: Review and perspectives. *Higher Education Studies, 7*(3), 132–147. doi:10.5539/hes.v7n3p132

Pierce, M. R. (1995, Winter). The university selection process: A Canadian perspective. *Info.*

Pounder, J. (1999). Institutional performance in higher education: Is quality a relevant concept? *Quality Assurance in Education, 7*(3), 156–165. doi:10.1108/09684889910281719

Pratasavitskaya, H., & Stensaker, B. R. (2010). Quality management in higher education: Towards a better understanding of an emerging field. *Quality in Higher Education, 16*(1), 37–50. doi:10.1080/13538321003679465

Roberts, P., & Tennant, C. (2003). Application of the Hoshin Kanri methodology at a higher education establishment in the UK. *The TQM Magazine, 15*(2), 82–87. doi:10.1108/09544780310461080

Rosa, M. J., Sarrico, C. S., & Amaral, A. (2012). *Implementing quality management systems in higher education institutions. University of Lisbon. Alberto Amaral.* Centre for Research in Higher Education Policies.

Sallis, E. (2002). *Total quality management in education* (3rd ed.). London: Stylus Publishing Inc.

Schargel, F. P. (1994). Total quality in education. *Quality Progress, 26*(10), 67–71.

Sintayehu, K. A. (2019). African higher education and the Bologna Process. *European Journal of Higher Education, 9*(1), 118–132. doi:10.1080/21568235.2018.1561313

Soomro, T. R., & Ahmad, R. (2012). Quality in Higher Education: United Arab Emirates perspective. *Higher Education Studies, 2*(4), 148–152. doi:10.5539/hes.v2n4p148

Srikanthan, G., & Dalrymple, J. (2003). Developing alternative perspectives for quality in higher education. *International Journal of Educational Management, 17*(3), 126–136. doi:10.1108/09513540310467804

Teixeria, P., Kim, S., Landoni, P., & Gilani, Z. (2017). *Rethinking the public-private mix in higher education: Global trends and National Policy Challenges*. Rotterdam, The Netherlands: Sense Publisher. doi:10.1007/978-94-6300-911-9

Toma, S. G., & Naruo, S. (2009). Quality assurance in the Japanese universities. *Amfiteatru Economic, 6*(26), 574–584.

University of Namibia (UNAM). (2015). *Quality assurance and management policy*. Windhoek, Namibia: Author.

Wiklund, H., Wiklund, B., & Edvardsson, B. (2003). Innovation and TQM in Swedish higher education institutions – possibilities and pitfalls. *The TQM Magazine, 15*(2), 99–107. doi:10.1108/09544780310461116

Winch, C. (1996). *Quality and education*. Oxford, UK: Blackwell Publisher.

World Bank. (2009). *Accelerating catch-up: Tertiary education for growth in sub-Saharan Africa*. Washington, DC: World Bank.

Zmas, A. (2015). Global impacts of the Bologna Process: International perspectives, local particularities. *Compare: A Journal of Comparative Education, 45*(5), 727–747. doi:10.1080/03057925.2014.899725

ADDITIONAL READING

Kadhila, N., & Iipumbu, N. (2019). Strengthening internal quality assurance as a lever for enhancing student learning experiences and academic success: Lessons from Namibia. *Quality in Higher Education, 24*(3), 1–17.

Kuria, M., & Marwa, S. M. (2017). *Shaping internal quality assurance from a triple heritage: Daystar University, Kenya. New Trends in Higher Education*. Paris: IIEP-UNESCO.

Lamagna, C., Villanueva, C. C., & Hassan, F. (2017). *The effects of internal quality assurance on quality and employability: American International University – Bangladesh. New Trends in Higher Education*. Paris: IIEP-UNESCO.

Lange, L., & Kriel, L. (2017). *Integrating internal quality assurance at a time of transformation: University of the Free State, South Africa. New Trends in Higher Education*. Paris: IIEP-UNESCO.

O'Sullivan, D. (2017). Evolution of internal quality assurance at one university – a case study. *Quality Assurance in Education, 25*(2), 189–205. doi:10.1108/QAE-03-2016-0011

Seyfried, M., & Pohlenz, P. (2018). Assessing quality assurance in higher education: Quality managers' perceptions of effectiveness. *European Journal of Higher Education, 8*(3), 258–271. doi:10.1080/21568235.2018.1474777

KEY TERMS AND DEFINITIONS

Accreditation: A process by which a higher education institution is authorized to conduct certification of conformity to prescribed standards.

Assessment: The act of determining the extent of compliance with requirements.

Certification: A process by which a product, process, person or organisation is deemed to meet special requirements.

Higher Education Institutions: In the Namibian context, these are institutions of higher learning offering qualifications beyond grade 12 at NQF level 5 and above.

Quality Assurance: Is the process of ensuring that a higher education institution develops, implements and maintains the quality of its provision through continuous evaluation and improvement.

Quality Management System: The set of interconnected and managed processes that function together to achieve the organization's quality goals.

Quality Standards: Is a set of requirements, specifications, characteristics and guidelines to be met for the product, service or process to fulfil its purpose.

Registration: A process of recording details of organizations of assessed capability that have satisfied prescribed results.

Regulatory Requirements: Requirements established by law pertaining to products, services, or processes.

Chapter 5
Leadership and Innovative Approaches in Higher Education

Sulaiman Olusegun Atiku
https://orcid.org/0000-0001-9364-3774
University of KwaZulu-Natal, South Africa

Richmond Anane-simon
Pentecost University College, Ghana

ABSTRACT

The place of leadership support for technological innovation in advancing quality management in higher education cannot be underrated in the fourth industrial revolution. This chapter examines the role of leadership in higher education and innovative teaching and learning methods for quality assurance in higher education system. The literature review approach and author observation were adopted to cross-examine the influence of leadership on innovative teaching/learning methods and quality assurance in higher education. This chapter shows that leadership support for innovative teaching and learning methods is a benchmark for quality assurance in higher education in recent times. Therefore, no meaningful change will happen in any higher institution without a strong leadership support for innovation and quality management. Policymakers in higher education should create a climate that promotes creativity and innovation by ensuring that transformational leaders are at the helm of affairs for quality management.

INTRODUCTION

The innovations in educational technology is transforming higher education institutions (HEIs) across the globe. This chapter focuses on the current and emerging innovative teaching and learning approaches available for human capital building in the HEIs across the globe. The leadership in higher education could be strategic by adopting ambidextrous approach, which is achievable by simultaneously exploiting current and future opportunities in the industry. For example, rather than being reactive to the current trends, an institution could be proactive in terms of knowledge creation by enhancing its teaching/learning approaches to meet both present and future labour market requirements.

DOI: 10.4018/978-1-7998-1017-9.ch005

Many public entities worldwide have correlated higher education reform strategies to the concept of "globalization" which embodies a variety of developments including the intensified integration of national economies, the continuous information technology and the development of Post-Fordism work practices (Heitor & Horta, 2016; Waters & Castells, 1995;1996). A new type of economy had emanated out of this perceived developments, the knowledge economy which led to a drastic shift from material production and manual work in advanced economies (nations). Notwithstanding the wide-ranging contestation over the exact meaning and existence of the term globalization (Hirst & Thompson, 2002), the capacity to compete on a global scene in this context has come to rely on the production of higher value-added products and services. Accordingly, the value-added products and services are dependent on knowledge, especially scientific and technical knowledge and continual innovation. It is obvious that higher education has been strategically placed as a relevant site for the transfer of economically productive knowledge, innovation and technology (Carnoy, 1994).

Leadership effectiveness has a positive influence on organisational efficiency or success, as organizations are not limited by their opportunities but by their leaders (Gumusluoglu & Ilsev, 2009). A leadership expert - John Maxwell, puts it that "everyone can steer the ship but it takes the leader to chart the course of the ship" (Maxwell, 2007). Indeed, for higher education to thrive and be highly effective, it would largely be depend on excellent leadership. There are various styles of leadership, which per discretion and for the general benefit of the organization may be adopted to meet organisational goals and objectives. The function of leadership then becomes the creation of systems, structures and environment where interaction and learning can occur (Allen, et al., 1998). In the Twenty-first century, leadership should be seen as learning and doing and not as an opportunity to increase personal aggrandizement. For example, a transformational leader sees a vision, communicate the vision to all stakeholders, estimates costs/benefits of program utility analysis, ensures stakeholders buy-in, and empowers all categories of staff, delegate and champions the transformational agenda.

Incorporating innovative teaching and learning approaches in the higher education requires management support and efforts of visionary leaders (Garrison & Vaughan, 2013). This implies that a transformational leader will exhibits a great level of effectiveness in propagating the benefits of innovative teaching and learning approaches in higher education. The benefits of innovative learning platforms include environmental, technological, pedagogical, psychosocial, and economic benefits (Mata, Lazar, Nedeff, & Lazar, 2013). This chapter examines the relationship between leadership and innovative approaches in human capital formation in higher education systems. This chapter also provides an insight on how innovative teaching and learning methods (e.g. Learning Management Systems) is being used for quality assurance or management in higher education system. By extension, corporate universities and training institutes need to consolidate their teaching and learning approaches with the level of automation and artificial intelligence driving the fourth industrial revolution. The next section provides useful insights on the background of innovative approaches in higher education.

BACKGROUND

The emergence of innovative teaching and learning approaches could be traced back to the evolution of blended learning approaches in higher education (Garrison & Kanuka, 2004; Garrison & Vaughan, 2013). Garrison and Vaughan (2013) submit that innovative approaches in higher education require clear organisational plans, transformational leadership effectiveness and strong stakeholders' commitment. With regards to blended learning, the University of Pennsylvania's Virtual Online Teaching (VOLT) certificate program equips instructors with the skill to critically evaluate the use of technology in the blended learning environment before implementing them (Adams, 2016). Furthermore, the advances in science and technology, automation and artificial intelligence have created some challenges and opportunities (Shapiro, Haahr, Bayer, & Boekholt, 2007) for the leadership of higher education systems across the globe (Franck & Galor, 2015). The change champions would like taking advantage of the opportunities by considering the benefits of technological innovation on key performance areas of higher education. Conversely, placing emphasis on the challenges; in terms of the huge investments and sacrifices required to migrate from the traditional approach into the state-of-the-art teaching and learning approaches is a major concern in developing countries (Atiku, 2018). The main challenges driving innovation in higher education are in three folds namely, (i) pressures from globalization; (ii) changing supply of and demand for higher education; and (iii) changes in higher education funding (Brennan, et al., 2014). Briefly, the gap between what higher education offers and what industry requires is of growing concern (Andolfi, 2016). However, managing an institution involves devising a set of strategies to overcome the challenges posed by vast technological innovations, and at the same time taking advantage of the inherent opportunities. The primary objective of innovative approaches in higher education systems is to enhance teaching and learning in line with the learners' needs and labour market requirements.

The bedrock for innovation is challenging the status-quo, creativity or doing new things. One of the emerging teaching and learning approaches is the Massive Open Online Courses (MOOCs), which have merited outstanding attention from the media, entrepreneurial vendors, technological enthusiasts and most importantly educational institutions of higher learning (Brennan, et al., 2014). The MOOCs ensures and provides free access, innovative courses that could drive down the cost of university-level education and potentially disrupt the existing modules of higher education. This has triggered elite institutions of higher learning to display their course online via setting up Open Learning platforms, such as edX. Other commercial startups have also been launched in collaboration with various universities offering online courses free or charging some reasonable amount for certification, which may or may not be part of the credit for the awards.

Pearson and Google are also are also planning to venture into the higher education sector as global service rendering organisations, and are likely to adopt a MOOCs (Yuan & Powell, 2013). The future learn has been launched by the Open University in the UK, to bring together a range of free, open online courses from the leading UK universities for learners around the world (Futurelearn, 2013). Kickstarting from open access to open education resources and more recently to open online courses, higher education institution have already developed an insatiable thirst for the "Open" movement. For example, the UK Open Educational Resources launched in 2009, have succesfully made significant amount of new and existing teaching and learning resources freely available worldwide, with copyright licenses that promote their use, reuse and re-purposing (JISC, 2013). Nevertheless it has become quite cumbersome to keenly pinpoint a sustainable approach to the development of the Open Educational Resources(OER). As sums of money invested begin to dwindle, critics have spelt out that the OERs have not affected traditional business models or daily teaching practices at some institutions of higher learning (Kortemeyer, 2013). In the current dispensation it is obvious that sitting down in front of chalkboard with spiral note book and pen will be one of the greatest educational jokes.

INNOVATION IN HIGHER EDUCATION

Many scholars and practitioners have conceptualized innovation in the last five decades. The attention on innovation is still ongoing in the era of innovative technology, which is the engine driving fourth industrial revolution. Thompson (1965, p. 2) cited in Baregheh, Rowley and Sambrook (2009), provides an early and straightforward definition of innovation as "the generation, acceptance and implementation of new ideas, processes, and products or services. Similarly, innovation was conceptualized as an effective application of processes and products new to the organisation and designed to benefit it and its stakeholders (West & Anderson, 1996; cited in Baregheh, Rowley, & Sambrook, 2009). Recently, Nick Skillicorn in the Community for Creativity and Innovation (n.d), states that innovation has to do with turning an idea into a solution that adds value from a customer's perspective. The customers in higher education industry that require innovative solutions include the university management, students, parents, employers of labour, government and quality assurance agencies.

The three stages of innovation identified in the literature include (1) innovation as a process, (2) innovation as a discrete item such as products, programs or services, and (3) innovation as an attribute of organisations (Baregheh, Rowley, & Sambrook, 2009). The foregoing suggests why innovation in higher education system involves the process of generating new ideas, development of new programs or services, and as an attribute of higher institution. Therefore, innovation is "the creation of new knowledge and ideas to facilitate new business outcomes, aimed at improving internal business processes and structures and to create market driven products and services (Plessis, 2007, p. 21). Accordingly, innovation involves both radical innovation (business process re-engineering) and incremental innovation (business process improvement).

The drivers of technological innovations in higher education are developments in information and communication technologies across the global (Garrison & Vaughan, 2013). These developments are vigorously reshaping teaching and learning strategies in higher education. For example, technical innovations in higher education have resulted into blended learning, e-learning, m-learning, s-learning, virtual learning (web-based learning), cloud-based learning management systems (Pappas, 2015), gamification, simulations and other wearable gadgets (Elton, 2017; Timothy, 2016). These innovative teaching and learning approaches have revolutionized the operations of higher education in recent times. Wearable gadgets also enhance learning experience with virtual reality (VR), and augmented reality (AR) by generating artificial objects in real environment for learners' interactions (Elton, 2017; Pappas, 2015; Timothy, 2016). The ongoing advances in technology will continue to revolutionise learning approaches, as such transformational leaders should make conscious efforts to embrace innovations in higher education.

Without management support for innovation in higher education, the institutional objectives may not be feasible in the digital age. Hence, the support for technological innovations by management of higher education is extremely important. There are enormous financial obligations that come in the quest for technological innovations in institutions of higher learning (Atiku, 2018; Bowen, 2018). Management has the sole responsibility of budgeting and investing heavily in this field. Studies have shown that top management support can have positive impact on innovation (Elkins & Keller, 2003). Organisational decision-making power is vested in top managers and their support would go a long way in advancing technological innovation.

The selection of faculty members in academic institutions has a long-lasting effect on institutions ability to fulfil its mission (Grandzon, 2005). Recently, the knowledge or competencies in innovative teaching and learning approaches are included in the selection criteria for appointing qualified faculty members in higher education (Bowen, 2018). Indeed, faculty competence cannot be overemphasized in higher educational process improvement. To improve the operational efficiency and reliability in higher education, stakeholders must embrace the latest innovative approaches and performance indicators, fitness for purpose, value added, peer review, total quality management and academic audit (Chung Sea Law, 2010). The students learning experience should also be at the center stage of the improvement process in higher education.

Innovative Approaches and Pro-Environmental Behaviour in Higher Education

Technology is essential in improving existing standards set by institution of higher learning. In the 21st century, process improvement would have almost been impossible without the advent of technology. The foundation to process improvement's dramatic results is information technology, a largely untapped resource but crucial enabler of process improvement (Davenport, 1993). Success of any institution of higher education depends on how well the institution meets the needs of its stakeholders (Noe, Hollenbeck, Gerhart, & Wright, 2006). On the side of students, technological tools play a dominant role in helping students develop statistical literacy and reasoning (Chance, Ben-ZVI, Garfield, & Medina, 2007). The success of workplace green initiatives depends on the pro-environmental behaviours (PEBs) of employees, not just the implementation of new technology and processes (Graves & Sarkis, 2018). PEB could be referred to as "behaviour that consciously seeks to minimize the negative impact of one's actions on the natural and built world" (Kollmuss & Agyeman, 2002, p. 240). Pro-environmental behaviour can be adopted in higher education as a commitment to effective workplace sustainability plans (Loverock & Newell, 2012).

The use of electronic-based teaching and learning approaches is related to PEB in higher education systems. Mata, Lazar, Nedeff, and Lazar (2013) put it that environmentally friendly materials and technological innovations in higher education will have a positive impact on environmental sustainability. The reason is that e-learning platforms will reduce the paper-and-pencil transactions of an institution leading to efficiency (cost reduction), as well as workplace green behaviour. The electronic-based teaching and learning platforms include m-learning, s-learning, virtual learning (web-based learning), cloud-based learning management systems, gamification, simulations and other wearable gadgets (Elton, 2017; Pappas, 2015; Timothy, 2016). These learning platforms have caused a drastic reduction in the paper-and-pencil transactions in higher education, which will have a positive impact on environmental sustainability. Adopting innovative learning approaches leading to huge reduction in the use of paper in higher education could be regarded as a workplace pro-environmental behaviour. For example, eco-innovative teaching and learning approaches in higher education will make a significant contribution to environmental sustainability (Mata, Lazar, Nedeff, & Lazar, 2013).

Furthermore, HEIs also sponsor research in science and technology for further development of eco-innovative approaches (Mata, Lazar & Lazar, 2016). This implies that the leadership in HEIs not only adopt e-learning methods but also invest in development of environmental friendly teaching and learning materials or platforms. Such pro-environmental behaviour should be exhibited at individual, group and organisational levels for workplace green behaviour effectiveness (Atiku, 2019). Hence, pro-environmental behaviour is subject to stakeholder's sensitization, empowerment and cultural values to support the initiatives for eco-innovative learning materials and assessment methods in higher education.

The assessment methods (formative and summative assessments) could be redesigned to reduce the paper-and-pencil transactions in higher education. For example, computer-based multiple choice tests (Lau, Lau, Hong, & Usop, 2011) as an innovative assessment method is effective in testing knowledge of facts, ideas, principles, laws, and quantitative processes in science and engineering (Bates, n.d). Similarly, simulations, gamification, and virtual worlds could be used as effective formative assessment methods to enhance students experience learning in the digital age (Bates, n.d). Automated Essay Scoring (AES) is effective in providing students with automatic, iterative and correct scores or feedback on their essays (Parachuri, 2013). There is no doubt that these innovative assessment methods have tremendously contributed to environmental sustainability by reducing the use of paper-and-pencil assessment methods in HEIs.

The sustainability of higher education for positive social, financial and environmental outcomes potentially depends on eco-innovation (Aguilera-caracuel & de-Mandojana, 2013; Fields & Atiku, 2017). Exhibiting green behaviours in HEIs include fusing green initiatives into their structures and technological innovations that save energy, prevent pollution, or enable waste recycling and support green products design and environmental management (Aguilera-caracuel & de-Mandojana, 2013). Most innovative approaches in higher education have less negative impact on the environment, unlike industrial innovation where there are emissions of toxic gasses, which turn to deplete ozone layer.

Innovation and Social Demand Approach

Social demand approach is highly utilized by educational planners for policy formulation. Government considers the population growth and provides education for the masses accordingly. Because educational resources are limited (Brennan, et al., 2014, educational planners are concerned with how to prioritize at every given stage of the educational process with the needs of the economy. For examples, many West African countries are confronted with the challenge of infrastructural facilities to support innovative approaches, as well as meeting the social needs of education in recent times (Atiku, 2018).

According to Aghenta (2001), social demand approach focuses on education as a service required by people just like any other social services. This means that institutions of higher learning have an obligation to provide schools with the right facilities in place for all prospective learners who are seeking admission. It therefore dawns on educators to employ stupendous innovation in meeting their social obligations. Therefore, the factors influencing social demand for higher education include; the cost of education, benefits accrued from education, government policy, distance or geographical proximity of higher education institution (no longer a challenge with various e-learning platforms), quality of school, demographic data, cultural factors, admission policies, among other (Cullinan, Flannery, Walsh, & McCoy, 2013). Such factors have high influence on higher education enrolment and should be carefully considered. Social innovation enhances the understanding and analysis of radical educational change (Loogma, Tafel-Viia, & Umarik, 2013).

Institutions of higher learning are being compelled and under incredible pressure to carefully reconsider their role in society and ensure that relationships with their various stakeholders, constituencies and communities is re-evaluated (Jongbloed, Enders, & Salerno, 2008). There has been a gradual shift in the past decades around the world among HEIs from environmental changes to enormous societal expectations, new public policies, and technological innovations, which poses a new set of challenge for institutions of higher learning (Gumport & Sporn, 1999). Therefore, interdisciplinary curricula and multi-disciplinary education are at the heart of the strategies by which many HEIs seek to train future innovators and leaders (OCED, 2014).

Innovation and Quality Management in Higher Education

The primary objective of quality assurance is to ensure that product or service of an organisation meets the already established standard and as well fit the purpose for which such product is meant to serve (Oduma, 2014). Accordingly, it has to do with monitoring and evaluating an organisation processes or activities involved in production process to maximize the probability that minimum standards are met. The quality assurance in education is a process of improving the general standard and value of education to profit the students or learners and the society at large (Oduma, 2014). Government usually champions the quality assurance in higher education and its agency (Ministry or Department of Education) in form of policy framework targeted at improving the quality of tertiary education within a country. Therefore, university management are mandated in many countries to comply with the educational reforms to improve the quality of higher education (Harvey & Williams, 2010). Quality assurance in higher education is positioned to enforce compliance with the standards of education, thereby meeting the micro and macro needs of education.

Quality assurance in the era of innovative technology requires the use innovative teaching and learning methods to improve students learning experience and outcomes (Mitchell, 2015). For example, the rationale behind development and adoption e-learning platforms is to enhance teaching and learning experience beyond the classroom (Atiku, 2018). E learning will enhance the quality of higher education through innovative methods by increasing the students' motivation, interest and engagement (Pavel, Fruth, & Neacsu, 2015). Accordingly, quality can be enhanced by facilitating the acquisition of skills and by improving instructor training, which will eventually improve communication and exchange of information. This could be used as a yardstick to explain the connection between technological advancement and quality management in higher education. There is no doubt that a positive relationship exists between innovation and quality assurance in higher education (Hoecht, 2006). Many developed and developing countries have incorporated audio-visual technology in the Lecture Theater (Atiku, 2018) as a standard for quality assurance in their higher education system.

Another innovative technology adopted to improve the quality of teaching and learning in higher education is Learning Management Systems (LMS). LMS is an innovative teaching and learning technology adopted by universities and made available for instructors and learners to enhance the quality of learning experience in the digital age (Atiku, 2018; Paulsen, 2003). Adoption of LMS can be regarded as a standard for quality improvement and management in higher education. For example, the students' evaluation report as a measure to improve the quality of instructors' delivery based on learners/students feedback is being conducted via LMS at the end of the each semester. This implies that LMS is an effective platform for quality review and management in higher education. The quality assurance departments of HEIs have incorporated LMS as one of the criteria for assessing the quality of teaching and learning experience in higher education (Dias & Diniz, 2014). Therefore, innovative methods in higher education play important role in enhancing students learning experience and outcomes, meeting labour market requirements and fulfilling social expectations of higher education system.

Innovative Approaches and Work-Life Balance in Higher Education

Research findings from several countries suggest that academic work has become comparatively stressful, with potentially serious consequence for the workforce and the quality of higher education (Kinman & Jones, 2008). Greenhaus and Allen (2011) define life balance as a multi-modal plan emerged from a sense of effectiveness and satisfaction in multiple life roles. Work-life balance can be referred to as a transition towards flexible and fluid boundaries between one's work and life outside of the workplace (Sorenson, 2017). This position corroborates the life balance definition most applicable to educators, the ability to manage external pressure from a competitive work environment with leisure or family (Khallash & Kruse, 2012). Casper, Vaziri, Wayne, DeHauw, and Greenhaus (2018) concluded that work-life balance is a self-evaluation of how best to combines work with non-work roles. Therefore, the university management and academics need to decide on the best approach in managing work and family demands to avoid role conflicts (Owens, Kottwitz, Tiedt, & Ramirez, 2018).

When role conflict occurs, employees tend to carry issues at home to work and issues at work to the house. According to Sullivan and Lewis (2006), schedule inflexibility increased depression in both men and women and increased physical distress such as insomnia, appetite problem, tension related aches and pains. Kinman and Jones (2008) reported that work related stress has increased in the educational sector. Managing work and family life is an emerging challenge for both employers and employees in the world of work (Fatimal & Sahibzada, 2012). When people are psychologically not positioned at the workplace they are unable to deliver or meet organisational expectations and this affects overall institutional efficiency and effectiveness.

In the era of online courses (MOOCs), the use of the internet increases the flexibility of academics. The internet and work flexibility are found to increase work-family conflict (Stra & dottir, 2010). As most institutions have gradually shifted to Massive Open-Online Course (MOOCs) and other internet based learning and teaching modules, extra care should be taken as it poses treat to work-life balance. Therefore, the emerging innovative teaching and learning approaches could be used as a work-life balance strategy (enhanced flexible work arrangement) in HEIs

LEADERSHIP IN HIGHER EDUCATION

Leadership is crucial in advancing an organisation towards the realization of its vision and mission statements. It involves channeling a path or strategy towards accomplishing the goals of an organisation, be it manufacturing or service rendering organisation. Leadership is all about influencing or motivating followers and other stakeholders towards the attainment of organisational goals (Bryman, 2007). For example, a visionary leader sees a vision, communicate the vision to all stakeholders, estimates costs/benefits of organisational development process, ensures stakeholders buy-in, and empowers all categories of staff to achieve desired organisational outcomes. Therefore, leadership in higher education system plays a huge role in enhancing university effectiveness (Bryman, 2007). The level of university effectiveness is subject to the leadership style(s) being adopted by the university management.

Taking insights from the literature on leadership effectiveness and behaviour of past or current business leaders in relation to organisational outcomes, there are several leadership styles. According to Achua and Lussier (2010), leadership styles relate to the combination of traits, skills, and behaviours that leaders use as they interact with followers. The leadership styles include autocratic leadership, democratic leadership, laissez-faire leadership, charismatic leadership, transactional leadership, transformational leadership, and among others (Achua & Lussier, 2010).

An authoritarian leader through which all decision-making powers are centralized in the leader usually exhibits autocratic leadership style. This leadership style is more prominent in the military, where followers have no options than to comply with the decisions reached by the superior officers. Autocratic leadership style is not an appropriate style to drive innovation in higher education, since university system is based on committee system in its decision making process, otherwise there will be frustration and anger (Bhatti, Maitlo, Shaikh, Hashmi, & Shaikh, 2012). Democratic leadership style favours decision-making by the group, a leader wins the cooperation of the group and can motivate followers effectively and positively towards informed decision. (Achua & Lussier, 2010; Bryman, 2007). Democratic style is exhibited in higher education in setting admission criteria for programmes, consideration of results and other administrative decision-making processes at departmental, faculty, college and university levels (Bryman, 2007). Laissez-faire leadership on the other hand, leaves the group entirely to itself; such a leader allows maximum freedom to subordinates (Achua & Lussier, 2010). For example, subordinates are given a free hand in deciding their own methods; which can be can be very useful in businesses where creative ideas are important in goal setting and meeting targets to drive organisational performance.

Charismatic leadership style was derived from the Greek word *charisma, which* means "divinely inspired gift" (Achua & Lussier, 2010). Such a leader influence followers based on followers' perceptions that the leader is endowed with the gift of divine inspiration or supernatural qualities. It appeals to people's emotional side. The followers' action are not based on rational likelihood of success, but on an effective belief in the extraordinary qualities of the leader. Due to the dark side charismatic leadership style, such leadership behaviour could be regarded as inappropriate based on the need to drive innovation in higher education. Transactional leadership centres on the exchanges that occur between leaders and followers (Achua & Lussier, 2010; Bass, 2008; McCleskey, 2014). The term "transactional" refers to the fact that this type of leader essentially motivates subordinates by exchanging rewards (extrinsic rewards) for performance (Achua & Lussier, 2010; McCleskey, 2014). Therefore, caution should be taken in adopting this leadership style in an attempt to influence professional or faculty members in higher education to avoid being construed as a carrot and stick approach. Transformational leaders on the other hand, stimulate and inspire their followers to achieve extraordinary outcomes and, in the process, develop their followers' leadership capability (Achua & Lussier, 2010; McCleskey, 2014). This chapter is of the view that the link between leadership and university effectiveness (Bryman, 2007), in terms of technological innovations can best be expressed through transformational leadership. The next subheading presents the interplay between transformational leadership and advancement in innovative teaching/learning approaches in higher education.

Transformational Leadership and Innovation in Higher Education

There is a positive relationship between strong leadership and adoption of innovative teaching and learning approaches in higher education (Garrison & Vaughan, 2013). Numerous challenges had confronted institutions of higher learning in the last decade; financial pressure, growth in technology, changing faculty roles, public scrutiny, changing demographics and the enormous rate of global change (Kezar & Ekel, 2002). Managing an institution in the midst of these challenges and volatilities in the global environment require the efforts of transformational leaders.

Burns introduced the concept of transformational leadership in 1978 (Gumusluoglu & Ilsev, 2009). Transformational leadership was later subdivided into four components; charismatic role modelling, individualized consideration, inspirational motivation, and intellectual stimulation (Bass & Avolio 1995, cited in Gumusluoglu & Ilsev, 2009). Accordingly, the authors found a significant positive relationship between transformational leadership and followers' creativity. A transformational leader sets clear organisational plans, build cultural values to embrace creativity, innovation and strong commitment (Garrison & Vaughan, 2013). The efforts of those in leadership positions will result to enhanced teaching and learning process in higher education (Garrison & Kanuka, 2004; Garrison & Vaughan, 2013). Institutions of higher learning in developing countries must be innovative enough to identify, analyze and improve standards already set to meet labour market requirements in the fourth industrial revolution (World Economic Forum, 2017). Running an education enterprise involves process improvement as a major driver for efficiency of the institution. As responsible business solutions continues to improve, probabilities for sustainability in the end becomes higher (Fields & Atiku, 2017).

Transformational leadership does not only inspire followers, but also challenges them to be creative (Achua & Lussier, 2010). Accordingly, transformational leaders inspire creativity and empower followers to do new things (innovation). Many factors have been found to account for organisational innovation of which leadership style of top managers is predominant (Jung, Chow, & Wu, 2003). Studies found that transformational leadership is the most promising approach to enhancing innovations (García-Morales, Jiménez-Barrionuevo, & Gutiérrez-Gutiérrez, 2012; Gumusluoglu & Ilsev, 2009; Moolenaar, Daly, & Sleegers, 2010). Undoubtedly, empirical studies revealed that transformational leadership positively correlates with innovation (García-Morales, et al., 2012; Gumusluoglu & Ilsev, 2009). In higher education where there is continuous teaching and learning, transformational leadership influences the innovative approaches. Teaching goes beyond disseminating information and learning goes beyond mere consumption of such information. Proper learning only takes place where an instructor inspires the learners to challenge the status quo with the information provided and come up with creative ideas leading to innovation. The inspirational motivation of leaders (Bass & Avolio 1995, cited in Gumusluoglu & Ilsev, 2009) in higher education increases follower's cognitive and behavioural patterns to accept challenging tasks and achieve desirable results (Garrison & Vaughan, 2013). This suggests that inspirational leaders have a role to play in ensuring sustainable competitive advantage in recent times. Higgs and Rowland (2011) identified five broad areas of leadership competency needed in the change process:

- Creating the case for change
- Creating structural change
- Engaging others in the process and building commitment
- Implementing and sustaining change
- Facilitating and developing capability

The following are essential in enhancing innovative teaching and learning approaches by leaders in HEIs (Reich, 2016).

- Building a strong support for research and development.
- Providing an enabling environment for knowledge sharing and experimentations.
- Creating opportunities for Knowledge transfer across learning communities.
- Guiding innovation with shared vision and shared instructional language.

According to Horth and Buchner (2014), leadership for innovation requires contemporary business leaders to create a conducive environment for other stakeholders to apply creative thinking to solve problems and develop new products and services. The authors submit that growing a culture of innovation, is not just by hiring a few creative individuals, but also by helping others to think differently and work in new ways to face challenges and stay ahead of the competition. Therefore, the stakeholders require the six innovative thinking skills in higher education systems.

Six Innovative Thinking Skills

The innovative thinking skills (Horth & Buchner, 2014) could be referred to as a set of skills in developing or adapting to innovative teaching and learning in the digital age. These skills should be inculcated by transformational leaders to followers or subordinates, as well as students in higher education for quality assurance as discussed below:

- **Paying attention**: The ability to pay attention to details is very important stage of the innovative thinking process (Horth & Buchner, 2014). This is a crucial stage of diagnostic approach to envisage new patterns (Truss, Mankin, & Kelliher, 2012). It becomes imperative to listening to new perspectives; consider different points of view and multiple inputs.
- **Personalizing:** The ability to tap into (seemingly unrelated) personal experiences and passions introduces fresh perspectives on challenges. The customer side of personalizing is the ability to understand customers in a full and real way. Deep customer knowledge leads to the new ideas, patterns, and insights that fuel innovation (Horth & Buchner, 2014).
- **Imaging**: Using one's imagination to answer the critical questions can lead to extraordinary images and possibilities. The imagery is a very good approach of assimilating and processing information for creativity and developing innovative products and services.
- **Serious Play:** Business thinking and routine work can become a rigid process. Innovation requires bending some rules, branching out, having some fun. To generate knowledge and insight through nontraditional ways — free exploration, improvisation, experimentation, levity and rapid prototyping, limit testing, work becomes challenging and interesting (Horth & Buchner, 2014).
- **Collaborative Inquiry**: Insights through thoughtful, nonjudgmental sharing of ideas are essential for creativity and innovation (Fields & Atiku, 2017). Collaborative inquiry is a process of sustained, effective dialogue with those who have a stake in an organisation (Horth & Buchner, 2014). For example, intellectual, affective and social engagement are three main dimensions of employee engagement (Truss et al., 2012) that are necessary for an enhanced innovative teaching and learning approaches across various disciplines in the higher education systems.
- **Crafting:** The test of a first-rate intelligence is the ability to hold two opposing ideas in the mind at the same time and retain the ability to function (Horth & Buchner, 2014). The practice of crafting allows work groups to resolve paradox and contradiction. Unlike the traditional analysis of business thinking, which requires a breakdown of problems into separate units, known facts, and current assumptions — crafting is about synthesis, integration, and possibility (Horth & Buchner, 2014). Through adductive reasoning, one can make intuitive connections among seemingly unrelated information and begin to shape order out of chaos.

RECOMMENDATIONS

Policy makers in higher education should create a climate that promotes creativity and innovation by ensuring that transformational leaders are at the helm of affairs for quality management. The findings presented in this chapter show that leadership support for innovation in higher education is a benchmark for quality assurance in higher education in recent times. Managing a higher education institution in the digital age requires a rethink on how educational systems work in the twenty-first century and how governments could prioritize to streamline the modeling of graduates in line with the labour market requirements.

As students are the key customers in higher education, policies should be drafted to enhance deeper learning outcomes with the aid of vast technological innovation as one of the focus of quality management. Student learning experiences should ultimately be enhanced. Instructors or lecturers should be dynamic by accepting mentorship and coaching roles. Regular lecture visits from key players in the industry to universities should be encouraged to breach the skills gap between universities and industry. Universities should also consider changing their administrative models to ones that are more responsive and nimble as well as developing teams that are dedicated to researching complex issues of sustainability and resilience (Robin, 2015). Policy makers should also hold work-life balance in high esteem as it also sparks innovation.

FUTURE RESEARCH DIRECTIONS

This chapter centres on leadership and innovative approaches in HEIs. Future studies may consider developing an operational framework on the link between leadership and innovation in higher education. An empirical analysis of a conceptual framework on this area of research would add value to the academic discourse. Action research should be conducted in developing countries to find a lasting solution to leadership problem and lack of infrastructural facilities to support innovative teaching and learning approaches in HEIs operating in African countries.

CONCLUSION

The main objective of this chapter was to examine the relationship between leadership and innovative teaching/learning approaches in HEIs. This chapter concludes that there is a positive relationship between transformational leadership and adoption of innovative approaches in higher education systems. However, vast technological innovations across the globe have created some challenges and opportunities for those in leadership positions. The main challenges driving innovation in higher education are pressures from globalization, changing supply of and demand for higher education and changes in higher education funding. In spite of these challenges, vast technological innovations also come up with some benefits such as environmental, technological, pedagogical, psychosocial, and economic benefits (Mata, Lazar, Nedeff, & Lazar, 2013). Therefore, institutions of higher learning should pay attention to the demands of students in an ever-evolving educational environment in adapting to the contemporary innovative approaches in higher education. Partnerships should also be a core mandate of higher education as organizations do not operate in a vacuum. To implement identifiable innovative approaches in higher education, institutions could team up with governments and other organizations of interest to secure the necessary funding for projects. Conclusively, no meaningful change will happen in any higher institution without a strong leadership support for innovation and quality management.

REFERENCES

Achua, C. F., & Lussier, R. N. (2010). *Effective leadership* (4th ed.). South-Western Cengage Learning.

Adams, J. L. (2016). *NMC Horizon Report*. Austin, TX: The New Media Consortium.

Aghenta, J. (2001). *Educational planning: A turning point in education and development in Nigeria*. Benin City: University of Benin City, Nigeria.

Aguilera-caracuel, J., & de-Mandojana, N. O. (2013). Green innovation and financial performance: An institutional approach. *Organization & Environment*, *26*(4), 365–385. doi:10.1177/1086026613507931

Allen, K. E., Bordas, J., Hickman, G. R., Matusak, L. R., Sorenson, G. J., & Whitemire, J. K. (1998). Leadership in the twenty-first century. Academy of Leadership Press.

Andolfi, G. (2016). Development and innovation management on higher education institutions. *European Journal of Social Sciences Studies*, *1*(1), 65–70.

Atiku, S. O. (2018). Reshaping human capital formation through digitalization. In *Radical Reorganization of Existing Work Structures through Digitalization* (pp. 52–73). Hershey, PA: IGI Global. doi:10.4018/978-1-5225-3191-3.ch004

Atiku, S. O. (2019). Institutionalizing social responsibility through workplace green behaviour. In *Contemporary Multicultural Orientations and Practices for Global Leadership* (pp. 183–199). Hershey, PA: IGI Global. doi:10.4018/978-1-5225-6286-3.ch010

Baregheh, A., Rowley, J., & Sambrook, S. (2009). Towards a multidisciplinary definition of innovation. *Management Decision*, *47*(8), 1323–1339. doi:10.1108/00251740910984578

Bass, B. M. (2008). *The Bass handbook of leadership: Theory, research, & managerial applications* (4th ed.). New York, NY: Free Press.

Bates, A. W. (n.d.). *A.8 Assessment of learning*. Retrieved 22 March 2019 from https://opentextbc.ca/teachinginadigitalage/chapter/5-8-assessment-of-learning/

Bhatti, N., Maitlo, G. M., Shaikh, N., Hashmi, M. A., & Shaikh, F. M. (2012). The impact of autocratic and democratic leadership style on job satisfaction. *International Business Research*, *5*(2), 192–201. doi:10.5539/ibr.v5n2p192

Bowen, H. (2018). *Investment in learning: The individual and social value of American higher education*. Routledge. doi:10.4324/9781351309929

Brennan, J., Broek, S., Durazzi, N., Kamphuis, B., Ranga, M., & Ryan, S. (2014). *Study on innovation in higher education*. Retrieved March 19, 2019 from http://www.lse.ac.uk/business-and-consultancy/consulting/assets/documents/study-on-innovation-in-higher-education.pdf

Bryman, A. (2007). Effective leadership in higher education: A literature review. *Studies in Higher Education*, *32*(6), 693–710. doi:10.1080/03075070701685114

Carnoy, M. (1994). *Faded dreams: The Economics and Politics of Race in America*. New York: Cambridge University Press. doi:10.1017/CBO9780511572166

Casper, W., Vaziri, H., Wayne, J., DeHauw, S., & Greenhaus, J. (2018). The jingle-jangle of work–nonwork balance: A comprehensive and meta-analytic review of its meaning and measurement. *The Journal of Applied Psychology*, *103*(2), 182–214. doi:10.1037/apl0000259 PMID:29016161

Chance, B., Ben-ZVI, D., Garfield, J., & Medina, E. (2007). *The role of technology in improving student learning of statistics*. Academic Press.

Chung Sea Law, D. (2010). Quality assurance in post-secondary education: Some common approaches. *Quality Assurance in Education*, *18*(1), 64–77. doi:10.1108/09684881011016007

Community for Creativity and Innovation. (n.d.). *What is innovation? 15 experts share their innovation definition*. Retrieved May 24, 2019 from https://www.ideatovalue.com/inno/nickskillicorn/2016/03/innovation-15-experts-share-innovation-definition/#nicks

Cullinan, J., Flannery, D., Walsh, S., & McCoy, S. (2013). Distance effects, social class and the decision to participate in higher education in Ireland. *The Economic and Social Review*, *44*(1), 19-51.

Davenport, T. H. (1993). *Process innovation: reengineering work through information technology*. Harvard Business Press.

Dias, S. B., & Diniz, J. A. (2014). Towards an enhanced learning management system for blended learning in higher education incorporating distinct learners' profiles. *Journal of Educational Technology & Society*, *17*(1), 307–319.

Elkins, T., & Keller, R. T. (2003). Leadership in research and development organizations: A literature review and conceptual framework. *The Leadership Quarterly*, *14*(4-5), 587–606. doi:10.1016/S1048-9843(03)00053-5

Elton, K. (2017). *Wearable tech in the classroom: Taking the education industry by storm*. Retrieved March 19, 2019 from https://elearningindustry.com/wearable-tech-in-the-classroom-taking-education-industry-storm

Fatimal, N., & Sahibzada, S. A. (2012). An empirical analysis of factors affecting work-life balance among university teachers: The case of Pakistan. *Journal of International Academic Research*, *12*(1), 16–29.

Fields, Z., & Atiku, S. O. (2017). Collective green creativity and eco-innovation as key drivers of sustainable business solutions in organisations. In *Collective Creativity for Responsible and Sustainable Business Practice* (pp. 1–25). Hershey, PA: IGI Global. doi:10.4018/978-1-5225-1823-5.ch001

Franck, R., & Galor, O. (2015). *The complementarity between technology and human capital in the early phase of industrialization*. Retrieved August 27, 2018 from http://d.repec.org/n?u=RePEc:bro:econwp:2015-3&r=his

Futurelearn. (2013). *Futurelearn Launches*. Retrieved from Futurelearn: http://futurelearn.com/feature/futurelearn-launches/

García-Morales, V. J., Jiménez-Barrionuevo, M. M., & Gutiérrez-Gutiérrez, L. (2012). Transformational leadership influence on organizational performance through organizational learning and innovation. *Journal of Business Research, 65*(7), 1040–1050. doi:10.1016/j.jbusres.2011.03.005

Garrison, D. R., & Kanuka, H. (2004). Blended learning: Uncovering its transformative potential in higher education. *The Internet and Higher Education, 7*(2), 95–105. doi:10.1016/j.iheduc.2004.02.001

Garrison, D. R., & Vaughan, N. D. (2013). Institutional change and leadership associated with blended learning innovation: Two case studies. *The Internet and Higher Education, 18*, 24–28. doi:10.1016/j.iheduc.2012.09.001

Grandzon, J. R. (2005). *Improving the faculty selection process in higher education: A case study for the Analytic Hierarchy Process*. Association for Institutional Research.

Graves, L. M., & Sarkis, J. (2018). The role of employees' leadership perceptions, values, and motivation in employees' proevironmental behaviours. *Journal of Cleaner Production, 196*, 576–587. doi:10.1016/j.jclepro.2018.06.013

Greenhaus, J. H., & Allen, T. D. (2011). Work–family balance: A review and extension of the literature. In J. C. Quick & L. E. Tetrick (Eds.), *Handbook of occupational health psychology* (2nd ed.). Washington, DC: American Psychological Association.

Gumport, P. J., & Sporn, B. (1999). Institutional Adaptation: Demand for management reform and university administration. Higher education: Handbook of theory and research, 103-145.

Gumusluoglu, L., & Ilsev, A. (2009). Transformational leadership, creativity, and organisational innovation. *Journal of Business Research, 62*(4), 461–473. doi:10.1016/j.jbusres.2007.07.032

Harvey, L., & Williams, J. (2010). Fifteen years of Quality in Higher Education. *Quality in Higher Education, 16*(1), 3–36. doi:10.1080/13538321003679457

Heitor, M., & Horta, H. (2016). Reforming higher education in Portugal in times of uncertainty: The importance of illities, as non-functional requirements. *Technological Forecasting and Social Change, 113*, 146–156. doi:10.1016/j.techfore.2015.09.027

Higgs, M., & Rowland, D. (2011). What does it take to implement change successfully? A study of the behaviours of successful change leaders. *The Journal of Applied Behavioral Science, 47*(3), 309–355. doi:10.1177/0021886311404556

Hirst, P., & Thompson, G. (2002). The Future of Globalization. *Journal of the Nordic International Studies Association*, 247-265.

Hoecht, A. (2006). Quality assurance in UK higher education: Issues of trust, control, professional autonomy and accountability. *Higher Education, 51*(4), 541–563. doi:10.100710734-004-2533-2

HomeRoom. (2015, october 14). *HomeRoom*. Retrieved February 17, 2019, from The official Blog US department of education: go.nmc.org/equip

Horth, D., & Buchner, D. (2014). *Innovation leadership: How to use innovation to lead effectively, work collaboratively, and drive results*. Center for Creative Leadership. Retrieved March 24, 2019 from https://www.ccl.org/wp-content/uploads/2015/04/InnovationLeadership.pdf

JISC. (2013). *Open Educational Resources Programme*. Retrieved from JISC: http:www.jisc.ac.uk/whatwedo/programmes//elearning/oer.aspx

Jongbloed, B., Enders, J., & Salerno, C. (2008). Higher education and its communities: Interconnections, interdependencies and research agenda. *Higher Education, 56*(3), 303–324. doi:10.100710734-008-9128-2

Jung, D., Chow, C., & Wu, A. (2003). The role of transformational leadership in enhancing organisational innovation: Hypothesis and some preliminary findings. *The Leadership Quarterly, 14*(4-5), 525–544. doi:10.1016/S1048-9843(03)00050-X

Kezar, A., & Ekel, P. D. (2002). The effect of institutional culture on change strategies in higher education: Universal principles or culturally responsive concepts. *The Journal of Higher Education, 73*(4), 435–460.

Khallash, S., & Kruse, M. (2012). The future of work and work–life balance 2025. *Futures, 44*(7), 678–686. doi:10.1016/j.futures.2012.04.007

Kinman, G., & Jones, F. (2008). A life beyond work? Job demands, work-life balance, and well-being in UK academics. *Journal of Human Behavior in the Social Environment, 17*(1-2), 41–60. doi:10.1080/10911350802165478

Kinman, G., & Jones, F. (2008). Effort-reward imbalance, over-commitment and work-life conflict: Testing an expanded model. *Journal of Managerial Psychology, 23*(3), 236–251. doi:10.1108/02683940810861365

Kollmuss, A., & Agyeman, J. (2002). Mind the gap: Why do people act environmentally and what are the barriers to pro-environmental behaviour? *Environmental Education Research, 8*(3), 239–260. doi:10.1080/13504620220145401

Kortemeyer, G. (2013, February 26). *Educause Review*. Retrieved February 18, 2019, from Educause: https://er.educause.edu/articles/2013/2/ten-years-later-why-open-educational-resources-have-not-noticeably-affected-higher-education-and-why-we-should-care

Lau, P. N. K., Lau, S. H., Hong, K. S., & Usop, H. (2011). Guessing, partial knowledge, and misconceptions in multiple-choice tests. *Journal of Educational Technology & Society, 14*(4), 99–110.

Loogma, K., Tafel-Viia, K., & Ümarik, M. (2013). Conceptualizing educational changes: A social innovation approach. *Journal of Educational Change, 14*(3), 283–301. doi:10.100710833-012-9205-2

Loverock, D. T., & Newell, R. (2012). *Pro-environmental behaviours in the workplace: Driving social change*. Interactive Case Studies in Sustainable Community Development.

Mata, L., Lazar, I., Nedeff, V., & Lazar, G. (2013). Ēno interactive whiteboards as an innovative eco-technology solution in teaching science and technological subjects. *APCBEE Procedia, 5*, 312–316. doi:10.1016/j.apcbee.2013.05.053

Maxwell, J. C. (2007). *21 irrefutable laws of leaderhsip.* Nashville TN: Thomas Nelson.

McCleskey, J. A. (2014). Situational, transformational, and transactional leadership and leadership development. *Journal of Business Studies Quarterly, 5*(4), 117–130.

Mitchell, T. (2015). *Innovation and quality higher education.* Retrieved May 26, 2019 from https://blog.ed.gov/2015/07/innovation-and-quality-in-higher-education/

Moolenaar, N. M., Daly, A. J., & Sleegers, P. J. (2010). Occupying the principal position: Examining relationships between transformational leadership, Social network position and school's innovative climate. *Educational Administrational Quarterly, 46*(5), 623-670.

Oduma, C. A. (2014). Quality assurance in education: The role of ICT and quality control measures in tertiary institutions in Nigeria. *AFRREV STECH: An International Journal of Science and Technology, 3*(2), 136–158. doi:10.4314tech.v3i2.9

OECD. (2014). *Innovation strategy for education and training.* Retrieved March 24, 2019 from http://www.oecd.org/education/ceri/IS%20Project_Conference%20Brochure_FINAL.pdf

Owens, J., Kottwitz, C., Tiedt, J., & Ramirez, J. (2018). Strategies to attain faculty work-life balance. *Building Healthy Academic Communities Journal, 2*(2), 58–73. doi:10.18061/bhac.v2i2.6544

Pappas, C. (2015). *The top learning management systems statistics and facts for 2015 you need to know.* Retrieved March 19, 2019 from https://elearningindustry.com/top-lms-statistics-and-facts-for-2015

Parachuri, V. (2013). *On the automated scoring of essays and the lessons learned along the way.* Retrieved March 22, 2019 from vicparachuri.com

Paulsen, M. F. (2003). Experiences with Learning Management Systems in 113 European Institutions. *Journal of Educational Technology & Society, 6*(4), 134–148.

Pavel, A. P., Fruth, A., & Neacsu, M. N. (2015). ICT and e-learning–catalysts for innovation and quality in higher education. *Procedia Economics and Finance, 23*, 704–711. doi:10.1016/S2212-5671(15)00409-8

Plessis, M. D. (2007). The role of knowledge management in innovation. *Journal of Knowledge Management, 11*(4), 20–29. doi:10.1108/13673270710762684

Reich, J. (2016). *Four ways school leaders can support innovation.* Retrieved March 24, 2019 from https://blogs.edweek.org/edweek/edtechresearcher/2016/11/four_ways_school_leaders_can_support_innovation.html

Robin, M. (2015, August 4). *Better future.* Retrieved August 4, 2015, from New Media Consortium: go.nmc.org/betterfuture

Shapiro, H., Haahr, J. H., Bayer, I., & Boekholt, P. (2007). *Background paper on innovation and education.* Danish Technological Institute and Technopolis for the European Commission, DG Education & Culture in the context of a planned Green Paper on innovation.

Stra, T. M. (2010). The Internet and academics workload and work-family balance. *The Internet and Higer Education, 13*(3), 158–163. doi:10.1016/j.iheduc.2010.03.004

Sullivan, C., & Lewis, S. (2006). Relationships between work and home life. In F. Jones, R. Burke, & M. Westman (Eds.), *Managing the work- home interface: A psychological perspective*. London: Taylor and Francis.

Timothy, A. (2016). *What you wear – 4 ways to use wearable tech in corporate training*. Retrieved March 19, 2019 from https://elearningindustry.com/4-ways-wearable-tech-in-corporate-training

Truss, C., Mankin, D., & Kelliher, C. (2012). *Strategic human resource management*. New York: Oxford University Press.

Waters, M., & Castells, M. (1995). Globalization; The Rise of the Network Society. New York: Routledge.

World Economic Forum. (2017). *System innovative on shaping the future of education gender and work*. Retrieved August 27, 2018 from https://www.weforum.org/system-initiatives/shaping-the-future-of-education-gender-and-work

Yuan & Powell. (2013). MOOCs and Open education: Implications for higher education. *JICS Cetis*, 1-5. Retrieved from academia.edu

KEY TERMS AND DEFINITIONS

Automated Essay Scoring: An innovative assessment method, which is effective in providing students with automatic, iterative and correct scores or feedback on their essays.

Curriculum Review: An ongoing process in educational institutions, which requires active participation of the faculty members in various disciplines, and employers for effective learning outcomes.

Innovation: A process of converting a creative idea into a solution that adds value to the products and services of an organisation from customer's perspective.

Inspirational Motivation: An inducement that increases follower's cognitive and behavioral patterns to accept challenging tasks and achieve desirable results.

Intellectual Stimulation: A leader's ability to instill innovative and creative capabilities into followers as a way of building their critical thinking and problem-solving skills.

Learning Outcomes: A set of capabilities displaying the quality of essential learning experience that learners have achieved in specific fields of study.

Quality Assurance: An evaluative process of assessing the quality of education and improving the general standard and value of education to benefit the students and the society.

Chapter 6
Quality Management and Academic Leadership

Joseph Ezale Cobbinah
https://orcid.org/0000-0001-5200-7093
University of Ghana, Ghana

Samuel Agyemang
Bia College of Education, Ghana

ABSTRACT

Quality management in higher education is one of the measures that institutions put in place to ensure that courses and programs that are offered meet international and accreditation standards. This chapter examines how academic leaders can promote and manage quality in higher education institutions. Higher education institutions and senior faculty members appear to improve performance by ensuring that quality assurance unit enforces effective delivery to increase students and parents' satisfaction. Promotion of quality and the management of quality is not about long service but an exhibition of effective leadership that will help higher education institutions to navigate through the turbulence of challenges facing higher education institutions today. To achieve this, the academic leader is supposed to assist institutions to pursue their vision and mission to enable them to effectively manage quality.

INTRODUCTION

The wind blowing around the world in higher education institutions has raised global concerns about a need to ensure that higher education institutions are well managed and responding to the quality needs of students, parents, employers and governments. The world is changing so are higher education institutions. The changing nature of higher education institutions also calls for educational administrators, human resources departments and heads of departments as well as program coordinators to ensure that the institutions also respond to the dynamic nature of our institutions. The changes taking place in higher education institutions in the recent times raise concerns about the issue of quality management and how academic leadership should respond to the changes while ensuring that quality is well managed in the

DOI: 10.4018/978-1-7998-1017-9.ch006

higher education institutions. The increasing demand for higher education by many people in several countries has put pressure on higher education institutions to introduce new programs and courses while others have mounted courses that could be studied on part time basis, through distance and online, as well as blended and even through sandwich mode. This initiatives have made providers of higher education to help meet the growing demand so as to allow those working but need higher education to take advantage. However the widening of participation through the introduction of different programs and different study modes cannot be compromised with quality delivery.

Paradoxically, promoting and managing quality cannot happen in a vacuum but needs effective academic leadership to help institutions navigate through such turbulence of change. Higher education institutions in many parts of the world are 'undergoing profound and rapid changes which force educational systems to respond to ensure that the quality of life' in our societies is improved (Maguad & Krone, 2012, p. 10). Institutions are responding to the changes to ensure that there is proper accountability, transparency and value for money for those who invest in higher education. Some countries response to the challenges facing higher education institutions by cutting down non-basic services, introduce part time work instead of full time, outsourcing some positions such as security, cleaners and laundry staff, among others. It is worth to note that there should be academic leaders to give direction to institutions and ensure there is effective management of any quality management initiative to enable the institutions achieve their objectives.

The training of skillful and knowledgeable workforce by higher education institutions to meet national development needs will be very difficult as far as creation of competitive edge for quality enhancement in higher education is concerned (Khan, 2008). This chapter is aimed at examining the concept of quality, and what is quality management in higher education institution? How could academic leaders promote and sustain quality management in their institutions so as to bring improvement? Answers to these questions will help deepen our understanding of quality management in higher education institutions and the role that educational leadership could play to make the quality initiatives in their institutions become a success. It will draw the attention of leaders of higher educational institutions to the importance of honesty and accountable for their stewardship. And to comprehend that to achieve quality, is a process, hence if institutions are to improve through best practices, then the issue of quality management should remain paramount in higher education institutions.

WHAT IS QUALITY MANAGEMENT?

To answer the above question, we will first of all look at the two concepts; quality and management in separate lenses, before examining the meaning of quality management and how it is viewed in higher education institutions. The concept of quality which will be examined in the first lens seem simple to explain but in reality means different to different people and also depends on the context in which the concept of quality is being viewed or perceived. According to Csizmadia (2006) explanation of the concept of quality has a range of overlapping meaning. Some critics view quality as a complex and multi-faceted construct that is very difficult to assign a single definition or interpretation to it (Cheng & Tam, 1997; Becket & Brookes, 2006), but even if an interpretation is offered it will depend on which institution wants quality and what quality agenda they are pursuing. On the contemporary agenda of many higher education institutions, the issue of quality is still an issue of debate in higher education (Csizmadia, 2006). Quality is also seen as a very slippery concept in higher education institutions in that the interpretation has depended on which aspect of higher education institution the emphasis of quality is being placed.

Quality in recent times has become mandatory in many organizations and even in educational institutions. If governments are to relent in their efforts to invest in higher education institutions while students' enrollment continue to increase then the challenge that remains is how to address quality in the institutions? The issue of quality management is to ensure that the available resources are used prudently to meet national demand. However, Hwang & Teo (2001) assert that it is difficult to deliver quality education, if the institutional agenda as well as the quality initiatives are not well managed. And that management for quality should replace management of quality; where as in respect of educational institutions the quality of education being given to students remain central to any quality management framework (Cruikshark, 2003). Higher education institutions in several countries have put in place quality assurance units and departments as a means to ensure institutions deliver quality education through effective monitoring and supervision of staff and administrators.

Quality has become the most salient factor in higher education worldwide (Rena, 2000). Nonetheless, the issue of quality is not about how higher education institution leaders promote efficiency and effectiveness in their institutions, but rather how they would effectively manage quality initiatives in their institutions so that there is value for money. Thus quality management in higher education institutions will help promote high quality academic delivery in higher education institutions and improve performance (Flynn, Schroeder & Sakakibara, 1995). Some critics have argued that, 'providing high-quality services could bring outstanding results for the organization' and also improve customers' satisfaction which forms the integral part of every organization's performance objectives (Sadeh & Garkaz, 2015, p. 1336). A nation could develop through improving economy, education and labor force and reduce poverty, inequality, social injustice and promote knowledge generation, and also help students to acquire new knowledge and skills through improved quality management in academic institutions.

The second lens examines the concept of management which according to Gill (2009) is about organizational efforts to achieve efficient, effective and stable delivery of services. Management is about controlling, problem solving, planning and budgeting for an organization. It is about path following but those in management position are supposed to ensure that things are done in the right way. Mullins (2013, p. 783) also views management as 'the process through which efforts of members of the organization are coordinated, directed and guided towards the achievement of organizational goals'. The work of managers are therefore supposed to ensure that organizations operational activities are enforced and sustained. Mullins (2013) have argued that management activities are variable. Organizations activities are not discrete but take place in deferent forms and at different levels. It is also important for the leader to be focused and act promptly to avoid problems before they get out of hand.

According to Gill (2009) quality management comes from the concept of Total Quality Management (TQM) which place emphasis on the management of change using variety of means by the organization. TQM gives 'attention to every aspect of organizational practice in pursuit of continuous improvement, the highest possible standards of practice, products, services and customer service' (Pettinger, 2007, p. 15). However, in their assessment of TQM some critics have observed that it is based on some assumptions (Lunenburg & Ornstein, 2008). According to Lunenburg and Ornstein when individuals decide to do their best to improve performance of their organization it becomes the responsibility of management to ensure that the work being done is improved so as to improve overall performance of the organization. Although there are some assumptions about what organizations want to achieve from TQM, it still means different for some corporate organizations, but it is still applicable in educational institutions such as universities, community colleges, high schools and even primary schools. The principles behind the application of TQM is to improve quality service delivery. Every organization is aimed at improving the quality of its service delivery so application of quality management (which is a subset of TQM) in higher education is very laudable.

According to the founder of TQM, William Edwards Deming, the effectiveness of TQM has provided a framework for schools and higher education institutions to be integrated into their performance management systems ways to improve their performance (Lunenburg & Ornstein, 2008). In schools, it is used as a positive development tool for 'team teaching, site-based management, cooperative learning, and outcome based education' (p. 49). Goetsch & Davis (2010) explained that total quality means institutions attempt to maximize its competitiveness through a continual improvement of the quality of its products, services, people, processes and environments. Therefore quality management as a concept can be looked at in two different dimensions; by focusing on quality and by ensuring that the quality is sustained in terms of human and material resources to meet the set goals of the institution. Focusing on quality is making sure that there is effective delivery, good programs are taught in the institutions, institutions quality standards are met and accreditation requirements are also satisfied. Sustaining quality means putting structures in place such that faculty members do not get exhausted, are well motivated, resources are made available and the leadership are well focused to meet the institutional, goals and objectives. Quality management has diverse interpretations to its meaning, however what constitute quality and how it should be managed also depends on the available resources and the needs of the institution. According to Michaela & Shreya (2017) quality management in higher education institutions is more often than not part of a written commitment to quality, laid down in a strategic plan or quality policy.

According to Goetsch & Davis (2014) organizations are dynamic so are our higher education institutions. Efficient management of institutional resources would also ensure quality is managed and sustained. They have outlined the following trends as factors affecting the future of quality management in higher education institutions; increasing global competition, increasing customer expectations, opposing economic pressures and new approaches to management. Goetsch & Davis (2014) have argued that there should be total commitment, it must be market driven, commitment to leading people taking into consideration customer satisfaction, cost leadership, effective human resource and integration and fundamental improvements.

Hargreaves & Javis (2001) have observed that it is important to develop and manage staff effectively to improve upon the work of the institution to contribute to its quality framework. As the work of the institution improves so will the quality of its activities. Effectiveness of higher education institution performance is a key to quality assurance, but it is pertinent to note that leaders develop and manage their organization and staff to ensure there is good performance. This forms an integral part of every higher education institution. Unfortunately, however, 'individuals often get left out of formal institutional leadership development initiatives because their role, on the organizational chart, is usually viewed as something' general that may automatically happen if staff are well monitored (Ladyshewsky & Flavell, 2011, p. 128). The work of staff must be monitored and evaluated to ensure there is quality in their performance. Ensuring quality management should be integrated with capacity building to enhance their performance and improve quality. Academic leadership responding to quality management cannot compromise with the organizations' quest to succeed and achieve quality, improve and sustain performance (Manoj, 2016). Higher education leaders are to encourage, motivate and organize their staffs and develop interest in their continuous professional development so as to improve and sustain the quality agenda.

Quality Management in Higher Education

'The term quality management refers to the policies, systems and processes designed to ensure the maintenance and enhancement of quality within an institution' (Csizmadia, 2006, p. 24). Managing an 'institution of higher education requires knowledge about the interaction of forces (individuals, schools, department, units, etc.) within the system' (Maguad & Krone, 2012, p. 87). It requires those in management to have a better understanding of the operational system within the institution with respect to how each unit or department works and how the whole system functions collectively. According to Sultan & Wong (2012) in a competitive environment, such as the education sector, institutions need to improve their service delivery by ensuring that there is quality in the education they deliver, but at the same time they need to also manage the quality of administrative structures which becomes an integral part of management of higher educational institutions.

Sadeh & Garkaz (2015, p. 1336) noted in their assessment of higher education quality management that providing 'high-quality services could bring outstanding results for the organization' so that customer satisfaction which is one of the main goals of many organizations could be achieved. Quality management is a very component in many institutions programs and courses delivery because it is the foundation for higher education institution's quality delivery system (Sultan & Wong, 2012). For the purpose of accreditation, public confidence, global acceptability purposes quality management becomes important. They further explained that in a competitive environment, higher education institutions are expected to improve performance and their service delivery so as to enhance customer satisfaction. In several universities around the world, there is a daunting task for institutions to ensure that there is quality in the delivery on lessons (Scott et al., 2008 as cited in Ladyshewsky & Flavell, 2011) so as to boost the confidence of students, parents, governments and employers.

In many higher education institutions, concerns about increase in students' intake and introduction of new programs and courses with different modes of delivery systems all border on quality. Giannakou (2006) observed that there are over 17, 000 higher education institutions in the world, yet every government is making efforts to increase access to higher education nonetheless they are not relenting on their efforts to ensure there is quality in the type of education they deliver to the citizens. Everyone who wishes to enroll into higher education institution looks for a good program that will enable him/her get the best job, the institution offers better teaching and research, availability of teaching and learning resources, adequate faculty to teach courses and the fees are affordable. Although the elite institutions charge higher fees there is still assumption that such institutions offer quality education so employers look for graduates from such elite institutions. All these constitute quality education that employers, governments, parents as well as students will want to see being delivered by institutions. Quality per se has been described by different people, but all point out to imply doing the right thing at the right time to achieve success.

Quality means a predictable degree of uniformity and dependability with standard that are suitable to the customer (Deming, 2000). It is an ever changing state that focuses on three elements of superior value: superior quality, superior cost and superior service (Goetsch & Davis, 2010). Literatures regarding quality management have focused on business organizations and companies, but it is worth noting that applying the best practices to higher education institutions is long overdue; hence quality has become a great and exciting challenge to higher education (Black, 2015). Durvasula, Lysonski & Madhavi (2011) asked the following questions; what does higher education institutions quality delivery mean to students and to the larger society? How does it impact on universities courses offerings and delivery? However in answering the above questions, Dlačić, Arslanagić, Kadić-Maglajlić, Marković & Raspor (2014) have pointed out that even though the term quality has broad and subjective meanings, in terms of standards, excellence, and academic fitness for purpose, there has been concerns about the nature of quality observed in our higher education institutions.

Csizmadia (2006) sees quality management as a means to an end not the end in itself. Quality management in higher education institutions involves ensuring that academic standards are met, making activities very transparent and accountable while ensuring that performance is enhanced. Meeting academic standards is by ensuring there is value for money in terms of what is being taught, employers and governments get high quality graduates, ensuring that lecturers and administrators are contributing to meet accreditation standards and also public expectations and demands. Universities also set standards for lecturers in terms of what they should teach, how they teach and assess students as part of its quality assurance and management process. However, Csizmadia (2006, p. 24) argued that management of quality is 'about getting things done as quickly, cheaply and effectively as possible – and usually about getting things done through other people'.

The management of quality in higher education institutions is envisaged as the most fundamental tool for verifying areas in institutions that require improvement. This supports Ganguly (2015) argument that quality management issues have become one of the most basic issues confronting institutions all over the world. Successful implementation of quality management requires that academic leaders identify problematic areas and address them to promote quality. According to Tari & Dick (2016) there exist few studies that provide literature on quality management. However it is the responsibilities and duties of higher education institutions to focus on best practices so as to yield positive results in respect of quality management. Maguad & Krone (2012, p.12) have observed that higher education institutions 'need to act proactively and initiate positive, quality-focused and learner-centered programs' to remain competitive. This could be done through constant review of the academic programs in terms of what is being taught in the lecture rooms, how students are taught and assessed, while ensuring that accreditation standards are met.

Looking at the concept of quality, placing 'emphasis on efficiency, effectiveness and accountability has forced higher education institutions to adopt structures, systems, mechanisms and models intended to enhance such objectives' (Csizmadia, 2006, p. 18). Although there is competition among institutions for both students so that higher education institutions can raise funds to run the institutions, the quest for quality from students, parents, governments and even employers will also be demanded from higher education institutions (Maguad & Krone, 2012) to ensure there is value for money. They further argued that with the demand for quality education, higher education institution cannot afford to continue to deliver courses and programs in the same orthodox way. Higher education institutions have to improve so as to meet the needs of students, employers and governments. Maguad & Krone (2012, p. 12) have observed that 'no matter how good these institutions are now, or how good they have been, they need to be even better in the future if they are to meet the needs of a rapidly changing world'.

A survey conducted by Michaela & Shreya (2017) has shown that quality management in higher education institutions across the world appear to be given priority in the overall policy framework, although emphasis is placed on teaching and learning. They observed that in Latin America and the Caribbean, institutional quality policy was based on the global average in terms of faculties or departments performance. However, there were less monitoring of students' success and fewer incentives for academic staff to take part in quality management. In the case of Asia and Pacific, the study noted that although quality management handbooks were seen to be common compared to Latin American and the Caribbean the purpose of quality management are just to monitor graduates employability rather than students' performance on their programs. In Europe, the study noted that many higher education institutions have quality policy, and over half of the countries had quality management handbook with well-structured quality management in place (Michaela & Shreya, 2017). In Africa many higher education institutions have plans in developing their institutional quality assurance policy while many too have quality assurance tools in place. In North America, it was observed from the study that higher education leaders are less involved in quality management, but concerned with community outreach and income generation (Michaela & Shreya, 2017). They further observed that the least used quality management tool to improve academic programs with focus on student workload assessment and student feedback on assessment at a lower rate.

Some countries are increasing their funding to support higher education delivery yet others are struggling with their limited budget so have limited support for higher education institutions (Giannakou, 2006). The question that needs to be answered is can government bear all the cost of financing higher education and ensure there is quality? Or should there be cost sharing as it is happening in some countries in the developed world? Higher education institutions contribute towards development of a nation's human capital, and educated citizens contribute to nations building nonetheless, if quality in higher education would become sustained individuals going through the education system must contribute towards education delivery. If quality would be maintained and improved, institutions cannot whatsoever place the whole burden on government but there should be cost sharing to promote quality and sustainability. Government endeavor to augment her investment and funding in higher education institutions, academic and administrative staff need to work assiduously with the available resources provided by government to enhance quality delivery so as to achieve good outcomes (Materu, 2007). The Organization for Economic Cooperation and Development (OECD) (2006) report pointed out that in majority of OECD countries; the expenditure on government for Higher Education institutions is declining in recent years. Nonetheless, Pounder (1999), Harvey (2005), Mok (2005), Dollery, Murray & Crase (2006) emphasize a need for government of every nation to use resources efficiently and effectively as a major priority for Higher Education institutions. Deming (2000) has suggested following factors that must be taking into consideration if higher education institutions can ensure quality management:

- Creation of constancy of purpose for improvement of product and service,
- Adopt new philosophy,
- Cease dependence on mass inspection,
- End the practice of awarding business on the basis of price tag alone,

- Improve constantly and forever the system of production and service,
- Institute training,
- Adopt and institute leadership,
- Eliminate slogans, exhortations, and targets for the work force,
- Eliminate numerical quotas for the work force and eliminate numerical goals for people management,
- Remove barriers that rob people of the pride of workmanship,
- Encourage education and self-improvement for everyone,
- Taking action to accomplish the transformation must be everybody's task.

For quality to be achieved, management of institution must set goals in accordance with the institutions goals, objectives and priorities. As Flyn, Schroeder & Sakakibara (1995) noted, different core quality management practices lead to success in different dimensions of quality, and that those dimension function differently. It is incumbent on management of a higher education institution to set priorities and ensure that the right decisions are taken to meet the institutions goals and objectives.

Leadership in Higher Education

The concept of leadership has been subjected to extensive study over a long time (Lunenburg & Ornstein, 2008). The study has led to evolution of many definitions of the concept of leadership. For example Dubrin (2010, p. 3) gave three different definitions to explain leadership:

'A process in which an individual influences a group of individuals to achieve a common goal';

'The act of influencing people by persuasion or example to follow a line of action',

'An effect to maintain control and power over others'.

Lussier & Achua (2010) have stated that there is no universal definition of the concept of leadership. That the concept of leadership is complex and has been 'studied in deferent ways that require different definitions' (p. 5). The definition of leadership has always been based on the activities of the individuals in charge of the organization and what they do to influence activities within the organization. According to Lussier & Achua (2010, p. 6) leadership will be defined as 'the influencing process of leaders and followers to achieve organizational objectives through change'. The influencing process is between the leadership and the followers and not one-sided where only the followers are influenced. Although the leaders are also influenced in one way or the other, those in leadership control power and authority. Higher education institutions are made up of individuals with different backgrounds, experiences, expectations and aspirations who must not be forced but allowed to voluntarily exercise their rights freely and willingly towards the achievement of the institutional goals. In the past decade, leadership seem to have been crucial in the administrative structures in higher education which previously focused more on management (Bush, 2008 as cited in Ladyshewsky & Flavell, 2011). Leadership is about 'increasing effectiveness through change and transformation' (Gill, 2009, p. 298). Although organizations can change even if there is no effective leadership, but the understanding of the concept indicates that the change must lead to transformation of the organizations.

The success of higher education institutions depends on what the leadership can do in terms of their capabilities and ability to exercise their influence and control. Leadership is the quality to lead others to accomplish the set goals of an organization or institution (Manoj, 2014). In this regard, it should be appropriate for a leader in a higher education institution, to ascertain what areas need improvement and what is going on well and what is not. It is therefore important for the academic leaders to comprehend about the challenges facing the institution, and employ best practices to transform behavior of the members within it and resources. In the light of the ability to communicate to the members the vision and mission of the organization making sure the members buy into the vision and contribute towards achieving better results. Thus, apart from the academic leader, faculty and non-teaching staff must also play their role together with the leadership to enable the institution succeeds.

Leadership is needed in every department and at all levels within the institution for universities to respond to the challenges they face and also very beneficial since it improves performance across all activities including teaching and research (Ball, 2007 as cited in Odhiambo, 2014; Hotho et al., 2008). Dubrin (2010, p. 3) explained that 'leadership is needed at all levels in an organization and can be practiced to some extent even by a person not assigned to a formal leadership position'. Higher education leaders must show concern for their staff and students in their departments and are supposed to ensure the welfare of their students and staff remain paramount (Manning & Curtis, 2009). According to Ladyshewsky & Flavell (2011, p.450) higher education leaders are supposed to give 'a group of people a clear vision and a clear sense of direction, trying to take them forward, as a collective and as individuals, in that direction and by initiating appropriate actions'. Leadership is associated with change so in the universities departments' leadership is seen as agent for the change amongst colleagues or subordinates and is viewed as being necessary for the responses to the change process in the department. Higher educational institutions are supposed to deliver courses to students. However Dlačić et al (2014) have indicated that with the high demand for higher education continuous to increase so is competition among the institutions also 'increasing without consideration of the knowledge gap identified' in some academic literature (p.141).

Observations made by Manoj (2014) showed that administrators, heads of departments, Deans of Faculties, program coordinators, unit heads leading the institutions are expected to promote quality in the institution. Promoting quality in an institution is about ensuring that there is quality teaching and learning as well as research while ensuring that products coming out of the institutions must have the skills needed by employers and government (Materu, 2007). Managing quality of the teaching staff and ensuring that students acquire the requisite knowledge and skills is another component of effective higher education leadership. The best quality practices must be adhered to ensure maintenance of organizational culture that is in conformity with the changing trends of the institutions. Quality needs decisive actions to be taken, implemented and evaluated in a processes to adhere to by academic leaders in order to achieve quality through commitment to manage all available resources (Deming, 2000).

Some critics have argued that in the United States there are leadership crisis in a number of higher education institutions because many college and universities presidents are over 50 years these are individuals that almost exiting from the workplace (Ebersole, 2014 as cited in Fassinger & Good, 2017). Yet little attention is given to the development of leaders and there are no leadership succession plans for institutions (Fassinger & Good, 2017). Achievement of quality would be difficult if there is no leadership. Lunenburg (2008) has argued that higher education leaders are supposed to be transformational and instructional. 'Transformational leaders raise organizational members' levels of personal commitment to achieve organizational goals, resulting in greater productivity' (p. 115). Lunenburg further explained that transformational leaders increase individuals' level of ethical aspirations. Leaders are supposed to transform their followers and give them hope. Being an instructional leadership is concerned with the 'effects of leadership behaviors on student achievement and other important school outcomes' (Lunenburg & Ornstein, 2008, p. 115). Lecturers in higher education engage students in activities through their daily lecturers and instructions. These activities affect the growth of students. Some critics also argue that 'being a leader in itself is a challenge since most organizations place leaders in a position in which they are responsible for carrying out several parallels, quite distinct and often superficially contradictory roles' (Odhiambo, 2014, p.188). Leaders in higher education institutions face a lot of challenges both internal and external and there are high expectations from students', parents, employers and government to deliver and as a result put pressure on management in terms of expertise, time, energies and emotional well-being.

Academic Quality Management and Effective Leadership

Academic quality could be achieved if there is strong and effective institutional leadership. Although higher educational leaders aim at ensuring there is effective teaching and learning, maintain high standards of achievement for every student, while ensuring that there is fitness value for money (Harvey & Green, 1993). Academic quality management will be difficult to be achieved without effective leadership. Thus making institutional leadership very significant in promotion and management of quality in the academic arena. In education institution, the leader is supposed to promote quality management, ensure that there is continuous improvement in the training being delivered to the students (Bolman & Deal, 1991). Quality management in higher education helps towards the preparation and training of a workforce for the 21st century and also broaden the knowledge base of the staff through changes that may occur as a result of accumulation of knowledge provided from the different expertise in higher education for effective working in this global age (The Task force on Higher Education and Society, 2000).

Gill (2009) explained that leadership in the context of quality management is not about power and authority, but about recognizing the work of the staff, empowering them, mentoring and coaching them to become effective and contribute towards organizational performance. Quality management is about taking a 'holistic view of the organization and its relations as well as a procedural approach by continuously developing all activities further in such a way as to increase customer satisfaction' (Maguad & Krone, 2012, p. 90). Quality management makes customer satisfaction remains central in the organizational agenda. According to Deming quality management could make sense in arena of cooperate organization but may mean different in educational sector (Lunenburg & Ornstein, 2008). Because when we read about quality management discourses they are ensuring products and services are of standards acceptable to the customer. In higher education the students become the customers, therefore quality management also remain significant in education delivery.

Ervay (2006, p. 78) has observed in his investigation that academic leadership has always been important in higher education institution 'because a lecturer's success is contingent on the professional culture in which he or she works, one that either encourages or discourages professional and scholastic growth'. Arguably, leaders of higher education institutions are responsible to hunt for new knowledge and skills as well as initiation of any changes that occur in an institution. The new knowledge economy calls for higher education leadership to ensure there is quality in what they deliver, but should ensure that quality must not be imposed from outside the institution, outside the team or outside the individual (Carr & Burnham, 1994). The quality must well be managed so as to benefit the institution as well as staff within the institution. Imposing quality could lead to resistant which could affect introduction of any change initiative that could bring improvement within the organisation. Dlačić et al (2014) have observed that higher education institutions are supposed to be involved in much more than just delivering of course materials and courses to students, but are supposed to deliver quality which must be well managed through effective leadership. According to More and Diamond (2000) quality management by academic leadership could be achieved through capacity building in respect of releasing and engaging human potential, sustaining change, which must come from within the academic unit of an institution per vision and mission and commitment of its academic leadership.

Ladyshewsky & Flavell (2011, p. 128) observed that 'one group of university staff who have a significant role to play in leading high quality teaching and learning outcomes is the program coordinator (PC)'. Siting an example from Australia, they explained that, the position of the PC is also referred to as course coordinator, program director or department chair whose main duties are to coordinate courses and programs within a department. They are also responsible for distribution of courses to tutors or lecturers and are to ensure that courses in the departments are taught. Unfortunately, Ladyshewsky & Flavell (2011, p. 128) has noted that 'these individuals often get left out of formal institutional leadership development (LD) initiatives because their role, on the organizational chart, is usually viewed as something between a general academic staff position and head of school/department'. They added that besides their enormous role in the delivery of courses and program in the departments, the challenge for the higher education program coordinator is that, in 'addition to having academic credibility they must lead and manage the course team without having any line management authority' (p. 128).

Dlačić et al (2014, p. 142) noted that maintenance of quality standards brings satisfaction to students and makes them 'less prone to move to other universities, thereby increasing the retention rate'. They further noted that when students are satisfied with what they learn, parents are also happy and that gives them hope and high expectation in their studies and future aspirations. Parents also become satisfied for their investments in their children's education. Promoting quality has a ripple effect on students, parents and the larger community. Dlačić et al (2014) observed that improving higher education also contributes towards development of human capital and overall productivity and household incomes. They further noted that quality education and training is not just about having impact on the lives of the students, but it is supposed to have effect on the overall society. Quality promotion also serves as a measure of the nature and level of effectiveness of leadership in higher education institutions (Ervay, 2006). Ervay added that academic leadership is also measured in terms of how compliant educational institutions and their leadership are meeting externally imposed standards and accreditation requirements so as to achieve courses and programs targets.

Effective management of higher education is a collective responsibility although the academic leadership a crucial role to play to ensuring that the quality agenda is pursued and managed. This includes all who matters at the top management level to be involved in the decision-making process. There are some strategies higher education institution leadership must employ to enhance quality management through motivation of staff, effective planning and implementing good policies and programs, resolution and management of institutional conflicts, solving institutions problem, and ensure there is good teamwork. Leadership in quality management requires that the leader's critical thinking needs a continuous cultural change as the followers are guided to embrace whatever change the leadership initiates (Sathye, 2004). An effective academic leader who intends to enhance management quality should have the ability to diagnose, adopt and communicate within and outside the institution. The academic leadership are supposed to be competent, innovative, creative, proactive and ready to take preventive measures. According to Manoj (2014) academic leaders need extraordinary ability and skills to maintain and continually manage the technical, financial and human resources to serve the academic mission of the institution.

It must be noted that effective leaders delegate to empower their followers to discharge their responsibilities and duties in a manner that results in quality management. The leaders are supposed to inspire, encourage, and motivate the followers in the institution. A leader must be a role model to his or her members and in all practices toe the line of the goals of the institution. Sathye (2004) observed that academic leaders can enhance quality management by delegation of clear tasks and monitoring performance plus sustaining staff interest and encouraging staff.

To succeed as an academic leadership in higher education there are some characteristics that should be demonstrated. Ramsden (1998) listed some of these characteristics as:

- Pedagogical leadership,
- Leadership in research,
- Strategic vision and networking,
- Collaborative and motivational leadership,
- Fair and efficient leadership,
- Development and recognition of performance and
- Good interpersonal skills.

The practiced of the above factors by academic leaders of higher education institutions can help address a number of challenges resulting in poor quality management in Higher Education institutions.

Leadership effectiveness is necessary in higher education but it shoulders dual responsibility (Durie & Beshir, 2016). The first responsibility is to develop skilled manpower through utilizing the tax payers' money and the second is to prioritize activities in the institution, use the resources appropriately and in accordance, including the institution's budget to improve performance (Durie & Beshir, 2016). Students going through any educational institutions are supposed to be equipped with the skills required on the job market, and are not to learn only theories, while ensuring that institutions improve performance. It is however argued that academic leaders are promoted not based on the skills and experience in higher education leadership but the number of articles, books, book chapters that are published in internationally reputable journals. The question that remain answered is does ability to publish mean individuals are competent in leading higher education institution? Although higher education institutions are supposed to demonstrate good leadership in teaching and research, ability to demonstrate does not mean one can be an effective leader. According to Durie & Beshir (2016) challenges facing academic leaders to make them ineffective include complex and dynamic, social, economic, and political contexts amid scarce resources. Pressure on academic leaders to publish, research and teach make them turn their attention onto those areas and neglect academic leadership responsibilities.

Black (2015) argues that leaders in higher education institutions are required to examine how to lead their institutions, and must also look for approaches which fit best in the higher education context. He posits further that there is a need for a leader to examine the benefits of leadership constructs within the higher education environment and compare the existing understanding of leadership within higher education alongside contemporary or postmodernism era of leadership theory and practice. Taking into account 'command and control' leadership – this is envisaged as unsuitable and unacceptable way of becoming an effective leader because it is counter-productive (Goffee & Jones, 2009), situational leadership-this is supported as worthwhile in that it seeks to address more complete considerations of human nature and motivation (Hersy & Bladchard, 1969), transactional-transformational leadership – this requires the academic leader to understand his or her followers, and building their self-worth and focus, credibility, vision, values, competence, judgement, experimentation and engagement of staff (Kouzes and Posner, 2007, Bennis, 2009) and 'system thinking'- with system thinking, a leader is expected to think critically with the aim to optimize links between manager behavior, rules, structure, decision-making, skills, methods and results (Senge, 1990; Oak-land, 2001).

Higher education leaders need a combination of leadership and management competencies in order to address the challenges facing the enterprise (Black, 2015). In this postmodernism era of ever changing world, effective leader must be both student and teacher (Kotter, 1996), ready to learn more always regarding how to enthuse, engage and empower the followers.

Black, Groombridge & Jones (2011) have considered challenges associated with current leadership approaches within Higher Education, which requires attention:

- Collaboration, partnership and interdisciplinary
- Enhancing the student experience (teaching, extra-curricular, employability,
- Learning communities and learner-centred approaches,
- Bureaucracy which stifles innovation and creates inefficiency and ineffectiveness,
- Efficient use of resources,
- Combined role (teacher/researcher/citizen),
- Collegial preference tending towards a self-serving culture,
- Transitional roles for academic leaders,
- Conflicts between the demands encountered in professional, Academic and improve the organization,
- Individualism and external loyalties,
- Leading diversity and inclusion,
- Globalization and internationalization,
- Governance

Following the discourse, it must be clear that as an academic leader your influence in the institution to ensure success is vital. In this regard, Sathye (2015) argues that academic leaders have to be specific about how they go about appraising their staff. Sathye further noted that academic leaders are supposed to provide leadership in research and must demonstrate their commitment and dedication to assigned roles and responsibilities, bearing in mind the distinct different of their leadership from those corporate governance.

Challenges Facing Academic Leaders in Public and Private Higher Education Institutions

The challenges facing leaders of academic institutions are complex. However in spite of these challenges, the growing demand for higher education has brought about an increase in the number of private higher education institutions in low and middle-income countries (Binelli & Rubio-Codina, 2013). Some critics have argued that the growing demand for higher education and lack of government resources to meet the demand through the provision of public higher education institutions have brought about the increasing numbers of private tertiary institutions in many countries (Jamshidi et al, 2012 as cited in Shaha, Vu & Stanford, 2019). This continuous growth of private higher education institutions is as a result of their flexible entry requirements, mode of a delivery being flexible, offer courses needed in the current job market and in most cases have manageable class sizes that promote better learning (Shah and Brown 2009).

A study undertaken by Oketch in some African countries shows that the growing number of private higher education has come to increase access to university education, and offering of certain courses and programs (Oketch, 2009 as cited in Bennett, Nair & Shah, 2012). For instance high demand courses such as Law and Nursing that is offered in a number of private higher education institutions are all contributing to widening access to higher education. Despite the widening of access the Polish experience suggests that private higher education also have negative impacts. They cited poor quality teaching, least qualified and experienced faculty to teach courses because they cannot afford to pay for the salaries of highly qualified lecturers, their focus always remains on maximizing profits and have a narrow focus on institutional governance (Jalowiecki 2001 as cited in Bennett et al, 2012). Many students also prefer to study in private higher education institutions 'because of their closer links with industry and more clearly defined career paths' (Bennett et al, 2012, p. 427).

Many nations are making efforts to widen access to education but there are a lot of challenges facing both public and private higher education institutions, although the challenges differ among institutions. According to Northouse (2004), some of the challenges may be attributed to a number of factors including leadership. Research conducted in the UK higher education clearly showed that 'there are a number of ways in which leadership could make a significant contribution to the task of 'reinventing higher education', both in relation to the process of change itself and in relation to the educational functions carried out within higher education' (Middlehurst, 1997, p. 188). Although the primary mandate of the leadership is 'to create the motivational climate in which students are stimulated to seek and create knowledge and understanding for themselves' (p. 189), it goes beyond these. Ineffective leadership could jeopardize members' efforts to contribute towards the achievement of those institutional goals. For instance the inability of public higher education institutions leadership to take certain decisions affect the day to day running of the institutions. In public higher education institutions, any planning has to be approved by a legislative body, the governing council which has government representatives unlike private institutions in which individuals or group of individuals lead and control affairs of the institution without any external interference (Farkas and Wetlaufer, 1996). In public higher education institutions, many leaders are subject to diffuse responsibilities because accountability and decision making may be challenged, although some critics also argue that centralized executives authority is vitally important for decision making in the private institution (Atieno, 2013).

In public educational higher institutions, there is no clear chain of command with regard to leadership direction in that there are external influences because of the presence of government representatives on their governing councils (Farkas and Wetlaufer, 1996; Starling, 1993). It is argued that with the public higher educational institutions there exists tenure of office which may be four or five years depending on the country's system of institutional governance. That is to say that public higher education institutions operate within a democratic political system in which the leadership is subject to change every four or five years. In private higher education institutions, the leaders do not have clearly defined term of office, so the leadership spend longer time working with the institution that ensures continuity and job security (Gordon and Milakovich, 1998., Farkas and Wetlaufer, 1996, Starling, 1993). However, this is changing because governments in many public educational higher institutions now charge fees for the provision of certain services. In spite of the differences leaders in both public and private must be competent in implementing shareholders and stakeholders regarding the goals and objectives of the institution (Gordon and Milakovich, 1998).

In implementing quality management in higher educational institutions, there are some impediments that may erupt to adversely affect quality. The culture of a higher educational institution, whether private or public, is one of the major causes of failures of institutional quality management (Kekale, 1998). According to Black (2003) organizational values, norms and its guiding principles demonstrate the kind of behavior employees will exhibit. Quality management, therefore, requires a change of culture which is notoriously uneasy to achieve and also takes time to implement (Sally, 2002). Another behavioral issue is the lack of commitment to the part of the staff within an institution. Any institution in which there is a lack of commitment on the part of senior management quality control and implementation becomes extremely difficult. Lack of vision of the leadership to effectively manage quality remain a challenge that must be addressed to improve and promote quality (Salaheldin, 2009).

Another challenge worth pointing out is the failure to continuously implement the principles of quality management by the leadership of the institution who are supposed to be responsible for products and services that are offered (Yusuf, Gunasekaran and Dan, 2007). Lack of ability to adapt to change is critical for an institution to succeed in this dispensation (Atieno, 2013). Some educational institutions do not include quality in their strategic plan, hence allocating little attention to quality management in their human, materials and financial resources. Managing change is another obstacle to the implementation of quality management practice (Anderson, Rungtusanatham, Schroeder & Devaraj, 1995). For example, management must ensure staff are abreast with any new technologies that could be used to support activities within the institution (Farell, 2007; Look, 2005). Zarei and Shaharaki (2011) are of the view that educational institutions must ensure staff realize their full potential through training and development of their workforce so as to maintain a conducive environment towards improvement of the institution.

Odhiambo (2014, p.189) observed that 'with the increase in student population and the decrease in government funding, there is the challenge arising from the tension between delivering quality pedagogy and research and the necessity to create efficiencies'. Institutions are responding to the funding reduction so some institutions have introduced cost-sharing mechanisms, as a means to raise funds and charge fees. Promoting cost-sharing comes with its own challenges. It increases the number of stakeholders and that dilutes the system of governance and exposes quality management systems to outside influence and control.

CONCLUSION

The demand for higher education in many countries around the world has compelled institutions to introduce several modes of delivering lessons to students. The traditional modes of delivering lessons by distance, through online, blended as well as sandwich to widen access and participation to higher education. Besides, institutions are introducing new programs and establishing new departments to meet demands and also train graduates that are suitable for the present job market. However, in spite of these, institutions need to ensure there is value for money by promoting quality assurance means to institutions in terms of programs on offer. In conclusion quality management and academic leadership practices if complied by individual institutions of higher learning academic leaders can result in quality management globally as far as higher education institutions are concerned.

REFERENCES

Anderson, J., Rungtusanatham, M., Schroeder, R., & Devaraj, S. (1995). A Path Analytic Model of a Theory of Quality Management Underlying the Deming Management Method: Preliminary Empirical Findings. *Decision Sciences*, *26*(5), 637–658. doi:10.1111/j.1540-5915.1995.tb01444.x

Atieno, A. J. (2013). *Challenges facing the implementation of total quality management practices in public secondary schools in Kenya* (Master's thesis). School of Business, Kenyatta University.

Becket, N., & Brookes, M. (2006). Evaluating Quality Management in University Departments. *Quality Assurance in Education*, *14*(2), 123–142. doi:10.1108/09684880610662015

Becket, N., & Brookes, M. (2007). Quality Management in higher education: A review of International issues and practice. *International Journal for Quality and Standards*. Retrieved from www.bsieducation.org/ijas

Bennett, L., Nair, C. S., & Shah, M. (2012). The emergence of private higher education in Australia: The silent provider. *European Journal of Higher Education*, *2*(4), 423–435. doi:10.1080/21568235.2012.730377

Bennis, W. (2009). *On Becoming a Leader* (Revised Edition). New York: Addison-Wesley Publishing.

Binelli, C., & Rubio-Codina, M. (2013). The Returns to Private Education: Evidence from Mexico. *Economics of Education Review*, *36*, 198–215. doi:10.1016/j.econedurev.2013.06.004

Black, R. J. (2003). *Organizational Culture: Creating the influence needed for Strategic Success*. London, UK: ISBN.

Black, S. A. (2015). Qualities of Effective Leadership in Higher Education. *Open Journal of Leadership*, *4*, 54–66. doi:10.4236/ojl.2015.42006

Black, S. A., Groombridge, J. J., & Jones, C. G. (2011). Biodiversity Conservation: Applying New Criteria to Assess Excellence. *Total Quality Management*, *22*(11), 1165–1178. doi:10.1080/14783363.2011.624766

Boaden, R. J. (1997). What is total quality management…and does it matter? *Total Quality Management*, *8*(4), 153–171. doi:10.1080/0954412979596

Bolman, L., & Deal, T. (1991). *Organisations*. San Francisco: Josses-Bass.

Carr, B., & Burnham, J. (1994). *Managing Quality in Schools. A Training Manual*. Harlow: Longman.

Cheng, Y., & Tam, W. (1997). Multi-Models of Quality in Education. *Quality Assurance in Education*, *5*(1), 22–30. doi:10.1108/09684889710156558

Cruickshank, M. (2003). Total Quality Management in the higher education sector a literature review from an international and Australian perspective. *TQM & Business Excellence*, *14*(10), 1159–1167. doi:10.1080/1478336032000107717

Csizmadia, T. G. (2006). *Quality Management in Hungarian higher education organisational responses to governmental policy*. Enschede: CHEPS/UT.

Deming, W. E. (2000). *Out of the Crisis, Institute of Technology*. MIT Press.

Dlačić, J., Arslanagić, M., Kadić-Maglajlić, S., Marković, S., & Raspor, S. (2014). Exploring perceived service quality, perceived value, and repurchase intention in higher education using structural equation modelling. *Total Quality Management & Business Excellence*, *25*(1-2), 1–2, 141–157. doi:10.1080/14783363.2013.824713

Dollery, B., Murray, D., & Crase, L. (2006). Knaves or knights, pawns or queens? An Evaluation of Australian higher education reform policy. *Journal of Educational Administration*, *44*(1), 86–97. doi:10.1108/09578230610642674

Dubrin, A. J. (2010). *Principles of Leadership (7th ed.)*. South-Western Cengage Learning.

Durie, A. D., & Beshir, E. S. (2016). Leadership effectiveness in Higher Education Institutions: The IPA Approach. Arabian, J. Bus. *Management Review*, *6*, 243.

Durvasula, S., Lysonski, S., & Madhavi, A. D. (2011). Beyond service attributes: Do personal values matter? *Journal of Services Marketing*, *25*(1), 33–46. doi:10.1108/08876041111107041

Ervay, S. (2006). Academic Leadership in America's Public Schools. *NASSP Bulletin*, *90*(2), 77–86. doi:10.1177/0192636506290175

Farell, G. M. (2007). *ICT in Education in Kenya ''Survey of ICT and education in Africa: Kenya Country Report*. Retrieved from www.infodev.org

Farkas, C. M., & Wetlaufer, S. (1996). The way chief executive officer leads. *Harvard Business Review*, *74*(3), 1–6.

Fassinger, R. E., & Good, G. E. (2017). Academic Leadership and Counseling Psychology: Answering the Challenge, Achieving the Promise. *The Counseling Psychologist*, *45*(6), 752–780. doi:10.1177/0011000017723081

Flynn, B. B., Schroeder, R.G., & Sakakibara, S. (1995). The impact of quality management practices on performance and competitive advantage. Decision Sciences. *Journal of Operations Management, International Journal of Production Research, 26*(5), 659-691. doi:10.1111/j.1540-995.tb1445.x

Flynn, B. B., Schroeder, R. G., & Sakakibara, S. (1995). The impact of quality management practices on performance and competitive advantage. Decision Sciences. *International Journal of Production Research, 26*(5), 659–691. doi:10.1111/j.1540-995.tb1445.x

Ganguly, A. (2015). Exploring Total Quality Management (TQM) Approaches in Higher Education Institutions in a Globalized Environment – case Analysis of UK and Sweden. *Brock Journal of Education, 3*(7). Available at http://www.eajournals.org/wp-content/uploads/Exploring-Total-Quality-Management-TQM-Approaches-in-Higher-Education-Institutions-in-a-Globalized-Environment-Case-Analysis-of-UK-and-Sweden.pdf

Giannakou, M. (2006) Chair's Summary, Meeting of OECD Ministers. Academic Press.

Gill, R. (2009). *Theory and Practice of Leadership.* London: Sage Publishing Ltd.

Goffee, R., & Jones, G. (2009). *Clever: Leadership Your Smartest Most Creative People.* Boston, MA: Havard Business Press.

Gordon, G. J., & Milakovich, M. E. (1998). *Public administration in America* (6th ed.). New York, NY: St. Martin's Press.

Hargreaves, P., & Javis, P. (2001). *The human resource development handbook.* London: Kogan Page Ltd.

Harvey, L. (2005). A history and critique of quality and evaluation in the UK. *Quality Assurance in Education, 13*(4), 263–276. doi:10.1108/09684880510700608

Harvey, L., & Green, D. (1993). Defining Quality. *Assessment and Evaluation in Higher Education, 18*(1), 9-34. doi:10.1080/0260293930180102

Hersey, P., & Blanchard, K. H. (1969). Life Cycle Theory of Leadership. *Training & Development, 23,* 26–34.

Hwang, H., & Teo, C. (2000). Translating Customers' Voices into Operational Requirements-AQFD application in higher education. *International Journal of Quality & Reliability Management, 18*(2), 195–220.

Kekale, T. (1998). *The effects of organizational culture on success and failures in implementation of some total quality management approaches. Towards a theory of selecting a culturally matching quality approach* (Ph.D. thesis). University of Vaasa, Acta Wasaennsia No. 65.

Kotter, J. P. (1996). *Leading Change.* Boston, MA: Harvard Business School Press.

Kouzes, J. M., & Posner, B. Z. (2007). *The Leadership Challenge* (4th ed.). San Francisco, CA: Jossey-Bass Publishers.

Ladyshewsky, R. K., & Flavell, H. (2011). Transfer of Training in an Academic Leadership Development Program for Program Coordinators. *Educational Management Administration & Leadership, 40*(1), 127–147. doi:10.1177/1741143211420615

Look, D. (2005). *Discussion Paper: Impact of Technology in Education*. PUSD Excellence Committee.

Lunenburg, F. C., & Ornstein, A. C. (2008). *Educational Administration: Concepts and Practices* (5th ed.). Belmont: Wadsworth Cengage Learning.

Lussier, R. N., & Achua, C. F. (2010). *Effective Leadership (5th ed.)*. South-Western Cengage Learning.

Maguad, B. A., & Krone, R. M. (2012). *Managing for quality in higher education: a system perspective*. Accessed at www.bookboon.com

Manning, G., & Curtis, K. (2009). *The Art of Leadership*. Boston: McGraw-Hill Education.

Manoj, K.V. (2016). *Importance of Leadership in Total Quality Management*. Vistas of Education. Mizoram University.

Materu, P. (2007). *Higher Education Quality Assurance in sub-Saharan Africa; status, challenges, opportunities and promising practices*. Washington, DC: The World Bank. doi:10.1596/978-0-8213-7272-2

Michaela, M., & Shreya, P. (2017). *Quality management in higher Education: development and drivers: results from an international survey*. International Institute for Educational Planning. Available at: https://unesdoc.unesco.org

Middlehurst, R. (1997). Reinventing Higher Education: The leadership challenge. *Quality in Higher Education, 3*(2), 183–198. doi:10.1080/1353832970030208

Mok, K. (2005). The quest for a world class university. *Quality Assurance in Education, 11*(3), 277–300. doi:10.1108/09684880510626575

Moore, M. R., & Diamond, M. A. (2000). *Academic Leadership: Turning Vision into Reality*. The Ernst and Young Foundation.

Mullins, L. J. (2013). *Management and Organizational Behaviour* (12th ed.). London: Pearson.

Northouse, P. G. (2004). *Leadership: Theory and Practice* (3rd ed.). Thousand Oaks, CA: Sage Publication.

Oakland, J. S. (2001). *Total Organizational Excellence: Achieving World Class Performance*. Oxford, UK: Butterworth-Heinemam. doi:10.1016/B978-0-7506-5271-1.50004-1

Odhiambo, G. (2014). The challenges and future of public higher education leadership in Kenya. *Journal of Higher Education Policy and Management, 36*(2), 183–195. doi:10.1080/1360080X.2014.884676

OECD. (2006). Quality Management in Higher Education: A review of International Issues and Practice. *The International Journal for Quality and Standards*.

Pettinger, R. (2007). *Introduction to Management* (4th ed.). Basingstoke, UK: Palgrave MacMillan. doi:10.1007/978-1-137-21899-5

Pounder, J. (1999). Institutional performance in higher education: Is quality a relevant concept? *Quality Assurance in Education, 7*(3), 56–127. doi:10.1108/09684889910281719

Ramsden, P. (1998). Managing the effective University. *Higher Education Research & Development, 17*(3), 347–370. doi:10.1080/0729436980170307

Rena, R. (2010). *Emerging Trend of Higher Education in Developing countries*. Scientific Annals of the 'Alexandru loan cuza' University of Iasi: Economic Sciences Series.

Sadeh, E., & Garkaz, M. (2015). Explaining the mediating role of service quality between quality management enablers and students' satisfaction in higher education institutes: The perception of managers. *Total Quality Management & Business Excellence*, 26(12), 1335–1356. doi:10.1080/14783363.2014.931065

Salahedin, S.I. (2009). Problems, sucessess factors and benefits of QCs implementation a case of QASCO. *Total Quality Management Journal*.

Sally, S. (2002). *Total Quality Management in education*. Stylus Publishing.

Sathye, M. (2004). *Leadership in Higher Education: A Qualitative Study*. Forum Qualitative Sozialfrschung/Forum: Qualitative. *Social Research*, 5(3), 26. Retrieved from http://nbn-resolving.de/urn:nbn:0114-fqs0403266

Senge, P. (1990). *The Fifth Discipline*. New York: Doubleday.

Shah, M., & Brown, G. (2009). The Rise of Private Higher Education in Australia: Maintaining Quality Outcomes and Future Challenges. *Proceedings of the Australian Universities Quality Forum*, 14350, 13.

Shaha, M., Vu, H. Y. & Stanford, S. (2019). *Perspectives: policy and practice in higher education*. Academic Press.

Srikanthan, G., & Dalrymple, J. (2004). A synthesis of a quality management model for Quality in Higher Education. *International Journal of Educational Management*, 18(4), 266–273. doi:10.1108/09513540410538859

Starling, G. (1993). Managing the public sector (4th ed.). Belmont, CA: Wadsworth Publishing Company.

Sultan, P., & Wong, H. (2012). Service quality in a higher education context: An integrated model. *Asia Pacific Journal of Marketing and Logistics*, 24(5), 755–784. doi:10.1108/13555851211278196

Tari, J. J., & Dick, G. (2016). Trends in quality management research in higher education institutions. *Journal of Service Theory and Practice*, 26(3), 273–294. doi:10.1108/JSTP-10-2014-0230

The Task Force on Higher Education & Society. (2000). Higher Education in Developing Countries: Peril and Promise. Washington, DC: The International Bank for Reconstruction and Development, the World Bank.

Yusuf, Y., Gunasekaran, A., & Dan, D. (2007). Implementation of TQM in China and organization Performance: An Empirical Investigation. *Total Quality Management & Business Excellence*, 18(5), 509–530. doi:10.1080/14783360701239982

Zarei, M., & Shaharaki. (2011). Article. *Society for Business and Management Dynamics Magazine*, 1(3), 1-12.

Chapter 7
Overcoming Complacency Through Quality Intelligence in Greek Higher Education:
The Critical Role of Academic Leadership

Loukas Anninos
University of Piraeus, Greece

ABSTRACT

During the last decade, an intensification of evaluation at the Greek universities has been noted, encouraged by the state and institutional initiatives aiming to reform, modernize, and cultivate a culture of excellence. The progress that has been reported was facilitated by global developments that gradually strengthened the cultural and scientific foundations of university performance evaluation and set the foundations for continuous institutional improvement and transformation. However, the role of academic leadership is crucial if universities wish to fully embrace the concept of excellence in their operations and services not from an obligatory, but from an evolutionary perspective that would allow them to learn and improve. As Greek universities are currently in the process of quality accreditation, the chapter briefly presents the framework for quality accreditation in Greek universities and underlines the critical role of academic leadership for achieving accreditation and establishing a culture for sustainable excellence.

INTRODUCTION

University institutions nowadays are being reorganized to respond effectively to several challenges such as global competition in the dawn of the 4th industrial revolution, the mass character of higher education, the appearance of new higher education providers, the multiplicity of customers (receivers of educational services), and the issue of accountability to state and society and the assurance of quality. These challenges along with the pursuit of excellence in mission attainment mark out quality as a basic goal, a reference criterion and a seal of efficient and effective university management and operation.

DOI: 10.4018/978-1-7998-1017-9.ch007

The effective management of higher education presupposes evaluation of achieved results at the institutional, departmental and study program level (undergraduate and postgraduate). The academic and organizational pillars of universities should be evaluated, in order to unveil potential weaknesses and deviations regarding goal achievements and mission and formulate the basis for continuous quality improvement. University performance evaluation offers objective data and criteria for state financing, teaching and research staffing and allows the comparison of performance (with similar institutions). This process is also a helpful instrument in the hands of students that helps them in making the right decisions for their studies. In addition, the process of university performance evaluation additionally facilitates the proper alignment and coordination among the higher education system and the job market. When evaluation is scientifically correct and is conducted systematically, it can contribute to noble competition among institutions and excellence.

Evaluation, in general, is a term used to denote the value, performance of something/someone based on specific criteria. It is a systematic process of critical analysis which allows the extraction of conclusions regarding the quality of the evaluated subject/object (Beywl, 2003, p.5), based on quantitative and qualitative evidence. In the context of higher education, performance evaluation should not be considered as a management fad, but as a necessary element in the management of any institution. The existence of an evaluation system/framework in higher education presupposes solid scientific foundations, organizational ability and institutional commitment for implementation, assurance of transparency and objectivity, publication of results and a dynamic design, so that the system can transform itself and thus adapt to changing circumstances (Anninos, 2010, p.235).

The comprehensive performance evaluation of higher education institutions is an issue of high significance and difficulty. The various evaluation objectives, the interactions among the performance constituents, the complexity and particularity of the educational environment and the unique character of each institution have contributed in the development of a variety of evaluation approaches and systems that can be implemented. The great challenge for scholars is the evaluation of suitability, compatibility and reliability of the suggested approaches and systems with reference to the achievement of their main purpose, which should be continuous improvement of institutional quality and provision of relevant information to stakeholders. According to literature, university performance evaluation is achieved through (Anninos, 2010, p.235):

1. **Typical Evaluation** that focuses on (Danish Evaluation Institute,2003, p.8):
    a. the quality of a subject in all study programs that the subject is taught (for example, the subject "total quality management" in a business administration study program)
    b. the study program itself
    c. the quality of an institution in every aspect of each operation (for example, educational or organizational) and
    d. the quality of a specific practice (e.g. internship programs)
2. **Accreditation** which refers to the procedure by which an independent agency/actor evaluates the quality of an institution or a study program in order to certify that it meets specific and pre-defined standards (Vlasceanu, Grunberg & Parlea, 2007, p.25)
3. **Audit**, which is the process by which the performance of institutional quality assurance systems and quality monitoring procedures is evaluated (Vlasceanu *et al.*,2007, p.31)

4. **Benchmarking** which constitutes a systematic method to collect and present information regarding the performance of organizational units and allow comparisons with the aim to establishing best practices, identifying performance strengths and weaknesses (Vlasceanu *et al.*,2007, p.34),
5. **Statistical techniques** like Data Envelopment Analysis (DEA) which constitutes a linear programming technique used when there are many inputs and outputs but no clear functional relationship between the two. DEA permits the analysis of multiple input and output factors at the same time (Rickards, 2003) and is a tool for evaluating relative efficiency (Kocher, Luptacik & Sutter, 2006),
6. **Ranking or Rating Systems** that are an established technique used to present the ranking (or rating in certain categories) of academic units in terms of their overall performance and/or a set of specific indicators (which according to each evaluation actor are critical parameters for excellence). They provide information to students, university administration and stakeholders regarding the quality of universities. Even though there are many problems regarding their methodology and the scientific base and validity of the systems, they are still popular and a means of initiating improvements within institutions.

BACKGROUND

During the last decade, the Greek higher education sector was hit by a multilevel and multifaceted crisis and consequent ill-prepared reforms with no clear reference points. Visionless and badly designed/executed higher education policies along with cultural distortions and false perceptions of the university system`s purpose and operation (e.g. accountability, policy decisions made on political promises and not real social and economic needs) have been impeding the higher education sector from realizing its full potential. The consequences (e.g. funding inadequacy, dysfunctional operation with unclear strategic planning, low competitiveness, introversion, demand-supply mismatch) are widely known and referred in bibliography (e.g. Livanos, 2010; Zmas, 2015). The weaknesses of Greek higher education (e.g. the outdated legislative framework (that limited for many years institutional autonomy, affected the sources of funding, university management and internationalization policies), the institutional politics and highly polarized academic cultures that often suppressed innovative ideas and change, the problematic awareness of "excellence", its evaluation and relation to meritocracy) had resulted in a kind of complacency (Anninos in Hall & Ogunmokun, 2018,p.12). Despite exceptions, this was translated into self-preservation mentalities combined with faded attention to the details of quality management, reactive and slow decision making, leaving institutions unprepared for an ever-changing global context.

As Greece slowly overcomes the aforementioned perennial crisis and tries to reshape and modernize its higher education sector, an increasing number of institutions and academic management boards are gradually adopting a systematic approach to quality and express their enthusiasm and pride when quality related milestones are being achieved (e.g. positive institutional evaluations, ranks in global league tables, accreditations).

University evaluations that were conducted in the previous years in Greece resulted in significant inferences for universities, highlighted strong points, indicated weakness areas and made recommendations for improvement. More specifically, the last year has been marked by the transcendence of institutions from evaluation to quality accreditation based on standards relevant to the academic and managerial operation of universities (Hellenic Quality Assurance and Accreditation Agency, 2018). It is worth pointing out that 8 Greek universities are currently included in the three most popular league tables (namely Quacquarelli Symonds-QS, Academic Ranking of World Universities-ARWU, Times Higher Education-THE).

The strong momentum for quality and excellence in universities in Greece which has been fueled by European, international developments and state initiatives is being amplified by the Hellenic Quality Assurance and Accreditation Agency (HQA) that began its operations in 2006 (and became a European Association for Quality Assurance in Higher Education -ENQA full member in 2015) as the safe keeper of quality in the Greek higher education. The HQA more specifically aims at the development and implementation of a unified quality assurance system that would be a reference point for universities` operations. The HQA (based on its overarching mission and among other responsibilities) periodically accredits the quality of the internal quality assurance systems of institutions of higher education and all kinds of study programs in the Greek higher education sector.

Quality accreditation enables institutions to adopt a robust approach towards continuous improvement and excellence, as it offers systematic self-assessment based on predefined criteria and processes. In addition, an accreditation seal leads to the gradual increase in the competitiveness of institutions and their study programs, secures academic qualifications of graduates and offers them more opportunities in the labour market and future career paths (through the recognition of accredited degrees in the European Higher Education Area).

It is expected that academic leaders primarily and responsible staff for quality assurance should be committed and competent enough on quality management issues for the successful implementation of quality assurance processes in universities. Otherwise, any institutionally legitimate attempt to design and implement systems and processes for the effective operation of educational and administrative services would meet considerable hurdles. Hence, the role of academic leadership becomes crucial for the effective and efficient operation of universities, especially at a time of financial pressures, globalization, demand for accountability, and increasing complexity of operation (Kiat Kok & Mc Donald, 2017).

The chapter provides a brief overview of the quality accreditation framework in Greek universities and underlines the critical role of academic leadership for achieving accreditation and establishing a culture for sustainable excellence (by suggesting specific actions).

THE QUALITY ACCREDITATION FRAMEWORK IN GREEK HIGHER EDUCATION

Total Quality Management is a (managerial) philosophy and structured approach for managing organizations (Dahlgaard, Chen, Jang, Banegas, & Dahlgaard-Park, 2013; Dahlgaard Park, Chen, Jang & Dahlgaard, 2013; Dahlgaard-Park, Reyes, & Chen, 2018). It was formed through the fusion of ideas from quality pioneers (e.g. W.A. Shewhart, W. Edwards Deming, Joseph M. Juran), their enthusiasm and commitment for excellence (Ritchie & Dale, 2000). In general, TQM is manifested by continuous improvements of products, services and processes, focus on processes, total employee participation and self-improvement, evidence-based thinking and decision making with the aim to exceed customers` expectations (Evans & Dean, 2000, p.13).

The successful implementation of quality strategies in various industry sectors and the need for a revolution in education contributed in numerous attempts to introduce quality concepts in higher education, in the late 1980s (Owlia & Aspinwall, 1996). Nevertheless, the quality assurance movement in higher education was initiated in the mid-1990s followed by the establishment of quality assurance agencies in Europe (European University Association, 2006, p.6).

In the context of higher education there seems to be no unanimity regarding the meaning of quality. It is very common to define quality based on our personal understanding of the concept of higher education. Quality can be related to institutional management or the educational functions of a university or both. (Lagrosen, Seyyed-Hashemi & Leitner, 2004). It can be considered as a key factor through which different perspectives and requirements by stakeholders are merged and translated into a well-articulated vision, mission and objectives. Dahlgaard, Kristensen & Kanji (1995) define quality in education as a culture that is characterized by increased customer satisfaction through continuous improvement, in which all employees and students actively participate. It can be depicted as the base of a conceptual model that drives university management through the quality principles to excel in teaching, research and social contribution. Quality is not static; it constantly changes as do needs and requirements in the global context. Nowadays, quality should be considered as a philosophy, an attitude, a behaviour that is people-centered, systemic, dynamic and transformative (managerial and epistemic). Quality can be culture sensitive or be defined through internal discussions in terms of each institution's unique profile (European University Association, 2006, p.9).

The pursuit of quality and excellence in higher education has been a well research subject in literature (e.g. Badri & Abdulla, 2004; Hides, Davies & Jackson, 2004; Osseo-Assare & Longbottom, 2005; Badri, Selim, Alshare, Grandon, Younis & Abdulla, 2006; Calvo-Mora, Leale & Roldan, 2006; Anninos, 2007). Some authors focus on the application of excellence models in universities (e.g. Osseo-Asare & Longbottom, 2002; Hides *et al.*, 2004; Calvo-Mora, Leale & Roldan, 2005; Tari & Juana-Espinosa, 2007) and examine ways to implement Total Quality Management in higher education (e.g. Asif, Awan, Khan & Ahmad, 2013; Rosa, Saraiva & Diz 2003; Sakthivel & Raju, 2006; Campatelli, Cittib & Meneghin, 2011, Bayraktar, Tatoglu & Zaim, 2008, Venkatraman, 2007; Kanji, Tambi & Wallace, 1999). In addition, other authors write about service quality in higher education which results from a systematic orientation towards quality (Yeo, 2008; Sultan & Wong (2012) Venkatraman, 2007; Cardona & Bravo, 2012; Calvo-Mora *et al.*, 2006; Tsinidou, Gerogiannis & Fitsilis, 2010 ; Khan & Matlay, 2009; Senthilkumar & Arulraj, 2011), while some of them are skeptical (e.g. Birnbaum, 2001, p.7).

Quality accreditation constitutes an approach of university performance evaluation (as said earlier). Accreditation focuses on the results of quality assurance, namely the attempts made by institutions to set their objectives and goals based on data, establish strategies with specific timeframes, develop processes to support the realization of strategies and improve. It further strengthens quality assurance and the effectiveness of universities.

The Hellenic Quality Assurance and Accreditation Agency (being responsible by its founding law and based on the European Standards Guidelines -ESG for quality accreditation) has developed its standards initially for the Internal Quality Assurance System of universities and undergraduate study programs. It defines accreditation as a process of external evaluation based on predefined and internationally accepted and published quantitative and qualitative criteria and indicators that comply with the principles and guidelines for quality assurance in the European higher education area (HQA website). The following table briefly presents the standards used for quality accreditation of the Internal Quality Assurance System (IQAS) and study programs of Greek universities.

Table 1. HQA Accreditation Standards

IQAS STANDARDS	UNDERGRADUATE STUDY PROGRAM STANDARDS
1. Institution policy for quality assurance 2. Provision and management of the necessary resources 3. Establishing goals for quality assurance 4. Structure, organization and operation of the IQAS 5. Self-assessment 6. Collection of quality data: measuring, analysis and improvement 7. Public information 8. External evaluation and accreditation of IQAS	1. Quality assurance policy 2. Design and approval of programmes 3. Student-centred learning, teaching and assessment 4. Student admission, progression, recognition and certification 5. Teaching staff 6. Learning resources and student support 7. Information management 8. Public Information 9. On-going monitoring and periodic internal review of programmes 10. Regular external evaluation of undergraduate programmes

Source: Hellenic Quality Assurance and Accreditation Agency, Available at https://www.adip.gr/el/basic-page/734/protypa-pistopoiisis *(accessed 12 February 2019)*

It is a strict precondition for an institution to have an accredited Internal Quality Assurance System before seeking accreditation of its study programs.

As a process, quality accreditation involves five consecutive steps, namely (HQA, 2017):

a) the submission of an accreditation proposal (following a call by HQA) which includes the preparation of a comprehensive report by the institution (a task undertaken by the institutional Quality Assurance Unit) that takes into consideration the standards and criteria set by HQA,
b) a site visit conducted by a team of experts (accreditation panel) selected by HQA. The accreditation panel reviews the report prepared by the institutions, examines all evidence presented, visits institutions and organizes interviews with members of the academic and administrative staff. Its judgements appear on the accreditation report draft, which includes a recommendation (full compliance with the standard`s requirements, substantial compliance, partial compliance, no compliance) to HQA.
c) the HQA forwards the accreditation report draft to the institutions for comments/feedback and,
d) the HQA board reviews the final accreditation report and decides on whether accreditation should be granted (institutions have the right to place an appeal). The result of the accreditation process is the awarding of a status, and a license to operate within a specific time frame (4 years).
e) the consistent follow-up of the internal quality assurance system/study program operation by the university`s Quality Assurance Unit (QAU).

An institution that manages to acquire the IQAS accreditation is introduced to the journey for excellence. In the case of undergraduate study programs there are benefits for students, institutions and employers. For example, an accredited study program bares an official proof that it conforms to the European standards for quality and becomes a platform for adopting the teachings and TQM practices.

Its competitiveness is increased and thus the value of its degrees in the European Higher Education Area is upgraded, something which is translated into more work and mobility opportunities for graduates. It is already common for global employers to prefer hiring graduates from accredited institutions and institutions which are high in ranking positions. This is explained by the fact that their qualifications are guaranteed through the program`s conformance to quality standards, something useful for professional organizations also. It is also pertinent to point out that transnational and international cooperation between institutions/departments in facilitated, hence their extroversion is improved. The continuous monitoring of study programs by the institutional Quality Assurance Unit guarantees that quality is maintained and improved.

A university that is fully committed to excellence is characterized by relevant values, attitudes and behaviours which are aligned to its strategies, policies and practices. University excellence is achieved through the interaction of the organizational and education pillar of institutions and the committed pursue for higher and higher levels of quality. Excellence primarily as a vision should also reflect the basic institutional ideals and priorities as far as the role of a modern university and diffuse internationalization as a basic academic objective in the educational and organizational pillar. It must inspire, act as a reference point and nourish commitment primarily by top institutional management. Its role in participating in global networks for best practice exchange and learning is critical for success. Thus, top university management should help developing a climate conducive to excellence.

The achievement of sustainable excellence in universities demands primarily an active and meaningful engagement of academic leadership that would undertake the task of developing a framework for quality management (system, processes, people and culture) and committing itself to the pursuit of quality. W. E Deming and J. Juran, two of the founders of Total Quality Management, agree regarding the role of top management and leadership of an organization in the integration of quality, the existence and frequent use of quality monitoring for improvement, the significance of customer (internal or external) satisfaction, continuous improvement, the use of scientific methods and techniques to control quality, training and development of human resources as well as their involvement in problem solving activities and decision making.

ROLE OF ACADEMIC LEADERSHIP IN QUALITY ASSURANCE CONTEXT: ISSUE OF CULTURE

Management is the systematic process of planning, organizing, leading and controlling of all available resources efficiently and effectively to achieve the desired goals (Daft, 2006, p.8). Leadership differs from management in a considerable degree. Management refers to the activities and functions of an organizations while leadership refers to all activities that develop human resources in order to help them attain organizational objectives.

According to Edgeman, Dahlgaard, Dahlgaard Park & Scherer, (1999) leadership constitutes a vision that stimulates hope and mission which transform hope into reality, courage to sacrifice personal or team goals for the greater community goal, consensus that drives unity of purpose, empowerment that grants permission to make mistakes, encourages the honesty to admit them and provides the opportunity to learn from them, and finally conviction that provides the stamina to continually strive toward business excellence. Warren Bennis defines leadership as the ability of an individual to translate a vision into reality (Bennis, 1989, p.139), something that implies influence. Thus, leadership can be theorized as an ability of exerting influence over others (colleagues or subordinates) in order to collectively achieve specific predetermined goals (Northouse, 2004, p.3). It is a dynamic process, which means that a leader's action would cause reaction by subordinates which in turn results in another action by the leader. The degree of influence though depends on him/her, the others and the specific situations in which the two sides interact. Hence, leadership is an ability, which is expressed by suitable behavior that can be learned and improved. As a relationship of influence, it is based on the power leaders hold and how/when they use it.

The significance of leadership for success in the implementation of Total Quality Management in any organization and context has been present in Deming`s 14 points for management transformation (Deming, 2000, p.54). It is indeed impossible for an organization to succeed in any quality assurance effort without a vision, committing itself to a set of (relevant to the vision) values and people involvement in continuous improvement efforts (Evans & Dean, 2000, p.277). A leader is expected to be capable of utilizing intellectual and emotional abilities to conceive a vision. During this process, it is important to engage human resources, so that they can express their ideas and beliefs. Having done so, it is then easier for a leader to communicate the vision to the organization, because it would be a result of dialogue and cooperation. The pursuit of vision presupposes certain values that primarily the leader and people would have to live by. Examples of such values might be continuous self-improvement, team working, cooperating for exceeding customer expectations. A leader is thus expected to lead by example and inspire people work and achieve things they believed to be impossible. It should be noted that TQM failures are often caused by inadequate attention, knowledge and profound understanding of the human dimension (Dahlgaard-Park, 2011).

In the academic context, leadership may also have various definitions (e.g. Ramsden, Prosser, Trigwell & Martin, 2007; Bryman, 2007; Vikinas, 2009). When seen within the academic context, leadership is a continuous struggle for balancing contrasting roles (e.g. managing vs leading, academic vs manager) with multiple reference levels, implies self-development for the pursuit of new ways for supporting, managing and developing colleagues, a power for qualitative transformation of institutions (Ramsden, 2000,p.126). Leaders` awareness of their own weaknesses and strengths as well as their collaboration and communication abilities are highly important for sucess.

Despite the on-going controversy on the fusion of management`s philosophies and educational values of higher education institutions, a significant portion of relative literature (regarding quality management in higher education) deals with the successful adoption and implementation of the Total Quality Management philosophy in higher education institutions, thus outlining critical success factors. All studies indicate the importance (among other constituents) of leadership commitment, top management engagement and process management (e.g. Asif *et al.,* 2013; O` Mahony & Garavan, 2012; Flumerfelt & Banachowski, 2011; Ahire, Golhar & Waller, 1996). According to Black (2015), the changing context in higher education globally demands academic leaders that would be capable of dealing also with managerial/organizational issues, which has caused mainly cultural and work practices conflicts among the romantics and the realists. It is thus advisable for academic leadership to be able to deal with complexity (namely manage), change (namely lead) and have the necessary competences, namely, to be "quality intelligent" to design the path for university excellence and engage in all necessary actions for its realization.

Quality intelligence can be theorized as a set of specific embraced mental and cognitive elements (e.g. values and attitudes, knowledge, vision and strategic intelligence, empathy and compassion, creativity and change, willingness for action and world/universal perspective) that motivate people to constantly pursue improvement. It could be considered as the "invisible hand" of excellence that guides institutions from the lowest level of maturity in quality (uncertainty) to the highest (certainty) (according to Crosby`s Quality Maturity Model).

Becoming a quality intelligent academic leader is not an easy task. Usually people receive training on a specific discipline, get qualified and enter the labor market. In the case of academic leadership this does not happen. Academics that are appointed to managerial positions are scientists with no training for successfully addressing tasks and challenges relevant to their positions (such as resolving a conflict, understanding a budget, diffusing a strategy, inspiring and motivating colleagues, exercising management and leadership) (Gmelch & Buller, 2015, p.2). It would not be easy for a philologist (for example) to think in the process logic as required by the quality management theory, implement the House of Quality to design a new course, understand Deming`s System of Profound Knowledge or choose a leadership style that matches contingencies and institutional staff characteristics so as to successfully lead an institution not only to comply with accreditation standards but also increase its collective consciousness regarding quality and excellence.

Ramsden (1998) in his book "Learning to lead in higher education" refers to some good and bad university leadership characteristics (p.87). The abilities to fight complacency, manage resources effectively, have a clear, open and flexible vision, have a strategic perspective, motivate and inspire people are some characteristics of good university leadership. On the contrary, being authoritarian, giving directions with no explanations, not having the respect of academic colleagues due to inadequate academic credibility constitute characteristics of bad university leadership.

In a recent article, academics that have been appointed in leadership positions in the past mark out the mastering of new skills (e.g. crisis management, financial management, governance, time management), collective work and authentic interest for staff, reliability and flexibility, influencing change and gaining an enriched awareness of the meaning of commitment to education (among other factors) as enablers for success (Beddington, Dirks, Price, Rand, Stolker, O`Sullivan & Yates, 2018).

Institutional leadership is responsible for creating the circumstances to embed a culture of quality and this is something that should be facilitated by "quality intelligent" academic leaders. It is both necessary and advisable for academic leaders to understand soft and hard quality issues (e.g. process perspective, lean approach, data-based thinking, quality diseases, quality function deployment). In those cases, in which academic leaders have a vague idea of what is management or how management is exercised, their actions and behaviors could result in misbalancing the whole system. This is a major issue for institutions, namely the need to have academic leaders that would not only be excellent in their respective disciplinary field but also have adequate knowledge of the quality management paradigm, development in education methodologies, managerial experience and specific personality characteristics. These factors constitute the "quintet" for success in academic leading and the progress of institution towards quality maturity. It is necessary for academic leaders to be role models of quality philosophy (committed to quality) and practice to inspire the members of academic community engage and participate in the quality journey. By developing quality practices (like quality circles for example), new (quality) values are being implemented, monitored and reinforced.

The global developments in higher education demand primarily visionary leaders that will manage to articulate compelling visions in their institutions consistent with unique institutional values, history, context and ambition. Leaders provide direction, instill commitment, promote strategy to human resources (academic and administrative) and external stakeholders by effective communication mechanisms, manage the relationships between academic and non-academic staff, motivate them and offer opportunities. The role of leadership is to sustain a vision of connectedness, make obvious for everyone how each process results in student satisfaction and create and sustain a culture of quality. A quality culture must be strong outlining a clear alignment among goals, structure, roles and strategies so that organizational transformation towards excellence is successful. Hence, it is easily deduced that cultural transformation would be the first step of an institution to become quality oriented.

Bearing in mind the fact that quality is primarily an issue of values that permeate organizations (Hellsten & Klefsjö, 2000), the first step towards quality integration should be the change of pre-existing values, to change attitudes and then behaviors first at the individual level and then at the collective level (Lagrosen, 2003). It is not possible to have organizational structures committed to excellence (and achieve sustainable excellence) by simply conforming to legal/bureaucratic obligations. This is a false starting point. Quality should not be viewed as a result of simply following a process (often seen as) imposed by an external actor. Quality must start from within, from each person`s heart and mind. It is highly significant for an academic leader to have insight, namely the ability to identify gaps between the current status quo and the future and eager to make the leap forward. Moreover, it should not be forgotten that excellence is a continuous journey that involves caring more, risking more, dreaming more and expecting more while engaging in doing common, everyday things (Dahlgaard Park, 2009). It is this process that leads people to realize their full potential. Having that in mind it is pertinent to underline that academic leaders should pay attention so that no one is marginalized. It is the degree of excellence`s within every individual that will eventually determine if and to what degree social/organizational structures will eventually thrive.

Quality in the management of a higher education institutions surely demands organizational changes (incremental or radical) based on the degree of readiness to become quality oriented. Internally a higher education institution should initially identify the need for quality. All processes and procedures related to university operation should be discussed and documented in a quality manual and quality values should be incorporated in institutional vision, mission, objectives and daily activities. This will help institutions develop a strategy on how to embed a culture of quality. According to Lagrosen *et al.,* (2004), the integration of quality in higher education can be problematic and be hampered by the lack of a shared vision and match between quality management and educational processes. The failure to embed quality can be ascribed either to lack of institutional preparation to embrace the quality philosophy, cultural reasons or the lack to create a holistic and unified approach to excellence.

Schein (1992, p.18) describes culture as a set of shared assumptions and beliefs of a group or an organization which have been developed during its adaptation to external environment or internal integration. Leaders are able to influence culture and they do it in various ways, such as by paying attention to things that represent their priorities and concerns, reacting to crises based on specific values, acting as role models of specific behaviors and values, managing human resources, designing systems, processes and structures or simply by making formal statements (Yukl, 2002, p.278).

Some researchers have argued that there is a constant interplay between organizational culture and leadership (Bass & Avolio, 1993; Schein, 1992, p.3), while a positive correlation among culture and performance (e.g. Marcoulides & Heck, 1993; Petty, Beadles, Lowery, Chapman & Connell, 1995) has been empirically documented in literature. Hence, it is easily deduced that culture at the organizational level influences objectives, individual and collective priorities, managerial practices, processes and the achievement of results. It is worth mentioning some characteristics of high performing organizations, as mentioned by Barrett (1998, pp.12-13), namely:

- Positive values` culture
- Commitment to learning

- Continuous adaptation and risk undertaking
- Formation of strategic alliances
- Balanced measurement of performance

Quality culture in the higher education context refers to a culture that aims to permanently transform quality and is characterized by (European University Association, 2006, p.10):

a) shared values, beliefs, expectations and commitment to quality which constitute the cultural / psychological element and
b) processes that improve quality, coordinate individual efforts and constitute the structural / managerial element. These elements are linked through effective communication and wide human resources participation at institutional level.

Deming has been quite clear when he said that quality is everyone's responsibility. Quality culture can is the collective personality of an institution (Trivellas & Dargenidou, 2009). The integration of a quality culture in a university begins gradually and takes years to complete depending on how mature an institution is regarding quality (e.g. Is there a quality policy? Are there clear quality objectives?, Has the institution clearly defined processes to monitor quality and initiate improvements?, Do criteria and indicators exist, according to which performance is evaluated and decisions are made? etc.). Quality values and principles must become part of institutional strategy and be adjusted to every organizational unit or university function. Top institutional management should be able to identify potential structural barriers and remove them (such as rigid policies or symbols), invest in human resources training and development and act bearing in mind the systemic nature of the university. Teambuilding, trust, openness and feedback, reliability, commitment, participation in teams, coaching, mentoring, conflict resolution, and improvement are some indicators of a quality culture. Attitudes and behaviors that will make these values permanent are required and be fostered. By embedding a culture of quality in a higher education institution, the first step towards excellence would have been achieved.

A higher education institution that is characterized by a quality culture is proactive, has a shared vision, aims at continuous improvement, instills trust and respect among its staff which is committed, reflective and monitors quality (Lomas, 2004). The main values that characterize a quality oriented higher education institution or organization are (Lagrosen, 2003):

- **Customer (receiver of services) orientation:** identification of needs and expectations, design of processes based on these needs and expectations, effective management of customer relationships, measurement of customer satisfaction and undertaking of necessary corrective actions.
- **Leadership commitment**: strong belief in quality, integration of quality with university objectives and daily activities, setting of high expectations, human resources' motivation, demonstration of personal involvement, inspiration through a student-oriented vision, provision of direction, encouragement of collective action, development and management of culture, learning and improvement support.
- **Staff full participation and team-working**: high employee involvement, use of suggestion schemes for improvement, reward and recognition schemes, team working and empowerment, investment in training and development (e.g. workshop for quality) and tracking of employee satisfaction.

- **Focus on processes**: thinking with the big picture in mind in an Input – Process – Output/Outcome logic with clear indications as to where value is added, provision of documentation so that everyone is aware and understand their roles and clear and how each one`s role fits in, commitment to kaizen (namely continuous marginal changes), institutional adaptations/transformation to support the process perspective (line of authority, flow of information etc.).
- **Measurements and management by facts**: development of meaningful performance indicators, use of comparative information for improvement, use of analytical methods, collection of reliable, accessible and visible data.
- **Continuous improvement and learning:** managerial mechanisms for organizational learning and processes for improvement whenever necessary (e.g. learning organization perspective).

However, as emphatically said earlier, quality is internalized at the personal level, it will never become rooted in the culture of an organization or a higher education institution. If someone embraces quality as a personal value, then it's highly likely to perform better than expected.

The implementation of quality culture is facilitated through active and full participation of all staff. Responsibilities should be apportioned, and ownership of certain processes must be strengthened. Beyond the existence and effective operation of the QAU which is institutionally responsible for quality assurance, it is advisable to have capable administrative staff helping towards the introduction of quality and academic staff that coordinate this attempt. In order to make everyone responsible for quality, the QAU could engage in the training of staff on TQM issues (e.g. meaning of quality in higher education, the significance of evidence-based thinking and strategy formulation with achievable objectives, timeframes, responsibilities and relation to KPIs). Training and development initiatives must be always present, and administrators should aim at motivating and helping towards quality awareness. Between academic and non-academic staff as well as between different departments and hierarchical levels there must be good communication and exchange of ideas must be encouraged (European University Association, 2006, p.16).

Institutional leadership can increase student participation in quality assurance by offering support to students, by providing them with opportunities to learn about quality assurance issues and how their evaluations are taken into consideration and included in the institutional knowledge mechanism. The participation of students must not be confined in filling out questionnaires (in e.g. teaching quality evaluation) but they can have a meaningful impact on decision making (European University Association, 2006, p.24). A major challenge for Greek universities is the utilization of students` course evaluation results. It is common for students to express their discomfort and discontent when they are asked to fill in a course evaluation questionnaire and this happens simply because they are not convinced about the degree and the method of utilization and/or they have not been formally initiated in quality assurance (which is a significant weakness of IQAS). The participation of alumni and professional organizations can also have a significant role in continuous improvement as their experience can act as a guide for institutions to redesign their programs and courses.

An institution cannot assess its progress towards the implementation of a quality culture without having processes and indicators to evaluate it. The evaluation system must be integrated in the institutional management system and be dynamic. All indicators should refer to strategic goals and be interpreted according to each institution's profile and context. Every evaluation attempt should not be perceived as a control mechanism but as an opportunity for improvement. Self-evaluations, peer review, external evaluation are practices widely used. Feedback is necessary for continuous improvement, learning and growth as well as sharing results information and disseminating best practice. The process of evaluation should be based on sound principles, rules and criteria should be based on consent. Quality should not be mere compliance but inspiration towards better performance. The role of academic and non-academic staff should be encouraged. Thus, institutional leadership has the power to influence key organizational factors like structure, strategy staff engagement in order to achieve quality in both the organizational and the academic pillar of a higher education institution.

CONCLUSION

It is now present more than ever before a compelling social need for reforming the higher education sector (which is also a state priority) and creating the circumstances, so that the Greek institutions of higher education are moved to the center stage of the economy and fuel growth. To achieve that, it is imperative to review the role of universities, to remove the barriers that restrict them from realizing their full potential and to develop a new model for growth, according to which universities form the core in a network of interactions among cooperating actors.

The pursuit of sustainable performance excellence and the increasing international focus present the two constituents upon which the future of the Greek higher education should be based. Quality, innovation, the strengthening of international collaboration in research and knowledge sharing constitute the basic strategic priorities of Greek institutions.

Quality culture is a basic prerequisite to integrate quality in a higher education institution. Inside universities, quality should constitute a way of life, a way of behaving so that individual and collective contribution towards "customer" satisfaction is maximized along with personal and organizational advancement through continuous improvement and learning. The development of suitable and academy – adjusted values which aim to create a dynamic process of organizational changes and improvements in the educational pillars of a university depends on leadership. Top university leadership style and commitment to quality values constitute a primary factor to embed quality culture in a university setting, improve quality and set the foundations for sustainable excellence.

SOLUTIONS AND RECOMMENDATIONS

University officials could actively participate in international quality assurance forums and conferences and thus broaden their exposure to international developments regarding the management of universities and the implementation of quality methodologies, be immersed in a multitude of international experiences and practices.

Furthermore, HQA could design and realize educational activities in which institutional quality assurance units and university officials could participate. An example could be a simulation (the Q Game) in which participants could enhance their knowledge on quality related issues, deepen their understanding on the implementation of IQAS processes and procedures and learn how to develop a consistent managerial approach of quality issues, as well as a methodology for finding best solutions to problems and making decisions. For example, a simulation could create hypothetical situations in a "safe" learning environment of escalating difficulty and complexity. In these situations, and more specifically at each stage of the simulation, evidence-based decisions would have to be made on the strategic, operational and functional level of universities. At the end of each stage of the simulation, the progress made by each

Table 2. The Q Game simulation roles

HQA	QAU
• Organizes and facilitates the process • Defines the simulation scenario in the field of European and Greek higher education • Evaluates the suggestions/recommendations of QAUs and monitors the progress of each QAU in the simulation • Rewards the winning QAU • Strengthens communication among external experts and QAUs and facilitates the exchange of ideas and knowledge regarding quality assurance	• Is taught basic TQM principles and concepts • Learns to combine evidence and data • Collaborates with and utilizes the experience of external experts • Is immersed into the process of quality development and learns to be self-evaluated • Combines managerial and technical skills • Evaluates the attempts/progress by other QAUs

QAU would be evaluated by both the HQA and peer QAUs. The registry of QAU of external experts/evaluators could also be utilized. A small number of external evaluators could undertake mentoring roles for QAUs. Participants would be able to combine strategic thinking, problem solving methodology, utilization of technical skills, teamworking and exercising of leadership. The following table provides an overview of roles:

FUTURE RESEARCH DIRECTIONS

Four future research directions are suggested in this chapter, namely:

- The global and national transformation of traditional universities (to network-based universities), their multiple roles in the modern global context and the subsequent increase in the degree of operational complexity is expected to pose new challenges in university performance evaluation and indicate new performance dimensions for university excellence. A relevant example is the European initiative for the establishment of European Universities, which is considered as a quantum leap in the European higher education. European Universities constitute alliances between universities that would further promote common European values and identity and improve the competitiveness of European higher education. Alliances are translated into interacting institutional systems whose interfaces must be also evaluated with specific criteria and indicators,
- The investigation of university learning mechanisms that defines if and how recommendations are embedded in institutional management systems. It is true that the transformation of universities into learning organizations is not an easy task due to the peculiarities of higher education, despite the benefits that follow (e.g. improved quality, increased competitiveness and innovation, strengthening of strategic sense). The learning organization is being described as an ideal or a philosophy towards which organizations should evolve to successfully respond to the challenges they face. Success when it comes to endeavors like that depends on issues like the time needed on behalf of staff, its personal development level and its subsequent support by the institutions (Senge, 1990, p.139; Senge, Kleiner, Ross, Roth & Smith, 1999; Bui & Baruch, 2010),
- The abundance of technological applications in institutional operation, the need for rapid integration of evaluation findings in the institutional knowledge repositories, the emphasis on graduates` learning outcomes, skills and competences (the collection and analysis of big data) and the evolution of management highlight the need for highly committed, knowledgeable and skillful

university administrators that will be able to identify institutional priorities and further develop the institutional quality assurance system

- The assurance of the flawless operation and autonomy of HQA and the strengthening of its` scientific contribution by enabling knowledge exchange among institutions through the organization of annual meetings and funding of specialized research projects.

REFERENCES

Ahire, S., Golhar, D., & Waller, M. (1996). Development and validation of TQM implementation constructs. *Decision Sciences*, *27*(1), 23–56. doi:10.1111/j.1540-5915.1996.tb00842.x

Anninos, L. N. (2007). The archetype of excellence in universities and TQM. *Journal of Management History*, *13*(4), 307–321. doi:10.1108/17511340710819561

Anninos, L. N. (2010). *Suitability and compatibility of university performance evaluation systems and processes in Greece* (Ph.D Thesis). University of Piraeus.

Anninos, L. N. (2018). Internationalizing the Greek higher education: A quest and a vision for excellence. In D. Hall & G. Ogunmokun (Eds.), *Management, leadership and marketing of universities* (pp. 11–30). Perth, Australia: Global Publishing House International.

Asif, M., Awan, M., Khan, M., & Ahmad, N. (2013). A Model for Total Quality Management in Higher Education. *Quality & Quantity*, *47*(4), 1883–1904. doi:10.100711135-011-9632-9

Badri, M., & Abdulla, M. (2004). Awards of excellence in institutions of higher education: An AHP approach. *International Journal of Educational Management*, *18*(4), 224–242. doi:10.1108/09513540410538813

Badri, M. A., Selim, H., Alshare, K., Grandon, E., Younis, H., & Abdulla, M. (2006). The Baldridge education criteria for performance excellence framework: Empirical test and validation. *International Journal of Quality & Reliability Management*, *23*(9), 1118–1157. doi:10.1108/02656710610704249

Barrett, R. (1998). *Liberating the corporate soul: Building a visionary organization*. Oxford, UK: Butterworth Heinemann.

Bass, B. M., & Avolio, B. J. (1993). Transformational leadership and organizational culture. *Public Administration Quarterly*, *17*(1), 112–121.

Bayraktar, E., Tatoglu, E., & Zaim, S. (2008). An instrument for measuring the critical factors of TQM in Turkish higher education. *Total Quality Management & Business Excellence*, *19*(6), 551–574. doi:10.1080/14783360802023921

Beddington, W., Dirks, N. B., Price, D., Rand, J., Stolker, C., O'Sullivan, H., & Yates, L. (2018). *What is it like to take a leadership role at a university?* Available at https://www.timeshighereducation.com/features/what-is-it-like-to-take-a-leadership-role-at-a-university

Bennis, W. (1989). *On Becoming a Leader*. New York: Addison-Wesley Publishing.

Beywl, W. (2003). *Selected comments to the standards for evaluation of the German Evaluation Society*. Cologne: DeGEval.

Birnbaum, R. (2001). *Management fads in higher education. San Francisco*: Jossey Bass.

Black, S. A. (2015). Qualities of Effective Leadership in Higher Education. *Open Journal of Leadership*, 4(2), 54–66. doi:10.4236/ojl.2015.42006

Bryman, A. (2007). Effective leadership in higher education: A literature review. *Studies in Higher Education*, 32(6), 693–710. doi:10.1080/03075070701685114

Bui, H., & Baruch, Y. (2010). Creating learning organizations: A systems perspective. *The Learning Organization*, 17(3), 208–227. doi:10.1108/09696471011034919

Calvo-Mora, A., Leal, A., & Roldan, J. (2006). Using enablers of the EFQM model to manage institutions of higher education. *Quality Assurance in Education*, 14(2), 99–122. doi:10.1108/09684880610662006

Calvo-Mora, A., Leal, A., & Roldán, J. L. (2005). Relationships between the EFQM model Criteria: A study in Spanish universities. *Total Quality Management & Business Excellence*, 16(6), 741–770. doi:10.1080/14783360500077708

Campatelli, G., Cittib, P., & Meneghin, A. (2011). Development of a simplified approach based on the EFQM model and Six Sigma for the implementation of TQM principles in a university administration. *Total Quality Management & Business Excellence*, 22(7), 691–704. doi:10.1080/14783363.2011.585755

Cardona, M., & Bravo, Y. (2012). Service quality perceptions in higher education institutions: The case of a Colombian university. *Estudios Gerenciales*, 28(125), 23–29. doi:10.1016/S0123-5923(12)70004-9

Daft, R. (2006). *The new era of management*. South Western.

Dahlgaard, J. J., Chen, C.-K., Jang, J.-Y., Banegas, L. A., & Dahlgaard-Park, S. M. (2013). Business excellence models: Limitations, reflections and further development. *Total Quality Management & Business Excellence*, 24(5–6), 519–538. doi:10.1080/14783363.2012.756745

Dahlgaard, J. J., Kristensen, K., & Kanji, G. K. (1995). TQM and education. *Total Quality Management & Business Excellence*, 6(5/6), 445–456.

Dahlgaard-Park, S. M. (2009). Decoding the code of excellence – for achieving sustainable excellence. *International Journal of Quality and Service Sciences*, 1(1), 5–28. doi:10.1108/17566690910945840

Dahlgaard-Park, S. M. (2011). The quality movement – where are you going? *Total Quality Management & Business Excellence*, 22(5), 493–516. doi:10.1080/14783363.2011.578481

Dahlgaard-Park, S. M., Chen, C. K., Jang, J. Y., & Dahlgaard, J. J. (2013). Diagnosing and prognosticating the quality movement – a review on the 25 years quality literature (1987–2011). *Total Quality Management & Business Excellence*, 24(1-2), 1–18. doi:10.1080/14783363.2012.756749

Dahlgaard-Park, S. M., Reyes, L., & Chen, C. K. (2018). The evolution and convergence of total quality management and management theories. *Total Quality Management & Business Excellence*, 29(9-10), 1108–1128. doi:10.1080/14783363.2018.1486556

Danish Evaluation Institute. (2003). *Quality procedures in European Higher Education*. European Network for Quality Assurance.

Deming, W. E. (2000). *Out of the crisis*. Cambridge, MA: MIT Press.

Edgeman, R., Dahlgaard, J. J., Dahlgaard-Park, S. M., & Scherer, F. (1999). On leaders and leadership. *Quality Progress*, *32*(10), 49–54.

European University Association. (2006). *Quality culture in European universities: A bottom-up approach: Report on the three rounds of the quality culture project 2002–2006*. Brussels: European University Association.

Evans, J. R., & Dean, J. W. (2000). *Total Quality: Management, Organization and Strategy*. South Western.

Evans, J. R., & Lindsay, W. M. (1999). *The management and control of quality*. South Western.

Flumerfelt, S., & Banachowski, M. (2011). Understanding leadership paradigms for improvement in higher education. *Quality Assurance in Education*, *19*(3), 224–247. doi:10.1108/09684881111158045

Gmelch, W. H., & Buller, J. L. (2015). *Building academic leadership capacity: A guide to best practices*. San Francisco: Jossey Bass.

Hellenic Quality Assurance Agency. (2017). *Guidelines for accreditation*. Retrieved from https://www.adip.gr/sites/default/files/pages/06/701-odigos_pistopoiisis_en.pdf

Hellenic Quality Assurance Agency. (2018). Annual report 2017. Athens: Author.

Hellsten, U., & Klefsjö, B. (2000). TQM as a management system consisting of values, techniques and tools. *The TQM Magazine*, *12*(4), 238–244. doi:10.1108/09544780010325822

Hides, M., Davies, J., & Jackson, S. (2004). Implementation of EFQM excellence model self-assessment in the UK higher education sector-lessons learned from other sectors. *The TQM Magazine*, *16*(3), 194–201. doi:10.1108/09544780410532936

Kanji, G. K., Tambi, A. M., & Wallace, W. (1999). A comparative study of quality practices in higher education institutions in US and Malaysia. *Total Quality Management*, *10*(3), 357–371. doi:10.1080/0954412997884

Khan, H., & Matlay, H. (2009). Implementing service excellence in higher education. *Education + Training*, *51*(8), 769–780. doi:10.1108/00400910911005299

Kiat Kok, S., & Mc Donald, C. (2017). Underpinning excellence in higher education- an investigation into the leadership, governance and management behaviours of high performing academic departments. *Studies in Higher Education*, *42*(2), 210–231. doi:10.1080/03075079.2015.1036849

Kocher, M. G., Luptacik, M., & Sutter, M. (2006). Measuring productivity of research in economics: A cross country study using DEA. *Socio-Economic Planning Sciences*, *40*(4), 314–332. doi:10.1016/j.seps.2005.04.001

Lagrosen, S. (2003). Exploring the impact of culture on quality management. *International Journal of Quality & Reliability Management*, *20*(4), 473–487. doi:10.1108/02656710310468632

Lagrossen, S., Seyyed-Hashemi, R., & Leitner, M. (2004). Examination of the dimensions of quality in Higher Education. *Quality Assurance in Education*, *12*(2), 61–69. doi:10.1108/09684880410536431

Livanos, H. (2010). The relationship between higher education and labour market in Greece: The weakest link? *Higher Education*, *60*(5), 473–489. doi:10.100710734-010-9310-1

Lomas, L. (2004). Embedding quality: The challenges for higher education. *Quality Assurance in Education*, *12*(4), 157–165. doi:10.1108/09684880410561604

Marcoulides, G. A., & Heck, R. H. (1993). Organizational culture and performance: Proposing and testing a model. *Organization Science*, *4*(2), 209–225. doi:10.1287/orsc.4.2.209

Northouse, P. G. (2004). *Leadership: theory and practice*. Los Angeles, CA: SAGE Publications, Inc.

O'Mahony, K., & Garavan, T. N. (2012). Implementing a quality management framework in a higher education organization. *Quality Assurance in Education*, *20*(2), 184–200. doi:10.1108/09684881211219767

Osseo-Asare, A. E., & Longbottom, D. (2002). The need for education and training in the use of the EFQM model for quality management in UK higher education institutions. *Quality Assurance in Education*, *10*(1), 26–36. doi:10.1108/09684880210416085

Osseo-Asare, A., Longbottom, D., & Murphy, W. (2005). Leadership best practices for sustaining quality in UK higher education from the perspective of the EFQM excellence model. *Quality Assurance in Education*, *13*(2), 148–170. doi:10.1108/09684880510594391

Owlia, M., & Aspinwall, E. (1996). Quality in higher education. *Total Quality Management*, *7*(2), 161–172. doi:10.1080/09544129650034918

Petty, M. M., Beadles, N. A. II, Lowery, C. M., Chapman, D. F., & Connell, D. W. (1995). Relationships between organizational culture and organizational performance. *Psychological Reports*, *76*(2), 483–492. doi:10.2466/pr0.1995.76.2.483 PMID:8559874

Ramsden, P. (2000). *Learning to lead in higher education*. London: Routledge.

Ramsden, P., Prosser, M., Trigwell, K., & Martin, E. (2007). University teachers' experiences of academic leadership and their approaches to teaching. *Learning and Instruction*, *17*(2), 140–155. doi:10.1016/j.learninstruc.2007.01.004

Rickards, R. C. (2003). Setting benchmarks and evaluating balanced scorecards with data envelopment analysis. *Benchmarking:an International Journal*, *10*(3), 226–245. doi:10.1108/14635770310477762

Ritchie, L., & Dale, B. (2000). Self-assessment using the business excellence model: A study of practice and process. *International Journal of Production Economics*, *66*(3), 241–254. doi:10.1016/S0925-5273(99)00130-9

Rosa, M. J. P., Saraiva, P. M., & Diz, H. (2003). Excellence in Portuguese higher education institutions. *Total Quality Management & Business Excellence*, *14*(2), 189–197. doi:10.1080/1478336032000051377

Sakthivel, P. B., & Raju, R. (2006). Conceptualizing total quality management in engineering education and developing a TQM Educational Excellence Model. *Total Quality Management & Business Excellence*, *17*(7), 913–934. doi:10.1080/14783360600595476

Schein, E. H. (1992). *Organizational culture and leadership*. San Francisco: Jossey-Bass.

Senge, P. (1990). *The fifth discipline: The art and practice of the learning organization*. New York: Doubleday.

Senge, P., Kleiner, A., Ross, R., Roth, G., & Smith, B. (1999). *The Dance of Change*. New York: Currency Doubleday.

Senthilkumar, N., & Arulraj, A. (2011). SQM-HEI – determination of service quality measurement of higher education in India. *Journal of Modelling in Management, 6*(1), 60–78. doi:10.1108/17465661111112502

Sultan, P., & Wong, H. (2012). Service quality in a higher education context: An integrated model. *Asia Pacific Journal of Marketing and Logistics, 24*(5), 755–784. doi:10.1108/13555851211278196

Tari, J., & Juana-Espinosa, S. (2007). EFQM model self-assessment using a questionnaire approach in university administrative services. *The TQM Magazine, 19*(6), 604–616. doi:10.1108/09544780710828449

Trivellas, P., & Dargenidou, D. (2009). Organisational culture, job satisfaction and higher education service quality: The case of Technological Educational Institute of Larissa. *The TQM Journal, 21*(4), 382–399. doi:10.1108/17542730910965083

Tsinidou, M., Gerogiannis, V., & Fitsilis, P. (2010). Evaluation of the factors that determine quality in higher education: An empirical study. *Quality Assurance in Education, 18*(3), 227–244. doi:10.1108/09684881011058669

Venkatraman, S. (2007). A framework for implementing TQM in higher education programs. *Quality Assurance in Education, 15*(1), 92–112. doi:10.1108/09684880710723052

Vikinas, T. (2009). *Improving the leadership capability of academic coordinators in postgraduate and undergraduate programs in business*. Australian Learning and Teaching Council.

Vlasceanu, L., Grunberg, L., & Parlea, D. (2007). *Quality Assurance and Accreditation: a Glossary of Basic Terms and Definitions*. Bucharest: UNESCO.

Yeo, R. K. (2008). Servicing service quality in higher education: Quest for excellence. *On the Horizon, 16*(3), 152–161. doi:10.1108/10748120810901459

Yukl, G. (2002). *Leadership in organizations*. Prentice Hall.

Zmas, A. (2015). Financial crisis and higher education policies in Greece:Between intra- and supranational pressures. *Higher Education, 69*(3), 495–508. doi:10.100710734-014-9787-0

ADDITIONAL READING

Altbach, P. G., & Salmi, J. (2011). *The road to academic excellence*. Washington: The World Bank.

Askling, B., & Stensaker, B. (2002). Academic leadership: Prescriptions, practices and paradoxes. *Tertiary Education and Management, 8*(2), 113–125. doi:10.1080/13583883.2002.9967073

Bowen, W. G., & Shapiro, H. T. (1998). *Universities and their leadership*. Princeton, New Jersey: Princeton University Press. doi:10.4159/9781400880096

Bryman, A. (2007). Effective Leadership in Higher Education: A Literature Review. *Studies in Higher Education, 32*(6), 693–710. doi:10.1080/03075070701685114

Bryman, A. (2009). *Effective leadership in higher education: Final report. Research and Development Series*. London: Leadership Foundation for Higher Education.

Jones, D. G. (2011). Academic leadership and departmental headship in turbulent times. *Tertiary Education and Management, 17*(4), 279–288. doi:10.1080/13583883.2011.605906

Knight, P., & Trowler, P. (2001). *Departmental leadership in higher education*. Buckingham: Open University Press.

Psomas, E., & Antony, J. (2017). Total quality management elements and results in higher education institutions: The Greek case. *Quality Assurance in Education, 25*(2), 206–223. doi:10.1108/QAE-08-2015-0033

Sattler, C., & Sonntag, K. (2018). Quality cultures in higher education Institutions-Development of the quality culture inventory. In P. Meusburger, M. Heffernan, & L. Suarsana (Eds.), *Geographies of the University* (pp. 313–327). Cham: Springer. doi:10.1007/978-3-319-75593-9_9

KEY TERMS AND DEFINITIONS

Accreditation: The procedure by the quality of an institution or a study program is evaluated by an independent agency in order to become certified that it conforms to specific and pre-defined standards.

Evaluation: Evaluation is a term used to denote the value, performance of something/someone based on specific criteria.

Leadership: Leadership can be theorized as an ability of exerting influence over others (colleagues or subordinates) in order to collectively achieve specific predetermined goals.

Quality Culture (in Higher Education): A combination of 1) shared values, beliefs, expectations and commitment to quality which constitute the cultural / psychological element and 2) processes that improve quality, coordinate individual efforts and constitute the structural/managerial element.

Quality in Higher Education: A kind of culture that is characterized by increased customer satisfaction through continuous improvement and involvement of all staff and students.

Quality Intelligence: A set of specific embraced mental and cognitive elements (e.g., values and attitudes, knowledge, vision and strategic intelligence, empathy and compassion, creativity and change, willingness for action, and world/universal perspective) that motivate people to constantly pursue improvement.

Total Quality Management: A (managerial) philosophy and structured approach for managing organizations striving for excellence.

University Excellence: University excellence is a continuous pursue for higher and higher levels of quality in the organizational and education pillar of institutions.

Chapter 8
Situational Leadership for Quality Graduate Research in Higher Education

Hylton James Villet
Namibia University of Science and Technology, Namibia

ABSTRACT

Quality postgraduate supervision is key in ensuring that postgraduate programs at institutions of higher learning produce quality graduates and in turn play an appropriate role in building a knowledge economy. In essence, the role of the supervisor is to support the postgraduate student to successfully complete specific tasks in line with the research process. Supervisors adopt a variety of styles to supervise students. Adopting an exploratory research approach the chapter deliberates the supervisor-student dyad through the lens of the situational leadership model.

INTRODUCTION

Sundać and Krmpotić (2011) state that there is continuing discussion in both academia and the business sector, advancing that an ideas-driven, global knowledge economy (KE) constitutes a promising scenario for the future. In this regard, institutions of higher learning and business alike should revisit their mandates. They state that institutions of higher learning are compelled to adopt strategies that will foster innovation and creativity. According to Hughes and Kitson (2012), universities and research centers constitute strategic factors in the Knowledge Economy, as a better-skilled population is needed in order to create new knowledge and transform research outcomes into innovative products. If universities and research centers are key in a Knowledge Economy, then quality postgraduate supervision is key in ensuring that postgraduate programs at institutions of higher learning produce quality graduates and in turn play its role in the Knowledge Economy (Cloete, et al., 2013). Universities are known as knowledge producers and, the centrality of research as a key function in the triad of teaching, research and community service cannot be overemphasized (Zhao, 2001). According to Chireshe (2012), postgraduate students' research is a vital component of a university's research output.

DOI: 10.4018/978-1-7998-1017-9.ch008

Several definitions of postgraduate supervision exist and the description of the postgraduate supervisor is varied. Kimani (2014) describes the postgraduate supervisor as a coach, a facilitator, or a coordinator. In essence, the role of the postgraduate supervisor is to assist the postgraduate student to successfully complete specific tasks in line with the research process. This process requires the postgraduate supervisor to provide leadership and guidance to the student, as well as to manage properly the research process (Sambrook, 2008). Supervisors also adopt a variety of styles and ways of providing supervision. Postgraduate supervisors, in general, will have preferred styles of interactions with students. Supervisors could adopt a master-apprentice role (Zeegers and Barron, 2012), offering structure to the relationship or, have a laissez-faire relationship with the student (Sambrook, 2008). The variations of supervisory styles coupled, with the number of students under supervision the variation in student developmental capacity and, the complexity of thematic areas students may research creates a challenge for both postgraduate supervisor and student. Sambrook (2008) advances that this diversity of student capacity and interest, the supervisors' areas of interest and research focus areas of both student and supervisors have the potential for mismatches in expectations between the supervisor and student. Despite this diversity, Sambrook (2008) asserts that there is consensus internationally that postgraduate supervision focusses on two key dimensions, i.e., the provision of technical and social support, which in turn, influence supervisory styles.

In this dyad of supervisor and student, it is possible that the preferred style of a supervisor does not match the capacity, expectation or preference of a student. This misalignment of student and supervisor can have various consequences. These consequences may include situations that could lead to potential conflict (i.e. personality clashes or philosophical disagreements) between the supervisor and student. This conflict episode can have multiple implications for the progress of the student in the research process. For example, the conflict could lead to a request to change supervisor, which in turn can lead to a delay in progress made by the student. There are no readymade prescriptions or perfect recipe of how supervisors and students should interact and there is thus no guarantee that the supervisor-student pairing will be a workable one. This chapter will view the Supervisor-Student dyad through the lens of the Situational Leadership Model. The Situational Leadership Model advocates that a supervisor must assess the personal development levels of students given a specific task. After such an assessment, the supervisor, in line with the prescriptions of the Situational Leadership Model, should adopt an appropriate and matching leadership/supervisor style in order to be effective. Postgraduate supervisors can apply the Situational Leadership Model in the supervisor-student dyad. This could lead to applying a more appropriate and structured supervisor style that matches the developmental level of the student.

The chapter is conceptual and exploratory in scope and has the following structure. First, it explores the elements and definition of Postgraduate Research Supervision. Second, the chapter discusses the various approaches, the roles, and responsibilities of postgraduate supervision. Third, the chapter will discuss Post Graduate Student Supervision and linking it to Student Management. Fourth, the chapter will draw parallels between Leadership and postgraduate supervision. Fifth, the chapter introduces the Situational Leadership Model and its linkage to postgraduate supervision and finally, offer suggestions for future research on the topic.

BACKGROUND

The key functions of most universities are teaching, research and community service. While each function has a unique role to fulfil in a university, these functions are also interrelated and complementary. Chireshe (2010) argues that research informs the teaching and community service activities at a university and thus place the research at the center in the university setting. The centrality of research in a university setting means that universities will be inclined to focus on research. This focus on research, according to Mutala (2009a), can be sustained by developing research capacity among graduate students through research supervision. Chen and Kenney (2007) support the notion that graduate students not only contribute to research but that they play a significant role in innovation and economic development in many countries. Kimani (2014) puts forth that if it is assumed that universities are capable of providing an adequate foundation for the complexities of the knowledge economy through postgraduate research then, the quality of supervision of postgraduate students becomes critical. The criticality and quality of research supervision cannot be overemphasized. However, the literature on research supervision reports multiple interpretations of what supervision is, what it is supposed to be, what form of supervision is best, what constitutes effective and successful supervision and, what type of supervision produces better quality and so on. In fact, Roberts and Watson (2016) opine that it is unclear what accounts for 'good supervision' as there is no standardized guideline for supervisory practice and there is no documented, precise definition of the supervisors' roles.

This chapter does not intend to answer all these diverse and sometimes conflicting views of research supervision. This chapter is conceptual and exploratory in scope. The chapter does not attempt to make value judgments on which supervisory approach is best rather; this chapter offers a practical and tested model from the Leadership domain called the Situational Leadership Model (SLM) to overlay the complexity of postgraduate supervision. The Situational Leadership Model offers guidelines that have the potential to sensitize postgraduate supervisors about the varied capacity of each of the students they supervise and the supervisors' adoption of an appropriate style of supervision, in accordance with the prescriptions of the Situational Leadership Model

Post Graduate Research Supervision: Eluding Definition

The definitions of graduate supervision are multiple and varied. Roberts and Watson (2016) posit that graduate supervision is the process of aiding students to become members of an academic community, it is managing students and their research and, guiding students toward the completion of tasks outlined as part of the research process.

It is well known that postgraduate student's research is an important part of the university's research effort. Chireshe (2012) who highlights that research informs the teaching and community service activities at a university and thus place the research at the center in the university setting supports this view. The centrality of postgraduate research in university settings does not mean that research is elevated to the same level as faculty research. Scholars put forward that postgraduate research and research supervision is an advanced form of teaching (Connel, 1985), where supervision, is a process of fostering and enhancing learning, research, and communication (Laske, Zuber-Skerritt, 1996). Kimani (2014) underscores this view by stating that postgraduate supervision is a complex style of teaching and learning. The supervisory process is thus crucial to the success of postgraduate students and it is central to the achievement of quality, effectiveness, and productivity of the research process (Zhao, 2001).

Research supervision requires an array of skills. Beasley (1999) states that good supervisors must have research knowledge as well as management and interpersonal skills. He states that good supervisors must be:

- Innovative;
- Creative problem solvers;
- Resource-oriented;
- Work focussed;
- Technically expert;
- Decisive; and
- Dependable

Deist (1990), on the other hand, sees the task of the supervisor as ensuring that:

- the topic on which a candidate embarks does indeed present a problem;
- the candidate has a clear understanding of the field in which the problem occurs and of the problem itself;
- the candidate uses the correct methods to solve the problem and does an extended literature study of appropriate sources; and
- the problem is solved according to the requirements of the methods employed

Zhao (2001) is of the opinion that the stakeholders to this process view research supervision differently. For example, supervisors see research supervision different from how students see research supervision. Lee (2007) found that the view of research supervisors of research supervision affect the way supervisors provide supervision to their students. The approach to research supervision also affects the way the research students operate and ultimately, the type of researcher that emerges at the end of the process. So too, does the conceptions of students of research, the research process and research supervision, affect their respective perceptions of the process and the engagement with their supervisors.

While the existence of varied explanations points to conceptual ambiguity in defining research supervision, there is a shared acknowledgment of graduate supervision as a process (Roberts and Watson, 2016). What exactly the process entails varies among scholars and underscores the uncertainty associated with the supervisory practice (Roberts and Watson, 2016). Given the complex nature of supervision, coupled with the conceptual ambiguity of what supervision is and, the uncertainty of what the process entails, this chapter aims to draw on the Situational Leadership Model as a framework to offer insights into the dynamics associated with the supervisor/student dyad.

Post Graduate Research Supervision: Approaches, Roles and Responsibilities

The approaches to postgraduate programs can vary from institution to institution and even from country to country. Zeegers and Barron (2012) in their review of the pedagogy of postgraduate research undertakings, raised concerns about the so-called Oxbridge approach to graduate supervision. The Oxbridge approach advances that the novice student researcher learns from an academic who is assigned as the principal or coordinating supervisor. The assignment of the role of the supervisor is based on discipline rather than teaching knowledge (Zeegers and Barron, 2012). In this relationship, Green and Lee (1995) suggest that supervision carry powerful overtones of overseeing, looking over and looking after, production and development with regard to academic knowledge and identity (p 218). Other approaches advance supervision as a master-apprentice relationship where the supervisor creates a rite of passage (Bartlett and Mercer, 2001). These approaches to research supervision reflect the student as ignorant and in some way does not align to the view that research supervision a complex form of teaching (Connel, 1985). In practice, research supervisors ignore their role as teachers and adopt a laisses-fair approach, ignoring the assertion that research supervision is a complex extension of teaching. In such situations, supervisors tend to expect students to have all the requisite skills to conduct research on the selected thematic area.

Lessing & Schulze (2002) is of the opinion that the role of the supervisor is to guide, advise, ensure scientific quality and provide emotional support to the student. There are varying views on the independence or dependence of the two parties in the postgraduate research process. Some supervisors view the postgraduate student as an independent researcher while others view the student as one dependent upon the supervisor. The latter view will in essence also dictate the manner in which the supervisor will engage the student and the way the student will respond to the preferred supervisory styles. In practice, some supervisors argue strongly against spoon-feeding or handholding students and put forth that their role to purely one of providing intellectual expertise and to facilitate and counsel the student (Sidhu, et.al, 2013). Supervisors are not only expected to provide support, make themselves available to the student, and provide encouragement but also to provide resources and information, feedback and guidelines of thesis writing (Sidhu, et.al. 2013). Sidhu, et.al. (2013) further argue that the role of supervisors is not only academic matters but also to support students with personal problems.

Within postgraduate research, certain roles and responsibilities on the part of the supervisor-student dyad exist and are documented. Relationships in this dyad are informed in part by the approaches to graduate supervision as explained in the above paragraph. For example, if a supervisor approaches graduate supervision from the Oxbridge paradigm, one can expect that the supervisor will assume the role of overseer or foreperson. This situation could lead to the development of a master-apprentice relationship. The student, on the other hand, may also have varied interpretations of the role of the supervisor. Chireshe (2012) found that students interpret supervision as ruthless, when supervisors were unapproachable, where supervisors harassed them or when supervisors discouraged them. Whereas good supervision, according to Chireshe (2012) is where the supervisor is knowledgeable, friendly, and informative, are good listeners and motivates the student. This brings into question the problem of mismatched expectations between the parties in the research supervision dyad. The incongruence of expectations have the potential for negative consequences and ultimately a potential breakdown in relationships between supervisor and student.

Sambrook (2018) investigated the psychological contract between supervisors and students, looking into the respective role expectations. The psychological contract is an unwritten agreement that exists between employees and employer, and in the context of this chapter, between supervisors and students. This contract addresses the reciprocal promises and obligations in the relationship (Robbins and Judge, 2013). In the supervisor-student dyad, Sambrook (2018) puts forth that greater awareness of the contractual arrangements in postgraduate supervision can help improve the quality of student experiences as well as enhance the research collaborations. Conversely, Lee (2008) states that postgraduate supervision has been a "private act between consenting adults" (p269). It is mostly when things go wrong, i.e., when a supervisor neglects to guide the student or when the student neglects to respond to the guidance of a supervisor, that this psychological contract is invoked. In such situations, students want to change supervisors or supervisors choose to discontinue the relationship. Sambrook (2018) suggest that in order to avoid this scenario, institutions should consider developing guidelines on managing the psychological contract.

While Sambrook's suggestion of managing the psychological contract within research supervision may bring structure and guidelines to the supervisor-student relationship, it may fall short of enhancing the quality of graduate supervision. The fact that contractual arrangements are in place, does not automatically lead to enhanced quality in graduate supervision. The observations by Chireshe (2012) reflects that various other factors of an interpersonal nature tend to have a significant impact on the student's perceptions of good or bad research supervision. Consideration should be given to the dynamics of the supervisor-student dyad and the possibility of how interventions at this level can enhance postgraduate supervision.

Post Graduate Student Supervision: Student Management

There are definite parallels between postgraduate supervision and general management. Managers get things done through people, specifically through the activities of planning, organizing, leading and controlling. In both contexts, there is a dyad that consists of an academic supervisor or business manager on the one hand and on the other hand, a student or subordinate. In both cases there is a task to be completed within a time frame, by one (the student or subordinate) and this task is supervised or overseen by another (the supervisor or manager). The research supervisor's role is not unlike that of a manager who strives for effective management through informed observation, sensitive analysis, and appropriate application of skills as a leader (Vilkinas, 2002).

If there were parallels between postgraduate supervision and management, one would expect postgraduate research supervisors to deploy the functions of management (planning, organizing, leading and control), to get the research project done. This is not always the case. Supervisors who adopt the Oxbridge approach will, as Green and Lee (1995) puts it, display powerful overtones of overseeing, looking over and looking after, the production and development with regard to academic knowledge and identity. The Oxbridge approach, by its nature, is contrary to the hands-on activities of planning, organizing, leading and controlling.

In pursuing the parallels between research supervision and management, Robbins and Judge (2016) identify specific management roles, as adopted by Henry Mintzberg. These are:

- **Interpersonal Role:** This role is identified by Chireshe (2012) as key in student perception of a good supervisor. Chireshe (2012) reports that students regarded a supervisor as good when he/she managed the supervision process well. Good supervisors are also those who are friendly, good listeners and who motivates students (Chireshe 2012).
- **Information Role:** Students reported that a supervisor is good if they are knowledgeable and informative (Chireshe 2012) and,
- **Decision Role:** Students are required to make decisions about a variety of aspects as it relates to their research. Whether such decisions are about the methodology, conclusions or suggesting future research, for example. Chireshe (2012) reports that perceptions of good supervisors are of those who assist students and taking decisions by providing clear research guidelines.

In order to execute the interpersonal-, information-, and decision roles, Robbins and Judge (2016) put forth that effective managers require the following skills:

- **Technical Skills:** The ability to apply specialized knowledge and expertise. Postgraduate supervisors are regarded to have the requisite expertise and specialized knowledge of the thematic area of the students they supervise. Sambrook (2012) states that some supervisors see their role as purely technical, i.e., providing structure and subject-specific knowledge.
- **Human Skills:** The ability to work with, being able to understand and being able to motivate other people. Postgraduate supervisors, as indicated by Chireshe (2012), should also have the capacity to motivate students and encourage them to complete the research process.
- **Conceptual Skills:** The mental capacity to analyze and diagnose complex situations. Supervisors are deemed as good supervisors if they can help students navigate the complexity of the research process successfully and even, as per Sidhu, et.al. (2013) assist the student with their personal problems.

The roles and skills of managers are also required for the postgraduate supervisor-student dyad. Supervisors fulfil these respective roles and display their respective skills at various times in the postgraduate transactions.

Viliknas (2002) advances that in both business and the postgraduate research setting the manager or research supervisor is required to be knowledgeable of the task. She posits that the academic supervisor needs to perform two important roles. These roles are that of a knowledge expert and that of supervisor/manager since the supervisor must know the subject matter well and must have the capacity and understanding to work within the parameters of the system (Vilkinas, 2002). Zeegers and Barron (2012), Green and Lee (1995), and Bartlett and Mercer (2001) view the role of knowledge expert of the research supervisor as a key skill set.

There is a paucity of research into the role of the postgraduate supervisor as manager. Supervisors, like business managers, must have the capacity to determine which supervisory qualities are required at which times during the process of supervision (Vilkinas, 2002).

In an attempt to link research supervision to management, Gatfield (2005) investigated postgraduate supervisory styles by adopting the Blake and Mouton managerial grid. The Managerial Grid stems from the era of leader behavior approaches and is concerned with depicting management styles. The objective of the Managerial Grid is to analyze and assign preferred management styles to individuals based on objective criteria. The Managerial Grid joins concern for people and concern for production in a model with two intersecting axes. The horizontal axes address the concern for people, i.e., the degree to which the manager is people-centered and concerned about good interpersonal relations and the vertical axes, is the concern for production, i.e., the degree to which the manager is concerned with getting the job done, ensuring procedures are followed and the overall volume of output. Eighty-one management styles are assigned to a manager according to the prescriptions of the Managerial Grid. Gatfield (2005) succeeded in clustering twelve academic supervisors on the Managerial grid, plotting their preferred styles when engaged in graduate research undertakings. Gatfield's (2005) conclusions show that most supervisors report both high concern for the task as well as a high concern for people. This means that supervisors are not unidimensional in their approach to supervision.

While Gatield's insights are useful, it falls short of offering clarity on the capacity and personal development level of the student in the postgraduate research dyad, and in particular the adoption of a supervisory style given the developmental level of the student. Similarly, Gu, He, and Liu (2017) adopted cognitive theory and leadership theory and set out to test a theoretical model linking supervisory styles with graduate student creativity. They specifically looked at supportive and directive supervisory styles and its link to graduate student creativity and report that creative self-efficacy and intrinsic motivation mediate the influences of supportive and directive supervisory styles on student creativity. Their results indicate a positive influence of directive supervisory style on graduate student creativity (Gu, He & Liu, 2017). While this study also offers good insights on how two different supervisory styles impact graduate student creativity, the findings of the relationship between leadership styles and creativity are mixed and inconclusive (Gu, He, & Liu, 2017).

The literature on linking student supervision to student management leads us closer to conceptualizing student supervision from a leadership angle. In this regard, this conceptual chapter puts forth that the Situational Leadership Model is an appropriate lens through which one can view how the personal development capacity of students (followers) influences the selection of an appropriate supervisor (leadership) style. This approach is more dynamic than the Managerial Grid of Blake and Mouton.

LEADERSHIP AND RESEARCH SUPERVISION

Leadership is the art of influence. According to Stogdill, (1974) leadership can be considered as the process (act) of influencing the activities of an organized group in its efforts toward goal setting and goal achievement. Rauch and Behling (1984) see leadership as the process of influencing the activities of an organized group toward goal achievement, while Northhouse (2004) view leadership as a process whereby an individual influences a group of individuals to achieve a common goal. While many other definitions of leadership exist, the above suffice for this chapter. Most definitions capture the following terms (Daft, 2017):

- **Influence:** That there is an active relationship between leaders and follower. What is also important to note here is that this influence is reciprocal i.e., that while leaders can influence followers, followers in turn also influence leaders.
- **Change:** Leadership involves creating change towards an outcome for both leader and follower.

Postgraduate supervision is also about influence and change. The supervisor with the requisite skills (technical, human and conceptual) aims through influence, to change the skills sets and enhance the subject-specific knowledge of the student. The process requires the supervisor to direct the student in research and with guidance, produce a final product, which is a Thesis. This process in itself is transformative to both the supervisor and the student and thus leads to change for both.

Situational Leadership Model

The Situational leadership Model focusses on leadership in various situations. The premise of the model is that different situations demand different kinds of leadership (Northhouse, 2019). This model developed by Paul Hersey and Ken Blanchard in 1969 and originated as the life-cycle theory of leadership

(Hersey and Blanchard 1969). The conceptual basis of the Situational leadership has been criticized (Graeff, 1983), and its major hypotheses remained largely untested (Vecchio, 1987). However, despite the critique, this model is, without doubt, one of the most popular leadership models for practitioners.

The Situational leadership Model advocates that a leader should adopt his/her leadership styles based on a combination of relationship (concern for people) and task (concern for production) behavior (Northouse, 2019). This combination maps with what Sambrook (2012) refers to as the technical and social support postgraduate supervisors' offer, which in turn influences their research supervisory styles.

The model flow from the assumption that there is a task to be completed and that there is a follower (s) who should execute those tasks and achieve the desired outcome, i.e., a completed thesis. The model advances that the leader first diagnose the development level of the follower for a specific task and thereafter determine the appropriate leadership style for the identified personal developmental levels of followers. The model proposes a taxonomy consisting of four leadership styles, ranging from directing to delegating, and a framework for matching each style to specific situations (Thompson and Glasø, 2014).

The Situational Leadership Model also postulates four levels of follower development levels. Roe (2014) states that a leader must consider a number of factors to assess correctly the personal development level of followers. These include task complexity, the skills the follower has in relation to the task, the drive, and energy to start and complete the task as well as other historical data i.e., how well they performed on similar tasks previously (Roe, 2014). For example, a new employee may take some time to understand the job and the how of certain tasks to complete within a specific context.

In relation to the postgraduate supervisor-student dyad, it is likely that a supervisor will have a student(s) who have varying levels of personal development capacity and in line with the prescriptions of the Situational leadership Model; the supervisor should consider this when supervising the student. This diagnostic approach is crucial to determine the appropriate style. A mismatch in this dyad may lead to negative consequences. For example, a postgraduate supervisor who believes that his/her role is only to offer technical skills and no social support may be missing the mark in terms of providing the holistic support the student may require.

Workings of the Situational Leadership Model

The core of the Situational Leadership Model is the interaction between the leadership style and the developmental capacity level of followers. In the case of the postgraduate supervisor-student dyad, the interaction between supervisor style and graduate student developmental capacity for a specific task, function or objective. The effective leader should adopt an appropriate leader style given the personal development level of the follower (Hersey, Blanchard & Johnson, 1996). According to this model, there is no one best leadership style. Effective leadership is determined by the leaders' capacity to adapt his or her style depending on the follower developmental capacity.

Categories of Follower Personal Development Level

The prescriptions of the Situational leadership Model indicate four categories of follower capacity or personal development level:

- **Developmental Level 1:** This follower is unable and insecure and, do not possess the necessary skills or drive to complete the task. A student, new to the process of graduate supervision could feel a sense of anxiety and be insecure to tackle the process. It is also possible that the student will not exactly know how and where to start.
- **Developmental Level 2:** This follower though unable to complete the task, displays a willingness to want to try to complete the task. While this follower may lack the knowledge, ability or skill, this follower is willing and is motivated. Students can display a willingness and be eager to tackle the process but may lack the technical expertise to start and proceed in the research process. This situation arises often when students do not fully understand the magnitude of the research process and mistakenly view the project as a class assignment.
- **Developmental Level 3:** This follower has the technical knowledge and skills to execute the task but may lack the motivation to do so. This follower may also be insecure or nervous about the task. Students can pose skills but may lack the motivation to start and continue with the process. The reasons for this state can be multiple. For example, the time slot for the research project is normally at the end of the coursework. This, coupled with the fact that some students are employed full time, can lead to a lack of motivation.
- **Developmental Level 4:** This follower is ready, willing and able to perform the task. The follower poses the required technical skills and is confident to complete the task. It is possible that some students are both skilled and motivated to tackle the research.

The above-listed categories of follower developmental levels can be applied to the postgraduate research dyad and in particular to the student developmental levels. Within a given cohort, one will find a mix of students at varying personal developmental levels. It is advantageous for a research supervisor to understand each student's developmental levels in order to adopt an appropriate supervisory style.

Categories of Leader Style

The Situational Leadership Model prescribes variations of leader styles based on a combination of relationship behavior and task behavior. Relationship behavior refers to the extent to which the leader engages in giving support, facilitating, communication, active listening and providing feedback (Hersey, Blanchard, and Johnson (1996). Task behavior refers to the extent to which the leader engages in defining roles, goal setting, organizing, establishing timelines, directing and controlling (Hersey, Blanchard and Johnson, 1996). The prescriptions of the Situational Leadership Model provide four categories of leader styles.

- Style 1: Directing/telling: this style is characterized by high task behavior and low relationship behavior. The typical behaviors of this leader will be systematic instructions and close supervision, with a clear task focus. For example, the leader with this style will give instructions on what and how a task must be completed while closely supervising followers.
- Style 2: Explaining/clarifying/persuading/coaching. This style is characterized by high task behavior and high relationship behavior. Typical behaviors will be that the leader will have a closer personal interaction with followers where the leader will reinforce good behavior. However, the task behavior is also part of the style and the leader will still address the "what" and "how" of task completion.

- Style 3: Encouraging/participating/collaborating. This style is characterized by low task and high relationship behavior. The typical leader behaviors are offering support with relatively less directive instruction.
- Style 4: Delegating/monitoring. This style is characterized by low task and low relationship behavior. The leader now delegates, and is hands-off while trusting that the follower will remain motivated and will get the task done.

The figure illustrates the interaction between task and relationship behaviour and how these two elements combine to prescribe each of the four leadership styles. The Situational Leadership Model postulates that the most appropriate leadership style is the one that matches the assessment of follower personal development level. For example, for the student at the developmental level one (D1), the suggested supervisory style is S1 or Directing Style, i.e., high task and high relationship behaviors. The opposite end of the spectrum displays a student who has high personal development, who has the appropriate knowledge and skills and who is confident to complete the task (D4). According to the prescriptions of the Situational Leadership Model, the appropriate supervisory style is S4 or Delegating Style, i.e., low task and low relationship behavior. The model is clear that it should not be no task or relationship behavior but low levels of interaction.

Figure 1. Adopted from Northouse (2019)

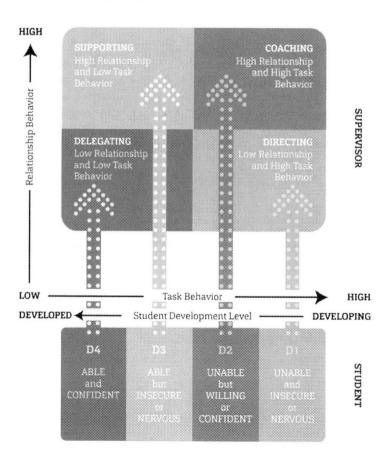

The Situational Leadership Model highlights the fact that leaders or supervisors must be attuned to the development levels of their students. It is also possible that a supervisor can make an inaccurate assessment of the student developmental level. For example, a student could be a D4 and the supervisor could adopt an S1 style. Such a condition could lead to a misunderstanding between a supervisor and the student and has the potential to lead to a conflict episode.

Future Areas of Research

This conceptual chapter draws attention to the application of the popular Situational Leadership Model. Practitioners in organizations use this model extensively as a training approach. The chapter suggests the application of this model to the postgraduate supervisor/student dyad. The model advocates that supervisors of postgraduate students be aware of the fact that students will be at varying developmental levels and those supervisors must diagnose these levels, in line with the prescriptions of the model, and then select an appropriate supervisory style for effective engagement of the student.

Future research should look into whether the prescriptions of the Situational Leadership Model will hold for the supervisor/student dyad in an academic environment. An interesting area for research may be the influence of gender, age and their likely impact on the supervisor's capacity to appropriately assess student developmental levels and select appropriate supervisory styles.

A further research focus could be to investigate if emotional intelligence of both student and supervisor in this dyad has an influence on the developmental levels of students and the adopted leadership style of supervisors. Lastly, a number of other leadership models or theories can be overlaid onto the supervisor/student dyad in order to gain better insights into the effectiveness of postgraduate supervision. For example, House's Path-Goal Theory may offer insights into the postgraduate research process. Another approach, for example, could be to apply Transactional analysis. Transactional analysis is a system of popular psychology based on the idea that one's behavior and social relationships reflect an interchange between parental (critical and nurturing), adult (rational), and childlike (intuitive and dependent) aspects of personality established early in life. This lens could be useful for investigating the dynamics of supervisors who adopt the Oxbridge approach.

CONCLUSION

Supervisor style and supervisor preference, have been well documented. For example, supervisors who subscribe to the Oxbridge paradigm, tend to see the supervisor-student dyad as a master-mentor relationship. Gatfield (2012), managed to apply the Blake and Mouton Managerial grid to plot preferred supervisory styles when engaging with students, while Vilkinas (2002) used the Competing Values Framework to illustrate the capabilities required for successful postgraduate supervision. These empirical endeavors are useful as they offer different insights into the postgraduate research supervision process and in particular to the dynamics in the process. However, the focus of these studies was on the supervisor role or what the supervisor did but did not take into account the developmental levels of students.

Empirical evidence also exists that report student perceptions of what good or bad supervision is. (Chireshe, 2012 &Sidhu, et.al, 2013). What is lacking from the readings is the recognition of the developmental level of students and how this may or may not impact supervisory styles and how these supervisors styles then is described as either good or bad

When considering the diverse approaches to supervision, the diverse expectations of postgraduate students of the supervision they receive, and when considering the diverse institutional requirements for successful supervision, it is evident that postgraduate research supervisors require training and regular upskilling on how to be successful at the postgraduate research activity. Such training should empower postgraduate research supervisors to have a clear understanding of their roles and responsibilities. Supervisors need to manage effectively the relationship with their students; they need to be friendly, open, approachable and supportive towards their students.

The application of the Situational Leadership Model to postgraduate supervision and in particular the dynamics of the supervisor-student dyad requires refinement and testing to establish if merit exists to make a case for training supervisors in this model. While the context of the Situational Leadership Model, its popularity and its extensive application in practice, stems from industry and business organizations, the views advanced in this paper promotes consideration for the Situational Leadership Model in the context of the supervisor-student dyad. From practical insights into the dynamics of the supervisor-student dyad, indicators exist that supervisors can benefit from the principles of the Situational Leadership Model when applied to postgraduate supervision. Observations support the notion that students feel frustrated and demotivated if their supervisor fails to understand their personal development level and respond to them with a firmly rooted and preferred style that does not match the student expectation. Where such situations exist, students tend to seek to change supervisors. This activity can lead to delays in the completion of the research project as well as the negative and unpleasant perception of postgraduate research. In practice, supervisors also at times seek not to further engage with a particular student. This situation arises where the supervisor views the student as not responding appropriately to his/her guidance. Supervisors need to be appropriately trained and sensitized to the fact that not all students are the same, in terms of personal developmental levels and, that varying levels of personal development require variations in supervisor style. Such awareness may contribute to enhanced collaboration between supervisor and student, ultimately leading to a better experience for both and perhaps a better quality output.

REFERENCES

Bartlett, A., & Mercer, G. (2001). Introduction. In A. Bartlett & G. Mercer (Eds.), *Postgraduate Research Supervision: Transforming Relations. Peter Lang*. doi:10.1007/978-1-4615-1637-8_2

Chen, K., & Kenney, M. (2007). Universities/Research Institutes and Regional Innovation Systems: The Cases of Beijing and Shenzhen. *World Development, 35*(6), 1056–1074. doi:10.1016/j.worlddev.2006.05.013

Chireshe, R. (2010). Why Articles Are Not Accepted For Publication: Guest Editorial Experiences. Consolidating Research, Innovation and Technology Platforms for a Knowledge-based Economy. *WSU Research Conference Proceedings*, 162-172.

Cloete, N., Maassen, P., & Teboho, M. (2013). *Higher Education and different notions of development. IIE Newsletter*. Institute of International Education.

Connell, R. (1985). How to supervise a Ph.D. *Vestes, 2*, 38–41.

Daft, R. L. (2018). *The Leadership experience* (7th ed.). Singapore: Cengage.

Deist, F. E. (1990). The role of the promoter. *Theologia Evangelica, 23*(3), 66–68.

Gatfield. (2005). An investigation into Ph.D. supervisory management styles: Development of a dynamic conceptual model and its managerial implications. *Journal of Higher Education Policy and Management,* 311-325.

Graeff, C. (1983). The Situational Leadership Theory: A critical view. *Academy of Management Review, 8*(2), 285–291. doi:10.5465/amr.1983.4284738

Green, B., & Lee, A. (1995). Conclusion. In A. Lee & B. Green (Eds.), *Postgraduate Studies/Postgraduate Pedagogy.* Sydney: University of Technology.

Gu, J., He, C., & Liu, H. (2017). Supervisory Styles and graduate student creativity: The mediating roles of creative self-efficacy and intrinsic motivation. *Studies in Higher Education, 42*(4), 721–742.

Hersey, P., & Blanchard, K. (1969). The life cycle theory of leadership. *Training and Development Journal.*

Hersey, P., Blanchard, K. H., & Johnson, D. E. (1996). *Management of Organizational behavior: Utilising human resources* (7th ed.). Upper Saddle River, NJ: Prentice Hall.

Hughes, A., & Kitson, M. (2012). Pathways to impact and the strategic role of universities: New evidence on the breadth and depth of university knowledge exchange in the UK and the factors constraining its development. *Cambridge Journal of Economics, 36*(3), 723–750. doi:10.1093/cje/bes017

Kimani, E. N. (2014). Challenges in Quality Control for postgraduate supervision.; *International Journal of Humanities Social Sciences and Education,* 63-70.

Laske, S., & Zuber-Skerrit, O. (1996). *Framework for Post Graduate Research and Supervision.* Lismore: Southern Cross University Press.

Lee, A. (2007). Developing effective supervisors: Concepts of research supervision. *South African Journal of Higher Education, 21*(4), 680–693.

Lee, A. (2008). How are doctoral students supervised? Concepts of doctoral research supervision. *Studies in Higher Education, 33*(3), 267–281. doi:10.1080/03075070802049202

Lessing, A. C., & Schulze, S. (2002). Postgraduate Supervision and Academic Support: Students' Perceptions. *South African Journal of Higher Education., 16*(2), 139–149. doi:10.4314ajhe.v16i2.25253

Mutula, S. M. (2009). Challenges of Postgraduate Research: Global Context, African Perspectives. Keynote Address Delivered at the University of Zululand. *10th DLIS Annual Conference.*

Nakabugo, M. G., & Ssebunga Masembe, C. (2004). Supervisor-Supervisee relationship: a rose without thorns? In Graduate studies at Makerere University: A book of readings. Nelson.

Northhouse, P. G. (2004). *Leadership: theory and practice* (3rd ed.). Thousand Oaks, CA: Sage.

Robbins, S. P., Timothy, A., & Judge, T. A. (2013). *Organizational Behavior* (15th ed.). Boston: Pearson.

Roberts, N., & Watson, D. (2016). Re-imagining graduate supervision. *Caribbean Teaching Scholar, 6,* 27–42.

Roe, K. (2014). *Leadership: Practice and perspectives*. Oxford University Press.

Sambrook, S. (2018). *Managing the psychological contract within Doctoral Supervisory relationships*. Research Gate.

Sidhu, G. K., Kaur, S Fook, C. Y., & Yunus, F. W. (2013). Postgraduate supervision: Comparing student perspectives from Malaysia and the United Kingdom. *Social and Behavioral Sciences, 123,* 151 – 159.

Stogdill, R. M. (1974). *Handbook on Leadership*. New York, NY: The Free Press.

Sundać, D., & Fatur Krmpotić, I. (2011). Knowledge economy factors and the development of the knowledge-based economy. *Croatian Economic Survey, 13*(1), 105–141.

Thompson, G., & Glaso, L. (2015, July 6). Situational leadership theory: A test from three perspectives. *Leadership and Organization Development Journal, 36*(5), 527–544. doi:10.1108/LODJ-10-2013-0130

Vecchio, R. P. (1987). Situational Leadership Theory: An examination of a prescriptive theory. *The Journal of Applied Psychology, 72*(3), 444–451. doi:10.1037/0021-9010.72.3.444

Vilkinas, T. (2002). The PhD process: The supervisor as manager. *Education + Training, 44*(3), 129–137. doi:10.1108/00400910210424337

Zeegers, M., & Barron, D. (2012). Pedagogical concerns in doctoral supervision: A challenge for pedagogy. *Quality Assurance in Education, 20*(1), 20–30. doi:10.1108/09684881211198211

Zhao, F. (2001). Postgraduate Research Supervision: A process of knowledge management. *ultiBASE Articles*. Retrieved from http://ultibase.rmit.edu.au/Articles/may/01/zhao1.htm

Chapter 9
Fair Process in Assessing the Quality of University Faculty

Denise A. D. Bedford
Georgetown University, USA

ABSTRACT

This chapter presents an exploratory research framework designed to support quality assessment of faculty in higher education. First, a neutral view of a university is developed which highlights five essential business capabilities, including teaching, research, advising, advocacy, and convening. Activity models are constructed for each capability – identifying inputs, activities, and outputs. Faculty preparation and contributions to inputs, activities, and outputs/outcomes are modeled and described. Deming's model of quality is applied to the five activity models. The quality model is applied to faculty (e.g., tenure and tenure-track, non-tenure track, adjunct, graduate students, clinical, and other specialized faculty). Finally, the research explores whether the current quality management processes are fair for faculty and effective for the university's stakeholders. The exploratory research offers six observations and recommendations. The most significant observation is that only one of the five business capabilities – research has a fair and effective quality process.

INTRODUCTION

Quality has always been an important factor in higher education. Quality of education is a competitive factor and a comparative advantage for universities. Over the past sixty years education has been within reach of a significant portion of the population. The demand for higher education has continued to increase. The increase is not limited to the traditional high school graduating base or traditional "college age" populations. In the first quarter of the 21st century, advanced learning is now understood to be both lifelong and lifewide. Who is learning has changed dramatically. The demand for higher education has been addressed not only by an increase in the number of colleges and universities, but in alternative forms and access. As a result, who is producing and who is consuming higher education has changed significantly.

DOI: 10.4018/978-1-7998-1017-9.ch009

Fair Process in Assessing the Quality of University Faculty

In this context of change, the concept of quality may also be shifting. This chapter focuses on the most important quality element of higher education – faculty – and considers how the definition and perspective on quality might be shifting. Who is delivering higher education and why will affect the criteria we use to judge quality. Who is paying for education will affect how quality is measured and judged. Who teaches and who learns will affect how quality is assessed. How we define and assess research quality will be judged by who conducts research. Who does what kinds of research will also affect the research literacies that faculty and researchers bring to the university. Will these reflect traditional research quality criteria? Where people are learning will affect the quality of delivery channels or learning environments. And, perhaps most important from a faculty perspective – how do these changes affect the quality and balance of competencies one faculty is expected to bring to higher education.

We care about these changes and their effect on quality because quality is defined by stakeholders, stakeholder expectations and the value we deliver to stakeholders. Where stakeholder shift, quality processes may also shift. We care about these changes because quality is defined by the context in which we deliver value. As the context changes, so will the definition and assessment of quality change. Finally, universities and colleges have had few competitors in the past. Quality has been defined by universities for their audiences and populations. With a broadening market, universities and colleges may need to consider how quality is being defined by players beyond their traditional boundaries.

Universities are and have always been complex operations – they do many things and serve many stakeholders. The expanding boundaries of higher education have highlighted the fact that faculty quality criteria and assessment have been focused primarily on research and teaching. As teaching is increasingly handed off to adjuncts, graduate students and specialized staff, quality increases focuses on research. This paper begins with the assumption that it is important to view quality more broadly – to consider quality for all of the roles that faculty play. In fact, we suggest that as the boundaries of higher education expand, the quality criteria and methods of higher education provided a strong foundation for assessing the quality of all providers.

Higher education quality management is a challenging question because universities and higher education ultimately produce and consume people – educated people and knowledge. We focus this chapter on the quality process as it pertains to one of the universities primary stakeholders and inputs – faculty. We consider faculty quality from the perspective of the primary business areas or capabilities that a university performs.

In 2019 the general public assumes that our higher education faculty represents the best and the brightest minds of the country. In order to maintain this stock of high quality intellectual capital colleges and universities must have rigorous and sustainable quality management processes in place for faculty – for recruiting, developing, leveraging and retaining faculty. This chapter is an exploration of what those processes are today and what they will need to be in the future. We begin by considering the nature of higher education business. Understanding higher education as a business is essential for applying widely accepted quality management models and methods. This chapter leverages the well-established quality assessment methods used in business and industry. The chapter also considers whether the quality assessment models an methods are fair and effective. We consider fairness in relation to the faculty who are being assessed. We consider effectiveness in relation to the college and university that is being assessed. We consider fairness and effectiveness at the business capability level. We also consider whether the current quality and fairness models likely to sustain in the changing context of higher education.

The chapter takes the form of thought paper intended to reframe how we think about, prepare for and assess the quality of higher education faculty. The chapter presents exploratory research. The chapter is organized into three broad sections. In the first section, we describe the context and exploratory research strategy. The second section forms the majority of the chapter and focuses on the research questions, their grounding in the literature, the models, methods and sources that supported the exploratory research. Each research question and its results are presented sequentially to accommodate for the dependencies across research questions. Finally, the third section offers exploratory observations and suggestions for reframing and enhancing the current quality management processes for faculty in higher education.

RESEARCH QUESTIONS AND RESEARCH CONTEXT

This chapter is exploratory and conceptual intended to frame a problem for further discussion and research. To support the research goals, we present and discuss seven exploratory research questions, including:

- **Research Question 1:** What are the core operational business capabilities of higher education?
- **Research Question 2:** What are the activity models – inputs, processes, outputs – that support each of these core business capabilities?
- **Research Question 3:** How does faculty support these activities models?
- **Research Question 4:** What are the quality management models for these activity models?
- **Research Question 5:** How do the quality management models vary by faculty status and role?
- **Research Question 6:** What does fair process tell us about the quality management model for each core business capability?
- **Research Question 7:** Are these quality and fairness models likely to sustain in the changing context of higher education?

To support and test the dependencies across the research questions we designed a three stage exploratory model (Figure 1). In Stage 1 we develop a neutral view of a university in terms of its essential business capabilities (Exploratory Question 1). For each capability model we present an activity or systems model to assist in identifying inputs, activities/processes and outputs/outcomes (Exploratory Question 2). In this context, we consider faculty activities and competencies to perform and support these capabilities (Exploratory Question 3).

In Stage 2 we establish a framework for managing the quality of faculty inputs, activities and outputs/outcomes of each capability (Exploratory Question 4). We consider how the framework is applied to different faculty roles and stakeholders (Exploratory Question 5). Finally, in Stage 3 we consider whether the current quality management processes are fair and effective for faculty and for the university's stakeholders. We define "fair" in terms of fair process elements including engagement, explanation and clarity of explanation (Exploratory Question 6). We define "effective" in terms of changes that we are likely to see in the future (Exploratory Question 7)

Fair Process in Assessing the Quality of University Faculty

Figure 1. Three Stage Exploratory Research Model

RESEARCH QUESTION 1: WHAT ARE THE CORE OPERATIONAL BUSINESS CAPABILITIES OF HIGHER EDUCATION?

Research Question 1 Literature Review

Higher education institutions, as knowledge-intensive organizations, have been in the knowledge business for a long time (Dumay, 2009) (Edvinsson and Malone, 1997) (Fazlagic 2007) (Guthrie, 2001) (Handzic and Ozlen 2009) (Hellstrom and Husted 2004) (Leitner 2002) (Sveiby 1997) (Sanchez and Elena 2006) (Sanchez Elena and Castrillo 2009) (Barnett 1997) (Knapp and Siegel 2009) (Rich 2006) (Carlson and Fleisher 2002).

Williams (2007) and Warhurst (2008) have suggested that intellectual capital is a university's most valuable and strategic capital asset. Attracting and retaining high quality intellectual capital – in the form of faculty - is vital to the university's ability to achieve quality outputs and outcomes (Handzic and Ozlen 2011).

Research Question 1 Model, Methodology and Source Data

To an outsider all colleges and universities appear to have similar goals, structures and management practices. Upon closer review, though, every higher education organization has its own cultures, history and strategies. They organize themselves around these essential elements. If we intend to do cross-organizational research on quality management of faculty we need a neutral framework.

This exploratory research leverages business capability modeling to provide a neutral framework of a college and university. A business capability is what the organization does to perform or produce something of value to the organization's stakeholders (Teece Pisano and Shuen 1997). A capability is expressed in terms of outcomes and services that provide value to stakeholders. Capabilities describe *what* the organization delivers as opposed to *how* the organization works or *how* (business process) it delivers the *what*. An organization's full repertoire of business capabilities takes the form of a Business on a Page (BOAP). A Business on a Page (Figure 2) organizes capabilities into three categories, including (1) strategic capabilities; (2) operational or core capabilities; and (3) enabling capabilities.

Figure 2. Research Model - University Represented as a Business on a Page

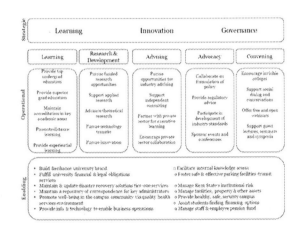

Strategic capabilities are those dedicated to setting the future direction and driving the organization. The university used as an example has three strategic capability areas – learning, innovation and governance.

Enabling capabilities are those which support the day to day functioning of the organization. These capabilities and their use of intellectual capital add value indirectly. For this university there are fourteen enabling capabilities. In five years working with the Business on a Page methodology, we have found that there is consistency in strategic and enabling capabilities.

It is *core or operational capabilities* that distinguish one organization from another. Operational or core capabilities are those that define the essential business of the organization. These capabilities must be – valuable, rare, costly to imitate, non-substitutable. Capabilities that help a firm exploit opportunities to create value for customers or to neutralize threats in the environment are Valuable. Capabilities that are possessed by few current or potential competitors are difficult to imitate, result from complex relationships that cannot be replicated - trust, teamwork, informal relationships, causal ambiguity (Rare). Capabilities that other firms cannot develop easily because of unique historical conditions, causal ambiguity or social complexity are Costly to Imitate. Capabilities that do not have strategic equivalents, such as firm-specific knowledge or trust-based relationship are Non-substitutable. This speaks directly to the use of intellectual capital assets.

The exploratory research was based on the earlier work reported by Bedford (2013). This work was based on an analysis of fifteen public and fifteen private research universities and fifteen public and fifteen private four-year colleges. To support this research, the five high level capabilities were further analyzed against the academic websites of fifteen two-year and community colleges.

Research Question 1 Exploratory Results

Based on previous cross-university research (Bedford 2013) we suggest that a typical university will have five core operational business capabilities, including:

(1) Teaching
(2) Research and Development
(3) Advising

(4) Advocacy
(5) Convening

These high level operational capability areas break down into 28 capabilities (Table 1). For each core capability we suggest a scope, explain why it is important to higher education and who the new competitors might be in a changing 21st century knowledge economy.

The *Teaching and Learning* capability includes undergraduate teaching, graduate teaching, teaching lifelong learners (sometimes referred to as continuing education), teaching intensive and short courses, teaching workshops, maintaining academic program accreditation, teaching distance and online courses, promoting experiential learning and coaching and mentoring students through extracurricular activities and learning. This capability is core to any college or university. It is also a source of increasing competition from other learning institutions and organizations today. It is critical that higher education maintains quality here as a competitive advantage in the education market.

The Research and Development capability includes conducting funded research, applied research, theoretical research and transdisciplinary research, innovative and exploratory research. This capability also includes moving research to production and development including technology transfer. It also includes all stages of the research life cycle from idea generation and methodology formulation to the conduct of research and the communication of research results. Higher education has long been the primary source of new knowledge and innovation for the nation – this capability has value to the university but also to the country as a whole. This capability has a rapidly expanding foundation (Agrawal 2001) (Anton and Yao 2005) (Arora 1995) (Arora 1996) (Bullen Fahey and Kenway 2006). With a more educated population, with companies becoming 'knowledge organizations' we increasingly find research

Table 1. Breakdown of Core and Operational Business Capabilities for a University

Teaching and Learning	Research and Development	Advising	Advocacy	Convening
Undergraduate Teaching	Conduct Funded Research	Advise Industry	Advocate for Policy	Organize Conferences and Meetings
Graduate Teaching	Conduct Applied Research	Engage in Consulting	Advocate for de facto and de jure standards	Participate in Invisible Colleges
Teaching Lifelong Learners (Continuing Education)	Conduct Theoretical Research	Collaborate with the Private Sector	Give Expert Testimony	Organize seminars and workshops
Teaching Short Courses and Workshops	Conduct Transdisciplinary Research	Support External Executive and Organizational Development	Sponsor Events and Conferences	Generate webinars and podcasts
Maintain Academic Accreditation	Engage in Innovative and Exploratory Research	Provide Regulatory Advice	Advocate for Non-Profit Organizations	
Teach Distance Learning Students	Engage in Technology Transfer			
Promote Experiential Education				
Coach and Mentor Extracurricular Learning				

being conducted in non-traditional environments. This means that universities may now be competing with research institutions, with private sector laboratories, with public sector laboratories and research institutes. Quality, credibility and trustworthiness will be competitive factors in this new environment.

The Advising capability has multiple audiences, including internal students and staff, external clients and consumers. Faculty have traditionally been responsible for both internal and external advising when enrolments were lower and where student to faculty ratios were low. However, as enrolments grow faculty time may not be used to best comparative advantage for advising. In these cases, advising may be handed off to staff and the advising capability may be more narrowly defined to meeting institutional requirements or certification criteria. This may impact quality – not only of student success but also of student career development. This is a capability where quality should be given greater faculty attention. Additionally, faculty time is valued for external advising – particularly to paying clients, external community leaders or as regulatory or legislative experts. In the advising capability universities may find themselves in direct competition with think tanks and other research institutes.

The Advocacy capability includes policy advocacy, advocating for de facto and de jure standards, providing expert testimony, advocating for non-profit or vulnerable groups. Advocacy also increasingly include political, social and economic advocacy. In this regard, quality is a distinguishing factor. Quality of advocacy may be judged by reliability and validity, trustworthiness and credibility. In this capability, university faculty increasingly find themselves pulled into other competitors as paid consultants. This may influence the quality of advocacy where faculty affiliate with think tanks and other advocacy groups that do not maintain the neutrality and standards promoted in higher education.

Finally, the Convening capability includes organizing conferences and meetings, developing the content for events, participating in invisible colleges, developing webinars or podcasts and generally building and supporting communities of practice and interest. Convening is an important capability for maintaining the health of academic and subject communities. Faculty quality is frequently assessed on participation in professional associations and major conferences. This is a representation of faculty stature in the general academic community.

RESEARCH QUESTION 2: WHAT ARE THE ACTIVITY MODELS – INPUTS, PROCESSES, OUTPUTS – THAT SUPPORT EACH OF THESE CORE BUSINESS CAPABILITIES?

Having established a neutral business capability framework in Research Question 1, Research Question 2 focuses on developing neutral activities models. Activity models are defined for all five capabilities.

Research Question 2 Literature Review

The higher education capabilities for which faculty are critical are not generally described or discussed as "systems". This may be because our perception of the work that faculty do for a college or university is "intellectual" in nature rather than "process". The fact that these capabilities presume a different set of inputs and processes does deny the fact that teaching, research, advising, advocacy and convening are all processes. This leaves faculty vulnerable to a less than rigorous review of whether the capability is well understood, is being fully supported, is appropriately assessed and is fair to all those involved. We cannot look to the literature of higher education for references. Rather, we translate and interpret the work of researchers in the management and engineering fields (Brits, Botha and Herselman 2006) (Homann, Levy, Merrifield, Appel, Davidson, Isaacs and Judah 2006) (Salviano and Figueiredo 2008) (Fleischer, Herm and Ude 2007) (Zott, Amit and Massa 2011) (Rajala and Westerlund 2007).

Research Question 2 Research Model, Methodology and Source Data

In this section we construct an activity model or a systems representation for each of the high level business capabilities. An activity model defines the inputs, the activities or processes that are carried out and the outputs and outcomes that are produced by the activity (Figure 3). This perspective is essential for considering whether quality management is rigorous and whether it is fair and effective to faculty and all other stakeholders. We need to understand what quality attributes faculty are expected to have for each capability, how they develop them, how they are used to perform the activity and how they do or do not produce quality outputs and outcomes.

The research methodology consisted of open ended questions posted to seventeen faculty representing tenured, tenure-track, non-tenure track, adjunct and administrative faculty. The questions included:

- What are the essential inputs for teaching? What are the essential activities involved in teaching? What are the outputs and outcomes of teaching?
- What are the essential inputs for research? What are the essential activities involved in research? What are the outputs and outcomes of research?
- What are the essential inputs for advising? What are the essential activities involved in advising? What are the outputs and outcomes of advising?
- What are the essential inputs for advocacy? What are the essential activities involved in advocacy? What are the outputs and outcomes of advocacy?
- What are the essential inputs for convening? What are the essential activities involved in convening? What are the outputs and outcomes of convening?

The responses were recorded as interview notes. The results were synthesized and are presented below.

Research Question 2 Exploratory Results

The inputs, processes and outputs-outcomes for each activity model for each of the five capabilities are described below (Tables 2, 3, 4, 5 and 6). The activity or systems model framework is important for understanding how we manage quality in all three elements. Current quality models of higher education tend to focus only on outputs and outcomes. While this is an important focus point, it is not sufficient for understanding the root or fundamental causes of quality challenges.

Figure 3. Activity or Systems Model

Table 2. Activity model for teaching and learning

System Component	Faculty Attributes
Inputs	• Subject Knowledge • Knowledge of Pedagogy • Emotional and Social Intelligence • Communication Skills • Mentoring and Coaching Skills • Curriculum Development • Knowledge of Learning Systems and Technologies
Processes	• Developing and delivering lectures • Knowledge transfer from faculty to students • Knowledge transfer from students to faculty • Mentoring and coaching students • Preparing courses • Instructor learning • Student learning • Grading and grade assignment
Outputs and Outcomes	• Accredited and Established Courses • Accredited and Established Curricula • Increased student knowledge • Increased faculty knowledge • New and improved courses

Table 3. Activity model for research and development

System Component	Faculty Attributes
Inputs	• Subject knowledge • Research literacy, skills and competencies • Research experience • Research agendas • Research questions and problems • Applied research needs • Theoretical research gaps
Processes	• Research problem identification and definition • Research focus and agenda definition • Research methodology formulation • Perform research • Assess research results • Record and report research results
Outputs and Outcomes	• Research publications • Research communications • Conference presentations • New research funding proposals • Research transfer to production and development

RESEARCH QUESTION 3: HOW DO FACULTY SUPPORT THESE ACTIVITY MODELS?

The exploratory results for Research Question 2 provide a set of activities models against which we can now define what faculty must do to support these capabilities. This is the most complete and rigorous framework for assessing quality of any business activity.

Table 4. Activity model for advising

System Component	Faculty Attributes
Inputs	• Communication skills and competencies • Listening skills and competencies • Empathy, engagement and supportive competencies • Relationship and social capital • Subject expertise • Analytical skills and competencies
Processes	• Assessing stakeholder goals • Assessing stakeholder choices • Assessing conditions and context • Designing solutions • Communicating recommendations • Receipt and interpretation of feedback
Outputs and Outcomes	• Successful students • Increased class enrolments • Satisfied clients • More learned and informed family • Strong graduation rates • Strong revenue models

Table 5. Activity model for advocacy

System Component	Faculty Attributes
Inputs	• Subject knowledge • Open research questions • Proven research methods and experiences • Need to translate theoretical to applied research • Opportunity to interpret research in real world contexts • Opportunity to explore real world challenges and problems from a scholarly or research perspective
Processes	• Formulate recommendations • Develop media campaigns • Public speaking • Lobbying • Commissioning • Commissioned research • Expressed research • Polling
Outputs and Outcomes	• Collective action • Issue group advocacy • Mass advocacy • Interest group advocacy • Expert advocacy • Legislation • Testimony • Political campaigns • Media campaigns • Safeguarded rights • Protecting vulnerable groups • Represented views

Table 6. Activity model for convening

System Component	Faculty Attributes
Inputs	• Audience identification • Venue development and configuration • Agenda development • Event publicity • Event materials preparation • Event funding • Sponsor coordination and development
Processes	• Meeting • Assembling • Congregating • Organizing • Uniting and coalescing • Summoning • Discussions and conversations
Outputs and Outcomes	• Conventions • Meetings • Conferences • Workshops • Seminars • Convocations • Webinars • Associations • New and renewed communities • Event publications

Research Question 3 Literature Review

For guidance on this research question, we must look to research that is focused on each of the five activities. In fact, there is little research on faculty learning and activities in any of these areas. The body of knowledge around pedagogy and the processes that support student learning is rich indeed. It is not unsurprising that faculty turn their focus on the learning processes of others – because faculty assessment and performance is judged indirectly – based on the learning of others.

Research Question 3 Research Model, Methodology and Source Data

To explore this research question we consider how faculty prepare for, develop and monitor quality of inputs, activities, outputs and outcomes. For us to assume there is an active quality process in place, we should be able to find evidence of quality in all three components of the activity model. The challenge that college and university faculty face is that there are a standard set of criteria established for recruitment, performance assessment and retention or rejection decisions.

The research methodology consisted of a set of five questions that were posed to seventeen faculty representing tenured, tenure-track, non-tenure track, adjunct and administrative faculty. The questions included:

- How did you learn how to teach? How did you learn how to learn?
- How did you learn to do research?

- How did you learn to advise students?
- How did you learn to advocate?
- How did you learn to convene?

The responses were recorded as interview notes and logs. The results were consistent across all those interviewed.

Research Question 3 Exploratory Results

We caution the reader that the narrative in this section of the chapter is derived from observation and experience from several different contexts. It represents common observations and typical experiences from private and public universities, large and small higher institutions of higher education and several different roles. These observations and experiences do not represent a scientific study. Rather, the observations may provide a description which can be further tested in future research.

How do faculty learn how to teach? How do faculty learn to learn?

These are not questions that are commonly asked of higher education faculty. We know how teachers are trained and credentialed for teaching in primary and secondary education. This training and these requirements, though, do not translate to higher education. Faculty are hired to teach in universities because of their research competencies. It is expected that new faculty will learn how to teach on the job in the college or university. So, how do faculty learn and develop these competencies? Faculty develop subject knowledge over time, through individualized study and learning. Faculty develop knowledge of pedagogy on the job, through coaching and mentoring and dedicated self-study. Not all faculty have an opportunity to learn pedagogy, though, particularly if teaching curricula and syllabi are developed by the department and taught by part-time or adjunct instructors. Faculty emotional and social intelligence is an inherent competency for which there is little mentoring or coaching provided by the organization. The majority of coaching and mentoring tends to be corrective in nature – we address the competency when it is lacking or insufficient. Communication skills are essential for quality teaching but these are individual competencies not typically trained for. In fact communication and language skills may be a challenge where the faculty member's native language is different from the language of learning. Mentoring and coaching competencies are also individual competencies. Curriculum development competencies are dependent upon assignments by the university and professional activities. Knowledge of learning systems and technologies are competencies which are learned through special assignments and opportunities. Some universities and colleges now offer formal instructional design courses that lead to faculty certification for online instruction. Developing and delivering lectures is another individual competency which may or may not be well developed particularly where standardized syllabi and curricula are required. Faculty competencies to share knowledge with students are dependent upon individual experiences and organizational rewards and recognition systems. It is also dependent upon student to teacher ratio and the time and opportunity an individual faculty has to devote to students. Course preparation and development competency development may be reserved for selected faculty and perhaps reserved for particular roles or levels of education.

How do faculty learn to monitor student learning? This may be a learned competency, though there are few formal learning opportunities for most higher education faculty. They frequently learn from colleagues or through trial and error. How do faculty learn how to assess learning and to develop and assign grading conventions? In many cases, faculty are given instructions by their school or department – instructions that align with syllabi, lectures, tests and grading rules.

In general, we observe that the quality of faculty teaching and learning is developed individually, on the job, through trial and error and may vary significantly depending on the environment. Where the department chairs, deans or senior faculty actively invest in the development and cultivation of junior faculty, quality will be high. Where there is high turnover or where other capabilities are more highly valued than teaching and learning, the opportunity to develop high competencies will be more challenging. Where junior faculty have opportunities to teach as graduate students, where universities provide pedagogical study communities, or where they provide and encourage teaching communities of practice, the opportunity to develop and cultivate these competencies and performance will be greater.

How do faculty learn to do research?

We acknowledge that research is generally supported by tenured, tenure track or specialized and dedicated faculty. It is heavily dependent upon advanced subject knowledge and specialized funding sources. Subject knowledge is developed individually and over time, through practice and experience. While research literacy, skills and competencies are taught in advanced coursework, learning how to apply these skills and competencies is achieved through continuous mentoring and coaching. An individual faculty may have developed research competencies in a particular type of research but may have little or no experience with other types. Research experience is gained through funding opportunities and is developed based on the work load allocations available to faculty. Research agenda development is typically afforded to tenure and tenure track faculty. However, the opportunity to craft and implement a faculty-specific research agenda may be limited in scope depending on the priorities of the department or school. The ability to develop research questions and problems is an independent competency developed by individual faculty. This competency is also heavily dependent upon coaching and mentoring. Some colleges and universities assign little or no value to applied research. Faculty may in fact be discouraged from engaging in applied research. This approach is a high risk in a changing research landscape. How we define quality research may need to shift if a college or university expects to remain engaged and relevant in this new landscape.

Faculty abilities to identify and cultivate research gaps in existing domains can be a critical success factor for new research discoveries and innovation. However, the opportunity to develop this competency is heavily dependent upon the culture and reward-recognition system of the organization. In many institutions, faculty are rewarded for following and supporting the research agendas of senior faculty rather than cultivating their own paths. In contrast, higher ranking and quality universities will encourage faculty to chart their own paths and focus on new and unique areas of research rather than adding to the stature of senior faculty.

In general, we observe that research competencies are developed through experience. Research experience begins with advanced degrees or through applied research experiences. Research competencies are developed over time and the course of a career. Coaching and mentoring by advanced researchers and learning through participation on research teams is an ideal environment for developing these competencies. Graduate students can gain these competencies if they have opportunities to work on funded research projects with advisors and senior faculty. Absent these opportunities, though, research competencies and skills may be challenging to develop. This capability is heavily dependent upon the culture of the department, school and university.

How do faculty learn to advise?

The competencies that support the Advising capability also pertain to other capabilities – some of which we have already addressed. Communication skills are important for advising – this is an individual competency for which there is little if any formal training. Listening skills are critical to delivering relevant advice. Empathy, engagement and emotional intelligence are also important advising and counselling competencies. Again, there are no formal relevant learning opportunities for faculty. Faculty may independently assess these competencies for their own professional development. Advisers and counsellors, though, may not be formally assessed on the quality of these competencies in higher education. Subject expertise, understanding student or client goals, understanding the range of choices and being able to craft individual action plans and solutions are critical quality success factors. A good adviser or counsellor will bring these competencies to the capability. They may not be assessed on these competencies, though. Advisers and counsellors must also be good receptors and interpreters of feedback. Ultimately, quality of this capability is judged on course enrolments, graduating students and revenue models. These indicators infer quality indirectly.

In general, we observe that advising competencies are gained through experience. Quality is most frequently assessed by adherence to guidance materials and checklists developed by schools and departments. Additionally, depending on the context, students may only receive formal academic guidance – and may gain this advice through static publishing of guidance materials. Smaller colleges and universities with lower student to faculty ratios may offer students more individualized coaching and mentoring for career and professional development.

How do faculty learn to advocate?

Faculty develop these competencies almost entirely dependent upon time and professional opportunities available to them. Where the college or university does not value this capability, those opportunities will be more limited. These competencies are likely to be highly correlated with external professional activities. Professional association activities will teach faculty how to formulate recommendations, to work in a community to develop strategies and media campaigns, to gain public speaking skills, to learn how to lobby. External engagements – perhaps working in support of mentors or coaches – can also teach faculty how to conduct polls, take or promote collective action, undertake issue group support, understand how to do advocacy in a way that is consistent with professional standards and ethics. Depending on a faculty's subject interests advocacy competencies may also involve developing a deep understanding of legislative or judicial procedures, supporting public hearings or offering expert advice to public media. The value of this capability to the university is often indirect. The value adds to the reputation and stature of the faculty member, which in turn reflects well on the reputation and stature of the institution. Advocacy is heavily influenced by mentoring and coaching. Professional associations and advocacy activities provide strong opportunities for faculty to develop external mentors and coaches.

How do faculty learn to convene?

The competencies that support the convening capability are often developed through extracurricular or community service activities. Professional association participation may also contribute to developing these competencies. They are, though, a specialized set of competencies which we do not assume a faculty member would have developed as part of developing their research or teaching abilities. They include audience identification, venue development and configuration, agenda development, event publicity and materials preparation, event funding, sponsor coordination and development, meeting agenda development, motivating attendance and organizing, delivering events and assessing the success of an event. In fact, the competencies that support convening strongly resemble administrative and management competencies. It is interesting to consider that faculty who are promoted to administrative positions might be assessed on the quality of their convening competencies. In fact, faculty are often promoted based on their faculty status and research track record.

In general, we note that convening competencies are learned through working with communities and professional engagements. The quality of these competencies is dependent upon the quality of competencies of those faculty learn from – professional colleagues, community leaders, administrators, extracurricular activities and role models.

RESEARCH QUESTION 4: WHAT ARE THE QUALITY MANAGEMENT MODELS FOR THESE ACTIVITY MODELS?

At this point in the research process, we have a strong foundation for applying quality criteria. Quality is generally defined as doing the right things right. A quality of products and processes is one that performs its intended function. Quality is measured as the degree to which anything meets or exceeds the expectations of its consumers. Quality is unique defined by each individual – and its meaning is best understood in a specific context. How do we define the context and how does the meaning emerge from the context? There are a variety of definitions of quality. Quality may be defined as doing the right things right, performing a process or producing a product that is said to have "quality", or the degree to which something meets or exceeds the expectations of its market. While all of these definitions are correct, meaning only attaches when we define the context in which quality will be assessed.

Research Question 4 Literature Review

There is a body of research focused on the question of what constitutes quality of higher education generally and indirectly through faculty promotion and tenure processes (Green, 1994) (Harvey and Green 1993) (Srikanthan and Dalrymptoe 2003) (Astin 2012) (Braskamp and Ory 1994) (Braskamp and Ory 1994) (Centra 1979) (Colbeck 2002) (Palomba and Banta 1999) (Seldin 1980). The research on quality management of faculty and faculty activities, though, is sparse. There is a reason this is an under-researched topic. Colleges and universities are complex organizations. There are many different ways to define, perceive, manage and measure quality because there are so many different processes at play in higher education. The bulk of the literature on quality assessment in higher education focuses on the quality of undergraduate teaching and the quality of learning and outcomes for students and stakeholders. This is an entirely legitimate perspective but it is not a comprehensive review the university's quality. This book and all of its chapters constitute an important contribution to the body of knowledge on this topic. An important element of this body of knowledge is the contribution that faculty make to the quality of universities and colleges.

Systematic quality management was originally developed in the manufacturing sector. One of the thought leaders in quality managers was W. Edward Deming. In his Out of the Crisis (Deming 1986) Deming gave us a simple model of the quality process – one that we could apply to any context (Figure 4). The model leverages the classic economic model of inputs-throughput-output. Deming's quality of process speaks to quality control – the method we use to review the quality of all the factors involved in process. Deming's model applies equally well to manufacturing, service provision and also to higher education. Deming reminds us that quality is dependent upon quality of the sources or inputs that are used in any process. He stresses the importance of managing variation. Variability in quality of inputs will have a significant impact on the quality of the process and of the result. While the majority of Deming's research focused on manufacturing processes, his basic systems and quality model applies to any business capability.

Quality is most often judged by quantitative outputs, managerial goals, quotas and financial incentives. Because the business goals of higher education are not profit oriented, we must identify a different focus for judging quality. Deming reminds us to assess quality for individuals based on those processes they control rather than factors that are under the control of others. This is an important consideration for higher education quality assessment where assessment typically focuses on student learning outcomes and graduation rates. Our core question then is what constitutes quality inputs, processes and outputs for the five business capabilities? We answer this question in two ways. First, how do we define quality today? Second, is the way that we currently define quality appropriate?

Deming's thinking is particularly appropriate to the question of quality of faculty. Deming reminds us to assess quality for individuals based on those processes they control rather than factors that are under the control of others. This is an important consideration for higher education quality assessment where assessment typically focuses on student learning outcomes and graduation rates.

Figure 4. Deming's Quality Process Model Applied to Activity Models

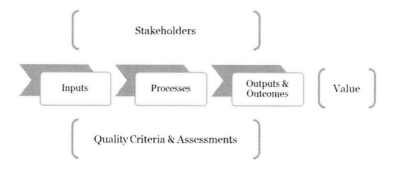

Research Question 4 Research Model, Methodology and Source Data

To consider quality in the spirit of Deming, we need to select a focus and then construct and apply a quality model similar to that proposed by Deming. Deming provides a basic systems model we can use to identify quality inputs, quality in processes and quality outputs and outcomes. These are the critical steps in managing and assessing quality in the five business capabilities of higher education.

Our modelling of the business capabilities of higher education provides a framework for applying Deming's quality management and control. Quality of process speaks to quality control – the method by which entities review and manage the quality of all the factors involved in a capability. The quality of a capability is assessed by its adherence to and variations from standards or expectations.

We approach this research question with the assumption that quality criteria and methods are unique and distinct for each of the five business capabilities. Each capability has a different set of quality considerations – different quality standards, different quality assessment and review processes and different expectations for the nature and quality of outputs and outcomes (Figure 5). Given a university or college's priorities, though, faculty may tend to be assessed for all capabilities in a single process. Given the changing landscape and a changing competitive environment, this one size fits all approach to quality may not be a good approach. We approached this research question by asking the seventeen faculty we interviewed about their experience with performance and assessment for each of the five business capabilities.

Research Question 4 Exploratory Results

How do we define and assess quality for the *Teaching and Learning* capability? This capability has several stakeholder groups. Each group has a role to play in assessing faculty performance. Faculty quality is assessed through peer review and evaluations from internal and external colleagues. It is also judged through external accreditation reviews and by external credentialing organizations. Students also provide feedback in the form of course evaluations. Grades can be seen as a quality metric where grades reflect the actual performance of students and the quality of their learning. Where grades reflect a simple expected bell curve, they are not good indicators of quality. The department will also consider faculty quality in terms of course enrollments and the revenue generated by courses, particularly where

Figure 5. Quality Criteria, Performance and Assessment for Each Capability

courses reflect the particular specializations or expertise of a faculty member. Colleges and universities, though, typically only become involved in assessing the quality of teaching and learning when faculty are eligible for contract renewal, for tenure awards or for promotion. Faculty teaching and learning quality criteria are most often applied and assessed at the school or department level.

How do we define and assess quality for *Research and Development*? This capability has several stakeholder groups including faculty peers and colleagues, research funding agencies and sources, the academic school or department and the college or university. Each group has a different role to play in assessing faculty performance though there is more consistency in quality criteria and methods than for other capabilities. Research and development quality is most often judged through peer review processes and through simple financial calculations. Peer review is a well-established and very rigorous process. While there are common procedures and ethics associated with peer review processes, peer review decisions and the factors that influence them will vary by subject area. Faculty who are well mentored through their research careers will understand what those factors are. They will also understand how to best leverage those factors to achieve quality performance standards. The simple truth is that research publications are the primary quality indicator of faculty research and publications in journals that have high impact factors. Ideally and theoretically, peer reviewed publications in high impact journals is an indication of high quality research. Book publishing is also important though it is less an indication of research quality and productivity than a reflection of research interests and interpretations. Publishing in conference proceedings is also important but of lower quality than peer-reviewed journals. In some fields, technical reports and manuals will be regarded an indication of quality. Quality criteria and methods developed for research and development are good practice models for all types of organizations engaged in research and development capabilities.

How do we define and assess quality for *Advising*? The stakeholder groups for advising are defined internally and externally. Internal stakeholders are students who have little influence in assessing faculty. If this activity is handed off to staff, the quality of advising is likely to be narrowed. And, the quality of faculty contributions will be diminished. Ironically, it is the personalized advising and mentoring that often distinguishes the higher ranked colleges and universities from others. Parents and students may be more drawn to colleges and universities where they have a greater chance of engaging with and being mentored by faculty. Willingness to pay for tuition may be directly related to the quality and availability of faculty advising. External advising is often judged by the level of satisfaction of the client. In this case the quality criteria for faculty are heavily dependent upon the reputation and stature of the client. Where the client is well respected in the subject area, a satisfied client reflects well on the advising and consulting work of the faculty.

How do we define and assess quality for *Advocacy*? This capability has a very broad set of stakeholders. Quality criteria and qualify performance of faculty would be judged by the degree of value and satisfaction of the advocacy group. This may include consulting clients for whose benefit and well-being the faculty member is advocating. It may also include joint or collaborative advocacy efforts on behalf of professional associations. Advocacy for civil societies, local communities, or vulnerable groups may also be valued by colleges and universities. Such activities, though, are likely to be considered of secondary importance – as community service or outreach – rather than primary faculty activities. Increasingly we find university faculty engaged with advocacy groups to promote scientific or research agendas. This may be an important activity that contributes to the health of the subject domain and to the funding of research and professional activities. Increasingly, though, we also see faculty engaged in advocacy associated with think tanks that have political, economic or social affiliations. These may affect the quality of the reputation of the faculty and are viewed with caution from a professional ethics perspective.

How do we define and assess quality for *Convening*? Convening is a capability which can be related to research and development. Historically, this capability was the purview of faculty engaged in professional associations and societies. With an expanding market for conferences, trade shows, meetings, online events and webinars, though, colleges and universities now may have dedicated staff to support these activities. Faculty roles may be focused more on delivering and contributing subject expertise and advice. Quality here is judged by peers, by peer communities, but schools and departments when these events result in publications or revenues. These may be considered indications of professional activities and contributions by faculty who are eligible for tenure awards or for promotion. These are unlikely to be quality factors for faculty of other status or roles, though. Colleges and universities needs to monitor these types of activities in their subject areas, though, as they are increasingly accepted as forms of continuing education or lifelong learning. To the extent colleges and universities do not participate in this capability; they may be losing comparative advantage and market share.

RESEARCH QUESTION 5: HOW DO THE QUALITY MANAGEMENT MODELS VARY BY FACULTY STATUS AND ROLE?

This research question considers variations in quality assessment methods based on faculty status (e.g., tenure and non-tenure tract, contract faculty, clinical and practitioner faculty, adjunct and part-time faculty, graduate student faculty-teaching assistants). While we may have consistent quality criteria, standards and processes defined for a core capability those criteria and methods may be applied differently depending on faculty status. While this may be appropriate to faculty status and higher education's commitment based on status, it may have an unintended impact on the overall quality of the university.

Research Question 5 Literature Review

There is a rich body of literature on faculty issues by different status and roles (Baldwin and Chronister 2001) (Diamond 1993) (Ehrenberg and Zhang 2005) (Feldman and Turnley 2001) (Gappa 2008) (Kezar 2012) (Kezar and Sam 2010) (Levin and Shaker 2011) (Levin and Shaker 2011) (Lubitz 1997) (Nestor and Leary 2000) (Purcell 2007) (Schrodt, Cawyer and Sanders 2003) (Stern, Choper, Gray and Wolfson 1981) (Jolson 1974) (Campbell Gaertner and Vecchio 1983) (Wolfgang Gupchup and Plake 1995) (Shapiro 2006). However, there research on faculty quality is largely concentrated on the tenure and promotion process for tenured- and tenure-track faculty. Every college and university has a faculty handbook that provides guidance on protocols and processes related to faculty governance. In many cases, these handbooks do not address protocols and processes for faculty in a position with another status.

Research Question 5 Model, Methodology and Source Data

Faculty is a complex group. Individuals in higher education who may be called faculty may include tenure track and tenured faculty, non-tenure track staff who may be hired on long term contracts, graduate students who are giving stipends for teaching or assisting in research projects, adjunct faculty who are affiliated only on a semester by semester course contract basis, visiting scholars and researchers and recently clinical and practitioner faculty. The source data for this exploratory research question were the faculty handbooks for 10 higher education institutions published to the web. In each case, we reviewed the source document to determine whether there was coverage of the activities included in our capability model.

Ideally, there is a distinct quality performance process in place for each of these faculty categories. And, the criteria used to assess performance will also vary by status. Where we found coverage, we assessed the importance of the activity and characterized the rigor of the process. The results of our exploratory analysis are presented below (Tables 7, 8, 9, 10, 11 and 12).

Research Question 5 Exploratory Results

Looking across all faculty categories the research and development capability appears to have the strongest quality support. We would also expect to find consistently high quality concern for Teaching and Learning, but this is not the case for all types of faculty. We also note that the most stringent quality criteria and methods are applied to tenured and tenure track faculty. This makes sense because the university makes the greatest investment and assumes the greatest risk in hiring faculty in this category. This is not an unexpected result.

Table 7. Quality models and methods for tenure and tenure track faculty

Business Capability	Relevance of Quality Criteria and Methods
Teaching and Learning	Mid Quality Priority, Sufficient Process
Research and Development	High Quality Priority, Rigorous Process
Advising	Low Quality Priority, Insufficient Process
Advocacy	Mid Quality Priority, Insufficient Process
Convening	Low Quality Priority, Insufficient Process

Table 8. Quality Models and Methods for Contract Faculty

Business Capability	Relevance of Quality Criteria and Methods
Teaching and Learning	High Quality Priority, Insufficient Process
Research and Development	Low Quality Priority for Teaching Faculty, High Quality for Clinical or Practitioner Faculty
Advising	Mid Quality Priority, Insufficient Process
Advocacy	No Quality Priority
Convening	No Quality Priority

Table 9. Quality models and methods for graduate student faculty

Business Capability	Relevance of Quality Criteria and Methods
Teaching and Learning	High Quality Priority, Insufficient Process
Research and Development	Mid Quality Priority, Rigorous Process
Advising	No Quality Priority
Advocacy	No Quality Priority
Convening	No Quality Priority

Table 10. Quality models and methods for adjunct faculty

Business Capability	Relevance of Quality Criteria and Methods
Teaching and Learning	High Quality Priority, Insufficient Process
Research and Development	No Quality Priority
Advising	No Quality Priority
Advocacy	No Quality Priority
Convening	No Quality Priority

Table 11. Quality models and methods for visiting scholars and researchers

Business Capability	Relevance of Quality Criteria and Methods
Teaching and Learning	No Quality Priority
Research and Development	High Quality Priority, Rigorous Process
Advising	No Quality Priority
Advocacy	No Quality Priority
Convening	No Quality Priority

Table 12. Quality models and methods for clinical and practitioner faculty

Business Capability	Relevance of Quality Criteria and Methods
Teaching and Learning	No Quality Priority
Research and Development	High Quality Priority, Rigorous Process
Advising	Mid Quality Priority, Insufficient Process
Advocacy	No Quality Priority
Convening	No Quality Priority

RESEARCH QUESTION 6: WHAT DOES FAIR PROCESS TELL US ABOUT THE QUALITY MANAGEMENT MODEL FOR EACH CORE BUSINESS CAPABILITY?

This research question considers the fairness of the quality management and assessment process. For us to trust the results of a quality assessment, we must have some confidence that the process is fair, relevant and effective. The exploratory research foundation established in Research Questions 1 through 5 provides a foundation for us to consider whether the processes that are in place today are in fact fair. This exploratory research question is dependent upon what we mean by "fair" and what evidence we can find that processes support this definition.

Research Question 6 Literature Review

The research landscape pertaining to this exploratory question is concentrated in two areas: explaining and advising prospective faculty on the criteria for success in the tenure and promotion process and senior faculty mentoring of junior faculty (Bower 1998) (Boyle and Boice 1998) (Darwin 2000) (Dobie, Smith and Robins 2010) (Eby, Allen, Evans, Ng and DuBois 2008) (Kogler Hill, Bahniuk and Dobos 1989) (Lumpkin 2011) (Lumpkin 2011) (Luna and Cullen 1995) (Palepu, Friedman, Barnett, Carr, Ash, Szalacha and Moskowitz 1998) (Ragins, Cotton and Miller 2000) (Sorcinelli and Yun 2007). While we can draw important observations and lessons from this research, it does not speak directly to how we might apply a quality management process to each of the capabilities for which faculty are assessed.

Research Question 6 Model, Methodology and Source Data

To fill this gap in the research, we look to the work of Kim and Mauborgne (1997) focused on "fair process". Fairness was defined as Fair Process as defined and widely accepted by Kim and Mauborgne (1997). Fair process is a concept that builds execution into strategy by creating people's buy-in up front. Fair process is important for quality management in higher education because – as our earlier review suggests – quality factors are heavily influenced by people, institutional strategies and cultures. When fair process is exercised people trust that a level playing field exists, inspiring cooperation, collaboration and mutual agreement in achieving goals. Kim and Mauborgne define Fair Process as three mutually reinforcing elements - commonly referred to as the three "E" principles - including engagement, explanation and clarity of expectation (Figure 6).

For this exploratory research question we looked for evidence in the faculty handbooks referenced above of engagement (i.e., involvement), explanation (i.e., detailed descriptions and examples) and specific references to criteria and requirements for achieving specific performance or assessment levels. The results are summarized in the narrative sections below.

Research Question 6 Exploratory Results

Fair Process through Engagement means involving individuals in decisions that affect them by soliciting their input and by allowing them to refute the merits of other's ideas and assumptions. Engagement communicates respect for individuals and their point of view. The result is better strategic decisions by management and genuine commitment from everyone involved in execution. Engagement is a core element of the tenure review and promotion process. How engagement is exercised may vary across

Figure 6. Fair Process Conceptual Model

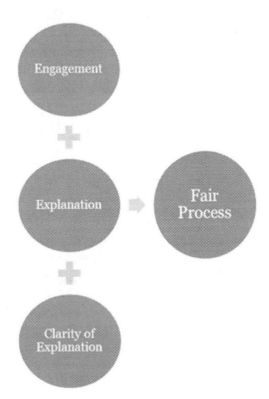

universities. It may be supported in a formal and rigid way where formal guidelines are made available to candidates and committees remotely consider applications and awards. It may be supported in a collegial and informal way where formal guidelines exist and committees conduct themselves in accordance with professional ethics. Informal approaches may also involve significant coaching and mentorship by school or department deans and directors. Where we find continuous coaching and mentorship faculty are more likely to succeed. Faculty are more likely to perform to quality expectations and contribute to the quality reputation and stature of the institution.

So much of the engagement factor is dependent upon the school or department culture and the stature of the leader within the university. As our exploration of the earlier research questions suggests, the quality of faculty and the quality of faculty contributions to the business of higher education is dependence upon individual development, coaching, mentoring, experience, learning by doing, learning with and from others and learning by trial and error. Where the culture supports this individual development – where engagement for faculty success is the norm – faculty quality will be high. Where the culture encourages competition and criticism, political or social alignments over common quality achievement – faculty quality will tend to be lower.

Fair Process through Explanation means that everyone involved and affected should understand why final decisions are made. An explanation of rationale engenders confidence among employees that managers have considered their opinions and have made decisions impartially in the overall interest of the company, even if their own ideas have been rejected. It also serves as a powerful feedback loop to enhance learning. We offer similar explanations for the influence of explanation on the development of quality faculty. Explanations are a core component of coaching and mentoring, of learning from and with others and learning from mistakes and small failures. Explanation becomes not only a rationale for making a decision but the core learning component. Strong cultures will leverage explanations as important learning tools.

Fair Process through Clarity of Explanation requires that when a process is set or a decision has been made, those in a position of author will clearly state the new rules of the game. While we have suggested in our earlier discussions that quality criteria may be clear and documented, this may not always be the case. In fact, there are many examples of performance assessments, tenure reviews and promotion review where all documented criteria were satisfied but the decision was negative. This is an indication that the full explanation has not been clearly stated. When this is the case it may be a signal that the quality review process was dependent upon subjective factors. As Deming reminds us quality review must be focused on those aspects of performance over which the individual has control. If the factors are political, social or economic – not related to the quality performance of those core business capabilities – the quality management process may have been corrupted. In this case the process may not be trusted or credible to other stakeholders. This element does not speak to the rigor of those criteria, but simply to whether they are explicitly and honestly stated and leveraged. Faculty must know up front the quality standards by which their work will be judged and the consequences of failure. When people clearly understand expectations, political maneuvering and social preferences will be minimized.

RESEARCH QUESTION 7: IS THE PROCESS EFFECTIVE FOR FACULTY

This research question considers whether the processes and protocols as currently defined are effective for faculty. While our observations are focused on fairness and effectiveness for faculty, the answer is relevant to the effectiveness of institutions of higher education in general. Are the quality criteria and management processes effective for the college or university? With the market for higher education expanding beyond the traditional college and university and the increasing fragmentation of faculty status and roles, what might an ineffective or an unfair process mean for the quality of higher education in general?

Research Question 7 Literature Review

The research and literature on the effectiveness of faculty quality is primarily focused on the rigor and results of faculty tenure review (Dooris and Guidos 2006) (Kezar 2012) (Lawrence, Celis and Ott 2014) (Lawrence, Celis, Kim, Lipson and Tong 2014) (Licata 1986) (McCartt 1983) (Prottas, Shea-Van Fossen, Cleaver and Andreassi 2017) (Schell 1998) (Whitman and Weiss 1982) (Wright 2006). While the research is informative, it only tells us that there is some concern about the process when tenure or promotion are not awarded, or when tenure and promotion are awarded disproportionately to certain categories of faculty. Rather than serving as a guide for exploring this research question, this body of research speaks to the need for a more rigorous and focused reference model.

Research Question 7 Model, Methodology and Source Data

The exploratory methodology for this research question was a synthesis and analysis of the results of the six previous research questions. The results represent the analysis conducted by the researcher. The results do not represent a scientifically rigorous result outside of the synthesis of the results of the earlier research questions.

Research Question 7 Exploratory Results

The critical dependency here appears to be faculty composition and assignment of different categories of faculty to the five core business capabilities. Where a school or department invests in the development of its faculty, where it hires with the intention of ensuring that all of its junior faculty can succeed and that all of its senior faculty will continuously learn and grow, quality processes will be effective for the university. Where faculty are recruited and hired for convenience, where the institution makes little investment into their success and attempts to "manage" through competition and criticism, the quality processes will not be effective for the university.

While all five core business capabilities may not carry equal weight they are all essential to a healthy academic, research and learning environment. Where faculty are differentiated based on status, where variable quality performance criteria are promoted and where quality assessment is not taken seriously, the institution as a whole will suffer. The literature reminds us that quality of teaching and learning is a primary ranking factor for higher education. Where teaching and learning is assigned to graduate students and adjunct faculty, quality assessments from stakeholders will be low.

Faculty are the essential quality factor for colleges and universities. The quality attributes of faculty have value beyond the physical boundaries of a college and university. As the markets for learning, research, advising, advocacy and convening expand, so do the quality attributes of faculty and the quality management processes developed for higher education. Rather than diminish these criteria and processes, we must adapt and improve them.

EXPLORATORY OBSERVATIONS AND RECOMMENDATIONS

The observations and recommendations offered in this chapter are indicative rather than definitive. They are based on observations from eight universities – some private and some public, some small and some large, some top tier and some second and third tier. The intent of sharing and formalizing these observations is to provide a framework for more targeted, quantitative and objective research in the future. Our three stage exploratory research model has produced __ observations.

Observation 1. Teaching is the weakest activity for quality management which presents a risk wherever teaching and learning is the most important of the five capabilities.

If this observation proves to be accurate, it suggests an area of high risk for higher education because the alternative sources and channels for teaching and learning continue to expand. It is high risk because alternatives may tend to be more cost effective for non-traditional stakeholders. The conceptual exercise suggests there are fewer quality criteria for teaching activity model inputs. The exploratory research suggests there are few if any criteria for faculty training for this activity and the quality criteria for outputs and outcomes are indirect. While there are standard methods for stakeholders to provide inputs (e.g., evaluation surveys, observation, review of teaching materials, etc.) the activity itself lacks up front quality criteria that relate directly to individual student outcomes. In addition, quality monitoring exhibits the greatest variation of all five capabilities. Some universities – particularly small colleges with low student to teacher ratios – pay more attention to this capability than do the larger universities. Where teaching is assigned to non-tenure track or non-tenured faculty, the quality management process is perhaps assigned the lowest priority.

Observation 2. Research is the activity which receives the highest quality management.

Our exploratory research suggests that not all institutions of higher education assign a high priority to research – particularly two and four year colleges which focus primarily on teaching. This will be a business capability with increased competition – an increasing number of players in the market and decreases resources to support research time and facilities. Quality for this capability is often measured directly and indirectly. It is measured directly in terms of publications and indirectly in terms of research funds procured. Stakeholder interest in research topics influences where they offer research funds. This in turn drives research agendas and interests. With shifts in research funding, this indicator may tend to be less objective and reliable than in the past. This may influence the quality of faculty based research. The quality criteria and assessment for research, though, are strong and rigorous quality models. The process should not be weakened but should instead be promoted beyond the college and university environment.

Observation 3. Advising presents an internal risk for quality management.

It is clear that faculty lack appropriate training for advising students. As a result we cannot expect they will perform well or to quality standards. The challenge here, though, is that we lack basic and objective quality criteria and models for advising and consulting success. It is also clear that this is a high risk area particularly where the student population continues to shift from the traditional high school graduating classes to lifelong and lifewide learners. Faculty who have not worked outside an academic environment will find it challenging to advise working adult students. This core capability may be shifted to non-faculty staff in the future which means that students are simply working through checklists for graduation rather than preparing for full careers and in particular preparing for different careers and career paths in the 21st century.

Observation 4. Advocacy has no apparent or consistent quality criteria or processes

Advocacy may be more highly valued for senior faculty than for junior faculty. Advocacy may be an indirect indicator of reputation and respect where that advocacy is not politically, socially or financially motivated. As a sanctioned activity for faculty, though, advocacy should have well established quality criteria. It should also be subjected to quality assessment processes. If advocacy is a valued competency, fair process models of engagement, explanation and clarity of explanation should be brought into the process.

Observation 5. Convening is only indirectly assessed for quality.

Like advocacy, convening is a sanctioned faculty activity. It may not be assigned a high value or priority for all faculties, though. Like advocacy, convening should have established and objective quality criteria and be supported by quality management processes.

Observation 6. Overall vulnerability of higher education Quality Criteria and Assessment

What is surprising is the general vulnerability that institutions of higher education have in relation to quality management. While there are some strong methods in place (e.g., research) the majority of the higher education institution's business capabilities are not well supported by quality criteria and processes. When we focus our research only on traditional ranking criteria and use them to judge quality, we may be overlooking these vulnerabilities. In a changing landscape it is essential that we address these vulnerabilities.

REFERENCES

Agrawal, A. (2001). University-to-industry knowledge transfer: Literature review and unanswered questions. *International Journal of Management Reviews, 3*(4), 285–302. doi:10.1111/1468-2370.00069

Anton, J., & Yao, D. (2005). Markets for partially contractible knowledge: Bootstrapping versus bundling. *Journal of the European Economic Association, 3*(2-3), 745–754. doi:10.1162/jeea.2005.3.2-3.745

Arora, A. (1995). Licensing tacit knowledge: Intellectual property rights and the market for know-how. *Economics of Innovation and New Technology, 4*(1), 41–60. doi:10.1080/10438599500000013

Arora, A. (1996). Contracting for tacit knowledge: The provision of technical services in technology licensing contracts. *Journal of Development Economics, 50*(2), 233–256. doi:10.1016/S0304-3878(96)00399-9

Astin, A. W. (2012). *Assessment for excellence: The philosophy and practice of assessment and evaluation in higher education*. Rowman & Littlefield Publishers.

Barnett, R. (1997). *Higher education: A critical business*. McGraw-Hill Education.

Bedford, D. (2013). Business Capability Modeling as a Foundation for Intellectual Capital Audits. In *Proceedings of the 10th International Conference on Intellectual Capital, knowledge Management and Organisational Learning: ICICKM 2013* (p. 60). Academic Conferences Limited.

Bower, D. J. (1998). Support-challenge-vision: A model for faculty mentoring. *Medical Teacher, 20*(6), 595–597. doi:10.1080/01421599880373

Boyle, P., & Boice, B. (1998). Systematic mentoring for new faculty teachers and graduate teaching assistants. *Innovative Higher Education, 22*(3), 157–179. doi:10.1023/A:1025183225886

Braskamp, L. A., & Ory, J. C. (1994). *Assessing Faculty Work: Enhancing Individual and Institutional Performance*. Jossey-Bass Higher and Adult Education Series.

Braskamp, L. A., & Ory, J. C. (1994). *Assessing Faculty Work: Enhancing Individual and Institutional Performance*. Jossey-Bass Higher and Adult Education Series.

Brits, J., Botha, G., & Herselman, M. (2006). *Conceptual framework for modeling business capabilities* (Doctoral dissertation). Tshwane University of Technology.

Bullen, E., Fahey, J., & Kenway, J. (2006). The knowledge economy and innovation: Certain uncertainty and the risk economy. *Discourse (Abingdon), 27*(1), 53–68. doi:10.1080/01596300500510286

Campbell, D. K., Gaertner, J., & Vecchio, R. P. (1983). Perceptions of promotion and tenure criteria: A survey of accounting educators. *Journal of Accounting Education, 1*(1), 83–92. doi:10.1016/0748-5751(83)90031-3

Carlson, P. M., & Fleisher, M. S. (2002). Shifting realities in higher education: Today's business model threatens our academic excellence. *International Journal of Public Administration, 25*(9-10), 1097–1111. doi:10.1081/PAD-120006127

Centra, J. A. (1979). *Determining Faculty Effectiveness*. Assessing Teaching, Research, and Service for Personnel Decisions and Improvement.

Colbeck, C. L. (2002). *Evaluating faculty performance*. Jossey-Bass.

Cox, M. D. (2004). Introduction to faculty learning communities. *New Directions for Teaching and Learning, 2004*(97), 5–23. doi:10.1002/tl.129

Crockett, D. S. (1978). Academic advising: A cornerstone of student retention. *New Directions for Student Services, 1978*(3), 29–35. doi:10.1002s.37119780306

Darwin, A. (2000). Critical reflections on mentoring in work settings. *Adult Education Quarterly, 50*(3), 197–211. doi:10.1177/07417130022087008

Deming, W. E. (1986). Out of the crisis. Massachusetts Institute of Technology.

Diamond, R. M. (1993). Changing priorities and the faculty reward system. *New Directions for Higher Education, 81*(81), 5–12. doi:10.1002/he.36919938103

Diamond, R. M. (1995). Preparing for Promotion and Tenure Review; A Faculty Guide. Anker Publishing Co., Inc.

Dillon, R. K., & Fisher, B. J. (2000). Faculty as part of the advising equation: An inquiry into faculty viewpoints on advising. *NACADA Journal, 20*(1), 16–23. doi:10.12930/0271-9517-20.1.16 PMID:11314371

Dobie, S., Smith, S., & Robins, L. (2010). How assigned faculty mentors view their mentoring relationships: An interview study of mentors in medical education. *Mentoring & Tutoring, 18*(4), 337–359. doi:10.1080/13611267.2010.511842

Dooris, M. J., & Guidos, M. (2006, May). Tenure achievement rates at research universities. In *Annual Forum of Association for Institutional Research. Sheraton Chicago Hotel and Towers* (Vol. 17). Academic Press.

Dumay, J. C. (2009). Intellectual capital measurement: A critical approach. *Journal of Intellectual Capital, 10*(2), 190–210. doi:10.1108/14691930910952614

Eby, L. T., Allen, T. D., Evans, S. C., Ng, T., & DuBois, D. L. (2008). Does mentoring matter? A multidisciplinary meta-analysis comparing mentored and non-mentored individuals. *Journal of Vocational Behavior, 72*(2), 254–267. doi:10.1016/j.jvb.2007.04.005 PMID:19343074

Edvinsson, L., & Malone, M. S. (1997). *Intellectual Capital: Realising Your Company's True Value by Finding Its Hidden Brainpower*, Judy Piatkus (Publishers), Ltd.

Fazlagic, A. (2007). *Measuring the Intellectual capital of a university*. In Conference on Trends in the Management of Human Resources in Higher Education. Accessed online on May 1,2013 at: http://www.oecd.org/edu/imhe/35322785.pdf

Fleischer, J., Herm, M., & Ude, J. (2007). Business Capabilities as configuration elements of value added networks. *Production Engineering, 1*(2), 187–192. doi:10.100711740-007-0012-1

Gordon, V. N., Habley, W. R., & Grites, T. J. (2008). *Academic advising: A comprehensive handbook.* John Wiley & Sons.

Green, D. (1994). What Is Quality in Higher Education? Taylor & Francis.

Guthrie, J. (2001). The management, measurement and the reporting of intellectual capital. *Journal of Intellectual Capital, 2*(1), 27–41. doi:10.1108/14691930110380473

Handzic, M., & Ozlen, K. (2009). Intellectual capital in universities: faculty and student perceptions. *Proceedings of the 12th International Conference on Knowledge Management, University of Passau Germany.*

Harvey, L., & Green, D. (1993). Defining quality. *Assessment & Evaluation in Higher Education, 18*(1), 9–34. doi:10.1080/0260293930180102

Hellstrom, T., & Husted, K. (2004). Mapping knowledge and intellectual capital in academic environments. *Journal of Intellectual Capital, 5*(1), 165–180. doi:10.1108/4691930410512987

Hemwall, M. K. (2008). Advising delivery: Faculty advising. *Academic advising: A comprehensive handbook, 2,* 68-84.

Homann, U., Levy, M., Merrifield, E., Appel, D., Davidson, E., Isaacs, S., & Judah, N. (2006). *U.S. Patent Application No. 11/076,142.* US Patent Office.

Jolson, M. A. (1974). Criteria for promotion and tenure: A faculty view. *Academy of Management Journal, 17*(1), 149–154.

Kezar, A. (2012). *Embracing non-tenure track faculty: Changing campuses for the new faculty majority.* Routledge. doi:10.4324/9780203828434

Kim, W., & Mauborgne, R. (1997). Fair process. *Harvard Business Review, 75,* 65–75. PMID:10168337

King, M. C. (1993). Advising models and delivery systems. *New Directions for Community Colleges, 82*(82), 47–54. doi:10.1002/cc.36819938206

Knapp, J. C., & Siegel, D. J. (Eds.). (2009). *The Business of Higher Education* (3 vols.). ABC-CLIO.

Kogler Hill, S. E., Bahniuk, M. H., & Dobos, J. (1989). The impact of mentoring and collegial support on faculty success: An analysis of support behavior, information adequacy, and communication apprehension. *Communication Education, 38*(1), 15–33. doi:10.1080/03634528909378737

Kreber, C., & Cranton, P. A. (2000). Exploring the scholarship of teaching. *The Journal of Higher Education, 71*(4), 476–495. doi:10.2307/2649149

Kukulska-Hulme, A. (2012). How should the higher education workforce adapt to advancements in technology for teaching and learning? *The Internet and Higher Education, 15*(4), 247–254. doi:10.1016/j.iheduc.2011.12.002

Lawrence, J. H., Celis, S., Kim, H. S., Lipson, S. K., & Tong, X. (2014). To stay or not to stay: Retention of Asian international faculty in STEM fields. *Higher Education, 67*(5), 511–531. doi:10.100710734-013-9658-0

Lawrence, J. H., Celis, S., & Ott, M. (2014). Is the tenure process fair? What faculty think. *The Journal of Higher Education, 85*(2), 155–192.

Leitner, K. H. (2002). *Intellectual capital reporting for universities: coneptual background and applications within the recognition of Austrian universities*. In The Transparent Enterprise. The Value of Intangibles, Madrid, Spain.

Licata, C. M. (1986). Post-Tenure Faculty Evaluation: Threat or Opportunity? ASHE-ERIC Higher Education Report No. 1. Association for the Study of Higher Education.

Lubitz, R. M. (1997). Guidelines for promotion of clinician-educators. *Journal of General Internal Medicine, 12*(S2), S71–S78. doi:10.1046/j.1525-1497.12.s2.10.x PMID:9127247

Lumpkin, A. (2011, October). A model for mentoring university faculty. *The Educational Forum, 75*(4), 357–368. doi:10.1080/00131725.2011.602466

Luna, G., & Cullen, D. L. (1995). Empowering the Faculty: Mentoring Redirected and Renewed. ASHE-ERIC Higher Education Report No. 3. ERIC Clearinghouse on Higher Education.

Mallinckrodt, B., Miles, J. R., & Levy, J. J. (2014). The scientist-practitioner-advocate model: Addressing contemporary training needs for social justice advocacy. *Training and Education in Professional Psychology, 8*(4), 303–311. doi:10.1037/tep0000045

McCartt, A. (1983). *The application of social judgment analysis to library faculty tenure decisions*. Academic Press.

Palepu, A., Friedman, R. H., Barnett, R. C., Carr, P. L., Ash, A. S., Szalacha, L., & Moskowitz, M. A. (1998). Junior faculty members' mentoring relationships and their professional development in US medical schools. *Academic Medicine: Journal of the Association of American Medical Colleges, 73*(3), 318-323.

Palomba, C. A., & Banta, T. W. (1999). Assessment Essentials: Planning, Implementing, and Improving Assessment in Higher Education. Jossey-Bass, Inc.

Prottas, D. J., Shea-Van Fossen, R. J., Cleaver, C. M., & Andreassi, J. K. (2017). Relationships among faculty perceptions of their tenure process and their commitment and engagement. *Journal of Applied Research in Higher Education, 9*(2), 242–254. doi:10.1108/JARHE-08-2016-0054

Radius, S. M., Galer-Unti, R. A., & Tappe, M. K. (2009). Educating for advocacy: Recommendations for professional preparation and development based on a needs and capacity assessment of health education faculty. *Health Promotion Practice, 10*(1), 83–91. doi:10.1177/1524839907306407 PMID:18381970

Ragins, B. R., Cotton, J. L., & Miller, J. S. (2000). Marginal mentoring: The effects of type of mentor, quality of relationship, and program design on work and career attitudes. *Academy of Management Journal, 43*(6), 1177–1194.

Rajala, R., & Westerlund, M. (2007). Business models–a new perspective on firms' assets and capabilities: Observations from the Finnish software industry. *The International Journal of Entrepreneurship and Innovation*, *8*(2), 115–125. doi:10.5367/000000007780808039

Rich, D. (2006). Academic leadership and the restructuring of higher education. *New Directions for Higher Education*, *2006*(134), 37–48. doi:10.1002/he.215

Salviano, C. F., & Figueiredo, A. M. C. (2008, July). *Unified Basic Concepts for Process Capability Models*. SEKE.

Sanchez, P. M., & Elena, S. (2006). Intellectual capital in universities. *Journal of Intellectual Capital*, *7*(4), 529–548. doi:10.1108/14691930610709158

Sanchez, P. M., Elena, S., & Castrillo, R. (2009). Intellectual capital dynamics in universities: A reporting model. *Journal of Intellectual Capital*, *10*(2), 307–324. doi:10.1108/14691930910952687

Schell, E. E. (1998). *Gypsy academics and mother-teachers: Gender, contingent labor, and writing instruction*. Portsmouth, NH: Boynton/Cook Publishers.

Schrodt, P., Cawyer, C. S., & Sanders, R. (2003). An examination of academic mentoring behaviors and new faculty members' satisfaction with socialization and tenure and promotion processes. *Communication Education*, *52*(1), 17–29. doi:10.1080/03634520302461

Seldin, P. (1980). *Successful Faculty Evaluation Programs. A Practical Guide to Improve Faculty Performance and Promotion/Tenure Decisions*. Academic Press.

Shapiro, H. N. (2006). Promotion & tenure & the scholarship of teaching & learning. *Change: The Magazine of Higher Learning*, *38*(2), 38–43. doi:10.3200/CHNG.38.2.38-43

Sorcinelli, M. D., & Yun, J. (2007). From mentor to mentoring networks: Mentoring in the new academy. *Change: The Magazine of Higher Learning*, *39*(6), 58–61. doi:10.3200/CHNG.39.6.58-C4

Srikanthan, G., & Dalrymple, J. (2003). Developing alternative perspectives for quality in higher education. *International Journal of Educational Management*, *17*(3), 126–136. doi:10.1108/09513540310467804

Stern, C. S., Choper, J. H., Gray, M. W., & Wolfson, R. J. (1981). The status of part-time faculty. *Academe*, *67*(1), 29–39. doi:10.2307/40248821

Sveiby, K. (1997). *The new organizational wealth: managing and measuring knowledge-based assets*. San Francisco: Berrett-Koehler.

Teece, D. J., Pisano, G., & Shuen, A. (1997). Dynamic capabilities and strategic management. *Strategic Management Journal*, *18*(7), 509–533. doi:10.1002/(SICI)1097-0266(199708)18:7<509::AID-SMJ882>3.0.CO;2-Z

Warhurst, C. (2008). *The knowledge economy, skills and government labour market intervention*. Policy. doi:10.1080/01442870701848053

Whitman, N., & Weiss, E. (1982). *Faculty Evaluation: The Use of Explicit Criteria for Promotion, Retention, and Tenure*. AAHE-ERIC/Higher Education Research Report No. 2.

Williams, P. J. (2007). *Valid Knowledge: The Economy and the Academy.* Springer Science + Business Media B.V.

Wiseman, C. S., & Messitt, H. (2010). Identifying components of a successful faculty-advisor program. *NACADA Journal, 30*(2), 35–52. doi:10.12930/0271-9517-30.2.35

Wolfgang, A. P., Gupchup, G. V., & Plake, K. S. (1995). Relative importance of performance criteria in promotion and tenure decisions: Perceptions of pharmacy faculty members. *American Journal of Pharmaceutical Education, 59*(4), 342–347.

Wright, C. J., Katcher, M. L., Blatt, S. D., Keller, D. M., Mundt, M. P., Botash, A. S., & Gjerde, C. L. (2005). Toward the development of advocacy training curricula for pediatric residents: A national Delphi study. *Ambulatory Pediatrics, 5*(3), 165–171. doi:10.1367/A04-113R.1 PMID:15913410

Wright, R. E. (2006). Student evaluations of faculty: Concerns raised in the literature, and possible solutions. *College Student Journal, 40*(2), 417.

Zott, C., Amit, R., & Massa, L. (2011). The business model: Recent developments and future research. *Journal of Management, 37*(4), 1019–1042. doi:10.1177/0149206311406265

Chapter 10
Quality Assurance for Teacher Education in Democratic Globalized World

Liphie Precious Pereira
University of Eswatini, Eswatini

ABSTRACT

In this chapter it is argued that when determining quality assurance in teacher education there is need to take into account not only what teachers are taught but also how they are taught. New perspectives on learning and teaching at school level and the changed nature of the role of the teacher form the basis for suggesting a focus on the "how" of teacher education in addition to or more than the "what." It draws on research underpinned by a critical realist philosophy to demonstrate the changed nature of the school system and the need to adopt a sociocultural approach to learning and teaching in teacher education.

INTRODUCTION

The school system has transformed in many parts of the world to ensure learners are provided with quality education. However, as many researchers have noted, the meaning of quality in education is contested and difficult to define. Quality of education may be understood from an economist perspective (Barratt, Chawla-Duggan, Lowe, Nikel, and Ukpo, 2006), also called a quantitative view (Motala, 2001). It can also be understood from a humanist perspective (Sanyal, 2013; Barratt et al, 2006), and termed a qualitative (Motala, 2001) or a reconceptualist view (Ornstein and Hunkins, 2004). The humanist view places emphasis on educational processes that occur in schools and in the classroom, while the economist view "is macro in focus" (Motala, 2001: 62), measuring educational quality in relation to the extent to which it is able to serve economic sector needs (Lotz-Sisitka, 2010; Barratt et al, 2006; Motala, 2001).

No matter which view is taken the idea of quality in education alters what should be taught and how it should be taught. The economic view is based on the assumption that the role of education is to prepare learners or students for the world of work that has changed. For example, education providers are expected to focus on academic knowledge as well as the development of 21st Century skills such as

DOI: 10.4018/978-1-7998-1017-9.ch010

creativity, problem solving, innovativeness, decision-making, and lifelong learning (Nikitina and Lapina, 2017; Lock, Kim, Koh, & Wilcox, 2018) which are crucial for the business world that the students will operate in as workers or owners of business. This calls for schools and institutions of higher learning to change what they teach and how learning and teaching is conducted (Baren, 2013) in order to increase the quality and relevance of graduates. The humanist approach is based on the understanding that socio-economic problems affect participation in education causing education to discriminate against some students and favour others who are often the affluent ones. Problems of unemployment, poverty, HIV and AIDS, geographical location and other socio-economic difficulties that many countries face threaten the right of the child to education that is of quality. Therefore, from a humanist approach quality education is one in which all, regardless of socio-economic status, have equal access to education and benefit equally from the education provided (Fredriksson, 2004; Komorowska, 2017).

To ensure relevance and equality of education, transformations have been made to global education systems. According to Fredriksson (2004), improving quality in education may be crucial to help teachers improve their teaching methodology and skills. The adoption of actively engaging methods of learning and teaching is viewed as important in ensuring quality in education. Education providers therefore have been called upon to adopt child-centred (in the case of primary schools), learner-centred (in the case of secondary schools) and student-centred (in the case of higher education) strategies of learning and teaching. Because they are capable of helping to produce the kind of person that can fit in the new socioeconomic world (Nikitina and Lapina, 2017). The ability of teachers to use such strategies of teaching is therefore critical in ensuring quality of the education learners receive in schools. Sanyal (2013, pp. 7) argues that, "Education policies, however well-intentioned and official curricula however well crafted, cannot succeed without the teacher, whose professional management of the teaching-learning process ensures that education really takes place". Curricula reforms, meant to improve quality in education, are therefore determined primarily by teacher competence which include his or her ability to teach in ways which enhance quality of the education learners receive in school. Ensuring that teachers can teach using new innovative strategies that actively engage learners in the learning and teaching process is therefore an important aspect of teacher education.

Teacher education refers to the preparation of teachers for effective participation in the school system. Teacher education therefore has to be of the highest quality to meet the demands of current education systems. Quality in teacher education therefore could be seen as the degree to which the teachers produced meet the requirements of the school system.

A number of studies have shown that qualified teachers in Asian (Ramen, Moazzam & Jugurnath, 2016; Nguyen et al., 2006) and African countries (summarised in Schweisfurth, 2013a & 2013b) are unable to teach using the methods which actively engage learners in the learning and teaching process. The studies indicate that qualified teachers who have gone through teacher education teach new learner-centred education systems using traditional approaches that do not help much in enhancing the quality of the education learners receive in schools. A number of useful explanations have been provided in literature for this lack of change at classroom level. Without blaming the teacher and learner, some studies have implied that the problem lies with the teacher, the learner, and their social environment. Others see new education systems themselves as the problem since they are considered foreign and not appropriate for the contexts where they are being implemented. Teacher education remains untouched in most of the explanations given.

While acknowledging all other explanations given in various studies this research views the persistence of traditional methods of learning and teaching in schools as indicating a problem with the quality of teacher education. It indicates that teacher education is not able to meet the demand high quality teachers expected in the school system. Sarita and Sonia (2016) argue that "teacher educators repeat and experiment their own training, which they received earlier upon their students" (2016, pp. 735). Therefore, teacher education programs are stagnant, behind and unable to fulfil the objectives of school education (Sarita and Sonia, 2016; Malek and Mishra, 2016). Sarita and Sonia therefore call for the transformation of teacher education in order to ensure it is quality oriented.

Number of studies that have also shown that teacher education is static and stagnant particularly where pedagogic change is concerned. Just like in school, education several studies have shown that regardless of the call for higher education to enhance the quality of the education they provide through adopting learner-centred methods of learning their teaching is still predominantly teacher focussed relying mostly on the traditional lecture based form of learning and teaching (Grunspan, Kline, and Brownell, 2018). Do these studies suggest that teacher education uses traditional methods to teach how to teach in non-traditional ways? Could they mean that teacher education is teaching "about" how to teach and not "how" to teach? Teacher education is mainly concerned with how to teach therefore that it is critical to ask such questions where teacher education is concerned.

Grunspan, Kline and Brownell (2018) developed a model that can help understand better historical constraints on pedagogical change particularly in higher education. It is a model that focuses on how past and current selection and social transmission processes perpetuate the dominance of the lecture method in higher education. By social transmission they mean "… the beliefs, practices and various artifacts of others that individuals acquire within the social and institutional contexts they experience throughout their careers in academia" (2017, pp. 2). By selection, they mean ongoing admission procedures that filter out some individuals from entering graduate school. They demonstrate that pedagogic processes used with undergraduate students in higher education are an early experience of enculturation. They argue that:

An undergraduate experience that includes primarily lecture classrooms may lead to undergraduates who passively adopt beliefs that college professors are supposed to lecture. While this experience is not the sole determinant of how these students may teach in the future if they later become instructors, studies have shown that one's own learning experiences can often inform future teaching decisions… A continued tradition of teaching undergraduates via straight lecture perpetuates an early normative belief into the population of potential future graduate students that lecture is both the preferred and accepted way to teach (2017: 5).

They further demonstrate that because of the dominance of the lecture method in undergraduate classroom the on-going selection process into graduate school favours students who succeeded in such classrooms and therefore students who have no reason to dislike the lecture method (ibid). On-going selection processes therefore in most cases has for generations created a cohort of graduate students who on average are inclined towards lecture (ibid). When such students become lecturers in universities they are most likely to adopt a lecture method, as that method worked for them. Students who struggled in the lecture-based classrooms, who otherwise would have succeeded in a different classroom, are sifted out. While their study was not focussed on teacher education, it helps in problematizing the adoption of lecture method in teacher education. Their model shows that the lecture experience that students are exposed to during teacher education may influence how they teach in the future when they become teachers. This may be especially so because their school experiences are mostly those of teacher centred learning and teaching.

In teacher education, one of the key dimensions of quality is curriculum design (Sarota and Sonia, 2016). Curriculum design as a measure of quality in teacher education is concerned with the knowledge constitutes the teacher education program (theory) and the ways in which the skills of teaching are developed in students (practicum) (ibid). Sarota and Sonia suggest that the practicum should include the adoption of actively engaging methods such as case studies, projects, simulations, community outreach activities. Yamuzumi (2016) proposes a model of pre-service teacher education that is underpinned by cultural-historical activity theory. The model marries theory with practice in such a way that the teacher educator and students collaborate in constructing new concepts and in implementing them in practice (ibid). The model connects course content with practice by practically implementing what they learn. These studies address one of the concerns of teacher education noted by Malek and Mishra (2016). They noted that theory in teacher education is not linked with practical work and the realities on the ground. While both studies are useful they both seem to consider theory as separate from practice therefore needing to be brought together through emphasising the practical aspect of theory. That is, by addressing theory thereafter put into practice the theory.

This research adds to such literature by problematizing the use of traditional methods to teach how to teach in learner-centred ways. It argues that what is likely to make a difference is teaching the theory using the methods that the students are expected to learn and adopt in the school system. Its purpose is to demonstrate that teacher education may not be adequately preparing student for the contemporary world of learning and teaching in which the students will be functioning in as teachers. It suggests that change should begin at teacher education level. It proposes a process of learning and teaching, derived from the work of James Paul Gee (2004) that is likely to contribute positively to the adoption of non-traditional methods at school level. Hence, it adds to the growing literature on pedagogical change at higher education in particular in teacher education.

The chapter starts by developing a deep understanding of pedagogic change by discussing mechanisms, which influenced the emergence of new ways of learning and teaching leading to shifts from traditional forms of curricula to mostly learner-centred forms. The implication of these new curriculum practices to teacher education is discussed. Finally, the need to adopt a cultural process (Gee, 2004) of training teachers to ensure quality in teacher education is demonstrated.

MECHANISMS INFLUENCING CURRICULUM CHANGE

The mechanisms discussed in this chapter are derived from a PhD study conducted by Pereira (2012) which explored the emergence of a new curriculum in the Kingdom of Eswatini. The study took a critical realist approach. Critical realists believe that experiences of people (*empirical*) and events of the world (*actual*) are generated by mechanisms that operate at a deeper level of reality, which they call the *real*. These mechanisms "…combine to generate the flux of phenomena that constitute the actual states and happenings of the world" (Bhaskar, 1975, p. 47). This means that, explanations of social phenomena cannot be derived from what people experience or observe but deeper meaning and explanation needs to be sought (Bhaskar, 1975). This reality level is likely to bring about a deeper understanding of the curricula change experienced in many parts of the world at school level. Exploring this layer of reality could help teacher education understand the kind of teacher to produce for fitness into the school system.

Archer's principle of analytical dualism complements critical realism in that it focuses on the level of real. It was used in the study as an analytical tool for exploring the deep-seated mechanisms responsible to changes in curriculum systems. Analytical dualism is a method that recognises that social reality consists of three elements, structure, culture (the parts) and agency (people). Structure and culture are the conditions that human beings as social agents confront in their everyday lives, conditions that are not of their making and which they are unable to avoid (Archer, 1995, 1996; Carter & New, 2004a, 2004b). Culture refers to ideational aspects such as values, beliefs, theories etc., while structure refers to the material aspects such as resources, positions, roles etc. Agency refers to the human aspects of social reality such as who is doing what to whom (ibid). Archer emphasises that these elements (structure, culture and agency) in real life are not separate entities but are intertwined, simultaneously influencing each other. They are separated for analytical purposes to help achieve a deeper understanding of their differences and influences on social reality. For the purpose of this chapter, the focus is on the culture and structure mechanisms that were identified.

In exploring the mechanisms, selected relevant literature was analysed using critical discourse analysis. Drawing on Kress (1988), discourse meant sets of statements that give expression to what is valued and practised in the global environment. Discourses within a critical realist framework can be seen to exist as mechanisms with emergent powers at the *level of the real*. Critical discourse analysis therefore is most convenient for critical realists because they are not only interested in finding out "what people really mean when they say this or that, or to discover the reality behind the discourse" (Phillips & Jorgensen, 2004, p. 21). However, they also seek to identify the powers that discourses have in shaping events and experiences of the world (the critical aspect of discourse analysis). The aim of critical discourse analysis in the study was to uncover discourses active at level of *real* in shaping curriculum events and practice and our experiences of it. As such, following Fairclough (2005) orders of discourse and sub discourses were identified in order to show the complex ways in which various discourses interact in shaping curriculum practice. An order of discourse was used to refer to a discourse that derives its meaning from various other discourses. It also referred to a discourse whose meanings differ in different periods therefore shaping education differently in the different periods. Discourses were viewed in the study as *cultural* mechanisms because they refer to the ideas, beliefs, values, and attitudes, which together condition what people, can or cannot do within a social group (Gee, 1996, 1999). While conducting the discourse analysis the researcher kept track of structural mechanisms. Structural analysis entailed identifying material properties seen as necessary in sustaining the operation of privileged discourses.

Cultural mechanisms that were identified consist of an order of discourse named the *discourse of economic development*, which draws from three basic discourses named the *discourse of modernisation*, the *discourse of competitiveness*, and the *discourse of democracy*. Three structural mechanisms were identified which were named the *globalisation structure*, the *education structure*, and the *production structure*. Together all these mechanisms played a significant role in influencing the nature of curriculum in schools. The identification and naming of these mechanisms was influenced by what the researcher know, have read about and have paid attention to. This suggests that another researcher could possibly identify and name the mechanisms differently (Quinn, 2012). Because of space the *discourse of economic development* and only the globalisation structure is discussed. These are enough to demonstrate what quality in teacher education means in today's world of learning and teaching.

Discourse of Economic Development

The discourse of economic development draws its meaning from three other basic discourses. These discourses all explain what causes poor economic conditions and how poor economic conditions could be improved. These are the *discourse of modernisation*, the *discourse of competitiveness*, and the *discourse of democracy*. All these have contributed in enabling the emergence of education systems that take a particular shape some of which are opposed and dichotomised such that countries have seen the need to transform their education systems.

The *modernisation discourse* was dominant in the period between the late 1940s (the early post-war period) and the 1970s or early 1980s (Robertson, Novelli, Dale, Tikly, Dachi, & Alphonce, 2007). It is underpinned by the belief that poor nations, which are most often African nations, are poor because they are not modernised like the Western rich countries. Economic development therefore, from a modernist perspective, requires nations to be modernised. This means modelling Western countries (Robertson et al., 2007). That is, they need to copy or adopt Western culture and practices. Western knowledge was thus considered superior to local traditional knowledge given the status of "modern standards" (Nguyen, Terlouw, & Pilot, 2006). It was based on the assumption that "certain kinds of knowledge have canonical status: that some knowledge is 'intrinsically' worthwhile and some is not" (Edwards & Usher, 2001, p. 278). Knowledge therefore in a modernist paradigm exists "out there", apart from the acquirer and waiting to be discovered (Frame, 2003).

Action that came out of this discourse was the emergence of modern school systems which followed prescribed curriculum programmes (Robertson et al., 2007; Nguyen, et al., 2006) and which focused on teaching learners the Western technical and cultural skills deemed appropriate for economic development (Robertson et al., 2007). Furthermore, it created enabling conditions for the practice of importing curriculum programmes from overseas countries, particularly Britain, to many African and Asian countries (Nguyen et al., 2006; Rizvi, 2000; Robertson et al., 2007; Tabulawa, 1997, 2003, 2009). The importation of Western educational programmes assumes that "what has been done successfully over *there* would produce similar outcomes *here*" (Walker & Dimmock, 2000 in Nguyen et al., 2006, p. 4; emphasis in original). This practice was technicity and premised on the assumption that:

The same curriculum, with the possibility of minor adaptations, is appropriate across any number of educational contexts, because the same laws about what to teach, how to teach, how learners learn and how to assess their learning, will apply (Frame, 2003, p. 20).

The modernist curriculum system therefore was based on the understanding that knowledge exists out there and can be transferred from where it is to those without it and therefore curriculum becomes the process of transferring knowledge.

In the 1970s a new social order emerged which required alternative modes of understanding and meaning making because the modernist tools were no longer adequate for this new social order (Edwards & Usher, 2001). This period was mostly referred to as postmodernism and extends to the current period. The postmodernist period is characterised as complex, rapidly changing, and unstable (Frame, 2003). Views about economic development in this period drew from two important discourses that the researcher calls the *discourse of international economic competitiveness* and the *discourse of democracy*. These two discourses underpin the postmodernist way of operating the economy. They fundamentally differ from the modernist conception of economic development.

The *discourse of international economic competitiveness* is underpinned by a belief in a free market economy. It is based on the assumption that economic competitiveness will occur if countries have access to the global market (competitive advantage). This view has been held since the economic crisis of the early 1970s (Robertson et al., 2007). Those subscribing to this discourse argue that "rather than protecting products from the world market . . . economic prosperity would emerge from more active engagement with the world market through free and unfettered trade" (Robertson et al., 2007, p. 38). The free market economy enables the free flow of capital in the global world and is viewed as a necessary condition for attracting foreign investment, often referred to as Foreign Direct Investment (FDI) (Tabulawa, 2009). In poor nations, such as African countries, the free market economy was promoted through Structural Adjustment Programmes (SAPs) by core governments (Europe and America) and aid agencies (e.g. the World Bank and International Monetary Fund – IMF) (Robertson et al., 2007; Tabulawa, 2009).

Postmodernists' construction of economic development is further drawn from a discourse, which the researcher named the *discourse of democracy*. There is a relationship between a free market economy and democracy. Operating a free market economy requires less government control and more autonomy of the institutions of a country. Hence a democratic environment in a necessary condition for the operation of a free market economy. This discourse is based on the assumption that economic development, particularly for poor nations such as African nations, is only possible if the political system of these nations has characteristics of Western democracies (Tabulawa, 2003; Robertson et al., 2007). While there are many ways in which democracy is explained, Western democracy values the freedom and autonomy of people such that it is sometimes referred to as "liberal" democracy (Tabulawa, 2003). It is underpinned by the belief that the people are supposed to rule themselves by making joint decisions through decision-making units (ibid). "These units must not only decide together but deliberate together" (ibid: 129). This discourse has influenced the trend in recent years for developing nations (under the influence of aid agencies such as the World Bank, IMF, UNICEF, World Vision, etc.) to emphasise democratic practices. The change to democratic societies require people with a voice, people who can adapt to change, share ideas, listen to others, respect others' views, critic, and make quick decisions which are important qualities for economic development of the postmodernist era. According to Ornstein and Hunkins, "the use of democratic school procedures was considered a prelude to community and social reform" (2004, p. 46).

Furthermore, emerging at the level of actual learning and teaching, from the *discourse of democracy*, is the development and adoption of curriculum systems that are progressive. Consistent with the democratic idea of joint deliberation, a progressive curriculum is weakly framed, emphasising joint planning of activities between the teacher and learner (even though the final decision lies with the teacher) and less domination of the learner by the teacher (e.g. the call for a student-centred and humanistic curriculum in the 1960s). It also exhibits weakly classified boundaries between the school and the real world. For example, the emergence of the discourses of a more *relevant* curriculum and a *humanistic* curriculum which emphasised student-centeredness in the 1960s and 1970s (Ornstein & Hunkins, 2004, 2009) seemed to be an attempt by progressivists to weaken the boundaries between the school and everyday life of the child that existed in established school structures. The idea of a more relevant and humanistic curriculum takes into account the interests, needs, growth, and freedom of the learner (ibid), addressing his or her survival needs in a democratic world. It relates to the view that teaching should build on real-life experiences of the learner and should include topics that are of concern to learners (ibid).

Progressive education focuses on the child as the learner rather than on the subject; that is, on *how* to think rather than *what* to think (Ornstein & Hunkins, 2004, 2009), hence it encourages active learning and independent thinking as opposed to learner passivity and teacher dominance. This transforms the teacher's role from transmitter of knowledge to facilitator of learner construction of knowledge (Huang & Asghar, 2018). As a facilitator, the teacher is expected to give learners more autonomy and opportunities to become actively involved in their own learning (ibid). The construction of the learner by progressivists as independent, active, participatory, wise, and knowledgeable, and the construction of the teacher as a facilitator, helper, or guide to student learning (ibid), indicate a concern with weakened boundaries (weak classification) between the teacher and the learner and hence weakly-framed pedagogic practice. Such pedagogical shifts and changes in views about teaching, learning, knowledge, the teacher, and the learner also significantly transform the focus of teacher education.

Globalisation Structure

Globalisation is discussed in this research as a structure rather than a discourse because it focuses on how the world is organised and operated rather than on the ideas and beliefs underpinning how the world is operated. When talking about the structure of the global world, ideas and belief may emerge in the discussion because as noted earlier in reality these elements of social life (structure and culture, including agency) are intertwined. Here they are being separated only for the purpose of understanding how each one of them work to influence what is privileged in education.

The global world is often described as constantly changing and unpredictable (Burbules & Torres, 2000). It is a world that requires flexibility and adaptability because of its ever-changing nature. People need to learn quickly, communicate with one another, make choices (products are no longer standardised) and make quick decisions. For the purpose of this research, globalisation was associated with post-industrialism and therefore understood as the interconnectedness and interdependence of the world (Cleveland, Laroche, Takahashi, 2015; Burbules & Torres, 2000). Interconnectedness and interdependence suggest that nations engage with each other either knowingly or unknowingly but they are not excluded from the rest of the world (Singh, 2004). Technological advancement has enabled this interconnectedness and interdependency of the world. According to Singh, people need not be present to have influence on others. The ideas and expertise of people in other places are present and influence the way of life of people without their physical presence in those places (ibid). For example the "time-space compression", as Singh (2004, p. 103) puts it, has led to new developments such as the sharing and importation of curriculum ideas including the popular progressivist ideas of learner-centeredness (Priestly, 2002; Nguyen et al., 2006). It has also led to the emergence of a multicultural society requiring that people to be able to tolerate, trust, and understand one another.

The globalised nature of the world has influenced educationists to rethink issues of curriculum, hence leading to the emergence of curriculum systems that focus on preparing learners for participation in this kind of environment. For example, a *Reconstructionist* (Ornstein & Hunkins, 2004) view of curriculum emerged that attempted to weaken the boundaries between the school and society. Reconstructionists were mainly concerned with problems faced by societies and wanted learners and teachers to be active in transforming their societies. The Reconstructionist view emerged in reaction to progressivism. Reconstructionists argued that progressive education ignored social problems such as poverty, unemployment, racial and class discrimination, inequality, computer technology, political oppression, war, environmental pollution, diseases, hunger, AIDS, and depletion of the earth's resources. They viewed the school as an agent of social change and as an institution of social reform (ibid).

Internationalists, who are a component of reconstructionist, argue that "our gross national product, standard of living, and security are connected with the world community and influenced by global activities" therefore they advocate a "world" or "universal core" curriculum that is sensitive to global issues and that focuses on understanding the economic system of the world and world problems (ibid: 51). For internationalists it is important that each nation promotes its own cultural values and its own political and economic system, but mainly in their curriculum, they are concerned with the acquisition of "knowledge and skills essential for global peace and cooperation" (ibid: 51).

Reconceptualists who are also a component of reconstructionist advocate for a curriculum that addresses problems of inequalities both within and outside the school (ibid). They attack traditional forms of curricular activity for perpetuating inequalities. Inequality in the reconceptualist view occurs when schooling outcomes for children of different races, backgrounds, and abilities, and from different schools are not the same (ibid). Therefore, equality, in their view, is achieved when schooling outcomes are similar for all children regardless of race, background, ability, etc. This is a view of equality that is different from the view that was held in the early twentieth century, which defined equality in terms of an equal start for all children (ibid).

Constructivists agree with progressivists' ideas of learner-centredness, relevance, and humanistic and radical school reforms (ibid). They are focused on developing attitudes and values such as self-realisation, active participation, freedom, autonomy, trust, love, self-direction, enjoyment, emancipation, and liberation of the learner (ibid). Because their curricula are concerned with community, national, and global problems, the ability to analyse, interpret, and evaluate problems are important skills that they promote and feel the school system should be able to develop.

Globalisation therefore as a structure that operates at a deeper level of reality has, together with other deep seated mechanisms like the discourses already discussed and others not identified and discussed in this chapter, conditioned the emergence of curriculum systems that are weakly classified and framed and often referred to as learner-centred.

IMPLICATIONS FOR TEACHER EDUCATION

The discourses and structures discussed up to this point indicate that those involved in education, including higher education, need to view learning and teaching differently from how they viewed it in the past. This is more so for teacher education whose business is to produce teachers who will be able to teach in the new emerging ways. The new school world requires teachers to be able to demonstrate teaching behaviour that allows learners to develop skills needed in democratic and globalised worlds. The role of teacher education therefore is to prepare teachers for 'fitness' in this 'new' non-traditional school world – where the work of the teacher is not to deliver knowledge to learners but to partner with learners in making meaning of abstract subject knowledge. A quality teacher education program therefore could most importantly be seen as one that has the ability and capacity to produce teachers who are able to produce classrooms that are learner focussed.

In preparation for this chapter a quick survey was conducted which explored learning and teaching practices in teacher education in the kingdom of Eswatini. The Kingdom of Eswatini is a low middle-income country situated in Southern Africa. In 2017, the growth rate in gross domestic product was estimated at 1.9% and was expected to decline by 0.4% in 2018 (Annual Economic Review Report, 2017/2018). It has a population of about 1.4 million (World Population Review, 2019) of which about

97% of the population are Africans with the majority of them being native and only about 3% being of European origin (World Fact Book, 2012). About 70% of the population live below poverty line and about 25% are extremely poor (WFP Eswatini Country Brief January 2019). This implies that the majority of the learners in Swazi public schools come from poor families. It is a member of many international organisations where declarations pertaining to access and quality of education such as Millenium Development Declaration (MDD) and Education For All (EFA) are made and signed.

The Swaziland National Curriculum Framework for General Education indicates that the Kingdom of Eswatini aims to provide "… accessible, affordable and relevant education of high quality for all learners" (2018: 2). Quality of education in Eswatini has continuously been strengthened through curriculum reviews at the various levels of education (The Swaziland Education For All Review Report, 2000-2015). For example, in 2006 a learner-centred curriculum was introduced at secondary school level. "Inclusive education principles which seek to ensure that every learner, regardless of age, gender, capacity to learn or level of achievement, benefits from curriculum delivery" are incorporated (Swaziland National Curriculum Framework For General Education, 2018:3). Furthermore, currently a competency-based curriculum is being implemented in Primary Education and is being developed for secondary education. The reviews are made to ensure that the education provided is more suitable for the people of Eswatini and is meeting international standards (ibid). The curriculum of Eswatini aim to develop a set of eight 21st Century skills which everybody needs in the current world which are listed as ICT, creativity and learning, numeracy, innovation, literacy and communication, thinking, social and personal skills, (ibid).

Indicated in the framework is vision of the teacher as someone who is a skilled facilitator, caring, exemplary role model and life-long learner. A skilled facilitator is "…resourceful and creative in devising and implementing appropriate ways of teaching learners which engage them in successful learning and assist them in developing core skills" (2018:32). Learner centred methods of learning and teaching are emphasised. Teachers are urged to ensure that they engage learners more actively and not compromise the learner- centred approach (ibid). Teacher training institutions are expected to align their curriculum so that it is in line with the realities of the school where the national curriculum is being implemented (ibid).

The purpose of the study was to find out if teaching practice in teacher education demonstrates a consistency with the requirements of the education system in the kingdom of Eswatini. The survey focussed on experiences of students in three of the five government supported teacher training institutions in the Kingdom of Eswatini. A questionnaire with closed ended questions was administered to final year students doing either a diploma or a bachelors' degree in secondary education. These students were purposively sampled because of the long exposure to learning and teaching in their respective colleges or universities, hence they were in a better position to provide reliable information that could be used to determine learning and teaching practices in the institutions. Due to time constraints no validation was made on the data collected by further observing actual classroom practices in the institutions. However, the closed nature of the questionnaire allowed validation of the information by requiring students to respond to seventeen statements that were probing the same information. Table 1 gives example with a few of the statements.

One of the seventeen statements was disregarded at analysis stage because member checking indicated that the statement did not clearly indicate a traditional or non-traditional approach to learning and teaching. Out of 214 students, only 162 (75.7%) questionnaires were returned. The responses the students gave (145/162) were mostly consistent (88.8%) than contradictory. Only 21 of the questionnaires contained

Table 1. Sample of Few Statements

	In all the classes	In most classes	In a few classes	In none of the classes
We are quiet most of the time				
We are always busy doing something				
We spend more time listening to the lecturer				
The lecturer is the one who talks most of the time				
We spend less time listening to the lecturer				
We are given the content by the lecturer				

responses that were inconsistent hence because of the confusing nature of the responses this data was not used ending up with a total of 124 out of the 145 (85.5%) questionnaires. The collected data was analysed by categorising the responses into traditional and non-traditional classroom practices. Frequencies were determined and percentages calculated. For example, in the statement - we are actively doing something – all the students (100%) selected *IN NONE OF THE CLASSES* indicating that a **traditional** approach to learning and teaching. Table 2 below presents the results that is students' responses to the sixteen statements.

Table 2. Results Presentation Based on Students' Responses

		Traditional (teacher-centred)		Non-traditional (student-centred)	
		Frequency	Percentage	Frequency	Percentage
1	We are quiet most of the time	66	53	58	49
2	We are actively doing something	124	100	0	0
3	We are told the content by our lecturer	124	100	0	0
4	We discuss with our lecturer the content	78	63	46	37
5	When we ask questions they are answered by our lecturer	115	93	9	7
6	When one of us ask a question we work together as a team in finding the answer to the question	113	91	11	8
7	We are not given notes, we make our own notes	115	93	9	7
8	Notes are detected to us or written on the board by the lecturer	112	90	10	10
9	Our lecturers makes us say something about the content	117	94	7	6
10	The lecturer is the one who talks	122	98	2	2
11	We listen to lecturers	115	93	9	7
12	We ask each other questions	112	90	10	10
13	We spend more time discussing or doing something	94	76	30	24
14	We spend less time discussing or doing something	124	100	0	0
15	We spend less time listening to the lecturer	124	100	0	0
16	We spend more time listening to the lecturer	124	100	0	0

There was need to do a follow up interview on the first statement (We are quiet most of the time) because how the students responded to this statement contradicted the rest of their responses. A focus group discussion with ten randomly selected students indicated that they understood this statement to mean they do not get a chance to talk in class. They claimed to speak in classes where lecturers ask them questions about what they learned previously and in cases where they want them to relate current lesson to what they learned previously. They also explained that some lecturers allowed them to ask questions, which give them the opportunity to talk. It is worth mentioning that the analysis was kept as is because not all participants had the opportunity to explain their responses (which was going to be impossible to do because for ethical reasons names of participants and of their institutions were not required). It appeared as if the talking largely referred to a traditional approach to learning and teaching than a non-traditional approach.

It is important to note that this focus on only one country limits the generalizability of the findings of the study to all teacher-training institutions. However, the reader may make his own decision based on what is presented here and how similar the case is to his or her own experiences. The findings as indicated in table 2 shows that teacher education in the Kingdom of Eswatini takes a more traditional approach in conducting lessons to students' training to be teachers. The findings are consistent with many others that show that learning and teaching in higher education is mostly lecture based (as noted in the introduction). They indicate that teachers are being prepared in very traditional ways to teach modern curricula. From a sociocultural perspective, in particular from the point of view of new literacy studies, this may constrain the students' ability to learn how to teach in a learner-centred way.

LEARNING PROCESSES

New literacy studies (NLS) refers to a line of research that adopts a socio-cultural view of literacy. Work developed by Street (1984, 2006), Scollon and Scollon (1981), Heath (1983), and Gee (1996, 1999) amongst others may be placed in this category. New literacy studies (NLS) make us aware that social practices, which include curriculum practices, are not value neutral but are influenced socially, culturally, and historically by life around us. They are critical of the role of discourse (however, they define discourse) and the way it influences the way people behave in social life. They also indicate how people's actions are most often an instantiation of, and hence a reinforcement of, established socio-cultural systems.

To demonstrate the problem of teaching to teach modern methods of learning and teaching using traditional methods this research draws mainly on James Paul Gee's understanding of learning processes in human development including his concepts of big D and small d discourse. Gee refers to three major types of learning processes, which he calls the natural, instructed and cultural processes.

The natural process is a type of learning that comes naturally because it is biologically supported. Gee provides are learning to walk and the acquisition of a first language. A learning process cannot work for skills that have not acquired the status of being biologically supported. That is "...if it is too new a process historically to have had the evolutionary time required to ... become "wired" into our human genetic structure" (2004, p. 9). Every normal person learning through a natural process the skills that are biologically supported succeeds in learning and learns well.

According to Gee, an instructed process of learning refers to the way in which formal school subjects such as physics are taught in schools. It is a type of learning that is not biologically supported. For example, according to Gee, "every human is built to learn a native language well; not everyone is built to learn physics well" (2004, p. 10). Instruction is done in stages, each stage leading to another (sequential). The skills are practiced outside contexts with people who are experts in the field (ibid). Gee argues that most humans are not very good at learning via an instructed process such that even children if they were to be taught playing game through a lot of overt instruction they would resist learning to play games. A few succeed very well and many succeed much less well when learning is instructed (ibid).

There is a difference between teaching to teach and teaching about teaching. The former is concerned with actual teaching behaviour while the latter is concerned with theory. In addition to other explanations provided in literature, the problem of failure to implement modern methods of learning and teaching also relates to how learning to teach happens in teacher training. It is assumed in this study that teacher training emphasises the adoption of modern methods of learning and teaching. It is doubted that teacher training teaches teachers to rely on traditional methods. However, studies show that many African teachers use traditional methods and they use them very well. Following Gee, it is argued in this research that it is because historically the traditional methods have been in place long enough (e.g. in Pereira, 2012 & Tabulawa, 1997) such that they have gained biological support. They are "wired" in the human genetic system (Gee, 2004, p. 9). No instruction of it is needed or helpful (ibid). Modern learning and teaching practices draw from Western cultures and are very new to African people to have gained that biological support. Learning how to teach using modern methods of learning therefore cannot assume a natural process.

Gee has argued that most humans are not very good at learning via an instructed process and that too few excel while the majority succeed much less well. Thus a process is neither easy nor effective (ibid). Teacher education in many African institutions often takes an instructed process in the form of lectures to teach how to teach. It may be one of the many reasons why most African teachers have found it hard to learn how to produce lessons that are non-traditional. While learning about how to teach may take an instructed process (though not easy for the student and not effective as argued by Gee), deep learning of how to teach may occur if teacher education takes a cultural process (ibid).

A cultural learning process is derived from the way in which cultural groups ensure that those who need to (Gee, 2004) learn what is important for their survival. It requires that the learner become a member of a cultural group, which Gee calls big D Discourse. He refers to two meanings of discourse, which he differentiates between by the use of big "D" and little "d". Little "d" discourse is a linguistic construction meaning a stretch of text or our use of language in different contexts. Big "D" Discourse "includes much more than language" (Gee, 1996: viii). It includes also what is non-language, such as ways of interacting, behaving, valuing, thinking, speaking, reading, and writing that particular groups of people accept as "instantiations of particular roles (or types of people)" (ibid: viii). It (Discourse) is therefore socially constructed because the group's needs, values, interests, ideas, and beliefs shape its form. Each Discourse type constructs in particular ways who is "inside" or "outside" the Discourse. It defines what "insiders" can/cannot do (i.e. how people talk, behave, dress, etc.). One may be seen as "normal" or an "insider" when he or she behaves in a manner judged as "appropriate" by members participating in the Discourse. He/she may also be seen as "abnormal" or an "outsider" when he/she behaves in a manner judged as "inappropriate" by the insiders. Learning appropriate ways of being in the Discourse involves observing experts perform important tasks. Experts for learners to learn model behaviour. While doing so they (experts) give talk that focuses the learner on what is important to note and focus on (Gee, 2004). The learner and the expert work together at the initial stage of learning. Verbal and behavioural feedback is continuously given to the learner for the effort he or she makes (ibid).

Gee (1996), views people as participating in multiple Discourses and have multiple literacies (ways of being). They slip in and out of roles. However, most often, these Discourses are not consistent and compatible with each other (ibid). They consist of conflicting sets of values and beliefs (conflicting discourses). People, therefore, in their everyday lives experience these conflicts. "Each of us lives and breathes these conflicts as we act out our various Discourses" (ibid: ix). Hence, every person brings to a *new* Discourse values, beliefs, and behaviours from other Discourses including the home Discourse that may or may not be consistent with each other. For example, the values and skills most African teachers acquire from their home Discourses are not recognised as appropriate in the new teaching Discourse. Authoritative practices which impose on the learner putting the teacher in a superior position that many African teacher acquired from their home lives and from the old teaching system (Pereira, 2012; Tabulawa, 1997) are 'deviant' and 'non-standard'" (Gee, 1996: ix) for the new teaching Discourse. Drawing on those Discourses makes the teachers to be viewed (in the *empirical world*) as 'failing' to teach 'appropriately' because those practices, skills, and values are not recognised in this new system. Therefore, for these teachers to succeed in teaching in the new school system they need to acquire the values and skills privileged in the new school system? However, Gee and others in the New Literacy movement caution that literacy is acquired after a long and intense process of socialisation into the accepted ways of being in a Discourse. As Boughey explains:

Membership of secondary Discourses and mastery of secondary literacies are . . . acquired (not taught) over time. The extent to which one can acquire membership of a secondary Discourse and mastery of a secondary literacy is then dependent on factors such as exposure to the target Discourse and on the "distance" between the primary Discourse and the target Discourse (2009, p. 7).

It is important that teacher education creates a 'smart' environment (ibid: 11) that provides the student teachers with experiences relevant to modern learning and teaching which they can draw on when learning to teach. Modern day teaching (whatever version of it depending on the context) should be an entrenched cultural practice in teacher education so that students can learn from within through experience and observations. Living it in everyday learning and teaching of their education courses could enhance learning of how to teach. Such an environment could make the student teachers see the adoption of modern approaches as an important aspect of being a teacher.

While microteaching (simulated classroom environment where students practice to teach under the supervision of a lecturer) and teaching practice (an extended period of actual teaching in real schools with real learners) are important, the cultural process provides much more opportunity to a lot more students to succeed well enough in learning to teach than microteaching and teaching practice could provide. Teaching practice and microteaching in most cases take an instructed process in that the role of the students is produce the teaching on their own drawing from theory taught in class, and the role of the lecturer (master or expert) is to observe critique and guide or instruct on how the lesson could be improved. In some situations due to financial constraints supervision of microteaching and teaching practice, become a mark collection exercise rather than learning and teaching experiences for the students. Students get to be seen by, or to interact with their lecturers too few times (mostly not more than four visits are made by lecturers) to impact on how they teach.

CONCLUSION

Teacher education does not appear to be providing an environment conducive for student teachers to experience and practice what they are expected to practice in the actual world of learning and teaching. Literature shows that other environments from which the many teachers participate do not prepare them for the kinds of practices and ways of valuing and behaving expected in the new kinds of schools. Teacher education seems to add to these 'deficient' environments by adopting strategies of learning and teaching that are traditional. The traditional learning and teaching approaches adopted in teacher education are inadequate in preparing teachers for the role they are expected to play in actual primary and secondary school classroom situations. The learning and teaching practices in teacher education weaken the quality of teachers who join the school system.

A cultural process to learning has potential to enhance the quality of teachers that are produced in teacher education. However, it is important to ask the question pertaining to the quality of teacher educators: Do teacher educators in teacher training institutions have the ability and capacity to adopt cultural processes in preparing teachers for the school system?

According to Aithal and Kumar (2016), lecturer quality has a direct relation to learning outcome to the extent that it is a major determinant of the overall quality index of the institution. It influences curriculum- its formulation, implementation and modification (ibid). Lecturers need to be responsive to both students' and society's needs (Maryam, Mohammad, & Mohammadreza, 2018). Machumu and Kisanga (2014) argue that it is only by implementing new learning paradigm that quality assurance practices in higher education can be enhanced. This research suggests that teacher educators may lack the ability to implement new learning systems, which are important in enabling a cultural process to learning how to teach in the current modern school systems. What other researchers found as constraining teachers from adopting new methods of teaching may apply to teacher educators including their past learning experiences (Grunspan, Kline and Brownell, 2018). It thus suggests the need for capacity development (Aithal & Kumar, 2016) and a focus on 'how' (Coates, 2005) of teacher education than just on 'what' to ensure quality in teacher education.

ACKNOWLEDGMENT

Kellogg Foundation [KSAL program] supported the initial PhD study from which this chapter mainly draws on.

REFERENCES

Aithal & Kumar. (2016). Maintaining teacher quality in higher education institutions. *International Journal of Current Research and Modern Education, 1*(1). Retrieved January 15, 2019, from www.rdmodernresearch.com

Annual, E. R. R. 2017/2018. (n.d.). Central Bank of Eswatini. Retrieve May 1, 2019, from http://www.centralbank.org.sz/about/annual/Annual_Economic_Review_2017-18.pdf

Archer, M. S. (1995). *Realist social theory: the morphogenetic approach*. Cambridge, UK: Cambridge University Press. doi:10.1017/CBO9780511557675

Archer, M. S. (1996). *Culture and agency: the place of culture in social theory*. Cambridge, UK: Cambridge University Press. doi:10.1017/CBO9780511557668

Baran, E. (2013). Connect, participate and learn: Transforming pedagogies in higher education. *Bulletin of the IEEE Technical Committee on Learning Technology, 15*(1), 9–12.

Barratt, A., Chawla-Duggan, R., Lowe, J., Nikel, J., & Ukpo, E. (2006). *The concept of quality in education: a review of the 'international' literature on the concept of quality in education*. Working Paper. EdQual RPC. (EdQual Working Paper No. 3)

Bhaskar, R. (1975). *A realist theory of science*. Brighton, UK: Harvester.

Bhaskar, R. (1978). *A realist theory of science*. Sussex, UK: Harvester.

Bhaskar, R. (1991). *Philosophy and the idea of freedom*. Oxford, UK: Blackwell.

Bhaskar, R. (1998). *The possibility of naturalism: a philosophical critique of the contemporary human sciences*. London: Routledge.

Boughey, C. A. (2009). *Meta-Analysis of teaching and learning at the five research intensive South African Universities not affected by mergers*. Pretoria: Council on Higher Education.

Burbules, N. C., & Torres, C. A. (Eds.). (2000). *Globalization and education: critical perspectives* (pp. 1–26). New York: Routledge.

Carter, B., & New, C. (Eds.). (2004a). *Making realism work: realist social theory and empirical research*. New York: Routledge.

Carter, B., & New, C. (2004b). *Realist social theory and empirical research*. Paper presented at ESA Social Theory Conference, Paris, France.

Cleveland, M., Laroche, M., & Takahashi, I. (2015). The Interplay of Local and Global Cultural Influences on Japanese Consumer Behavior. In C. Campbell (Ed.), *Marketing in Transition: Scarcity, Globalism, & Sustainability. Developments in Marketing Science: Proceedings of the Academy of Marketing Science*. Springer. doi: 10.1007/978-3-319-18687-0_158

Coates, H. (2005). The value of student engagement for higher education quality assurance. *Quality in Higher Education, 11*(1), 25-36. Doi:10.1080/13538320500074915

Edwards, R., & Usher, R. (2001). Lifelong learning: A postmodern condition of education? *Adult Education Quarterly, 51*(4), 273–287. doi:10.1177/07417130122087296

Eswatini Country Brief January, W. F. P. (2019). World Food Program. Retrieved May 1, 2019, from https://reliefweb.int/sites/reliefweb.int/files/resources/WFP-0000103024.pdf

Fairclough, N. (2005). Discourse analysis in organization studies: The case for critical realism. *Organization Studies, 26*(6), 915–939. doi:10.1177/0170840605054610

Frame, J. (2003). Theorising curriculum. In M. Coleman, M. Graham-Jolly, & D. Middlewood (Eds.), *Managing the curriculum in South African schools* (pp. 17–35). London: Commonwealth Secretariat.

Fredriksson, U. (2004). *Quality Education: The key role of teachers*. Education International Working Papers No. 14. Brussels: Education International.

Gee, J. P. (1996). *Social linguistics and literacies: ideology in discourses*. London: Routledge Falmer.

Gee, J. P. (1999). *Discourse analysis: theory and method*. London: Routledge.

Gee, J. P. (2004). *Situated language and learning: a critique of traditional schooling*. Routledge, Taylor & Francis Group. Retrieved January 23, 2019, from http://networkedlearningcollaborative.com/wp-content/uploads/2015/07

Grunspan, D. Z., Kline, M. A., & Brownell, S. F. (2018). The Lecture Machine: A Cultural Evolutionary Model of Pedagogy in Higher Education. *CBE Life Sciences Education, 17*(6), 1–11. doi:10.1187/cbe.17-12-0287 PMID:29953324

Heath, S. B. (1983). *Ways with words: language, life, and work in communities and classrooms*. Cambridge, UK: Cambridge University Press. doi:10.1017/CBO9780511841057

Hossain, B. (2017). Factors Affecting Higher Education Quality in Bangladesh: An Attempt to Improve Higher Education Quality in Bangladesh through HEQEP. *International Journal of Science and Business, 1*(1), 47–59.

Huang, Y. S., & Asghar, A. (2018). Science education reform in Confucian learning cultures: Teachers' perspectives on policy and practice in Taiwan. *Cultural Studies of Science Education, 13*(1), 101–131. doi:10.100711422-016-9762-4

Komorowska, H. (2017). Quality assurance in teacher education. *Glottodidactica, XLIV*(1), 28–38.

Kress, G. (1988). *Linguistic processes in sociocultural practice*. Oxford, UK: Oxford University Press.

Lock, J., Kim, B., Koh, K., & Wilcox, G. (2018). Navigating the Tensions of Innovative Assessment and Pedagogy in Higher Education. *The Canadian Journal for the Scholarship of Teaching and Learning, 9*(1), 1–20. doi:10.5206/cjsotl-rcacea.2018.1.8

Lotz-Sisitka, H. (2010). *Conceptions of quality and learning as connections: teaching for relevance*. Retrieved November 19, 2011 from http://www.fgcu.edu/CESE/images/Lotz-Sisitka-Learning-as-Connection.pdf

Machumu, H. J., & Kisanga, S. H. (2014). Quality Assurance Practices in Higher Education Institutions: Lesson from Africa. *Journal of Education and Practice, 5*(16), 144–156.

Maryam, Y., Mohammad, S., & Mohammadreza, S. (2018). What factors affect education quality in higher education? *International Journal of Management and Applied Science, 4*(2), 85–88.

Motala, S. (2001). Quality and indicators of quality in South African education: A critical appraisal. *International Journal of Educational Development, 21*(1), 61–78. doi:10.1016/S0738-0593(00)00014-6

Neihart, M. F., & Ling, L. (2017). Quality assurance in teacher education in Singapore. In O. S. Tan, W. C. Liu, & E. L. Low (Eds.), *Teacher Education in the 21st Century*. Singapore: Springer. doi:10.1007/978-981-10-3386-5_16

Nguyen, P., Terlouw, C., & Pilot, A. (2006). Culturally appropriate pedagogy: The case of group learning in a Confucian Heritage Culture context. *Intercultural Education*, *17*(1), 1–19. doi:10.1080/14675980500502172

Nikitina, T., & Lapina, I. (2017). Overview of Trends and Developments in Business Education. *Proceedings of the 21st World Multi-Conference on Systemics, Cybernetics and Informatics (WMSCI 2017)*, 2, 56-61.

Ornstein, A. C., & Hunkins, F. P. (2004). *Curriculum foundations, principles, and issues* (4th ed.). Boston: Pearson Education, Inc.

Ornstein, A. C., & Hunkins, F. P. (2009). *Curriculum foundations, principles, and issues* (5th ed.). Boston: Pearson Education, Inc.

Pereira, L. (2012). *A critical realist exploration of the implementation of a new curriculum in Swaziland* (Doctoral Thesis). Rhodes University, Grahamstown. Available from South East Academic Libraries Systems (SEALS Digital Commons), http://hdl.handle.net/10962/d1003365

Phillips, L., & Jorgensen, M. W. (2004). *Discourse analysis: as theory and method*. London: SAGE.

Priestley, M. (2002). Global discourse and national reconstruction: The impact of globalisation on curriculum policy. *Curriculum Journal*, *13*(1), 121–138. doi:10.1080/09585170110115295

Quinn, L. (2012). Understanding resistance: An analysis of discourses in academic. *Studies in Higher Education*, *37*(1), 69–83. doi:10.1080/03075079.2010.497837

Ramen, M., & Jugurnath, B. (2016). Accounting teaching techniques with the advent of technology: Empirical evidence from Mauritius. *Proceedings of the Fifth Asia-Pacific Conference on Global Business, Economics, Finance and Social Sciences*. Retrieved from www.globalbizresearch.org

Rizvi, F. (2000). International education and the production of global imagination. In N. C. Burbules & C. A. Torres (Eds.), *Globalization and education: critical perspectives* (pp. 205–225). New York: Routledge.

Robertson, S., Novelli, M., Dale, R., Tikly, L., Dachi, H., & Alphonce, N. (2007). *Globalisation, education and development: ideas, actors and dynamics*. DFID Publications. Retrieved February 24, 2009, from http://www.dfid.gov.uk/pubs/files/global-education-dev-68.pdf

Sanyal, B. C. (2013). *Fundamentals of teacher education development 5: quality assurance of teacher education in Africa*. Addis Ababa: UNESCO: International Institute for Capacity Building in Africa.

Sarita & Sania. (2016). Quality assurance in teacher education: a critical issue. *International Journal of Applied Research*, *2*(8), 735-739.

Sayer, A. (2000). *Realism and social science*. London: Sage Publications. doi:10.4135/9781446218730

Schweisfurth, M. (2013a). Learner-Centred education in international perspective. *Journal of International and Comparative Education, 2*(1), 1–8. doi:10.14425/00.45.70

Schweisfurth, M. (2013b). *Learner-centered education in international perspective: Whose pedagogy for whose development?* London: Routledge. doi:10.4324/9780203817438

Scollon, R., & Scollon, Z. (1981). *Narrative, literacy and face in interethnic communication*. Norwood, MA: Ablex Publishing Corporation.

Singh, P. (2004). Globalization and education. *Educational Theory, 54*(1), 103–115. doi:10.1111/j.0013-2004.2004.00006.x

Street, B. V. (1984). *Literacy in theory and practice*. Cambridge, UK: Cambridge University Press.

Street, B. V. (2006). *Autonomous and ideological models of literacy: approaches from New Literacy Studies*. Paper presented at European Association of Social Anthropologists (EASA), Media Anthropology Network. Retrieved November 17, 2011, from http://www.media-anthropology.net

Tabulawa, R. (1997). Pedagogical classroom practice and the social context: The case of Botswana. *International Journal of Educational Development, 17*(2), 189–204. doi:10.1016/S0738-0593(96)00049-1

Tabulawa, R. (2003). International aid agencies, learner-centred pedagogy and political democratisation: A critique. *Comparative Education, 39*(1), 7–26. doi:10.1080/03050060302559

Tabulawa, R. (2009). Education reform in Botswana: Reflections on policy contradictions and paradoxes. *Comparative Education, 45*(1), 87–107. doi:10.1080/03050060802661410

The Swaziland Education For All Review Report, 2000-2015. (n.d.). Mbabane: Ministry of Education and Training.

The Swaziland National Curriculum Framework for General Education. (2018). *National Curriculum Centre*. Ministry of Education and Training.

World Fact Book. (2012). Retrieved April 24, 2012, from http://www.theodora.com/wfbcurrent/swaziland

World Population Review. (2019). *Swaziland Population 2019*. Retrieved May 1, 2019, from http://worldpopulationreview.com/countries/swaziland-population/

Yamuzumi, K. (2016). Quality assurance in teacher education: implications for promoting student learning. In C. Ng, R. Fox, & M. Nakano (Eds.), *Reforming Learning and Teaching in Asia-Pacific Universities. Education in the Asia-Pacific Region: Issues, Concerns and Prospects* (Vol. 33). Singapore: Springer. doi:10.1007/978-981-10-0431-5_18

ADDITIONAL READING

Archer, M., Bhaskar, R., Collier, A., Lawson, T., & Norrie, A. (1997). *Critical realism: essential readings*. London: Routledge.

Archer, M. S. (1995). *Realist social theory: the morphogenetic approach*. Cambridge: Cambridge University Press. doi:10.1017/CBO9780511557675

Archer, M. S. (1996). *Culture and agency: the place of culture in social theory*. Cambridge: Cambridge University Press. doi:10.1017/CBO9780511557668

Bernstein, B. (1971). Primary socialization, language and education: class, codes and control, volume 1, theoretical studies towards a sociology of language. London: Routledge & Kegan Paul. doi:10.1177/001312457100400111

Bernstein, B. (1975). Class, Codes & Control Vol III: towards a theory of educational transmissions. London: Routledge & Kegan Paul. doi:10.4324/9780203011430

Bhaskar, R. (1975). *A realist theory of science*. Brighton: Harvester.

Bhaskar, R. (1978). *A realist theory of science*. Sussex: Harvester.

Bhaskar, R. (1991). *Philosophy and the idea of freedom*. Oxford: Blackwell.

Bhaskar, R. (1998). *The possibility of naturalism: a philosophical critique of the contemporary human sciences*. London: Routledge.

Fairclough, N. (1989). *Language and power*. London: Longman.

Frame, J. (2003). Theorising curriculum. In M. Coleman, M. Graham-Jolly, & D. Middlewood (Eds.), *Managing the curriculum in South African schools* (pp. 17–35). London: Commonwealth Secretariat.

Schweisfurth, M. (2013). *Learner-centred education in international perspective: Whose pedagogy for whose development?* London: Routledge. doi:10.4324/9780203817438

KEY TERMS AND DEFINITIONS

Critical Realism: It is a way of conducting research that helps acquire a deep understanding of life's events and experiences such as the emergence of new systems of education.

Cultural Learning Process: It is a learning process that has the ability to enable all to learn well enough what is needed to be learned for effective implementation of new curricula systems. It requires that one live (be part of) in a community of people who teach in the modern ways to be able to learn from their practices what is needed to be learned.

Discourse: A Discourse is an environment with people who are basically the same because they share the same interests, values, principles and ways of behaving. It allows learning from within through being a participating member of the Discourse.

Instructed Learning: It is a process of learning that is not effective for learning how to teach in modern ways because it is a step by step instruction that most human beings find difficult and therefore often reject. Learning to teach does not require memorization or following of steps. It requires that one live (be part of) in a community of people who teach in the modern ways.

Natural Learning: It is a process of learning that cannot work when learning how to teach in modern ways because the modern ways of learning and teaching have not been around long enough to acquire the status of being genetically supported.

Quality Assurance: It is what teacher education do to ensure that teachers produced in the institution meet the current standards of teaching that are expected in the school system.

Social Realism: Expands critical realism by distinguishing between the types of mechanisms that operate at the deeper layer of reality into cultural, structural and agential mechanisms. It can operate as an analytical tool when exploring mechanisms responsible to the emergence of certain events and experiences.

Teacher Education: It is the department in institutions of higher learning responsible for the training of teachers for teaching at school level.

Teacher Quality: It is the ability to produce teachers who meet the standards of teaching expected by the ministry of education at school level.

Chapter 11
Professional Integrity for Educational Quality in Management Sciences

José G. Vargas-Hernández
University of Guadalajara, Mexico

ABSTRACT

The objective of this chapter is to analyze the importance of professional integrity as the improvement concept and ethics in the development of professionals in administration and management sciences. The research method employed is the ethnographic, documental, and life histories, complemented with field work supported by in-depth interviews and analyzed using a comparative method. The outcomes of the research on the application in management education demonstrate that the drama of economic efficiency is centered on dysfunctional professional integrity. This chapter provides a sound professional philosophy that empowers professionals to act with integrity, increases the probability for long-term success and professional fulfillment. The results provide also the basis to develop a code of conduct and regulation policies to sustain management education for professional integrity that can positively impact on business culture through influencing the behavior of key actors.

INTRODUCTION

Professional integrity as an improvement concept to the actual values and virtues has meaningful managerial capabilities and attitudes to assume any professional task. The objective of this paper is to analyze the importance of professional integrity as the improvement concept and ethics in the development of professionals in administration and management sciences. The paper also pretends to present some suggestions of ethical and integrity program based in professional integrity that can lead the manager to a more ethical and humanistic practice based on a case at University Centre for Economic and Managerial Sciences, University of Guadalajara.

DOI: 10.4018/978-1-7998-1017-9.ch011

Economic and political conditions of the globalization processes carry with them the elements toward the multinational integration which implies a higher professional competitiveness. Professionals have to be prepared for a global market constrained by time and resources for their basic developments. Thus, there is a need for optimizing the resources applied to the development of the new professionals. The most important change facing the new demands of education is the task of personal and professional integrity formation for the performance of citizenship and productive capabilities. Smith and Oakley (1994) concluded that personal integrity and ethical values of honesty were negatively correlated with formal education, not confirming the findings of previous research. Llano (1997) makes reference to a divorce between professional formation and the real labor market as the product of nonexistent but necessary synchronization, between the graduated professionals from Universities and technological institutes and the requirements of employers that have resulted to be devastating for the social responsibility that the organizations must fulfill. The integrity of managerial education empowers professionals to take "informed decisions and responsible actions for environmental integrity, economic viability and a just society, for present and future generations, while respecting cultural diversity" (UNESCO, 2014, p.12; Schulz, 2016).

The manager's success in the provision of services to individuals and society depends to a certain extent in the degree of knowledge, skills and experiences obtained in the classroom and the professional performance. Moreover, it depends of the achieved level of personal qualities development that distinguishes him/her as an individual, such as the professional integrity, independence, ethics, and so forth (AICPA, 1980: 16). There is a peremptory need to recover credibility, integrity and respect in the management profession through a truth reconstruction of the ethical and integrity fundamentals. Professional formation and development in management sciences conducted in Universities must specify the required behaviors for the professional integrity. The formation of professional integrity at University programs, more than the added value must be the inherent value expected to grant to the organizations and society as a whole.

NOTION OF INTEGRITY

Integrity is important to build a good society, a reason that makes necessary to define with precision the origin and sense of the term. Srivastva and Associates (1988) describe integrity with an emphasis on congruence, consistency, morality, universality and concern for others. Kerr (1988: 126-127) lists the Ten Commandments of Executive Integrity. Covey (1992) describes integrity as honestly matching words and feelings with thoughts and actions for the good of others. A key component of integrity is the consistency between actions and words. Integrity is defined by the Webster's New World Dictionary (1994) as: "1. the quality or state of being complete; unbroken condition; wholeness; entirety; 2. the quality or state of being unimpaired; perfect condition; soundness; and 3. the quality or state of being of sound moral principle; uprightness, honesty, and sincerity". Integrity is a state or condition of being whole, complete, unbroken, unimpaired, sound, perfect condition.

The word integrity suggests the wholeness of the person in such a way that can be said that person with integrity are whole as human beings. The term integrity refers to honesty, playing by the rules and not necessarily following the rules, which means setting aside in situations where people may be victimized.

Becker (1998) conceptually distinguishes integrity from honesty and fairness. However, the empirical research conducted by Hooijberg and Lane (2005) shows those managers and their direct reports, peers, and bosses do not distinguish integrity from honesty and fairness. Integrity in the context of other values that are in the eye of the beholder is an implicit model to evaluate the meaning of integrity. Becker (1998) found no standard definition of integrity because it is treated as synonymous with other values such as honesty and fairness, which makes very difficult to measure it. The theory of Human Values (Gorgievski, Ascalon & Ute (2011) argue on Business Owners' success criteria and human values. This theory departs from Schwartz' value theory (2005), turning to 10 value orientations and then derive predictions based on success criteria. Among these value orientations are benevolence, tradition, (p-213). Findings of the research conducted by Longenecker, Moore, Petty, Palich and McKinney (2006) reveal the extent to which business integrity has gained or lost ground and varied in importance within large and small companies.

Integrity means honesty or stating what one really thinks even if the honest person runs the risk of hurting relationships and getting the organization in trouble. The condition of integrity must emerge at the heart of the person, people and organizations as the distinctive seal in all actions, decisions, determinations, etc. Simons (1999) defines Behavioral Integrity (BI) as the perceived degree of congruence between the values expressed by words and those expressed through action. Integrity is primarily a formal relation one has to oneself. Integrity refers to the wholeness, intactness or purity of a thing, meanings that are sometimes, applied to people (Cox, La Caze and Levine, 2005).

"What is it to be a person of integrity? Ordinary discourse about integrity involves two fundamental intuitions: first, that integrity is primarily a formal relation one has to oneself or between parts or aspects of one's self; and second, that integrity is connected in an important way to acting morally, in other words, there are some substantive or normative constraints on what it is to act with integrity. How these two intuitions can be incorporated into a consistent theory of integrity is not obvious, and most accounts of integrity tend to focus on one of these intuitions to the detriment of the other." (Cox, La Caze, and Levine, 2005).

Erhard, Jensen and Zaffron (2010) combine the two intuitions of integrity developed by Cox, La Caze, and Levine (2005), the second becoming a logical implication of the first, in one consistent theory. Integrity is the integration of self, the maintenance of identity and standing for something. Professionals are active in building their own work-identity to achieve integrity instead of subjugating their identity to achieve work-identity (Pratt, Rockmann, K. W., et al. 2006). Authenticity as a career driver is related to the expression of integrity. Professionals require a "jewel of integrity" integrated into one's career with "authenticity work" (Svejenova, 2005), although some individuals achieve identity integrity in their professional identity (Pratt et al. 2006). (O'Neil and Ucbasaran 2010) found that entrepreneurship offers a means not only to enact desired entrepreneurial identities but also to express one's authenticity and inwardly-derived values.

Personal integrity, defined as honoring one's word, becomes predictable with first-hand reliable and accurate information (Erhard, et al., 2007). Integrity is the base to trust to people because it guarantees the subject consistency in making decisions and in how he/she relates to others. Trust and ethics are terms related to the concept of integrity. Integrity is a guarantee of being ready to repair any threat to honesty. Integrity is defined as honoring one's word in a positive model developed by Erhard, Jensen and Zaffron (2008) revealing the causal link between integrity and performance. There is not a consistent and validated framework of integrity. Erhard, Jensen and Zaffron (2010) define integrity as: *a state or condition of being whole, complete, unbroken, unimpaired, sound, perfect condition.* Personal integrity has to do with the wholeness and completeness of that person's word. Personal integrity is one of the personal qualities. The Oxford Dictionary (2011) defines integrity as "the quality of being honest and having strong moral principles", "the state of being whole and undivided".

Integrity has different meanings to different respondents. Integrity is for an individual, group, or organization as honoring one's word.

At an individual level, integrity is the matter of that person's word "being whole and complete". Personal integrity has to do with the wholeness and completeness of that person's word (Erhard, Jensen and Zaffron, 2010). A person's word may consist of what is said, known, expected, is said is so, stands for, and the social moral, group ethical and governmental legal standards. Integrity is a matter of a human entity's word being whole and complete. One's word is not a matter of being obligated or not, being willing or not willing to fulfill the expectations of others. To be a person of integrity is honoring one's word and not a matter of keeping one's word. Simons (2002) defines integrity as keeping one's word. Honoring one's word is defined by Erhard, Jensen and Zaffron (2010) as keeping or not keeping the word on time when it is impossible, saying to everyone impacted if the conditions are not met and cleaning up any consequences.

Keeping the word is doing what it is said will be done and on time. Keeping the word is doing what it is known to do and doing the way it was meant to be done, and on time, unless it has been said it would not so be doing what others expect to be done. It is congruent to define integrity to the capability to rationalize without interest's influences or particular sensations. Even if it has been never said it would not be done, and doing it on time, unless it has been said it would not have been done and it has been made expectations of others clear to them by making explicit requests being willing to held accountable when it is asserted something that others would accept the evidence on the issue as valid.

Considered as a positive phenomenon, independent of normative value judgments, integrity is defined as honoring one's word. Honoring the one's word to oneself provides a solid foundation for self-discipline as a way to maintain one whole and complete as a person that empowers him/her to deal with the matter with integrity. One may create trust by others when honoring one's word although fails to *keep* one's word. Honoring the word maintains integrity when it is not possible or appropriate to keep the word or to choose not to keep the word. The concept of integrity as Honoring One's Word includes a way to maintain integrity when one is for any reason not going to keep one's word. Integrity is a guarantee of being ready to repair any threat to honesty. However, for Kaizer and Hogan (2010), integrity is a moral attribution that we place on the behavior of another person, in such a way that integrity is in the eyes of the beholder rather than consistency of that person's words and actions.

Argyris (1991) contends that people consistently act inconsistently; unaware of the contradiction between the way they think they are acting and the way they really act. Simons (1999) argues that behavioral integrity is the perceived degree of congruence between the values expressed by words and those expressed through action that he terms "wordaction". However, while keeping the words is not always possible, honoring the word, and thus, to be a person of integrity, whole and complete, is always possible. Honoring one's word when failing to keep it provides behavior that can generate substantial benefits. It is the interpretation of one's body, emotions and thoughts in the own words that are said, which ultimately defines who is one is for self.

Authenticity means being and acting consistent with which you hold yourself out to be for others, and who you hold yourself to be for yourself. Being authentic is "being willing to discover, confront, and tell the truth about yours in authenticities" (Erhard, W. and Jensen, M., 2009). Argyris (1991) argues that "people consistently act inconsistently; unaware of the contradiction between their espoused theory and their theory-in-use, between the way they think they are acting, and the way they really act."

For a group or organizational entity, Erhard, Jensen and Zaffron (2010) define integrity as that group's or organization's word being whole and complete. Organizational integrity as any human system is an organization that honors whole and complete its word to its members and to outsiders. Respondents refuse to answer questions related to identify integrity issues and behaviors of managers lacking integrity besides the difficulties to observe and rate them.

Honoring one's word to another creates a whole and complete relationship. One's word is constituted by what literally one person says in words, in the "speaking" of his/her actions and in what these actions say to others. Being in-integrity leaves one person whole and complete outside or inside the relationship with other person who may be out-of integrity. Shakespeare (1914) said, "This above all: to thine own self be true, it must follow, as the night the day, thou can't not be false to any man." When one is true to one's word, which is being true to one's self, one cannot be but true to any man. Being in-integrity allows one person to continue to be effective and workable in the relationship with other or others.

The terms integrity, morality, ethics, and legality are confused by the common usage. Morality, ethics and legality exist in a normative realm of virtues while integrity exists in a positive real. Erhard, Jensen and Zaffron (2010:1) distinguish the domain of integrity "as the objective state or condition of an object, system, person, group, or organizational entity." Integrity is within the positive realm and its domain is one of the objective state or condition. The virtue phenomena of morality and ethics are related to integrity as a positive phenomenon.

The Oxford Dictionary (2011) defines morals as "standards of behavior or beliefs concerning what is and is not acceptable to do". Morality exists in the social virtue domain in the normative realm. Morality is the generally accepted standards of what is desirable and undesirable; of right and wrong conduct, and what is considered by that society as good behavior and what is considered bad behavior of a person, group, or entity. Integrity cannot be falsified because it is, by its own nature, the truthiness, what avoids the fragmentation of persons and the cracking down of moral strengthens.

The Oxford Dictionary (2011) defines ethics as "moral principles that govern a person's or group's behavior" (Sic). Ethics refers to the set of values and behaviors defined by society as desirable in such a way that any action can be judged as "good or bad" (Pojman, 1995). Ethics exists in the group virtue domain in the normative realm. Ethics is defined as in a given group (the benefits of inclusion in which group a person, sub-group, or entity enjoys), ethics is the agreed on standards of what is desirable and undesirable; of right and wrong conduct; of what is considered by that group as good and bad behavior of a person, sub-group, or entity that is a member of the group, and may include defined bases for discipline, including exclusion.

Integrity as the condition of being whole and complete is a necessary condition for workability. Workability is defined as the state or condition that constitutes the available opportunity for something or somebody or a group or an organization to function, operate or behave to produce an intended outcome, i.e., to be effective; or the state or condition that determines the opportunity set from which someone or a group or an organization can choose outcomes, or design or construct for outcomes (Erhard, Jensen and Zaffron, 2010). The resultant level of workability determines the available opportunity set for superior performance. Integrity provides access for superior performance and competitive advantage for individuals, groups, organizations, and societies. Erhard, Jensen and Zaffron (2010) conclude that the way in which integrity is defined for individuals, groups and organizations reveals the impact of integrity on workability and trustworthiness, and consequently on performance.

Variations in personal behavior depending on situations may be interpreted as lack of integrity. Lack of integrity is compatible with a multiplicity of interests that are in collision among each other. Lack of integrity implies a gap between what is said and what is thought, between what is considered a proper conduct and what is finally done, between what is morally fair and what it appears to result from pressure of circumstances. The lack of integrity goes beyond and has effects far away the sphere of the specific activity in each organization, even impact the society's rules of the game. Personal as well as professional integrity in firms declines more and more in an environment of global economy, leading to a decrease in performance.

Moral and ethical values may guide human action and interactions shaping professional integrity and determining performance. Professional integrity derives its substance from the fundamental goals or mission of the profession (McDowell, D., 2010).

Legality exists in governmental virtue domain in the normative realm. Legality is defined as the system of laws and regulations of right and wrong behavior that are enforceable by the state (federal, state, or local governmental body in the U.S.) through the exercise of its policing powers and judicial process, with the threat and use of penalties, including its monopoly on the right to use physical violence.

Honoring the standards of the three virtue phenomena of morality, ethics and legality and its relationships with performance, including being complete as a person and the quality of life, raises the likelihood to shape human behavior.

PROFESSIONAL INTEGRITY

One of the first documents that treat on professional integrity is the Hippocratic Oath. The thesis behind is that professionals have to aspire to excellence. Personal integrity is directly related to professional integrity. Personal integrity and professional integrity are generally interdependent and compatible. Professional integrity is related to, but different from personal integrity. Professional integrity is an attribute although philosophically the term integrity relates to general character. Professional integrity derives its substance from the fundamental goals or mission of the profession (McDowell D. 2010) Professional integrity is sustained on the principle of moral integrity and ethical principles centered in transparency, honesty, sincerity, moral consciousness, loyalty, truthiness and reality in the functions performed adhered to legality. Professional integrity is the set of principles and commitments to improve the results of the manager's activities, to maximize autonomy, to create relationships characterized by integrity, the ethical practice, social justice and team work.

Different aspects of professional integrity are derived from the basic functions of each profession. The professional integrity includes the role-specific obligations and responsibilities of a particular profession. Well-established professions often spell out and stand on the role-specific principles of professional integrity. Professional integrity derives its substance from the mission and fundamental goals of the profession. Where the stakes for society are so high, professional integrity must be first over personal loyalties of friendships. Professional integrity is based on value integrity first, service before self, and excellence in all that we do. When a professional commit himself /herself to "integrity first" is that he or she understands the importance of both personal integrity and professional integrity, and through his/her efforts to keep them compatible, he or she best provides the crucial professional functions and activities to the society. Firms develop cooperative strategies stressing personal integrity in a more competitive environment (Solomon, 1999).

A clash between personal integrity and professional integrity leads to integrity dilemmas which are present in some situations such as for example a professional refuse to participate on moral grounds because it is not morally obligatory even though it is legally permitted. In any professional role it may be possible to live up to high standards of competence and conduct but not to sustain professional integrity outside the professional realm and context by living entirely different, opposed, conflicting or contradictory moral values in private life. It reveals a direct conflict between personal integrity and professional integrity. Culpable incompetence is clearly violation of professional integrity.

At the times when professional integrity is most valuable, there is an excuse to avoid the obligation to be in integrity. To be in professional integrity when it is most valuable to others, means to bear the costs. Professional integrity may be sacrificed to avoid some costs imposed on others, such as to protect institutional reputation. Based on integrity, it is build the personal reputation, and also as an extension the institutional reputation, when these are liberated according to the integrity criteria. The value of good reputation has been manifested several times in management. With violations of the public trust by actions of authority are serious breaches of professional integrity. When the stakes are so high in a profession, the breach of professional integrity could be devastating to society. Mayor challenges to professional integrity are the misuse of science, research and evidence in policymaking (McDowell, D. 2010).

The concept of professional integrity is separated from normative concepts to understand it as a "purely positive phenomenon that plays a foundational role" in economic performance. The issue of competence is directly relevant to professional integrity. The duties of competent professionals can be carried out by professional practices, functions and actions constrained by moral, ethical and legal restraints on professional integrity. "Ethical implies conformity with an elaborated, ideal code of moral principles, sometimes, specifically, with the code of a particular profession" (*Webster's New World Dictionary*).

The codes of conduct support the profession's conception of professional integrity. A code of professional ethics allows to norm a more ethical and humanistic professional practice and the commitment with individuals and society, the actions that must be guided not only by the speculation but for the necessity to act with justice, responsibility, discretion, honesty, etc. Von Kimakowitz, Pirson, Spitzech, Dierksmeier, and Amann (2010) present some business cases and analyze that their success in the context of global competitive environment managed as an integrated and responsive generation of social benefits rather than maximum business profits supported by a humanistic management approach. A myopic vision of professional integrity and ethic is reduced to a catalogue of things that are good and that are bad, and that there are not considered under a wider vision as the set of principles that serve to the human beings to achieve perfection and plenitude which is an arduous task. Changes on environment and the actual life can originate the loss of a clear vision of the limits between the honest and what is not, where it finishes the dignity and where begins the non-dignity and what are the moral principles that must rule professional behavior.

Professional integrity is formed by social responsibility and some other social elements that professionals inherit to maintain high standards of competence and conduct in the entire full range of professional activities and not just for themselves. Professional integrity has as an effect a major consistency of one person on himself/herself and produces greater social cohesion. Honest members of society strengthen the links of the structure and make advancements toward the own end, the common good. Professional integrity involves competences shared by all members of the profession and joint responsibilities for conduct. Integrity in communication is the pillar in trusting interpersonal networks building as a condition for the cooperation among human beings.

PROFESSIONALISM

Professionalism has integrity as the essential and defining element. Professionalism is an ethical movement defined by essential elements of professional good will and good doing and reflects on values, actions and curricular implications. Business management curricula is under review focusing more on business ethics, morality and corporate social responsibility (Ghoshal,2005), issues that cannot be separated from human intentionality despite the claim that ethics and moral prescription should be denied in any science, theory and any practice of business management. Professionalism as an aspect of a person's life is an attribute of integrity.

MANAGERIAL INTEGRITY

Organizational activities include regular issues of professional managerial integrity (Thompson et al., 2008) Professional management integrity is defined as a "leadership competency and measures it using co-worker ratings of observed ethical behavior" (Sic). Professional managers displaying integrity are more concerned about the welfare of others (Brown & Trevino, 2006). Managerial integrity acknowledges responsiveness among one another, receptivity and creative efforts to understand other's perspectives while at the same time articulating their own (Levinson, 1988: 318).

Perceived managerial integrity is central to managers – stakeholder's relations as it is for leaders in the role of leader-follower relations, although it is questionable as to what extent integrity is important for various stakeholders. A manager would like to be able to look at themselves as someone who has integrity, is fair and honest. Kerr (1988) argues about the difference between the conceptual work on integrity and the realities faced by management practitioners. Kerr truly explored the meaning of integrity for real managers. As Kerr (1988: 138) states that the author's prescriptions about how to behave with ethics and integrity, were far away from the managerial practice in everyday organizational life. When the mistakes and incompetency of managers are buried instead of being exposed and removed from their practice, the managerial authorities fall short of their responsibilities to the mission and goals of the profession. Managers act with integrity to stay true to themselves (Levinson, 1988: 268).

The environment under which the role of management takes place include managerial integrity, honesty and in safeguarding the integrity of the management system. Trust may create a "transformation in relational logic" which produces differential interaction effects for personal and professional integrity trust and capability trust (Bigley and McAllister, 2002) in professionals. Professional managers must have high integrity in order to be trusted by other stakeholders, as leaders by followers. There are negative as well as the positive effects on public managerial integrity caused by the introduction of businesslike methods in the public service Kolthoff, Huberts, and Heuvel (2003). However, global perceptions of supervisor integrity are a function of discrete, and primarily destructive, supervisor behaviors (Craig and Gustafson 1998, p.134).

Moral philosophers agreed that integrity is linked to personality psychology and also Allport (1937) recognized this connection which can be measured directly through integrity testing. In organizational life, managerial integrity and other related competencies can be measured and evaluated through structured interviews, background checks, assessment centers, and other methods such as high-fidelity simulations and strategically designed assessment exercises that are other more valid and reliable methods for measuring integrity. Little effort has been made to link ethical theory to management behavior (Fritzche and Becker (1984: 166). Becker (1998: 159) suggests obtaining assessments of integrity from supervisors or peers because integrity tests invoke social desirability responses with an emphasis on action. One important instrument to assess managerial integrity is the Diamond of Managerial Integrity model was developed by Kaptein (2003) to assess and improve the integrity of managers.

Leslie & Fleenor (1998) reported 24 popular assessment instruments that are similar in content to other competency instruments used by organizations that were compared and analyzed by Kaiser and Hogan (2010) who found several weaknesses centered on the lack of clarification of the integrity domain. Moreover, the instruments define low integrity by the absence of high integrity rather than by the presence of devious behaviors, and were found used for rating the integrity of managers only focusing on the positive desirable integrity construct but not on a lack of integrity or unethical behavior. Minor breaches of integrity are not rated as violations against serious violations of integrity that are usually covert.

However, Kaiser and Hogan (2010) measure managerial integrity framed by personality theory to identify the integrity of managers, drawing on the concepts of reputation and the influence of "weak" situations on the expression of dark-side tendencies. According to Kaiser and Hogan (2010) self assessments of managerial integrity are dubious sources of information because the manipulation and deceit of persons lacking integrity. Managers who lack integrity hardly recognize themselves as that and observers may identify questionable integrity behaviors of managers. Thus, subordinates are likely to be a prime and the best source of information about the personal and professional integrity of managers (Brown & Trevino, 2006). Kaiser and Hogan (2010) found that competency ratings do not identify managers with integrity issues. Ratings of an integrity competency are heavily skewed favoring managers who receive high ratings for integrity and are unlikely to identify managerial misconduct. Respondents refuse to answer questions related to identify integrity issues and behaviors of managers lacking integrity besides the difficulties to observe and rate them.

Firms may be concerned with effectively preventing declines in managerial integrity. Erhard, Jensen, and Zaffron (2007) assume that the decision of a firm to appoint a previous CEO, relies to a greater extent on firm-specific information on personal and professional integrity. In the case of the integrity of the previous CEO, firms promote an insider and hire an outsider in the case of a former dishonest CEO. However, it is not enough to be trusted in terms of managerial integrity to predict OCB.

Ratings of managerial integrity always favor managers and rarely identify the ones who may lack integrity. Kaiser and Hogan (2010) contend that competency ratings are unlikely to identify managerial integrity issues. They propose an alternative method, referred as the dubious reputation approach, to identify managers with potential integrity problems focusing on the lower level of the integrity, not relying on ratings of observed behavior but estimating the likelihood those managerial engagements in unethical behaviors. Ratings focused on the undesirable behaviors of the integrity domain of managers may identify their integrity problems. The dubious reputation approach involves personal integrity evaluations of the dark side of managers' personalities. This method proves to identify and assess levels of managerial integrity and effective competency.

The epitome of the dubious reputation method developed by Kaiser and Hogan (2010) is the Perceived Leader Integrity Scale (PLIS) developed by Craig and Gustafson (1998) which identifies low integrity of managers. An empirical research conducted by Kaiser and Hogan (2011) found that the PLIS yielded variability and higher incidence of low scores of managerial integrity than the integrity competency scale. Perceived integrity as a variable is more highly correlated with Consideration than Initiating Structure. Also the research concluded that as the strongest predictor, Perceived Integrity as a variable is more highly correlated to Perceived Effectiveness. This result is consistent with the notion that integrity is concerned with the needs and rights of other people.

INTEGRITY AND PERFORMANCE

The ontological law of integrity states that "To the degree that integrity is diminished, the opportunity for performance (the opportunity set) is diminished" (Erhard, Jensen and Zaffron, 2010). There is a relationship between integrity and performance, where integrity is a necessary condition for performance. Integrity not only exists as a virtue but rather than as a necessary condition for performance. Performance is defined as "the manner in which something or somebody functions, operates, or behaves; the effectiveness of the way somebody does his or her job" (Encarta Dictionary, 2004). To maintain management performance centered in the human and ethical values is always an issue that requires being subject to pressures and tensions for the same nature of the management profession. Perceptions of the manager's integrity determine how much to trust the manager which, in turn, influences attitudes and performance. Medlin and Green (2003) investigated the differences in ethical attitudes and perceptions of small business managers and owners finding that they expressed attitudes more alike between them rather ethical than unethical attitudes and perceptions.

Competency models that include integrity as a dimension are used by organizations to identify managerial performance capabilities (Boyatzis, 1982) use subordinate ratings focusing on behaviors to evaluate the integrity of managers. Perceptions of manager's behavioral integrity created collective trust and were related to customer satisfaction and profitability which translated into higher performance (McLean Parks, 1997). Behavioral ratings of observed ethical behavior by co-workers' measures integrity defined as a leadership competency suggests that only a small proportion of managers may have integrity issues without distinguishing high- from low-performing managers (Kaiser and Hogan, 2010).

When nobody has an incentive to invest in firm-specific knowledge, the managerial integrity drops, and consequently the performance of the firm also drops, such as the case of external hires who step up the regression of integrity in firms (Rost et al., 2008). Regression of integrity in firms may result in the prevalence of outside hires. When followers believe their leader cannot be trusted because the leader is perceived not to have integrity, they divert energy diminishing work performance (Mayer and Gavin, 1999). Assuming that the integrity of the previous CEO has no effects on performance, Erhard, Jensen and Zaffron, (2007) found that the managerial integrity of a former CEO pays off improving the performance of a firm at the time when the leadership change is stable.

Kaiser and Hogan (2010) conducted an empirical study of ratings on a competency-based integrity scale with psychometric properties to test the expectation that few managers are rated as lacking integrity, to prove that ratings of integrity fail to identify individuals at the low level and not predict managerial performance. The integrity competency analysis use subordinate ratings of integrity to predict overall performance. Subordinate ratings of a professional managerial integrity competency are consistent with performance ratings in organizations. Results of a research conducted by Kaiser and Hogan (2010) show that ratings on the integrity competency are unrelated to managerial performance. The proposed method by Kaiser and Hogan (2010) based on subordinate expectations about the likelihood that professional managers would misbehave and have unethically behaviors suggests that a larger proportion of managers may have professional integrity issues without distinctions performance.

Kaiser and Hogan (2010) found in their empirical research that manager's competency integrity is highly correlated with building talent showing concern for subordinates, although does not distinguish the level of management performance concluding that integrity competency does not predict performance. This finding is consistent with the definition of integrity as sensitivity for the needs and rights of other people. The empirical research conducted by Kaiser and Hogan (2010) found that the levels of manager's integrity is not correlated with the level of performance. This finding contradicts the research showing that personal integrity is a prerequisite for effective leadership.

INTEGRITY AND LEADERSHIP EFFECTIVENESS

Regarding integrity, most leaders follow a more Machiavellian view who wrote that a prince should appear a man of integrity (Machiavelli, 1981: 101). Integrity as other values has an impact on effectiveness. The argument that leaders need integrity to function effectively is supported by Covey (1992:61 and 108), who contends that followers become guarded of leaders with low level of integrity.

There are few empirical studies conducted to explore the role that integrity plays in leadership effectiveness. There is a lack of empirical research to analyze the relationship between integrity, leadership behaviors and effectiveness. The study of the impact that integrity has for effectiveness has not been clarified because integrity is to a greater or lesser extent being perceived as more effective when having honesty and fairness. Few empirical studies examine the relationship between integrity and leader effectiveness but not the impact integrity has on leader effectiveness. What may be good for the sense of integrity may not improve effectiveness. Direct reports have association between integrity and leadership effectiveness and are concerned about indicators of integrity of managers because of the need for consistent behavior (Staw, et al., 1980).

The assumption that integrity has a positive effect on leader and organizational effectiveness is questionable when research on leadership emphasizes behavioral approaches rather than integrity and actions that lack integrity can lead to success (Jackall, 1988). Morgan (1989) developed a leadership assessment scales on integrity to analyze the relationship to leader effectiveness and found that integrity as a variable is related to trust. Trust reflects the integrity or capability of another party, thus trust in a leader's integrity may inspire followers because of the leader's adherence to certain values (McAllister, 1995). Research on integrity and leadership effectiveness suggests a positive relationship. Badaracco and Ellsworth (1990) and Covey (1992) argue integrity has an impact for leadership effectiveness. Followers believing in the integrity of their leaders are more comfortable engaging in risky behaviors (Mayer, Davis, & Schoorman, 1995). Hooijberg, Hunt and Dodge (1997) call for the role of integrity as a value in leadership research.

Craig and Gustafson (1998) developed the Perceived Leader Integrity Scale (PLIS) to measure employee's perceptions of their leader's integrity and job satisfaction and found positive correlation. Craig and Gustafson (1998) provide a large pool of items. The global indicators of integrity (Craig and Gustafson, 1998: 134) account for 81% of the variance in perceptions of integrity. Becker (1998: 160) argues high personal integrity make excellent candidates for leadership positions. Simons (1999) used the concept of behavioral integrity and leader effectiveness and found that there is a significant positive correlation between perceived integrity and leader effectiveness. Morrison (2001: 65) states that integrity is necessary for managers to engender the goodwill and trust required for an effective leadership. Parry and Proctor-Thomson (2002) revised the PLIS to analyze the relationship.

Integrity is a cognitive form operating via different processes on outcomes such as the organizational citizenship behavior (OCB). Thus, Dirks and Skarlicki (2004) argue that integrity may be a predictor of OCB and the leader may be seen as being with high integrity. This idea, according to the authors implies that integrity predicts employee OCB although the main effects for benevolence and integrity on OCB were not significant at low and moderate levels, however the authors found that when benevolence is high the relationship between integrity and OCB is positive. Mayer and Davis' (1999) trustworthiness scales assess trust in managers in terms of integrity and benevolence. Behavioral integrity and competence impact trust, although Salam (2000) argues that integrity and competence are not sufficient to increase trust for other parties.

Hooijberg and Lane (2005) examine the impact integrity has on people's perceptions of effectiveness and found that integrity has a small relevance for leadership effectiveness. To test the relationship between leadership behaviors, integrity, and managerial effectiveness, Hooijberg and Lane, N (2005) included in his research values associated with integrity and values in conflict with integrity. Hooijberg and Lane (2005) reported that is partially confirmed for all evaluators that integrity has a positive association with effectiveness for managers and their peers. Melé (2009, p. 198- 224) focuses on "Human Virtues in Leadership of Organizations" and he speaks of moral character in leadership on wisdom and integrity intended as wholeness of virtue; on humility and authenticity, justice, honesty, loyalty, self-discipline, courage, patience and being positive.

However, between integrity and direct reports or bosses' perceptions of effectiveness, they did not find a significant association between integrity and effectiveness. The results show a statistically significant association for the managers themselves and their peers, but there is not statistically significant association between Integrity and effectiveness for the direct reports and bosses. Their results also confirm that bosses associate goal-oriented behaviors had the strongest association, but not integrity with leadership effectiveness. These values have a stronger association with effectiveness than integrity, honesty, and fairness do. Integrity affects perceptions of managerial effectiveness when managers strongly associate being goal-oriented, monitoring and facilitation. Perceived competence and integrity are character-based factors make individuals willing to take the risk toward a common goal. Goal-oriented behaviors of managers are associated with effectiveness, but not integrity. Integrity as a key ingredient for effectiveness may be hard to maintain.

Competency ratings of integrity are not capable to identify managers who may lack integrity because there is an assumption that managers are at risk for misbehaving. Competency rating methods assume integrity in terms of desirable observed ethical behaviors in such a way that to identify managerial integrity underestimates the number of managers with integrity issues. Definitively, when an organization is led by managerial integrity, interior life develops with integrity and generates an exemplar effect for all involved in the activities.

Kaiser and Hogan (2010) suggest that organizations conducting character and integrity audits consider other alternative approaches for detecting integrity such as simulations, assessment centers, enhanced background checks, specially designed interviews and rely on more than just competency ratings of integrity. There is the possibility to replace competency ratings with ratings based on the dubious reputation methods, the PLIS scale is in the public domain, by focusing on subordinates' expectations or create hybrid scales. The PLIS scale, a measure of the dubious reputation method identifies managers' integrity at the unethical end of the continuum. The dubious reputation analysis use subordinate ratings of integrity to predict ratings of job satisfaction and perceived effectiveness. Kaiser and Hogan (2010) propose the dubious reputation method to evaluate the integrity of managers based on expectations that managers behave unethically. The dubious reputation method is intended to replace the competency ratings to identify and evaluate the integrity of managers. Results of using PLIS are consistent with prior findings that leader integrity is determinant of leadership perceptions.

Integrity and ethics concern one's relationships with other people. The absence of ethics and integrity precluded leadership. Hooijberg, and Lane, (2005) examine the impact of some values including integrity on leadership behaviors and effectiveness finding that the value of integrity has a significant impact on effectiveness. The findings of Hooijberg, R. and Lane, N (2005) do not support the notion that integrity is essential for leadership. They did not find a statistically significant association between integrity and effectiveness

Personal integrity also plays a central role in transformational as well as charismatic leadership highlighted by research. Thus, Personal integrity is a prerequisite for leadership (Cohen, 2009). Followers' perceptions of a leader's integrity are related to transformational leadership (Parry & Proctor-Thomson, 2002). However, competency ratings do not measure low level of personal and managerial integrity because leadership research focuses on positive qualities (Padilla, Hogan & Kaiser, 2007).

MATERIAL AND METHODS / EXPERIMENTAL DETAILS / METHODOLOGY

The hypothesis of this research considers that there are some economic, social and cultural factors which appear to pressure management education to far outweigh to maintain professional integrity. This hypothesis is proved empirically confirmed by the finding that significant importance is placed on the professional's reputation for integrity, economic efficiency strength, organizational social capital, and a compliance ethical culture. This paper outlines an approach in which professional integrity in management education is understood in the context of honesty, as having an ethical background, building trust and maintaining credibility. The chapter concludes by presenting a model of management education for professional integrity that can used to prescribe a more sensitive and dynamic human-ethical environment.

The research method employed is the ethnographic, documental and life's histories, complemented with field work supported by in-depth interviews and analyzed using a comparative method. Participants described several dimensions of professional integrity in management education. Discussion focuses on integrity as the basic principle of professionalism in management education to guide complex ethical reasoning, as well as the need for creating and sustaining professional integrity environments through ethical modeling and relational behaviors promoted by integrity as the essential element. This methodology puts in evidence that there is an urgent need to develop a model to approach professional integrity in economic and managerial careers.

In our own research conducted with information units involving teachers and students to determine the existence of program content oriented toward teaching ethics and professional integrity in the administration major at the university level as well as the existence of behavior codes as a frame of reference. For managerial students, it is essential to make the concepts of integrity, fairness, and corruption tangible, stressing that students must a personal interest in honest in obtaining legitimate qualifications to compete in the tight job market complement appeals to integrity (Gainer, 2015). Results indicated that all the teachers coincide in affirming the need to incorporate a transversal program axis that would permeate the curriculum, oriented toward teaching ethics and professional integrity in the administration schools. Therefore, the study recommended setting up cooperation networks to implement common axes for teaching ethics at the national universities.

The outcomes of the research on the application in management education demonstrate that the drama of economic efficiency is centered on a dysfunctional professional integrity. This chapter provides a sound professional philosophy that empowers professionals to act with integrity, increases the probability for long-term success and professional fulfillment. The chapter offers practitioners, managers, leaders, etc., skills and moral frameworks of professional integrity that can be shared across and within professions, and used to compare and evaluate their professional practice. The results provide also the basis to develop a code of conduct and regulation policies to sustain management education for professional integrity which, can positively impact on business culture through influencing the behavior of key actors.

RESULTS AND DISCUSSION

In general, there is a consensus that now a day it is required professionals with the capacity to live and share in harmony with others, sociability, self-control, professional integrity and adaptability in cultural diversity. To develop this type of professional, it is necessary to institute, teach and share with an example the values of the organization to the personnel on the basis of congruence between the word and the action of executives. The teaching of ethical professional based on the integrity must consider teaching at the university as an educative responsibility to satisfy the professional development programs. The ultimate end of any educative process is that human being achieve its plenitude to be capable to build everyday a fairer and equalitarian society where justice, tolerance and participation and of course, respect to others must prevail over any other interest. Being that, the economic progress will be possible on the behalf of human being integrity.

Personal sustainable development and success requires getting, restoring and maintaining professional integrity. To have, restore and maintain professional integrity behavior for individuals, groups and organizations where it doesn't exist or it has been diminished requires a development program of professional integrity. As it has been signaled by Batteman y Snell (2001) ethics programs must be based on integrity and to go beyond to avoid illegality, to worry for the law, but also to inculcate on the people a personal responsibility for ethical behavior. Ethical problems based on personal integrity, besides the legal aspects consider necessary to inculcate in the student personal responsibility for his/her ethical behavior. Behaviors are manifestations and expressions of a value scale. As Humboldt had said: If we want to have professionals with ethics, we have to teach to be and how to be.

Professional development must inculcate the habits of professional integrity, in such a way to create confidence that those habits of professional integrity will be practiced by these same individuals when they become licensed professionals. However, determination to work in an ethical way and to be an integrity person is an individual process. The teaching of professional ethics and integrity is a factor contributed to an elemental human development in the global realm (Kliksberg, 2002 and Etkin, 1993). Professional ethics determine the essential bases of behaviors, to make decisions on the grounds of moral values and professional acts and keep on the relationship with vocation. The business ethics has an incidence in professional integrity. In this way, institutions of higher education must attend the specific needs of professional formation and development that society merits to the aim to guarantee the positioning of professionals in labor markets.

Learning models must integrate a holistic vision of professional managerial integrity formation and development, the institutions of higher education must foster formation and development of professional integrity of organizational administration according to the existent needs, achieving the requests by why they were created. The characteristics of professional integrity as part of the graduate profile of universities must be screened by the mechanisms of personnel selection of organizations and vice versa, according to the environment needs. It is required the existence of a major coordination between business organizations and the university to have an incidence in the formation and development of the managerial cadres in educative institutions as a product of this synchronization.

It has been under the study the need to achieve some changes centered on the formation and development of professional integrity in the professional practice (Rodríguez Ordoñez, 2004). The components of the professional's moral integrity and their influence in the development of activities such as the academic formation and how it complements with learned values in the family nucleus which will generate in the professional an indisputable added value. Professional integrity of the manager's action in the development of competencies and capabilities are related to corporate social responsibility (CSR) that has a fundamental part in corporative governance. Hemingway and Maclagan (2004) among others, justify the notion that managerial values and attitudes towards corporate social responsibility (CSR) in organizational settings are likely to influence firm-level CSR outcomes. Stead & Stead (2004) interpret context sustainability-oriented business as multidimensional and normative social, ecological and economic concerns. Since the natural environment provides organizations with some crucial resources in which business is conducted, a research agenda connects the business model research and strategic sustainability management (Stead & Stead, 2004).

An analysis of professional integrity and values across cultures and their interrelationships to increase or reduce human welfare is a new field of research. In this sense, Managers constantly associated integrity with honesty, merit and fairness but differ with other values. In some training situations penalties for tolerating lapses of integrity may be ameliorated, the same which may be fully enforced in the professional context. However, professional integrity must be so crucial in training situations where the stakes are not too high and some failures may be tolerated.

Some proposals can be implemented in the management teaching programs development addressed to the application of integrity and ethical values at the same level of knowledge, searching for coherent professional behaviors in order to avoid the forced interpretation of normative. Otherwise, when the occasion comes, it allows to treason without scrupulous the spirit of the norm, looking for meeting only the personal interests that nothing have to do with the pretended public interest that is equivalent to collective welfare of a community of persons and institutions served by the professional manager. The point to make here is that trust in his/her objectivity and integrity is vital to sustain the adequate functioning of the organizational activity.

Management's curriculum must be oriented towards the future and to must be enriched to include student's development in a systematic and ordered way of attitudes, attributes and personal qualities, such as professional integrity and independence, among others. All of these must be aligned with the concept of integral development, moreover because they are consubstantial to the successful practice of the profession (AICPA, 1980: 16).

IMPLICATIONS FOR MANAGEMENT EDUCATION

Professions exist to serve society's needs through professionals using morally decent means to provide values and services. Professionals in administration and management must be able to effectively cultivate an image of personal integrity. When integrity-based trust in management professionals is high, organizations that espouse ethical and moral values are more willing to trust more important and crucial responsibilities and activities. The professional ethical principles give substance to different forms of professional behavior included in the actions, such as how to focus justice to human beings, responsibility in performance of professional activities, discretion in information management and honesty in each one of his/her actions.

An individual maintains its professional integrity as long as it remains uncorrupted. Professionals that distort their essential service functions to society toward unreasonable profits, power, or greed, they may lose the trust and respect of their communities. Gregg, S. & Stoner, J.R. (Eds.) (2008) analyze the relationship between virtue and profit drawing from and applying natural law and virtue ethics approaches in the context of business management education and business practice, that the authors find compatible despite that they appear to be centered on modern individualism. The authors recommend the cultivation of virtues for the business management education. Ruisi, M., Fasone, V. Paternostro, S. (2009) also confirm the same approach that they call binomial to support the creation of an entrepreneurial model. Bucar and Hisrich (2004) found that managers more than entrepreneurs may sacrifice their personal values to those of the company, but entrepreneurs consistently demonstrate higher ethical attitudes.

The character-based perspective focusing on concerns about the managerial integrity, suggests that the referent trusted predicts the response or concern toward a specific individual integrity. The negligent professional manager in his/her actions despite that having necessary information to execute his/her functions, expose his/her professional integrity. In the case of conflicting duties, professional integrity tells us that the highest duty is to avoid harming others. Simons (1999) "... proposes that the divergence between words and deeds has profound costs as it renders managers untrustworthy and undermines their credibility and their ability to use their words to influence the actions of their subordinates." The manager must have and show absolute mental independence and criteria regarding to any interest, which can be considered incompatible with integrity and objectivity principles that can be affected without an application of autonomous and neutral criteria.

Management's professional must act with integrity which is achieved taking into account that must be immerse in each one of his/her functions, tasks and components of personal activities. The most important and significant aspects of management's professional services towards clients, customers and general public, cannot be defined as knowledge and experiences but in less precise terms, such as professional integrity, sense, wise, perception, imagination, circumspection, service to others, professional stability, personal benefits, professional honesty, respect to personal dignity, vocation, and so forth. Beyond the technological financial and of any other type aspects, the management's professional must have as a central axis his action and behavior toward other human beings.

A reconstruction of professional ethics and integrity is necessary to recover credibility and respect of management's profession. According to the competencies of knowing to be and knowing to share, the attitudes, values, qualities, habits and dispositions imprinted in the citizens and professionals' character, make managers builders of a better society. Being capable of make sense on managerial knowledge and practices it is expected from personal integrity.

Society provides the necessary resources and opportunities for carrying out the professional integrity functions, the authority to act on its behalf and the autonomy required to provide social trust. Failures of social trust are related to breaches of professional integrity. Violations of the trust based on the relationship and on the authority to act on behalf of the entire society, are serious breaches of professional integrity. To refuse a professional assignment in such a way that breaks faith with all other members of the profession and the social interest, it may be considered a first-order violation of professional integrity. It is the equivalent of a manager to manage or abandoning managerial assignments that can be devastating to and organization and society. Manager's professional reputation and integrity in his/her relationships to other persons and stakeholder groups are important. The commitment to social welfare and preservation of environment is getting anchored in all managerial and economic fields' professions.

In conclusion to value integrity as a relevant aspect to individuals, is possible to work effectively for personal goodness and for the common good.

Recommendations for assessing professional managerial integrity in practice must urge the professional managers to consider the prevalence and impact of managerial misconduct. All the professions and management is not the exception, are ruled under social principles of honesty, integrity and collective responsibility that must be developed at the workplace. Integrity and responsibility must be part of the manager's professional life. This means that a good professional must know his / her legal, labor and entrepreneurial limitations which are aligned with the ethical values that generate a higher level of transparency. This issue is confirmed by other studies reporting that integrity to the entrepreneur is supported by the role of identity drivers of individuals involved in sustainable entrepreneurship and authenticity emerging as an identity condition leading to triggering entrepreneurial activity (O'Neil and Ucbasaran 2010). Sustainable entrepreneurship is defined as the process of discovering, evaluating, and exploiting economic opportunities that are present in market failures which detract from sustainability, including those that are environmentally relevant (Dean and McMullen, 2007). Lester, D. & Mullane, J. (2010) argue that sustainable entrepreneurship educational programs prepare university students for the creation of successful enterprises promoting sustainability as an outcome, for both their students' entrepreneurial efforts and their own academic programs. The management's professional is committed to carry on his/her functions with transparency and integrity generating a better quality of life.

It is necessary to promote a managerial culture to rescue the values and the attention to human being as a key factor to have organizations that every day achieves higher levels of development and productivity.

It is necessary to strengthen and consolidate plans and programs on management study with the ethical and human formation either in the teaching of specific courses strengthen them with the action of academic and administrative authorities.

Future research on professional and managerial integrity could conduct a more anthropological study and collect not only quantitative assessments but also qualitative assessments.

REFERENCES

Adler, N. J., & Bird, F. B. (1988). International dimensions of executive integrity: Who is responsible for the world? In S. Srivastva & ... (Eds.), *Executive Integrity: The Search for High Human Values in Organizational Life*. San Francisco, CA: Jossey-Bass.

AICPA (American Institute of Certified Public Accountants AICPA). (1980). *Accounting for your Future*. New York: Author.

Allport, G. W. (1937). *Personality: A psychological interpretation*. New York: Henry Holt & Company.

Argyris, C. (1991, May). Teaching Smart People How to Learn. *Harvard Business Review*, 99–109.

Badaracco, J. L., & Ellsworth, R. R. (1990). Quest for integrity. *Executive Excellence*, 7, 3–4.

Batteman, T. S., & Snell, S. A. (2001). Administración una ventaja competitiva. Editorial McGraw Hill.

Becker, T. (1998). Integrity in organizations: Beyond honesty and conscientiousness. *Academy of Management Review*, 23(1), 154–161. doi:10.5465/amr.1998.192969

Bigley, G., & McAllister, D. (2002). *Transformations in Relational Logic: How Types of Supervisory Trust Interact to Predict Subordinate OCB*. Unpublished manuscript. University of Washington.

Boyatzis, R. E. (1982). *The competent manager: A model for effective performance*. New York: Wiley.

Brown, M. E., & Trevino, L. K. (2006). Ethical leadership: A review and future directions. *The Leadership Quarterly*, 17(6), 595–616. doi:10.1016/j.leaqua.2006.10.004

Bucar, B., & Hisrich, R. D. (2004). Ethics of business managers vs. entrepreneurs. *Journal of Developmental Entrepreneurship*, 61(1), 59–82.

Cohen, W. A. (2009). *Drucker on leadership*. San Francisco: Jossey-Bass.

Covey, S. R. (1992). *Principle-Centered Leadership*. New York: Simon & Schuster.

Cox, D., La Caze, M., & Levine, M. (2005). Integrity. In *The Stanford Encyclopedia of Philosophy*. Accessed April 9, 2006 at: http://plato.stanford.edu/archives/fall2005/entries/integrity/

Craig, S. B., & Gustafson, S. B. (1998). Perceived leader integrity scale. *The Leadership Quarterly, 9*(2), 127–145. doi:10.1016/S1048-9843(98)90001-7

Dean, T., & McMullen, J. (2007). Toward a theory of sustainable entrepreneurship: Reducing environmental degradation through entrepreneurial action. *Journal of Business Venturing, 22*(1), 50–76. doi:10.1016/j.jbusvent.2005.09.003

Dirks, K. T., & Skarlicki, D. (2004). Trust in Leaders: Existing Research and Emerging Issues. In R. Sage (Ed.), Trust and distrust in organizations: Dilemmas and approaches. Academic Press.

Erhard, W., Jensen, M., & Zaffron, S. (2007). *A New Model of Integrity: Without Integrity Nothing Works. Negotiation, Organizations and Markets Research Papers*. Harvard.

Erhard, W., Jensen, M. C., & Zaffron, S. (2008). *Integrity: A Positive Model that Incorporates the Normative Phenomena of Morality, Ethics and Legality*. Harvard Business School NOM Working Paper No. 06-11; Barbados Group Working Paper No. 06-03; Simon School Working Paper No. FR 08-05. Available at SSRN: http://ssrn.com/abstract=920625

Erhard, W., Jensen, M. C., & Zaffron, S. (2010). *Integrity: A Positive Model that Incorporates the Normative Phenomena of Morality, Ethics, and Legality - Abridged (English Language Version)*. Harvard Business School NOM Unit Working Paper No. 10-061; Barbados Group Working Paper No. 10-01; Simon School Working Paper No. 10-07. Available at SSRN: http://ssrn.com/abstract=1542759

Erhard, W., Jensen, M. C., & Zaffron, S. (2011). *Integridad: Un Modelo Positivo Que Incorpora Fenomenos Normativos de Moral, Etica y Legalidad - Abreviado* [Integrity: A Positive Model that Incorporates the Normative Phenomena of Morality, Ethics, and Legality - Abridged]. Harvard Business School NOM Unit Working Paper No. 10-061; Barbados Group Working Paper No. 10-01; Simon School Working Paper No. 10-07. Available at SSRN: http://ssrn.com/abstract=1756285

Etkin, J. (1993). *La doble moral de las organizaciones*. Mc Graw Hill.

Fritzche, D. J., & Becker, H. (1984). Linking management behavior to ethical philosophy: An empirical investigation. *Academy of Management Journal, 27*, 166–175.

Gainer, M. (2015). *Shaping Values for a New Generation: Anti-Corruption Education in Lithuania, 2002-2006*. Princeton University. Retrieved from https://successfulsocieties.princeton.edu/sites/successfulsocieties/files/MG_NORMS_Lithuania_1.pdf

Ghoshal, S. (2005). Bad management. Theories are destroying good management practices. *Academy of Management Learning & Education, 4*(1), 75–91. doi:10.5465/amle.2005.16132558

Gorgievski, M. J., Ascalon, M. E., & Ute, S. (2011). Small business owners' success criteria, a values approach to personal differences. *Journal of Small Business Management, 49*(2), 207–232. doi:10.1111/j.1540-627X.2011.00322.x

Gregg, S., & Stoner, J. R. (Eds.). (2008). Rethinking Business Management. Examining the Foundations of Business Education. Witherspoon Institute.

Hemingway, C. A., & Maclagan, P. W. (2004). Managers' personal values as drivers of corporate social responsibility. *Journal of Business Ethics, 50*(1), 33–44. doi:10.1023/B:BUSI.0000020964.80208.c9

Hernández, R., Silvestri, K., & Álvarez, A. (2007). Enseñanza de la ética en la formación gerencial. *Revista de Ciencias Sociales, 13*(3).

Hooijberg, R., Hunt, J. G., & Dodge, G. E. (1997). Leadership complexity and development of the leaderplex model. *Journal of Management, 23*, 375–408. doi:10.1177/014920639702300305

Hooijberg, R., & Lane, N. (2005). *Leader effectiveness and integrity: Wishful thinking? IMD 2005-1 IMD*. International Institute for Management Development.

Jackall, R. (1988). *Moral Mazes*. New York, NY: Oxford University Press, Inc.

Jensen, M. C. (2009). Integrity: Without it Nothing Works. *Rotman Magazine: The Magazine of the Rotman School of Management*, 16-20. Available at SSRN: http://ssrn.com/abstract=1511274

Jensen, M. C., Granger, K. L., & Erhard, W. (2010). *A New Model of Integrity: The Missing Factor of Production. (PDF file of Keynote and PowerPoint Slides.* Harvard Business School NOM Unit Working Paper 10-087; Barbados Group Working Paper No. 10-03. Available at SSRN: http://ssrn.com/abstract=1559827

Kaiser, R. B., & Hogan, R. (2010). How to (and how not to) assess the integrity of managers. *Consulting Psychology Journal: Practice and Research American Psychological Association, 62*(4), 216–234. doi:10.1037/a0022265

Kaptein, M. (2003). The diamond of managerial integrity. *European Management Journal, 21*(1), 98–108. doi:10.1016/S0263-2373(02)00157-3

Kerr, S. (1988). Integrity in effective leadership. In *Executive Integrity: The search for high human values in organizational life*. San Francisco, CA: Jossey-Bass.

Kliksberg, B. (2002). *Ética y Desarrollo, La Relación Marginada (con los premios Nóbel de Economía Amartya Sen, Joseph Stiglitz y otros)*. El Ateneo.

Kolthoff, E., Huberts, L., & Heuvel, H. (2003). The Ethics of New Public Management: Is Integrity at Stake? EGPA Study Group "Ethics and Integrity of Governance" Oeiras, Portugal.

Leslie, J. B., & Fleenor, J. W. (1998). *Feedback to managers: A review and comparison of multi-rater instruments for management development*. Greensboro, NC: Center for Creative Leadership.

Lester, D., & Mullane, J. (2010). Sustainable entrepreneurship education: a comparative approach. *Small Business Institute, National Conference Proceedings*, 34(1).

Levinson, H. (1988). To thine own self be true: Coping with the dilemmas of integrity. In S. Srivastva & ... (Eds.), *Executive Integrity: The Search for High Human Values in Organizational Life*. San Francisco, CA: Jossey-Bass.

Llano, C. (1997). *Empleo, Educación y Formación Permanente. Lo mejor de Executive Excellence*. Panorama Editorial.

Longenecker, J. G., Moore, C. W., Petty, J. W., Palich, L. E., & McKinney, J. A. (2006). Ethical attitudes in small business & large corporations: Theory & empirical findings from a tracking study planning three decades'. *Journal of Small Business Management, 2*(44), 167–183. doi:10.1111/j.1540-627X.2006.00162.x

Machiavelli, N. (1981). *The Prince* (G. Bull, Trans.). New York, NY: Penguin Books.

Mayer, R., & Gavin, M. (1999). *Trust for management and performance: Who minds the shop while the employees watch the boss?* Paper presented at the Annual Meeting of the Academy of Management, Chicago, IL.

Mayer, R. C., & Davis, J. H. (1999). The effect of the performance appraisal system on trust for management: A field quasi-experiment. *The Journal of Applied Psychology, 84*(1), 123–136. doi:10.1037/0021-9010.84.1.123

Mayer, R. C., Davis, J. H., & Schoorman, F. D. (1995). An integrative model of organizational trust. *Academy of Management Review, 20*(3), 709–734. doi:10.5465/amr.1995.9508080335

McAllister, D. J. (1995). Affect- and cognition-based trust as foundations for interpersonal cooperation in organizations. *Academy of Management Journal, 38*, 24–59.

McDowell, D. (2010). *Core Values and Professional Integrity*. Retrieved from http://www.mncap.org/protocol/CoreValues_ProfIntegrity.pdf

McLean, P. (1997). The fourth arm of justice: The art and science of revenge. In Research on Negotiation in Organizations. JAI Press.

Medlin, B., & Green, K.W., Jr. (2003). Ethics in small business: attitudes and perceptions of owners/managers. *Academy of Entrepreneurship Journal, 6*, 513-518.

Melé, D. (2009). *Business Ethics in Action. Seeking Human Excellence in Organizations*. Hampshire, UK: Palgrave Macmillan. doi:10.1007/978-1-137-07468-3

Morgan, R. B. (1989). Reliability and validity of a factor analytically derived measure of leadership behavior and characteristics. *Educational and Psychological Measurement, 49*(4), 911–919. doi:10.1177/001316448904900414

Morrison, A. (2001). Integrity and global leadership. *Journal of Business Ethics, 31*(1), 65–76. doi:10.1023/A:1010789324414

O'Neil, I., & Ucbasaran, D. (2010). *Individual identity and sustainable entrepreneurship: The role of authenticity*. London: Institute of Small Business & Entrepreneurship Conference.

Oxford Dictionaries. (2011) Retrieved from http://oxforddictionaries.com

Padilla, A., Hogan, R., & Kaiser, R. B. (2007). The toxic triangle: Destructive leaders, vulnerable followers, and conducive environments. *The Leadership Quarterly, 18*(3), 176–194. doi:10.1016/j.leaqua.2007.03.001

Paladino, M., Debeljuh, P. & Del Bosco, P. (2005). *Integridad: respuesta superadora a los dilemas éticos del hombre de empresa*. Academic Press.

Parry, K., & Proctor-Thomson, S. B. (2002). Perceived integrity of transformational leaders in organizational settings. *Journal of Business Ethics, 35*(2), 75–96. doi:10.1023/A:1013077109223

Pojman, L. P. (1995). *Ethical theory: Classical and contemporary readings* (2nd ed.). Belmont, CA: Wadsworth.

Pratt, M. G., Rockmann, K. W., & Kaufmann, J. B. (2006). Constructing Professional Identity: The Role of Work and Identity Learning Cycles in the Customization of Identity Among Medical Residents. *Academy of Management Journal, 49*(2), 235–262. doi:10.5465/amj.2006.20786060

Rodríguez Ordoñez, J. A. (2004). Hacia la integralidad de la enseñanza y la práctica profesional en geotecnia. *Ing. Univ. Bogotá, 8*(2), 159-171.

Rost, K., Salomo, S., & Osterloh, M. (2008). CEO appointments and the loss of firm-specific knowledge - putting integrity back into hiring decisions. *Corporate Ownership and Control, 5*(3), 86–98. doi:10.22495/cocv5i3p10

Ruisi, M., Fasone, V., & Paternostro, S. (2009). *Respect and hope a binomial relationship supporting the creation of a true entrepreneurial model*. Paper presented at the European SPES Forum, Respect and Economic Democracy, Catania.

Salam, S. (2000). Foster trust through competence, honesty, and integrity. In E. Locke (Ed.), *Handbook of principles of organizational behavior* (pp. 274–288). Malden, MA: Blackwell.

Schulz, W. (2016), *Becoming Citizens in a Changing World: IEA International Civic and Citizenship Education Study 2016 International Report*. IEA. Retrieved from http://iccs.iea.nl/fileadmin/user_upload/Editor_Group/Downloads/ICCS_2016_International_report.pdf

Shakespeare, W. (1914). *The Oxford Shakespeare: The complete works of William Shakespeare. Hamlet, Act II*. London: Oxford University Press.

Simons, T. L. (1999). Behavioral Integrity as a Critical Ingredient for Transformational Leadership. *Journal of Organizational Change Management, 12*(2), 89-104.

Simons, T. L. (2002). Behavioral Integrity: The Perceived Alignment Between Manager's Words and Deeds as a Research Focus. *Organization Science, 13*(1), 18–35. doi:10.1287/orsc.13.1.18.543

Smith, P. L., & Oakley, E. F. III. (1994). A Study of the Ethical Values of Metropolitan and Nonmetropolitan Small Business Owners. *Journal of Small Business Management, 32*(4), 17–27.

Solomon, R. C. (1999). *A Better Way to Think About Business: How Personal Integrity Leads to Corporate Success*. New York: Oxford University Press.

Srivastva, S., & ... (1988). *Executive Integrity: The Search for High Human Values in Organizational Life*. San Francisco, CA: Jossey-Bass.

Staw, B. M., & Ross, J. (1980). Commitment in an experimenting society: A study of the attribution of leadership from administrative scenarios. *The Journal of Applied Psychology, 65*(3), 249–260. doi:10.1037/0021-9010.65.3.249

Stead, W., & Stead, J. (2004). *Sustainable Strategic Management*. Armonk, NY: ME Sharpe.

Svejenova, S. (2005). The Path with the Heart: Creating the Authentic Career. *Journal of Management Studies*, *42*(5), 947–974. doi:10.1111/j.1467-6486.2005.00528.x

Thompson, A. D., Grahek, M., Phillips, R. E., & Fay, C. L. (2008). The search for worthy leadership. *Consulting Psychology Journal: Practice and Research*, *60*(4), 366–382. doi:10.1037/1065-9293.60.4.366

UNESCO. (2014). *Unesco roadmap for implementing the Global Action Program on education for sustainable development*. Paris, France: UNESCO.

Von Kimakowitz, E., Pirson, M., Spitzech, H., Dierksmeier, C., & Amann, W. (2010). *Humanistic Management in Practice*. New York: Palgrave Macmillan.

Webster's. (1994). *Webster's New World Dictionary on PowerCD version 2.1, based on Webster's New World Dictionary* (Edition 1994). Third College.

KEY TERMS AND DEFINITIONS

Integrity: Integrity means the totality of a person, including the physical dimension, that is, the body. As a human value, integrity is a personal choice and a commitment to consistency with honoring ethics, values and principles. The moral dimension, including the way of being and the values. In general, the concept applies to human rights, but also to the values that a person may have. In ethics, integrity considers the veracity and transparency of personal actions, therefore, is opposed to falsehood or deception.

Leadership: Consists of the ability or ability of a person to influence, induce, encourage or motivate others to carry out certain objectives, with enthusiasm and of their own will.

Management Education: Is one discipline of higher education by which students are taught to be business leaders, directors, managers, executives, and administrators.

Managerial Integrity: Is a holistic management approach that makes prudent and ethical decisions in managerial positions relating to functional areas of organizations such as finance, operations, marketing, human resources as well as manufacturing by adhering to the highest standards of product quality, open and clear communication.

Organizational Performance: Capacity of the organization that harmonizes the individual group results and of the own organization; that stimulates performance; recognizes the perceptions of workers; and expresses the characteristics of the competencies that it has.

Professional Integrity: Degree of identification of the behavior of a professional with the ethical requirements of their profession.

Professionalism: The professionalism is the way or the way to develop certain professional activity with a total commitment, moderation and responsibility, according to their specific formation and following the pre-established guidelines socially.

Chapter 12
Ethics Courses Teaching Linkage to Quality Management Education

Damini Saini
University of Lucknow, India

Sunita Singh Sengupta
University of Delhi, India

ABSTRACT

Almost every management institution in India has an ethics course in their curriculum that is focused upon inculcating the value set in an individual. To understand the role of ethical education in accelerating the quality of management education, this chapter provides a discussion of implications of the questions of quality, dilemma, and pedagogy of ethical training. In the introduction, the authors emphasize on the reasons of focusing upon the ethical education, then give a brief history of ethics education in Indian management institutions. In order to show the significance, authors also show the place of ethics course in top 10 business institutions in India. Further, the authors describe the main focus of the chapter that is the contribution of ethics in management education.

INTRODUCTION

Why a course on ethics? This can be an important quest in era where almost every sphere is actually neglecting the ethics and values. People are actually running behind so many things in life and without being aware of the consequences they are taking decisions. There are so many areas where ethics can get fit and provide required rationality. Nevertheless in this chapter we will precisely talk about the higher education in management field and it's correlation with ethics and values. Importance and requirement of ethics in management related courses is not new, more than two decades earlier the courses focused on ethics has been introduced in the management institutions of global importance.

DOI: 10.4018/978-1-7998-1017-9.ch012

Ethics Courses Teaching Linkage to Quality Management Education

In point of fact management is the main force that operates in the organization, spreads the value and seeds the morality in the environment and business leaders are the main role models to whom the employee look up. The never-ending list of failed corporations caught in scams and the magnitude of their leader's desire for profit maximization with complete disregard to well beings of their employees and common shareholders indicate the sidelined importance of values and ethics in business Being the torchbearers whether in the case of a nation or a corporation, leaders show the path to their followers and set examples. Henceforth the related perspective phenomenon of values and ethics in the management education carries a huge importance in today's corporate world. In the last few decades there are so many unethical activities happened in the corporate front in all over the world by which left the other people stunned. Then the leadership and the business schools were questioned about the prevalent practices and focus upon ethics in management has been intensified. Researchers worked persuasively upon business ethics and its consequences, organizational ethical climate and ethical leadership since then. Business colleges ought to be pioneers in delivering not "only" financial development and imperativeness additionally moral and socially dependable conduct; and along these lines business colleges ought to, and must, deliver business pioneers who can effectuate positive, esteem expanding change on a worldwide premise.

In the introduction of the chapter authors emphasize on the reasons of focusing upon the ethical education, then give a brief history of ethics education in Indian management institutions because of its focus on ethics courses in management. In order to show the significance of the course authors also list down the place of ethics course in top 10 business institution in India. Further they describe the main focus of the chapter that is contribution of ethics course in the quality management education. The chapter revolves around the related concept of ethics for instance responsibility, authenticity, self-reflection and spirituality of the top management in the various areas of organization which directly or indirectly affect their ethical instance of behavior and actions and highlights the importance of ethical education. Further the chapter is also consisting a single case which intensifies the dearth of a holistic approach of teaching ethics in universities. A few research propositions on the course of ethics and values also surfaced from this case. In the end we propose an idea of ethics and value related courses to show and how it complements and fits in the present education scenario.

LITERATURE REVIEW

Trevino (1986) speculated that since unethical practices cost the industries billions of dollars a year and damage the images of corporations, the emphasis on ethical behavior in organizations has increased over the recent years. Every individual has his own values but when the leader demonstrates the morality in actions the employees follow the blueprints and organization also gets recognition for its ethicality towards society. Henceforth the related perspective phenomenon of ethicality carries a huge importance in creating a morally healthy business environment for social and economic growth. Ethical behavior in business is a complex interaction of organizational factors, personality characteristics, and societal information cues which have a positive effect on long-term profitability (Neil C. Herndon, Jr. John P. Fraedrich, Quey-Jen Yeh, 2001). Ethical problems occur when the individual values and the social norms conflict with each other. Often, due to conflicting interests of different stakeholders, managers in organizations face the dilemma of identifying the righteous decision as perceived by these stakeholders, the task of determining what is ethical or not is not easy (Fritzsche & Tsalikis, 1989).Hence, it is important to guide managers — by articulating and communicating unambiguously — regarding what is right and what is not (Ganesh & Maheshwari, 2006). Initially Jansen and Von Glinow (1985) pointed out that corporate ethical values help in establishing and maintain the standards that describe the 'right' thing to do and the things 'worth doing'. In the similar vein Hunt et al. (1989) indicate that the ethical values of the company promote the establishment and maintenance of standard that trace "good" things to do and "bad" things to avoid and allow the organization to set normative standards for employees.

Poulton (2005) noted that, it is a society's quest for defining and understanding what constitutes "the good life" or "the good [that] has rightly been declared to be that at which all things aim" (Aristotle, 350BC). Ethics is the philosophy that ideally, rationally and reasonably determines right from wrong, good from bad, moral from immoral and just from unjust actions, conducts and behavior. According to Merriam-Webster's Online Dictionary, ethics is "the discipline dealing with what is good and bad and with moral duty and obligation", "a set of moral principles" or "A set of moral issue or aspect." More specifically, Poulton (2005) defined ethics as, "a societal discussion of what ought to be considered for overall human well-being, including the broader concepts of fairness, justice and injustice, what rights and responsibilities are operable under certain situations, and what virtues a society admires and wants to emphasize (p.4)."

The concerns related ethics and values have lately acquired a huge attention in the post Enron period due to the never-ending lists of unethical incidents happening in the corporations. Unethical practices are affecting every size and type of business organization from multinationals to small sized native firms. These degradations have surprised the stakeholders and they lost their faith in the corporations. From Enron to Anderson, Satyam to 2G every scandal is a disclosure of misdeeds by our own respected business leaders and their political counterparts (Saini, 2017). Individual and groups both can lead to unethical behavior and causes could be the pressures, conflict of interest, greed, opportunistic behavior and other phenomenon. Indian corporations have also recieved prevalent undesirable rankings in various global, regional and national surveys on corporate integrity and administrative integrity in recent decades. In 2017, the Corruption Perception Index of Transparency International ranked India very low (81 out of 180 countries) with a score of 40 (*The Indian Express*, 2018).

There are numerous ideas and solutions offered by the researchers and scholars to implement the ethical values in the organization (Lloyd & May, 2010; Sheshadri, Raghavan & Hegde, 2007; Driscoll & McKee, 2007). Various organizations have already put those ideas into action; there are certain rules and regulations, laws that abide. For instance Sheshadri et al. (2007) proposed some ideas for a company's ethics policy to be successfully implemented:

- The code of ethics is clearly communicated to employees.
- Employees are formally trained in it.
- They are told how to deal with ethical challenges.
- The code is implemented strongly.
- The code is contemporary.
- The company leadership adheres to the highest ethical standards.

Except the given last key, all other ideas are indirectly dependent upon the top leadership as they are who frame the guidelines and policies and make sure to implement them for the organization. To implement ethical values in the organization scholars and practitioners suggested various assisting resolutions.

To cope up with the problem individual training in business ethics is required in management education, so that the future managers would be able to find solutions in the situations of ethical dilemmas, they will have tools and techniques which can direct them in dark zones and it also induce the integrity in their personal characters (Saini, 2017). In the current scenario, it becomes imperious for instructors to incorporate ethical decision making into their curricula in an effort to help equip future leaders with tools or strategies that can be used to navigate shadowy areas (Wankel, 2011). Especially while dealing with integrity in management education we have to move beyond the economic view of integrity and teach students of management a broader ethical concept of integrity (Palmer, 2015). Numerous expert and exchange affiliations proclaim codes of morals, and sticking to a moral code is one of the characterizing components of a calling.

Higher education is facing rising demand among learners for improved accessibility and convenience that should be in tandem with quality assurance practices. Higher education in India and the world over is undergoing a paradigm shift. Indian governments is increasingly recognizing education as responsible and essential for the progress of contemporary societies. While talking about quality if higher education, ethical education cannot be surpassed as it contains the power to transform the entire conduct of the individual in any context. Personal ethics and values is associated with so many other behavioral exhibits for e.g. Trustworthiness and promise-keeping are "foundational values" for most successful business relationships (Donaldson& Dunfee, 1999). Honesty, authenticity, responsibility, integrity, self-refection, courage and transparency etc. develop with the correct instillation of values in the personality of the individual. All these virtues are required to be a good decision maker in the organization specially to conduce the value based environment in organization. This is how a well drafted and implemented ethics and value courses can surely contribute in the quality of management education in India.These reviews strongly present the effectiveness of ethics and responsibility in the management education and in the coming section we will consider on a brief history of ethics courses in management education in India and its challenges.

A Brief History of Ethics Courses in Indian Management Education

Currently, Business ethics has been a part of the curriculum of major global professional institutes. And Indian institutions are no behind anyway in involve the theme in the core courses. Almost every management institution is having an ethics courses in their curriculum in India, which is focused upon inculcating the value set in an individual. To understand the role of ethical education in accelerating the quality of management education this chapter provides a discussion of implications of the questions of quality, dilemma and pedagogy of ethical training. Few years ago, right after the slowdown, Indian Institute of Management-Calcutta included business ethics a compulsory course. Now it is developing up a discrete division proceeding business ethics and communication. IIM Calcutta is well recognized for the subject and strongly supports the inclusion of ethics throughout the course and curriculum along with a biannual journal dedicated to human values. The number and quality of required and elective business ethics courses have grown, as have the extra-curricular offerings and the recognition by another faculty that ethics is a core business discipline. An increase found in the number of stand-alone ethics courses offered to 25% of respondents, up from 5% in a 1988 study by a survey from the Financial

Table 1. Place of ethical course in the top ten Indian business schools in 2018

S.N	Business schools	Place	Label
1	IIM Ahmadabad	First Year Courses (All Compulsory)	Managing ethically
2	Indian Institute Of Management, Bangalore	PGPEP	Corporate Governance and Ethics
3	Indian Institute Of Management, Calcutta	Term 3 Qualifying noncredit course	Business ethics
4	Indian Institute Of Management, Lucknow	Second year Core course	Corporate Governance & Strategy
5	Indian Institute Of Management, Indore	Skill Development Courses (SDC) Term 2	Ethics and CSR
6	XLRI Jamshedpur	General management Core course	Managerial Ethics
7	Faculty Of Management Studies (Fms), Delhi	Semester 3	Business Ethics & Corporate Social Responsibility
8	Indian Institute Of Management, Kozhikode	First year Core course	Business Ethics
9	SPJMIR Mumbai	Foundation course	Ethics in Business (spread across semesters)
10	MDI Gurgaon	Term 3 Values Based Education (Learning Goal)	Business ethics

(Source: institutional websites)

Times top 50 business schools focused on ethics, sustainability, and corporate social responsibility programs (Christensen, Peirce, Hartman, Hoffman, & Jamie Carrier, 2007). Correspondingly Srinivasan, Srinivasan, and Anand (2012) clinched and probed that the status of the teaching of ECCE courses in business schools in India is quite strong with an overwhelming 90% of the schools having a course in this area but are we able to produce ethically and morally profound managers? Fisman and Galinsky (2012) specified that the ethics curriculum at business schools can best be described as an unsuccessful work-in-progress. In the next section of the chapter we will be focusing upon the place of ethics course in top business schools in India.

Place of Business Ethics in the Syllabus of Top Business Schools

Many leading corporations already accepted the legitimacy of role and importance of ethics, rather, they are finding new ways to put ethics into practice, forecasting says that the ethical encounters will be even greater for the coming leaders. To impart concrete knowledge to students about ethical philosophy and frameworks for analysis, help students to develop a set of skills for integrating ethical concepts into business decision making and management practices and move learners to greater self-awareness by inspiring individual reflection and values clarification on the individual, organizational, and societal levels. Nonetheless, it is even challenging itself to implement. To effectively integrate ethics at the fundamental level, business schools must remove significant problems like no support for ethics as a core discipline.

In a Bloomberg article Himsel (2014) alleged business schools of not producing ethical graduates though accepted that they are trying to improve ethical teaching and training. In the list the author has also tried to illustrate the place of ethics course in the MBA curriculum according to the precedence in top ten Indian B Schools according to a survey of financial express in 2018(Top MBA Colleges).

A wide moral structure of an organization is unrealistic to be powerful unless it has a champion at the largest amount and is supported by an establishment's representing body. The leader of the organization would be the undeniable decision as champion, in spite of the fact that the seat of governors might be more proper at times. It is additionally basic that senior champions set a sample with their own particular conduct by "living" the organization's moral standards and practices. The foundation's qualities ought to support everything that it does. It is vital that any moral system develops out of and is reliable with existing institutional mission and qualities proclamations.

Challenges /Barriers in in Implementation of Ethical Education

The reason behind introducing the ethical education might be the increased unethical behavior in the organizations. The review of literature has established that all over the world including India there is a steep increase in introduction of courses related to ethics (Christensen et al, 2007; Srinivasan et al, 2012). Though a number of researchers supported the fact that the ethics related education advances ethical and fair attitude (Oddo, 1997; Burton, Johnston & Wilson, 1991), few for instance Stephens and Stephens (2008) scrutinized the problem well and determined that the ethics courses offered not taken seriously are the prime cause. On the other hand Cragg (1997) claimed that ethics is something which cannot be taught and further a study conducted by Bishop (1992) braced the fact by saying that as long as we have laws that dictate what is permissible; we do not need courses in ethics". Therefore we have in fact different contrasting views in support and against the inclusion of ethics in curriculum. Mostly ethics courses emphasizing upon hypothetical decision-making and defining that what the right thing to do is. Though there is a difference between knowing and doing the same and ethical decisions making is something which is a more than knowing and doing, which is being and that creates all the difference.

In general curriculum of business education revolves around the financial education, though according to Giacalone and Thompson (2006), to advance ethics in management education, one must ground the curriculum in a worldview that takes well-being as a priority, making ethics the main concern rather than the backfill of the curriculum. A famous saying from Buddha is that, "what we think we become", somehow fits here completely in the foresaid situation as when our mind will constantly revolves around the generation of money, soon the similar thinking pattern lead to self-centeredness and self-involvement (Gini&Marcocx,2009; Murtaza,2011),which results in unethical behavior and greed. There are so many areas apart from finance for e.g. Human resources, production management where the ethics and morality is similarly relevant and significant. The major focus is not upon what are the grey areas and how should we take decisions while in dilemma but how to nurture the personalities of students that we can give rise to the virtues in them. They must develop as in more empathetic, altruism, compassion, honesty, fair benevolent, supportive, helping, and justice oriented and grounded individuals.

A Case

A case encompassed in this chapter demonstrates the importance of ethics course in education system. As a research method, case study methodology is well established in the Social Sciences.It is a type of research inquiry that examines a real life contemporary phenomenon(Yin, 2009).Case studies constitute an important research tool in the field of management. In fact, case studies have been the source of some of the most trailblazing concepts in the field (Lobo, Moeyaert, Cunha &Babik, 2017).Typically *Case studies* refer to a broad array of approaches most often used for observing an individual and reporting on their interactions with variables of interest (e.g., life events, psychological intervention, and so on). (Nock, Michel & Photos, 2007). Although case studies can provide valuable information, as commonly used they lack the methodological requirements to draw valid inferences about the relations among variables (Kazdin, 1981). Certainly, case studies typically do not include design features such as objective assessment, systematic data collection or analysis, specified manipulation of the independent variable, or replication of treatment effects.

Nock, Michel and Photos (2007) specified four significance of single case research designs:

1. Single-case research designs can demonstrate clear fundamental relations between intervention and behavior change with much more efficiency than large-sample designs.
2. Single-case research designs offer much more flexibility in the implementation and evaluation of interventions than large-sample designs.
3. The assessment methods used in single case research designs provide for the evaluation of individual change patterns in the data.
4. Most of these statistical or methodological problems are avoided or remedied through the use of single-case research designs

The following case study is about a teacher in management who perceived that the ethics education adopted in management institutions is only followed on a surface level. The original objectives of the courses on ethics and values is, to inculcate the value set and instill ethics in the individuals. Which is not at all met at present situation.

Why Ethics for Us?

On a warm Friday afternoon in a class of organizational behavior in business administration department Dr. Maya asked students about their understanding of values and ethics while discussing personality. The answers she got were like the basic idea behind ethics is the differentiation from good to bad and wright from wrong. She was amazed to understand that no student was able to relate the personal ethics with business or with personal life properly. The second question she threw was why you are learning ethics and values and do you really need it. Again students were not having any concrete answer, though they have learned the subject related to ethics and values with deeper dimensions in the first semester still they were ignorant about it. This made her think about that management students must be knowing about the reasons associated with the introduction of this particular course. They must know about the endless list of the unethical activities happened in the corporations in the last few decades. Though the students might know about the scams and scandals happened in Indian corporations but not in details and in relation to ethics which actually creates a gap. They had some understanding about CSR and business ethics but no clue about why they are reading all the Indian scriptural lessons, Purushastras and Patanjali yoga sutra. Dr. Maya was extremely astonished by this approach of students, because she was herself devoted much towards this subject in her doctoral thesis. She was also having a good realization of spiritual principles and interconnection of ethics and values. So, why ethics in management education is already answered by many but why ethics from students perspective, is still not taken into consideration. Further how does this subject is increasing the level of management education is also important. The pedagogy, linkage, gaps and effectiveness of teaching are few questions which remain unanswered till now. On the basis of this awareness we have come up with a few propositions, which are given below:

Proposition 1: Knowing the antecedents of ethics course is likely to enhance the intent of learning the course.
Proposition 2: Knowing the interrelationship of course content is likely to enhance the intent of learning the course.

Contribution of Ethics Course Towards the Quality of Management Education

A business educator must help students in becoming more socially responsible and ethically sensitive in order to fulfill the substantive part of their responsibility as they prepare a new generation of business practitioners (Giacalone & Thompson, 2006). Ethics is a core discipline of business and an essential competency for the next generation of managers but Business schools aren't doing enough to build ethics as a foundation course and part of other disciplines into their curricula (Saini, 2017). Business schools, must lead the path in raising business to, and holding business to, the moral measures of a calling. It is additionally vital that institution take a more extensive partner approach and teach the idea of the social obligation of business. The purposes of management colleges are not "just" to deliver financially fruitful graduates but rather business pioneers who will make a superior society (Saini, 2017).

By identifying the significance of supervisory influence and accountability on ethical behaviour and decision- making, the framework insists on the need for a high level of commitment among the top-level executives towards organizational ethics (Maheshwari &Ganesh,2006). Trivino (2006) said that ethical decision making is influenced by moral reasoning .Moral intensity is a characteristic of the moral issue itself. It is a major factor in influencing the ethical awareness, ethical decision-making, and behavior of the employees (Jones, 1991). Ethical decision making is the survivor while in the interpersonal work value conflict. To make a decision ethical is challenging task. The decision maker should take care of everyone including company, shareholders, society and customers and for that the grounds for the consideration should be highly dependent on the moral approach.

Business, being an essential part of our lives, is an essential aspect of living consciously and a conscious business leader bring awareness of truth, good, human nature, moral imperatives to the business and promotes mindfulness. By increased self-awareness, self-regulation and positive modeling, authentic leaders nurtures the development of truthfulness in followers, in turns followers authenticity contributes to their well-being and attainment of sustainable and veritable performance (Avolio &Gardner,2005). Generally unethical activities in an organization are associated with a number of undesirable outcomes for organizations and their stakeholders around the world. In this connection, there has been a call for managers to practise ethics and better management of ethical and moral behaviour in organizations (Brown, Treviño, & Harrison, 2005). Brown and Trevino, (2006) also specified that self-awareness; openness, transparency, and consistency are at the core of authentic leadership. They also found that conscientious individuals are responsible and dependable, consistent with credibility which enhances model effectiveness according to social learning theory. Deliberating the keys for authentic leadership de George (2011) said that self-reflection as a necessary antidote for leaders, he said that before taking a leadership role, one should ask himself the reason behind it, if the answers are power, prestige and money they are at risk of relying external gratification for fulfillment. External gratification rather than inner fulfillment leads to lose their foundation. In addition to greater self-awareness, there is a need of discussion of the kinds of structural solutions that force people to confront ethics rather than leaving them in the background. This will help the students with their own ethical lapses *and* help them in their roles as future business leaders (Fisman &Galinsky, 2012). To avoid unethicality in organizations it is imperative that institutions engaged in imparting higher learning to the younger generation inculcate and instill in them a value system which will teach them the importance of practicing ethics in all walks of life (Nair, 2014). So there is a requirement of an education which can develop the sense of awareness and self-refection in the young minds and there should be a scope that they can get specific advice whenever required in state of dilemma. So, the contribution of ethics teaching in the management courses should be more than just written rules and regulations and more focused on living the values. Visibly this discussion has shown that the main areas in which ethics course contribute and the provide strong foundations of morals and ethics in future business leaders. The next section provides a general ideas, model practices and programs for the amplification of ethics related courses in management education.

Model Practices, Ideas, and Programs

The faculty community play a significant role in imparting knowledge on ethics to the student fraternity and they are also required to maintain a high academic integrity while teaching and also hold high moral and ethical standards while doing scholarly work and other services (Nair, 2014). Because of the challenges in ethics teaching, experts in ethical teaching should be preferred for imparting the ethical education because it is more than saying and doing, it is being. Pedagogy seems to be one crucial area for ethics course as when Weber (2007) suggested to raise sensitivity to the pedagogical approach, an insightful approach is apt to meet the benchmarks. Apart from lectures and talks, vignettes and case studies are the most common techniques for teaching ethics. According to a survey, the use of vignettes is one way to measure aspects of ethical sensitivity, but more study is required to clarify what is being measured (Hébert, Meslin, Dunn, Byrne, and Reid,1990). Further Husu (2003) claimed that case study method is getting more popular in ethics teaching, as it provides a vehicle for teacher to find out how the ethical judgment comes up in specific situations and it also gives a real dilemma feel to the students which train them that what type of ethical problems could be . Consequently, case reports can offer instructional forums to the teacher to learn moral reasoning and dialogue. Business ethics cases also facilitate the development of deductive, inductive and critical reasoning skills (Falkenberg & Woiceshyn, 2008) of students. Active discussions in the class and development of syllabus focusing upon ethics that acknowledge academic integrity have been suggested as effective means of encouraging student learning about uprightness and ethics (Gynnild & Gotschalk, 2008).

In the area of ethical education self-regulated learning could be a blessing in disguise and it can be of greater usage. There are a variety of definitions of self-regulated learning, but three components seem especially important for classroom performance. First, self-regulated learning includes students' metacognitive strategies for planning, monitoring, and modifying their cognition. Second is students' management and control of their effort on classroom academic tasks has been proposed as another important component. For example, capable students who persist at a difficult task or block out distractors (i.e., noisy classmates) maintain their cognitive engagement in the task, enabling them to perform better. The last but not the least is the actual cognitive strategies that students use to learn, remember, and understand the material such as rehearsal, elaboration etc (Pintrich & De Groot,1990).

According to Cassidy (2011) in self-regulated learning, there is harmony regarding the central role played by student perceptions of themselves as learners. Further Cassidy establishes that self-regulated learning is relevant and valuable concept in higher education and it promote the study of those constituent elements considered most likely to develop the understanding beyond a mere description of those processes thought to be involved in self-regulated learning. There are certain requirements to establish self-regulated learning in the institutions, which can be implemented to the ethical education:

- An 'enabling environment' including the physical setting, material resources and social interaction.
- Positive support from teachers and peers.
- There is a particular emphasis on information communication technologies.
- Involves a new role for teachers which focuses on process-orientated teaching with students actively involved in the learning process.

Student involvement in self-regulated learning is meticulously secured to students' efficacy beliefs about their capability to perform classroom tasks and to their beliefs that these classroom tasks are interesting and worth learning (Pintrich & De Groot,1990). Therefore the institutions should focus upon the relevant ideas to make the ethics education interesting and make students understand the fact that what is the reason behind this learning and how these areas will be supportive in their professional future.

Implementation Framework

Various related literature reviewed which form the basis of the current status of courses of business ethics in India in various management institutions along with a listing and a case let which unearth the research issues leading to the research questions of: If the clarity about the requirement of ethics courses in management are helpful to attract and increase the bent of learning in students? If the proper knowledge of the course content (how does it interrelate) act as an arbitrator for the increase the bent of learning ethics and values in students?

The approach of teaching ethics in management courses should be integral in nature and it must encompass self-reflection and it must explore that what are their own personal values. Moreover code of ethics and an ethics process is identified as an inter-subjective practice.

The literature review provided the requirement of revision of ethics and values course which has been required to cope up with turbulent times of corrupt corporates. This indications to the description of business ethics researches related to it done by prominent researchers. An overview of the literature on ethics has highlighted ways which can transform the current state of the courses of values and ethics in university system. The research issues identified the importance of the base building before throwing the course content to the management students.

CONCLUSION AND RECOMMENDATIONS

The chapter has a call for ethical training which can help growing the moral level of individuals which is required to pursue the ethically precise environment in the organization and the hardships to maintain the ethical culture in the organizations. It began by reviewing the history of ethics related courses in India and various other dimensions required in ethically responsible education for understanding the phenomena. The theme of this chapter revolves around the ethical education in the management discipline, its significance and its challenges. The author also underwritten a case about the scenario of ethical education especially in the universities. Consequently, the author has tried to find out the gaps in teaching ethical and moral courses in management courses. Firstly the authors concluded that there is a huge requirement to focus upon the base building for the ethics courses in business as the students can not relate to the subject. Secondly they found that the course content should have more clarity in the interrelationship of topics mentioned which will provide foundation to the progression of the course. Last but not the least the ethics is something which is pervasive in nature and a student well trained in ethics and values will obviously contribute in quality of management education in Indian universities.

Recommendation

The effectiveness and usefulness of teaching ethics and values in management education depends upon the active participation of every business institute. An equal emphasis on structural courses, techniques, and faculty factors might help to provide the answers and help educators to identify the facilitating and inhibiting factors which influence the success of ethical teachings in management. Apart from well-designed syllabus, which is well knitted with real life examples, along with proven teaching tactics we need to make students learn introspection, self-discipline and self-awareness to develop and cultivate values in oneself. We strongly recommend self-regulate learning for ethics related education as this is something that you learn and develop within yourself. And nobody but individual has to develop their values themselves.

Limitation and Future Scope of the study

Apart from the numerous strengths there are few limitations to the study that need to be considered. Limitations are discussed in the areas of the design of the research method, which is a single case study which has its own limitations for example design features such as objective assessment, systematic data collection or analysis, specified manipulation of the independent variable. The scope of study can be extended to a qualitative study, taking students as respondents followed by a quantitative research study. Which will provide the opportunity to explore the meticulous underlying problems in the course of ethics and values in universities. Which will definitely enhance the level and the quality of management education in India.

REFERENCES

Aristotle. (350 BC). *Nichomachean Ethics* (W. D. Ross, Trans.). Retrieved from The Internet Classic Archive: http://classics.mit.edu

Avolio, B. J., & Gardner, W. L. (2005). Authentic leadership development: Getting to the root of positive forms of leadership. *The Leadership Quarterly, 16*(3), 315–338. doi:10.1016/j.leaqua.2005.03.001

Brown, M. E., Trevino, L. K., & Harrison, D. A. (2005). Ethical leadership: A social learning perspective for construct development and testing. *Organizational Behavior and Human Decision Processes, 97*(2), 117–134. doi:10.1016/j.obhdp.2005.03.002

Burton, S., Johnston, M. W., & Wilson, E. J. (1991). An experimental assessment of alternative teaching approaches for introducing business ethics to undergraduate business students. *Journal of Business Ethics, 10*(7), 507–517. doi:10.1007/BF00383349

Cassidy, S. (2011). Self-regulated learning in higher education: Identifying key component processes. *Studies in Higher Education, 36*(8), 989–1000. doi:10.1080/03075079.2010.503269

Christensen, L. J., Peirce, E., Hartman, L. P., Hoffman, W. M., & Carrier, J. (2007). Ethics, CSR, and sustainability education in the Financial Times top 50 global business schools: Baseline data and future research directions. *Journal of Business Ethics, 73*(4), 347-368.

Cragg, W. (1997). Teaching business ethics: The role of ethics in business and in business education. *Journal of Business Ethics, 16*(3), 231–245. doi:10.1023/A:1017974908203

De George, R. T. (2011). *Business ethics*. Retrieved from http://books.google.co.in/books?id=jwQB_XWs0TkC&printsec=frontcover&source=gbs_ge_summary_r&cad=0#v=onepage&q&f=false

Donaldson, T., & Dunfee, T. W. (1999). *Ties that bind: A social contracts approach to business ethics*. Academic Press.

Driscoll, C., & McKee, M. (2007). Restoring a culture of ethical and spiritual values: A role for leader storytelling. *Journal of Business Ethics, 73*(2), 205–221. doi:10.100710551-006-9191-5

Falkenberg, L., & Woiceshyn, J. (2008). Enhancing business ethics: Using cases to teach moral reasoning. *Journal of Business Ethics, 79*(3), 213–217. doi:10.100710551-007-9381-9

Fisman, R., & Galinsky, G. (2012). *We need a new way to teach ethics to business school students*. Retrieved January 2016 from http://www. slate. com/articles/business/the_dismal_science/2012/09/business_school_and_ethics_can_we_train_mbas_to_do_the_right_thing_. html

Fritzsche, D. J., & Tsalikis, J. (1989). Business Ethics: A Literature Review with a Focus on Marketing Ethics. *Journal of Business Ethics, 8*(9), 695–744. doi:10.1007/BF00384207

Giacalone, R. A., & Thompson, K. R. (2006). From the guest co-editors: Special issue on ethics and social responsibility. *Academy of Management Learning & Education, 5*(3), 261–265. doi:10.5465/amle.2006.22697015

Gini, A., & Marcoux, A. M. (2009). Malden Mills: When being a good company isn't good enough. *Proceedings of the Good Company. Sixth International Symposium on Catholic Social Thought and Management Education.*

Gynnild, V., & Gotschalk, P. (2008). Promoting academic integrity at a Midwestern University: Critical review and current challenges. *International Journal for Educational Integrity, 4*(2).

Hébert, P., Meslin, E. M., Dunn, E. V., Byrne, N., & Reid, S. R. (1990). Evaluating ethical sensitivity in medical students: Using vignettes as an instrument. *Journal of Medical Ethics, 16*(3), 141–145. doi:10.1136/jme.16.3.141 PMID:2231639

Herndon, N. C. Jr, Fraedrich, J. P., & Yeh, Q. J. (2001). An investigation of moral values and the ethical content of the corporate culture: Taiwanese versus US sales people. *Journal of Business Ethics, 30*(1), 73–85. doi:10.1023/A:1006493907563

Himsel, D. (2014). Business schools aren't producing ethical graduates. *Bloomberg Business*. Retrieved from http://www.bloomberg.com/bw/articles/2014-08-06/business-schools-dont-teach-ethics-effectively

Hunt, S. D., Wood, V. R., & Chonko, L. B. (1989). Corporate ethical values and organizational commitment in marketing. *Journal of Marketing, 53*(3), 79–90. doi:10.1177/002224298905300309

Husu, J. (2003). Constructing ethical representations from the teacher's pedagogical practice: A case of prolonged reflection. *Interchange, 34*(1), 1–21. doi:10.1023/A:1024595600952

Jansen, E., & Glinow, M. A. V. (1985). Ethical Ambivalence and Organizational Reward Systems. *Academy of Management Review, 1*(10), 4814–4822.

Maheshwari, S., & Ganesh, M. P. (2006). Ethics in organizations: The case of tata steel. *Vikalpa, 31*(2), 77–87. doi:10.1177/0256090920060205

Murtaza, N. (2011). Pursuing self-interest or self-actualization? From capitalism to a steady-state, wisdom economy. *Ecological Economics, 70*(4), 577–584. doi:10.1016/j.ecolecon.2010.10.012

Nair, S. R. (2014). Ethics in higher education. In *Handbook of research on higher education in the MENA Region: Policy and practice* (pp. 230–260). IGI Global. doi:10.4018/978-1-4666-6198-1.ch011

Nock, M. K., Michel, B. D., & Photos, V. I. (2007). Single-case research designs. Handbook of research methods in abnormal and clinical psychology, 337-350.

Oddo, A. R. (1997). A framework for teaching business ethics. *Journal of Business Ethics, 16*(3), 293–297. doi:10.1023/A:1017951729585

Palmer, D. E. (2015). *Handbook of research on business ethics and corporate responsibilities*. IGI Global. doi:10.4018/978-1-4666-7476-9

Pintrich, P. R., & De Groot, E. V. (1990). Motivational and self-regulated learning components of classroom academic performance. *Journal of Educational Psychology, 82*(1), 33–40. doi:10.1037/0022-0663.82.1.33

Poulton, M. S. (2005). Organizational storytelling, ethics and morality: How stories frame limits of behavior in organizations. *EJBO-Electronic Journal of Business Ethics and Organization Studies*. Retrieved from http://classics.mit.edu

Saini, D. (2017). Relevance of teaching values and ethics in management education. In *Management Education for Global Leadership* (pp. 90–111). IGI Global. doi:10.4018/978-1-5225-1013-0.ch005

Seshadri, D. V. R., Raghavan, A., & Hegde, S. (2007). Business ethics: The next frontier for globalizing indian companies. *Vikalpa, 32*(3), 61–79. doi:10.1177/0256090920070305

Srinivasan, P., Srinivasan, V., & Anand, R. V. (2012). *Status of ethics, corporate governance, CSR and environment education in business schools in India: An exploratory study.* Corporate Governance, CSR and Environment Education in Business Schools in India: An Exploratory Study. IIM Bangalore Research Paper, 362.

The Indian Express. (2018). *India ranks 81st in global corruption index.* Retrieved from http://indianexpress.com/ article/india/india-ranks-81st-in-global-corruption-perception-index-5073800/

Top MBA Colleges in India 2018. (2018). Retrieved on November 2018 from https://www.financialexpress.com/education-2/top-mba-colleges-in-india-2018-these-are-best-100-b-schools-iim-ahmedabad-is-1-full-list-is-here/1100128/

Trevino, L. K. (1986). Ethical decision making in organizations: A person-situation interactionist model. *Academy of Management Review, 11*(3), 601–617. doi:10.5465/amr.1986.4306235

Wankel, C. (Ed.). (2011). *Teaching arts and science with the new social media.* Emerald Group Publishing Limited. doi:10.1108/S2044-9968(2011)3

Weber, J. A. (2007). Business ethics training: Insights from learning theory. *Journal of Business Ethics, 70*(1), 61–85. doi:10.100710551-006-9083-8

Chapter 13
Higher Education Quality Improvement Strategies Through Enriched Teaching and Learning

Idahosa Igbinakhase
https://orcid.org/0000-0003-4667-2809
University of KwaZulu-Natal, South Africa

Vannie Naidoo
University of KwaZulu-Natal, South Africa

ABSTRACT

This chapter focuses on the critical analysis of evidence of higher education improvement strategies in improving teaching and learning in higher education institutions. Several higher education improvement strategies such as preparation for accreditation and student learning assessment has been utilized in the area of teaching and learning in higher education institutions with diverse outcomes. Overall and despite some recorded successes, there still exist some situations where improvement strategies create challenges and conflicts in the institutions as a result of the improvement strategies not serving their defined purpose. Some of these challenges are ineffective teacher professional development initiatives and lack of specifically developed programs designed for specific students' needs. In order to resolve higher education improvement challenges, decision makers in higher educational institutions must be willing to involve key stakeholders in designing the right approach to quality assurance in higher educational institutions.

DOI: 10.4018/978-1-7998-1017-9.ch013

INTRODUCTION

Higher education is known to take place after secondary school education and is delivered in higher institutions of learning which include universities (Jongbloed, Enders, & Salerno, 2008), colleges (Brubacher, 2017) and institutes of technology (Altbach, 2015). Higher education improvement strategies have become very necessary as key stakeholders globally expect improvement of outcomes in higher education which is in line with total quality management in education (Sallis, 2014; Sherr & Lozier, 1991). According to Fishman, Ludgate and Tutak (2017) college graduation is an uncertainty to some undergraduates due to their inability to cope with the higher education system and this has led to an increase in dropout rates of students who desire higher education qualifications. This concern further stresses the need for continuous educational change with a focus of improving teaching and enhancing student learning as required by universities (D'Andrea & Gosling, 2005), in an ever evolving society. To achieve the critical outcomes of improved teaching and enhanced learning in universities, the role of human designated participants in the initiation, implementation, continuation and outcome of change in education (Ellsworth, 2001; Fullan, 1982) cannot be overemphasised.

Higher education improvement strategies are required to achieve stakeholders' expectation of higher education. It is important to add that decision makers in higher institutions are beginning to promote educational practices that will lead to the realisation of their institutional objectives and the attainment of the highest level of accountability to stakeholders (Rice & Taylor, 2003), and higher education improvement strategies are some of the steps taken to position higher institutions in the right direction of accomplishments and quality service delivery. There are several higher education improvement strategies in existence. This chapter focuses on critically analyzing higher education improvement strategies for teaching (Wright, 1995) and learning in higher education. Some of the strategies considered in this chapter are strategies for improving student retention (Bowles & Brindle, 2017; Crosling, Heagney, & Thomas, 2009; Gazza & Hunker, 2014), strategies for improving graduation rates (Schargel &Smink, 2014) and strategies for improving laboratory teaching (Gibbs & Jenkins, 2014) among other higher education improving strategies for teaching and learning in higher education.

This chapter aims to investigate higher education improvement strategies in order to identify the evidence of higher education improvement strategies in improving teaching and learning in higher education. In order to achieve the chapter's aim, the following are the objectives of this chapter:

1) To identify higher education improvement strategies.
2) To critically analyze evidence of higher education improvement strategies in improving teaching and learning in higher education institutions.
3) To determine the effects of higher education improvement strategies for teaching and learning in higher education institutions.
4) To critically analyze the challenges associated with higher education improvement strategies for teaching and learning in higher education institutions.
5) To identify if any improvements are required to facilitate the adoption of more effective higher education improvement strategies to improve learning and teaching outcomes in higher education institutions.
6) To make recommendations to improve higher education improvement strategies to facilitate effective teaching and learning in higher education institutions.

Research Methodology

The research methodology adopted for this chapter is the Comprehensive Literature Review (CLR) approach by Onwuegbuzie and Rebecca (2016). According to Onwuegbuzie and Rebecca (2016), CLR involves an integrative review, using a combination of narrative review (a comprehensive, critical and objective analysis of the current knowledge on a topic) and systematic review (a review carried out using focused research questions with narrow parameters, and it is done by assessing the quality of studies and generates a conclusion relating to the focused research questions). Key information utilized in this chapter was from secondary sources, documents, expert opinions, media and authors' observations. The CLR has a seven-step methodology and they are:

Step 1: Exploring Beliefs and Topics;
Step 2: Initiating the search;
Step 3: Storing and Organizing Information;
Step 4: Selecting/Deselecting Information;
Step 5: Expanding the Search to Include One or More MODES (Media, Observation(s), Documents, Expert(s), Secondary Data);
Step 6: Analyze and Synthesize Information; and
Step 7: Present the CLR Report (Onwuegbuzie & Rebecca, 2016, p.54).

The CLR process has three phases, and they are steps' 1-5 (the exploratory phase), step 6 (the interpretation phase) and step 7 (the communication phase).

Lastly, the aforementioned seven steps are "multidimensional, interactive, emergent, iterative, dynamic, holistic and synergistic" (Onwuegbuzie & Rebecca, 2016, p.54).

BACKGROUND

Higher education provides an opportunity for high school leavers continue their postsecondary education/third-level education in a higher educational institution of their choice. In defining higher education, Cortese (2003) notes that higher education refers to education that student receive in a higher educational institution of learning such as a university (Kerr, 2001). Furthermore, Cortese (2003) affirms that the general practice of higher education involves a system where education, research, university operations and relationship with external community are interlinked, and this provides an enabling environment that supports teaching and learning activities. In addition, Levine (2018) describes higher education as a postsecondary education system and notes that there are several post-secondary education providers such as colleges and universities. Based on these existing definitions of higher education, higher education can be seen as post-secondary education that results in further acquisition of knowledge and skills at a tertiary institution of learning that enables students to make positive contributions to the development of the society(Douglass, 2018).

Many positive contributions to the society can be linked to higher education. According to Leslie and Brinkman (1988) who investigated the economic value of higher education, there is evidence that higher education significantly contribute economic value to all stakeholders (students, colleges and societies) locally and nationally. Similarly, Cortese (2003) notes that higher education can have a positive effect on the sustainability drive of a society through several environmental and sustainability literacy, curriculum incorporating environmentally sustainable design on campuses, curriculum involving improvement in local communities and expanding and improving architectural education. Furthermore, evidence by Marginson (2011) supports the assertion that higher education contributes to the public good through their involvement in research and teaching activities. Thus, higher education remains an important tool in the development of progressive societies.

In order to get more positive benefits of higher education for all stakeholders, quality standards must be enshrined in higher educational institutions. To identify suitable quality standards for higher educational institutions, some scholars have opened the debate on what is quality in higher education? Green (1994) posits the question- what is quality in higher education? While the term "quality" has given rise to several debates in a bid to provide an acceptable meaning and explanation for the term by scholars focusing on higher education and quality debates (Parri, 2002), higher education quality remains a necessary component of the activities higher education providers in order to achieve their mandate in the society.

In Order to expand the discussion of quality in higher education in this chapter, a traditional concept of quality is provided based on Green (1994) description of quality- quality is "associated with the notion of providing a product or service that is distinctive and special, and which confers status on the owner or user"(Green, 1994, p.23). In addition, Green (1994) suggests a second opinion about "quality" as "conformance to a specification or standard" (p.23). Green (1994, p.25) further notes that in higher education, analyst and policy makers see quality as "fitness for purpose", and this definition is hinged on the purpose of the product or service being provided. It is important to note that despite the several definitions of quality, the definition of quality still varies across different stakeholders and societies (Green, 1994, p.27). Historical evidence on the discourse on higher education quality suggests that the subject area is a well researched area (Barnett, 1992; Lewis & Smith, 1994; Newman, Trimmer, & Padró, 2019; Wit & Knight, 1999). Also, the debates on higher education quality have led to policy implications such as the establishment of quality code for higher education in some developed countries (Jackson, 1997). A typical example is the UK quality code for higher education(Brown, 2004) which protects the UK higher education systems, caters for both public and student interests and allows the UK to maintain its reputation as a destination for quality Higher education(Quality Assurance Agency[QAA]-The UK's quality body for higher education, 2019). According to QAA (2019), The UK's quality code consists of important elements that enable the promotion of effective quality assurance, and these elements are Expectations, Core practices, Common practices and advice and guidance. The UK quality code is an indication that the UK as a progressive society is determined to protect its higher education system and its reputation, and this essence is captured by a notable contribution by Seymour (1992) who provides a practical and general picture of what quality is to higher institutions and stakeholders in the higher education sector by stating that "college and university education as a quality-oriented service with students, parents, and legislators as customers demanding quality". This aforementioned expression underscores the importance of quality in higher education and the need to continually improve upon the quality standards of higher educational institutions to satisfy all stakeholders.

The need for strategies to enable higher educational institutions to achieve their educational objectives cannot be over emphasized. According to Davis (1993), there is a tendency for teachers in higher educational institutions to get stuck with a particular method of teaching regardless of the teaching outcome without proper guidance. When this situation occurs, student learning can be affected and the objective of the higher institution is defeated. Also, Robert and Mary (1995), notes that societies expect quality teaching and learning outcomes in terms of graduates that can contribute positively to the society.

Competent and quality graduates are a necessity in the development of progressive societies (O'Regan, 2002). Furthermore, IIyasin (2017) investigated the balance scorecard focusing on the strategy for the quality improvement of Islamic higher education and noted that the focus of improving higher education (for religious and non religious education service providers) is to enable the higher education institutions to achieve its stated mission and goals in a dynamic business environment and with a growing complex demands of stakeholders. Thus, improvement strategies remain a valuable contribution to the development of effective teaching and learning outcomes that serves the needs of all stakeholders in a society.

Having identified the importance of higher education improvement strategies, there is a need for an analysis of higher education improvement strategies. Higher education improvement strategies are planned approaches adopted by higher institutional managers to continually that their institutions conform to set standards of quality. According to Rice and Taylor (2003), continuous improvement strategies in the form of quality implementation strategies in higher education are being utilized by higher educational institutions' management and decision makers, and they include process improvement, continuous improvement, institutional effectiveness, student learning assessment, preparation for accreditation, Baldrige methodology, state quality award preparation, balanced scorecard and quality-based cost accounting. It is important to state that the focus of this chapter is on improving higher education strategies in the area of teaching and learning. Notable studies have focused on higher education improvement strategies with specific focus on teaching. According to Berk (2005) who investigated a survey of 12 strategies to measure teaching effectiveness and they are student ratings, peer ratings, self-evaluation, videos, student interviews, alumni ratings, employer ratings, administrator ratings, teaching scholarship, teaching awards, learning outcome measures and teaching portfolios. Also, Bidabadi, Isfahani, Rouhollahi, and Khalili (2016) investigated effective teaching methods in higher education and focused on requirements and barriers. Bidabadi et al. (2016) noted that the most effective teaching method is the mixed method which is student centred and teacher centred in addition to educational planning and prior readiness. Furthermore, Eaton (2001) investigated distance learning with a focus on academic and political challenges of higher education accreditation and found out that the aim of distance learning teaching and learning is not ending the traditional classroom activities but to create alternative models of teaching and learning. It is important to add that the distance learning model has enabled some higher education institutions to achieve their educational objectives of effective teaching and learning.

With respect to higher education improving strategies focusing on learning, there are some strategies utilized by higher institutions to improve learning outcomes. According to Rust (2002), the focus on student-centred outcomes-based approaches are receiving global attention and it is becoming necessary for key departments in higher education institutions to develop appropriate assessment strategies and learner-centred assessment practice which meets the Quality Assurance Agency (QAA) (Ryan, 2015) general principles of assessment.

Previous studies on higher improvement strategies have focused on strategies that contribute to the continuous quality improvement of higher education. Ramsden (1987) investigated improving teaching and learning higher education focusing on the case for relational perspective. According to Ramsden (1987), a relational perspective associates "the improvement of the professional practice of teaching with research into student learning". He further notes that a relational perspective involves an investigation into and reflection on how students learn particular subjects in a defined context. This approach enables policy decision makers in higher institutions to make changes in teaching and assessment which often leads to staff development and quality of teaching in higher education (Ramsden, 1987). Furthermore, Crosling, Heagney and Thomas (2009) investigated Improving student retention in higher education with a focus on improving teaching and learning, and found out students need to be engaged effectively in their studies to boost students' retention rates in higher institutions. Also and recently, looney (2011) investigated developing high-quality teachers with a focus on improving teacher evaluation and noted that having quality teachers remains a priority for countries that ensure that their students maintain academic excellence.

Despite several studies dedicated to the investigation of higher education improvement strategies in the past, very few studies focused on analyzing the outcomes of these strategies in improving higher education. In this regard, a study by Razinkina, Pankova, Trostinskaya, Pozdeeva, Evseeva and Tanova (2018), investigated student satisfaction as an element of education quality monitoring in an innovative higher education institution and found out that in monitoring education quality, student feedback plays a significant role in enhancing the process of education quality monitoring. Furthermore, this chapter addresses a critical aspect of higher education improvement strategies with respect to outcomes of higher education improvement strategies by focusing on evidence of higher education improvement strategies in improving teaching and learning in higher education institutions.

MAIN FOCUS OF THE CHAPTER

Higher Education Quality Improvement Strategies

Higher education quality improvement strategies are actionable plans designed to achieve the overall aim of higher education in the society. The overall aim of higher education in the society can only be achieved when there is a consistent offering of quality higher education by higher education institutions. According to Trayner and Mkrtchyan (2010), the quality of higher education represents the full features and characteristics of an education service that is awarded by means of a document of a higher education provider and satisfies the exact knowledge demands of the consumer. In order to maintain the quality of higher education provided by higher institutions, individual institutions design plans that are in line with national quality assurance systems. According to Trayner and Mkrtchyan (2010, 2520), the national quality assurance system includes:

- Establishing the responsibility of organizations and institutions taking part in educational processes;
- Evaluating, both internal and external, of the universities' programs;
- A system of accreditation, certification and other procedures;
- Evidence of evaluation of international cooperation and network programs.

It is important to add that higher education quality improvement strategies (Petrovskiy & Agapova, 2016) are similar to other topics such as quality assurance in higher education (Ulewicz, 2017) and continuous improvement in higher education (Rice & Taylor, 2003) used in similar studies and as a result concepts such as "Total Quality management" (Mohammed, Alotibie & Abdulaziz, 2016) and continuous improvement (Rice & Taylor, 2003) are used in studies dedicated to quality in higher education. Several higher education improvement strategies exist (both external and internal), and some of them include accreditation, audit and assessment which are classed as external practices (Swanzy & Potts, 2017, p.101) while others, such as admission criteria, teacher appraisal, programme review, examination moderation and rules and regulations are classed as internal strategies in the form of procedures adopted by higher education institutions (Swanzy & Potts, 2017, p.101). Other higher education improvement strategies take the form of process improvement, continuous improvement, institutional effectiveness, student learning assessment, and preparation for accreditation, Baldrige methodology, state quality award preparation, balance scorecard and quality-based cost accounting (Rice & Taylor, 2003, p.6).

There are key stakeholders playing important roles in quality improvement in higher education institutions. According to Becket and Brookes (2008), higher education stakeholders are divided into internal and external stakeholders. Furthermore, Ulewicz (2017) investigated the role of stakeholders in quality assurance in higher education and noted that internal stakeholders consist of students and higher education institutions' (universities, colleges and other higher education institutions) employees while external stakeholders consist of employers, graduates, government bodies and the general public, with each stakeholder having specific roles to play in the quality assurance activities of the higher education institution. For example, in Europe and Nordic countries (Finland), evidence by Alaniska, Codina, Bohrer, Dearlove, Eriksson, Helle and Wiberg (2006) indicate that students in the academic community are part of the tripartite system (a system that involves students, professors and other staff in university decision making) in university decision making. The student roles in quality assurance are divided into four groups: students as an information provider, student as an actor, student as an expert and student as a partner (Alaniska et al., 2006). The students are able to contribute to the quality assurance process through the academic community, student union and student association at subject level (Alaniska et al., 2006). This view is supported by Ulewicz (2017) who affirm that students are able to provide important contributions in the quality assurance process using feedback provided by students. To illustrate the role of external stakeholders (employers) in quality assurance in higher education institutions, evidence by Ulewicz (2017) noted that employers (external stakeholders) are able to provide feedback on the quality assurance of higher institutions based on the performance of graduate of the higher education institutions employed by the employers. Other stakeholders such as higher education institutions' employees, graduates, government bodies and the general public contribute specifically to the quality assurance process to improve the quality of higher education (Ulewicz, 2017).

Thus higher education institution's stakeholders are very relevant in higher education quality assurance process and outcomes as their feedbacks can determine the higher education quality improvement strategies adopted by higher education institutions.

Since the 19th century, debates to improve higher education quality have been increasing. According to Becket and Brookes (2008, p.40), "in many countries and many cultures the issue of quality management has been firmly on the agenda of Higher Education Institutions (HEIs) for quite some time. Furthermore Matei and Iwinska (2016) affirm that challenges with regards to quality in higher education are a global trend present in all countries with higher education institutions, and these challenges have continuously been addressed. Matei and Iwinska (2016) further pointed that in the United States quality improvement practices existed since the 1900, in Europe discussions on quality improvement and reforms related to higher education took place in the 1980s, with the rest part of the world carrying out various reforms in their respective higher education institutions. Thus, higher education quality improvement activities have been in existence for a long time and continue to be an important issue at this time and remains part of higher education processes and activities.

Quality improvement strategies are applied in all the processes in a higher education institution. According to Kahveci, Uygun, Yurtsever, IIyas (2012), quality assurance is an activity that covers all the processes in a higher education institution with the intention of meeting the accepted quality standard needs of all stakeholders. Kahveci et al. (2012) further opined that some key areas where quality assurance activities are required in higher education institutions include strategic management, process management and measuring monitoring system. Furthermore, Swanzy and Potts (2017) noted that quality assurance strategies are applied externally and internally by higher education institutions in order to maintain, monitor and achieve quality outcomes which are in line with the institution's goals. For instance, higher education institutions set admission criteria to ensure that they admit students that can cope with the rigours of academic activities, and this procedure serves as an internal measure and strategy to maintain quality in the admission system (Swanzy & Potts, 2017). Therefore, quality assurance strategies are part of higher education system as it carries out its mandate in the society.

Role of Higher Education Quality Improvement Strategies in Improving Teaching in Higher Education Institutions

Higher education quality improvement strategies play important roles in teaching in higher education institutions. Below are higher education improvement strategies designed to improve teaching in some higher education institutions and their roles as identified by Swanzy and Potts (2017):

- **Transparent and Merit-based Staff Recruitment:** The main role of a transparent and merit based staff recruitment strategy is to employ qualified academic staff to achieve the higher education institution's teaching objectives. The process of recruiting academic staff is rigorous and it is based on the institution's recruitment policy, and managed by an appointment and promotion board/committee set up by the institution (Swanzy & Potts, 2017).
- **Staff Induction:** The main role of staff induction in improving teaching in higher education institutions is to inform newly recruited staff about the institution's quality culture and also to provide information about the institution's history, mission, vision, core values and approved method of teaching and assessment of the institution (Swanzy & Potts, 2017).
- **Staff Rules and Regulations:** Higher education institutions have rules and regulations governing all areas concerning their processes, procedures and activities in order to provide quality education for their students. Higher education institutions utilize the staff rules and regulations to guide staff conduct and activities (Swanzy & Potts, 2017).
- **Staff Formal Appraisal Methods:** These appraisals are done by the administering of questionnaires through students and departmental heads to appraise staff job knowledge and personal conduct against the institution's standards (Swanzy & Potts, 2017). The role of this strategy is to ensure that staff job knowledge meets the expected needs of the students, and also meets the expected standards of the departments and the institution (Swanzy & Potts, 2017).
- **Staff Workshops and Seminars:** The role of staff workshops and seminars in improving teaching in higher education institutions is to ensure that academic staffs are constantly aware of the current developments in teaching effectively and academic staff requirements for teaching effectively in a dynamic academic environment (Swanzy & Potts, 2017).
- **Further Studies for Staff:** The role of further studies for staff is to encourage academic personal and professional development to enable the academic staff to effectively carry out assigned tasks that contribute to the achievement of the institution' quality mandate (Swanzy & Potts, 2017).

Role of Higher Education Quality Improvement Strategies in Improving Learning in Higher Education Institutions

There are several higher education quality improvement strategies designed to improve learning in higher education institutions. According to Swanzy and Potts (2017), the following are some higher education quality improvement strategies designed and utilized by some higher education institutions to improve learning and their specific roles:

- **Transparent and Merit-based Students Recruitment:** The role of a transparent and merit-based students' recruitment strategy is to ensure that qualified students are recruited based on set criteria that determines their suitability for the academic program that the students are recruited to study (Swanzy & Potts, 2017).
- **Student Orientation:** The role of student orientation as a quality improvement strategy in higher education institution is to provide information on the institution's mission, values, norms, teaching, employability and what to expect in the academic environment (Swanzy & Potts, 2017). The student orientation also presents an opportunity for the students to be informed about the institution's rules and regulations (Swanzy & Potts, 2017).
- **Simulated Work Place for Students:** The role of this strategy is to provide students with the needed experience and exposure about workplace environments (Swanzy & Potts, 2017). This strategy enables students to learn about workplace culture and the demands of working in a workplace environment (Swanzy & Potts, 2017).
- **Student Academic Counselling:** The role of student academic counselling in improving learning in higher education institutions is to provide students with sound academic advice and strategies to cope with the rigours of academic activities (Swanzy & Potts, 2017).
- **Student Department-based Associations:** The role of this strategy in improving learning in higher education institutions is to improve the quality of students' learning experience through peer associations where students are mentored by senior peers, and are exposed to further specialist knowledge of their academic disciplines (Swanzy & Potts, 2017).
- **Student Graduation Ceremonies:** The role of this strategy is to ensure that students who have successfully completed the requirements of their degrees are presented with their certificates confirming their professional status (Swanzy & Potts, 2017). These events are usually well attended by academic staff, students and other invited guests and stakeholders.
- **Alumni Tracer Studies:** The role of this strategy in improving the quality of learning in higher education is to ensure that the graduates of higher education institutions are monitored to ensure that the graduates are job market ready and the higher education institution's curriculum meets the job market demands thereby improving and maintaining the quality of education provided by the higher education institution. (Swanzy & Potts, 2017).

FUTURE RESEARCH DIRECTIONS

Higher education improvement strategies are a well research area with diverse focus. Several studies focusing on higher education improvement strategies have focused on continuous quality improvement in higher education (Ellis, 2018; Mahdiuon, Masoumi, & Farasatkhah, 2017; O'Neill & Palmer, 2004;

Roffe, 1998).Some studies have focused on teaching improvement practices (Bergsmann, Schultes, Winter, Schober, & Spiel, 2015;Darling-Hammond, 2017;Lueddeke, 2003). Other notable studies such as Brown and Knight (2012) focused on assessing learners in higher education, Moxley, Najor-Durack and Dumbrigue (2013) focused on keeping students in higher education using successful practices and strategies for retention, and Jaggars and Xu (2016) investigated how does online course design features influence student performance? These studies were all carried out with diverse outcomes. In order to continue the discourse of higher education improvement strategies and expand our knowledge of the subject area, future studies on higher education improvement strategies should focus on identifying the factors that affect higher education strategies in both developing and developed societies, and also identify the different role of stakeholders in the higher education improvement process in various higher institutions' geographical locations.

CONCLUSION

Higher education improvement strategies remain an important approach towards creating higher education value for all stakeholders in the society. With the establishment of a quality monitoring mechanism such as a Quality Assurance Agency (UK) to ensure quality improvements in higher institutions of learning in the UK, stakeholders are now championing efforts to enable higher institutions of learning to deliver the needed quality graduates that can contribute positively to the society.

Although higher education improvement strategies are designed to improve the situation of things in the higher education system, not all higher education strategies are effective and non-problematic. In achieving accreditation status, such as AACSB accreditation, some higher institutions face challenges such as staff qualification. Also, in organizing faculty development workshops, college instructors do not familiarize themselves with the important features of the instructional strategy that is being adopted by the college instructor thereby creating a knowledge gap that hinders effective teaching. Furthermore, there exist other higher education improvement strategies' challenges associated with students and student learning assessment such as the lack of effect of student assessment outcomes on student learning and development and other key areas that are beneficial to the student.

In order to resolve higher education improvement strategies, practical solutions such stakeholder involvement in the design of higher improvement strategies and the piloting of strategies in a limited area before replicating the strategies in a wider area are recommended, among other solutions, to enable managers of higher education institutions to achieve their institutional goals in the society.

REFERENCES

Alaniska, H., Codina, E. A., Bohrer, J., Dearlove, R., Eriksson, S., Helle, E., & Wiberg, L. K. (2006). *Student involvement in the processes of quality assurance agencies.* Helsinki: European Association for Quality Assurance in Higher Education.

Altbach, P. (2015). Why branch campuses may be unsustainable. *International Higher Education*, (58).

Astin, A. W. (1984). Student involvement: A developmental theory for higher education. *Journal of College Student Personnel*, 25(4), 297–308.

Barnett, R. (1992). *Improving higher education: Total quality care*. Open University Press.

Becket, N., & Brookes, M. (2008). Quality management practice in higher education-What quality are we actually enhancing? *Journal of Hospitality, Leisure, Sports and Tourism Education, 7*(1), 40.

Bejan, A. S., Damian, R. M., Leiber, T., Neuner, I., Niculita, L., & Vacareanu, R. (2018). Impact evaluation of institutional evaluation and programme accreditation at Technical University of Civil Engineering Bucharest (Romania). *European Journal of Higher Education, 8*(3), 319–336. doi:10.1080/21568235.2018.1474780

Bergsmann, E., Schultes, M. T., Winter, P., Schober, B., & Spiel, C. (2015). Evaluation of competence-based teaching in higher education: From theory to practice. *Evaluation and Program Planning, 52*, 1–9. doi:10.1016/j.evalprogplan.2015.03.001 PMID:25847854

Berk, R. A. (2005). Survey of 12 Strategies to Measure Teacher Effectiveness. *International Journal on Teaching and Learning in Higher Education, 17*(1), 48–62.

Bidabadi, N. S., Isfahani, A. N., Rouhollahi, A., & Khalili, R. (2016). Effective teaching methods in higher education: Requirements and barriers. *Journal of Advances in Medical Education & Professionalism, 4*(4), 170. PMID:27795967

Borko, H. (2004). Professional development and teacher learning: Mapping the terrain. *Educational Researcher, 33*(8), 3–15. doi:10.3102/0013189X033008003

Boud, D., & Falchikov, N. (2006). Aligning assessment with long-term learning. *Assessment & Evaluation in Higher Education, 31*(4), 399–413. doi:10.1080/02602930600679050

Bowles, T. V., & Brindle, K. A. (2017). Identifying facilitating factors and barriers to improving student retention rates in tertiary teaching courses: A systematic review. *Higher Education Research & Development, 36*(5), 903–919. doi:10.1080/07294360.2016.1264927

Boyle, D. M., Carpenter, B. W., & Hermanson, D. R. (2014). The accounting faculty shortage: Causes and contemporary solutions. *Accounting Horizons, 29*(2), 245–264. doi:10.2308/acch-50967

Brink, K. E., Palmer, T. B., & Costigan, R. D. (2018). Business school learning goals: Alignment with evidence-based models and accreditation standards. *Journal of Management & Organization, 24*(4), 474–491. doi:10.1017/jmo.2017.35

Brown, G. A., Bull, J., & Pendlebury, M. (2013). *Assessing student learning in higher education*. Routledge.

Brown, R. (2004). *Quality assurance in higher education: The UK experience since 1992*. Routledge. doi:10.4324/9780203416327

Brown, S., & Knight, P. (2012). *Assessing learners in higher education*. Routledge.

Brubacher, J. (2017). *Higher education in transition: History of American colleges and universities*. Routledge. doi:10.4324/9780203790076

Chappell, K. B., Sherman, L., & Barnett, S. D. (2018). An interactive faculty development workshop designed to improve knowledge, skills (competence), attitudes, and practice in interprofessional continuing education. *Medical Teacher, 40*(9), 896–903. doi:10.1080/0142159X.2018.1481286 PMID:29969328

Corona, R. (2018). The Challenges for AACSB Accreditation at CEIPA Business School: Adapting New Standards for a Continuous Improvement Process. *International Journal of Business and Social Science, 9*(2).

Cortese, A. D. (2003). The critical role of higher education in creating a sustainable future. *Planning for Higher Education, 31*(3), 15–22.

Crosling, G., Heagney, M., & Thomas, L. (2009). Improving student retention in higher education: Improving teaching and learning. *Australian Universities' Review. The, 51*(2), 9.

D'Andrea, V., & Gosling, D. (2005). *Improving teaching and learning in higher education: a whole institution approach: a whole institution approach*. McGraw-Hill Education.

Dancy, M., Henderson, C., & Turpen, C. (2016). How faculty learn about and implement research-based instructional strategies: The case of peer instruction. *Physical Review Physics Education Research, 12*(1), 010110. doi:10.1103/PhysRevPhysEducRes.12.010110

Darling-Hammond, L. (2008). Teacher learning that supports student learning. *Teaching for Intelligence, 2*(1), 91-100.

Darling-Hammond, L. (2017). Teacher education around the world: What can we learn from international practice? *European Journal of Teacher Education, 40*(3), 291–309. doi:10.1080/02619768.2017.1315399

Darling-Hammond, L., & Richardson, N. (2009). Research review/teacher learning: What matters. *Educational Leadership, 66*(5), 46–53.

Davis, J. R. (1993). *Better Teaching, More Learning: Strategies for Success in Postsecondary Settings. American Council on Education Series on Higher Education*. Oryx Press.

Douglass, G. K. (2018). Economic returns on investments in higher education. In *Investment in Learning* (pp. 359–387). Routledge. doi:10.4324/9781351309929-15

Eaton, J. S. (2001). *Distance learning: Academic and political challenges for higher education accreditation*. Washington, DC: Council for Higher Education Accreditation.

Ellis, R. (2018). Quality assurance for university teaching: Issues and approaches. In *Handbook of Quality Assurance for University Teaching* (pp. 21–36). Routledge. doi:10.4324/9781315187518-1

Ellsworth, J. B. (2000). *Surviving changes: A survey of Educational change models*. Syracuse, NY: ERIC Clearinghouse.

Falchikov, N. (2013). *Improving assessment through student involvement: Practical solutions for aiding learning in higher and further education*. Routledge.

Fishman, T. D., Ludgate, A., & Tutak, J. (2017). Success by design: Improving outcomes in American higher education. *Deloitte Insights*. Accessed from https://www2.deloitte.com/insights/us/en/industry/public-sector/improving-student-success-in-higher-education.html

Friedlander, J., & Serban, A. M. (2004). Meeting the challenges of assessing student learning outcomes. *New Directions for Community Colleges*, *2004*(126), 101–109. doi:10.1002/cc.158

Fullan, M. (1982). *The meaning of educational change*. New York: Teachaers College Press.

Gazza, E. A., & Hunker, D. F. (2014). Facilitating student retention in online graduate nursing education programs: A review of the literature. *Nurse Education Today*, *34*(7), 1125–1129. doi:10.1016/j.nedt.2014.01.010 PMID:24529796

Gibbs, G., & Jenkins, A. (2014). *Teaching large classes in higher education: How to maintain quality with reduced resources*. Routledge. doi:10.4324/9781315041384

Graham, M. J., Frederick, J., Byars-Winston, A., Hunter, A. B., & Handelsman, J. (2013). Increasing persistence of college students in STEM. *Science*, *341*(6153), 1455–1456. doi:10.1126cience.1240487 PMID:24072909

Green, D. (1994). What Is Quality in Higher Education? Taylor & Francis.

Hanover Research. (2014). *Strategies for improving student retention*. Hanover Research-Academy Administration Practice. Available from https://www.hanoverresearch.com/media/Strategies-for-Improving-Student-Retention.pdf

Hayward, C. N., Kogan, M., & Laursen, S. L. (2016). Facilitating instructor adoption of inquiry-based learning in college mathematics. *International Journal of Research in Undergraduate Mathematics Education*, *2*(1), 59–82. doi:10.100740753-015-0021-y

Ilyasin, M. (2017). Balanced Scorecard: A Strategy for the Quality Improvement of Islamic Higher Education. *DinamikaIlmu*, *17*(2), 223–236.

Jackson, N. (1997). Internal academic quality audit in UK higher education: Part II-implications for a national quality assurance framework. *Quality Assurance in Education*, *5*(1), 46–54. doi:10.1108/09684889710156585

Jaggars, S. S., & Xu, D. (2016). How do online course design features influence student performance? *Computers & Education*, *95*, 270–284. doi:10.1016/j.compedu.2016.01.014

Jongbloed, B., Enders, J., & Salerno, C. (2008). Higher education and its communities: Interconnections, interdependencies and a research agenda. *Higher Education*, *56*(3), 303–324. doi:10.100710734-008-9128-2

Kahveci, T. C., Uygun, Ö., Yurtsever, U., & İlyas, S. (2012). Quality assurance in higher education institutions using strategic information systems. *Procedia: Social and Behavioral Sciences*, *55*, 161–167. doi:10.1016/j.sbspro.2012.09.490

Kerr, C. (2001). *The uses of the university*. Harvard University Press.

Lea, S. J., Stephenson, D., & Troy, J. (2003). Higher education students' attitudes to student-centred learning: Beyond 'educational bulimia'? *Studies in Higher Education*, *28*(3), 321–334. doi:10.1080/03075070309293

Leslie, L. L., & Brinkman, P. T. (1988). The Economic Value of Higher Education. American Council on Education/Macmillan Series on Higher Education. Macmillan Publishing.

Levine, A. (2018). Privatization in higher education. In *Privatizing education* (pp. 133–148). Routledge. doi:10.4324/9780429498015-6

Lewis, R. G., & Smith, D. H. (1994). *Total Quality in Higher Education. Total Quality Series*. St. Lucie Press.

Looney, J. (2011). Developing High-Quality Teachers: Teacher evaluation for improvement. *European Journal of Education, 46*(4), 440–455. doi:10.1111/j.1465-3435.2011.01492.x

Lueddeke, G. R. (2003). Professionalising teaching practice in higher education: A study of disciplinary variation and 'teaching-scholarship'. *Studies in Higher Education, 28*(2), 213–228. doi:10.1080/03075070320000558082

Mahdiuon, R., Masoumi, D., & Farasatkhah, M. (2017). Quality Improvement in Virtual Higher Education: A Grounded Theory Approach. *Turkish Online Journal of Distance Education, 18*(1), 111–131. doi:10.17718/tojde.285720

Marginson, S. (2011). Higher education and public good. *Higher Education Quarterly, 65*(4), 411–433. doi:10.1111/j.1468-2273.2011.00496.x

Matei, L., & Iwinska, J. (2016). *Quality Assurance in Higher Education: A practical handbook*. Academic Press.

Mohammed, K., Alotibie, B. A., & Abdulaziz, A. (2016). Total Quality Management in Saudi Higher Education. *International Journal of Computers and Applications, 135*(4), 6–12. doi:10.5120/ijca2016908245

Mooring, Q. E. (2016). Recruitment, advising, and retention programs—Challenges and solutions to the international problem of poor nursing student retention: A narrative literature review. *Nurse Education Today, 40*, 204–208. doi:10.1016/j.nedt.2016.03.003 PMID:27125174

Moxley, D., Najor-Durack, A., & Dumbrigue, C. (2013). *Keeping students in higher education: Successful practices and strategies for retention*. Routledge. doi:10.4324/9780203062401

Newman, T., Trimmer, K., & Padró, F. F. (2019). The Need for Case Studies to Illustrate Quality Practice: Teaching in Higher Education to Ensure Quality of Entry Level Professionals. In *Ensuring Quality in Professional Education* (Vol. 1, pp. 1–17). Cham: Palgrave Macmillan. doi:10.1007/978-3-030-01096-6_1

O'Neill, M. A., & Palmer, A. (2004). Importance-performance analysis: A useful tool for directing continuous quality improvement in higher education. *Quality Assurance in Education, 12*(1), 39–52. doi:10.1108/09684880410517423

O'Regan, K. (2002). Producing competent graduates: The primary social responsibility of law schools. *South African Law Journal, 119*, 242.

Okojie, J. A. (2008, June). *Licensing, accreditation and quality assurance in Nigerian Universities: Achievements and challenges*. Paper presented at a session of the 2008 Council of Higher Education Accreditation (CHEA) summer workshop.

Onwuegbuzie, A. J., & Rebecca, F. (2016). Seven Steps to a Comprehensive Literature Review: A Multimodal and Cultural Approach. *Sage (Atlanta, Ga.)*.

Parri, J. (2002). Quality in higher education. Vadyba Management.

Petrovskiy, I. V., & Agapova, E. N. (2016). Strategies of Raising the Quality of Higher Education and Attaining Equality of Educational Opportunities. *International Journal of Environmental and Science Education, 11*(9), 2519–2537.

Ramsden, P. (1987). Improving teaching and learning in higher education: The case for a relational perspective. *Studies in Higher Education, 12*(3), 275–286. doi:10.1080/03075078712331378062

Rice, G. K., & Taylor, D. C. (2003). Continuous –Improvement strategies in Higher Education: A progress Report. *EDUCAUSE-Centre for Applied Research.* Available from http://assessment.tcu.edu/wp-content/uploads/2016/06/ERB0320.pdf

Robert, V. H., & Mary, C. H. (1995). Continuous Quality Improvement in Higher Education. *International Statistical Review, 63*(1), 35–48. doi:10.2307/1403776

Roffe, I. M. (1998). Conceptual problems of continuous quality improvement and innovation in higher education. *Quality Assurance in Education, 6*(2), 74–82. doi:10.1108/09684889810205723

Rust, C. (2002). The impact of assessment on student learning: How can the research literature practically help to inform the development of departmental assessment strategies and learner-centred assessment practices? *Active Learning in Higher Education, 3*(2), 145–158. doi:10.1177/1469787402003002004

Ryan, T. (2015). Quality assurance in higher education: A review of literature. *Higher Learning Research Communications., 5*(4), 1–12. doi:10.18870/hlrc.v5i4.257

Sallis, E. (2014). *Total quality management in education.* Routledge. doi:10.4324/9780203417010

Schargel, F., & Smink, J. (2014). *Strategies to help solve our school dropout problem.* Routledge. doi:10.4324/9781315854090

Seymour, D. T. (1992). On Q: Causing quality in higher education. Macmillan Publishing Company.

Sherr, L. A., & Gregory Lozier, G. (1991). Total quality management in higher education. *New Directions for Institutional Research, 1991*(71), 3–11. doi:10.1002/ir.37019917103

Srinnivasan, L. E. (2018). *Why educational improvement strategies always disappoint.* Carnegie Corporation of New York: https://www.carnegie.org/news/articles/why-education-improvement-strategies-always-disappoint/

Swanzy, P., & Potts, A. (2017). Quality assurance strategies in higher education: The case of Ghanaian Polytechnics. *Education Research and Perspectives, 44*, 100–127.

Traynev, V. A., Mkrtchyan, S. A., & Saveliev, A. Y. (2010). *Improving the quality of higher education and the Bologna process.* Moscow: AST.

Ulewicz, R. (2017). The role of stakeholders in quality assurance in higher education. *Human Resources Management & Ergonomics, 11*(1).

Vaughn, J. (2002). Accreditation, commercial rankings, and new approaches to assessing the quality of university research and education programmes in the United States. *Higher Education in Europe*, *27*(4), 433–441. doi:10.1080/0379772022000071913

Vlăsceanu, L., Grünberg, L., & Pârlea, D. (2004). *Quality assurance and accreditation: A glossary of basic terms and definitions*. Bucharest: Unesco-Cepes.

Wit, H. D., & Knight, J. A. (1999). *Quality and internationalisation in higher education*. Academic Press.

Wolpert, J. (1965). *Behavioral aspects of the decision to migrate*. Papers in Regional.

Wright, G. B. (2011). Student-centered learning in higher education. *International Journal on Teaching and Learning in Higher Education*, *23*(1), 92–97.

Wright, W. A. (1995). Teaching Improvement Practices: Successful Strategies for Higher Education. Anker Publishing Co., Inc.

ADDITIONAL READING

Al-rahmi, W. M., Othman, M. S., & Musa, M. A. (2014). The improvement of students' academic performance by using social media through collaborative learning in Malaysian higher education. *Asian Social Science*, *10*(8), 210–221.

Al Shobaki, M. J., & Naser, S. S. A. (2017). The Role of the Practice of Excellence Strategies in Education to Achieve Sustainable Competitive Advantage to Institutions of Higher Education-Faculty of Engineering and Information Technology at Al-Azhar University in Gaza a Model. *International Journal of Digital Publication Technology*, *1*(2), 135–157.

Ghemawat, P. (2017). Strategies for higher education in the digital age. *California Management Review*, *59*(4), 56–78. doi:10.1177/0008125617717706

Kuh, G. D., Ikenberry, S. O., Jankowski, N., Cain, T. R., Hutchings, P., & Kinzie, J. (2015). *Using evidence of student learning to improve higher education*. John Wiley & Sons.

Liu, S. Y., Tan, M., & Meng, Z. R. (2015). Impact of quality assurance on higher education institutions: A literature review. *Higher Education Evaluation and Development*, *9*(2), 17–34.

Ramsden, P. (2003). *Learning to teach in higher education*. Routledge. doi:10.4324/9780203507711

Thomas, L., & Jamieson-Ball, C. (2011). *Engaging students to improve student retention and success in higher education in Wales*. York: Higher Education Academy.

Venkatraman, S. (2007). A framework for implementing TQM in higher education programs. *Quality Assurance in Education*, *15*(1), 92–112. doi:10.1108/09684880710723052

KEY TERMS AND DEFINITION

College Instructor: A person who teaches a subject or skill at the postsecondary level.

Dropout Rate: This refers to the percentage of students who are unable to complete a particular school or college course within a defined time frame.

Graduation Rate: This refers to the percentage of students that are able to successfully complete a particular school or college course within a defined time frame.

Higher Education: A post-secondary school education that occurs at a college or university.

Learning: A deliberate acquisition of knowledge, skills, and behaviors through studying.

Quality Education: An education that is well designed to provide the recipient with an all round development of skills and potential to achieve success in their future endeavors in a society.

Teaching Strategies: This refers to a plan of activities designed to help students learn particular course contents to achieve success in line with defined academic standards.

Chapter 14
Mentoring for Quality Enhancement and Fostering Industry-Ready Graduates in Higher Education

Rajka Presbury
Torrens University, Australia

Madalyn A. Scerri
Torrens University, Australia

ABSTRACT

Mentoring programs play a valuable role in higher education. Formal mentoring processes and relationships increase the overall perceived quality of an educational program and the professional success of new hotel management graduates. To evaluate an established mentoring program in higher education, a single case study of the Blue Mountains International Hotel Management School at Torrens University Australia (BMIHMS @TUA) was developed and that is presented and discussed in this chapter. The evaluation of the mentoring program found that mentoring relationships enable mentees to build knowledge and skills, develop networking opportunities, build confidence, and gain self-reflection abilities. The chapter offers insights and recommendations for higher education institutions to consider when setting up mentoring programs. The knowledge gained through this research will assist higher education institutions to better prepare students for a transition to work through mentoring whilst enhancing the quality of educational courses.

DOI: 10.4018/978-1-7998-1017-9.ch014

INTRODUCTION

The service industry has emerged as a significant economic driver that plays an important role in the development of national and regional wealth (United Nations 2017). In the past ten years, world output and employment have grown from around 65.8% to 68.2% and employment from 54.5 to 60.8% respectively and show no sign of slowing down (International Labor Office, 2015). Significant future employment will be in the service industry as more countries develop their hospitality and tourism capacity.

In particular, the hotel sector in Australia has seen major growth. 2013-14 saw the opening of seventeen properties in Darwin, Canberra, Brisbane and Melbourne which added around 1, 700 new rooms to the existent supply of 87, 795 rooms (Australia Tourism, 2015). Additionally, the national occupancy rate grew 1.5 percentage points to 66.9% at the end of 2014. In 2015, occupancy rate increased to 74.4%, the average daily rate growth 2.1%, and the revenue per available room was 3.7% more (STR Global, 2015). By the end of 2017, Australia's occupancy rate was 81.3%, the average daily rate is $152.12, and the revenue per available room is $123.73 (STR Global, 2017). These figures suggest the Australian accommodation sector is performing well, and it is projected that accommodation properties will continue to perform well financially (Deloitee Access Economics, 2017). Therefore, employment in the hotel sector will provide many opportunities for quality higher education graduates.

Employment in the hotel sector requires specific skills, knowledge and capabilities to service diverse needs and wants of customers. However, corporations (such as hotels, retail outlets, financial services and design houses) lack direct control over delivery quality by service employees (Scerri, Jenkins, & Lovell, 2017). Rather than using the traditional in house "apprenticeship" style training, service corporations largely depend on higher education institutions for formal qualifications and training of their employees (Fitzsimmons & Fitzsimmons, 2008). In turn, higher education institutions can develop relationships and processes with industry, including industry-employed alumni, to strengthen the quality and currency of education. Mentoring programs are one-tool institutions can utilise to develop and sustain high-quality education programs.

This chapter explores the role mentoring programs play in higher education programs. An evaluation of the Blue Mountains International Hotel Management School @ Torrens University Australia (BMIHMS @ TUA) mentoring program is developed to offer insights and recommendations for the establishment of mentoring in higher education institutions.

NEED FOR WORK READY GRADUATES

The corporation, educational service provider and the student or graduate operate in a triadic service relationship. The global employment environment, combined with the growth of knowledge industries, demands services graduates who are technically skilled and ready for work. Employment of such work-ready graduates is high on the agendas of governments in many developed countries, which are strengthening the role of higher education institutions to contribute to the national economy by meeting the needs of employers and the industry (Shah, Nair & Wilson, 2011). Employers expect that, on graduation, students will have a well-developed understanding of the business world (Jackson, Ferns, Rowbottom & McLaren, 2015). A report from the Grattan Institute in 2018 stated, "Although new graduate employment has improved since its 2014 low point, the labour market is still tough for younger graduates".

The Australian Trade and Investment Commission (2016) highlighted the direct correlation between skills and employment, namely the development of soft skills involving communication, change management, self and other leadership, presentation, flexibility and application. Additionally the Commission also reported a perceived disconnect between formal industry training and employer needs. They concluded that there is a perception that the tourism industry does not offer long-term careers, a view that is underpinned by lack of clear education pathways into the industry, thus advocating the need to develop relevant education programs that produce job- and industry-ready graduates.

Graduates face other challenges with career development and growth. Opportunities for new graduates to enter management is often limited and graduates become dispirited when they are unable to secure high level positions that they envisaged they would be in after graduation. Newly employed graduates often expect more responsibility than they are able to handle and initial employment in roles above the perceived inferior entry-level positions they are given upon commencement of employment. Even management trainee programs that only take the best students consist essentially of operational experiences (Raybould & Wilkins, 2005). Therefore, graduates can be lost to other industries where they can immediately use their academic skills in roles and where they may not require specific operational skills to do the job, and sometimes in higher-level roles. Equally, graduates may remain employed in the hospitality sector as demotivated employees (Raybould & Wilkins, 2005).

In the Australian higher education system, there is increasing debate and emphasis on employability and industry-identified desired graduate attributes. The Australian Higher Education Review (Bradley, Noonan, Nugent, & Scales, 2008) consolidated discussion by recommending that all higher education curricula must provide learning and teaching that equip the student with "technical skills and generic employability skills (such as communication and language skills)" (Bradley et al., 2008, p. 210).

In recognition of the importance of this shift, universities in Australia and New Zealand, as well as elsewhere, offer programs designed to meet the needs of employers in the service industry (Patrick, Peach, Pocknee, Webb, Fletcher & Pretto, 2009). The new direction for the Australian higher education system matches institutional interest in Work Integrated Learning (WIL) and has resulted in the development of WIL programs at university level and the creation of agencies such as the Australian Collaborative Education Network (ACEN) at the national level (Cooper, Orrell and Bowden, 2010; Smigiel & Harris, 2007). However, as WIL can be perceived as complex, challenging and costly to operate, Australian universities have implemented a diverse range of programs and services that are predominantly additions to their core curricula (Jackson et al., 2015; Kennedy, Billett, Gherardi & Grealish, 2015).

Institutions have provided industry contacts; resume writing, interview techniques and placement support for proactive students in preparing for, and participating in, WIL. There are also dedicated corporate partnerships and institution-funded on-campus programs such as the *Hatchery* at UTS, which has Apple, co-founder Steve Wozniak as its Founding Professor (Gilbert, 2016; Head, 2014). University-Industry collaborating, according to Juhari and Thomas (2013) has the potential to enhance knowledge generation and build the talent that comes from universities. Alternatively, formal or informal mentoring programs can be adopted to support the development of graduates' knowledge and skills and help students effectively transition into the labour market (Gannon & Maher, 2012).

Transition Through Mentoring

Mentoring is described as a management development technique that involves an experienced individual teaching and training someone with less knowledge in a particular area (Dessler, Lloyd-Walker & Griffiths, 2007). Mentoring involves close relationships between experienced staff and mentees (learners or protégés). Mentees observe, question and explore, whilst mentors demonstrate, explain and model (Kaye & Jacobson, 1996). Through mentoring, an aspiring manager can acquire skills and knowledge by interacting with more experienced managers (Cieri & Kramar, 2003).

Veale (1996) argues that mentoring should be part of a human resource development strategy, and that the goal of mentoring relationships is to help the mentee understand the industry within which they work. Additionally, Veale (1996) suggests that mentoring allows mentees to understand how things are done whilst building their confidence. Mentors provide vital learning for how to do jobs effectively in complex and continually changing circumstances (Eby, McManus, Simon & Russell, 2000). Kaye and Jacobson (1996) see mentoring as promoting intentional learning through the development of the mentee's capabilities while Orpen (1997) argues that mentoring enables mentees to perform their jobs better and advance their careers faster. Most importantly, mentoring enables a mentee to discuss and analyse failures, identify what went wrong and then learn from the experience in a process of self-reflection (Clutterbuck, 2014).

Research has shown that mentoring programs are a popular support mechanism for young managers, especially those belonging to minority groups (Noe, 2005). As early as 1985, Kram pointed to evidence that mentors provide both career support (establishing the mentee as an independent and successful professional) and psychosocial support (enhancing the mentee's sense of competence and effectiveness). Furthermore, Kram asserted that individuals who had experienced mentoring relationships were promoted more quickly, gained higher incomes and enjoyed greater satisfaction. Various writers have also concluded that mentoring benefits the whole career of managers (Coffey & Anderson, 1998; Rutherford & Wiegenstein, 1985). The influence of mentors and the acquisition of social capital are have been reported by scholars as significant. For example Yuen (1995) argued that mentor presence and mentor career support is positively related to managers' promotion in early career.

Mentoring has also been associated with transition and in particular it is argued that mentoring enables a process of socialization into new environments (Pensiero & McIlveen, 2006). Researchers have identified mentoring as being useful for transitioning students into the world of work (Poulsen, 2006). Mentoring also allows for the enrichment of students' education experience, through the connections they make, the introductions to the real industry, beyond the classroom (Hill & Sawatzky, 2011). Additionally Revis (2008) argued that the hospitality industry bears a great cost due to high turnover of talent and thus a dedicated strategy to retain young talent is now accepted practice. Appropriate transition through mentoring may reduce the reported high attrition levels by young and potential managers in the hospitality industry.

Mentoring relationships often develop informally because of shared interests or values between mentors and their mentees (Cieri & Kramar, 2003), however such relationships can also be planned. Formal mentoring programs are generally modelled on concepts from social learning theory (Robbins, Marsh, Cacioppe & Millet, 1994). Mentors are 'role models' and as such convey knowledge as well as the attitudes and behaviour that the organisation embraces.

There are advantages in establishing formal mentoring programs. Generally, because this ensures access to mentors for all and the participants in such programs are made aware of what is expected of them (Cieri & Kramar, 2003). There are also specific advantages for potential mentees. Mentors may advance the career of a mentee by: nominating them for promotion, introducing them to a range of management contacts, helping them make more informed decisions about progression, providing counselling on work related issues, and by suggesting coping strategies for problems within the workplace (Stone, 2002). The major reported benefit of mentoring is that it allows the protégé to make difficult decisions with greater confidence while under the protection of a mentor. It helps expand their natural abilities and help them reflect on their personal strengths and weaknesses.

Quality enhancement is a major concern for higher education institutions (Biggs, 2003), including accountability to various stakeholders and ensuring that, teaching programs produce results for students and the industry they serve. Evaluating established formal mentoring programs used in higher education can provide useful insights into the outcomes and challenges of mentoring to inform quality enhancement. Following a review of studies on undergraduate mentoring, Gershenfeld (2014) recommended that mentoring evaluations should include details of programmatic information, mentoring functions and operational components of the program.

Project Design

This project sought to evaluate an existing mentoring program in a higher education setting. A single case study methodology with a field-based approach was applied to share in-depth knowledge of a particular context with a wider education community. The mentoring program at the Blue Mountains International Hotel Management School @ Torrens University Australia (BMIHMS@TUA) was selected as the case study as it offers valuable insights into an established formal mentoring program. The framework advised by Gershenfeld (2014) has been used to report on the BMIHMS@TUA mentoring program.

A case study approach in its simplest format is a study of one thing in its entirety. An examination of the whole situation in detail is essential, and as such the idea is to look at a large number of inter-related features of a particular case (Yin, 2013).

Five stages of data collection were integrated:

1. Communication documents in the form of letters, emails, agendas, announcements, meeting minutes, proposals, and written progress reports pertaining to the mentoring program.
2. Discussions with the staff who were involved in the project to ascertain how the process occurred, their opinions about events along the way, insights into milestones.
3. Two focus groups held with both undergraduate and postgraduate students to ascertain their views on: how the promotion of the Mentoring Program was received; their general motivation for joining the program; their views on mentor and mentee allocation/matching; what expectations they had of their mentors; their views on how the program was working and suggestions for future improvement of the program.
4. Semi-structured interviews with the Alumni Board members who were enlisted to be the first mentors in the program.

5. A questionnaire survey administered to ascertain students' views on how the mentoring program was presented and initiated. This survey was distributed to all classes with final year students (undergraduate and postgraduate) in Term 2 of 2014.
6. Two surveys and multiple semi-structured interviews over two evaluation periods (2014-2015 and 2016-2017) were conducted.

Primary data in the first evaluation captured the views of 75 stakeholders and was compiled using student (mentees) focus groups, students (mentees and non-mentees) questionnaires and semi-structured interviews with senior managers (mentors). In the second evaluation, the data collected captured the views of 48 mentees and 14 mentors, representing just under 50% of total participants in the program.

When reporting a case study, it is important to illustrate why certain decisions were made, how they were applied, and what the outcomes were (Yin, 2013). The following sections illuminate these details of the BMIHMS@TUA mentoring program. From this evaluation, a number of recommendations for other institutions' mentoring programs are presented.

Context: The BMIHMS@TUA Mentoring Program

The BMIHMS@TUA offers a 2.5-year undergraduate degree program with two industry practicums: one in food and beverage and the other in rooms' division operations. To date the program has been able to boast great success in the placement of students and in a high level of graduate employment. Similarly, the BMIHMS@TUA Master's program is a 2-year degree with one industry practicum in a hotel. Both programs are delivered across four (4) terms per year, each term being 12 weeks in duration. All WIL subjects have credit points attached towards the qualification and students are required to complete paid work placements, managed by University staff, which complement students' reflective learning journals and employer reports (Presbury, 2015).

BMIHMS@TUA alumni, who are now spread globally in positions of hotel management and managers of other hospitality services, are active in the school's decision-making and add much to the discussions on enhancing quality in program development. In July 2014, the BMIHMS Alumni Board proposed the launching of a mentoring program. The primary purpose of the program was to serve better undergraduate and postgraduate final year students in preparation for their transition to industry. The design of the BMIHMS@TUA mentoring program recognised that hotel management graduates are increasingly being lost to other industries because graduates and employers have a range of expectations in the workplace and at times, these can be in conflict. This can occur for a range of reasons, such as lack of communication, misunderstanding, and lack of experience, disinterest and a lack of development.

It was hypothesized that access to mentoring by seasoned practitioners would enable new hospitality graduates to develop their career potential. In addition, it was anticipated that a mentoring program would serve as an effective tool for managing new graduate and employer expectations as to what is practical, possible and achievable in the development of the graduate in the workplace. Table 1 identifies the major milestones of the BMIHMS@TUA mentoring program.

Mentoring for Quality Enhancement and Fostering Industry-Ready Graduates

Table 1. Major Milestones

Date	Action	Detail	Student Participants
2012 June	Alumni Board proposes mentoring program discussion	Focus group ideas, limitations, working party established	
2014 June	Mentoring Panel Established		
2014 July	Alumni Mentoring Programme Pilot	Mentees: 1st Year Alumni or 3rd Year students Commitment: minimum 3 F2F meetings and monthly email	6
2014 September	Alumni Mentoring Policy and Procedure developed	Giving a definition of who could be invited to be a mentor; responsibility of mentors; responsibilities of mentees; and how the program would function.	12
2014 Term 4	Mentoring Programme intake begins	GPP students are given automatic entry to Mentor Programme	
2015 Term 2	Mentoring Programme intake 2	Short presentation developed along with classroom session to induct students into programme	9
2015 Terms 3 & 4	Evaluation of the program Focus groups with mentees and interviews with mentors. Report submitted to Alumni Board	Recommendations: • Change the promotion and timing of advertising the program • Matching mentees and mentors • Capping number of mentees to mentors • Better communication with students and a more streamlined application process • Create and provide tools to help mentors	
2015 August	Official coordinator of program appointed	Direct responsibility for the management of the mentoring program and liaison between mentors and mentees.	
2015 Term 4	Mentoring Programme intake 3	• Promotion of programme through on-Campus e-monitors, postcards, promotional posters in student "break out" areas, group emails/reminder • Online application process created • Only open to students in last 6-months on-campus	9
2015 October	Alumni Board Meeting approves further changes	• Agreed to increase the programme to quarterly (each term) rather than twice a year. Aim to capture word of mouth support from students still engaged. • Support material developed for Mentors and added to the Alumni website. • Welcome Letter developed for Mentees as a welcome to the programme from the President of the Alumni Board.	
2016 -January	Detailed steering document produced	Giving a clear definition of who could be invited to be a mentor; responsibility of mentors; responsibilities of mentees; and how the program would function.	
2016 Term 1	Promotion through Orientation, TV screens, postcards, Posters, Careers team going into classes, group email. Contact mentors on list and request additional assistance.	Students orientated into the program by coordinator.	19 2 drop out
2016 Term 2	Promotion as above		9
Term 2	Promotion as above	Starting to see benefit of word-of-mouth support for programme	17
2016 Term 3	Promotion as above		13
2016 Term 4	Promotion as above		12
2017 Term 1	New selection criteria and procedure based on Alumni Board feedback, students required to complete short panel interview with 2 x Career Dept. team members.	40% of those students who applied were successful, in comparison to previous groups where almost 100% of students were successful	16
T2 2017	Promotion as above and interviews held	22 applications, 16 successful (73% success rate)	16
T3 2017	Promotion as above and interviews held	9 applications, all successful	9
T4 2017	Promotion as above and interviews held	8 applications, 5 successful (62.5% success rate)	5
T1 2018	Promotion as above and interviews held	12 applications, 6 successful (50% Success rate)	6
T2 2018	Promotion as above and interviews held	9 applications, 7 successful (78% Success rate)	7
T3 2018	Promotion as above and interviews held	10 applications, 7 successful (70% Success rate)	7
T4 2018	Promotion as above and interviews held	7 applications, 2 successful (some students not eligible as not in final term of studies, some need work on objectives and chose to reapply in the next term)	2

Promotion of the Program

Initial promotion and advertising of the mentoring program took place from Week 2 of 2014. The promotion was through direct email to those students who would be eligible (students in their final 6-months on campus), TV screen advertising throughout the campus; promotional postcards and posters. Applications were accepted up until the end of Week 7, allowing students five weeks to complete their application e-forms. Students were asked to complete an application e-form outlining their reason for applying to the programme, departments or subjects they are interested in, proudest achievements, areas they wish to improve on and future goals. Additionally students were asked to attach a current resume. As Table 1 indicates, a small number (6) and then twelve (12) students participated in the program in the first year.

As per stage 4 of the study's data collection, all classes with final year students were visited (undergraduate and postgraduate) in term 4, 2014. A questionnaire survey was administered to ascertain students' views on how the mentoring program was presented and initiated. The survey sought to discover if students remembered the launching of the mentoring program, and why or why not they decided to participate. Additional information was sought from students on their preferred communication for such a promotion, what value they saw in the program, and their preference for mentor mentee matching. Seventy-one (71) responses were received from students who were eligible to enter the program at that time.

Students were able to discern anticipated benefits of such a program (see Figure 1), including benefits for setting career goals and fostering career advancement. However, when asked about their recollections on the launching of the mentoring program the results were very surprising.

Sixty one percent (61%) of student respondents did not recall receiving an email promoting the mentoring program. This means that 39% did remember receiving the email but chose not to engage in the program. Furthermore, students stated that the presentation of the program lacked impact and thought

Figure 1. Anticipated benefits of the mentoring program

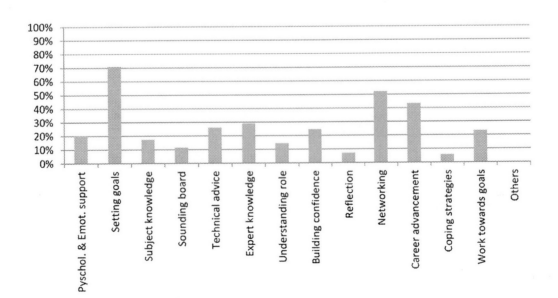

the "*emails were probably overlooked by most students.*" All agreed that limited information about the mentoring program was made available to students. Opportunities for questions were not available in any formal way and students were confused about the program and what it had to offer. Students commented:

i. "Sending the emails was "not enough…"
ii. "there were plenty of questions but no answers"
iii. "how is it going to help me was not answered"
iv. "some students are not interested and don't care therefore they don't read emails or engage in the activities offered"
v. "some people are doing it to gain a visa/stay longer in Australia. Not interested in a career in hospitality"
vi. "it is sometimes hard to engage students…as they don't live on campus…..those in the SRC are more engaged"
vii. "students are not aware of what is available on…campus…"
viii. "*a lot of students in their last year just want to get the course finished and don't engage in other activities*"

Thus, it was recognised almost immediately that the promotion of the program needed further attention and structure. Detailed communication with students about the program is essential at the point of promotion, and an opportunity to discuss the program with the program administers would be prudent. Additionally, there was a need to concentrate on the credibility and benefits of the program, including from mentoring success stories. It was clear that one avenue of communication (email) was not enough and in the next launch of the mentoring program, multiple communication methods should be used. Additionally, it was decided that the mentoring program ought to be treated as a normal part of the school activities and communicate in orientation, on the institution's website, during classes, and on the notice boards at the campus/s.

Matching mentors and mentees

Mentors in the program are defined as a group of established individuals who are graduates from the school who agree to be on the list of available mentors who may provide mentoring and support for current and future students at the BMIHMS @ Torrens. **Mentees** in the program are defined as those students who are in their final 6 months of study in an undergraduate or postgraduate program. All students who entered the program self-select to participate, receive no direct course benefit associated with credit points, and participate in their own time.

The quality of a mentoring relationship between mentors and mentees is recognised as an important part of establishing and maintaining a successful mentoring program, with trust and interpersonal comfort as key components (Simmons & Lupi, 2010). However, scholars differ as to the best way of matching mentors and mentees. Poulsen (2006) refers to the mentoring relationship as a learning alliance, where the mentor has experience and skills that are relevant to the mentee and the mentee is not offered a solution but rather encouraged to reflect and build solutions from the mentors guidance and experience in the field.

Initially, the BMIHMS@TUA mentoring program utilised a simple process of matching facilitated by the program administers. The literature shows that the institution as a third party (Crisp & Cruz 2009) often establishes mentoring relationships in educational settings. In the evaluation of the mentoring program in 2014, BMIHMS@TUA students agreed that a third party, that is, best did allocation of mentors by the institution itself. However, they also expressed concern regarding how they would handle a situation if they did not like their allocated mentor, and were wary about entering into the program with no knowledge of available mentors. As a result, mentees desired some form of interaction with mentors or insights to the mentors before allocation was finalised, potentially through profiles of suitable mentors selected by the institution. It was agreed that mentors really could not make a decision on mentees because they did not have enough information on the student.

It was further suggested that capabilities of mentors were more closely aligned to the needs of the mentees through matching. As a result, the mentoring coordinator was asked to take the above into consideration and in the refined program, process did include the following statement "Where possible, mentors and students will be profiled and matched according to personality profile, aptitude and area of interest/specialization."

In the 2016-17 evaluation, both mentors and mentees were in favour of a better process of matching. This was largely to do with further ensuring compatibility and alignment between the mentor's skillset and the potential mentee has needs, however mentors and mentees were not advocating for stringent or complicated matching processes. Recommended improvements to the matching process could include opportunities for alternative mentor allocations if either party were dissatisfied with the allocation. Matching capabilities of mentors to the needs of the mentees, which is currently used, is encouraged, however a mentee should also have the opportunity to identify their own development needs, thus specifically identifying a mentor that would be most effective for individual students' needs.

Future development of the mentoring program can enhance the process further. Matching may need to include a number of people who know both students and mentors and can better align two people for a successful relationship. It is further recommended that a closer look at the student profile information is scrutinised and may be adjusted to help in the matching process. It is also recommended there be investigation into some simple psychometric testing tools that may be completed quickly and easily and may be used for this purpose.

Roles of mentors and mentees

Mentoring others is a voluntary activity demonstrating prosocial, altruistic behaviour that benefits others (Gannon & Maher, 2012). In general, BMIHMS@TUA mentors emphasised the role of mentoring as a service to the school and its current student body, and was an important role alumni could assume to '*give back*' to the school community. When asked about their role, mentors reported a range of explanations as to what motivates them to participate (Table 2).

These findings are consistent with other research conducted on mentoring and show that the mentors have a clear understanding that mentoring relationships are focussed on the growth and accomplishments of an individual or community (Allen, 2003). The perceived role of mentoring also involved several essential attributes identified in the literature, including support, teaching learning, reflection opportunities, career development and personal development (e.g. Crisp & Cruz 2009). Mentors believed that their role helps mentees grow and succeed in their careers, including providing students with access to advice beyond the normal curricula contexts whilst maintaining the formal education context.

Table 2. Excerpts of mentor's motivations and perceptions of the mentoring role

Motivation for taking part as a mentor	Role as a mentor
Make a difference to the careers of students	To provide a platform of trust and listen to their needs away from the pressure of school
Help the kids, especially international students who don't have as much confidence	To be able to give mentees the information they need, especially where there are gaps, and to continue the connection between education, school, and industry
Help parents to see benefits of the education	Being a sounding board for students problems, opinions, concerns
Make the school stronger	Introduce students to industry through networking
Create a stronger Alumni	Act as facilitator to help students reach their immediate and also long term goals with respect to their careers
Challenge leadership skills	As Alumni offer empathy, understanding and a kick start
Pass on experience, knowledge, passion	Set the framework for the relationship
Provide students with connection with the Alumni	Helping them to redefine themselves as graduates

Some BMIHMS@TUA mentors identify and use a number of strategies to foster the mentoring process. The literature shows that the first stage of the mentoring relationship is to build a relationship with the mentee, because a mentoring relationship can only work if there is trust and a feeling of comfort to be honest (Kram, 1985; McDowall-Long, 2004; Evans, 2005). An important part of this first stage is to understand the mentee, particularly what they are looking for and what they hope to get out of the mentoring program. For example, one mentor suggested that they "*let the mentee set the initial conversation. I am available and provide appropriate feedback or guidance.*" This initial stage is crucial and has the potential to make or break the relationship. It is important to establish the framework of the relationship and ensure that both mentee and mentor understand how long the relationship will be, how often they want to meet, what formats they want to meet in and generally understand their expectations. BMIHMS@TUA mentors believed this stage is best conducted face-to-face.

The second stage is to build clear goals and action plans on how the mentee hopes to achieve them. The mentor's role in this processes it to provide a structure around those goals. Help the mentee be realistic and in many cases assist to align personal and career goals. During this stage email, communication is more than adequate. Once the goals are set all communication henceforth should be around those goals. The relationship in the BMIHMS@TUA mentoring program is short (6 months) and thus needs be more formal and structured to facilitate effective outcomes.

The third stage is where the mentee gains independence and only needs to check back with the mentor on their progress. If the mentee has challenges then the mentor may offer advice, including in the role of professional coach or empathetic counsellor. The fourth and final stage is when the partnership is redefined into a new and different relationship, such as when the individuals become colleagues; enter into a reporting relationship or informally '*remain in contact*' outside of the mentoring program. Alternatively, the relationship ends and both parties move on. For the mentor, they may be allocated a new mentee in the next round of the program and the cycle begins again.

Mentees recognised the important potential of the program and a list of motivations for joining the program were identified:

i. Networking in the industry and advice from those with greater experience.
ii. To "help me in the future"
iii. Access to industry as it is "…hard to meet other (more experienced) people in the industry
iv. Meet and know others who have "been there" and to understand what others have done.
v. Sounding boards to check "am I going in the right direction"
vi. Someone to talk to who understands the business….find out their perspective on something in particular
vii. Check with others on how to progress in the industry
viii. Advice on how to proceed strategically
ix. Helping sort out some "my doubts"
x. Get information on the paths I could take….information on skills….information on networks etc.

Overall student mentees expressed a genuine feeling that they were "*lucky*" to have access to such a program and recognised there were no "*certainties in life*" but wanted advice from mentors about career advice and opportunities. They did not have any expectations that the mentor would find them a job but really help them with their career development.

Specific comments by students of expectations were:

i. Gain specific knowledge. Students recognise 'gaps' in specific aspects of their industry knowledge.
ii. Understanding of what those in the industry have done and how they have done it, and to obtain ideas for their futures.
iii. Advice on industry areas such as cruise ships and associated career progression.
iv. No expectation of mentor to 'find you a job,' or be a counsellor on personal issues.
v. A pathway to identify goals, objectives, and an understanding of career development.
vi. Information on industry, where to go for information, and help me with my doubts.

In addition to career development, the literature on mentoring also suggests that there is a second important component of mentoring. In Kram's (1985) work on mentoring, she introduces the very important psychosocial function, which is argued to help the novice with respect to their emotional well-being. Counselling, role modelling, talking through dilemmas and acceptance being some of the support mechanisms associated with the psychosocial function. Foster and MacLeod (2004) as an important component of mentoring relationships also discuss emotional support. Such support has been described as listening, providing moral support, identifying problems and providing encouragement (Crisp & Cruz, 2009). When BMIHMS@TUA mentees were asked about their mentor's qualities that they most valued, they reported the following: "*friendly, inspirational and empathetic; honesty and easy to talk with; willingness to help; kindness and prompt replies; open to any sort of conversation- personal and professional; took time to understand what I wanted and what I needed to be where I want to be; willingness to understand me as a person more, before giving away any suggestion; transparency; perseverance; tenacity and determination; sharing personal experiences; good listener.*"

The above psychosocial mechanisms could go a long way in helping mentees with the various anxieties associated with starting a career and transitioning to industry. Mentees explained some of the benefits in the following ways:

"I am more certain what I want to do with my career."

"The program helped me develop both professionally and personally... she provided extensive knowledge and assistance toward creating future goals and building self-confidence."

"I did get some excellent solutions to various situational problems and I am very grateful for the advice I did get."

"Gave me broader idea as to what I want to achieve in the future."

Perceived Challenges of the Mentoring Program

The perceived challenges faced by both mentors and mentees stem from conflicts in personality, commitment levels and structural issues. Prevalent throughout literature is the disempowerment present in the matching process, leading to conflicts in personality (Eby, Allen, Evans, Ng & DuBois, 2008; Fagenson-Eland, Baugh & Lankau, 2005; Simmonds & Zammit Lupi, 2010). The lack of 'chemistry' between mentor and mentee can also lead to dysfunctional and unfulfilling relationships (Cameron & Jesser, 1994; Hunt & Michael, 1983). As explained above, the Alumni Board were in favour of simplicity in matching as depicted in this comment:

"If you [the mentor] who have certain skills are matched with a student/s who is interested in those things in particular or that profile [of the mentor] then just match them up. Two motivated people should be able to work it out and if things change well we deal with it."

According to the mentoring program coordinator very few cases of personality issues occurred, however a number of relationships fail due to unrealistic expectations and lack of commitment. Both mentors and mentees viewed commitment levels as critical to the successful outcome of the relationship. Previous studies have illuminated neglect from mentors as significant to the perception of the relationship (Eby & Lockwood, 2005). In the first evaluation of the program 50% of mentees reported frustration and confusion mainly due to a lack of appreciation around time and initiative in establishing meetings. Mentees expressed concern with a lack of interest or commitment from their mentor, or poor relational skills such as not listening to or understanding the mentee. For example *"I felt that my mentor lacked interest in how I was doing. I did get meetings every time I requested, however, during the meetings it was strictly only answering the questions I had. There was no voluntary input or advice."*

The mentees' expectation on what was a reasonable timeframe for the mentor to get back to them was very different to the mentors, who were senior executives in a fast-paced industry. Whilst mentees appeared to show empathy with the very busy schedules of mentors, they still felt that if mentors volunteered to be a mentor they had accepted a responsibility to the mentee. Most mentees felt strongly that frequent communication with mentors is necessary for any real benefits to be realised. For mentors, the most important expectation is that mentees are self-motivated and lead the mentoring process. Other expectations centred on the student being prepared, articulating their needs, making a commitment to the process, and fostering mutual respect. These expectations are depicted in this statement:

"I commit my time, so my expectation is that they commit their time in return, allocate their efforts, if for some reason they cannot come that they give me fair warning, and that they come to meetings prepared for our conversations, have their goals sorted out so that we can start to plan for the achievement of that goal. I understand of course that those goals may change, but they need to articulate what they need or the path they want to take, ask questions."

To be perceived as mutually beneficial, the mentoring relationship has to satisfy the expectations of both the mentor and the mentee. The factors involved in achieving this narrow balance are dependent on individual sensitivities and can thus be difficult to gauge. Eby and Lockwood (2005) suggest developing comprehensive and methodological mentoring frameworks that encapsulate the needs of both individuals to facilitate program's success. Poulsen (2006) argues that another risk is that the mentee will not be receptive to this kind of mentor behaviour and will react negatively to the mentor, resulting in a dysfunctional mentoring relationship. This could give the mentoring program a bad reputation in the organization as well as lead to participants dropping out of the program.

Lawson (1992) and Long (1997) articulated the lack of training provided to mentors, and lack of guidance as being key determinants where the relationship has failed to meet expectations, can often lead to a rise of negative emotions. Whilst mentors generally saw mentoring relationships as positive, there were identified stresses associated with the partnerships. Some mentors alluded to being over-burdened or fatigued by the cyclical nature of the mentoring program, and thus the repeated initiation and development of new mentoring relationships. Long (1997) listed the overuse of mentors as a concern often ignored or misunderstood in the mentoring process. As the altruistic giving of time and added responsibility can take its toll on the mentor, a challenge of the BMIHMS@TUA mentoring program is having adequate numbers of available alumni to facilitate breaks in mentor allocations. One alternative could be to extend the participation to junior alumni, making for a peer-to-peer mentoring program opportunity.

Moreover, enabling opportunities for administers of the program to reflect on the program development is extremely important. Reflective processes were described in the following ways:

"At every meeting of the [Alumni] Board we need to have a very frank discussion on how it's gone for everybody and we then need to adjust a few small things to make it right."

"If we start to make it too structured, formal and costly it will make it less accessible. Let's accept the slips through the cracks as part of the learning process."

Perceived Outcomes of the Mentoring Program

When asked about the overall value in the program at the second evaluation, mentors reported having a sense of personal satisfaction and self-reflection on their own experiences because of the program. They also reported combined gains of personal satisfaction, improved managerial skills, improved communication skills and self-reflection. Similarly, Ragins and Scandura (1999) observed that several important rewards could be identified from being a participant in a mentoring program: rewarding experiences, improved job performance, loyal base of support, recognition by others, and a feeling that one leaves a legacy for the future.

Personal satisfaction largely emerged from the mentor's enjoyment of helping others, which is an altruistic form of satisfaction related to 'other-focused' motives for joining the program The following quotes describe the value mentors perceive from providing opportunities to help students specifically:

"It is always nice to help the next generation."

"Satisfaction through hopefully assisting someone in a hugely pivotal and exciting time in their lives."

"I find the program very rewarding when the students build a connection and grown."

"The personal satisfaction knowing I can help others succeed."

Pensiero and McIlveen (2006) advocated that mentorship is a form of learning that supports students and outlined a considerable body of evidence where mentoring has positive benefits for development and growth. BMIHMS@TUA mentees reported that being part of the mentoring relationship has provided them professional networking, job opportunities, industry insight, an on-going professional contact in the industry, or an introduction to different career paths. Mentees comments validate these:

"The exposure to a network allowed me to be more proactive in making connections with leaders of the industry."

"Getting to know one more person in the industry, which may, as a result, open more doors for me in the future. Had the opportunity to visit my mentor's workplace and experience corporate life."

"I gained a job in a new part of the industry and moved out from food and beverage to front office; this change in direction has made me more confident. It also helps in working towards my future goal of being a GM one day."

"Looking at alternate career paths instead of the obvious one."

Collectively, these findings infer a belief that mentoring can positively enhance students' career success. Positive outcomes for mentors are also enabled, particularly when challenges of mentor fatigue are considered and mentors perceive the students' self-motivation in the mentoring process.

RECOMMENDATIONS FOR SETTING UP A MENTORING PROGRAM

The mentoring program has now been in place for 5 years, and almost 200 mentees and 50 mentors have participated. Two formal evaluations have been completed and many small but important changes have been made along the way. From this evaluation and reflection, the authors make a number of suggestions to other institutions.

Commitment to the Relationship

Maintaining a commitment to the mentoring relationship is a key contributing factor to successful mentoring. A mentoring program must begin by selecting both mentors and mentees who have a clear commitment to the process. This should mean that both parties commit to scheduled meeting times, communicate clear objectives and engage with frank discussions of what is hoped will be achieved. Maintaining these commitments can result in mutually beneficial outcomes for mentors and mentees. As was evidenced from the views of the mentors and mentees, mentoring relationships often lead to mutual learning and development. Other recent studies (Allen & Eby, 2008; Ragins, 2016) of mentoring relationships discuss care, concern, responsiveness, emotional connection and commitment as drivers.

Promotion of the Mentoring Program

Compelling promotion of a mentoring program is required to foster interest in the program, particularly when it is first launched. It is clear that one avenue of communication and promotion is not enough. Multiple communication methods include direct email, school social media sites, audio and visual materials on campus, as well as introductions to the program through orientation or professional development programs. More importantly, potential benefits of the program can be communicated. Photographs and biographical details of senior managers who are prepared to mentor students should be available for students to view. Success stories can be collected and shared with students in short videos and presentations by mentees who have gone through the program.

Matching Mentors and Mentees

The matching process used to establish mentor and mentee relationships should be carefully considered, reviewed and improved. Matching capabilities of mentors to the needs of the mentees has been discussed extensively in the literature (e.g. Cieri & Kramar, 2003; McDowall-Long 2004; Clutterbuck 2006). However, there is no universal agreement on how best to do this or if formal or informal mentoring programs should include structured matching. Benefiting from an experienced manager in the field that the student is interested in pursuing is the ultimate goal. However, from the views of the participants in this case it is recommended that mentees and mentors should have the opportunity to identify, along with their development needs, their preferences. The program coordinator needs to be mindful not to overburden any one mentor. The process may need to include a number of people who know both the student and the senior manager. Whilst a formal, structured program may benefit from using psychometric testing, this may result in costly and complex processes and take additional time. However, simple psychometric tools, easily available, can be employed to help with this challenge. This is the next iteration of the BMIHMS@TUA mentoring program.

Preparation of both Mentee and Mentors

Although the mentoring process includes different stages of activities, preparation of the mentee and the mentor is essential. Outlining roles and responsibilities is an important element for successful implementation of a mentoring program (Poulsen, 2006). A clear understanding of what is expected for both parties helps to foster structure in the program. The encouragement or development of interpersonal skills such as giving feedback, active listening and questioning is vital for both parties. Mentees would benefit from additional workshops that incorporate aspects of personal reflection and self-awareness, as well as setting expectations and goals. This may be part of the career development department role. It is not recommended that this be in a purely written format and consequently distributed to students via email. Students have a variety of learning styles and thus information should be disseminated in a variety of ways, including both formal and informal mechanisms.

A toolbox of activities for mentors to use may be developed and made available to participating mentors. A student platform, such as SharePoint or Blackboard, can be dedicated to the mentoring program for quick and easy access for mentors to share and receive information. Guides for expectation setting, goal setting and action planning could be developed to foster key activities in the mentoring relationship. An overall checklist of the mentoring process could be made available to both parties.

Support Mechanisms

The backbone of any mentoring program is a dedicated coordinator who is responsible for the mentoring program. The program coordinator needs to remain in touch with all stakeholders and can consider all the relevant aspects of the mentoring program's structure. The program coordinator must be able to help both mentees and mentors with information, have access to the established information portal and have overall responsibility for matching and maintaining up-to-date information, record keeping and collection of data. The university accepts the responsibility for the organisation of the program with administrative support from the university-wide mentor scheme coordinator, which is considered established practice (Theobald & Mitchell, 2002).

Recording Stories

Evaluation and continual improvement of the mentoring program is essential to ensure programs meet anticipated objectives and positively contribute to the quality of education programs. Feedback mechanisms include the distribution and analysis of evaluative survey questionnaires at the completion of each mentoring cycle. Perceived benefits and challenges of the mentoring process can be ascertained, including feedback on functional aspects such as mentor-to-mentee matching. Additional feedback can be sought as part of the program's promotional activities. Recording stories of mentees and mentors can be used to communicate benefits of the mentoring program and encourage further engagement within the institution.

Limitations and Future Direction

This chapter presented a single case study of a mentoring program used in a higher education setting. Consequently, this research is context bound and the findings cannot be generalised. The findings add to the building blocks of research on how mentoring programs can be embedded in higher education institutions and what part they play in building graduates and serving the industry.

Future research can track mentored students' career progress as a longitudinal study. This research would expand the perceived benefits proposed by mentees in this case study. Moreover, the interviews with mentors revealed that broadening the base of possible mentors was an important next step. Further research with this broader group of mentors may yield more wide-ranging results. Finally, comparative studies of mentoring programs in different educational settings may expand the recommendations offered in this study.

CONCLUSION

This case study has highlighted that a mentoring program has a number of benefits for an institution, its students, its alumni community and its industry partners. Whilst career development was never the goal for the introduction of the mentoring program by the Alumni Board, many students are reporting booth career and personal successes because of the program.

It is evident that there is not one single 'right' way to operationalise a mentoring program. It is important that students be offered choices to enrich their educational experience and their transitional process to industry. This may be a choice to engage with academic pursuits, work integrated learning, professional development opportunities, internships or a mentoring program. All or some of these activities, together with their formal educational program, will give students the attributes they need to transition to a fruitful and rewarding career in the industry they have chosen.

FUNDING STATEMENT

This research was supported by the Professor Susan Holland Fellowship grant offered through Laureate Universities.

ACKNOWLEDGMENT

The authors of this chapter acknowledge the assistance given by other BMIHMS @TUA staff involved in this project, in particular Dr Zelko Livaic. The input of other stakeholders is also acknowledged including the Alumni Board.

REFERENCES

Allen, T. D. (2003). Mentoring others: A dispositional and motivational approach. *Journal of Vocational Behavior*, *62*(1), 134–154. doi:10.1016/S0001-8791(02)00046-5

Allen, T. D., & Eby, L. T. (2008). Mentor commitment in formal mentoring relationships. *Journal of Vocational Behavior*, *72*(3), 309–316. doi:10.1016/j.jvb.2007.10.016

Australian Trade and Investment Commission. (2019). *Annual Report 2017–18*. Retrieved from https://www.austrade.gov.au/About/Corporate-Information/Annual-Report/Austrade-Annual-Report

Bradley, D., Noonan, P., Nugent, H., & Scales, B. (2008). *Review of Australian Higher Education: Discussion Paper.* Canberra, Australia: Department of Education, Employment and Workplace Relations.

Cameron, L., & Jesser, P. (1994). Mentoring can add extra value to the training dollar. In R. Stone (Ed.), *Readings in Human Resource Management* (Vol. 2, pp. 128–130). Brisbane, Australia: Wiley.

Cieri, D., & Kramar, R. (2003). *Human resource management in Australia: Management in strategy, people, and performance*. North Ryde, Australia: McGraw Hill.

Coffey, B. S., & Anderson, S. E. (1998). Career issues for women association executives: Mentors, pay equity, and boards of directors. *The Cornell Hotel and Restaurant Administration Quarterly*, *39*(4), 34–39. doi:10.1177/001088049803900106

Cooper, L., Orrell, J., & Bowden, M. (2010). *Work integrated learning: A guide to effective practice*. New York, NY: Taylor & Francis.

Crisp, G., & Cruz, I. (2009). Mentoring college students: A critical review of the literature between 1990 and 2007. *Research in Higher Education*, *50*(6), 525–545. doi:10.100711162-009-9130-2

Dessler, G., Lloyd-Walker, B., & Griffiths, J. (2007). *Human resource management* (3rd ed.). Frenchs Forest, Australia: Pearson Education.

Eby, L. T., Allen, T. D., Evans, S. C., Ng, T., & DuBois, D. L. (2008). Does mentoring matter? A multidisciplinary meta-analysis comparing mentored and non-mentored individuals. *Journal of Vocational Behavior*, *72*(2), 254–267. doi:10.1016/j.jvb.2007.04.005 PMID:19343074

Eby, L. T., Allen, T. D., Hoffman, B. J., Baranik, L. E., Sauer, J. B., Baldwin, S., & Evans, S. C. (2013). An interdisciplinary meta-analysis of the potential antecedents, correlates, and consequences of protégé perceptions of mentoring. *Psychological Bulletin*, *139*(2), 441–476. doi:10.1037/a0029279 PMID:22800296

Eby, L. T., & Lockwood, A. (2005). Protégés' and mentors' reactions to participating in formal mentoring programs: A qualitative investigation. *Journal of Vocational Behavior*, *67*(3), 441–458. doi:10.1016/j.jvb.2004.08.002

Eby, L. T., McManus, S. E., Simon, S. A., & Russell, J. E. (2000). The protégé's perspective regarding negative mentoring experiences: The development of a taxonomy. *Journal of Vocational Behavior*, *57*(1), 1–21. doi:10.1006/jvbe.1999.1726

Evans, T. (2005). How does mentoring a disadvantaged young person impact on the mentor. *International Journal of Evidence Based Coaching and Mentoring*, *3*(2), 17–29.

Fagenson-Eland, E. A., Baugh, S., & Lankau, M. J. (2005). Seeing eye to eye: A dyadic investigation of the effect of relational demography on perceptions of mentoring activities. *Career Development International*, *10*(6/7), 460–477. doi:10.1108/13620430510620557

Foster, S., & MacLeod, J. (2004). The role of mentoring relationships in the career development of successful deaf persons. *Journal of Deaf Studies and Deaf Education*, *9*(4), 442–458. doi:10.1093/deafed/enh053 PMID:15314017

Gershenfeld, S. (2014). A review of undergraduate mentoring programs. *Review of Educational Research*, *84*(3), 365–391. doi:10.3102/0034654313520512

Gilbert, P. (2016, December 31). Campus evolution: Teaching students to become entrepreneurs. *The Sydney Morning Herald*. Retrieved from http://www.smh.com.au/national/education/campus-evolution-teaching-students-to-become-entrepreneurs-20161231-gtk7v2.html

Head, B. (2014, November 18). With Wozniak on board, as UTS launches Hatchery to breed better tech start-ups. *The Sydney Morning Herald*. Retrieved from http://www.smh.com.au/national/education/campus-evolution-teaching-students-to-become-entrepreneurs-20161231-gtk7v2.ggshtml

Hill, L. A., & Sawatzky, J. A. V. (2011). Transitioning into the nurse practitioner role through mentorship. *Journal of Professional Nursing*, 27(3), 161–167. doi:10.1016/j.profnurs.2011.02.004 PMID:21596356

Hunt, D. M., & Michael, C. (1983). Mentorship: A career training and development tool. *Academy of Management Review*, 8(3), 475–485. doi:10.5465/amr.1983.4284603

Jackson, D., Ferns, S., Rowbottom, D., & McLaren, D. (2015). *Working together to achieve better work integrated learning outcomes: Improving productivity through better employer involvement*. Retrieved from http://acen.edu.au/wp-content/uploads/2016/06/Working-together-to-achieve-better-WIL-outcomes.pdf

Kaye, B., & Jacobson, B. (1996). Reframing mentoring. *Training & Development*, 50(8), 44.

Kennedy, M., Billett, S., Gherardi, S., & Grealish, L. (Eds.). (2015). *Practice-based learning in higher education: Jostling cultures*. Springer. doi:10.1007/978-94-017-9502-9

Kram, K. E. (1985). *Mentoring at work: Developmental relationships in organisational life*. Glenview, IL: Scott, Foresman.

Lawson, H. A. (1992). Beyond the new conception of teacher induction. *Journal of Teacher Education*, 43(3), 163–172. doi:10.1177/0022487192043003002

Long, J. (1997). The dark side of mentoring. *Australian Educational Researcher*, 24(2), 115–133. doi:10.1007/BF03219650

Mitchell, M., & Theobald, K. (2002). Mentoring: Improving transition to practice. *The Australian Journal of Advanced Nursing*, 20(1), 27. PMID:12405280

Noe, R. (2005). *Employee training and development*. New York, NY: McGraw-Hill/Irwin.

Orpen, C. (1997). The effects of formal mentoring on employee work motivation, organizational commitment and job performance. *The Learning Organization*, 4(2), 53–60. doi:10.1108/09696479710160906

Pensiero, D., & McIlveen, P. (2006). Developing an integrated approach to graduates' transition into the workforce. In *Proceedings of the 2nd Biennial Conference of the Academy of World Business, Marketing and Management Development: Business Across Borders in the 21st Century* (Vol. 2). Academy of World Business, Marketing and Management Development.

Poulsen, K. M. (2006). Implementing successful mentoring programs: Career definition vs mentoring approach. *Industrial and Commercial Training*, 38(5), 251–258. doi:10.1108/00197850610677715

Ragins, B. R. (2016). From the ordinary to the extraordinary. *Organizational Dynamics*, 45(3), 228–244. doi:10.1016/j.orgdyn.2016.07.008

Ragins, B. R., Cotton, J. L., & Miller, J. S. (2000). Marginal mentoring: The effects of type of mentor, quality of relationship, and program design on work and career attitudes. *Academy of Management Journal, 43*(6), 1177–1194.

Raybould, M., & Wilkins, H. (2005). Over qualified and under experienced: Turning graduates into hospitality managers. *International Journal of Contemporary Hospitality Management, 17*(3), 203–216. doi:10.1108/09596110510591891

Robbins, S., Marsh, T., Cacioppe, R., & Millet, B. (1994). *Organisational behaviour: Concepts, controversies and applications*. New York, NY: Prentice Hall.

Rutherford, D. G., & Wiegenstein, J. (1985). The mentoring process in hotel managers' careers. *The Cornell Hotel and Restaurant Administration Quarterly, 25*(4), 16–23. doi:10.1177/001088048502500406

Scerri, M. A., Jenkins, J. M., & Lovell, G. (2017). A grounded theory model of service language in Australia's luxury hotels. *Journal of Hospitality and Tourism Management, 33*, 82–92. doi:10.1016/j.jhtm.2017.09.003

Simmonds, D., & Zammit Lupi, A. M. (2010). The matching process in e-mentoring: A case study in luxury hotels. *Journal of European Industrial Training, 34*(4), 300–316. doi:10.1108/03090591011039063

Smigiel, H., Harris, J., & Hannah, J. (2007). *Bringing it all Together: An overview of the delivery of key work-integrated learning (WIL) initiatives at Flinders University*. Paper presented at the Australian Collaborative Education Network, Geelong, Australia. Retrieved from http://acen.edu.au/2012conference/wp-content/uploads/2012/11/64_Bringing-it-all-Together.pdf

Veale, D. J. (1996). Mentoring and coaching as part of a human resource development strategy: An example at Coca-Cola Foods. *Leadership and Organization Development Journal, 17*(3), 16–20. doi:10.1108/01437739610116948

Yin, R. K., & Campbell, D. T. (2013). *Case study research: design and methods* (5th ed.). Thousand Oaks, CA: SAGE.

ADDITIONAL READING

Allen, T. D. (2003). Mentoring others: A dispositional and motivational approach. *Journal of Vocational Behavior, 62*(1), 134–154. doi:10.1016/S0001-8791(02)00046-5

Allen, T. D., Eby, L. T., Poteet, M. L., Lentz, E., & Lima, L. (2004). Career benefits associated with mentoring for protégés: A meta-analysis. *The Journal of Applied Psychology, 89*(1), 127–136. doi:10.1037/0021-9010.89.1.127 PMID:14769125

Australian Hotels Association (AHA). (2009). *Australian hotels more than just a drink and a flutter: An overview of the Australian hotels industry*. Retrieved from http://aha.org.au/wp-content/uploads/2011/04/PWC-Hotel-Industry-Report-20092.pdf

Chi, C. G., & Gursoy, D. (2009). How to help your graduates secure better jobs? An industry perspective. *International Journal of Contemporary Hospitality Management, 21*(3), 308–322. doi:10.1108/09596110910948314

Clutterbuck, D. (2014). *Everyone needs a mentor* (5th ed.). London, UK: Chartered Institute of Personnel and Development.

Clutterbuck, D. (n.d.). *Evaluating Mentoring*. Retrieved from https://www.davidclutterbuckpartnership.com/wp-content/uploads/Evaluating-Mentoring.pdf

Cox, E. (2005). For better, for worse: The matching process in formal mentoring schemes. *Mentoring & Tutoring, 13*(3), 403–414. doi:10.1080/13611260500177484

Daloz, L. A. (2012). *Mentor: Guiding the journey of adult learners*. Somerset, NJ: Wiley.

Deloitte Access Economics. (2017). *Business Outlook Q4 2017*. Retrieved from https://www2.deloitte.com/au/en/pages/media-releases/articles/business-outlook.html

Doherty, N., Viney, C., & Adamson, S. (1997). Rhetoric or reality: Shifts in graduate career management? *Career Development International, 2*(4), 173–179. doi:10.1108/13620439710173661

Dominguez, N., & Hager, M. (2013). Mentoring frameworks: Synthesis and critique. *International Journal of Mentoring and Coaching in Education, 2*(3), 171–188. doi:10.1108/IJMCE-03-2013-0014

DuBois, D. L., Portillo, N., Rhodes, J. E., Silverthorn, N., & Valentine, J. C. (2011). How effective are mentoring programs for youth? A systematic assessment of the evidence. *Psychological Science in the Public Interest, 12*(2), 57–91. doi:10.1177/1529100611414806 PMID:26167708

Gannon, J. M., & Maher, A. (2012). Developing tomorrow's talent: The case of an undergraduate mentoring programme. *Education + Training, 54*(6), 440–455. doi:10.1108/00400911211254244

Garavan, T. N., O'Brien, F., & O'Hanlon, D. (2006). Career advancement of hotel managers since graduation: A comparative study. *Personnel Review, 35*(3), 252–280. doi:10.1108/00483480610656685

Glaser, B. G., Strauss, A. L., & Strutzel, E. (1968). The discovery of grounded theory; strategies for qualitative research. *Nursing Research, 17*(4), 364. doi:10.1097/00006199-196807000-00014

Grima, F., Paillé, P., Mejia, J. H., & Prud'homme, L. (2014). Exploring the benefits of mentoring activities for the mentor. *Career Development International, 19*(4), 469–490. doi:10.1108/CDI-05-2012-0056

Hay, J. (2000). Developmental mentoring: Creating a healthy organisational culture. *Journal of Communication Management, 4*(4), 378–384. doi:10.1108/eb023534

Insala. (2011). *5 Best practices for successful matching and pairing in a mentoring program*. Retrieved from https://www.insala.com/whitepapers/08-09-2011-matching-and-pairing-in-mentoring.pdf

Jauhari, V., & Thomas, R. (2013). Developing effective university-industry partnerships: An introduction. *Worldwide Hospitality and Tourism Themes, 5*(3), 238–243. doi:10.1108/WHATT-02-2013-0006

Lincoln, Y. S., & Guba, E. G. (1985). *Naturalistic Inquiry*. Beverly Hills, CA: SAGE. doi:10.1016/0147-1767(85)90062-8

McDowall-Long, K. (2004). Mentoring relationships: Implications for practitioners and suggestions for future research. *Human Resource Development International, 7*(4), 519–534. doi:10.1080/1367886042000299816

Peach, D., Moore, K., Campbell, M., Winchester-Seeto, T., Ferns, S., Mackaway, J., & Groundwater, L. (2016).*Building institutional capacity to enhance access participation and progression in Work Integrated Learning (WIL): Final report 2015.* Retrieved from http://eprints.qut.edu.au/98925/1/98925.pdf

Philip, K., & Hendry, L. B. (2000). Making sense of mentoring or mentoring making sense? Reflections on the mentoring process by adult mentors with young people. *Journal of Community & Applied Social Psychology, 10*(3), 211–223. doi:10.1002/1099-1298(200005/06)10:3<211::AID-CASP569>3.0.CO;2-S

Pogrebin, M. (Ed.). (2003). *Qualitative approaches to criminal justice: Perspectives from the field.* Thousand Oaks, CA: SAGE Publications.

Ragins, B. R., & Scandura, T. A. (1999). Burden or blessing? Expected costs and benefits of being a mentor. *Journal of Organizational Behavior, 20*(4), 493–509. doi:10.1002/(SICI)1099-1379(199907)20:4<493::AID-JOB894>3.0.CO;2-T

Rekha, K. N., & Ganesh, M. P. (2012). Do mentors learn by mentoring others? *International Journal of Mentoring and Coaching in Education, 1*(3), 205–217. doi:10.1108/20466851211279466

Scandura, T. A. (1992). Mentorship and career mobility: An empirical investigation. *Journal of Organizational Behavior, 13*(2), 169–174. doi:10.1002/job.4030130206

Scott, B., & Revis, S. (2008). Talent management in hospitality: Graduate career success and strategies. *International Journal of Contemporary Hospitality Management, 20*(7), 781–791. doi:10.1108/09596110810897600

Tesone, D. (2004). Whole brain leadership development for hospitality managers. *International Journal of Contemporary Hospitality Management, 16*(6), 363–368. doi:10.1108/09596110410550806

Turban, D., & Lee, F. (2008). The role of personality in mentoring relationships: formation, dynamics, and outcomes. In B. R. Ragins & K. E. Kram (Eds.), *The handbook of mentoring at work: Theory, research, and practice* (pp. 21–50). Thousand Oaks, CA: SAGE. doi:10.4135/9781412976619.n2

United Nations Intergovernmental Group of Experts on Competition Law and Policy. (2017). *Item 3 of the provisional agenda: Meeting on Trade, Services and Development, fifth session, Geneva, 18–20 July 2017.* Retrieved from https://unctad.org/en/pages/MeetingDetails.aspx?meetingid=1435

Veal, A. (2005). *Business Research Methods: A Managerial Approach.* Frenchs Forest, Australia: Pearson.

Weinberg, F. J., & Lankau, M. J. (2011). Formal mentoring programs: A mentor-centric and longitudinal analysis. *Journal of Management, 37*(6), 1527–1557. doi:10.1177/0149206309349310

KEY TERMS AND DEFINITIONS

Alumni Board: A group formed by the alumni association to advise on ways to promote and engage alumni nationally and internationally.

Mentees: Students who are in their final 6 months of study in an undergraduate or postgraduate program at BMIHMS @Torrens. All students who enter the mentoring program self-select to participate, receive no direct course benefit associated with credit points, and participate in their own time.

Mentors: A group of established individuals who are graduates from the school and currently hold positions in senior management. Mentors agree to be on the list of available mentors who may provide mentoring and support for current and future students at the BMIHMS @ Torrens.

WIL: Learning which takes place in a work setting, where students engage in work experiences to advance their professional understanding in a chosen career.

Chapter 15
Quality Assurance and Institutional Research for University Strategic Management:
A Case Study

Ngepathimo Kadhila
University of Namibia, Namibia

Gilbert Likando
University of Namibia, Namibia

ABSTRACT

Strategic management in higher education (HE) has become data-reliant. Most higher education institutions (HEIs) all over the world have implemented quality assurance (QA) and institutional research (IR) with the purpose of generating data that that would assist in evidence-based decision making for better strategic management. However, data generated through QA and IR processes have to be integrated and streamlined in order to successfully inform strategic management. One of the challenges facing higher education institutions is to integrate the data generated by QA and IR processes effectively. This chapter examines examples of good practice for integrating the data generated by these processes for use as tools to inform strategic management, using the University of Namibia as a reference point. The chapter offers suggestions on how higher education institutions may be assisted to overcome challenges when integrating the outcomes of QA and IR processes in order to close the quality loop through effective strategic management.

DOI: 10.4018/978-1-7998-1017-9.ch015

INTRODUCTION

Higher education institutions (HEIs) should contribute to the development and support of economic, social and cultural progress of any given country in the world (D'Andrea & Gosling, 2005). In order to make a meaningful contribution, HEIs have to respond to the demands of changing and evolving societal conditions, and have to develop the internal structures required to accomplish their vision (Kahveci & Taskin, 2013). These conditions produce challenges for HEIs which include a mixed profile in the student population as a result of massification, the emergence of new competitors, globalisation and internationalisation, a knowledge-based economy, a technology-driven society, new horizons in education, and increasing external demands for accountability and transparency (Kahveci & Taskin, 2013). Addressing these changes and challenges has meant finding ways to align organisational capacities with environmental demands and opportunities, as well as immense responsibilities for governance and management at institutional level. However, higher education (HE) systems and institutions are being faced with an unprecedented number of challenges, which call for new and innovative approaches to educational planning and decision-making. Strategic management has, accordingly, been widely acknowledged as a tool that can help to prepare HEIs to face these emerging challenges.

Quality assurance (QA) and institutional research (IR) can be inherently embedded in all a university's practices to achieve the strategic goals effectively (Weeks-Kaye, 2004). Quality assurance is a holistic approach which covers all processes in a HEI. The success of a QA system depends on the support of management, hence, QA should also cover strategic management, which is a primary responsibility of senior leadership (Kahveci, Uygun, Yurtsever, & Ilyas, 2012). Through QA an institution aims to assure an agreed standard for all activities, not only through established procedures and processes but also through a commitment to understanding and attempting to meet the expectations of students and others. Quality improvement adds a further step, with a commitment to continuous and proactive improvement in academic programmes and services.

In addition to Internal Quality Assurance (IQA,) many HEIs all over the world have introduced IR. Such IR has become central for integration in the QA system to support the strategic management process. However, compared to IR, formal QA systems in HE are a fairly new phenomenon (Geyser & Murdoch, 2016). According to the Southern African Association for Institutional Research (SAAIR), IR refers to research that is designed to generate information that serves planning, policy development, resource allocation, and management or evaluation decisions in all functional areas (SAAIR, 2019). Klemenčič and Brennan (2013) define IR as research conducted within an HEI to provide information which supports institutional planning, policy formation and decision making. IR is not merely conducted for the advancement of knowledge about higher education in general but is also applied research directed by specific planning, policy or decision situations.

It is clear that QA and IR play a complementary role, both generating data intended to inform external stakeholders regarding the accountability and institutional strategic management of quality enhancement (QE). However, according to Geyser and Murdoch (2016), the relationship between the QA and IR in informing institutional strategic management has not been clearly articulated. Therefore, collaboration and integration of the use of such data appears to be unclear. In this chapter, using the University of Namibia (UNAM) as a case study, the authors conduct a critical literature analysis to explore the challenges faced by HEIs in integrating QA and IR processes to effectively inform evidence-based decision making and strategic management. The purpose of the chapter is to identify examples of good practice and offer suggestions as to how to improve current practice. In this chapter, the authors argue that HEIs should put measures in place to integrate data generated by QA and IR processes so as to close the quality loop through effective strategic management.

BACKGROUND

HE in general is facing increasing pressure concerning effectiveness, accountability and responsiveness in the face of changing national and institutional environments (Geyser & Murdoch, 2016). HEIs are also faced with unprecedented challenges related to budget allocation, staffing and improving quality delivery within constrained infrastructural environments. These challenges are exacerbated by external factors such political unrest, which impact on the student experience. The pressures from stakeholders such as governments, industry, labour unions and civil society have prompted HEIs to put in place measures for supporting and informing strategic management to ensure public accountability and QE. As a result, in the 21st century, where universities are faced with new opportunities and new risks resulting from globalisation and the increasing role of human factors, strategic management has become one of the most promising management mechanisms for HE development (Yureva, 2016). Today, many Namibian HEIs, both large and small, have begun to implement their own development strategies, reflecting the vision of the institutional development prospects. The need for effective institutional management and QE has given rise to the implementation of QA and IR processes as tools to inform evidence-based decision making and strategic planning and management. Both QA and IR generate data that play a vital role in informing this process. However, instead of playing complementary roles, the two initiatives often operate in isolation. Currently, there have been calls for collaboration between IR and QA to provide data on institutional effectiveness and efficiency, as is evident in the literature (Yureva, 2016). This collaboration and/or integration of QA and IR has been further promoted by the need for IR data to inform external programme reviews for accreditation by national QA agencies and/or professional bodies (Geyser & Murdoch, 2016).

There is evidence in the literature of successful QA and IR integration to inform evidence-based decision making and strategic management, and the accompanying benefits, particularly in Europe (Kahveci et al., 2012; Kahveci & Taskin, 2013). In Namibia, despite the call for collaboration between QA and IR, where it does exist the relationship can still be regarded as ad hoc. Geyser and Murdoch (2016) observe that often one-way communication of data from IR to QA is implied, while the scope of the data is limited to the requirements of a particular quality review. Although this observation was done in South Africa, the authors contend that the situation is similar in Namibia as it also seems as if IR often excludes QA or that QA operates in isolation from IR. This is perhaps due to the fact that the core functions of QA and IR seem to differ. For example, QA focuses mainly on quality reviews of different units of analysis, i.e. institutions, programmes and/or modules. Conventional IR, on the other hand, is the sum of all activities directed at empirically describing the full spectrum of functions (educational, administrative and support) that is used for the purposes of institutional planning, policy development and decision making. Although the focus of IR has shifted in recent years, from reporting to active involvement in strategic positioning of the institution, references to IR do not necessarily include QA (Geyser & Murdoch, 2016). Thus, there is limited evidence of progress towards more strategic and integrated approaches to QA and IR. This chapter uses UNAM as a case study to advocate the need for a relationship between QA and IR as a point of departure for effective strategic management of HEIs. However, the nature and scope of the collaboration and/or integration require further exploration though in-depth research.

QUALITY ASSURANCE AND INSTITUTIONAL RESEARCH EMERGENCE

As has been alluded to in the introduction and background sections, the world is currently experiencing drastic expansion in the field of HE due to advancement, needs and development, and HE has been acknowledged as being key to socioeconomic development. Higher education provision in the 21st century has also become competitive, as HEIs have to compete with each other by providing quality education. This challenge has seen the introduction of formalised QA systems in HE education at both national and institutional levels, particularly since the 1980s. Accordingly, institutions are obliged to evaluate their activities regularly and participate in external evaluations (Kettunen, 2008). Thus, quality has become a central theme in higher education (Haris, 2013) and has, ultimately, given rise to the need for quality assurance (QA) initiatives at both the national and institutional levels. QA refers to the systematic internal and external management procedures and mechanisms by which HEIs assure stakeholders of the quality of their systems, processes, products and outcomes and their ability to manage the maintenance and enhancement of quality (Harvey, 2005). It is now widely acknowledged that QA plays a vital role in facilitating continuous improvement and QE in all the activities of HE systems. To date, most countries in the world have established national QA agencies that audit HEIs and provide accreditation. Thus, every country has its own QA systems and processes. Some countries have external review agencies to ensure quality in all HEI activities and some have government agencies that carry out these quality audits.

QA may be referred to as national QA, external quality assurance (EQA) or internal quality assurance (IQA). EQA refers to a range of quality monitoring and procedures that is undertaken by bodies (professional bodies or QA agencies) outside an HEI in order to determine whether the institution meets the agreed or predetermined quality standards (Pitsoe & Maila, 2017). On the other hand, IQA encompasses all the activities that an HEI must carry out internally in order to maintain and improve their quality. It refers to the internal policies and mechanisms of an HEI intended to ensure that it is fulfilling its purposes, as well as meeting the standards that apply to HE in general, or to the profession or discipline in particular. In this context, IQA mechanisms may include external moderation and examination systems, self-assessment (usually followed by external peer assessment for validation), benchmarking and stakeholder feedback (Martin & Stella, 2007).

Generally speaking, an EQA system has two main purposes, namely, quality improvement and external accountability. Furthermore, EQA denotes the actions of an external body, which may be a QA agency or anybody other than the institution, which assesses its operation or that of its programmes in order to determine whether it is meeting the agreed or predetermined standards (Martin & Stella, 2007). The agency or the government organisation defines the set of policies and procedures that HEIs should meet with respect to local and international requirements. Hence, they define QA and the audit framework that is suited to the nation. These are internationally benchmarked at various stages (Alkhafaji & Sriram, 2012).

In the Namibian context, EQA involves the registration of HEIs, accreditation by professional bodies and/or QA agencies, and institutional audits. There are three statutory QA agencies, namely, the Namibia Qualifications Authority (NQA) (Act No. 29 of 1996), the Higher Education Act – National Council for Higher Education (NCHE) (Act No. 26 of 2003), and the Namibia Training Authority (NTA) (Act No. 1 of 2008) (Government of Republic of Namibia, 2008). To ensure quality in all the activities of an HEI and to inform the public of this for accountability purposes, national QA agencies conduct quality audits according to respective national QA frameworks. The HEIs in Namibia are subjected to quality audits, and institutional and/or programme accreditation processes either by the Namibia Qualifications Authority (NQA) or the National Council for Higher Education (NCHE). Audit reports generate important data that may be used to inform evidence-based decision making and strategic management at national and institutional levels. For example, at national level, data generated by quality audits can be used to inform funding for HEIs, budget allocation and staffing, and improving quality delivery. At institutional level, the same data can be used to inform programme development and review.

Apart from EQA, most HEIs have also implemented IQA systems to ensure continuous QE in all their activities (Alkhafaji & Sriram, 2012). In the Namibian context, most HEIs have established QA units which assist the institution in implementing, enhancing and maintaining quality in all their activities. Such QA develops review systems and carries them out in the form of institutional and academic programme and support unit audits and reviews, which include peer evaluation. Furthermore, QA helps to ensure that quality improvement is entrenched in all academic work at institutions so as to continuously increase effectiveness and efficiency. In particular, HEIs have different types of QA processes which they have to undergo to maintain and improve quality in their quest to provide quality education. These are internationally benchmarked to ensure that the graduates become highly competitive. In most systems, HEIs prepare annual reports, among others, to support their activities during the academic year (Martin & Stella, 2007; World Bank (2009).

In addition to QA units, most HEIs the world over have established IR units with the purpose of meeting both internal and external responsibilities and the demands for data to inform evidence-based decision making and strategic management. Such IR supports strategic planning, and the analysis of institutional and other data to support university planning, management, operations, evaluation and decision making. This function involves regular surveys among staff and students in order to produce useful information about the institution. This information is intended to aid planning and point to areas where there is a need for action. In addition, IR develops and maintains planning support models. According to Haskell (2017), all over the world, the need for collecting and disseminating data about HEIs has grown rapidly. New technologies, new software, new analytical methodologies and new approaches combine to create the potential for exponentially larger amounts and types of data that may be used to inform all interested parties. Simultaneously, external demands for information about HEIs have expanded tremendously. Governments require more and better information about institutional performance and outcomes. Accrediting bodies seek data to improve their capacity for oversight, verification and QA. Prospective students and their families look for information about programmes, costs and what their investments will purchase. Employers seek greater alignment of student capabilities and employer needs. This confluence of expanding capabilities and increasing demands puts great pressure on those tasked with gathering and analysing data and reporting results to stakeholders (Haskell, 2017).

Despite HEIs having put in place QA and IR processes, whether or not data generated through the two processes are used effectively is not clear. There is therefore a need to improve institutional effectiveness in higher education in terms of the generation and use of data to inform strategic management.

STRATEGIC MANAGEMENT IN HIGHER EDUCATION INSTITUTIONS

Higher education systems and institutions are being faced with unprecedented challenges, which call for new innovative approaches to educational planning and decision making. A major challenge emerged with the phenomenal increase in the demand for higher education and the associated massive expansion of HE systems in the 21st century (Menon, Terka, & Gibbs, 2014). Today, in confronting these challenges, HEIs are called on to consider multiple concepts such as strategy, quality, process and the like in order to manage in an integrated manner. In particular, strategic management has recently been considered in many HEIs all over the world. Strategic management serves as a mechanism for giving long-term direction to HEIs and at the same time for allocating resources in line with this direction. It is a tool for forecasting the future and placing the institution in the best possible position for future success (Kahveci & Taskin, 2013). It is concerned with basic decisions about what the institution is now, and what it is to be in the future. Furthermore, it allows the institution to analyse the present conditions and to consider all stakeholders in order to create and sustain competitive advantage.

By implementing strategic management, HEIs focus on strategic and operational goals, objectives and strategies based on organisational policies, programmes and actions designed to achieve the institution's aims and desired results. The success of the institution is derived from the correct implementation of strategic plans. As a result of the current economic downturn, HEIs are under pressure to further cut costs while doing more with fewer resources than ever before by maintaining their attractiveness to prospective students through high quality education provision. In this context, HEIs are called upon to adopt QA and IR as tools to inform evidence-based decision making, strategic planning and management processes in addressing the needs of a larger, more diverse student body. For some of these reasons, most HEIs the world over, including UNAM, have started to place greater emphasis on QA, IR and strategic planning in an attempt to maintain their positions in an increasingly competitive HE market. There is also a call for HEIs to use effective performance indicators in the planning and management of HE.

To understand strategic planning in HEIs, Nickel (2011) addresses key components of this subject, namely, *strategic management* as a core component of every HEI that understands itself as an autonomous actor. It gives managers ideas and tools for strategic planning, implementation and control that are suitable for the specific organisational conditions in HEIs. In addition, strategic management typically involves three processes, namely, *planning, operationalisation and implementation*, and *controlling*. The planning process involves environmental scanning, SWOT (strengths, weaknesses, opportunities and threats) analysis, strategic decision making, and agreeing on strategic objectives and measures. This is an engaging process which involves everybody within an institution. Operationalisation and implementation involve the execution of the strategy after the plan has been approved by the university structures. This process requires cooperation between all institutional members. Controlling is a continuous task that supports strategic planning, as well as the implementation of the strategies, monitoring and reporting of the achievements on a regular basis.

According to Shawyun (2016), in the dynamics of planning and quality management, strategic planning can no longer be separated from QA, nor can strategic planning or quality management work in an information vacuum. Shawyun (2016) identifies three key questions that should be addressed in strategic planning and management within the HEI context:

1. **Where we are now and where are we going?** This should address our current and past performance based on an analysis of the internal and external environment to come to an understanding of the current position of the HEI in the staked-out education industry based on its capability. This current performance evaluation, based on the analysis, will determine whether the previously set vision, mission, goals and objectives have been achieved and where the institution will be going based on its current resources and capability.
2. **Where do we want to go or where could we be going?** This question addresses where the institution wants to chalk out a future position in the education industry and what product or service offerings and stakeholder groups the institution intends to compete. This would be based on the internal and external analysis, which determines what is deficient, what is needed in the existing capabilities, or that should be created to achieve that future staked out position.
3. **How do we get there?** This will address the resources, capabilities that the institution needs to create or build to execute its chosen strategies in order to achieve the envisaged position, and the outcomes that it intends to achieve. It also addresses the issue of what to do and how to do it in terms of the implementation of the strategies selected. It goes into the realms of building a capable and competitive organisation in the education industry through capability and capacity building to achieve its mission and goals.

These three questions highlight the main aspects that should be dealt with strategically. In order to answer these questions, there is a need for HEIs to integrate QA with strategic planning. In addition, the strategic planning and management must be developed within the QA context. However, the authors' analysis of institutional documents did not yield any evidence of such a practice at UNAM.

Quality Assurance and Institutional Research Implementation at University of Namibia

The focus of teaching and learning at the University of Namibia (UNAM) is on preparing graduates who will make a significant contribution to national development by ensuring that students are exposed as much as possible to opportunities that will mould them into fully rounded citizens. Such citizens will be empowered to participate fully in the economic, social and cultural advancement of the country and be able to engage competitively in diverse activities locally, nationally and at a global level (UNAM, 2016). However, what could set UNAM apart from other HEIs in the world is the quality of the education it provides. As a result, UNAM has established two units responsible for QA and IR, namely the Centre for Quality Assurance and Management (CEQUAM), and the Physical and Strategic Planning Unit (PSPU).

The CEQUAM is responsible for the implementation of a robust QA system incorporating the generation of data through quality audits/reviews. The PSPU coordinates the strategic planning process. Strategic planning commences with the leadership's annual analysis of the internal and external environment for the purposes of aligning or realigning the institution through planning (Nickel, 2011; Shawyun, 2016). As an outcome of this process, strategic priorities are identified that provide the parameters guiding institutional and faculty level planning. The continuous quest for quality and excellence permeates the academic core functions of teaching/learning, research and community engagement. This process has led to the identification of quality and excellence as one of the strategic priorities within the ambit of the institutional challenges of the institution. For UNAM, quality and excellence involve a continuous process aimed at identifying and addressing gaps in quality in all core functions and activities of the institution within a continuous cycle of planning, acting, evaluating and improving. The feedback and other information about the achievement of quality targets are used to develop the process and challenges.

Part of the functions of PSPU at UNAM is IR. Like QA, IR generates data intended to inform evidence-based decision making and strategic management. As Geyser and Murdoch (2016) and Yureva (2016) point out, to ensure effective strategic management and QE, there is a need for HEIs to link their QA with IR processes. However, although UNAM boasts of having implemented both QA and IR processes, it is not clear how it integrates data generated by the two processes to inform evidence-based decision making and ensure effective strategic management.

Strategic Direction of the University of Namibia

The University of Namibia (UNAM) is a public HEI which was established by an Act of Parliament on 31 August 1992 (University of Namibia Act 18 of 1992). The University of Namibia has an enrolment of over 26 000 students in its various academic programmes across its twelve campuses and eight regional centres countrywide. This enrolment figure includes on-campus full-time and part-time students, as well as distance students learning through the Centre for Open, Distance and eLearning (CODeL). The focus of a traditional university such as UNAM is on creating knowledge through research and disseminating knowledge to students. In its vision statement UNAM aspires "to be a beacon of excellence and innovation through teaching, research and community services" (UNAM Strategic Plan, 2016–2020, p. 1). This vision statement clearly indicates the commitment of the university to quality teaching, research and community engagement activities.

In line with its vision, the mission of UNAM is "to provide quality higher education through teaching, research and advisory services to our customers with the view to produce productive and competitive human resources capable of driving public and private institutions towards a knowledge-based economy, economic growth and improved quality of life" (UNAM Strategic Plan, 2016–2020, p. 1). Consistent with its vision and mission, UNAM has formulated a strategic plan for the period 2016 to 2020, which sets out the University's strategic direction for a period of five years. To achieve its vision and mission, a number of institutional policies which are benchmarked on national institutional legislative frameworks have been developed to guide the institution's practices. These include, notably, the quality assurance and management policy, teaching and learning policy, assessment policy, staff development policy and other related policies.

Successful quality management requires one to understand the context of the HEI mission, which represents its "reason for existence" or the very purpose of the HEI (Shawyun, 2016). According to Shawyun (2016), quality management systems (QMSs) implemented under a paucity of planning management systems (PMS) and information management systems (IMS) that are not aligned have resulted in the death of most QA systems, which at best pay lip-service to QA or merely go through annual or five-year audit and assessment cycles that do not bring about improvements and innovations. Furthermore, QA without improvements and innovations, or that does not bring about learning and integration with other systems, is a poor system at best that is not well planned and is lacking an evidence-based system. Therefore, QA at UNAM should be linked to the planning and information management systems through the strategic performance management framework, thus laying the foundation for continuous improvement and innovation based on evidence-based decision making and strategic management.

Quality Assurance System at the University of Namibia

Legislation requires that all HEIs, be it public or private, should have in place QA procedures aimed at improving the quality of the education and related services they provided. In line with this requirement, UNAM has the responsibility to assure its stakeholders and the public at large that the educational services it provides are of a quality which is accepted and recognised by employers and other educational institutions nationally, regionally and internationally; hence, the development of the Quality Assurance and Management Policy (2019). Against this background, the establishment of the Centre Quality Assurance and Management (CEQUAM) in 2010 signified the UNAM's intent to respond to national and international quality imperatives with regard to institutional QA mechanisms, and at the same time develop UNAM's capabilities in the area of QA in order to improve quality and enhance the capacity for continuous development. Some of our main activities include (UNAM, 2018 p. 1)

- Providing quality standards and measures for all programmes, centres and departments.
- Coordinating the internal and external review processes for the university itself, as well as all divisions (both academic and administrative) and programmes.
- Monitoring the implementation of the recommendations of internal and external reviews.
- Organising seminars and capacity-building training workshops in the area of QA for the University's staff and students.
- Promoting a culture of quality in every aspect of the university.
- Coordinating registration of qualifications on the National Qualifications Framework (NQF) and Programme Accreditation.
- Linking UNAM with external quality assurance agencies.

The Centre is instrumental in designing and implementing QA mechanisms and systems to ensure that students receive high quality and relevant education, and that their academic qualifications are widely recognised. Such recognition is seen as essential not only by national government and employers but also by other universities and employers on a global scale. Based on UNAM's Quality Assurance Framework, the decision to establish CEQUAM is on the premise of importance of a coordinated system of QA that should be applied consistently across the institution to allow for dialogue and sharing of good practices from different sections (UNAM, 2011).

The UNAM QA system is informed by the university's mission, vision, values and objectives, which are part of the university's routine operations. The main purpose for QA at UNAM is to ensure continuous improvement in the university's core business, namely, teaching and learning, research and community engagement. Accordingly, quality is the responsibility of everyone at institutional level (UNAM, 2011). Hence, QA at UNAM has adopted the national and international approach to QA as follows (UNAM, 2018 p. 1):

- *Fitness for purpose*. The core activities of the university are in relation to the vision and mission of the institution and on how well the various divisions at UNAM and the academic programmes are aligned to the vision of the university.
- *Fitness of purpose.* The university is discharging its functioning with regard to the manner and extent to which an institution's mission and academic activities are responsive to national priorities and needs.
- *Customer satisfaction.* The degree to which the university meets its customers' needs of which students are the main clientele.
- *Value for money.* The institution is judged in relation to the full range of higher education purposes set out in the various national policies. In addition, the effectiveness and efficiency of provision will depend on the quality and relevance of the education and training.
- *Transformation*: The development and capacity of the individual learners for personal, social and economic enrichment.

The University's approach to QA and QE is set out in its Quality Assurance and Management Policy. In accordance with this Policy, the QA system is based mainly on self-reviews, operating in all areas of the institution at different levels on a periodic cyclical basis focused on continuous improvement or QE (UNAM, 2015). The QA procedures at UNAM include a review of each department, faculty, programme and service provided by the university, which is conducted through self-review and validation through peer review. Self-review is the process by which a division under review reflects on its objectives and critically analyses the activities it engages in to achieve these objectives. It provides an evaluation of the division's performance, of its functions, its services, and its support activities. The self-review should be self-critical and analytical as it serves as the basis for a dialogue between the division under review and the review panel.

The planning for the cyclical institutional review and auditing is regarded as an important opportunity to take stock of quality management and assurance at the institution in a systematic, reflective and self-evaluative manner in order that the quest for continuous quality improvement may be bolstered. The review process involves the following four major steps (UNAM, 2018):

Step 1: Self-assessment:
- Of academic/administrative departments.
- Assessment by students/stakeholders.

Step 2: Peer review through site visits to validate the self-assessment report by"
- National experts.
- International experts.
- Stakeholders:

Step 3: Review report
- Publication of findings.

Step 4: Implementation of recommendations
- Agree a quality improvement plan of action with timescales and deliverables.
- Follow-up.

Since the inception of CEQUAM at UNAM, a number of quality reviews have been undertaken which have covered external audits and internal reviews/evaluations, namely

- Governance.
- Curriculum design and review.
- Student admission, progress and achievements.
- Teaching/learning and assessment.
- Student support services.
- Physical facilities.
- Staff.
- Research, extension and innovation.
- Process of quality management and continuous improvement (UNAM, 2015).

The outcome of a quality review culminates in a review report outlining recommendations for improvement. The recommendations of quality reviews are converted to self-improvement plans (SIPs) to be developed and implemented by the institution, faculty or department that underwent the quality review. The SIP specifies actions: designated responsibilities and timeframes to address the requirements and recommendations of the review reports for the purpose of follow-up, validation and closing the quality loop by the institution, faculty or department (see Table 1).

Improvement and enhancement planning and strategies need to be articulated with institutional structures and quality processes at different levels to ensure planned and strategically directed improvement. To monitor effectively the implementation of the SIP, UNAM has established an Implementation, Monitoring and Evaluation Committee (IMEC) within its committee structure.

It is evident from the literature that UNAM has implemented a robust QA system in an attempt to ensure strategic management and QE. To achieve this, a variety of internal and external evaluation processes have been developed and implemented. Ideally, data generated through QA processes such as audits and reviews should be complemented by data generated through IR processes to ensure an integrated approach and effective strategic management (Shawyun, 2016). However, the authors' analysis of institutional documents yielded no evidence of such a practice at UNAM. Connecting the outcomes of these QA evaluations with the outcomes of IR has often proved challenging owing to factors arising from organisational complexity.

Table 1. Self-improvement Plan Template

Recommendations	Actions needed	Responsible office/person	Overseeing person (monitor or sign off)	Resources required (human, physical, financial)	Timeframe for completion (month & year)	Evidence for completion
1.						
2.						
3.						
etc.						

Source: UNAM (2018)

Institutional Research Generated Data Usage to Inform Strategic Management

In the 21st century, the strategic management process, with its focus on improving HE practice, has become increasingly data-reliant (Thomas, Turjansky, & Jones & Williams, 2016). A major shift has occurred towards strategic management activities focused on data and information relating to students outcomes, rather than the processes operated by departments or institutions. Data, both qualitative and quantitative, is a fact of life for everyone in HEIs, and UNAM is no exception. In addition to data generated by QA processes, HEIs use data generated by IR processes to support and inform strategic management, and evidence-based decision making. According to Hazell and Guy (2016), internal and external data lead to HEIs taking a more data-driven approach to strategic decision making. Thomas et al. (2016, p. 6) identified specific IR activities and the data that inform them as follows:

Programme Development and Approval: Programme development and delivery costs balanced against projected intake numbers based on market research.

Programme Monitoring and Review

- **Student Recruitment:** Number/percentage of applications against programme targets; offers conversions and enrolments.
- **Retention Rate:** Number/percentage of students registered on a programme who return to it the following academic year.
- **Progression Rate:** Number/percentage of students that passed a particular year out of the total who obtained a result, i.e. students who have successfully completed the programme or have qualified to proceed to its next stage.
- **Graduation Rate:** Number/percentage of students who graduate within record time of the duration of programme.

Student Satisfaction Rates: External and internal student surveys.
Graduate Employability: Destination of leavers from higher education survey.

In line with Thomas et al. (2016), UNAM uses internal and external data (qualitative and quantitative) in many ways to improve the students' learning experience, for example when developing new programmes and monitoring and reviewing existing programmes. Qualitative data include feedback from students, external examiners and staff. Quantitative data, on the other hand, cover student recruitment, attainment, retention, progression, graduation and graduate destinations. The UNAM also uses data generated though IR to inform improvement in teaching and learning practice, assessment approaches, strategic decision making, infrastructural development, and key performance indicators (UNAM, 2018).

The UNAM generates data from various internal and external sources to ensure that internal academic monitoring and review processes are heavily data-reliant. However, Thomas et al. (2016, p. 6) identify frequent challenges facing HEIs and UNAM is no exception in this regard:

- Generating data that are meaningful, timely, reliable and integrated.
- Achieving consistency of data over time, location and mode of delivery.
- Developing flexibility to cope with non-standard provision.
- Meeting multiple requirements of multiple stakeholders.

- Securing user confidence in data at all levels.

Establishing effective institutional strategic management requires HEIs to integrate data generated from a broad variety of sources that are fundamental to enabling decision-making, communication and organisational processes between different stakeholders as well as the realisation of activities (Thomas et al., 2016). In light with this, UNAM uses data from a variety of sources such as internal and external QA processes and institutional research to inform strategic management. However, the authors' literature analysis has shown that there is little evidence as to how data generated from various sources such as QA and IR are integrated to ensure efficiency and effectiveness in institutional strategic management.

Challenge of Integrating Quality Assurance and Institutional Research to Support Strategic Management

The unequivocal roles HEIs play in responding to national imperatives and government expectations, for instance "economic progress and social well-being, including desirable outcomes such as poverty reduction, increased income equality, improved health, civic participation, good governance and the protection of human rights" (Oketch, McCowan & Schendel, 2014, p. 9, cited in Nel, 2016, p. 99), have raised the prominence of IR in strategic planning. Similar to QA, IR generates data about the institution that are important for informing evidence-based decision making through strategic planning and management. In this regard, both QA and IR are seen as playing a complementary role. However, according to Van der Westhuizen (2009), one of the urgent challenges for HEIs is to integrate data generated from QA and IR processes and connect them to the longer-term goals of the institution (contained in the strategic planning) and the annual outcomes and targets (contained in the quality reports and operational planning – strategic planning) to culminate in the achievement of these goals. Traditionally, the purpose of the strategic planning was to provide a framework for defining the institution's mission, vision and goals, while continuous quality improvement provides the principles and tools for guiding the planning and improvement processes. The other challenge has to do with the generation of timely and reliable data. One of the most important debates relating to the use of data generated from QA and IR concerns the measurement of quantity rather than quality. This leads to HEIs drawing false or unjustified conclusions in their decision making (Kahveci & Taskin, 2013). There is sometimes an assumption that data, especially numerical statistics, are "right" and therefore have some inherent authority, without recognising that such data require an appropriate methodology (Menon et. al., 2014). As a result, the risks associated with ineffective solutions to problems have increased both at the institutional and the systemic level (Menon et al., 2014). Educational policy makers and administrators are called on to select the "right" alternatives, aiming for both efficiency and effectiveness in delivered outcomes. In this context, decision makers strive to make informed decisions, based on a thorough examination and analysis of relevant data. It is widely accepted that integrating QA and IR would help to combine the strengths of the data generated by the two processes and eliminate the shortcomings of each.

In examining the UNAM context, it clear that emphasis is placed on data collection as a critical role of IR in supporting strategic planning, while the element of knowledge creation seems to gain less prominence. However, for QA and IR to meaningfully inform strategic planning, the data gathered must be transformed into information and information into knowledge (Nel, 2016). It is only once the knowledge is well packaged that it becomes a powerful tool for providing institutional intelligence.

To conduct a thorough analysis and arrive to an informed conclusion, the authors asked the following question: Is there synergy between QA and IR as tools to inform strategic management? Nel (2016) locates the answer to this question in Klemenčič, Šćukanec, and Komljenovič's (2015, p. 8) argument, "the emergence of strategic planning in higher education has been prompted by pressures from governments through performance-based funding models, quality assurance and accreditation regimes, and increased global competition". Thus, HEIs have adopted strategic planning and management as a tool to address the challenges associated with these developments in HE. In order to give prominence to the role of IR in strategic planning three questions are always asked:

- *Where we are now?*
- *Where are we going? and*
- *Where do we want to go or where could we be going?*

While the first two questions address the institution's current and past performance and capabilities based on an analysis of both the internal and external environments, the last question addresses where the institution wants to stake out a future position in the educational landscape (Nel, 2016). These questions were useful in informing the development of the UNAM Strategic Plan (2016–2020) and the ongoing revision of the current plan.

While the authors acknowledge that the UNAM has QA and IR policies and structures in place to support strategic planning and management processes, there are notable challenges with regard to the integration of QA and IR processes that hamper effective strategic management. The authors noted earlier that in most HEIs (and UNAM is no exception) there seems to be disconnect between setting institutional longer-term goals, annual outcomes and targets and how QA and IR processes jointly inform the achievement of these goals. In other words, HEIs in general (particularly those with QA systems in place) and UNAM in particular have not been effective in linking the outcomes of the QA audits with IR data in the implementation of the institutional strategic plan. Nel, (2016, p. 99) argue that "the resource allocation process acts like a filter that determines which intended and/or emergent initiatives get funding and pass through, and which initiatives are denied resources". In resource allocation and prioritisation, institutional leadership's preference in resource allocation is a determining factor in the implementation of the institutional strategic plan (Messah & Mucai, 2011). Unfortunately, the UNAM has not been able to balance its resource allocations and this has affected the realignment of the budget to strategy and thus the implementation of activities identified in the QA SIPs and IR data.

MODEL FOR INTEGRATION OF QUALITY ASSURANCE AND INSTITUTIONAL RESEARCH PROCESSES

The direction that an institution aspires to take is underpinned by its vision and mission which are further unpacked systematically through a strategic planning process. QA and IR may thus become paramount as tools for informing strategic management. For QA and IR to be effective, there is a need for the integration of, and/or collaboration between, the two. According to Geyser and Murdoch (2016), if an underpinning principle of QA, namely that it is developmental (i.e. improving quality), is taken into consideration, the collaboration/interaction between QA and IR becomes multidimensional. Both IR and QA should inform decision making but their contributions differ; their approaches to data collection differ and the kinds

Figure 1. Model for Strategic Management Process at UNAM
Source: Adapted from Deming (1986); Kettunen (n. d); UNAM (2018) and Van der Westhuizen (2009)

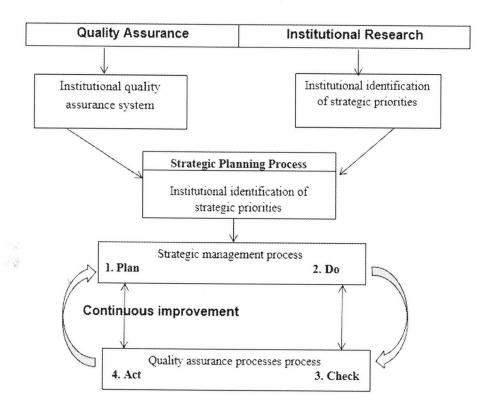

of data/intelligence that they produce are different (Geyser & Murdoch, 2016). Therefore, collaboration between IR and QA is necessary to provide data on institutional effectiveness and efficiency. The process of integrating QA and IR to inform strategic management may follow a model as suggested in Figure 1.

This model for the integration of QA and IR to inform strategic management is based on the principle of the Deming Cycle (Deming, 1986). The model can best be described as the middle ground between a "top-down" (strategic planning) and "bottom-up" (self-study) process (Van der Westhuizen, 2009). Quality is most efficient when it is situated at the grassroots level and if the staff members and students alike are committed to high quality (Kettunen, n.d.). According to Kettunen (n.d.), a major challenge of QA and IR in HEIs is to bring them close to teaching and learning, research and development, community engagement, and other activities. As can be seen in Figure 1, both QA and IR generate important data to inform evidence-based decision making and strategic planning and management. The institution identifies strategic priorities during the strategic planning phase, which in turn are implemented during the strategic management process. Both the IQA and EQA processes evaluate the effectiveness of strategic management. Ideally, there is continuous interface between QA, IR and strategic management processes.

As illustrated in Figure 1, the quality cycle includes the sequential phases of "plan", "do", "check" and "act" (Deming, 1986). These phases are explained as follows:

- **Plan:** The purpose of "plan" phase is to establish the objectives and processes necessary to deliver results in accordance with the specifications. It includes strategic plans, action plans, human resources plans, budgets, curricula, work plans for academics, process descriptions and operational rules (Kettunen, n.d.). In addition, this phase involves defining indicators to facilitate monitoring the attainment of these goals and objectives.
- **Do:** The purpose of "do" is to implement the plans. The essential aspect of implementation is the establishment of procedures to ensure the attainment of the goals and objectives. These procedures may vary considerably at an institutional level, for example in terms of the development of the operational system and the organisational structure, resource collection, involvement of stakeholders, or development of partnerships.
- **Check:** The purpose of the "check" phase is to monitor and evaluate the process and report on the outcomes. Evaluation and assessment encompass the evaluation of the higher education provided and the assessment of the achievement of outcomes at both system and individual levels. In general, the evaluation and assessment phase comprise two parts – firstly, the collection and processing of data and discussions and, secondly, the evaluation mechanism. This second part involves defining the scope of the evaluation as well as providing information on the results of the evaluation.
- **Act:** The purpose of the "act" phase is to apply actions to the outcome for the necessary improvement. This process forms part of a systematic and goal-oriented process which is used to amend plans and to develop operations in order to achieve the targeted outcomes and set new objectives. Furthermore, the aim of this phase is to learn from the information acquired, such as discussing and analysing the results with key stakeholders.

At the heart of the Deming Cycle is the principle of continuous improvement. Interaction is the basic principle for "closing the quality loop" and repeating the cycle can bring about continuous quality improvement, as every next cycle translates into better quality. Repeating the cycle can bring the managers close to perfect operation and output (Kettunen, n.d.). This is done through cyclical quality reviews. The reviews are guided by key questions, which are based on a "fitness for (and of) purpose" approach, namely (University of Namibia, 2018):

- What is the university trying to do?
- How is the university trying to do it?
- How does it know it works?
- How does the university change in order to improve?

There is consensus in the literature (Kettunen & Kantola, 2007) that in order to be effective, strategic planning and management has to engage with the academic heartland and, therefore, the extent of a consultative process is a major factor in process design in HE. In line with the good practice, the focus of the internal reviews moves beyond QA to support enhancement effectively, providing the basis for a robust QA function. The reviews also play an increasingly significant role in the institutional management of such enhancement by articulating more effectively with institutional enhancement strategies and with faculty/school/college plans, as well as being regarded as a key mechanism by staff and more beneficial than earlier compliance-based approaches (Van der Westhuizen, 2009).

It should be noted that the results of internal and external monitoring processes are not merely temporary adjustments but should result in lasting improvement. This leads to a cyclical process for creating a holistic and integrated planning culture that is able to link strategic and operational planning at departmental, faculty and administrative levels with the university's high-level goals, strategies, operational targets and performance indices. According to Harvey (2005), the initial impact of quality activities fades away quickly if there is no significant connection between internal and external processes, thus it seems important that the information generated by the QA process, both from internal and external sources, should provide one source of input in the strategic planning process. Even the development of the institutional quality system must be integrated with the strategic management. The action plan of the institution should outline the activities to be undertaken in implementing the strategic plan and the long- and short-term quality initiatives (Kettunen & Kantola, 2007).

To assure success in the linking of institutional QA and IR activities and results and to inform effectively institutional strategic planning and management processes with QE as their purpose, it is important to take note of the following desirable processes:

- The development and implementation of an enhancement-led approach by the top management (e.g. vice-chancellor, executive management, or equivalent).
- The existence of a robust institutional QA and IR system (policies, structures, mechanisms and processes) that includes a process for aligning the internal strategic planning processes with institutional reflection on enhancement or improvement activities.
- A widespread institutional committee or similar structure to facilitate better strategic linkages and strengthen the strategic drive synergy between QA and IR, as well as to promote more effective communication to support development and QE.
- A process for the operation of the institution's enhancement or improvement strategies with a hierarchy of senior managers at institutional level and middle managers located within faculties, schools and colleges, supported by administrative officers at different levels (both in terms of "top-down" and "bottom-up" processes) with a key role in promoting consistency of policy and practices across the institution.
- The existence of faculty or school-based structures (middle manager or faculty/school/group with a deliberate function) for implementing the QA and IR strategies and facilitating the implementation of the institutional strategic enhancement goals (Van der Westhuizen, 2009, p. 7).

The above desirable processes serve to underpin and make explicit the linkage between QA and IR, and thereby strengthen the strategic drive for QE. According to Van der Westhuizen (2009, p. 7), these activities involve staff (academic and support staff), students and other role players at all levels; the search for and use of information and data that reflect the needs of all the stakeholders; a look beyond the immediate day-to-day concerns to the future; a process to address limitations, barriers and weaknesses, as well as strengths in goals and objectives; set priorities to guide the focus of efforts; and show collaboration and integration of resources across the institution.

Solutions and Recommendations

This chapter makes the recommendation, as suggested in Figure 1, that HEIs should take a conscious and deliberate decision to integrate QA and IR processes to avoid duplication of effort and ensure efficiency and effectiveness in strategic management. Integration of QA with IR processes would also help to generate the timely and quality data much needed for strategic management and decision making.

There is also a need to appreciate that, although there is a need for collaboration between QA and IR as both generate data to inform decision making and strategic management, collaboration/interaction should take into consideration that the contributions, approaches to data collection, and the kinds of data/intelligence that the two initiatives produce are different.

Areas for Future Research

This chapter also recommends that the best ways for collaborating and integrating data generated by QA and IR to support the institution in achieving its strategic goals should further be explored through research not only institutionally but also nationally and internationally.

CONCLUSION

Efficient and effective strategic management of HEIs requires synergy between QA and IR. Similar to QA, IR generates data about the institution that is important to inform evidence-based decision making through strategic planning and management. In this regard, QA and IR are seen as playing a complementary role. Worldwide, most HEIs have implemented both QA and IR systems and structures; however, the challenge is for HEIs to integrate effectively QA with IR processes to make a meaningful contribution to strategic management. Instead of playing complementary roles, QA and IR processes generally operate in isolation. Another challenge is concerned with the generation of data, which is often not timely, or of a high quality. Therefore, there is a need for collaboration between IR and QA to provide data to inform efficient and effective strategic management. This means that QA and IR processes should begin to articulate more effectively with the wider institutional strategies and processes to support the strategic management of continuing improvement and the accompanying QA mechanisms.

Strategically integrated outcome-measurement efforts can give institutions a competitive advantage over organisations that only use outcomes tactically. However, the setback that most HEIs face (including UNAM) is how to integrate the data generated from QA activities, IR to inform strategic planning, and strategic management through evidence-based decision-making. Where there is collaboration between QA and IR, it tends to happen on an ad hoc basis, despite the fact that both initiatives depend on the same institutional financial resources, which are generally constrained. Other challenges facing HEIs include inadequate financial resources to finance strategic initiatives owing to challenges arising from the economic downturn, which have led to a sharp decrease in government funding for HE.

REFERENCES

Alkhafaji, S., & Sriram, B. (2012). Higher Education Institution Quality Assurance Management System: Modelling and design. *EXCEL International Journal of Multidisciplinary Management Studies*, 2(7), 18–31.

D'Andrea, V., & Gosling, D. (2005). *Improving teaching and learning in higher education: A whole institutional approach*. Glasgow, UK: Society for Research into Higher Education/Open University Press/Bell and Brain.

Deming, W. E. (1986). *Out of the crisis*. Cambridge, MA: MIT Centre for Advanced Engineering Study.

Geyser, H., & Murdoch, N. (2016). Quality assurance and institutional research. In J. Botha & N. Muller (Eds.), *Institutional research in South African higher education*. Stellenbosch: Sun Press. doi:10.18820/9781928357186/08

Government of Republic of Namibia (GRN). (2008). *Vocational Education and Training Act, Act No. 1 of 2008*. Windhoek: GRN.

Haris, I. (2013). Assessment on the implementation of internal quality assurance at higher education: An Indonesian report. *Journal of Educational and Institutional Studies in the World*, *3*(4), 41–49.

Harvey, L. (2005). A history and critique of quality evaluation in the United Kingdom. *Quality Assurance in Education*, *13*(4), 263–276. doi:10.1108/09684880510700608

Haskell, C. D. (2017). Institutional research as a bridge: Aligning institutional internal data needs and external information requirements a strategic view. *Higher Education Evaluation and Development*, *11*(1), 2–11. doi:10.1108/HEED-08-2017-001

Hazell, P., & Guy, M. (2016). *Data, quality assurance and improving student experience. Quality Assurance Agency for Higher Education (QAAHE)*. Retrieved from https://elearning.jiscinvolve.org/wp/2016/11/09/data-quality-assurance-and-improving-the-student-experience/

Kadhila, N., & Iipumbu, N. (2019). Strengthening internal quality assurance as a lever for enhancing student learning experiences and academic success: Lessons from Namibia. *Quality in Higher Education*, *24*(3), 1–17.

Kahveci, T. C., & Taskin, H. (2013). Integrated enterprise management system for higher education institutions based on strategic and process management: The case study of Sakarya University. *Procedia: Social and Behavioral Sciences*, *103*, 1505–1513. doi:10.1016/j.sbspro.2013.12.170

Kahveci, T. C., Uygun, O., Yurtsever, U., & Ilyas, S. (2012). Quality assurance in higher education institutions using strategic information systems. *Perspectives: Policy and Practice in Higher Education*, *55*, 161–167.

Kettunen, J. (2008). Integration of strategic management and quality assurance. In *Proceedings of 11th Annual Convention of the Strategic Management Forum*. Indian Institute of Technology.

Kettunen, J. (n.d.). *Integrating strategic management and quality assurance*. Turku: Turku University of Applied Science.

Kettunen, J., & Kantola, M. (2007). Strategic planning and quality assurance in the Bologna Process. Perspectives. *Policy and Practice in Higher Education*, *11*(3), 67–73. doi:10.1080/13603100701428205

Klemenčič, M., & Brennan, J. (2013). Institutional research in a European context: A forward look. *European Journal of Higher Education*, *3*(3), 265–279. doi:10.1080/21568235.2013.823726

Klemenčič, M., Šćukanec, N., & Komljenovič, J. (2015). Decision support issues in Central and Eastern Europe. In K. L. Webber & A. J. Calderon (Eds.), *Institutional research and planning in higher education: Global themes and context*. New York: Routledge. Retrieved from http://www.routledge.com/books/details/9781138021433/

Martin, M., & Stella, A. (2007). *External quality assurance in higher education: Making choices*. Paris: UNESCO International Institute for Educational Planning.

Menon, M. E., Terka, D. G., & Gibbs, P. (2014). *Using data to improve higher education: Research, policy and practice. Global perspectives on higher education* (Vol. 29). Sense Publishers. doi:10.1007/978-94-6209-794-0

Messah, B. O., & Mucai, P. G. (2011). Factors affecting implementation of strategic plans in government tertiary institution: Survey of selected technical training institutions. *European Journal of Business and Management, 3*(3), 85–105.

Nel, H. (2016). The role of institutional research in support of strategic planning. In J. Botha & N. Muller (Eds.), *Institutional research in South African higher education*. Stellenbosch: Sun Press. doi:10.18820/9781928357186/06

Nickel, S. (2011). *Strategic management in higher education institutions: Approaches, processes and tools*. Centre for Higher Education Development.

Pitsoe, V. J., & Maila, M. W. (2017). Quality and quality assurance in open distance learning (ODL) discourse: Trends, challenges and perspectives. *The Anthropologist, 18*(1), 251–258. doi:10.1080/09720073.2014.11891542

Shawyun, T. (2016). Strategic planning as an essential for quality assurance. *Journal of Institutional Research South East Asia, 14*(1), 42–70.

Southern African Association for Institutional Research (SAAIR). (2019). *The role of institutional research in strategic planning*. Retrieved from http://www.saair-web.co.za/

Thomas, H., Turjansky, A., Jones, L., & Williams, D. (2016). Report on the use of management data to support academic quality assurance. *Quality Strategy Network (QSN)*. Retrieved February 15, 2019, from http://qualitystrategynetwork.org.uk/

University of Namibia (UNAM). (2011). *Quality assurance framework*. Windhoek, Namibia: Author.

University of Namibia (UNAM). (2015). *Quality assurance manual*. Windhoek, Namibia: Author.

University of Namibia (UNAM). (2016). Strategic plan 2016–2020. Windhoek: Author.

University of Namibia (UNAM). (2018). *Centre for Quality Assurance and Management (CEQUAM)*. Windhoek: Author. Retrieved from http://www.unam.edu.na/cequam/quality-assurance-process

Van der Westhuizen, L. J. (2009). *Challenges to apply quality assurance as a strategic tool for higher education institutions*. Paper presented at the 31st Annual EAIR Forum, Vilnius, Lithuania.

Weeks-Kaye, B. (2004). Ensuring institutional quality through the strategic planning framework. In *Proceedings of the Australian Universities Quality Forum 2004: Quality in a time of change*. Melbourne: AUQA.

World Bank. (2009). *Higher education quality assurance in Sub-Saharan Africa*. Washington, DC: World Bank.

Yureva, O. Y. (2016). Strategic management in higher education system: Methodological approaches. *Electronic Business Journal*, *15*(10), 424–428.

ADDITIONAL READING

Brennan, J., & Shah, T. (2000). *Managing quality in higher education: An international perspective on institutional assessment and change*. Buckingham: Open University Press/Organisation for Economic Development.

Calderon, A., & Mathies, C. (2013). Institutional research in the future: Challenges within higher education and the need for excellence in professional practice. *New Directions for Institutional Research*, *157*(157), 77–90. doi:10.1002/ir.20040

Calderon, A., & Webber, K. L. (2015). Institutional research, planning, and decision support in higher education today. In K. Webber & A. Calderon (Eds.), *Institutional research and planning: global themes and contexts*. New York: Routledge/Taylor & Francis.

Cullen, J., Joyce, J., Hassal, T., & Broadbent, M. (2003). Quality in higher education: Moving from monitoring to management. *Quality Assurance in Education*, *11*(1), 5–14. doi:10.1108/09684880310462038

Keenerly, M., & Neely, A. (2002). A framework of the factors affecting the evolution of performance measurement systems. *International Journal of Operations & Production Management*, *22*(11), 1222–1245. doi:10.1108/01443570210450293

Knight, W. E. (2015). *Developing the integrated institutional effectiveness office*. Association for Higher Education Effectiveness: Webinar April 2015.

Shawyun, T. (2005). Quality assurance and strategic implementation in educational institutions: A holistic alliance? *Journal of Institutional Research South East Asia*, *3*(1), 39–50.

Tezcan-Unal, B., Winston, K., & Qualter, A. (2018). Learning-oriented quality assurance in higher education institutions. *Quality in Higher Education*, *24*(3), 221–237. doi:10.1080/13538322.2018.1558504

Welch, J. F., & Dey, S. (2002). Quality measurement and quality assurance in higher education. *Quality Assurance in Education*, *10*(1), 17–25. doi:10.1108/09684880210416076

Woodhouse, D. (2003). Quality improvement through quality audit. *Quality in Higher Education*, *9*(2), 133–139. doi:10.1080/13538320308156

KEY TERMS AND DEFINITIONS

Controlling: A continuous task that supports strategic planning as well as the implementation of the strategies, monitoring and the reporting of the achievements on a regular basis.

Operationalization and Implementation: Involves the execution of the strategy after the plan has been approved by the university structures. This process requires cooperation between all different institutional stakeholders.

Planning Process: As adopted in the UNAM Strategic Plan, it involves environmental scanning, SWOT (strengths, weaknesses, opportunities, and threats) analysis, strategic decision making, and agreeing on strategic objectives and measures.

Self-improvement Plan: Specifies actions, designated responsibilities and timeframes in order to address the requirements and recommendations of the review reports for the purpose of follow-up, validation and closing the quality loop by the institution, faculty, or department.

Strategic Management: As adopted in this chapter refers to a core component for every higher education institution which understands itself as an autonomous actor. It gives managers ideas and tools for strategic planning, implementation and control that are suitable for the specific organizational conditions in higher education institutions.

Compilation of References

Achua, C. F., & Lussier, R. N. (2010). *Effective leadership* (4th ed.). South-Western Cengage Learning.

Adams, J. L. (2016). *NMC Horizon Report*. Austin, TX: The New Media Consortium.

Adeinat, I., & Kassim, N. (2019). Extending the service profit chain: The mediating effect of employee productivity. *International Journal of Quality & Reliability Management, 36*(5), 797–814. doi:10.1108/IJQRM-03-2018-0064

Adie, L., Lloyd, M., & Beutel, D. (2013). Identifying discourses of moderation in higher education. *Assessment & Evaluation in Higher Education, 38*(8), 968–977. doi:10.1080/02602938.2013.769200

Adler, N. J., & Bird, F. B. (1988). International dimensions of executive integrity: Who is responsible for the world? In S. Srivastva & ... (Eds.), *Executive Integrity: The Search for High Human Values in Organizational Life*. San Francisco, CA: Jossey-Bass.

Afsar, B., Shahjehan, A., Shah, S. I., & Wajid, A. (2019). The mediating role of transformational leadership in the relationship between cultural intelligence and employee voice behavior: A case of hotel employees. *International Journal of Intercultural Relations, 69*, 66–75. doi:10.1016/j.ijintrel.2019.01.001

Aghenta, J. (2001). *Educational planning: A turning point in education and development in Nigeria*. Benin City: University of Benin City, Nigeria.

Agrawal, A. (2001). University-to-industry knowledge transfer: Literature review and unanswered questions. *International Journal of Management Reviews, 3*(4), 285–302. doi:10.1111/1468-2370.00069

Aguilera-caracuel, J., & de-Mandojana, N. O. (2013). Green innovation and financial performance: An institutional approach. *Organization & Environment, 26*(4), 365–385. doi:10.1177/1086026613507931

Ahire, S., Golhar, D., & Waller, M. (1996). Development and validation of TQM implementation constructs. *Decision Sciences, 27*(1), 23–56. doi:10.1111/j.1540-5915.1996.tb00842.x

Ahn, J., Lee, C.-K., Back, K.-J., & Schmitt, A. (2019). Brand experiential value for creating integrated resort customers' co-creation behavior. *International Journal of Hospitality Management, 81*, 104–112. doi:10.1016/j.ijhm.2019.03.009

AICPA (American Institute of Certified Public Accountants AICPA). (1980). *Accounting for your Future*. New York: Author.

Aithal & Kumar. (2016). Maintaining teacher quality in higher education institutions. *International Journal of Current Research and Modern Education, 1*(1). Retrieved January 15, 2019, from www.rdmodernresearch.com

Alaniska, H., Codina, E. A., Bohrer, J., Dearlove, R., Eriksson, S., Helle, E., & Wiberg, L. K. (2006). *Student involvement in the processes of quality assurance agencies*. Helsinki: European Association for Quality Assurance in Higher Education.

Al-Atiqi, I. M., & Deshpande, P. B. (2009). *Transforming US Higher Education with Six Sigma*. Abu Dhabi: International Network of Quality Assessment Agencies in Higher Education.

Alkhafaji, S., & Sriram, B. (2012). Higher Education Institution Quality Assurance Management System: Modelling and design. *EXCEL International Journal of Multidisciplinary Management Studies, 2*(7), 18–31.

Allen, K. E., Bordas, J., Hickman, G. R., Matusak, L. R., Sorenson, G. J., & Whitemire, J. K. (1998). Leadership in the twenty-first century. Academy of Leadership Press.

Allen, T. D. (2003). Mentoring others: A dispositional and motivational approach. *Journal of Vocational Behavior, 62*(1), 134–154. doi:10.1016/S0001-8791(02)00046-5

Allen, T. D., & Eby, L. T. (2008). Mentor commitment in formal mentoring relationships. *Journal of Vocational Behavior, 72*(3), 309–316. doi:10.1016/j.jvb.2007.10.016

Allport, G. W. (1937). *Personality: A psychological interpretation*. New York: Henry Holt & Company.

Al-Tarawneh, H. A., & Mubaslat, M. M. (2011). The Implementation of Total Quality Management (TQM) On the Higher Educational Sector in Jordan. *International Journal of Industrial Marketing, 1*(1), 1–10.

Al-Tarawneh, H., & Mubaslat, M. (2011). The implementation of total quality management (TQM) on the higher educational sector in Jordan. *International Journal of Industrial Marketing, 1*(1), 1–10.

Altbach, P. (2015). Why branch campuses may be unsustainable. *International Higher Education*, (58).

Alzhrani, K. M., Alotibie, B. A., & Abdulaziz, A. (2016). Total Quality Management in Saudi Higher Education. *International Journal of Computers and Applications, 135*(4), 6–12. doi:10.5120/ijca2016908245

Anane, G. K., & Addaney, M. (2016). Managing quality assurance in higher education: The case of the University of Energy and Natural Resources, Ghana. *Journal of Education and Practice, 7*(22), 41–46.

Anderson, J., Rungtusanatham, M., Schroeder, R., & Devaraj, S. (1995). A Path Analytic Model of a Theory of Quality Management Underlying the Deming Management Method: Preliminary Empirical Findings. *Decision Sciences, 26*(5), 637–658. doi:10.1111/j.1540-5915.1995.tb01444.x

Andolfi, G. (2016). Development and innovation management on higher education institutions. *European Journal of Social Sciences Studies, 1*(1), 65–70.

Anninos, L. N. (2010). *Suitability and compatibility of university performance evaluation systems and processes in Greece* (Ph.D Thesis). University of Piraeus.

Anninos, L. N. (2007). The archetype of excellence in universities and TQM. *Journal of Management History, 13*(4), 307–321. doi:10.1108/17511340710819561

Anninos, L. N. (2018). Internationalizing the Greek higher education: A quest and a vision for excellence. In D. Hall & G. Ogunmokun (Eds.), *Management, leadership and marketing of universities* (pp. 11–30). Perth, Australia: Global Publishing House International.

Annual, E. R. R. 2017/2018. (n.d.). Central Bank of Eswatini. Retrieve May 1, 2019, from http://www.centralbank.org.sz/about/annual/Annual_Economic_Review_2017-18.pdf

Anton, J., & Yao, D. (2005). Markets for partially contractible knowledge: Bootstrapping versus bundling. *Journal of the European Economic Association, 3*(2-3), 745–754. doi:10.1162/jeea.2005.3.2-3.745

Compilation of References

Antony, J., Krishan, N., Cullen, M., & Kumar, M. (2012). Lean six sigma for higher education institutions (heis): Challenges, barriers, success factors, tools/techniques. *International Journal of Productivity and Performance Management*, *61*(8), 940–948. doi:10.1108/17410401211277165

Archer, M. S. (1995). *Realist social theory: the morphogenetic approach*. Cambridge, UK: Cambridge University Press. doi:10.1017/CBO9780511557675

Archer, M. S. (1996). *Culture and agency: the place of culture in social theory*. Cambridge, UK: Cambridge University Press. doi:10.1017/CBO9780511557668

Argyris, C. (1991, May). Teaching Smart People How to Learn. *Harvard Business Review*, 99–109.

Aristotle. (350 BC). *Nichomachean Ethics* (W. D. Ross, Trans.). Retrieved from The Internet Classic Archive: http://classics.mit.edu

Arora, A. (1995). Licensing tacit knowledge: Intellectual property rights and the market for know-how. *Economics of Innovation and New Technology*, *4*(1), 41–60. doi:10.1080/10438599500000013

Arora, A. (1996). Contracting for tacit knowledge: The provision of technical services in technology licensing contracts. *Journal of Development Economics*, *50*(2), 233–256. doi:10.1016/S0304-3878(96)00399-9

Asif, M., Awan, M., Khan, M., & Ahmad, N. (2013). A Model for Total Quality Management in Higher Education. *Quality & Quantity*, *47*(4), 1883–1904. doi:10.100711135-011-9632-9

Astin, A. W. (1984). Student involvement: A developmental theory for higher education. *Journal of College Student Personnel*, *25*(4), 297–308.

Astin, A. W. (2012). *Assessment for excellence: The philosophy and practice of assessment and evaluation in higher education*. Rowman & Littlefield Publishers.

Atieno, A. J. (2013). *Challenges facing the implementation of total quality management practices in public secondary schools in Kenya* (Master's thesis). School of Business, Kenyatta University.

Atiku, S. O. (2018). Reshaping human capital formation through digitalization. In *Radical Reorganization of Existing Work Structures through Digitalization* (pp. 52–73). Hershey, PA: IGI Global. doi:10.4018/978-1-5225-3191-3.ch004

Atiku, S. O. (2019). Institutionalizing social responsibility through workplace green behaviour. In *Contemporary Multicultural Orientations and Practices for Global Leadership* (pp. 183–199). Hershey, PA: IGI Global. doi:10.4018/978-1-5225-6286-3.ch010

Australian Trade and Investment Commission. (2019). *Annual Report 2017–18*. Retrieved from https://www.austrade.gov.au/About/Corporate-Information/Annual-Report/Austrade-Annual-Report

Avolio, B. J., & Gardner, W. L. (2005). Authentic leadership development: Getting to the root of positive forms of leadership. *The Leadership Quarterly*, *16*(3), 315–338. doi:10.1016/j.leaqua.2005.03.001

Azizaman, N., Ariff, M., Zakuan, N., & Ismail, K. (2014). ISO 9001:2008 implementation in higher education: Does it contributes to student satisfaction? The Role of Service in the Tourism and Hospitality Industry. *Proceedings of the 2nd International Conference on Management and Technology in Knowledge, Service, Tourism and Hospitality, SERVE 2014*, 45-50.

Badaracco, J. L., & Ellsworth, R. R. (1990). Quest for integrity. *Executive Excellence*, *7*, 3–4.

Badri, M. A., Selim, H., Alshare, K., Grandon, E., Younis, H., & Abdulla, M. (2006). The Baldridge education criteria for performance excellence framework: Empirical test and validation. *International Journal of Quality & Reliability Management*, *23*(9), 1118–1157. doi:10.1108/02656710610704249

Badri, M., & Abdulla, M. (2004). Awards of excellence in institutions of higher education: An AHP approach. *International Journal of Educational Management*, *18*(4), 224–242. doi:10.1108/09513540410538813

Bagheri, S., Kusters, R. J., & Trienekens, J. J. M. (2019). Customer knowledge transfer challenges in a co-creation value network: Toward a reference model. *International Journal of Information Management*, *47*, 198–214. doi:10.1016/j.ijinfomgt.2018.12.019

Bakotić, D., & Rogošić, A. (2017). Employee involvement as a key determinant of core quality management practices. *Total Quality Management & Business Excellence*, *28*(11-12), 1209–1226. doi:10.1080/14783363.2015.1094369

Baporikar, N. (2014). Introduction. In N. Baporikar (Ed.), *Handbook of Research on Higher Education in the MENA Region: Policy and Practice* (pp. 1–7). Hershey, PA: IGI Global. doi:10.4018/978-1-4666-6198-1.ch001

Baporikar, N. (2015). Quality Facets in Educational Process for Enhanced Knowledge Creation. *International Journal of Service Science, Management, Engineering, and Technology*, *6*(4), 1–15. doi:10.4018/IJSSMET.2015100101

Baporikar, N. (2016). Stakeholder Approach for Quality Higher Education. In W. Nuninger & J. Châtelet (Eds.), *Handbook of Research on Quality Assurance and Value Management in Higher Education* (pp. 1–26). Hershey, PA: Information Science Reference. doi:10.4018/978-1-5225-0024-7.ch001

Baporikar, N. (2018a). Educational Leadership for Quality Teacher Education in Digital Era. In N. P. Ololube (Ed.), *Handbook of Research on Educational Planning and Policy Analysis* (pp. 241–255). Port Harcourt: Pearl Publishers.

Baporikar, N. (2018b). Policy Perspectives for Technology Usage in Higher Education. In N. P. Ololube (Ed.), *Handbook of Research on Educational Planning and Policy Analysis* (pp. 295–313). Port Harcourt: Pearl Publishers.

Baran, E. (2013). Connect, participate and learn: Transforming pedagogies in higher education. *Bulletin of the IEEE Technical Committee on Learning Technology*, *15*(1), 9–12.

Barcia, K. F., & Hidalgo, D. S. (2006). Implementación de una Metodología con la Técnica 5S para Mejorar el Área de Matricería de una Empresa Extrusora de Aluminio. *Revista Tecnológica ESPOL*, *18*(1), 69–75.

Baregheh, A., Rowley, J., & Sambrook, S. (2009). Towards a multidisciplinary definition of innovation. *Management Decision*, *47*(8), 1323–1339. doi:10.1108/00251740910984578

Barnett, R. (1992). Improving higher education: Total quality care. Open University Press.

Barnett, R. (1997). *Higher education: A critical business*. McGraw-Hill Education.

Barratt, A., Chawla-Duggan, R., Lowe, J., Nikel, J., & Ukpo, E. (2006). *The concept of quality in education: a review of the 'international' literature on the concept of quality in education*. Working Paper. EdQual RPC. (EdQual Working Paper No. 3)

Barrett, R. (1998). *Liberating the corporate soul: Building a visionary organization*. Oxford, UK: Butterworth Heinemann.

Bartlett, A., & Mercer, G. (2001). Introduction. In A. Bartlett & G. Mercer (Eds.), *Postgraduate Research Supervision: Transforming Relations*. Peter Lang. doi:10.1007/978-1-4615-1637-8_2

Bass, B. M. (2008). *The Bass handbook of leadership: Theory, research, & managerial applications* (4th ed.). New York, NY: Free Press.

Compilation of References

Bass, B. M., & Avolio, B. J. (1993). Transformational leadership and organizational culture. *Public Administration Quarterly, 17*(1), 112–121.

Bass, K., Dellana, S., & Herbert, F. (1996). Assessing the use of total quality management in the business school classroom. *Journal of Education for Business, 72*(4), 339–343. doi:10.1080/08832323.1996.10116809

Bates, A. W. (n.d.). *A.8 Assessment of learning.* Retrieved 22 March 2019 from https://opentextbc.ca/teachinginadigitalage/chapter/5-8-assessment-of-learning/

Bathie, D., & Sarkar, J. (2002). Total Quality Marketing (TQMk) – A Sympiosis. *Managerial Auditing Journal, 17*(5), 241–244. doi:10.1108/02686900210429650

Batteman, T. S., & Snell, S. A. (2001). Administración una ventaja competitiva. Editorial McGraw Hill.

Bayraktar, E., Tatoglu, E., & Zaim, S. (2008). An instrument for measuring the critical factors of TQM in Turkish higher education. *Total Quality Management & Business Excellence, 19*(6), 551–574. doi:10.1080/14783360802023921

Becker, T. (1998). Integrity in organizations: Beyond honesty and conscientiousness. *Academy of Management Review, 23*(1), 154–161. doi:10.5465/amr.1998.192969

Becket, N., & Brookes, M. (2007). Quality Management in higher education: A review of International issues and practice. *International Journal for Quality and Standards*. Retrieved from www.bsieducation.org/ijas

Becket, N., & Brookes, M. (2008). Quality management practice in higher education-What quality are we actually enhancing? *Journal of Hospitality, Leisure, Sports and Tourism Education, 7*(1), 40.

Becket, N., & Brookes, M. (2006). Evaluating quality management in university departments. *Quality Assurance in Education, 14*(2), 123–142. doi:10.1108/09684880610662015

Becket, N., & Brookes, M. (2008). Quality management in higher education: What quality are we actually enhancing? *Journal of Hospitality, Leisure, Sport and Tourism Education, 7*(1), 40–54. doi:10.3794/johlste.71.174

Beddington, W., Dirks, N. B., Price, D., Rand, J., Stolker, C., O'Sullivan, H., & Yates, L. (2018). *What is it like to take a leadership role at a university?* Available at https://www.timeshighereducation.com/features/what-is-it-like-to-take-a-leadership-role-at-a-university

Bedford, D. (2013). Business Capability Modeling as a Foundation for Intellectual Capital Audits. In *Proceedings of the 10th International Conference on Intellectual Capital, knowledge Management and Organisational Learning: ICICKM 2013* (p. 60). Academic Conferences Limited.

Bejan, A. S., Damian, R. M., Leiber, T., Neuner, I., Niculita, L., & Vacareanu, R. (2018). Impact evaluation of institutional evaluation and programme accreditation at Technical University of Civil Engineering Bucharest (Romania). *European Journal of Higher Education, 8*(3), 319–336. doi:10.1080/21568235.2018.1474780

Bennett, L., Nair, C. S., & Shah, M. (2012). The emergence of private higher education in Australia: The silent provider. *European Journal of Higher Education, 2*(4), 423–435. doi:10.1080/21568235.2012.730377

Bennis, W. (2009). *On Becoming a Leader* (Revised Edition). New York: Addison-Wesley Publishing.

Bergman, B., & Klefsjö, B. (2004). *Quality – from customer needs to customer satisfaction.* Lund, Sweden: Studentliteratur.

Bergquist, B., & Edgeman R. L. (2003). Six Sigma and Total Quality Management: Different day, same soup? *International Journal of Six Sigma and Competitive Advantage., 2*(2), 162–178.

Bergsmann, E., Schultes, M. T., Winter, P., Schober, B., & Spiel, C. (2015). Evaluation of competence-based teaching in higher education: From theory to practice. *Evaluation and Program Planning*, *52*, 1–9. doi:10.1016/j.evalprogplan.2015.03.001 PMID:25847854

Berk, R. A. (2005). Survey of 12 Strategies to Measure Teacher Effectiveness. *International Journal on Teaching and Learning in Higher Education*, *17*(1), 48–62.

Beywl, W. (2003). *Selected comments to the standards for evaluation of the German Evaluation Society*. Cologne: DeGEval.

Bhaskar, R. (1975). *A realist theory of science*. Brighton, UK: Harvester.

Bhaskar, R. (1991). *Philosophy and the idea of freedom*. Oxford, UK: Blackwell.

Bhaskar, R. (1998). *The possibility of naturalism: a philosophical critique of the contemporary human sciences*. London: Routledge.

Bhatti, N., Maitlo, G. M., Shaikh, N., Hashmi, M. A., & Shaikh, F. M. (2012). The impact of autocratic and democratic leadership style on job satisfaction. *International Business Research*, *5*(2), 192–201. doi:10.5539/ibr.v5n2p192

Bidabadi, N. S., Isfahani, A. N., Rouhollahi, A., & Khalili, R. (2016). Effective teaching methods in higher education: Requirements and barriers. *Journal of Advances in Medical Education & Professionalism*, *4*(4), 170. PMID:27795967

Bigley, G., & McAllister, D. (2002). *Transformations in Relational Logic: How Types of Supervisory Trust Interact to Predict Subordinate OCB*. Unpublished manuscript. University of Washington.

Binelli, C., & Rubio-Codina, M. (2013). The Returns to Private Education: Evidence from Mexico. *Economics of Education Review*, *36*, 198–215. doi:10.1016/j.econedurev.2013.06.004

Birnbaum, R. (2001). *Management fads in higher education*. San Francisco: Jossey Bass.

Black, R. J. (2003). *Organizational Culture: Creating the influence needed for Strategic Success*. London, UK: ISBN.

Black, S. A. (2015). Qualities of Effective Leadership in Higher Education. *Open Journal of Leadership*, *4*, 54–66. doi:10.4236/ojl.2015.42006

Black, S. A., Groombridge, J. J., & Jones, C. G. (2011). Biodiversity Conservation: Applying New Criteria to Assess Excellence. *Total Quality Management*, *22*(11), 1165–1178. doi:10.1080/14783363.2011.624766

Boaden, R. J. (1997). What is total quality management…and does it matter? *Total Quality Management*, *8*(4), 153–171. doi:10.1080/0954412979596

Bolman, L., & Deal, T. (1991). *Organisations*. San Francisco: Josses-Bass.

Borko, H. (2004). Professional development and teacher learning: Mapping the terrain. *Educational Researcher*, *33*(8), 3–15. doi:10.3102/0013189X033008003

Boswijk, A. (2013). The power of the economy of experiences: New ways of value creation. In J. Sundbo & F. Sørensen (Eds.), *Handbook on the Experience Economy* (pp. 171–176). Edward Elgar Publishing. doi:10.4337/9781781004227.00014

Boud, D., & Falchikov, N. (2006). Aligning assessment with long-term learning. *Assessment & Evaluation in Higher Education*, *31*(4), 399–413. doi:10.1080/02602930600679050

Boughey, C. A. (2009). *Meta-Analysis of teaching and learning at the five research intensive South African Universities not affected by mergers*. Pretoria: Council on Higher Education.

Compilation of References

Bounds, G., Yorks, L., Adam, M. G., & Ranney, G. (2004). *Beyond Total Quality Management: towards the emerging paradigm*. New York: McGraw-Hill.

Bowen, H. (2018). *Investment in learning: The individual and social value of American higher education*. Routledge. doi:10.4324/9781351309929

Bower, D. J. (1998). Support-challenge-vision: A model for faculty mentoring. *Medical Teacher*, *20*(6), 595–597. doi:10.1080/01421599880373

Bowles, T. V., & Brindle, K. A. (2017). Identifying facilitating factors and barriers to improving student retention rates in tertiary teaching courses: A systematic review. *Higher Education Research & Development*, *36*(5), 903–919. doi:10.1080/07294360.2016.1264927

Boyatzis, R. E. (1982). *The competent manager: A model for effective performance*. New York: Wiley.

Boyle, D. M., Carpenter, B. W., & Hermanson, D. R. (2014). The accounting faculty shortage: Causes and contemporary solutions. *Accounting Horizons*, *29*(2), 245–264. doi:10.2308/acch-50967

Boyle, P., & Boice, B. (1998). Systematic mentoring for new faculty teachers and graduate teaching assistants. *Innovative Higher Education*, *22*(3), 157–179. doi:10.1023/A:1025183225886

Bradley, D., Noonan, P., Nugent, H., & Scales, B. (2008). *Review of Australian Higher Education: Discussion Paper*. Canberra, Australia: Department of Education, Employment and Workplace Relations.

Brady, J. A., & Allen, T. T. (2006). Six Sigma Literature: A review and agenda for future research. *Quality and Reliability Engineering International*, *22*(3), 335–336. doi:10.1002/qre.769

Braskamp, L. A., & Ory, J. C. (1994). *Assessing Faculty Work: Enhancing Individual and Institutional Performance*. Jossey-Bass Higher and Adult Education Series.

Brennan, J., Broek, S., Durazzi, N., Kamphuis, B., Ranga, M., & Ryan, S. (2014). *Study on innovation in higher education*. Retrieved March 19, 2019 from http://www.lse.ac.uk/business-and-consultancy/consulting/assets/documents/study-on-innovation-in-higher-education.pdf

Brink, K. E., Palmer, T. B., & Costigan, R. D. (2018). Business school learning goals: Alignment with evidence-based models and accreditation standards. *Journal of Management & Organization*, *24*(4), 474–491. doi:10.1017/jmo.2017.35

Brits, J., Botha, G., & Herselman, M. (2006). *Conceptual framework for modeling business capabilities* (Doctoral dissertation). Tshwane University of Technology.

Brookes, M., & Becket, N. (2007). Quality management in higher education: A review of international issues and practice. *International Journal of Quality and Standards*, *1*(1).

Brown, G. A., Bull, J., & Pendlebury, M. (2013). *Assessing student learning in higher education*. Routledge.

Brown, M. E., & Trevino, L. K. (2006). Ethical leadership: A review and future directions. *The Leadership Quarterly*, *17*(6), 595–616. doi:10.1016/j.leaqua.2006.10.004

Brown, M. E., Trevino, L. K., & Harrison, D. A. (2005). Ethical leadership: A social learning perspective for construct development and testing. *Organizational Behavior and Human Decision Processes*, *97*(2), 117–134. doi:10.1016/j.obhdp.2005.03.002

Brown, R. (2004). *Quality assurance in higher education: The UK experience since 1992*. Routledge. doi:10.4324/9780203416327

Brown, S., & Knight, P. (2012). *Assessing learners in higher education*. Routledge.

Brubacher, J. (2017). *Higher education in transition: History of American colleges and universities*. Routledge. doi:10.4324/9780203790076

Bryman, A. (2007). Effective leadership in higher education: A literature review. *Studies in Higher Education*, *32*(6), 693–710. doi:10.1080/03075070701685114

Bucar, B., & Hisrich, R. D. (2004). Ethics of business managers vs. entrepreneurs. *Journal of Developmental Entrepreneurship*, *61*(1), 59–82.

Bui, H., & Baruch, Y. (2010). Creating learning organizations: A systems perspective. *The Learning Organization*, *17*(3), 208–227. doi:10.1108/09696471011034919

Bullen, E., Fahey, J., & Kenway, J. (2006). The knowledge economy and innovation: Certain uncertainty and the risk economy. *Discourse (Abingdon)*, *27*(1), 53–68. doi:10.1080/01596300500510286

Burbules, N. C., & Torres, C. A. (Eds.). (2000). *Globalization and education: critical perspectives* (pp. 1–26). New York: Routledge.

Burgelman, R. A. (1983). Corporate entrepreneurship and strategic management: Insight from a process study. *Journal of Manufacturing Science and Engineering*, *29*(12), 1349–1365.

Burton, S., Johnston, M. W., & Wilson, E. J. (1991). An experimental assessment of alternative teaching approaches for introducing business ethics to undergraduate business students. *Journal of Business Ethics*, *10*(7), 507–517. doi:10.1007/BF00383349

Butcher, N., Hoosen, S., & Chetty, Y. (2017). *State of play: Regional quality assurance in Southern Africa (SADC)*. DAAD.

Calvo-Mora, A., Leal, A., & Roldan, J. (2006). Using enablers of the EFQM model to manage institutions of higher education. *Quality Assurance in Education*, *14*(2), 99–122. doi:10.1108/09684880610662006

Calvo-Mora, A., Leal, A., & Roldán, J. L. (2005). Relationships between the EFQM model Criteria: A study in Spanish universities. *Total Quality Management & Business Excellence*, *16*(6), 741–770. doi:10.1080/14783360500077708

Cameron, L., & Jesser, P. (1994). Mentoring can add extra value to the training dollar. In R. Stone (Ed.), *Readings in Human Resource Management* (Vol. 2, pp. 128–130). Brisbane, Australia: Wiley.

Campanella, J. (1999). Principles of quality costs: Principles, implementation, and use. *ASQ World Conference on Quality and Improvement Proceedings*, 59.

Campatelli, G., Cittib, P., & Meneghin, A. (2011). Development of a simplified approach based on the EFQM model and Six Sigma for the implementation of TQM principles in a university administration. *Total Quality Management & Business Excellence*, *22*(7), 691–704. doi:10.1080/14783363.2011.585755

Campbell, D. K., Gaertner, J., & Vecchio, R. P. (1983). Perceptions of promotion and tenure criteria: A survey of accounting educators. *Journal of Accounting Education*, *1*(1), 83–92. doi:10.1016/0748-5751(83)90031-3

Cardona, M., & Bravo, Y. (2012). Service quality perceptions in higher education institutions: The case of a Colombian university. *Estudios Gerenciales*, *28*(125), 23–29. doi:10.1016/S0123-5923(12)70004-9

Cardoso, S., Rosa, M. J., & Stensaker, B. (2016). Why is quality in higher education not achieved? The view of academics. *Assessment & Evaluation in Higher Education*, *41*(6), 950–965. doi:10.1080/02602938.2015.1052775

Compilation of References

Carlson, P. M., & Fleisher, M. S. (2002). Shifting realities in higher education: Today's business model threatens our academic excellence. *International Journal of Public Administration*, *25*(9-10), 1097–1111. doi:10.1081/PAD-120006127

Carnoy, M. (1994). *Faded dreams: The Economics and Politics of Race in America*. New York: Cambridge University Press. doi:10.1017/CBO9780511572166

Carr, B., & Burnham, J. (1994). *Managing Quality in Schools. A Training Manual*. Harlow: Longman.

Carter, B., & New, C. (2004b). *Realist social theory and empirical research*. Paper presented at ESA Social Theory Conference, Paris, France.

Carter, B., & New, C. (Eds.). (2004a). *Making realism work: realist social theory and empirical research*. New York: Routledge.

Casper, W., Vaziri, H., Wayne, J., DeHauw, S., & Greenhaus, J. (2018). The jingle-jangle of work–nonwork balance: A comprehensive and meta-analytic review of its meaning and measurement. *The Journal of Applied Psychology*, *103*(2), 182–214. doi:10.1037/apl0000259 PMID:29016161

Cassidy, S. (2011). Self-regulated learning in higher education: Identifying key component processes. *Studies in Higher Education*, *36*(8), 989–1000. doi:10.1080/03075079.2010.503269

Centra, J. A. (1979). *Determining Faculty Effectiveness*. Assessing Teaching, Research, and Service for Personnel Decisions and Improvement.

Chakrabarty, T. K. C., & Chuan Tan, K. (2007). The Current State of Six Sigma Application in Services. *Managing Service Quality*, *17*(2), 194–208. doi:10.1108/09604520710735191

Chance, B., Ben-ZVI, D., Garfield, J., & Medina, E. (2007). *The role of technology in improving student learning of statistics*. Academic Press.

Chappell, K. B., Sherman, L., & Barnett, S. D. (2018). An interactive faculty development workshop designed to improve knowledge, skills (competence), attitudes, and practice in interprofessional continuing education. *Medical Teacher*, *40*(9), 896–903. doi:10.1080/0142159X.2018.1481286 PMID:29969328

Cheng, Y. C., & Tam, W. M. (1997). Multi-models of quality in education. *Quality Assurance in Education*, *5*(1), 22–31. doi:10.1108/09684889710156558

Chen, K., & Kenney, M. (2007). Universities/Research Institutes and Regional Innovation Systems: The Cases of Beijing and Shenzhen. *World Development*, *35*(6), 1056–1074. doi:10.1016/j.worlddev.2006.05.013

Chireshe, R. (2010). Why Articles Are Not Accepted For Publication: Guest Editorial Experiences. Consolidating Research, Innovation and Technology Platforms for a Knowledge-based Economy. *WSU Research Conference Proceedings*, 162-172.

Christensen, L. J., Peirce, E., Hartman, L. P., Hoffman, W. M., & Carrier, J. (2007). Ethics, CSR, and sustainability education in the Financial Times top 50 global business schools: Baseline data and future research directions. *Journal of Business Ethics*, *73*(4), 347-368.

Chung Sea Law, D. (2010). Quality assurance in post-secondary education: Some common approaches. *Quality Assurance in Education*, *18*(1), 64–77. doi:10.1108/09684881011016007

Cieri, D., & Kramar, R. (2003). *Human resource management in Australia: Management in strategy, people, and performance*. North Ryde, Australia: McGraw Hill.

Cleveland, M., Laroche, M., & Takahashi, I. (2015). The Interplay of Local and Global Cultural Influences on Japanese Consumer Behavior. In C. Campbell (Ed.), *Marketing in Transition: Scarcity, Globalism, & Sustainability. Developments in Marketing Science: Proceedings of the Academy of Marketing Science.* Springer. doi: 10.1007/978-3-319-18687-0_158

Cloete, N., Maassen, P., & Teboho, M. (2013). *Higher Education and different notions of development. IIE Newsletter.* Institute of International Education.

Coates, H. (2005). The value of student engagement for higher education quality assurance. *Quality in Higher Education, 11*(1), 25-36. Doi:10.1080/13538320500074915

Coffey, B. S., & Anderson, S. E. (1998). Career issues for women association executives: Mentors, pay equity, and boards of directors. *The Cornell Hotel and Restaurant Administration Quarterly, 39*(4), 34–39. doi:10.1177/001088049803900106

Cohen, W. A. (2009). *Drucker on leadership.* San Francisco: Jossey-Bass.

Colbeck, C. L. (2002). *Evaluating faculty performance.* Jossey-Bass.

Community for Creativity and Innovation. (n.d.). *What is innovation? 15 experts share their innovation definition.* Retrieved May 24, 2019 from https://www.ideatovalue.com/inno/nickskillicorn/2016/03/innovation-15-experts-share-innovation-definition/#nicks

Connell, R. (1985). How to supervise a Ph.D. *Vestes, 2,* 38–41.

Conti, T. (2006). Quality Thinking and Systems Thinking. *The TQM Magazine, 18*(3), 297–308. doi:10.1108/09544780610660013

Cooper, L., Orrell, J., & Bowden, M. (2010). *Work integrated learning: A guide to effective practice.* New York, NY: Taylor & Francis.

Corona, R. (2018). The Challenges for AACSB Accreditation at CEIPA Business School: Adapting New Standards for a Continuous Improvement Process. *International Journal of Business and Social Science, 9*(2).

Cortese, A. D. (2003). The critical role of higher education in creating a sustainable future. *Planning for Higher Education, 31*(3), 15–22.

Covey, S. R. (1992). *Principle-Centered Leadership.* New York: Simon & Schuster.

Cox, D., La Caze, M., & Levine, M. (2005). Integrity. In *The Stanford Encyclopedia of Philosophy.* Accessed April 9, 2006 at: http://plato.stanford.edu/archives/fall2005/entries/integrity/

Cox, M. D. (2004). Introduction to faculty learning communities. *New Directions for Teaching and Learning, 2004*(97), 5–23. doi:10.1002/tl.129

Cragg, W. (1997). Teaching business ethics: The role of ethics in business and in business education. *Journal of Business Ethics, 16*(3), 231–245. doi:10.1023/A:1017974908203

Craig, S. B., & Gustafson, S. B. (1998). Perceived leader integrity scale. *The Leadership Quarterly, 9*(2), 127–145. doi:10.1016/S1048-9843(98)90001-7

Crisp, G., & Cruz, I. (2009). Mentoring college students: A critical review of the literature between 1990 and 2007. *Research in Higher Education, 50*(6), 525–545. doi:10.100711162-009-9130-2

Crockett, D. S. (1978). Academic advising: A cornerstone of student retention. *New Directions for Student Services, 1978*(3), 29–35. doi:10.1002s.37119780306

Compilation of References

Crosling, G., Heagney, M., & Thomas, L. (2009). Improving student retention in higher education: Improving teaching and learning. *Australian Universities' Review. The, 51*(2), 9.

Cruickshank, M. (2003). Total Quality Management in the higher education sector a literature review from an international and Australian perspective. *TQM & Business Excellence, 14*(10), 1159–1167. doi:10.1080/1478336032000107717

Csizmadia, T. G. (2006). *Quality Management in Hungarian higher education organisational responses to governmental policy.* Enschede: CHEPS/UT.

Cullen, J., Joyce, J., Hassall, T., & Broadbent, M. (2003). Quality in higher education: From monitoring to management. *Quality Assurance in Education, 11*(1), 5–14. doi:10.1108/09684880310462038

Cullinan, J., Flannery, D., Walsh, S., & McCoy, S. (2013). Distance effects, social class and the decision to participate in higher education in Ireland. *The Economic and Social Review, 44*(1), 19-51.

D'Andrea, V., & Gosling, D. (2005). *Improving teaching and learning in higher education: a whole institution approach: a whole institution approach.* McGraw-Hill Education.

D'Andrea, V., & Gosling, D. (2005). *Improving teaching and learning in higher education: A whole institutional approach.* Glasgow, UK: Society for Research into Higher Education/Open University Press/Bell and Brain.

Daft, R. (2006). *The new era of management.* South Western.

Daft, R. L. (2018). *The Leadership experience* (7th ed.). Singapore: Cengage.

Dahlgaard, J. J., K., K., & Kanji, G. (2009). *Fundamentals of Total Quality Management.* Nelson Thornes.

Dahlgaard, J. J., Chen, C.-K., Jang, J.-Y., Banegas, L. A., & Dahlgaard-Park, S. M. (2013). Business excellence models: Limitations, reflections and further development. *Total Quality Management & Business Excellence, 24*(5–6), 519–538. doi:10.1080/14783363.2012.756745

Dahlgaard, J. J., Kristensen, K., & Kanji, G. K. (1995). TQM and education. *Total Quality Management & Business Excellence, 6*(5/6), 445–456.

Dahlgaard-Park, S. (2009). The Evolution Patterns of Quality Management: Some reflections on the quality movement. *Total Quality Management, 10*(4&5), 473–480.

Dahlgaard-Park, S. M. (2009). Decoding the code of excellence – for achieving sustainable excellence. *International Journal of Quality and Service Sciences, 1*(1), 5–28. doi:10.1108/17566690910945840

Dahlgaard-Park, S. M. (2011). The quality movement – where are you going? *Total Quality Management & Business Excellence, 22*(5), 493–516. doi:10.1080/14783363.2011.578481

Dahlgaard-Park, S. M., Chen, C. K., Jang, J. Y., & Dahlgaard, J. J. (2013). Diagnosing and prognosticating the quality movement – a review on the 25 years quality literature (1987–2011). *Total Quality Management & Business Excellence, 24*(1-2), 1–18. doi:10.1080/14783363.2012.756749

Dahlgaard-Park, S. M., Reyes, L., & Chen, C. K. (2018). The evolution and convergence of total quality management and management theories. *Total Quality Management & Business Excellence, 29*(9-10), 1108–1128. doi:10.1080/14783363.2018.1486556

Dancy, M., Henderson, C., & Turpen, C. (2016). How faculty learn about and implement research-based instructional strategies: The case of peer instruction. *Physical Review Physics Education Research, 12*(1), 010110. doi:10.1103/PhysRevPhysEducRes.12.010110

Danish Evaluation Institute. (2003). *Quality procedures in European Higher Education*. European Network for Quality Assurance.

Darling-Hammond, L. (2008). Teacher learning that supports student learning. *Teaching for Intelligence, 2*(1), 91-100.

Darling-Hammond, L. (2017). Teacher education around the world: What can we learn from international practice? *European Journal of Teacher Education, 40*(3), 291–309. doi:10.1080/02619768.2017.1315399

Darling-Hammond, L., & Richardson, N. (2009). Research review/teacher learning: What matters. *Educational Leadership, 66*(5), 46–53.

Darwin, A. (2000). Critical reflections on mentoring in work settings. *Adult Education Quarterly, 50*(3), 197–211. doi:10.1177/07417130022087008

Davenport, T. H. (1993). *Process innovation: reengineering work through information technology.* Harvard Business Press.

Davis, J. R. (1993). *Better Teaching, More Learning: Strategies for Success in Postsecondary Settings. American Council on Education Series on Higher Education.* Oryx Press.

De George, R. T. (2011). *Business ethics*. Retrieved from http://books.google.co.in/books?id=jwQB_XW s0TkC&printsec=frontcover&source=gbs_ge_summary_r&cad=0#v=onepage&q&f=false

Dean, T., & McMullen, J. (2007). Toward a theory of sustainable entrepreneurship: Reducing environmental degradation through entrepreneurial action. *Journal of Business Venturing, 22*(1), 50–76. doi:10.1016/j.jbusvent.2005.09.003

Deist, F. E. (1990). The role of the promoter. *Theologia Evangelica, 23*(3), 66–68.

Deming, W. E. (1986). Out of the crisis. Massachusetts Institute of Technology.

Deming, W. E. (2000). *Out of the Crisis, Institute of Technology.* MIT Press.

Deming, W. E. (2000). *Out of the crisis.* Cambridge, MA: MIT Press.

Dessler, G., Lloyd-Walker, B., & Griffiths, J. (2007). *Human resource management* (3rd ed.). Frenchs Forest, Australia: Pearson Education.

Dew, J. (2009). Quality issues in higher education. *Journal for Quality and Participation, 32*(1), 4–9.

Diamond, R. M. (1995). Preparing for Promotion and Tenure Review; A Faculty Guide. Anker Publishing Co., Inc.

Diamond, R. M. (1993). Changing priorities and the faculty reward system. *New Directions for Higher Education, 81*(81), 5–12. doi:10.1002/he.36919938103

Dias, S. B., & Diniz, J. A. (2014). Towards an enhanced learning management system for blended learning in higher education incorporating distinct learners' profiles. *Journal of Educational Technology & Society, 17*(1), 307–319.

Dicker, R., Garcia, M., Kelly, A., & Mulrooney, H. (2018). What does "quality" in higher education mean? Perceptions of staff, students and employers. *Studies in Higher Education*, 1–14. doi:10.1080/03075079.2018.1445987

Dillon, R. K., & Fisher, B. J. (2000). Faculty as part of the advising equation: An inquiry into faculty viewpoints on advising. *NACADA Journal, 20*(1), 16–23. doi:10.12930/0271-9517-20.1.16 PMID:11314371

Dirks, K. T., & Skarlicki, D. (2004). Trust in Leaders: Existing Research and Emerging Issues. In R. Sage (Ed.), Trust and distrust in organizations: Dilemmas and approaches. Academic Press.

Compilation of References

Dlačić, J., Arslanagić, M., Kadić-Maglajlić, S., Marković, S., & Raspor, S. (2014). Exploring perceived service quality, perceived value, and repurchase intention in higher education using structural equation modelling. *Total Quality Management & Business Excellence*, *25*(1-2), 1–2, 141–157. doi:10.1080/14783363.2013.824713

Do Nascimento, N. M., Moro-Cabero, M. M., & Valentim, M. L. P. (2018). The adoption of ISO standards in Brazil, Iberian Peninsula and the United Kingdom in information and documentation: A comparative study. *Records Management Journal*, *28*(3), 305–324. doi:10.1108/RMJ-04-2018-0009

Dobie, S., Smith, S., & Robins, L. (2010). How assigned faculty mentors view their mentoring relationships: An interview study of mentors in medical education. *Mentoring & Tutoring*, *18*(4), 337–359. doi:10.1080/13611267.2010.511842

Dollery, B., Murray, D., & Crase, L. (2006). Knaves or knights, pawns or queens? An Evaluation of Australian higher education reform policy. *Journal of Educational Administration*, *44*(1), 86–97. doi:10.1108/09578230610642674

Donaldson, T., & Dunfee, T. W. (1999). *Ties that bind: A social contracts approach to business ethics*. Academic Press.

Dooris, M. J., & Guidos, M. (2006, May). Tenure achievement rates at research universities. In *Annual Forum of Association for Institutional Research. Sheraton Chicago Hotel and Towers* (Vol. 17). Academic Press.

Douglass, G. K. (2018). Economic returns on investments in higher education. In *Investment in Learning* (pp. 359–387). Routledge. doi:10.4324/9781351309929-15

Driscoll, C., & McKee, M. (2007). Restoring a culture of ethical and spiritual values: A role for leader storytelling. *Journal of Business Ethics*, *73*(2), 205–221. doi:10.100710551-006-9191-5

Dubrin, A. J. (2010). *Principles of Leadership (7th ed.)*. South-Western Cengage Learning.

Dumay, J. C. (2009). Intellectual capital measurement: A critical approach. *Journal of Intellectual Capital*, *10*(2), 190–210. doi:10.1108/14691930910952614

Durie, A. D., & Beshir, E. S. (2016). Leadership effectiveness in Higher Education Institutions: The IPA Approach. Arabian, J. Bus. *Management Review*, *6*, 243.

Durvasula, S., Lysonski, S., & Madhavi, A. D. (2011). Beyond service attributes: Do personal values matter? *Journal of Services Marketing*, *25*(1), 33–46. doi:10.1108/08876041111107041

Eaton, J. S. (2001). *Distance learning: Academic and political challenges for higher education accreditation*. Washington, DC: Council for Higher Education Accreditation.

Eby, L. T., Allen, T. D., Evans, S. C., Ng, T., & DuBois, D. L. (2008). Does mentoring matter? A multidisciplinary meta-analysis comparing mentored and non-mentored individuals. *Journal of Vocational Behavior*, *72*(2), 254–267. doi:10.1016/j.jvb.2007.04.005 PMID:19343074

Eby, L. T., Allen, T. D., Hoffman, B. J., Baranik, L. E., Sauer, J. B., Baldwin, S., & Evans, S. C. (2013). An interdisciplinary meta-analysis of the potential antecedents, correlates, and consequences of protégé perceptions of mentoring. *Psychological Bulletin*, *139*(2), 441–476. doi:10.1037/a0029279 PMID:22800296

Eby, L. T., & Lockwood, A. (2005). Protégés' and mentors' reactions to participating in formal mentoring programs: A qualitative investigation. *Journal of Vocational Behavior*, *67*(3), 441–458. doi:10.1016/j.jvb.2004.08.002

Eby, L. T., McManus, S. E., Simon, S. A., & Russell, J. E. (2000). The protégé's perspective regarding negative mentoring experiences: The development of a taxonomy. *Journal of Vocational Behavior*, *57*(1), 1–21. doi:10.1006/jvbe.1999.1726

Edgeman, R., Dahlgaard, J. J., Dahlgaard-Park, S. M., & Scherer, F. (1999). On leaders and leadership. *Quality Progress*, *32*(10), 49–54.

Edvardsson, B., & Gustafsson, A. (2008). Quality in the Development of New Products and Services. In B. Edvardsson & A. Gustafsson (Eds.), *The Nordic School of Quality Management*. Studentliteratur.

Edvinsson, L., & Malone, M. S. (1997). *Intellectual Capital: Realising Your Company's True Value by Finding Its Hidden Brainpower*, Judy Piatkus (Publishers), Ltd.

Edwards, R., & Usher, R. (2001). Lifelong learning: A postmodern condition of education? *Adult Education Quarterly*, *51*(4), 273–287. doi:10.1177/07417130122087296

Elkins, T., & Keller, R. T. (2003). Leadership in research and development organizations: A literature review and conceptual framework. *The Leadership Quarterly*, *14*(4-5), 587–606. doi:10.1016/S1048-9843(03)00053-5

Ellis, R. (2018). Quality assurance for university teaching: Issues and approaches. In *Handbook of Quality Assurance for University Teaching* (pp. 21–36). Routledge. doi:10.4324/9781315187518-1

Ellsworth, J. B. (2000). *Surviving changes: A survey of Educational change models*. Syracuse, NY: ERIC Clearinghouse.

Elton, K. (2017). *Wearable tech in the classroom: Taking the education industry by storm*. Retrieved March 19, 2019 from https://elearningindustry.com/wearable-tech-in-the-classroom-taking-education-industry-storm

Erhard, W., Jensen, M. C., & Zaffron, S. (2008). *Integrity: A Positive Model that Incorporates the Normative Phenomena of Morality, Ethics and Legality*. Harvard Business School NOM Working Paper No. 06-11; Barbados Group Working Paper No. 06-03; Simon School Working Paper No. FR 08-05. Available at SSRN: http://ssrn.com/abstract=920625

Erhard, W., Jensen, M. C., & Zaffron, S. (2010). *Integrity: A Positive Model that Incorporates the Normative Phenomena of Morality, Ethics, and Legality - Abridged (English Language Version)*. Harvard Business School NOM Unit Working Paper No. 10-061; Barbados Group Working Paper No. 10-01; Simon School Working Paper No. 10-07. Available at SSRN: http://ssrn.com/abstract=1542759

Erhard, W., Jensen, M. C., & Zaffron, S. (2011). *Integridad: Un Modelo Positivo Que Incorpora Fenomenos Normativos de Moral, Etica y Legalidad - Abreviado* [Integrity: A Positive Model that Incorporates the Normative Phenomena of Morality, Ethics, and Legality - Abridged]. Harvard Business School NOM Unit Working Paper No. 10-061; Barbados Group Working Paper No. 10-01; Simon School Working Paper No. 10-07. Available at SSRN: http://ssrn.com/abstract=1756285

Erhard, W., Jensen, M., & Zaffron, S. (2007). *A New Model of Integrity: Without Integrity Nothing Works. Negotiation, Organizations and Markets Research Papers*. Harvard.

Eriksen, S. D. (1995). TQM and the transformation from an elite to a mass system of higher education in the UK. *Quality Assurance in Education*, *3*(1), 14–29. doi:10.1108/09684889510146795

Ervay, S. (2006). Academic Leadership in America's Public Schools. *NASSP Bulletin*, *90*(2), 77–86. doi:10.1177/0192636506290175

Eswatini Country Brief January, W. F. P. (2019). World Food Program. Retrieved May 1, 2019, from https://reliefweb.int/sites/reliefweb.int/files/resources/WFP-0000103024.pdf

Etkin, J. (1993). *La doble moral de las organizaciones*. Mc Graw Hill.

Etzioni, A. (1967). Mixed-Scanning: A 'Third' Approach to Decision-Making. *Public Administration Review*, *27*(5), 385–392. doi:10.2307/973394

Eurofund. (2016). *Employee involvement and participation at work: Recent research and policy developments revisited*. Brussels: European Foundation for the Improvement of Living and Working Conditions.

Compilation of References

European University Association. (2006). *Quality culture in European universities: A bottom-up approach: Report on the three rounds of the quality culture project 2002–2006*. Brussels: European University Association.

Evans, J. R., & Dean, J. W. (2000). *Total Quality: Management, Organization and Strategy*. South Western.

Evans, J. R., & Lindsay, W. M. (1999). *The management and control of quality*. South Western.

Evans, J., & Dean, J. J. (2003). *Total Quality: Management Organisation and Strategy* (3rd ed.). New York: Thomson South Western.

Evans, T. (2005). How does mentoring a disadvantaged young person impact on the mentor. *International Journal of Evidence Based Coaching and Mentoring*, *3*(2), 17–29.

Fagenson-Eland, E. A., Baugh, S., & Lankau, M. J. (2005). Seeing eye to eye: A dyadic investigation of the effect of relational demography on perceptions of mentoring activities. *Career Development International*, *10*(6/7), 460–477. doi:10.1108/13620430510620557

Fairclough, N. (2005). Discourse analysis in organization studies: The case for critical realism. *Organization Studies*, *26*(6), 915–939. doi:10.1177/0170840605054610

Falchikov, N. (2013). *Improving assessment through student involvement: Practical solutions for aiding learning in higher and further education*. Routledge.

Falkenberg, L., & Woiceshyn, J. (2008). Enhancing business ethics: Using cases to teach moral reasoning. *Journal of Business Ethics*, *79*(3), 213–217. doi:10.100710551-007-9381-9

Fang, J., Tang, L., Yang, J., & Peng, M. (2019). Social interaction in MOOCs: The mediating effects of immersive experience and psychological needs satisfaction. *Telematics and Informatics*, *39*, 75–91. doi:10.1016/j.tele.2019.01.006

Farell, G. M. (2007). *ICT in Education in Kenya ''Survey of ICT and education in Africa: Kenya Country Report*. Retrieved from www.infodev.org

Faria, J. R., Mixon, F. G., & Upadhyaya, K. P. (2019). Alumni donations and university reputation. *Education Economics*, *27*(2), 155–165. doi:10.1080/09645292.2018.1527895

Farkas, C. M., & Wetlaufer, S. (1996). The way chief executive officer leads. *Harvard Business Review*, *74*(3), 1–6.

Fassinger, R. E., & Good, G. E. (2017). Academic Leadership and Counseling Psychology: Answering the Challenge, Achieving the Promise. *The Counseling Psychologist*, *45*(6), 752–780. doi:10.1177/0011000017723081

Fatimal, N., & Sahibzada, S. A. (2012). An empirical analysis of factors affecting work-life balance among university teachers: The case of Pakistan. *Journal of International Academic Research*, *12*(1), 16–29.

Fazlagic, A. (2007). *Measuring the Intellectual capital of a university*. In Conference on Trends in the Management of Human Resources in Higher Education. Accessed online on May 1, 2013 at: http://www.oecd.org/edu/imhe/35322785.pdf

Feigenbaum, A. (2016). Total Quality Control. *Harvard Business Review*, *34*(6), 93–101.

Feigenbaum, A. (2016). *Total Quality Control*. New York: McGraw-Hill.

Fields, Z., & Atiku, S. O. (2017). Collective green creativity and eco-innovation as key drivers of sustainable business solutions in organisations. In *Collective Creativity for Responsible and Sustainable Business Practice* (pp. 1–25). Hershey, PA: IGI Global. doi:10.4018/978-1-5225-1823-5.ch001

Fishman, T. D., Ludgate, A., & Tutak, J. (2017). Success by design: Improving outcomes in American higher education. *Deloitte Insights*. Accessed from https://www2.deloitte.com/insights/us/en/industry/public-sector/improving-student-success-in-higher-education.html

Fisman, R., & Galinsky, G. (2012). *We need a new way to teach ethics to business school students.* Retrieved January 2016 from http://www. slate. com/articles/business/the_dismal_science/2012/09/business_school_and_ethics_can_we_train_mbas_to_do_the_right_thing_. html

Fleischer, J., Herm, M., & Ude, J. (2007). Business Capabilities as configuration elements of value added networks. *Production Engineering*, *1*(2), 187–192. doi:10.100711740-007-0012-1

Flumerfelt, S., & Banachowski, M. (2011). Understanding leadership paradigms for improvement in higher education. *Quality Assurance in Education*, *19*(3), 224–247. doi:10.1108/09684881111158045

Flynn, B. B., Schroeder, R.G., & Sakakibara, S. (1995). The impact of quality management practices on performance and competitive advantage. Decision Sciences. *Journal of Operations Management, International Journal of Production Research*, *26*(5), 659-691. doi:10.1111/j.1540-995.tb1445.x

Foster, S. T. (2017). *Mnaging Quality: Integrating the Supply Chain*. Cape Town: Pearson.

Foster, S., & MacLeod, J. (2004). The role of mentoring relationships in the career development of successful deaf persons. *Journal of Deaf Studies and Deaf Education*, *9*(4), 442–458. doi:10.1093/deafed/enh053 PMID:15314017

Frame, J. (2003). Theorising curriculum. In M. Coleman, M. Graham-Jolly, & D. Middlewood (Eds.), *Managing the curriculum in South African schools* (pp. 17–35). London: Commonwealth Secretariat.

Franck, R., & Galor, O. (2015). *The complementarity between technology and human capital in the early phase of industrialization.* Retrieved August 27, 2018 from http://d.repec.org/n?u=RePEc:bro:econwp:2015-3&r=his

Fredriksson, U. (2004). *Quality Education: The key role of teachers.* Education International Working Papers No. 14. Brussels: Education International.

Freeman, R. (1993). Quality assurance in training and education. *British Journal of Educational Studies*, *41*(3), 309–311. doi:10.2307/3122295

Friedlander, J., & Serban, A. M. (2004). Meeting the challenges of assessing student learning outcomes. *New Directions for Community Colleges*, *2004*(126), 101–109. doi:10.1002/cc.158

Fritzche, D. J., & Becker, H. (1984). Linking management behavior to ethical philosophy: An empirical investigation. *Academy of Management Journal*, *27*, 166–175.

Fritzsche, D. J., & Tsalikis, J. (1989). Business Ethics: A Literature Review with a Focus on Marketing Ethics. *Journal of Business Ethics*, *8*(9), 695–744. doi:10.1007/BF00384207

Fullan, M. (1982). *The meaning of educational change*. New York: Teachaers College Press.

Futurelearn. (2013). *Futurelearn Launches.* Retrieved from Futurelearn: http://futurelearn.com/feature/futurelearn-launches/

Gainer, M. (2015). *Shaping Values for a New Generation: Anti-Corruption Education in Lithuania, 2002-2006.* Princeton University. Retrieved from https://successfulsocieties.princeton.edu/sites/successfulsocieties/files/MG_NORMS_Lithuania_1.pdf

Ganguly, A. (2015). Exploring Total Quality Management (TQM) Approaches in Higher Education Institutions in a Globalized Environment – case Analysis of UK and Sweden. *Brock Journal of Education*, *3*(7). Available at http://www.eajournals.org/wp-content/uploads/Exploring-Total-Quality-Management-TQM-Approaches-in-Higher-Education-Institutions-in-a-Globalized-Environment-Case-Analysis-of-UK-and-Sweden.pdf

Ganguly, A. (2015). Exploring Total Quality Management (TQM) Approaches in Higher Education Institutions in a Globalized Environment-Case Analysis of UK and Sweden. *Brock Journal of Education*, *3*(7), 83–106.

García-Morales, V. J., Jiménez-Barrionuevo, M. M., & Gutiérrez-Gutiérrez, L. (2012). Transformational leadership influence on organizational performance through organizational learning and innovation. *Journal of Business Research*, *65*(7), 1040–1050. doi:10.1016/j.jbusres.2011.03.005

García-Torres, D. (2019). Distributed leadership, professional collaboration, and teachers' job satisfaction in U.S. schools. *Teaching and Teacher Education*, *79*, 111–123. doi:10.1016/j.tate.2018.12.001

Garrison, D. R., & Kanuka, H. (2004). Blended learning: Uncovering its transformative potential in higher education. *The Internet and Higher Education*, *7*(2), 95–105. doi:10.1016/j.iheduc.2004.02.001

Garrison, D. R., & Vaughan, N. D. (2013). Institutional change and leadership associated with blended learning innovation: Two case studies. *The Internet and Higher Education*, *18*, 24–28. doi:10.1016/j.iheduc.2012.09.001

Gatfield. (2005). An investigation into Ph.D. supervisory management styles: Development of a dynamic conceptual model and its managerial implications. *Journal of Higher Education Policy and Management*, 311-325.

Gazza, E. A., & Hunker, D. F. (2014). Facilitating student retention in online graduate nursing education programs: A review of the literature. *Nurse Education Today*, *34*(7), 1125–1129. doi:10.1016/j.nedt.2014.01.010 PMID:24529796

Gee, J. P. (2004). *Situated language and learning: a critique of traditional schooling*. Routledge, Taylor & Francis Group. Retrieved January 23, 2019, from http://networkedlearningcollaborative.com/wp-content/uploads/2015/07

Gee, J. P. (1996). *Social linguistics and literacies: ideology in discourses*. London: Routledge Falmer.

Gee, J. P. (1999). *Discourse analysis: theory and method*. London: Routledge.

Gershenfeld, S. (2014). A review of undergraduate mentoring programs. *Review of Educational Research*, *84*(3), 365–391. doi:10.3102/0034654313520512

Geyser, H., & Murdoch, N. (2016). Quality assurance and institutional research. In J. Botha & N. Muller (Eds.), *Institutional research in South African higher education*. Stellenbosch: Sun Press. doi:10.18820/9781928357186/08

Ghicajanu, M. (2019). Techniques to continually improve business quality and performance. *Quality-Access to Success*, *20*, 503–506.

Ghoshal, S. (2005). Bad management. Theories are destroying good management practices. *Academy of Management Learning & Education*, *4*(1), 75–91. doi:10.5465/amle.2005.16132558

Giacalone, R. A., & Thompson, K. R. (2006). From the guest co-editors: Special issue on ethics and social responsibility. *Academy of Management Learning & Education*, *5*(3), 261–265. doi:10.5465/amle.2006.22697015

Giannakou, M. (2006) Chair's Summary, Meeting of OECD Ministers. Academic Press.

Gibbs, G., & Jenkins, A. (2014). *Teaching large classes in higher education: How to maintain quality with reduced resources*. Routledge. doi:10.4324/9781315041384

Gilbert, P. (2016, December 31). Campus evolution: Teaching students to become entrepreneurs. *The Sydney Morning Herald*. Retrieved from http://www.smh.com.au/national/education/campus-evolution-teaching-students-to-become-entrepreneurs-20161231-gtk7v2.html

Gill, R. (2009). *Theory and Practice of Leadership*. London: Sage Publishing Ltd.

Gini, A., & Marcoux, A. M. (2009). Malden Mills: When being a good company isn't good enough. *Proceedings of the Good Company. Sixth International Symposium on Catholic Social Thought and Management Education*.

Gmelch, W. H., & Buller, J. L. (2015). *Building academic leadership capacity: A guide to best practices*. San Francisco: Jossey Bass.

Goffee, R., & Jones, G. (2009). *Clever: Leadership Your Smartest Most Creative People*. Boston, MA: Havard Business Press.

Goleman, D. (2018). *La inteligencia emocional*. Barcelona, Spain: Ediciones B.

Gordon, G. J., & Milakovich, M. E. (1998). *Public administration in America* (6th ed.). New York, NY: St. Martin's Press.

Gordon, V. N., Habley, W. R., & Grites, T. J. (2008). *Academic advising: A comprehensive handbook*. John Wiley & Sons.

Gorgievski, M. J., Ascalon, M. E., & Ute, S. (2011). Small business owners' success criteria, a values approach to personal differences. *Journal of Small Business Management*, *49*(2), 207–232. doi:10.1111/j.1540-627X.2011.00322.x

Govender, J. P., Veerasamy, D., & Noel, D. T. (2014). The service quality experience of International students: The case of a selected higher education institution in South Africa. *Mediterranean Journal of Social Sciences*, *5*(8), 465–473.

Government of Republic of Namibia (GRN). (1996). Namibia Qualifications Authority Act, Act No. 29 of 1996. Windhoek: Namibia.

Government of Republic of Namibia (GRN). (2008). *Vocational Education and Training Act, Act No. 1 of 2008*. Windhoek: GRN.

Government of Republic of Namibia (GRN). (2008). Vocational Education and Training Act, Act No. 1 of 2008. Windhoek: Namibia.

Government of the Republic of Namibia (GRN). (2003). Higher Education Act, Act. No. 26 of 2003. Windhoek: Namibia.

Government of the Republic of Namibia (GRN). (2004). Vision 2030. Windhoek: Namibia.

Graeff, C. (1983). The Situational Leadership Theory: A critical view. *Academy of Management Review*, *8*(2), 285–291. doi:10.5465/amr.1983.4284738

Graham, M. J., Frederick, J., Byars-Winston, A., Hunter, A. B., & Handelsman, J. (2013). Increasing persistence of college students in STEM. *Science*, *341*(6153), 1455–1456. doi:10.1126cience.1240487 PMID:24072909

Grandzon, J. R. (2005). *Improving the faculty selection process in higher education: A case study for the Analytic Hierarchy Process*. Association for Institutional Research.

Graves, L. M., & Sarkis, J. (2018). The role of employees' leadership perceptions, values, and motivation in employees' proevironmental behaviours. *Journal of Cleaner Production*, *196*, 576–587. doi:10.1016/j.jclepro.2018.06.013

Green, D. (1994). What Is Quality in Higher Education? Taylor & Francis.

Green, B., & Lee, A. (1995). Conclusion. In A. Lee & B. Green (Eds.), *Postgraduate Studies/Postgraduate Pedagogy*. Sydney: University of Technology.

Compilation of References

Greenhaus, J. H., & Allen, T. D. (2011). Work–family balance: A review and extension of the literature. In J. C. Quick & L. E. Tetrick (Eds.), *Handbook of occupational health psychology* (2nd ed.). Washington, DC: American Psychological Association.

Gregg, S., & Stoner, J. R. (Eds.). (2008). Rethinking Business Management. Examining the Foundations of Business Education. Witherspoon Institute.

Grover, R., Dalal, S., & Singh, A. (2016). Impact of 5S implementation. *Proceedings of the International Conference on Industrial Engineering and Operations Management*, 699-721.

Grunspan, D. Z., Kline, M. A., & Brownell, S. F. (2018). The Lecture Machine: A Cultural Evolutionary Model of Pedagogy in Higher Education. *CBE Life Sciences Education, 17*(6), 1–11. doi:10.1187/cbe.17-12-0287 PMID:29953324

Gu, J., He, C., & Liu, H. (2017). Supervisory Styles and graduate student creativity: The mediating roles of creative self-efficacy and intrinsic motivation. *Studies in Higher Education, 42*(4), 721–742.

Gumport, P. J., & Sporn, B. (1999). Institutional Adaptation: Demand for management reform and university administration. Higher education: Handbook of theory and research, 103-145.

Gumusluoğlu, L., & Ilsev, A. (2009). Transformational leadership, creativity, and organisational innovation. *Journal of Business Research, 62*(4), 461–473. doi:10.1016/j.jbusres.2007.07.032

Guryanova, A. V., Krasnov, S. V., & Frolov, V. A. (2020). Human transformation under the influence of the digital economy development. *Advances in Intelligent Systems and Computing, 908*, 140–149. doi:10.1007/978-3-030-11367-4_14

Guthrie, J. (2001). The management, measurement and the reporting of intellectual capital. *Journal of Intellectual Capital, 2*(1), 27–41. doi:10.1108/14691930110380473

Gynnild, V., & Gotschalk, P. (2008). Promoting academic integrity at a Midwestern University: Critical review and current challenges. *International Journal for Educational Integrity, 4*(2).

Hallencreutz, J., & Turner, D. (2011). Exploring organizational change best practice: Are there any clear-cut models and definitions. *International Journal of Quality and Service Sciences, 3*(1), 60–68. doi:10.1108/17566691111115081

Handzic, M., & Ozlen, K. (2009). Intellectual capital in universities: faculty and student perceptions. *Proceedings of the 12th International Conference on Knowledge Management, University of Passau Germany*.

Hanover Research. (2014). *Strategies for improving student retention*. Hanover Research-Academy Administration Practice. Available from https://www.hanoverresearch.com/media/Strategies-for-Improving-Student-Retention.pdf

Hargreaves, P., & Javis, P. (2001). *The human resource development handbook*. London: Kogan Page Ltd.

Haris, I. (2013). Assessment on the implementation of internal quality assurance at higher education: An Indonesian report. *Journal of Educational and Institutional Studies in the World, 3*(4), 41–49.

Harry, M., & Crawford, D. (2005). Six Sigma – the next generation. *Machine Design, 77*(4), 126–130.

Harvey, L. (2005). A history and critique of quality and evaluation in the UK. *Quality Assurance in Education, 13*(4), 263–276. doi:10.1108/09684880510700608

Harvey, L., & Green, D. (1993). Defining quality. *Assessment & Evaluation in Higher Education, 18*(1), 9–34. doi:10.1080/0260293930180102

Harvey, L., & Green, D. (1993). Defining Quality: Assessment and Evaluation in Higher Education. *The Quality Management Journal, 18*(1), 9–34.

Harvey, L., & Knight, P. T. (1996). *Transforming Higher Education*. Buckingham, UK: SRHE and Open University Press.

Harvey, L., & Williams, J. (2010). Fifteen years of Quality in Higher Education. *Quality in Higher Education*, *16*(1), 3–36. doi:10.1080/13538321003679457

Haskell, C. D. (2017). Institutional research as a bridge: Aligning institutional internal data needs and external information requirements a strategic view. *Higher Education Evaluation and Development*, *11*(1), 2–11. doi:10.1108/HEED-08-2017-001

Hayward, C. N., Kogan, M., & Laursen, S. L. (2016). Facilitating instructor adoption of inquiry-based learning in college mathematics. *International Journal of Research in Undergraduate Mathematics Education*, *2*(1), 59–82. doi:10.100740753-015-0021-y

Hazell, P., & Guy, M. (2016). *Data, quality assurance and improving student experience. Quality Assurance Agency for Higher Education (QAAHE)*. Retrieved from https://elearning.jiscinvolve.org/wp/2016/11/09/data-quality-assurance-and-improving-the-student-experience/

Head, B. (2014, November 18). With Wozniak on board, as UTS launches Hatchery to breed better tech start-ups. *The Sydney Morning Herald*. Retrieved from http://www.smh.com.au/national/education/campus-evolution-teaching-students-to-become-entrepreneurs-20161231-gtk7v2.ggshtml

Heath, S. B. (1983). *Ways with words: language, life, and work in communities and classrooms*. Cambridge, UK: Cambridge University Press. doi:10.1017/CBO9780511841057

Hébert, P., Meslin, E. M., Dunn, E. V., Byrne, N., & Reid, S. R. (1990). Evaluating ethical sensitivity in medical students: Using vignettes as an instrument. *Journal of Medical Ethics*, *16*(3), 141–145. doi:10.1136/jme.16.3.141 PMID:2231639

Heitor, M., & Horta, H. (2016). Reforming higher education in Portugal in times of uncertainty: The importance of illities, as non-functional requirements. *Technological Forecasting and Social Change*, *113*, 146–156. doi:10.1016/j.techfore.2015.09.027

Hellenic Quality Assurance Agency. (2017). *Guidelines for accreditation*. Retrieved from https://www.adip.gr/sites/default/files/pages/06/701-odigos_pistopoiisis_en.pdf

Hellenic Quality Assurance Agency. (2018). Annual report 2017. Athens: Author.

Hellsten, U. K., & Klefsjö, B. (2000). TQM as a management system consisting values, techniques, and tools. *The TQM Magazine*, *12*(4), 238–24. doi:10.1108/09544780010325822

Hellstrom, T., & Husted, K. (2004). Mapping knowledge and intellectual capital in academic environments. *Journal of Intellectual Capital*, *5*(1), 165–180. doi:10.1108/4691930410512987

Hemingway, C. A., & Maclagan, P. W. (2004). Managers' personal values as drivers of corporate social responsibility. *Journal of Business Ethics*, *50*(1), 33–44. doi:10.1023/B:BUSI.0000020964.80208.c9

Hemwall, M. K. (2008). Advising delivery: Faculty advising. *Academic advising: A comprehensive handbook*, *2*, 68-84.

Hernández, R., Silvestri, K., & Álvarez, A. (2007). Enseñanza de la ética en la formación gerencial. *Revista de Ciencias Sociales*, *13*(3).

Hernández, H., Martínez, D., & Rodríguez, J. (2017). Management of quality applied in the improvement of the university sector. *Espacios*, *38*(20), 29–41.

Herndon, N. C. Jr, Fraedrich, J. P., & Yeh, Q. J. (2001). An investigation of moral values and the ethical content of the corporate culture: Taiwanese versus US sales people. *Journal of Business Ethics*, *30*(1), 73–85. doi:10.1023/A:1006493907563

Compilation of References

Hersey, P., & Blanchard, K. (1969). The life cycle theory of leadership. *Training and Development Journal*.

Hersey, P., & Blanchard, K. H. (1969). Life Cycle Theory of Leadership. *Training & Development*, *23*, 26–34.

Hersey, P., Blanchard, K. H., & Johnson, D. E. (1996). *Management of Organizational behavior: Utilising human resources* (7th ed.). Upper Saddle River, NJ: Prentice Hall.

Hides, M., Davies, J., & Jackson, S. (2004). Implementation of EFQM excellence model self-assessment in the UK higher education sector-lessons learned from other sectors. *The TQM Magazine*, *16*(3), 194–201. doi:10.1108/09544780410532936

Higgs, M., & Rowland, D. (2011). What does it take to implement change successfully? A study of the behaviours of successful change leaders. *The Journal of Applied Behavioral Science*, *47*(3), 309–355. doi:10.1177/0021886311404556

Hill, L. A., & Sawatzky, J. A. V. (2011). Transitioning into the nurse practitioner role through mentorship. *Journal of Professional Nursing*, *27*(3), 161–167. doi:10.1016/j.profnurs.2011.02.004 PMID:21596356

Himsel, D. (2014). Business schools aren't producing ethical graduates. *Bloomberg Business*. Retrieved from http://www.bloomberg.com/bw/articles/2014-08-06/business-schools-dont-teach-ethics-effectively

Hirst, P., & Thompson, G. (2002). The Future of Globalization. *Journal of the Nordic International Studies Association*, 247-265.

Hoecht, A. (2006). Quality assurance in UK higher education: Issues of trust, control, professional autonomy and accountability. *Higher Education*, *51*(4), 541–563. doi:10.100710734-004-2533-2

Hok-Chun, K., Dennis. (2002). Quality Education through a Post Modern Curriculum. *Hong Kong's Teachers Centre Journal*, *1*(1), 56–73.

Homann, U., Levy, M., Merrifield, E., Appel, D., Davidson, E., Isaacs, S., & Judah, N. (2006). *U.S. Patent Application No. 11/076,142*. US Patent Office.

HomeRoom. (2015, october 14). *HomeRoom*. Retrieved February 17, 2019, from The official Blog US department of education: go.nmc.org/equip

Hong, J., Liao, Y., Zhang, Y., & Yu, Z. (2019). The effect of supply chain quality management practices and capabilities on operational and innovation performance: Evidence from Chinese manufacturers. *International Journal of Production Economics*, *212*, 227–235. doi:10.1016/j.ijpe.2019.01.036

Hooijberg, R., Hunt, J. G., & Dodge, G. E. (1997). Leadership complexity and development of the leaderplex model. *Journal of Management*, *23*, 375–408. doi:10.1177/014920639702300305

Hooijberg, R., & Lane, N. (2005). *Leader effectiveness and integrity: Wishful thinking? IMD 2005-1 IMD*. International Institute for Management Development.

Horth, D., & Buchner, D. (2014). *Innovation leadership: How to use innovation to lead effectively, work collaboratively, and drive results*. Center for Creative Leadership. Retrieved March 24, 2019 from https://www.ccl.org/wp-content/uploads/2015/04/InnovationLeadership.pdf

Hossain, B. (2017). Factors Affecting Higher Education Quality in Bangladesh: An Attempt to Improve Higher Education Quality in Bangladesh through HEQEP. *International Journal of Science and Business*, *1*(1), 47–59.

Huang, Y. S., & Asghar, A. (2018). Science education reform in Confucian learning cultures: Teachers' perspectives on policy and practice in Taiwan. *Cultural Studies of Science Education*, *13*(1), 101–131. doi:10.100711422-016-9762-4

Hughes, A., & Kitson, M. (2012). Pathways to impact and the strategic role of universities: New evidence on the breadth and depth of university knowledge exchange in the UK and the factors constraining its development. *Cambridge Journal of Economics*, *36*(3), 723–750. doi:10.1093/cje/bes017

Hunt, D. M., & Michael, C. (1983). Mentorship: A career training and development tool. *Academy of Management Review*, *8*(3), 475–485. doi:10.5465/amr.1983.4284603

Hunt, S. D., Wood, V. R., & Chonko, L. B. (1989). Corporate ethical values and organizational commitment in marketing. *Journal of Marketing*, *53*(3), 79–90. doi:10.1177/002224298905300309

Husu, J. (2003). Constructing ethical representations from the teacher's pedagogical practice: A case of prolonged reflection. *Interchange*, *34*(1), 1–21. doi:10.1023/A:1024595600952

Hwang, H., & Teo, C. (2000). Translating Customers' Voices into Operational Requirements-AQFD application in higher education. *International Journal of Quality & Reliability Management*, *18*(2), 195–220.

Ibeh, K. I. N., Uduma, I. A., Makhmadshoev, D., & Madichie, N. O. (2018). Nascent multinationals from West Africa: Are their foreign direct investment motivations any different? *International Marketing Review*, *35*(4), 683–708. doi:10.1108/IMR-08-2016-0158

Ilyasin, M. (2017). Balanced Scorecard: A Strategy for the Quality Improvement of Islamic Higher Education. *DinamikaIlmu*, *17*(2), 223–236.

Isaksson, R. (2019). A proposed preliminary maturity grid for assessing sustainability reporting based on quality management principles. *The TQM Journal*, *31*(3), 451–466. doi:10.1108/TQM-12-2017-0167

Ishikawa, K. (2008). *What is Total Quality Control? – the Japanese way*. Prentice-Hall.

Jackall, R. (1988). *Moral Mazes*. New York, NY: Oxford University Press, Inc.

Jackson, D., Ferns, S., Rowbottom, D., & McLaren, D. (2015). *Working together to achieve better work integrated learning outcomes: Improving productivity through better employer involvement*. Retrieved from http://acen.edu.au/wp-content/uploads/2016/06/Working-together-to-achieve-better-WIL-outcomes.pdf

Jackson, N. (1997). Internal academic quality audit in UK higher education: Part II-implications for a national quality assurance framework. *Quality Assurance in Education*, *5*(1), 46–54. doi:10.1108/09684889710156585

Jaggars, S. S., & Xu, D. (2016). How do online course design features influence student performance? *Computers & Education*, *95*, 270–284. doi:10.1016/j.compedu.2016.01.014

Jansen, E., & Glinow, M. A. V. (1985). Ethical Ambivalence and Organizational Reward Systems. *Academy of Management Review*, *1*(10), 4814–4822.

Jensen, M. C. (2009). Integrity: Without it Nothing Works. *Rotman Magazine: The Magazine of the Rotman School of Management*, 16-20. Available at SSRN: http://ssrn.com/abstract=1511274

Jensen, M. C., Granger, K. L., & Erhard, W. (2010). *A New Model of Integrity: The Missing Factor of Production. (PDF file of Keynote and PowerPoint Slides*. Harvard Business School NOM Unit Working Paper 10-087; Barbados Group Working Paper No. 10-03. Available at SSRN: http://ssrn.com/abstract=1559827

JISC. (2013). *Open Educational Resources Programme*. Retrieved from JISC: http:www.jisc.ac.uk/whatwedo/programmes//elearning/oer.aspx

Jolson, M. A. (1974). Criteria for promotion and tenure: A faculty view. *Academy of Management Journal*, *17*(1), 149–154.

Jongbloed, B., Enders, J., & Salerno, C. (2008). Higher education and its communities: Interconnections, interdependencies and research agenda. *Higher Education*, *56*(3), 303–324. doi:10.100710734-008-9128-2

Jung, D., Chow, C., & Wu, A. (2003). The role of transformational leadership in enhancing organisational innovation: Hypothesis and some preliminary findings. *The Leadership Quarterly*, *14*(4-5), 525–544. doi:10.1016/S1048-9843(03)00050-X

Juran, J. (2014). Why Quality Initiatives Fail. *The Journal of Business Strategy*, *14*(4), 35–38. doi:10.1108/eb039571 PMID:10127318

Kadhila, N. (2012). *Quality assurance mechanisms in higher education institutions in Namibia* (Unpublished doctoral dissertation). University of the Free State, Bloemfontein, South Africa.

Kadhila, N., & Iipumbu, N. (2019). Strengthening internal quality assurance as a lever for enhancing student learning experiences and academic success: Lessons from Namibia. *Quality in Higher Education*, *24*(3), 1–17.

Kahveci, T. C., & Taskin, H. (2013). Integrated enterprise management system for higher education institutions based on strategic and process management: The case study of Sakarya University. *Procedia: Social and Behavioral Sciences*, *103*, 1505–1513. doi:10.1016/j.sbspro.2013.12.170

Kahveci, T. C., Uygun, O., Yurtsever, U., & Ilyas, S. (2012). Quality assurance in higher education institutions using strategic information systems. *Perspectives: Policy and Practice in Higher Education*, *55*, 161–167.

Kahveci, T. C., Uygun, Ö., Yurtsever, U., & İlyas, S. (2012). Quality assurance in higher education institutions using strategic information systems. *Procedia: Social and Behavioral Sciences*, *55*, 161–167. doi:10.1016/j.sbspro.2012.09.490

Kaiser, R. B., & Hogan, R. (2010). How to (and how not to) assess the integrity of managers. *Consulting Psychology Journal: Practice and Research American Psychological Association*, *62*(4), 216–234. doi:10.1037/a0022265

Kalusi, J. I. (2001). Teacher quality for quality education. *Nigerian Journal of Educational Philosophy*, *8*(2), 62–72.

Kanji, G. K., Tambi, A. M., & Wallace, W. (1999). A comparative study of quality practices in higher education institutions in US and Malaysia. *Total Quality Management*, *10*(3), 357–371. doi:10.1080/0954412997884

Kaptein, M. (2003). The diamond of managerial integrity. *European Management Journal*, *21*(1), 98–108. doi:10.1016/S0263-2373(02)00157-3

Kaye, B., & Jacobson, B. (1996). Reframing mentoring. *Training & Development*, *50*(8), 44.

Kekale, T. (1998). *The effects of organizational culture on success and failures in implementation of some total quality management approaches. Towards a theory of selecting a culturally matching quality approach* (Ph.D. thesis). University of Vaasa, Acta Wasaennsia No. 65.

Kennedy, M., Billett, S., Gherardi, S., & Grealish, L. (Eds.). (2015). *Practice-based learning in higher education: Jostling cultures*. Springer. doi:10.1007/978-94-017-9502-9

Kerr, C. (2001). *The uses of the university*. Harvard University Press.

Kerr, S. (1988). Integrity in effective leadership. In *Executive Integrity: The search for high human values in organizational life*. San Francisco, CA: Jossey-Bass.

Kettunen, J. (n.d.). *Integrating strategic management and quality assurance*. Turku: Turku University of Applied Science.

Kettunen, J. (2008). Integration of strategic management and quality assurance. In *Proceedings of 11th Annual Convention of the Strategic Management Forum*. Indian Institute of Technology.

Kettunen, J., & Kantola, M. (2007). Strategic planning and quality assurance in the Bologna Process. Perspectives. *Policy and Practice in Higher Education*, *11*(3), 67–73. doi:10.1080/13603100701428205

Kezar, A. (2012). *Embracing non-tenure track faculty: Changing campuses for the new faculty majority*. Routledge. doi:10.4324/9780203828434

Kezar, A., & Ekel, P. D. (2002). The effect of institutional culture on change strategies in higher education: Universal principles or culturally responsive concepts. *The Journal of Higher Education*, *73*(4), 435–460.

Khallash, S., & Kruse, M. (2012). The future of work and work–life balance 2025. *Futures*, *44*(7), 678–686. doi:10.1016/j.futures.2012.04.007

Khan, H., & Matlay, H. (2009). Implementing service excellence in higher education. *Education + Training*, *51*(8), 769–780. doi:10.1108/00400910911005299

Kiat Kok, S., & Mc Donald, C. (2017). Underpinning excellence in higher education- an investigation into the leadership, governance and management behaviours of high performing academic departments. *Studies in Higher Education*, *42*(2), 210–231. doi:10.1080/03075079.2015.1036849

Kimani, E. N. (2014). Challenges in Quality Control for postgraduate supervision.; *International Journal of Humanities Social Sciences and Education*, 63-70.

Kim, W., & Mauborgne, R. (1997). Fair process. *Harvard Business Review*, *75*, 65–75. PMID:10168337

King, M. C. (1993). Advising models and delivery systems. *New Directions for Community Colleges*, *82*(82), 47–54. doi:10.1002/cc.36819938206

Kinman, G., & Jones, F. (2008). A life beyond work? Job demands, work-life balance, and wellbeing in UK academics. *Journal of Human Behavior in the Social Environment*, *17*(1-2), 41–60. doi:10.1080/10911350802165478

Kinman, G., & Jones, F. (2008). Effort-reward imbalance, over-commitment and work-life conflict: Testing an expanded model. *Journal of Managerial Psychology*, *23*(3), 236–251. doi:10.1108/02683940810861365

Klefsjö, B., Wiklund, H., & Edgeman, R. (2001). Six Sigma Seen as a Methodology for Total Quality Management. *Measuring Business Excellence*, *5*(1), 31–35. doi:10.1108/13683040110385809

Klemenčič, M., & Brennan, J. (2013). Institutional research in a European context: A forward look. *European Journal of Higher Education*, *3*(3), 265–279. doi:10.1080/21568235.2013.823726

Klemenčič, M., Šćukanec, N., & Komljenovič, J. (2015). Decision support issues in Central and Eastern Europe. In K. L. Webber & A. J. Calderon (Eds.), *Institutional research and planning in higher education: Global themes and context*. New York: Routledge. Retrieved from http://www.routledge.com/books/details/9781138021433/

Kliksberg, B. (2002). *Ética y Desarrollo, La Relación Marginada (con los premios Nóbel de Economía Amartya Sen, Joseph Stiglitz y otros)*. El Ateneo.

Knapp, J. C., & Siegel, D. J. (Eds.). (2009). *The Business of Higher Education* (3 vols.). ABC-CLIO.

Knight, J. E., Allen, S., & Tracy, D. L. (2010). Using six sigma methods to evaluate the reliability of a teaching assessment rubric. *The Journal for American Academy of Research Cambridge*, *15*(1), 1–6.

Kocher, M. G., Luptacik, M., & Sutter, M. (2006). Measuring productivity of research in economics: A cross country study using DEA. *Socio-Economic Planning Sciences*, *40*(4), 314–332. doi:10.1016/j.seps.2005.04.001

Kogler Hill, S. E., Bahniuk, M. H., & Dobos, J. (1989). The impact of mentoring and collegial support on faculty success: An analysis of support behavior, information adequacy, and communication apprehension. *Communication Education*, *38*(1), 15–33. doi:10.1080/03634528909378737

Kollmuss, A., & Agyeman, J. (2002). Mind the gap: Why do people act environmentally and what are the barriers to pro-environmental behaviour? *Environmental Education Research*, *8*(3), 239–260. doi:10.1080/13504620220145401

Kolthoff, E., Huberts, L., & Heuvel, H. (2003). The Ethics of New Public Management: Is Integrity at Stake? EGPA Study Group "Ethics and Integrity of Governance" Oeiras, Portugal.

Komorowska, H. (2017). Quality assurance in teacher education. *Glottodidactica*, *XLIV*(1), 28–38.

Kondo, Y. (2003). *Company Wide Quality Control*. Tokyo, Japan: 3A Corporation.

Kortemeyer, G. (2013, February 26). *Educause Review*. Retrieved February 18, 2019, from Educause: https://er.educause.edu/articles/2013/2/ten-years-later-why-open-educational-resources-have-not-noticeably-affected-higher-education-and-why-we-should-care

Kotter, J. P. (1996). *Leading Change*. Boston, MA: Harvard Business School Press.

Kouzes, J. M., & Posner, B. Z. (2007). *The Leadership Challenge* (4th ed.). San Francisco, CA: Jossey-Bass Publishers.

Kram, K. E. (1985). *Mentoring at work: Developmental relationships in organisational life*. Glenview, IL: Scott, Foresman.

Kreber, C., & Cranton, P. A. (2000). Exploring the scholarship of teaching. *The Journal of Higher Education*, *71*(4), 476–495. doi:10.2307/2649149

Kress, G. (1988). *Linguistic processes in sociocultural practice*. Oxford, UK: Oxford University Press.

Kukreja, A., Ricks, J. M. Jr, & Meyer, J. A. (2009). Using Six Sigma for performance improvement in business curriculum: A case study. *Performance Improvement*, *48*(2), 9–25. doi:10.1002/pfi.20042

Kukulska-Hulme, A. (2012). How should the higher education workforce adapt to advancements in technology for teaching and learning? *The Internet and Higher Education*, *15*(4), 247–254. doi:10.1016/j.iheduc.2011.12.002

Kwak, Y. H., & Anbarib, F. T. (2006). Benefits, obstacles, and future of six sigma approach. *Technovation*, *26*(5-6), 708–715. doi:10.1016/j.technovation.2004.10.003

Ladyshewsky, R. K., & Flavell, H. (2011). Transfer of Training in an Academic Leadership Development Program for Program Coordinators. *Educational Management Administration & Leadership*, *40*(1), 127–147. doi:10.1177/1741143211420615

Lagrosen, S. (2003). Exploring the impact of culture on quality management. *International Journal of Quality & Reliability Management*, *20*(4), 473–487. doi:10.1108/02656710310468632

Lagrossen, S., Seyyed-Hashemi, R., & Leitner, M. (2004). Examination of the dimensions of quality in Higher Education. *Quality Assurance in Education*, *12*(2), 61–69. doi:10.1108/09684880410536431

Laske, S., & Zuber-Skerrit, O. (1996). *Framework for Post Graduate Research and Supervision*. Lismore: Southern Cross University Press.

Lau, P. N. K., Lau, S. H., Hong, K. S., & Usop, H. (2011). Guessing, partial knowledge, and misconceptions in multiple-choice tests. *Journal of Educational Technology & Society*, *14*(4), 99–110.

Lawrence, J. H., Celis, S., Kim, H. S., Lipson, S. K., & Tong, X. (2014). To stay or not to stay: Retention of Asian international faculty in STEM fields. *Higher Education*, *67*(5), 511–531. doi:10.100710734-013-9658-0

Lawrence, J. H., Celis, S., & Ott, M. (2014). Is the tenure process fair? What faculty think. *The Journal of Higher Education, 85*(2), 155–192.

Lawson, H. A. (1992). Beyond the new conception of teacher induction. *Journal of Teacher Education, 43*(3), 163–172. doi:10.1177/0022487192043003002

Lea, S. J., Stephenson, D., & Troy, J. (2003). Higher education students' attitudes to student-centred learning: Beyond'educationalbulimia'? *Studies in Higher Education, 28*(3), 321–334. doi:10.1080/03075070309293

Lee, A. (2007). Developing effective supervisors: Concepts of research supervision. *South African Journal of Higher Education, 21*(4), 680–693.

Lee, A. (2008). How are doctoral students supervised? Concepts of doctoral research supervision. *Studies in Higher Education, 33*(3), 267–281. doi:10.1080/03075070802049202

Lee, E. K., Avgar, A. C., Park, W.-W., & Choi, D. (2019). The dual effects of task conflict on team creativity: Focusing on the role of team-focused transformational leadership. *International Journal of Conflict Management, 30*(1), 132–154. doi:10.1108/IJCMA-02-2018-0025

Leitner, K. H. (2002). *Intellectual capital reporting for universities: coneptual background and applications within the recognition of Austrian universities*. In The Transparent Enterprise. The Value of Intangibles, Madrid, Spain.

Leslie, L. L., & Brinkman, P. T. (1988). The Economic Value of Higher Education. American Council on Education/Macmillan Series on Higher Education. Macmillan Publishing.

Leslie, J. B., & Fleenor, J. W. (1998). *Feedback to managers: A review and comparison of multi-rater instruments for management development*. Greensboro, NC: Center for Creative Leadership.

Lessing, A. C., & Schulze, S. (2002). Postgraduate Supervision and Academic Support: Students' Perceptions. *South African Journal of Higher Education., 16*(2), 139–149. doi:10.4314ajhe.v16i2.25253

Lester, D., & Mullane, J. (2010). Sustainable entrepreneurship education: a comparative approach. *Small Business Institute, National Conference Proceedings, 34*(1).

Levine, A. (2018). Privatization in higher education. In *Privatizing education* (pp. 133–148). Routledge. doi:10.4324/9780429498015-6

Levinson, H. (1988). To thine own self be true: Coping with the dilemmas of integrity. In S. Srivastva & ... (Eds.), *Executive Integrity: The Search for High Human Values in Organizational Life*. San Francisco, CA: Jossey-Bass.

Lewis, R. G., & Smith, D. H. (1994). *Total Quality in Higher Education. Total Quality Series. St. Lucie Press*.

Licata, C. M. (1986). Post-Tenure Faculty Evaluation: Threat or Opportunity? ASHE-ERIC Higher Education Report No. 1. Association for the Study of Higher Education.

Linderman, K., Schroeder, R., Zaheer, S., Liedtke, C., & Choo, A. (2004). Integrating Quality Management Practices with Knowledge Creation Process. *Journal of Operations Management, 23*(6), 589–607. doi:10.1016/j.jom.2004.07.001

Livanos, H. (2010). The relationship between higher education and labour market in Greece: The weakest link? *Higher Education, 60*(5), 473–489. doi:10.100710734-010-9310-1

Llano, C. (1997). *Empleo, Educación y Formación Permanente. Lo mejor de Executive Excellence*. Panorama Editorial.

Lock, J., Kim, B., Koh, K., & Wilcox, G. (2018). Navigating the Tensions of Innovative Assessment and Pedagogy in Higher Education. *The Canadian Journal for the Scholarship of Teaching and Learning*, *9*(1), 1–20. doi:10.5206/cjsotl-rcacea.2018.1.8

Lomas, L. (2004). Embedding quality: The challenges for higher education. *Quality Assurance in Education*, *12*(4), 157–165. doi:10.1108/09684880410561604

Longenecker, J. G., Moore, C. W., Petty, J. W., Palich, L. E., & McKinney, J. A. (2006). Ethical attitudes in small business & large corporations: Theory & empirical findings from a tracking study planning three decades'. *Journal of Small Business Management*, *2*(44), 167–183. doi:10.1111/j.1540-627X.2006.00162.x

Long, J. (1997). The dark side of mentoring. *Australian Educational Researcher*, *24*(2), 115–133. doi:10.1007/BF03219650

Loogma, K., Tafel-Viia, K., & Ümarik, M. (2013). Conceptualizing educational changes: A social innovation approach. *Journal of Educational Change*, *14*(3), 283–301. doi:10.100710833-012-9205-2

Look, D. (2005). *Discussion Paper: Impact of Technology in Education*. PUSD Excellence Committee.

Looney, J. (2011). Developing High-Quality Teachers: Teacher evaluation for improvement. *European Journal of Education*, *46*(4), 440–455. doi:10.1111/j.1465-3435.2011.01492.x

Lotz-Sisitka, H. (2010). *Conceptions of quality and learning as connections: teaching for relevance*. Retrieved November 19, 2011 from http://www.fgcu.edu/CESE/images/Lotz-Sisitka-Learning-as-Connection.pdf

Loverock, D. T., & Newell, R. (2012). *Pro-environmental behaviours in the workplace: Driving social change*. Interactive Case Studies in Sustainable Community Development.

Lubitz, R. M. (1997). Guidelines for promotion of clinician-educators. *Journal of General Internal Medicine*, *12*(S2), S71–S78. doi:10.1046/j.1525-1497.12.s2.10.x PMID:9127247

Luckett, K. (2007). The introduction of external QA in South African HEIs: An analysis of stakeholder response. *Quality in Higher Education*, *13*(2), 97–116. doi:10.1080/13538320701629129

Lueddeke, G. R. (2003). Professionalising teaching practice in higher education: A study of disciplinary variation and 'teaching-scholarship'. *Studies in Higher Education*, *28*(2), 213–228. doi:10.1080/0307507032000058082

Lumpe, C. (2019). Public beliefs in social mobility and high-skilled migration. *Journal of Population Economics*, *32*(3), 981–1008. doi:10.100700148-018-0708-x

Lumpkin, A. (2011, October). A model for mentoring university faculty. *The Educational Forum*, *75*(4), 357–368. doi:10.1080/00131725.2011.602466

Luna, G., & Cullen, D. L. (1995). Empowering the Faculty: Mentoring Redirected and Renewed. ASHE-ERIC Higher Education Report No. 3. ERIC Clearinghouse on Higher Education.

Lunenburg, F. C., & Ornstein, A. C. (2008). *Educational Administration: Concepts and Practices* (5th ed.). Belmont: Wadsworth Cengage Learning.

Lussier, R. N., & Achua, C. F. (2010). *Effective Leadership (5th ed.)*. South-Western Cengage Learning.

Luyten, H., & Bazo, M. (2019). Transformational leadership, professional learning communities, teacher learning, and learner-centred teaching practices; Evidence on their interrelations in Mozambican primary education. *Studies in Educational Evaluation*, *60*, 14–31. doi:10.1016/j.stueduc.2018.11.002

Machiavelli, N. (1981). *The Prince* (G. Bull, Trans.). New York, NY: Penguin Books.

Machumu, H. J., & Kisanga, S. H. (2014). Quality Assurance Practices in Higher Education Institutions: Lesson from Africa. *Journal of Education and Practice, 5*(16), 144–156.

Madu, C. N., & Kuei, C. H. (1993). Dimensions of quality teaching in higher institutions. *Total Quality Management, 4*(3), 325–338. doi:10.1080/09544129300000046

Maguad, B. A., & Krone, R. M. (2012). *Managing for quality in higher education: a system perspective.* Accessed at www.bookboon.com

Mahdiuon, R., Masoumi, D., & Farasatkhah, M. (2017). Quality Improvement in Virtual Higher Education: A Grounded Theory Approach. *Turkish Online Journal of Distance Education, 18*(1), 111–131. doi:10.17718/tojde.285720

Maheshwari, S., & Ganesh, M. P. (2006). Ethics in organizations: The case of tata steel. *Vikalpa, 31*(2), 77–87. doi:10.1177/0256090920060205

Maleyeff, J., & Kaminsky, F. (2002). Six sigma and introductory statistics education. *Education + Training, 44*(2), 82–89. doi:10.1108/00400910210419982

Mallinckrodt, B., Miles, J. R., & Levy, J. J. (2014). The scientist-practitioner-advocate model: Addressing contemporary training needs for social justice advocacy. *Training and Education in Professional Psychology, 8*(4), 303–311. doi:10.1037/tep0000045

Manning, G., & Curtis, K. (2009). *The Art of Leadership.* Boston: McGraw-Hill Education.

Manoj, K.V. (2016). *Importance of Leadership in Total Quality Management.* Vistas of Education. Mizoram University.

Marcoulides, G. A., & Heck, R. H. (1993). Organizational culture and performance: Proposing and testing a model. *Organization Science, 4*(2), 209–225. doi:10.1287/orsc.4.2.209

Marginson, S. (2011). Higher education and public good. *Higher Education Quarterly, 65*(4), 411–433. doi:10.1111/j.1468-2273.2011.00496.x

Martens, E., & Prosser, M. (1998). What constitutes high quality teaching and learning and how to assure it? *Quality Assurance in Education, 6*(1), 28–36. doi:10.1108/09684889810200368

Martin, M., & Parik, S. (2017). *Quality management in higher education: Developments and drivers: Results from an international survey.* Paris, France: International Institute for Educational Planning, UNESCO.

Martin, M., & Stella, A. (2007). *External quality assurance in higher education: Making choices.* Paris: UNESCO International Institute for Educational Planning.

Maryam, Y., Mohammad, S., & Mohammadreza, S. (2018). What factors affect education quality in higher education? *International Journal of Management and Applied Science, 4*(2), 85–88.

Mata, L., Lazar, I., Nedeff, V., & Lazar, G. (2013). Eno interactive whiteboards as an innovative eco-technology solution in teaching science and technological subjects. *APCBEE Procedia, 5*, 312–316. doi:10.1016/j.apcbee.2013.05.053

Matei, L., & Iwinska, J. (2016). *Quality Assurance in Higher Education: A practical handbook.* Academic Press.

Materu, P. (2007). *Higher Education Quality Assurance in sub-Saharan Africa; status, challenges, opportunities and promising practices.* Washington, DC: The World Bank. doi:10.1596/978-0-8213-7272-2

Maxwell, J. C. (2007). *21 irrefutable laws of leaderhsip.* Nashville TN: Thomas Nelson.

Mayer, R., & Gavin, M. (1999). *Trust for management and performance: Who minds the shop while the employees watch the boss?* Paper presented at the Annual Meeting of the Academy of Management, Chicago, IL.

Mayer, R. C., & Davis, J. H. (1999). The effect of the performance appraisal system on trust for management: A field quasi-experiment. *The Journal of Applied Psychology*, *84*(1), 123–136. doi:10.1037/0021-9010.84.1.123

Mayer, R. C., Davis, J. H., & Schoorman, F. D. (1995). An integrative model of organizational trust. *Academy of Management Review*, *20*(3), 709–734. doi:10.5465/amr.1995.9508080335

McAdam, R., & Bannister, A. (2001). Business Performance Measurement and Change within a TQM Framework. *International Journal of Operations & Production Management*, *21*(1/2), 88–107. doi:10.1108/01443570110358477

McAllister, D. J. (1995). Affect- and cognition-based trust as foundations for interpersonal cooperation in organizations. *Academy of Management Journal*, *38*, 24–59.

McCartt, A. (1983). *The application of social judgment analysis to library faculty tenure decisions*. Academic Press.

McCleskey, J. A. (2014). Situational, transformational, and transactional leadership and leadership development. *Journal of Business Studies Quarterly*, *5*(4), 117–130.

McCormick, B. W., Guay, R. P., Colbert, A. E., & Stewart, G. L. (2019). Proactive personality and proactive behaviour: Perspectives on person-situation interactions. *Journal of Occupational and Organizational Psychology*, *92*(1), 30–51. doi:10.1111/joop.12234

McDowell, D. (2010). *Core Values and Professional Integrity*. Retrieved from http://www.mncap.org/protocol/CoreValues_ProfIntegrity.pdf

McKinnon, K. R., Walker, S. H., & Davis, D. (2000). *Benchmarking: A manual for Australian universities*. Canberra, Australia: Department of Education, Training and Youth Affairs, Higher Education Division.

McLean, P. (1997). The fourth arm of justice: The art and science of revenge. In Research on Negotiation in Organizations. JAI Press.

Medlin, B., & Green, K.W., Jr. (2003). Ethics in small business: attitudes and perceptions of owners/managers. *Academy of Entrepreneurship Journal*, *6*, 513-518.

Mehra, S., Hoffman, J., & Sirias, D. (2001). TQM as a Management Strategy for The Next Millenia. *International Journal of Operations & Production Management*, *21*(5/6), 855–876. doi:10.1108/01443570110390534

Melé, D. (2009). *Business Ethics in Action. Seeking Human Excellence in Organizations*. Hampshire, UK: Palgrave Macmillan. doi:10.1007/978-1-137-07468-3

Menon, M. E., Terka, D. G., & Gibbs, P. (2014). *Using data to improve higher education: Research, policy and practice. Global perspectives on higher education* (Vol. 29). Sense Publishers. doi:10.1007/978-94-6209-794-0

Messah, B. O., & Mucai, P. G. (2011). Factors affecting implementation of strategic plans in government tertiary institution: Survey of selected technical training institutions. *European Journal of Business and Management*, *3*(3), 85–105.

Michaela, M., & Shreya, P. (2017). *Quality management in higher Education: development and drivers: results from an international survey*. International Institute for Educational Planning. Available at: https://unesdoc.unesco.org

Middlehurst, R. (1997). Reinventing Higher Education: The leadership challenge. *Quality in Higher Education*, *3*(2), 183–198. doi:10.1080/1353832970030208

Mitchell, T. (2015). *Innovation and quality higher education*. Retrieved May 26, 2019 from https://blog.ed.gov/2015/07/innovation-and-quality-in-higher-education/

Mitchell, M., & Theobald, K. (2002). Mentoring: Improving transition to practice. *The Australian Journal of Advanced Nursing, 20*(1), 27. PMID:12405280

Mitra, A. (2004). Six-sigma education: A critical role for academia. *The TQM Magazine, 16*(4), 293–302. doi:10.1108/09544780410541963

Mok, K. (2005). The quest for a world class university. *Quality Assurance in Education, 11*(3), 277–300. doi:10.1108/09684880510626575

Moolenaar, N. M., Daly, A. J., & Sleegers, P. J. (2010). Occupying the principal position: Examining relationships between transformational leadership, Social network position and school's innovative climate. *Educational Administrational Quarterly, 46*(5), 623-670.

Moore, M. R., & Diamond, M. A. (2000). *Academic Leadership: Turning Vision into Reality*. The Ernst and Young Foundation.

Mooring, Q. E. (2016). Recruitment, advising, and retention programs—Challenges and solutions to the international problem of poor nursing student retention: A narrative literature review. *Nurse Education Today, 40*, 204–208. doi:10.1016/j.nedt.2016.03.003 PMID:27125174

Morgan, R. B. (1989). Reliability and validity of a factor analytically derived measure of leadership behavior and characteristics. *Educational and Psychological Measurement, 49*(4), 911–919. doi:10.1177/001316448904900414

Morrison, A. (2001). Integrity and global leadership. *Journal of Business Ethics, 31*(1), 65–76. doi:10.1023/A:1010789324414

Motala, S. (2001). Quality and indicators of quality in South African education: A critical appraisal. *International Journal of Educational Development, 21*(1), 61–78. doi:10.1016/S0738-0593(00)00014-6

Moxley, D., Najor-Durack, A., & Dumbrigue, C. (2013). *Keeping students in higher education: Successful practices and strategies for retention*. Routledge. doi:10.4324/9780203062401

Mullins, L. J. (2013). *Management and Organizational Behaviour* (12th ed.). London: Pearson.

Murtaza, N. (2011). Pursuing self-interest or self-actualization? From capitalism to a steady-state, wisdom economy. *Ecological Economics, 70*(4), 577–584. doi:10.1016/j.ecolecon.2010.10.012

Mutula, S. M. (2009). Challenges of Postgraduate Research: Global Context, African Perspectives. Keynote Address Delivered at the University of Zululand. *10th DLIS Annual Conference*.

Nadim, Z. S., & Al-Hinai, A. H. (2012). Critical Success Factors of TQM in Higher Education Institutions. *International Journal of Applied Sciences and Management, 2*(12), 19–32.

Nair, S. R. (2014). Ethics in higher education. In *Handbook of research on higher education in the MENA Region: Policy and practice* (pp. 230–260). IGI Global. doi:10.4018/978-1-4666-6198-1.ch011

Nakabugo, M. G., & Ssebunga Masembe, C. (2004). Supervisor-Supervisee relationship: a rose without thorns? In Graduate studies at Makerere University: A book of readings. Nelson.

National Council for Higher Education (NCHE). (2009). *Quality assurance system for higher education in Namibia*. Windhoek, Namibia.

National Planning Commission Secretariat. (2004). *Vision 2030*. Windhoek, Namibia: National Planning Commission, GRN.

Neihart, M. F., & Ling, L. (2017). Quality assurance in teacher education in Singapore. In O. S. Tan, W. C. Liu, & E. L. Low (Eds.), *Teacher Education in the 21st Century*. Singapore: Springer. doi:10.1007/978-981-10-3386-5_16

Nel, H. (2016). The role of institutional research in support of strategic planning. In J. Botha & N. Muller (Eds.), *Institutional research in South African higher education*. Stellenbosch: Sun Press. doi:10.18820/9781928357186/06

Newman, T., Trimmer, K., & Padró, F. F. (2019). The Need for Case Studies to Illustrate Quality Practice: Teaching in Higher Education to Ensure Quality of Entry Level Professionals. In *Ensuring Quality in Professional Education* (Vol. 1, pp. 1–17). Cham: Palgrave Macmillan. doi:10.1007/978-3-030-01096-6_1

Nguyen, P., Terlouw, C., & Pilot, A. (2006). Culturally appropriate pedagogy: The case of group learning in a Confucian Heritage Culture context. *Intercultural Education*, *17*(1), 1–19. doi:10.1080/14675980500502172

Nickel, S. (2011). *Strategic management in higher education institutions: Approaches, processes and tools*. Centre for Higher Education Development.

Nikitina, T., & Lapina, I. (2017). Overview of Trends and Developments in Business Education. *Proceedings of the 21st World Multi-Conference on Systemics, Cybernetics and Informatics (WMSCI 2017)*, 2, 56-61.

Nock, M. K., Michel, B. D., & Photos, V. I. (2007). Single-case research designs. Handbook of research methods in abnormal and clinical psychology, 337-350.

Noe, R. (2005). *Employee training and development*. New York, NY: McGraw-Hill/Irwin.

Northouse, P. G. (2004). *Leadership: Theory and Practice* (3rd ed.). Thousand Oaks, CA: Sage Publication.

Northouse, P. G. (2004). *Leadership: theory and practice*. Los Angeles, CA: SAGE Publications, Inc.

O'Mahony, K., & Garavan, T. N. (2012). Implementing a quality management framework in a higher education organization. *Quality Assurance in Education*, *20*(2), 184–200. doi:10.1108/09684881211219767

O'Neil, I., & Ucbasaran, D. (2010). *Individual identity and sustainable entrepreneurship: The role of authenticity*. London: Institute of Small Business & Entrepreneurship Conference.

O'Neill, M. A., & Palmer, A. (2004). Importance-performance analysis: A useful tool for directing continuous quality improvement in higher education. *Quality Assurance in Education*, *12*(1), 39–52. doi:10.1108/09684880410517423

O'Regan, K. (2002). Producing competent graduates: The primary social responsibility of law schools. *South African Law Journal*, *119*, 242.

Oakland, J. (2008). *Total Quality Management*. Oxford, UK: Heinemann Professional Publishing.

Oakland, J. S. (2001). *Total Organizational Excellence: Achieving World Class Performance*. Oxford, UK: Butterworth-Heinemam. doi:10.1016/B978-0-7506-5271-1.50004-1

Oddo, A. R. (1997). A framework for teaching business ethics. *Journal of Business Ethics*, *16*(3), 293–297. doi:10.1023/A:1017951729585

Odhiambo, G. (2014). The challenges and future of public higher education leadership in Kenya. *Journal of Higher Education Policy and Management*, *36*(2), 183–195. doi:10.1080/1360080X.2014.884676

Oduma, C. A. (2014). Quality assurance in education: The role of ICT and quality control measures in tertiary institutions in Nigeria. *AFRREV STECH: An International Journal of Science and Technology*, *3*(2), 136–158. doi:10.4314tech.v3i2.9

Oduro, G. K., & Dachi, H. (2008). *Educational Leadership and Quality Education in Disadvantaged Communities in Ghana and Tanzania*. The Commonwealth Council for Educational Administration & Management Conference, International Convention Centre, Durban, South Africa.

OECD. (2006). Quality Management in Higher Education: A review of International Issues and Practice. *The International Journal for Quality and Standards*.

OECD. (2014). *Innovation strategy for education and training*. Retrieved March 24, 2019 from http://www.oecd.org/education/ceri/IS%20Project_Conference%20Brochure_FINAL.pdf

OECD. (2016). Education at a glance 2016: Indicator B1 and B5. Paris, France: OECD.

Oh, H. (2009). Service Quality, Customer Satisfaction, and Customer Value: A holistic perspective. *Hospital Management*, *18*(1), 67–82. doi:10.1016/S0278-4319(98)00047-4

Okojie, J. A. (2008, June). *Licensing, accreditation and quality assurance in Nigerian Universities: Achievements and challenges*. Paper presented at a session of the 2008 Council of Higher Education Accreditation (CHEA) summer workshop.

Oldfield, B., & Baron, S. (1998). *Is the service scape important to student perceptions of service quality?* (Research Paper). Manchester Metropolitan University.

Onwuegbuzie, A. J., & Rebecca, F. (2016). Seven Steps to a Comprehensive Literature Review: A Multimodal and Cultural Approach. *Sage (Atlanta, Ga.)*.

Ornstein, A. C., & Hunkins, F. P. (2004). *Curriculum foundations, principles, and issues* (4th ed.). Boston: Pearson Education, Inc.

Orpen, C. (1997). The effects of formal mentoring on employee work motivation, organizational commitment and job performance. *The Learning Organization*, *4*(2), 53–60. doi:10.1108/09696479710160906

Osseo-Asare, A. E., & Longbottom, D. (2002). The need for education and training in the use of the EFQM model for quality management in UK higher education institutions. *Quality Assurance in Education*, *10*(1), 26–36. doi:10.1108/09684880210416085

Osseo-Asare, A., Longbottom, D., & Murphy, W. (2005). Leadership best practices for sustaining quality in UK higher education from the perspective of the EFQM excellence model. *Quality Assurance in Education*, *13*(2), 148–170. doi:10.1108/09684880510594391

Ost, J. H., & Da Silveira, C. G. (2018). Evaluation of the transition process from ISO 9001:2008 to ISO 9001:2015: A study focused on chemical companies in the State of Rio Grande do Sul, Brazil. *Gestão & Produção*, *25*(4), 726–736. doi:10.1590/0104-530x4089-17

Owens, J., Kottwitz, C., Tiedt, J., & Ramirez, J. (2018). Strategies to attain faculty work-life balance. *Building Healthy Academic Communities Journal*, *2*(2), 58–73. doi:10.18061/bhac.v2i2.6544

Owlia, M., & Aspinwall, E. (1996). Quality in higher education. *Total Quality Management*, *7*(2), 161–172. doi:10.1080/09544129650034918

Oxford Dictionaries. (2011) Retrieved from http://oxforddictionaries.com

Padilla, A., Hogan, R., & Kaiser, R. B. (2007). The toxic triangle: Destructive leaders, vulnerable followers, and conducive environments. *The Leadership Quarterly*, *18*(3), 176–194. doi:10.1016/j.leaqua.2007.03.001

Page, R., & Curry, A. (2000). TQM – a holistic view. *The TQM Magazine*, *12*(1), 11–18. doi:10.1108/09544780010287159

Compilation of References

Paladino, M., Debeljuh, P. & Del Bosco, P. (2005). *Integridad: respuesta superadora a los dilemas éticos del hombre de empresa.* Academic Press.

Palepu, A., Friedman, R. H., Barnett, R. C., Carr, P. L., Ash, A. S., Szalacha, L., & Moskowitz, M. A. (1998). Junior faculty members' mentoring relationships and their professional development in US medical schools. *Academic Medicine: Journal of the Association of American Medical Colleges, 73*(3), 318-323.

Palmer, D. E. (2015). *Handbook of research on business ethics and corporate responsibilities.* IGI Global. doi:10.4018/978-1-4666-7476-9

Palomba, C. A., & Banta, T. W. (1999). Assessment Essentials: Planning, Implementing, and Improving Assessment in Higher Education. Jossey-Bass, Inc.

Papanthymou, A., & Darra, M. (2017). Quality management in higher education: Review and perspectives. *Higher Education Studies, 7*(3), 132–147. doi:10.5539/hes.v7n3p132

Pappas, C. (2015). *The top learning management systems statistics and facts for 2015 you need to know.* Retrieved March 19, 2019 from https://elearningindustry.com/top-lms-statistics-and-facts-for-2015

Parachuri, V. (2013). *On the automated scoring of essays and the lessons learned along the way.* Retrieved March 22, 2019 from vicparachuri.com

Parker, S. C. (2009). *Intrapreneurship or Entrepreneurship*. IZA Discussion Paper, 4195. Bonn, Germany: Forschungsinstitut zur Zukunft der Arbeit.

Parri, J. (2002). Quality in higher education. Vadyba Management.

Parry, K., & Proctor-Thomson, S. B. (2002). Perceived integrity of transformational leaders in organizational settings. *Journal of Business Ethics, 35*(2), 75–96. doi:10.1023/A:1013077109223

Paulsen, M. F. (2003). Experiences with Learning Management Systems in 113 European Institutions. *Journal of Educational Technology & Society, 6*(4), 134–148.

Pavel, A. P., Fruth, A., & Neacsu, M. N. (2015). ICT and e-learning–catalysts for innovation and quality in higher education. *Procedia Economics and Finance, 23*, 704–711. doi:10.1016/S2212-5671(15)00409-8

Pensiero, D., & McIlveen, P. (2006). Developing an integrated approach to graduates' transition into the workforce. In *Proceedings of the 2nd Biennial Conference of the Academy of World Business, Marketing and Management Development: Business Across Borders in the 21st Century* (Vol. 2). Academy of World Business, Marketing and Management Development.

Pereira, L. (2012). *A critical realist exploration of the implementation of a new curriculum in Swaziland* (Doctoral Thesis). Rhodes University, Grahamstown. Available from South East Academic Libraries Systems (SEALS Digital Commons), http://hdl.handle.net/10962/d1003365

Perry, L. (2004). Instructional effectiveness: A real-time feedback approach using statistical process control (spc). *Proceedings of the 2004 American society for engineering education annual conference & exposition.*

Petrovskiy, I. V., & Agapova, E. N. (2016). Strategies of Raising the Quality of Higher Education and Attaining Equality of Educational Opportunities. *International Journal of Environmental and Science Education, 11*(9), 2519–2537.

Pettinger, R. (2007). *Introduction to Management* (4th ed.). Basingstoke, UK: Palgrave MacMillan. doi:10.1007/978-1-137-21899-5

Petty, M. M., Beadles, N. A. II, Lowery, C. M., Chapman, D. F., & Connell, D. W. (1995). Relationships between organizational culture and organizational performance. *Psychological Reports*, *76*(2), 483–492. doi:10.2466/pr0.1995.76.2.483 PMID:8559874

Phillips, L., & Jorgensen, M. W. (2004). *Discourse analysis: as theory and method*. London: SAGE.

Pierce, M. R. (1995, Winter). The university selection process: A Canadian perspective. *Info*.

Pifer, M. J., Baker, V. L., & Lunsford, L. G. (2019). Culture, colleagues, and leadership: The academic department as a location of faculty experiences in liberal arts colleges. *Review of Higher Education*, *42*(2), 537–564.

Pinchot, G. (1985). *Intrapreneuring: Why You Don't Have to Leave the Corporation to Become an Entrepreneur*. New York: Harper & Row.

Pintrich, P. R., & De Groot, E. V. (1990). Motivational and self-regulated learning components of classroom academic performance. *Journal of Educational Psychology*, *82*(1), 33–40. doi:10.1037/0022-0663.82.1.33

Pitsoe, V. J., & Maila, M. W. (2017). Quality and quality assurance in open distance learning (ODL) discourse: Trends, challenges and perspectives. *The Anthropologist*, *18*(1), 251–258. doi:10.1080/09720073.2014.11891542

Plessis, M. D. (2007). The role of knowledge management in innovation. *Journal of Knowledge Management*, *11*(4), 20–29. doi:10.1108/13673270710762684

Pojman, L. P. (1995). *Ethical theory: Classical and contemporary readings* (2nd ed.). Belmont, CA: Wadsworth.

Poulsen, K. M. (2006). Implementing successful mentoring programs: Career definition vs mentoring approach. *Industrial and Commercial Training*, *38*(5), 251–258. doi:10.1108/00197850610677715

Poulton, M. S. (2005). Organizational storytelling, ethics and morality: How stories frame limits of behavior in organizations. *EJBO-Electronic Journal of Business Ethics and Organization Studies*. Retrieved from http://classics.mit.edu

Pounder, J. (1999). Institutional performance in higher education: Is quality a relevant concept? *Quality Assurance in Education*, *7*(3), 156–165. doi:10.1108/09684889910281719

Pratasavitskaya, H., & Stensaker, B. R. (2010). Quality management in higher education: Towards a better understanding of an emerging field. *Quality in Higher Education*, *16*(1), 37–50. doi:10.1080/13538321003679465

Pratt, M. G., Rockmann, K. W., & Kaufmann, J. B. (2006). Constructing Professional Identity: The Role of Work and Identity Learning Cycles in the Customization of Identity Among Medical Residents. *Academy of Management Journal*, *49*(2), 235–262. doi:10.5465/amj.2006.20786060

Priestley, M. (2002). Global discourse and national reconstruction: The impact of globalisation on curriculum policy. *Curriculum Journal*, *13*(1), 121–138. doi:10.1080/09585170110115295

Prottas, D. J., Shea-Van Fossen, R. J., Cleaver, C. M., & Andreassi, J. K. (2017). Relationships among faculty perceptions of their tenure process and their commitment and engagement. *Journal of Applied Research in Higher Education*, *9*(2), 242–254. doi:10.1108/JARHE-08-2016-0054

Putra, E. D., & Cho, S. (2019). Characteristics of small business leadership from employees' perspective: A qualitative study. *International Journal of Hospitality Management*, *78*, 36–46. doi:10.1016/j.ijhm.2018.11.011

Quinn, L. (2012). Understanding resistance: An analysis of discourses in academic. *Studies in Higher Education*, *37*(1), 69–83. doi:10.1080/03075079.2010.497837

Radius, S. M., Galer-Unti, R. A., & Tappe, M. K. (2009). Educating for advocacy: Recommendations for professional preparation and development based on a needs and capacity assessment of health education faculty. *Health Promotion Practice*, *10*(1), 83–91. doi:10.1177/1524839907306407 PMID:18381970

Ragins, B. R. (2016). From the ordinary to the extraordinary. *Organizational Dynamics*, *45*(3), 228–244. doi:10.1016/j.orgdyn.2016.07.008

Ragins, B. R., Cotton, J. L., & Miller, J. S. (2000). Marginal mentoring: The effects of type of mentor, quality of relationship, and program design on work and career attitudes. *Academy of Management Journal*, *43*(6), 1177–1194.

Raifsnider, R., & Kurt, D. (2004). *Lean Six Sigma in higher education: Applying proven methodologies to improve quality, remove waste, and quantify opportunities in colleges and universities.* Xerox The Document Company, White paper.

Rajala, R., & Westerlund, M. (2007). Business models–a new perspective on firms' assets and capabilities: Observations from the Finnish software industry. *The International Journal of Entrepreneurship and Innovation*, *8*(2), 115–125. doi:10.5367/000000007780808039

Rajesh, B. (2008). Study on Indian Higher Education: A TQM Perspective. *Researchers World: Journal of Arts, Science and Commerce*, *4*(2), 53–65.

Ramen, M., & Jugurnath, B. (2016). Accounting teaching techniques with the advent of technology: Empirical evidence from Mauritius. *Proceedings of the Fifth Asia-Pacific Conference on Global Business, Economics, Finance and Social Sciences.* Retrieved from www.globalbizresearch.org

Ramesh, N., & Ravi, A. (2016). The 5S route for safety management. *International Journal of Business Excellence*, *10*(3), 283–300. doi:10.1504/IJBEX.2016.10000125

Ramsden, P. (1987). Improving teaching and learning in higher education: The case for a relational perspective. *Studies in Higher Education*, *12*(3), 275–286. doi:10.1080/03075078712331378062

Ramsden, P. (1998). Managing the effective University. *Higher Education Research & Development*, *17*(3), 347–370. doi:10.1080/0729436980170307

Ramsden, P. (2000). *Learning to lead in higher education*. London: Routledge.

Ramsden, P., Prosser, M., Trigwell, K., & Martin, E. (2007). University teachers' experiences of academic leadership and their approaches to teaching. *Learning and Instruction*, *17*(2), 140–155. doi:10.1016/j.learninstruc.2007.01.004

Raybould, M., & Wilkins, H. (2005). Over qualified and under experienced: Turning graduates into hospitality managers. *International Journal of Contemporary Hospitality Management*, *17*(3), 203–216. doi:10.1108/09596110510591891

Razaki, K. A., & Aydin, S. (2011). The Feasibility of Using Business Process Improvement Approaches to Improve an Academic Department. *Journal of Higher Education Theory and Practice*, *11*(2), 19–32.

Reich, J. (2016). *Four ways school leaders can support innovation*. Retrieved March 24, 2019 from https://blogs.edweek.org/edweek/edtechresearcher/2016/11/four_ways_school_leaders_can_support_innovation.html

Rena, R. (2010). *Emerging Trend of Higher Education in Developing countries*. Scientific Annals of the 'Alexandru Ioan cuza' University of Iasi: Economic Sciences Series.

Rice, G. K., & Taylor, D. C. (2003). Continuous –Improvement strategies in Higher Education: A progress Report. *EDUCAUSE-Centre for Applied Research*. Available from http://assessment.tcu.edu/wp-content/uploads/2016/06/ERB0320.pdf

Rich, D. (2006). Academic leadership and the restructuring of higher education. *New Directions for Higher Education*, *2006*(134), 37–48. doi:10.1002/he.215

Rickards, R. C. (2003). Setting benchmarks and evaluating balanced scorecards with data envelopment analysis. *Benchmarking:an International Journal*, *10*(3), 226–245. doi:10.1108/14635770310477762

Ritchie, L., & Dale, B. (2000). Self-assessment using the business excellence model: A study of practice and process. *International Journal of Production Economics*, *66*(3), 241–254. doi:10.1016/S0925-5273(99)00130-9

Rizvi, F. (2000). International education and the production of global imagination. In N. C. Burbules & C. A. Torres (Eds.), *Globalization and education: critical perspectives* (pp. 205–225). New York: Routledge.

Robbins, S. P., Timothy, A., & Judge, T. A. (2013). *Organizational Behavior* (15th ed.). Boston: Pearson.

Robbins, S., Marsh, T., Cacioppe, R., & Millet, B. (1994). *Organisational behaviour: Concepts, controversies and applications*. New York, NY: Prentice Hall.

Roberts, N., & Watson, D. (2016). Re-imagining graduate supervision. *Caribbean Teaching Scholar*, *6*, 27–42.

Robertson, S., Novelli, M., Dale, R., Tikly, L., Dachi, H., & Alphonce, N. (2007). *Globalisation, education and development: ideas, actors and dynamics*. DFID Publications. Retrieved February 24, 2009, from http://www.dfid.gov.uk/pubs/files/global-education-dev-68.pdf

Roberts, P., & Tennant, C. (2003). Application of the Hoshin Kanri methodology at a higher education establishment in the UK. *The TQM Magazine*, *15*(2), 82–87. doi:10.1108/09544780310461080

Robert, V. H., & Mary, C. H. (1995). Continuous Quality Improvement in Higher Education. *International Statistical Review*, *63*(1), 35–48. doi:10.2307/1403776

Robin, M. (2015, August 4). *Better future*. Retrieved August 4, 2015, from New Media Consortium: go.nmc.org/betterfuture

Rodríguez Ordoñez, J. A. (2004). Hacia la integralidad de la enseñanza y la práctica profesional en geotecnia. *Ing. Univ. Bogotá*, *8*(2), 159-171.

Roe, K. (2014). *Leadership: Practice and perspectives*. Oxford University Press.

Roes, K. C., & Dorr, D. (1997). Implementing statistical process control in service processes. *International Journal of Quality Science*, *2*(3), 149–166.

Roffe, I. M. (1998). Conceptual problems of continuous quality improvement and innovation in higher education. *Quality Assurance in Education*, *6*(2), 74–82. doi:10.1108/09684889810205723

Roopa, M.S., Pattar, S., & Buyya, R., Iyengar, S.S., & Patnaik, L.M. (2019). Social Internet of Things (SIoT): Foundations, thrust areas, a systematic review, and future directions. *Computer Communications*, *139*, 32–57. doi:10.1016/j.comcom.2019.03.009

Rosa, M. J. P., Saraiva, P. M., & Diz, H. (2003). Excellence in Portuguese higher education institutions. *Total Quality Management & Business Excellence*, *14*(2), 189–197. doi:10.1080/1478336032000051377

Rosa, M. J., Sarrico, C. S., & Amaral, A. (2012). *Implementing quality management systems in higher education institutions*. University of Lisbon. Alberto Amaral. Centre for Research in Higher Education Policies.

Rost, K., Salomo, S., & Osterloh, M. (2008). CEO appointments and the loss of firm-specific knowledge - putting integrity back into hiring decisions. *Corporate Ownership and Control*, *5*(3), 86–98. doi:10.22495/cocv5i3p10

Ruisi, M., Fasone, V., & Paternostro, S. (2009). *Respect and hope a binomial relationship supporting the creation of a true entrepreneurial model*. Paper presented at the European SPES Forum, Respect and Economic Democracy, Catania.

Rust, C. (2002). The impact of assessment on student learning: How can the research literature practically help to inform the development of departmental assessment strategies and learner-centred assessment practices? *Active Learning in Higher Education*, *3*(2), 145–158. doi:10.1177/1469787402003002004

Rutherford, D. G., & Wiegenstein, J. (1985). The mentoring process in hotel managers' careers. *The Cornell Hotel and Restaurant Administration Quarterly*, *25*(4), 16–23. doi:10.1177/001088048502500406

Ryan, T. (2015). Quality assurance in higher education: A review of literature. *Higher Learning Research Communications.*, *5*(4), 1–12. doi:10.18870/hlrc.v5i4.257

Sadeh, E., & Garkaz, M. (2015). Explaining the mediating role of service quality between quality management enablers and students' satisfaction in higher education institutes: The perception of managers. *Total Quality Management & Business Excellence*, *26*(12), 1335–1356. doi:10.1080/14783363.2014.931065

Saini, D. (2017). Relevance of teaching values and ethics in management education. In *Management Education for Global Leadership* (pp. 90–111). IGI Global. doi:10.4018/978-1-5225-1013-0.ch005

Sakthivel, P. B., & Raju, R. (2006). Conceptualizing total quality management in engineering education and developing a TQM Educational Excellence Model. *Total Quality Management & Business Excellence*, *17*(7), 913–934. doi:10.1080/14783360600595476

Salahedin, S.I. (2009). Problems, sucessess factors and benefits of QCs implementation a case of QASCO. *Total Quality Management Journal*.

Salam, S. (2000). Foster trust through competence, honesty, and integrity. In E. Locke (Ed.), *Handbook of principles of organizational behavior* (pp. 274–288). Malden, MA: Blackwell.

Sallis, E. (2002). *Total quality management in education* (3rd ed.). London: Stylus Publishing Inc.

Sallis, E. (2002). *Total Quality Management in Education*. Kogan Page Publishers.

Sally, S. (2002). *Total Quality Management in education*. Stylus Publishing.

Salviano, C. F., & Figueiredo, A. M. C. (2008, July). *Unified Basic Concepts for Process Capability Models*. SEKE.

Sambrook, S. (2018). *Managing the psychological contract within Doctoral Supervisory relationships*. Research Gate.

Sanchez, P. M., & Elena, S. (2006). Intellectual capital in universities. *Journal of Intellectual Capital*, *7*(4), 529–548. doi:10.1108/14691930610709158

Sanchez, P. M., Elena, S., & Castrillo, R. (2009). Intellectual capital dynamics in universities: A reporting model. *Journal of Intellectual Capital*, *10*(2), 307–324. doi:10.1108/14691930910952687

Sanyal, B. C. (2013). *Fundamentals of teacher education development 5: quality assurance of teacher education in Africa*. Addis Ababa: UNESCO: International Institute for Capacity Building in Africa.

Sarita & Sania. (2016). Quality assurance in teacher education: a critical issue. *International Journal of Applied Research*, *2*(8), 735-739.

Sathye, M. (2004). *Leadership in Higher Education: A Qualitative Study*. Forum Qualitative Sozialfrschung/Forum: Qualitative. *Social Research*, *5*(3), 26. Retrieved from http://nbn-resolving.de/urn:nbn:0114-fqs0403266

Sayer, A. (2000). *Realism and social science*. London: Sage Publications. doi:10.4135/9781446218730

Scerri, M. A., Jenkins, J. M., & Lovell, G. (2017). A grounded theory model of service language in Australia's luxury hotels. *Journal of Hospitality and Tourism Management, 33*, 82–92. doi:10.1016/j.jhtm.2017.09.003

Schargel, F. P. (1994). Total quality in education. *Quality Progress, 26*(10), 67–71.

Schargel, F., & Smink, J. (2014). *Strategies to help solve our school dropout problem*. Routledge. doi:10.4324/9781315854090

Schein, E. H. (1992). *Organizational culture and leadership*. San Francisco: Jossey-Bass.

Schell, E. E. (1998). *Gypsy academics and mother-teachers: Gender, contingent labor, and writing instruction*. Portsmouth, NH: Boynton/Cook Publishers.

Schrodt, P., Cawyer, C. S., & Sanders, R. (2003). An examination of academic mentoring behaviors and new faculty members' satisfaction with socialization and tenure and promotion processes. *Communication Education, 52*(1), 17–29. doi:10.1080/03634520302461

Schulz, W. (2016), *Becoming Citizens in a Changing World: IEA International Civic and Citizenship Education Study 2016 International Report*. IEA. Retrieved from http://iccs.iea.nl/fileadmin/user_upload/Editor_Group/Downloads/ICCS_2016_International_report.pdf

Schweisfurth, M. (2013a). Learner-Centred education in international perspective. *Journal of International and Comparative Education, 2*(1), 1–8. doi:10.14425/00.45.70

Schweisfurth, M. (2013b). *Learner-centered education in international perspective: Whose pedagogy for whose development?* London: Routledge. doi:10.4324/9780203817438

Scollon, R., & Scollon, Z. (1981). *Narrative, literacy and face in interethnic communication*. Norwood, MA: Ablex Publishing Corporation.

Seldin, P. (1980). *Successful Faculty Evaluation Programs. A Practical Guide to Improve Faculty Performance and Promotion/Tenure Decisions*. Academic Press.

Senge, P. (1990). *The Fifth Discipline*. New York: Doubleday.

Senge, P. (1990). *The fifth discipline: The art and practice of the learning organization*. New York: Doubleday.

Senge, P., Kleiner, A., Ross, R., Roth, G., & Smith, B. (1999). *The Dance of Change*. New York: Currency Doubleday.

Senthilkumar, N., & Arulraj, A. (2011). SQM-HEI – determination of service quality measurement of higher education in India. *Journal of Modelling in Management, 6*(1), 60–78. doi:10.1108/17465661111112502

Seshadri, D. V. R., Raghavan, A., & Hegde, S. (2007). Business ethics: The next frontier for globalizing indian companies. *Vikalpa, 32*(3), 61–79. doi:10.1177/0256090920070305

Seymour, D. T. (1992). On Q: Causing quality in higher education. Macmillan Publishing Company.

Shaha, M., Vu, H. Y. & Stanford, S. (2019). *Perspectives: policy and practice in higher education*. Academic Press.

Shah, M., & Brown, G. (2009). The Rise of Private Higher Education in Australia: Maintaining Quality Outcomes and Future Challenges. *Proceedings of the Australian Universities Quality Forum, 14350*, 13.

Shakespeare, W. (1914). *The Oxford Shakespeare: The complete works of William Shakespeare. Hamlet, Act II*. London: Oxford University Press.

Shalender, K., & Yadav, R. K. (2019). Strategic Flexibility, Manager Personality, and Firm Performance: The Case of Indian Automobile Industry. *Global Journal of Flexible Systems Management, 20*(1), 77–90. doi:10.100740171-018-0204-x

Shapiro, H., Haahr, J. H., Bayer, I., & Boekholt, P. (2007). *Background paper on innovation and education.* Danish Technological Institute and Technopolis for the European Commission, DG Education & Culture in the context of a planned Green Paper on innovation.

Shapiro, H. N. (2006). Promotion & tenure & the scholarship of teaching & learning. *Change: The Magazine of Higher Learning, 38*(2), 38–43. doi:10.3200/CHNG.38.2.38-43

Shawyun, T. (2016). Strategic planning as an essential for quality assurance. *Journal of Institutional Research South East Asia, 14*(1), 42–70.

Sherr, L. A., & Gregory Lozier, G. (1991). Total quality management in higher education. *New Directions for Institutional Research, 1991*(71), 3–11. doi:10.1002/ir.37019917103

Sidhu, G. K., Kaur, S Fook, C. Y., & Yunus, F. W. (2013). Postgraduate supervision: Comparing student perspectives from Malaysia and the United Kingdom. *Social and Behavioral Sciences, 123,* 151 – 159.

Simmonds, D., & Zammit Lupi, A. M. (2010). The matching process in e-mentoring: A case study in luxury hotels. *Journal of European Industrial Training, 34*(4), 300–316. doi:10.1108/03090591011039063

Simonova, A. A., & Fomenko, S. L. (2017). Evolution of integrated quality management system at higher school. *Quality-Access to Success, 18*(161), 126–134.

Simons, T. L. (1999). Behavioral Integrity as a Critical Ingredient for Transformational Leadership. *Journal of Organizational Change Management, 12*(2), 89-104.

Simons, T. L. (2002). Behavioral Integrity: The Perceived Alignment Between Manager's Words and Deeds as a Research Focus. *Organization Science, 13*(1), 18–35. doi:10.1287/orsc.13.1.18.543

Singh, J., Rastogi, V., & Sharma, R. (2014). Implementation of 5S practices: A review. *Uncertain Supply Chain Management, 2*(3), 155–162. doi:10.5267/j.uscm.2014.5.002

Singh, P. (2004). Globalization and education. *Educational Theory, 54*(1), 103–115. doi:10.1111/j.0013-2004.2004.00006.x

Sintayehu, K. A. (2019). African higher education and the Bologna Process. *European Journal of Higher Education, 9*(1), 118–132. doi:10.1080/21568235.2018.1561313

Smigiel, H., Harris, J., & Hannah, J. (2007). *Bringing it all Together: An overview of the delivery of key work-integrated learning (WIL) initiatives at Flinders University.* Paper presented at the Australian Collaborative Education Network, Geelong, Australia. Retrieved from http://acen.edu.au/2012conference/wp-content/uploads/2012/11/64_Bringing-it-all-Together.pdf

Smith, P. L., & Oakley, E. F. III. (1994). A Study of the Ethical Values of Metropolitan and Nonmetropolitan Small Business Owners. *Journal of Small Business Management, 32*(4), 17–27.

Solomon, R. C. (1999). *A Better Way to Think About Business: How Personal Integrity Leads to Corporate Success.* New York: Oxford University Press.

Soomro, T. R., & Ahmad, R. (2012). Quality in Higher Education: United Arab Emirates perspective. *Higher Education Studies, 2*(4), 148–152. doi:10.5539/hes.v2n4p148

Sorcinelli, M. D., & Yun, J. (2007). From mentor to mentoring networks: Mentoring in the new academy. *Change: The Magazine of Higher Learning, 39*(6), 58–61. doi:10.3200/CHNG.39.6.58-C4

Southern African Association for Institutional Research (SAAIR). (2019). *The role of institutional research in strategic planning.* Retrieved from http://www.saair-web.co.za/

Srikanthan, G., & Dalrymple, J. (2003). Developing alternative perspectives for quality in higher education. *International Journal of Educational Management*, *17*(3), 126–136. doi:10.1108/09513540310467804

Srikanthan, G., & Dalrymple, J. (2004). A synthesis of a quality management model for Quality in Higher Education. *International Journal of Educational Management*, *18*(4), 266–273. doi:10.1108/09513540410538859

Srinivasan, P., Srinivasan, V., & Anand, R. V. (2012). *Status of ethics, corporate governance, CSR and environment education in business schools in India: An exploratory study*. Corporate Governance, CSR and Environment Education in Business Schools in India: An Exploratory Study. IIM Bangalore Research Paper, 362.

Srinnivasan, L. E. (2018). *Why educational improvement strategies always disappoint*. Carnegie Corporation of New York: https://www.carnegie.org/news/articles/why-education-improvement-strategies-always-disappoint/

Srivastva, S., & ... (1988). *Executive Integrity: The Search for High Human Values in Organizational Life*. San Francisco, CA: Jossey-Bass.

Starling, G. (1993). Managing the public sector (4th ed.). Belmont, CA: Wadsworth Publishing Company.

Staw, B. M., & Ross, J. (1980). Commitment in an experimenting society: A study of the attribution of leadership from administrative scenarios. *The Journal of Applied Psychology*, *65*(3), 249–260. doi:10.1037/0021-9010.65.3.249

Stead, W., & Stead, J. (2004). *Sustainable Strategic Management*. Armonk, NY: ME Sharpe.

Stern, C. S., Choper, J. H., Gray, M. W., & Wolfson, R. J. (1981). The status of part-time faculty. *Academe*, *67*(1), 29–39. doi:10.2307/40248821

Stogdill, R. M. (1974). *Handbook on Leadership*. New York, NY: The Free Press.

Stoner, J. F., Freeman, R. E., & Gilbert, D. R. (2009). *Management*. London: Pearson.

Stra, T. M. (2010). The Internet and academics workload and work-family balance. *The Internet and Higer Education*, *13*(3), 158–163. doi:10.1016/j.iheduc.2010.03.004

Street, B. V. (2006). *Autonomous and ideological models of literacy: approaches from New Literacy Studies*. Paper presented at European Association of Social Anthropologists (EASA), Media Anthropology Network. Retrieved November 17, 2011, from http://www.media-anthropology.net

Street, B. V. (1984). *Literacy in theory and practice*. Cambridge, UK: Cambridge University Press.

Sullivan, C., & Lewis, S. (2006). Relationships between work and home life. In F. Jones, R. Burke, & M. Westman (Eds.), *Managing the work- home interface: A psychological perspective*. London: Taylor and Francis.

Sultan, P., & Wong, H. (2012). Service quality in a higher education context: An integrated model. *Asia Pacific Journal of Marketing and Logistics*, *24*(5), 755–784. doi:10.1108/13555851211278196

Sundać, D., & Fatur Krmpotić, I. (2011). Knowledge economy factors and the development of the knowledge-based economy. *Croatian Economic Survey*, *13*(1), 105–141.

Sveiby, K. (1997). *The new organizational wealth: managing and measuring knowledge-based assets*. San Francisco: Berrett-Koehler.

Svejenova, S. (2005). The Path with the Heart: Creating the Authentic Career. *Journal of Management Studies*, *42*(5), 947–974. doi:10.1111/j.1467-6486.2005.00528.x

Swanzy, P., & Potts, A. (2017). Quality assurance strategies in higher education: The case of Ghanaian Polytechnics. *Education Research and Perspectives*, *44*, 100–127.

Compilation of References

Tabulawa, R. (1997). Pedagogical classroom practice and the social context: The case of Botswana. *International Journal of Educational Development*, *17*(2), 189–204. doi:10.1016/S0738-0593(96)00049-1

Tabulawa, R. (2003). International aid agencies, learner-centred pedagogy and political democratisation: A critique. *Comparative Education*, *39*(1), 7–26. doi:10.1080/03050060302559

Tabulawa, R. (2009). Education reform in Botswana: Reflections on policy contradictions and paradoxes. *Comparative Education*, *45*(1), 87–107. doi:10.1080/03050060802661410

Takalo, S. K., Abadi, A. R. N. S., Vesal, S. M., Mizaei, A., & Nawaser, K. (2013). Fuzzy Failure Analysis: A New Approach to Service Quality Analysis in Higher Education Institutions. *International Education Studies*, *6*(9), 93–106.

Tari, J. J., & Dick, G. (2016). Trends in quality management research in higher education institutions. *Journal of Service Theory and Practice*, *26*(3), 273–294. doi:10.1108/JSTP-10-2014-0230

Tari, J., & Juana-Espinosa, S. (2007). EFQM model self-assessment using a questionnaire approach in university administrative services. *The TQM Magazine*, *19*(6), 604–616. doi:10.1108/09544780710828449

Tatikonda, L. (2007). Applying Lean Principles to Design Teach, and Assess Courses. *Management Accounting Quarterly*, *8*(3), 27–38.

Teece, D. J., Pisano, G., & Shuen, A. (1997). Dynamic capabilities and strategic management. *Strategic Management Journal*, *18*(7), 509–533. doi:10.1002/(SICI)1097-0266(199708)18:7<509::AID-SMJ882>3.0.CO;2-Z

Teixeria, P., Kim, S., Landoni, P., & Gilani, Z. (2017). *Rethinking the public-private mix in higher education: Global trends and National Policy Challenges*. Rotterdam, The Netherlands: Sense Publisher. doi:10.1007/978-94-6300-911-9

Tenji, T., & Foley, A. (2019). Testing the readiness of an organisational culture profile to a TQM implementation. *The TQM Journal*, *31*(3), 400–416. doi:10.1108/TQM-01-2018-0002

The British Assessment Bureau. (2018). *Quality Management Principles-ISO*. Retrieved from https://www.iso.org/files/live/sites/isoorg/files/archive/pdf/en/pub100080.pdf

The Indian Express. (2018). *India ranks 81st in global corruption index*. Retrieved from http://indianexpress.com/article/india/india-ranks-81st-in-global-corruption-perception-index-5073800/

The Swaziland Education For All Review Report, 2000-2015. (n.d.). Mbabane: Ministry of Education and Training.

The Swaziland National Curriculum Framework for General Education. (2018). *National Curriculum Centre*. Ministry of Education and Training.

The Task Force on Higher Education & Society. (2000). Higher Education in Developing Countries: Peril and Promise. Washington, DC: The International Bank for Reconstruction and Development, the World Bank.

Thomas, H., Turjansky, A., Jones, L., & Williams, D. (2016). Report on the use of management data to support academic quality assurance. *Quality Strategy Network (QSN)*. Retrieved February 15, 2019, from http://qualitystrategynetwork.org.uk/

Thompson, A. D., Grahek, M., Phillips, R. E., & Fay, C. L. (2008). The search for worthy leadership. *Consulting Psychology Journal: Practice and Research*, *60*(4), 366–382. doi:10.1037/1065-9293.60.4.366

Thompson, G., & Glaso, L. (2015, July 6). Situational leadership theory: A test from three perspectives. *Leadership and Organization Development Journal*, *36*(5), 527–544. doi:10.1108/LODJ-10-2013-0130

Timothy, A. (2016). *What you wear – 4 ways to use wearable tech in corporate training*. Retrieved March 19, 2019 from https://elearningindustry.com/4-ways-wearable-tech-in-corporate-training

Toma, S. G., & Naruo, S. (2009). Quality assurance in the Japanese universities. *Amfiteatru Economic, 6*(26), 574–584.

Top MBA Colleges in India 2018. (2018). Retrieved on November 2018 from https://www.financialexpress.com/education-2/top-mba-colleges-in-india-2018-these-are-best-100-b-schools-iim-ahmedabad-is-1-full-list-is-here/1100128/

Trąbka, J. (2015). Quality management support systems (QMSS)–definition, requirements, and scope. *Lecture Notes in Business Information Processing, 232*, 45–58. doi:10.1007/978-3-319-24366-5_4

Tracy, J. L., Cheng, J. T., Robins, R. W., & Trzesniewski, K. H. (2009). Authentic and hubristic pride: The affective core of self-esteem and narcissism. *Self and Identity, 8*(2–3), 196–213. doi:10.1080/15298860802505053

Traynev, V. A., Mkrtchyan, S. A., & Saveliev, A. Y. (2010). *Improving the quality of higher education and the Bologna process*. Moscow: AST.

Treacy, M., & Wiersema, F. (2013). Customer Intimacy and Other Value Disciplines. *Harvard Business Review, 71*(1), 84–93.

Trevino, L. K. (1986). Ethical decision making in organizations: A person-situation interactionist model. *Academy of Management Review, 11*(3), 601–617. doi:10.5465/amr.1986.4306235

Trivellas, P., & Dargenidou, D. (2009). Organisational culture, job satisfaction and higher education service quality: The case of Technological Educational Institute of Larissa. *The TQM Journal, 21*(4), 382–399. doi:10.1108/17542730910965083

Truss, C., Mankin, D., & Kelliher, C. (2012). *Strategic human resource management*. New York: Oxford University Press.

Tsinidou, M., Gerogiannis, V., & Fitsilis, P. (2010). Evaluation of the factors that determine quality in higher education: An empirical study. *Quality Assurance in Education, 18*(3), 227–244. doi:10.1108/09684881011058669

Tutida, L. (2019). ISO 9001: Comparisons, quality of life and results. *Espacios, 40*(1), 23–34.

Ulewicz, R. (2017). The role of stakeholders in quality assurance in higher education. *Human Resources Management & Ergonomics, 11*(1).

UNESCO. (2014). Unesco roadmap for implementing the Global Action Program on education for sustainable development. Paris, France: UNESCO.

University of Namibia (UNAM). (2011). *Quality assurance framework*. Windhoek, Namibia: Author.

University of Namibia (UNAM). (2015). *Quality assurance and management policy*. Windhoek, Namibia: Author.

University of Namibia (UNAM). (2015). *Quality assurance manual*. Windhoek, Namibia: Author.

University of Namibia (UNAM). (2016). Strategic plan 2016–2020. Windhoek: Author.

University of Namibia (UNAM). (2018). *Centre for Quality Assurance and Management (CEQUAM)*. Windhoek: Author. Retrieved from http://www.unam.edu.na/cequam/quality-assurance-process

Van der Westhuizen, L. J. (2009). *Challenges to apply quality assurance as a strategic tool for higher education institutions*. Paper presented at the 31st Annual EAIR Forum, Vilnius, Lithuania.

Vaughn, J. (2002). Accreditation, commercial rankings, and new approaches to assessing the quality of university research and education programmes in the United States. *Higher Education in Europe, 27*(4), 433–441. doi:10.1080/0379772022000071913

Veale, D. J. (1996). Mentoring and coaching as part of a human resource development strategy: An example at Coca-Cola Foods. *Leadership and Organization Development Journal, 17*(3), 16–20. doi:10.1108/01437739610116948

Vecchio, R. P. (1987). Situational Leadership Theory: An examination of a prescriptive theory. *The Journal of Applied Psychology*, *72*(3), 444–451. doi:10.1037/0021-9010.72.3.444

Venkatraman, S. (2007). A framework for implementing TQM in higher education programs. *Quality Assurance in Education*, *15*(1), 92–112. doi:10.1108/09684880710723052

Vikinas, T. (2009). *Improving the leadership capability of academic coordinators in postgraduate and undergraduate programs in business*. Australian Learning and Teaching Council.

Vilkinas, T. (2002). The PhD process: The supervisor as manager. *Education + Training*, *44*(3), 129–137. doi:10.1108/00400910210424337

Vlăsceanu, L., Grünberg, L., & Pârlea, D. (2004). *Quality assurance and accreditation: A glossary of basic terms and definitions*. Bucharest: Unesco-Cepes.

Vlasceanu, L., Grunberg, L., & Parlea, D. (2007). *Quality Assurance and Accreditation: a Glossary of Basic Terms and Definitions*. Bucharest: UNESCO.

Von Kimakowitz, E., Pirson, M., Spitzech, H., Dierksmeier, C., & Amann, W. (2010). Humanistic Management in Practice. New York: Palgrave Macmillan.

Wang, Z., Xu, S., Sun, Y., & Liu, Y. (2019). Transformational leadership and employee voice: An affective perspective. *Frontiers of Business Research in China*, *13*(1), 2–13. doi:10.118611782-019-0049-y

Wankel, C. (Ed.). (2011). *Teaching arts and science with the new social media*. Emerald Group Publishing Limited. doi:10.1108/S2044-9968(2011)3

Warhurst, C. (2008). *The knowledge economy, skills and government labour market intervention*. Policy. doi:10.1080/01442870701848053

Waters, M., & Castells, M. (1995). Globalization; The Rise of the Network Society. New York: Routledge.

Weber, J. A. (2007). Business ethics training: Insights from learning theory. *Journal of Business Ethics*, *70*(1), 61–85. doi:10.100710551-006-9083-8

Webster's. (1994). *Webster's New World Dictionary on PowerCD version 2.1, based on Webster's New World Dictionary* (Edition 1994). Third College.

Weeks-Kaye, B. (2004). Ensuring institutional quality through the strategic planning framework. In *Proceedings of the Australian Universities Quality Forum 2004: Quality in a time of change*. Melbourne: AUQA.

Weinhardt, J. M., & Sitzmann, T. (2019). Revolutionizing training and education? Three questions regarding massive open online courses (MOOCs). *Human Resource Management Review*, *29*(2), 218–225. doi:10.1016/j.hrmr.2018.06.004

Weinstein, L. B., Petrick, J., Castellano, J., & Vokurka, R. J. (2008). Integrating Six Sigma concepts in an MBA quality management class. *Journal of Education for Business*, *83*(4), 233–238. doi:10.3200/JOEB.83.4.233-238

Whitman, N., & Weiss, E. (1982). *Faculty Evaluation: The Use of Explicit Criteria for Promotion, Retention, and Tenure*. AAHE-ERIC/Higher Education Research Report No. 2.

Wiklund, H., Wiklund, B., & Edvardsson, B. (2003). Innovation and TQM in Swedish higher education institutions – possibilities and pitfalls. *The TQM Magazine*, *15*(2), 99–107. doi:10.1108/09544780310461116

Wiklund, H., & Wiklund, P. S. (2007). Widening the Six Sigma concept: An approach to improve organizational learning. *Total Quality Management*, *13*(2), 233–239. doi:10.1080/09544120120102469

Williams, P. J. (2007). *Valid Knowledge: The Economy and the Academy.* Springer Science + Business Media B.V.

Winch, C. (1996). *Quality and education.* Oxford, UK: Blackwell Publisher.

Wiseman, C. S., & Messitt, H. (2010). Identifying components of a successful faculty-advisor program. *NACADA Journal, 30*(2), 35–52. doi:10.12930/0271-9517-30.2.35

Wit, H. D., & Knight, J. A. (1999). *Quality and internationalisation in higher education.* Academic Press.

Wolfgang, A. P., Gupchup, G. V., & Plake, K. S. (1995). Relative importance of performance criteria in promotion and tenure decisions: Perceptions of pharmacy faculty members. *American Journal of Pharmaceutical Education, 59*(4), 342–347.

Wolpert, J. (1965). *Behavioral aspects of the decision to migrate.* Papers in Regional.

Womack, J., & Jones, D. T. (2006). Beyond Toyota: How to root out waste and pursue perfection. *Harvard Business Review, 74*(5), 55–65.

World Bank. (2009). *Accelerating catch-up: Tertiary education for growth in sub-Saharan Africa.* Washington, DC: World Bank.

World Bank. (2009). *Higher education quality assurance in Sub-Saharan Africa.* Washington, DC: World Bank.

World Economic Forum. (2017). *System innovative on shaping the future of education gender and work.* Retrieved August 27, 2018 from https://www.weforum.org/system-initiatives/shaping-the-future-of-education-gender-and-work

World Fact Book. (2012). Retrieved April 24, 2012, from http://www.theodora.com/wfbcurrent/swaziland

World Population Review. (2019). *Swaziland Population 2019.* Retrieved May 1, 2019, from http://worldpopulationreview.com/countries/swaziland-population/

Wright, W. A. (1995). Teaching Improvement Practices: Successful Strategies for Higher Education. Anker Publishing Co., Inc.

Wright, C. J., Katcher, M. L., Blatt, S. D., Keller, D. M., Mundt, M. P., Botash, A. S., & Gjerde, C. L. (2005). Toward the development of advocacy training curricula for pediatric residents: A national Delphi study. *Ambulatory Pediatrics, 5*(3), 165–171. doi:10.1367/A04-113R.1 PMID:15913410

Wright, G. B. (2011). Student-centered learning in higher education. *International Journal on Teaching and Learning in Higher Education, 23*(1), 92–97.

Wright, R. E. (2006). Student evaluations of faculty: Concerns raised in the literature, and possible solutions. *College Student Journal, 40*(2), 417.

Yamuzumi, K. (2016). Quality assurance in teacher education: implications for promoting student learning. In C. Ng, R. Fox, & M. Nakano (Eds.), *Reforming Learning and Teaching in Asia-Pacific Universities. Education in the Asia-Pacific Region: Issues, Concerns and Prospects* (Vol. 33). Singapore: Springer. doi:10.1007/978-981-10-0431-5_18

Yanar, B., Amick, B. C. III, Lambraki, I., D'Elia, T., Severin, C., & Van Eerd, D. (2019). How are leaders using benchmarking information in occupational health and safety decision-making? *Safety Science, 116*, 245–253. doi:10.1016/j.ssci.2019.03.016

Yang, H., & Yang, J. (2019). The effects of transformational leadership, competitive intensity and technological innovation on performance. *Technology Analysis and Strategic Management, 31*(3), 292–305. doi:10.1080/09537325.2018.1498475

Compilation of References

Yeo, R. K. (2008). Servicing service quality in higher education: Quest for excellence. *On the Horizon, 16*(3), 152–161. doi:10.1108/10748120810901459

Yeung, E., & Shen, W. (2019). Can pride be a vice and virtue at work? Associations between authentic and hubristic pride and leadership behaviors. *Journal of Organizational Behavior*, 1–20. doi:10.1002/job.2352

Yin, R. K., & Campbell, D. T. (2013). *Case study research: design and methods* (5th ed.). Thousand Oaks, CA: SAGE.

Yoon, K. (2014). Transnational youth mobility in the neoliberal economy of experience. *Journal of Youth Studies, 17*(8), 1014–1028. doi:10.1080/13676261.2013.878791

Yuan & Powell. (2013). MOOCs and Open education: Implications for higher education. *JICS Cetis*, 1-5. Retrieved from academia.edu

Yu, B. T. W., To, W. M., & Lee, P. K. C. (2012). A quality management framework for public management decision making. *Management Decision, 50*(3), 420–438. doi:10.1108/00251741211216214

Yukl, G. (2002). *Leadership in organizations*. Prentice Hall.

Yureva, O. Y. (2016). Strategic management in higher education system: Methodological approaches. *Electronic Business Journal, 15*(10), 424–428.

Yusuf, Y., Gunasekaran, A., & Dan, D. (2007). Implementation of TQM in China and organization Performance: An Empirical Investigation. *Total Quality Management & Business Excellence, 18*(5), 509–530. doi:10.1080/14783360701239982

Zahn, D. (2003). What influence is the six-sigma movement having in universities? What influence should it be having? *ASQ Six-Sigma Forum, 3*(1). Retrieved from http://asq.org/pub/ sixsigma/past/vol3issue1/youropinion.html

Zarei, M., & Shaharaki. (2011). Article. *Society for Business and Management Dynamics Magazine, 1*(3), 1-12.

Zeegers, M., & Barron, D. (2012). Pedagogical concerns in doctoral supervision: A challenge for pedagogy. *Quality Assurance in Education, 20*(1), 20–30. doi:10.1108/09684881211198211

Zhang, W., Hill, A. V., & Gilbreath, G. H. (2011). A research agenda for Six Sigma Research. *The Quality Management Journal, 18*(1), 39–53. doi:10.1080/10686967.2011.11918301

Zhao, F. (2001). Postgraduate Research Supervision: A process of knowledge management. *ultiBASE Articles*. Retrieved from http://ultibase.rmit.edu.au/Articles/may/01/zhao1.htm

Zmas, A. (2015). Financial crisis and higher education policies in Greece:Between intra- and supranational pressures. *Higher Education, 69*(3), 495–508. doi:10.100710734-014-9787-0

Zmas, A. (2015). Global impacts of the Bologna Process: International perspectives, local particularities. *Compare: A Journal of Comparative Education, 45*(5), 727–747. doi:10.1080/03057925.2014.899725

Zott, C., Amit, R., & Massa, L. (2011). The business model: Recent developments and future research. *Journal of Management, 37*(4), 1019–1042. doi:10.1177/0149206311406265

About the Contributors

Neeta Baporikar is currently Professor (Management) at Harold Pupkewitz Graduate School of Business (HP-GSB), Namibia University of Science and Technology, Namibia. Prior to this, she was Head-Scientific Research, with Ministry of Higher Education CAS-Salalah, Sultanate of Oman, Professor (Strategic Management and Entrepreneurship) at IIIT Pune and BITS India. With more than a decade of experience in the industry, consultancy, and training, she made a lateral switch to research and academics in 1995. Prof Baporikar holds D.Sc. (Management Studies) USA, Ph.D. in Management, the University of Pune INDIA with MBA (Distinction) and Law (Hons.) degrees. Apart from this, she is also an external reviewer, Oman Academic Accreditation Authority, Accredited Management Teacher, Qualified Trainer, Doctoral Guide and Board Member of Academics and Advisory Committee in accredited B-Schools. She has to her credit many conferred doctorates, is international and editorial advisory board member and reviewer for Emerald, IGI, Inderscience refereed journals, published numerous refereed research papers, and authored books in the area of entrepreneurship, strategy, management, and higher education.

Michael Sony is at present Faculty at Namibia University of Science & Technology, Windhoek, Namibia. He received the PhD Degree from Goa University, India in the year 2015. He holds a Master of Engineering in Industrial Engineering from Goa University. He was a University topper in the year 2008 at the Master of Engineering with a Distinction. He is also a certified Energy Manager and Energy Auditor, from Bureau of Energy Efficiency India, Lean Six Sigma Black Belt & TPM trainer. He has Industrial Experience in Goa Electricity Department, Government of Goa, India etc. He also has consulting experience in the area of quality management in various multinationals in India. He has to his credit more than 35 international journal articles, 10 conference papers, two books and has guided students at Bachelor and Master of Engineering & Master of Business Administration level. His research interest includes Quality Management, Industry 4.0, Productions & Operations Management.

* * *

Samuel Agyemang has a Bed (Hons) from the University of Cape Coast, an MA from University of Huddersfield and an EdD from the University of Sheffield.

Richmond Anane-Simon is an Open-minded person and a critical thinker who has been on the fore front of youth leadership for almost a decade. His analytical skills coupled with his ability to quickly grasp concepts, landed his current role as an Actuarial Scientist at Pentecost University College.

About the Contributors

Loukas N. Anninos received his Ph.D in Business Administration from the University of Piraeus. His research portfolio includes publications in peer reviewed journals, books and presentations in numerous national and international conferences. He has taught management, organizational behavior and human resources management (undergraduate and postgraduate level) and serves as a reviewer in journals and conferences.

Dileep Baragde is currently Head of Department /Professor (Computer/Management) at the G.S. Moze College, affiliated to Savitribai Phule pune University, India. With more than a 10 Years of experience in teaching. Dr. Baragde holds PhD in Management, Savitribai Phule Pune University INDIA with MBA (Computer Management) and MSc (Computer Science) degrees. Apart from this, He is also Reviewer for international journals, several written research papers and authored Chapters in books in the area of Information Technology, Business Innovation, Entrepreneurship, Management and Higher Education.

Denise Bedford is currently an Adjunct Professor, Georgetown University's Communication Culture and Technology program; adjunct faculty at the Schulich School of Business, York University; Visiting Scholar at the University of Coventry, and a Distinguished Practitioner/Virtual Fellow with the U.S. Department of State. In 2010, Dr. Bedford retired as Senior Information Officer, World Bank. In 2015, she retired from her role as Goodyear Professor of Knowledge Management, Kent State University. Dr. Bedford has also worked for Intel Corporation, NASA, University of California Systemwide Administration, and Stanford University. She currently serves as an Associate Editor of the Journal of Knowledge Management. Her educational background includes a B.A. triple major in Intellectual History, Russian Language, and German Language; an M.A. in Russian and East European History; an M.S. in Information Science; and a Ph.D. in Information Science with focus on Systems Analysis and Design, and Economics of Information.

Joseph Cobbinah is a lecturer with over 15 years of teaching experience. He obtained his BEd(Hons) degree from the University of Nottingham, an MSc from the Open University, UK; an MPhil from Fitzwilliam College, University of Cambridge; PGDip and a Ph.D. from the University of Bradford, UK. Joseph is also reading a Doctor of Education (EdD) degree from the University of Bath in the UK.

Idahosa Igbinakhase received his PhD in Entrepreneurship from the University of KwaZulu-Natal. In 2011 he was hired by the Federal Ministry of Education Nigeria to teach Technical Subjects in Federal Unity Colleges in Nigeria. His current research interests include family entrepreneurship, technology management, service quality, strategic management, and sustainable development. He is very passionate about management research and strongly believes that sound management practices hold the key to a sustainable society.

Selma M. Iipinge holds a Master of Financial Management from AMITY University in India, Postgraduate Certificate in Higher Education from Namibia University of Science and Technology and a Bachelor of Entrepreneurship Honours from Polytechnic of Namibia. She is currently a Junior Lecture for Business Simulation at the Namibia University of Science and Technology. Her research interest lies in the areas of Business management, youth entrepreneurship, SME development, cooperative education and teaching and learning in higher education.

Ngepathimo Kadhila holds a Bachelor of Education and Master of Education (Curriculum, Instructional and Assessment Studies) from the University of Namibia; Postgraduate Diploma in Higher Education (for Academic Developers) from Rhodes University in South Africa; and PhD in Higher Education Studies (with the focus on Quality Assurance) from the University of the Free State in South Africa. He currently serves as Quality Assurance Director at the University of Namibia. His research work lies in the areas of academic development, curriculum development, teaching and learning in higher education, assessment in higher education, and quality assurance in higher education.

Gilbert Likando holds a PhD in Education and an Associate Professor. He has authored a number of articles, book chapters, and co-edited books in the field of education. His research interest in the area of education encompasses: higher education, educational leadership; teaching and learning paradigms; adult education and, higher education.

Vannie Naidoo is a senior academic in the School of Management, IT and Governance at University of KwaZulu-Natal. She has a PhD (Management) from University of KwaZulu-Natal, SA. She has taught at both undergrad and post-grad modules in Corporate Strategy, Project management, Entrepreneurship, Contemporary Issues in Marketing and Research Methodology. Dr Naidoo is an international researcher who has attended numerous conference in SA and abroad. In 2017 she was keynote speaker at the conference-Emerging Trends in Academic Research ETAR-2017, November 27-28, 2017 Bali, Indonesia. She has published in various local and international journals and many book chapters in various interdisciplinary fields of study. Her field of research is in areas of strategy, entrepreneurship, marketing, service quality, ICT's in education, workplace dynamics and management.

Liphie Pereira was born and raised in the Kingdom of Eswatini. She started her education career in 1987. She has taught for 8 years at secondary school level teaching Accounting and Commerce in the Kingdom of Eswatini. Liphie is currently a lecturer at the University of Eswatini teaching Curriculum Studies in Accounting to students who are training to become Accounting teachers at secondary school level. She has been teaching this course for 11 years. Her contribution to Accounting education includes also the writing of Accounting textbooks used at secondary school level in the Kingdom of Eswatini.

Rajka Presbury is an Associate Professor at Torrens University Australia. Her PhD is on the topic of service quality in the hotel sector. Her research interest has predominantly been in service quality and service experience, exploring perceptions of customers, managers and employees in hotels. More recently she has become fascinated by the triadic service relationship of educational institutions, corporate service providers and students as current and future employees of the hospitality industry. Thus exploring topics such as Work Integrated Learning and Mentoring.

Damini Saini is working as an Assistant Professor and a key member of library and research committee at Institute of Management Sciences in University if Lucknow. Damini has received her PhD degree from Faculty of Management Studies (FMS), University of Delhi in HRM (OB). She holds her MBA and Graduation Degree from IET Lucknow and Lucknow University respectively and passed UGC–NET and has also been awarded UGC's Junior and Senior Research Fellowship. Damini has been awarded for the Best research paper award twice, at International Conference on, Vedic Foundations

About the Contributors

of Indian Management, organized by VFIM(2013) and PRMEs International Conference "Responsible Management Education, Training and Practice"(2015). Her scholarly interests are leadership and ethics, values and spiritual foundations for developing leadership etc. Damini has contributed to nationally and internationally acclaimed journals and conferences.

Jose Manuel Saiz-Alvarez Ph.D. with Honors, Economics and Business Administration, Autonomous University of Madrid (Spain), Ph.D. with Honors, Political Science and Sociology, Pontifical University of Salamanca (Spain). Research Professor, EGADE Business School, Tecnológico de Monterrey (Mexico). Visiting Professor, The Catholic University of Santiago de Guayaquil (Ecuador) and Autonomous University of Manizales (Colombia). He was Director of the BA Doctoral Program, Nebrija University (Spain) and Director of the Master in Microcredits and Social Inclusion, Pontifical University of Salamanca (Spain, and Guatemala). Member of GEM Jalisco and Academic Leader at Tecnológico de Monterrey. Diploma of recognition, House of Representatives of the Capitol of Puerto Rico. Diploma of Honor, Valahia University of Targoviste (Romania). Honorary Professor, Autonomous University of Madrid (Spain). International Advisor, Institute of Social Innovation BOSTAN (Turkey) and the Catholic University of Santiago de Guayaquil (Ecuador). He is accredited in Spain by the National Agency for the Evaluation of Quality and Accreditation, the National System of Researchers of Mexico, and the Mexican Academy of Sciences. He has published more than 300 publications in five languages and has supervised 74 doctoral theses. Scientific committees' member of indexed journals in Europe, America, and Asia. Who's Who in the World from 2011.

Madalyn Scerri is a Senior Lecturer at Torrens University Australia. Her research focuses on the dynamics of service language and interaction, primarily in the context of Australian hotels. With an interest in the complexity of customer service, Dr Scerri is applying this unique hospitality knowledge to research different service settings such as health care and peer-to-peer accommodation in the sharing economy. Her other research interests focus on teaching and learning pedagogy, graduate employability and qualitative research methodologies. She has presented her research at national and international conferences and in peer-reviewed publications.

Steven Sena Senior Lecturer University of Zimbabwe and Researcher with Zimbabwe National Defence University Graduated with a PhD in Commerce (Business Management) Nelson Mandela Metropolitan University (NMMU) (RSA); MSc Strategic Management Chinhoyi University of Technology (Zimbabwe); BA Media Studies Zimbabwe Open University.

Sunita Sengupta is currently heading Faculty of Management Studies, University of Delhi. She is a recipient of distinguished Homi Bhabha Fellowship, has authored 25 books and more than 6 dozen articles in national and international journals of repute. She is a widely travelled scholar and has lectured in USA, UK and France. Her area of research interests include Rethinking Management Education, Value Based Management, Corporate Social Responsibility, Women Leadership in Organizations, Business Transformation Through Spiritual Leadership, Indigenous Management, Global Climate Change and Eco System Management: Insights from Wisdom Traditions, Indian Culture Philosophy and Management, Social Unity and Harmony for Global Economic Development, Generating Happiness at Workplace,, Ethical and Spiritual Foundations of Organizational Development, and Vedic Foundations of Management.

Anna Shimpanda is a Junior Lecturer at the Namibian University of Science and Technology (NUST). She holds a master's degree in international business from Amity University and a post-graduate certificate in higher education from NUST. She is passionate about teaching and education and believes that education is indeed an equalizer. Her research interests are on business, entrepreneurship and education.

José Vargas-Hernández Research Professor Professor José G. Vargas-Hernández, M.B.A.; Ph.D. Member of the National System of Researchers of Mexico and a research professor at University Center for Economic and Managerial Sciences, University of Guadalajara. Professor Vargas-Hernández has a Ph. D. in Public Administration and a Ph.D. in Organizational Economics. He has undertaken studies in Organisational Behaviour and has a Master of Business Administration, published four books and more than 200 papers in international journals and reviews (some translated to English, French, German, Portuguese, Farsi, Chinese, etc.) and more than 300 essays in national journals and reviews. He has obtained several international Awards and recognition.

Hylton Villet has 34 plus years of Organisational experience at various levels, including the Executive level. He has over 17 years' experience in the consulting arena where he was engaged with Large Corporate Organisations, not-for-profit Organisations, State Owned Enterprises, SMME's and Local authorities. Dr. Villet has facilitated workshops for Strategic Planning and Development, Strategic Review, Business, and Operational Planning, Organisation Development, Change and Transformation, Organisational Culture and Climate re-alignment, Organisational Conflict Resolution as well as various stakeholders' engagement in different economic sectors of Namibia and the continent, in Kenya, Tanzania, Rwanda, Botswana and South Africa. He honed his skills as a founding member of the Mineworkers Union of Namibia, as the MD of two medium-sized ICT companies, he served as a non-executive director on many of the largest financial and insurance companies in Namibia. He still has an interest in the Technology Sector and is engaged in Social Entrepreneurship through Mydigitalbridge Foundation, serving as non-executive Chairman. This Foundation works with stakeholders to promote access to connectivity for rural communities. Dr. Villet currently serves as the Director of the Harold Pupkewitz Graduate School of Business at the Namibia University of Science and Technology.

Index

5S 7-8, 16, 21

A

academic 3, 9-10, 16, 25-27, 33, 35, 39, 41-42, 62, 66-68, 70-71, 73, 75, 87, 90, 94, 101-103, 105-107, 109-114, 116, 121-124, 127-130, 132-133, 143-147, 152, 160-162, 169, 173, 180-181, 188, 223, 226, 240-241, 250-253, 262, 265, 280, 288, 291, 294-295, 298, 302-303
accreditation 29, 58, 62-63, 65, 67-71, 75, 78, 82, 101, 104-106, 111, 121, 124-126, 129, 140, 161, 172, 246, 250-252, 255, 289-291, 300
ACTIVITY MODELS 156, 162, 164, 170-171
advising 156, 162, 169, 173, 177, 180-181
advocacy 156, 162, 169, 173-174, 180-181
Alumni Board 268, 275, 280, 286
assessment 4, 11, 26, 34, 42, 51, 53-54, 56, 65, 71-72, 82, 88, 100, 103, 105, 107, 142, 151-152, 156-157, 166, 170-172, 174, 177, 180-181, 217, 219, 221, 238, 242, 246, 250-252, 255, 290, 294, 298
Automated Essay Scoring 88, 100

B

benchmarking 30, 54, 65, 72-73, 290

C

certification 1, 9, 56, 82, 85, 162, 167
classification 3, 9, 47, 195
client 1-3, 10, 12, 14-15, 25, 29, 32, 169, 173
College Instructor 255, 262
competition 3, 10, 17, 38, 63, 66, 72, 93, 104, 106, 109, 121-122, 161-162, 178, 180-181, 300
continuous improvement 1-2, 5-7, 9-10, 14, 16-17, 44-45, 54, 65-66, 72, 103, 110, 122, 124-125, 127-128, 131-133, 140, 250-252, 290, 295-296, 302
controlling 103, 127, 146, 150, 292, 308
convening 156, 162, 170, 174, 180-181
critical realism 192, 207-208
Cultural Learning Process 200, 207
CURRICULUM CHANGE 191
Curriculum Review 100
Customer Focus 1, 3, 43
customer satisfaction 3-4, 40-41, 47, 54, 58, 66, 104-105, 110, 125, 140, 218

D

discourse 94, 113, 192-195, 199-201, 207, 211, 249, 255
discourse analysis 192
DMAIC 27, 33-34
Dropout Rate 262

E

education system 24, 57, 62, 68, 72-73, 83-84, 86, 89-90, 107, 122, 197, 238, 247-249, 253, 255, 265
educational objectives 249-250
Employee Voice 5, 21
ethics 48, 169, 173-174, 178, 209-211, 213-216, 221-225, 231-242
ethics education 232-233, 238, 241
evidence-based decision making 1, 11, 13-14, 22, 45, 287-289, 291-292, 294-295, 298-299, 301, 304

F

Faculty competencies 167
faculty quality 157, 162, 172, 174, 178-179
Flow 32-33, 50, 149, 194

G

Graduation Rate 26, 262

H

higher education 23-25, 31, 33-34, 38, 42, 57-58, 61-73, 75-76, 78, 82-95, 101-116, 121-126, 128-133, 140-141, 156-159, 161-163, 167-172, 174-175, 177-181, 189-191, 196, 199, 202, 223, 231-232, 235, 241, 246-255, 262-265, 267, 279, 287-288, 290-292, 294, 300, 308

higher education institutions 23, 33, 57-58, 62-73, 75, 78, 82-83, 101-116, 122, 128, 130, 159, 175, 246, 250-255, 263-264, 267, 279, 287-288, 292, 308

hospitality 264-266, 268

I

innovation 2, 10-11, 16, 66, 78, 83-86, 88-89, 91-95, 100, 133, 141, 143, 160-161, 168, 197, 294-295

inspirational motivation 92, 100

institution 14-15, 17, 41, 56-58, 63, 65, 68, 70-73, 76, 82-83, 85-88, 91-92, 94-95, 102-106, 108-115, 122, 125-126, 129-133, 140, 144, 169, 178, 180-181, 195, 202, 208, 232-233, 235, 239, 248-249, 251-253, 271-272, 279-280, 288, 290-297, 299-301, 303-304, 308

Institutional Research 287-288, 290, 293, 298-300

Instructed Learning 207

integrity 40, 57, 70, 209-226, 231, 234-235, 240

Intellectual Stimulation 92, 100

K

kaizen 2, 5, 7-8, 10, 14, 16-17, 22

L

leadership 1-2, 4-6, 11-15, 17, 22, 26, 34, 43, 51, 83-85, 87, 90-95, 101-102, 104-105, 108-116, 121, 124, 127-130, 132-134, 140-144, 148-153, 216, 218-221, 231, 233-234, 239-240, 265, 288, 293, 300

leadership effectiveness 84, 90, 112, 219-220

learning outcomes 30, 94, 100, 111, 171, 249-250

learning strategies 86

M

management education 209, 221-222, 224, 231-233, 235, 237, 239-240, 242

managerial integrity 216-219, 221, 223-226, 231

mentees 263, 266-268, 271-272, 274-279, 286

mentoring 110, 131, 134, 161, 167-169, 173, 177-179, 263-268, 270-280, 286

mentors 169, 266-268, 271-280, 286

N

Namibia Qualifications Authority 62, 291
National Council for Higher Education 62, 291
Natural Learning 208

O

Operationalization and Implementation 308
organizational performance 38, 110, 231

P

planning process 40, 50, 292-293, 300, 303, 308

postgraduate supervision 141-143, 145-146, 148, 152-153

professional integrity 209-210, 214-217, 219, 221-225, 231

professionalism 6, 216, 222, 231

profitability 51, 218, 233

Q

quality assurance 24, 40-42, 46, 54, 57-58, 61-71, 73, 75-76, 78, 82-84, 86, 89, 93-94, 100-101, 103-104, 106-107, 116, 124-128, 132-133, 188, 202, 208, 235, 246, 249-253, 255, 287-288, 290, 293-296, 299-300

quality audit 55-58, 70

quality control 25, 40-42, 46, 54, 65, 67, 115, 171-172

quality culture 24, 34, 45, 65, 73, 130-133, 140

quality education 16, 65, 103, 105-106, 111, 188-189, 262, 290-292

quality improvement 2, 25, 35, 39-41, 43, 45-46, 50, 52-55, 65, 69, 89, 122, 246, 250-254, 288, 290-291, 296, 299, 302

quality in higher education 24, 61, 64-65, 68-69, 73, 78, 101, 106-107, 125, 130, 132, 140, 249, 251-252

Quality Intelligence 121, 128, 140

quality management 1, 7, 13, 17, 22-26, 28-29, 34, 38-43, 46, 50-51, 56, 58, 61-68, 70-71, 73-75, 82-83, 87, 89, 94-95, 101-108, 110-112, 115-116, 123-125, 127-130, 140, 156-159, 163, 170-172, 174, 177, 179-181, 232-233, 247, 251-252, 293-294, 296

Index

Quality Management System 56, 82
quality models 62, 163, 181
quality planning 40-41, 54, 65
quality standards 10, 25, 40, 57, 65, 67, 69, 73, 82, 104, 111, 126, 172, 179, 181, 249, 290

R

registration 62-63, 65, 68-69, 78, 82, 291
Regulatory Requirements 57, 82
Relationships Management 22
reputation 3-7, 9-11, 13, 15-17, 169, 173-174, 178, 181, 215, 217-218, 221, 225, 249, 276

S

Self-improvement Plan 308
Sigma 8, 23-35
Situational Leadership 141-144, 148-153
Social Realism 208
stakeholder 22, 40, 42, 45, 58, 61, 65, 73, 88, 157, 172-173, 181, 216, 225, 252, 255, 290
strategic management 45, 50, 253, 287-292, 294-295, 297-301, 303-304, 308

strategic planning 45, 58, 123, 289, 291-293, 299-304, 308
Student Management 142, 146, 148

T

teacher education 188-192, 195-197, 199-202, 208
Teacher Quality 208
Teaching Strategies 262
Total Quality Management 7, 22, 24-26, 28, 39, 41, 46, 58, 87, 103, 124-125, 127-128, 140, 247, 251
transformational leadership 2, 5, 11-12, 22, 84, 91-92, 94, 221

U

University excellence 127-128, 140
University of Namibia 62, 287-288, 293-295, 302

W

WIL 265, 268, 286

Purchase Print, E-Book, or Print + E-Book

IGI Global's reference books are available in three unique pricing formats:
Print Only, E-Book Only, or Print + E-Book.
Shipping fees may apply.

www.igi-global.com

Recommended Reference Books

ISBN: 978-1-5225-9348-5
© 2019; 454 pp.
List Price: $255

ISBN: 978-1-5225-7763-8
© 2019; 253 pp.
List Price: $175

ISBN: 978-1-5225-7531-3
© 2019; 324 pp.
List Price: $185

ISBN: 978-1-5225-7802-4
© 2019; 423 pp.
List Price: $195

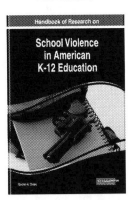

ISBN: 978-1-5225-6246-7
© 2019; 610 pp.
List Price: $275

ISBN: 978-1-5225-2998-9
© 2018; 352 pp.
List Price: $195

Do you want to stay current on the latest research trends, product announcements, news and special offers?
Join IGI Global's mailing list today and start enjoying exclusive perks sent only to IGI Global members.
Add your name to the list at **www.igi-global.com/newsletters**.

Publisher of Peer-Reviewed, Timely, and Innovative Academic Research

www.igi-global.com | Sign up at www.igi-global.com/newsletters | facebook.com/igiglobal | twitter.com/igiglobal | linkedin.com/igiglobal

Ensure Quality Research is Introduced to the Academic Community

Become an IGI Global Reviewer for Authored Book Projects

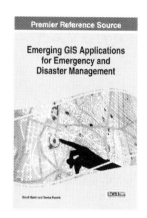 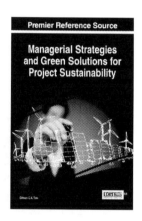  

The overall success of an authored book project is dependent on quality and timely reviews.

In this competitive age of scholarly publishing, constructive and timely feedback significantly expedites the turnaround time of manuscripts from submission to acceptance, allowing the publication and discovery of forward-thinking research at a much more expeditious rate. Several IGI Global authored book projects are currently seeking highly-qualified experts in the field to fill vacancies on their respective editorial review boards:

Applications and Inquiries may be sent to:
development@igi-global.com

Applicants must have a doctorate (or an equivalent degree) as well as publishing and reviewing experience. Reviewers are asked to complete the open-ended evaluation questions with as much detail as possible in a timely, collegial, and constructive manner. All reviewers' tenures run for one-year terms on the editorial review boards and are expected to complete at least three reviews per term. Upon successful completion of this term, reviewers can be considered for an additional term.

If you have a colleague that may be interested in this opportunity, we encourage you to share this information with them.

IGI Global Proudly Partners With eContent Pro International

Receive a 25% Discount on all Editorial Services

Editorial Services

IGI Global expects all final manuscripts submitted for publication to be in their final form. This means they must be reviewed, revised, and professionally copy edited prior to their final submission. Not only does this support with accelerating the publication process, but it also ensures that the highest quality scholarly work can be disseminated.

English Language Copy Editing

Let eContent Pro International's expert copy editors perform edits on your manuscript to resolve spelling, punctuaion, grammar, syntax, flow, formatting issues and more.

Scientific and Scholarly Editing

Allow colleagues in your research area to examine the content of your manuscript and provide you with valuable feedback and suggestions before submission.

Figure, Table, Chart & Equation Conversions

Do you have poor quality figures? Do you need visual elements in your manuscript created or converted? A design expert can help!

Translation

Need your documjent translated into English? eContent Pro International's expert translators are fluent in English and more than 40 different languages.

Hear What Your Colleagues are Saying About Editorial Services Supported by IGI Global

"The service was very fast, very thorough, and very helpful in ensuring our chapter meets the criteria and requirements of the book's editors. I was quite impressed and happy with your service."

– Prof. Tom Brinthaupt,
Middle Tennessee State University, USA

"I found the work actually spectacular. The editing, formatting, and other checks were very thorough. The turnaround time was great as well. I will definitely use eContent Pro in the future."

– Nickanor Amwata, Lecturer,
University of Kurdistan Hawler, Iraq

"I was impressed that it was done timely, and wherever the content was not clear for the reader, the paper was improved with better readability for the audience."

– Prof. James Chilembwe,
Mzuzu University, Malawi

Email: customerservice@econtentpro.com

www.igi-global.com/editorial-service-partners

www.igi-global.com

Celebrating Over 30 Years of Scholarly Knowledge Creation & Dissemination

InfoSci®-Books

A Database of Over 5,300+ Reference Books Containing Over 100,000+ Chapters Focusing on Emerging Research

GAIN ACCESS TO **THOUSANDS** OF REFERENCE BOOKS AT **A FRACTION** OF THEIR INDIVIDUAL LIST **PRICE**.

InfoSci®-Books Database

The **InfoSci®-Books** database is a collection of over 5,300+ IGI Global single and multi-volume reference books, handbooks of research, and encyclopedias, encompassing groundbreaking research from prominent experts worldwide that span over 350+ topics in 11 core subject areas including business, computer science, education, science and engineering, social sciences and more.

Open Access Fee Waiver (Offset Model) Initiative

For any library that invests in IGI Global's InfoSci-Journals and/or InfoSci-Books databases, IGI Global will match the library's investment with a fund of equal value to go toward **subsidizing the OA article processing charges (APCs) for their students, faculty, and staff** at that institution when their work is submitted and accepted under OA into an IGI Global journal.*

INFOSCI® PLATFORM FEATURES

- No DRM
- No Set-Up or Maintenance Fees
- A Guarantee of No More Than a 5% Annual Increase
- Full-Text HTML and PDF Viewing Options
- Downloadable MARC Records
- Unlimited Simultaneous Access
- COUNTER 5 Compliant Reports
- Formatted Citations With Ability to Export to RefWorks and EasyBib
- No Embargo of Content (Research is Available Months in Advance of the Print Release)

*The fund will be offered on an annual basis and expire at the end of the subscription period. The fund would renew as the subscription is renewed for each year thereafter. The open access fees will be waived after the student, faculty, or staff's paper has been vetted and accepted into an IGI Global journal and the fund can only be used toward publishing OA in an IGI Global journal. Libraries in developing countries will have the match on their investment doubled.

To Learn More or To Purchase This Database:
www.igi-global.com/infosci-books

eresources@igi-global.com • Toll Free: 1-866-342-6657 ext. 100 • Phone: 717-533-8845 x100

www.igi-global.com